Red Coats
On The Prairies
THE NORTH-WEST MOUNTED POLICE 1886-1900

Thorough and entertaining ... I have yet to read a book about the Mounted Police that is as comprehensive and interesting as this one. In my view, all serving members of the RCMP should add it to their reading list.

Supt. John E. Religa (RCMP – Rtd.)
The Beaver – Canada's   National   History Society

clarence Kapay
1997

Red Coats
On The Prairies

THE NORTH-WEST MOUNTED POLICE 1886-1900

William Beahen
and Stan Horrall

Centax Books
PrintWest Publishing Services
Regina, Saskatchewan

Red Coats On The Prairies

by
William Beahen and Stan Horrall

First Printing – June 1998

Canadian Cataloguing in Publication Data
Beahen, William, 1946–

    Red coats on the Prairies

    Published also in French under title: Les tuniques rouges dans la Prairie
    Includes bibliographical references and index.
    ISBN 1-894022-01-7 (bound)   ;   ISBN 1-894022-08-4 (pbk.)

1. North-West Mounted Police (Canada)–History.
2. Northwest, Canadian–History–1870-1905. I. Horrall, Stan, 1934–
   II. Title.

FC3216.2.B4 1998   363.2'0971   C98-920074-4
F1060.9.B4 1998

French Translation by Daniel Poliquin
Cover painting by Clarence Kapay
Cover and page design by Brian Danchuk, Brian Danchuk Design

Designed, Printed, and Published in Canada by:
Centax Books/PrintWest Publishing Services
Publishing Director – Margo Embury
1150 Eighth Avenue, Regina, Saskatchewan, Canada S4R 1C9
Telephone (306) 525-2304   Fax: (306) 757-2439

Dedication

This book is dedicated to

Joan, Megan and Katie Beahen,

and

to the memory of Matthew J. Beahen,

to

Ruth, Sean, Andrew and Caitlin Horrall,

and

to the memory of Sally Horrall.

Red Coats On the Prairies
The North-West Mounted Police 1886-1900

Contents

Part I: Taming the Frontier

Part II: All Sorts and Conditions of Men

Foreword

The Royal Canadian Mounted Police and their predecessors, the Royal Northwest Mounted Police and the North-West Mounted Police have attracted the attention of historians from the early days of their existence. Those in command of the Force were quick to recognize the importance of publicity and their receptiveness to writers led to many books, aimed mainly at the British and American markets. Some of these early works were written by talented writers who cared about accuracy and balance; many of them were not. John Peter Turner, a journalist who developed a life-long interest in the history of the Mounted Police, effectively became the official historian of the Force with the publication of his two-volume history by the Canadian government in 1950. Turner, who died before his books were published, could hardly be called a critical historian but he was a tireless collector of information and his work, which covers the first twenty years of the NWMP, is still useful as a reference. The decade of the 1950s was one of very rapid expansion for the RCMP and, perhaps understandably, they did not take the logical step of appointing an official historian to continue Turner's work until the late 1960s.

In retrospect, the timing was good. By the late 1960s there was a rapidly growing pool of professionally trained historians in Canada. The RCMP was extraordinarily fortunate that among these scholars was a former constable in the Force, Stan Horrall. Stan went on to write a number of books and numerous articles which were on a par with the best Canadian historical scholarship of the late twentieth century. His work has been ably carried on since his retirement by his successor, Bill Beahen. It is hard to think of any other organization in North America with a comparable record of sponsoring independent writing about its past.

I started writing a Ph.D. thesis on the NWMP about the same time that Stan Horrall was appointed RCMP historian. The thesis subsequently became a book, *The North West Mounted Police and Law Enforcement, 1873-1905*, published by the University of Toronto Press in 1976. I had the great advantage of being the first historian to go systematically through the Mounted Police papers after they were turned over to the national archives in the 1960s. It meant that I got to impose my ideas about what was important in the many thousands of pages of documents covering the period to 1905 without having to take much account of what earlier writers, who had not had access to those documents, had to say. I was well aware at the time that I was not writing a comprehensive history of the NWMP in the period. For various reasons I never returned to writing about the Mounted Police in the late nineteenth century but it was not because I though that the subject was exhausted. I was delighted to hear that Bill Beahen and Stan Horrall were working on a history of the NWMP for the period when L. W. Herchmer was Commissioner. I was even more pleased when I read it and saw what a fine job they had done. The Herchmer years were, I believe, the most critical period in the evolution of the newly created Mounted Police. It was this period that established the Force in the public mind as representing the best features of the emerging Canadian confederation. This book will be of absorbing interest to anyone with an interest in either the history of law enforcement or the history of western Canada. I would have been proud to have written this book.

R. C. Macleod
University of Alberta

Photograph Captions

1. Sergeant of the North-West Mounted Police in full dress uniform, 1898 (Ralph-Clark-Stone Ltd., painting by Tom McNeely).

2. Lawrence Herchmer, Commissioner, North-West Mounted Police, 1886-1900.

3. The presence of the NWMP added colour and ceremony to official state and civic occasions. Here a mounted escort for the Governor General and Countess of Aberdeen waits while their Excellencies enjoy the sporting events put on for their visit to Calgary in October 1894.

4. Church Parade, Regina, 1890. Once around the square led by the band and into the chapel.

5. Winter travel in Regina, 1895. A four-in-hand cutter with sleigh bells.

6. Clowning about in the pharmacy at Regina in the 1880s. The surgeon seems to be prescribing something that might put some life back into the skeleton.

7. 9 pounder gun drill at Fort Macleod, 1894. Both the guns and the two mortars between them were taken west by the police in 1874.

8. Almighty Voice, Kah-kee-say-mane-too-wayo, the Cree Indian who shot and killed Sgt. Colin Colebrook in October 1895.

9. $500 reward notice for the capture of Almighty Voice, Kah-kee-say-mane-too-wayo. After killing Colebrook, the young Cree Indian managed to elude police patrols for over a year.

10. Sgt. Colin Colebrook, a former shop clerk from London, England, endeavoured to apprehend Almighty Voice, Kah-kee-say-mane-too-wayo, without resorting to violence.

11. Ida Colebrook, the widow of the slain Sergeant, was one of the first women to be employed by the Mounted Police as a matron.

12. Mounted Police field guns shelling the bluff where Almighty Voice, Kah-kee-say-mane-too-wayo, and his companions were trapped in May 1897.

13. In 1891, teams from Winnipeg, Moosomin and the NWMP played off against each other for the Hamilton Cup in the first challenge for the rugby football championship of Manitoba and the North-West Territories. The Winnipeg football club emerged as the winner. The games were played at the NWMP barracks in Regina.

14. The NWMP rugby football club, 1891, known locally as the "Rough Riders", was captained by Insp. A. C. Macdonell (later Major General Sir A. C. Macdonell) seen here holding the ball.

15. Group of NWMP commissioned officers, ca. 1894. Sitting from left to right: Supt. A. B. Perry (later Commissioner), Assistant Commissioner J. H. McIllree, Commissioner L. W. Herchmer, Supt. S. Gagnon, Insp. C. Starnes (later Commissioner). Standing from left to right: Veterinary Surgeon J. F. Burnett, Assistant Surgeon P. Aylen, Insp. M. Baker, Insp. W. M. deRay Williams, Insp. R. Belcher, Insp. W. H. Irwin.

16. NWMP detachment teams leaving Regina for Wood Mountain in May 1895. In the background are the two 2-storey barrack buildings erected in 1887 and henceforth known as "A" Block and "B" Block.

17. Members of the NWMP Sergeants' Mess, Regina, 1896. Sitting from left to right: S/Sgts. H. Ayre and S. Bates; Sgts. Major F. Harper and J. F. Stewart, S/Sgts. B. E. Lasswitz, W. D. Bruce and Cochrane. Middle row: Sgts. J. Turnbull, Nicholson and Service; S/Sgts. Walker and M. H. E. Hayne; Sgts. F. B. Hyles, R. Featherstone, P. Walters and C. Corneil. Rear: Sgts. Henderson, G. Birchall and Alfred Howe.

18. Headquarters NWMP band playing outside Commissioner Herchmer's house on the barrack square at Regina, 1890 (National Archives, C-18997).

19. "D" Division under Supt. Sam Steele, wearing white helmet, on the march from Fort Steele to Fort Macleod, August 1888.

20. Supt. Samuel Benfield Steele.

21. Supt. Joseph Howe's funeral at Macleod in 1902. The firing party at the slow march with rifles reversed leads the gun carriage carrying the body to the grave site.

22. "The Tampered Brand" by Canadian artist Arthur Heming. Stealing cattle by changing their brands was a common offence. This black and white drawing is now at the RCMP Academy, Regina.

23. "Home Sweet Home". A barrack room at Battleford, 1898. From left to right: Cst. C. Draycott, Cpl. George Alleger, the Division librarian, Cpl. Jackson, 15-year-old bugler, F. J. Burke, Sgt. A. H. Richardson, who would later win the Victoria Cross in South Africa, Cst. J. Allen, Cst. Bob Prissick and Cst. Brennan.

24. A montage of police photographs put together by Steele & Co. of Winnipeg to be sold as a greeting card for Christmas and New Years.

25. NWMP mounted band at Regina, 1890, under Sgt. Harry Walker (left foreground). The sound of the music sometimes had a frightened horse going in one direction and the bandsmen in another. Mounted bands did not last very long because of the damage to instruments.

26. Sketches of the Canadian Mounted Police by the American artist Frederic Remington.

27. Remington's drawing of the charge of the NWMP Musical Ride which appeared in *Harper's Weekly* on 24 December 1887.

28. S/Sgt. Pat Mahoney "was a wonderful foot drill instructor" recalled a recruit. "One of the old school" who used a "little rough talk". "No kid glove handling methods with Pat." (Glenbow-Alberta Institute, NA-307-2).

29. A social afternoon for the officer class at Macleod, 1899. Standing left to right: Mrs. C. E. D. Wood, Insp. J. O. Wilson, unknown, John Cowdry, one of the first bankers in the NWT, Mr. C. E. D. Wood, ex-Constable of the NWMP, publisher of the *Macleod Gazette* and a frequent critic of Herchmer. Sitting: Insp. Z. T. Wood, a relative of the publisher, Mrs. Z. T. Wood, Mrs. J. O. Wilson and Emily Horn, the maid.

30. Members of the Stand Off detachment on the Blood Reserve, 1890. Back row: Scout Hunbury, Interpreter Jerry Potts. Middle row: Scout Cecil Denny (former Inspector), S/Sgt. C. Hilliard and Sgt. G. Cotter. Front row: Scouts Black Eagle and Elk.

31. Group of constables at Battleford in 1895 in typical everyday working attire.

32. NWMP cricket team, "E" Division, Calgary, 1890s.

33. The imposing riding school in Regina. In this building the first NWMP musical rides were performed in the winter of 1887.

34. NWMP town station, Regina, 1895. Once described as having holes in the floor, a cracked stove, no storm door and no toilet.

35. NWMP badge.

36. Fred White, Comptroller in charge of the Mounted Police, 1878-1913.

37. Ten Mile detachment in the Cypress Hills, 1891. The police kept lots of dogs, especially large ones, that went with them on patrol.

38. Writing on Stone detachment. A lonely and isolated post close to the American border from which desertions sometimes occurred.

39. Boundary Creek detachment, 1887. Log walls chinked with mud and a sod roof. Hospital S/Sgt. J. F. Foster, mounted.

40. Graburn detachment in the Cypress Hills about 1890 was named after Cst. Marmaduke Graburn who was murdered nearby in 1879 by a person or persons unknown. One of the first cases in which the Mounties "did not get their man".

41. Winchester model 1876 .45/75 calibre carbine in service with the police from 1878 to 1914.

42. Lee-Metford bolt action .303 calibre carbine in service from 1895 to 1914.

43. Mark II Enfield .476 calibre revolver in service with the police 1882 to 1905.

44. On patrol in "prairie dress", Maple Creek, 1890.

45. Aylesworth Bowen Perry who succeeded Herchmer as Commissioner of the NWMP in 1900.

46. Blood Indian Charcoal, or Si'k-Okskitis, who was hanged at Macleod in 1897 for the murder of Sgt. W. B. Wilde (Glenbow-Alberta Institute).

47. S/Sgt. C. Hilliard and Blood Indian scouts at Fort Macleod in 1894. Some of these had an outstanding and courageous role in the pursuit of Charcoal two years later. They are from left to right: Hilliard, Calf Tail, Many White Horses, Black Eagle, Meat Mouth, Many Mules, Tailfeathers and Big Rib.

48. With their "prairie suits", "cowboy hats", bandoliers, Winchester carbines and revolvers at the cross draw, members of the NWMP at the Queen's Diamond Jubilee looked like just the kind of resourceful, mobile men of action that were needed to keep the peace on the far flung corners of the Empire.

49. Members of the Jubilee contingent in London, 1897. From left to right: S/Maj. A. E. C. McDonell, Cst. H. Cobb, S/Sgt. Fred Bagley, Supt. A. B. Perry, Sgt. H. G. Joyce, Cpl. E. Harris, Sgt. S. W. Davis.

50. The "E" Division band under S/Sgt. Fred Bagley (seated centre in front of the bass drum) at Banff in 1888 to play at the newly opened Banff Springs Hotel.

51. NWMP contingent at Queen Victoria's Diamond Jubilee in London, 1897. Their proud bearing and workman-like dress caught the imagination of the crowds in the capital of the British Empire. The "very beau ideal of a soldier," said the *Montreal Star*. Their "picturesque and soldier-like appearance," reported the *London Times*, "excited great enthusiasm."

52. Information for applicants for engagement in the NWMP, 1897.

53. The oath of office and the oath of allegiance required to be attested to by all recruits since the organization of the Force in 1873. Those of non-British origin were considered to be eligible for engagement once they had sworn allegiance to Her Majesty Queen Victoria.

54. Menu card for Christmas dinner at "F" Division, Prince Albert, 1888.

55. The discharge certificate issued to all members. This one is for Cpl. J. G. Donkin, the author of *Trooper and Redskin*.

56. An example of the notorious liquor permits required to import alcohol into the NWT. This one is made out to Commissioner Irvine for one barrel of beer for domestic purposes and is signed by the Governor, Edgar Dewdney.

57. Schedule of free kit issued to new recruits.

58. Diagram showing how to lay kit out on the bed for inspection.

59. Recruiting poster for the NWMP, 1893.

60. Constables on patrol were required to visit every settler they passed on their route and ask them if they had any complaints. The settler was then asked to sign this patrol slip indicating that he had been visited and asked the question.

61. NWMP detachment, Pincher Creek, 1895, with Sgt. W. B. Wilde, who was murdered by Charcoal a year later, seated centre (Glenbow-Alberta Institute).

Acknowledgments

There simply is not enough room to acknowledge and thank all of the many individuals and institutions who made this publication possible. The contribution of some, however, was so substantial as to merit their recognition. We owe a great debt to Malcolm Wake, the former Director of the RCMP Centennial Museum in Regina, and his staff who freely placed the resources of the Museum at our disposal, gave willingly of their expert knowledge on numerous subjects and gladly answered our many questions. A special thanks goes to Constable Sean Murphy who spent many eye-straining hours reading newspapers on microfilm. We are grateful to Chief Superintendents John Bentham, Jim Walker, Jacques Lemay and Dawson Hovey for the administrative support and encouragement they provided over many years.

Stan Hansen and Doug Bocking of the Saskatchewan Archives Board in Saskatoon were very helpful in facilitating access to the records available in their custody. We are indebted also to Glen Gordon of the RCMP Historical Section. His extensive knowledge of RCMP records enabled him to ferret out many a file and fact that greatly reduced the burden of research for us. Glenn Wright provided constructive criticism and literary editing for the original manuscript. His professional assistance added much value to the book.

We thank Denis Smail and Al Nicholson of PrintWest Publishing Services for accepting this book for publication, and also thank the co-publishers, Friends of the Museum, and IKON Office Solutions for their commitment to the project. Thank you to Lori Bateman for providing copy edit, to Iona Glabus for proofing and coordinating and to Margo Embury of Centax Books for production management. We thank also Paul Edmondson and Dan Marce of PrintWest for their assistance in production and distribution.

This study would not have been possible without access to the indispensable services and resources of the National Archives of Canada and its staff. Joanne Frodsham was especially helpful with her expert advice on the large collection of NWMP records held there.

The translation of this work into French was expertly accomplished by Daniel Poliquin with the assistance of terminologist Mario Gagne. Collaboration with these two consummate professionals was always a pleasure and we are proud of the French edition of our history. Louis King provided copy edit for the French edition.

Finally and especially, the authors would like to acknowledge the support received from the members of their families, Joan, Megan and Katie Beahen and Sarah, Ruth, Sean, Andrew and Caitlin Horrall.

Authors

William Beahen

William Beahen has been employed for eighteen years in the Historical Branch, becoming the RCMP Historian in 1992. He was previously employed as a researcher with the Canadian War Museum, an intelligence analyst with the Communications Security Establishment and an historian with Parks Canada.

Bill was born in Ottawa and pursued his studies in English Literature and History at the University of Ottawa, obtaining his doctorate in 1980. Bill and his wife, Joan, are the parents of two girls, Megan and Katie.

Stan Horrall

Stan Horrall was RCMP Historian for almost twenty-five years, until his retirement in 1992. During that time, he was the author of numerous works on the history of Canada's famous police force.

Born in England, he emigrated to Canada in 1954. Following service as a constable in both the RCMP and Metropolitan Toronto Police, he studied history at Carleton University in Ottawa, the University of Toronto and University College, Dublin. The father of three grown children, Stan lives with his wife, Ruth, in Braeside, Ontario.

General Introduction

The Royal Canadian Mounted Police has a long and interesting history of service in Canada. Founded in 1873 as the North-West Mounted Police it was the arm of the federal government in a succession of frontiers on the prairies, the Yukon and the Arctic. Renamed the Royal Northwest Mounted Police in 1904, it assumed provincial police duties the following year in Alberta and Saskatchewan. In 1920, the RCMP absorbed the Dominion Police and became a national law enforcement agency with its jurisdiction extended from sea to sea to sea. Over the years new duties of federal, provincial and municipal law enforcement have been continually added to the mandate of the Force.

Detailing the history of this complex organization has always offered a special challenge to scholars and writers. Fortunately, since the beginning of the Force its exploits had been recorded in the Annual Reports of the Commissioner published in the *Parliamentary Sessional Papers*. This has provided ready reference to generations of researchers. For those wishing to go beyond published sources, there are several hundred yards of Mounted Police records in the National Archives of Canada. However, very little of this material deals with the period 1873 to 1886 because these records were destroyed in a fire in the NWMP office in Ottawa in 1897. But for the years after 1886, this material is formidable in volume. There is also Mounted Police-related archival material in most of the provincial archives in Canada, especially in Alberta and Saskatchewan.

The Royal Canadian Mounted Police has for many years employed historians to interpret the history of the organization for its own officers and for the general public. Until recently the Historical Branch has consisted of two historians, an historical researcher and a photograph archivist in Ottawa and four professional museologists at the RCMP Museum in Regina. For the most part this small group was kept busy answering questions about the Force's past and helping others to explore it through study of its material heritage and recording events in publications and on film. Restructuring of the RCMP has resulted in reducing the size of the Historian's office in Ottawa to one professional historian.

There have been many books written about Mounted Police history and an annotated bibliography is included in this volume. However, very few of these works have dealt with the subject in a scholarly fashion, meaning professional historians applying critical study of original documents. There are four notable exceptions to this rule. S. W. Horrall's *The Pictorial History of the Royal Canadian Mounted Police* (McGraw-Hill Ryerson 1973) is an excellent comprehensive overview of Force history. *The North West Mounted Police and Law Enforcement, 1873-1905* (University of Toronto Press 1976) by R. C. Macleod is a groundbreaking critical appreciation of the development of the Mounted Police in its social and political context. Keith Walden's *Vision of Order: The Canadian Mounties in Symbol and Myth* (Butterworth Press 1983) is an intellectual study of the Force's place in the consciousness of Canadians. And, also worthy of mention is William R. Morrison's *Showing the Flag: The Mounted Police and Canadian Sovereignty in the North, 1894-1925* (University of British Columbia Press 1985).

But to date nobody has tried to produce a comprehensive and scholarly account of what the Force was and what it did. A previous RCMP historian, J. P. Turner, tackled this task to a degree with his two-volume *The North-West Mounted Police, 1873-1893* (King's Printer 1950). But this work was a chronicle of NWMP doings, heavily reliant on the published annual reports, and with virtually no critical appreciation. Therefore, the two RCMP historians, William Beahen and Stan Horrall, received permission from their superiors to embark on a history of the period of Commissioner Lawrence Herchmer, 1886 to 1900, to delineate the important frontier period of the Mounted Police in the West. The co-authors divided the project into two parts because the material suggested such a division was natural and because this simplified the research and writing. In general, Part I is the work of William Beahen and Part II that of Stanley Horrall, but there is a cross-over in the contributions of the authors. They have restricted themselves to the Mounted Police activities on the prairie frontier for this volume. The NWMP in the Yukon and South Africa were not covered in this volume.

One question which will surely arise in the minds of many readers is the use of the term "Indians" throughout this book. Though the terms "Aboriginal people" and "First Nations" are more familiar to the modern reader they were unknown in the nineteenth century about which the authors are writing. Therefore the documents from which the authors quote always use the term "Indians" and so for the sake of consistency in the text and to better reflect the nineteenth century usage they retain this word throughout. No slight is in any way intended to Aboriginal peoples and the authors hope that their respect for them is demonstrated in the sensitivity they show to the changes Aboriginal peoples endured in this difficult period in their history. Similarly the occasional use of the outmoded term "half-breed" is in no way intended to demean the people of Métis origin who contributed so significantly to the success of the NWMP.

There is some peril in the occupation of official historians. There is a common perception that even scholarly histories produced in such circumstances are rightly suspect. The organization which supported the project may place preconditions on the authors or may vet the manuscript produced. Or the authors wishing to please their superiors and colleagues may consciously or unconsciously downplay the organization's shortcomings and overpraise its achievements. In the case of this volume there were no preconditions and no vetting. The authors tried to overcome a confessed admiration of the RCMP with an objective story, warts and all. How well they achieved this is up to the reader to judge.

Part I: Taming the Frontier

Introduction

In 1886, the Canadian government was reeling from a major failure in its policy of western development. The previous year a substantial number of Métis and Indian people in the West had violently rejected the government's method of accommodating them in the new West. The uprising had been suppressed with violence and peace achieved by military defeat and punishment of the rebel leaders. The prospect of further trouble between the Aboriginal people and the incoming settlers from the East and from Europe seemed likely.

Once again the government turned to the North-West Mounted Police as its principal instrument in ensuring the orderly transition of the western frontier. The Force had accomplished much between 1874 and 1885 to win the confidence of the Aboriginal people. Largely because of this most of the Indians chose not to participate in the North-West Rebellion. The government hoped that by doubling the size of the NWMP from 500 to 1,000 and by appointing a new leader, the Force would solve any future difficulties.

Prime Minister John A. Macdonald had a number of candidates available from which to choose a new Commissioner for the NWMP in 1886. There were several excellent officers already in the Force and also British Army officers who could be enticed to assume the command. Instead, Macdonald picked Lawrence Herchmer, a politically well-connected official of the Indian department. Herchmer had distinct advantages in that he was an experienced westerner and knew the Aboriginal people. But he had limited experience in the military and knew nothing of police work. His tenure as Commissioner would be an interesting and dynamic period for the NWMP.

Part I of this book, entitled "Taming the Frontier", will deal with how the Force faced the challenge of ensuring the orderly development of a society in transition of monumental proportions. In the first few years, the largely white male settlers and transient labourers had expectations and appetites which were not always legal or in accordance with the community standards the government wanted established in the West. This put them in conflict with the principal law enforcement agents, the Mounted Police. Later immigrants, many from Europe, were eager but unprepared to take up a homestead role on the frontier. The police were tasked with ensuring their security.

The existence of a lengthy border between the west of Canada and the United States added an interesting aspect to controlling the transition of the frontier. Although much mythologized, it is true that the American West was more violent than that of Canada. The NWMP were vigilant in ensuring that this criminal behaviour would not cross the border. The Force was also charged with regulating border crossing through enforcement of customs, agriculture and immigration regulations.

Inevitably, of course, crime came with increasing frequency as the population of the West increased. The range of crime ran the entire gamut of human weakness and depravity. The NWMP responded in a manner which won them a justifiable reputation for efficiency. They may not have gotten their man every time, but they were a formidable force against criminal activity.

Chapter 1

A New Commissioner, A New Order

On 15 July 1870, the new Dominion of Canada acquired sovereignty over the territory that would eventually comprise the provinces of Manitoba, Saskatchewan and Alberta. Two centuries earlier King Charles II of England granted this vast area to The Governor and Company of Adventurers of England Trading into Hudson's Bay, or the Hudson's Bay Company, as it was later called. The Company called its trading empire "Rupert's Land". To Canadians in the mid-nineteenth century it was known as the "North-West", and they developed a compelling interest in obtaining jurisdiction over it. To the men who created the new nation of Canada on 1 July 1867 the union of Ontario, Quebec, New Brunswick and Nova Scotia was just a beginning. The Fathers of Confederation hoped to unite all the British colonies in North America from the Atlantic to the Pacific. The acquisition of Rupert's Land was absolutely vital if British Columbia was to be a part of this "dominion from sea to sea". With the agreement of the British government, the Hudson's Bay Company was financially compensated for its rights and sovereignty over the area was transferred to Canada in 1870. That same year, a small part of it, the settlements along the banks of the Red River and its tributaries, became the new province of Manitoba. The remainder was designated the North-West Territories.

The area had not changed much in the two centuries it had been under suzerainty of the Hudson's Bay Company. The latter had discouraged white settlement. The population largely consisted of nomadic Indian nations whose culture was based upon fishing and hunting, particularly the enormous herds of buffalo that inhabited the vast open prairie grass lands to the south, and the Métis peo-

ple, the descendants of Native women and white traders. In the minds of most eastern Canadians the territory was perceived as a lawless frontier where drunken and savage Indians murdered and scalped settlers. Their suspicions were confirmed by a British officer, Lt. William Butler, who was commissioned by the government to survey the country in 1871. Butler dubbed it the "Great Lone Land", and reported that "The institutions of Law and Order, as understood in civilized communities, are wholly unknown".

Sir John A. Macdonald's answer to the problem of disorder and the threat of Indian violence in the North-West Territories was to organize a force of "Mounted Riflemen, trained to act as cavalry, but also instructed in the Rifle exercise". This body, Canada's first Prime Minister conceived, "should not be expressly Military but should be styled Police, and have the military bearing of the Irish Constabulary." It would proceed to the western plains, establish law and order and reach a peaceful understanding with the Indian nations about their future and that of their traditional hunting grounds in advance of settlement. In this manner Canada would avoid the armed conflict associated with expansion on the American frontier, the prairies would be peacefully opened up to white settlers and the railway could be built that would link eastern Canada with British Columbia.

Recruiting for the 300-man force began in the fall of 1873. The following year, under the command of Comm. George A. French, the North-West Mounted Police made its epic march from Manitoba to the foothills of the Rocky Mountains. Dressed in red tunics so that it would be readily identifiable to the Native people as British and not American, the Force's immediate task was to stop the whisky trade that was disrupting the Indian way of life and establish posts from which justice could be administered. During the years that followed, the Mounted Police, through their impartial enforcement of the law, played a significant role in gaining the trust of Native leaders, and induced them to make treaties with the Canadian government and to settle on reserves. Unfortunately, with the rapid disappearance of the buffalo and the coming of white settlers and government officials, the good relations that had existed earlier between the police and the Indians turned somewhat sour.

The reputation of the NWMP was considerably enhanced when it attracted international attention by its successful handling of the Sioux under Sitting Bull. In 1876, the warriors of this band had sent shock waves around the world following their annihilation of an American military force under Col. George A. Custer at the Battle of the Little Big Horn. Fearing retaliation by a larger concentration of American troops, the Sioux fled across the border into Canada. Here a small band of Mounted Police in the Cypress Hills had the difficult task of preventing them from continuing their war with the Americans on Canadian soil, ensuring that they did not disrupt the Canadian bands, and inducing them to surrender peacefully to United States' authorities.

The problem of finding a compatible and competent Commissioner to command the Force had plagued successive governments since 1873. George French, who had been responsible for the initial organization of the NWMP and had led the March West, refused to take orders from bureaucrats in Ottawa who he believed were ill-informed as to the actual conditions prevailing in the West. In 1876, the Liberal government of Alexander Mackenzie forced French to resign, and he returned to his career in the British Army. His successor was James F. Macleod, a qualified lawyer, who had been second in command to French until he resigned from the Force in January 1876 to fill the post of stipendiary magistrate for the North-West Territories. Now, seven months later, Macleod returned to the Mounted Police as Commissioner. He subsequently played a decisive role in convincing the chiefs of the Blackfoot Confederacy to agree to the terms of Treaty No. 7, but his financial management of the Force was a disaster. For this reason, Macdonald (who had returned to power in 1878) removed him from office in September 1880; Macleod was succeeded by his second in command, Acheson G. Irvine, Assistant Commissioner of the Force since 1876. Irvine was a more pliant individual than either of his predecessors, a situation that undoubtedly pleased Macdonald. However, to ensure that the future management of the Mounted Police was on a sound footing, a Comptroller was appointed in Ottawa to assume some of the Commissioner's administrative and financial responsibilities.

Irvine's incumbency, however, was undermined by the growing unrest among Métis and Indians for a redress of their grievances that would eventually lead to the outbreak of rebellion. In March 1885, a force of Métis under Gabriel Dumont seized the trading post and its stores at Duck Lake, and called upon Supt. Lief N. F. Crozier of the Mounted Police to surrender his post at Fort Carleton. The latter, with a party of police and civilian volunteers from Prince Albert, set out to confront the Métis, hoping that bold action would nip the rebellion in the bud. In the skirmish that ensued, however, Crozier's force was outnumbered and outgunned, and hastily beat a retreat suffering 12 killed and 11 wounded. After several engagements the rebellion was finally crushed in May 1885 by a military force from eastern Canada under the command of Major General F. D. Middleton.

By the fall of 1885 Irvine's future as Commissioner of the NWMP had been settled. Macdonald had decided that he had to go.[1] It was ironic that one of the few to recognize that trouble was brewing in the North-West and to urge Ottawa to do something should be used as a scapegoat by his political masters. Irvine's problems were partly of his own making, however. He had been too submissive with both his superiors and his subordinates. Some of his senior officers needed to be firmly handled. Discipline and efficiency in the Force had suffered. Even before the rebellion the *Regina Leader* and the *Toronto Globe* had begun a campaign for his removal, citing his lack of leadership and the absence of discipline.[2] The truth was that "Old Sorrel Top" was well liked but too good-natured to command effectively.

It was the rebellion and General Middleton that actually triggered his downfall. Irvine had remained in Prince Albert waiting for orders to come that would give him a chance to make his mark in the campaign. Instead, Middleton had ignored him. His "High Mightiness"[3] then added insult to injury by accusing him of running scared into the town and hiding there behind "hastily and imperfectly" erected fortifications.[4] The General's contempt was quickly picked up by eastern troops and the press. The Mounted Police were labelled "gophers".[5] Middleton was quoted in the *Regina Leader* as having said, "I must go to Prince Albert and get that gopher [meaning Irvine] out of his hole."[6] In spite of the impressive march he had led from Regina to Prince Albert, the damage had been done. Nicholas Flood Davin, the editor and owner of the *Regina Leader*, now had all the ammunition he needed to get rid of the Commissioner. The paper repeatedly called on Irvine to explain why he had kept 350 men sitting idle for a month in the middle of the troubled area; it described him as a "light weight" and insinuated that he was a coward.[7] Irvine could have defended himself, but he characteristically refused to enter into controversy. Requests from journalists for a statement were turned down.[8] He was satisfied merely to state his case dutifully in his official annual report for 1885.[9] This, however, was not made public until several months later. By then it was too late. Detachments of mounted police under Supts. Sam Steele, A. B. Perry and William Herchmer had served creditably elsewhere in the military campaign. Nevertheless, Irvine's seemingly inexplicable inaction, coupled with Crozier's retreat at Duck Lake, resulted in the reputation of the NWMP being seriously impaired and shook public confidence in its ability.[10] Things were not as bad as Middleton painted them when he claimed that the Mounted Police "have lost all prestige with the whites",[11] but Macdonald was left little choice but to seek a change in command.

The Prime Minister's first inclination was to find an experienced and reputable British army officer to take over. In May 1885, he offered the command to Lord Melgund, one of Middleton's staff officers. The future Earl of Minto, Governor General of Canada from 1898 to 1904 and first Honourary Commissioner of the Force, turned down the proposal.[12] During the summer, Middleton urged the government to reorganize the Mounted Police into a corps of mounted infantry under the Department of Militia and Defence,[13] but Macdonald apparently ignored the suggestion. Supt. R. B. Deane is probably right in stating that the Prime Minister resented the General's criticisms of the Force;[14] after all, as the responsible minister, Middleton's criticisms reflected upon him too.

It was common knowledge by the fall of 1885 that the search for a successor to Irvine was underway. Deane heard from a "man in the know" that there were three names in the running: Col. E. T. H. Hutton, a British Army officer; L. W. Herchmer, Indian Agent; and himself.[15] At least two other candidates offered their services including Lt. Colonel W. Osborne Smith, who had been Commissioner temporarily in 1873, and Maj. Gen. T. B. Strange, a retired British officer who had taken up ranching near Calgary.[16] Both men had served with the Canadian Militia, and both were experienced westerners. Maj. Samuel L. Bedson, the warden of Stony Mountain Penitentiary, was also mentioned[17] as a possible successor to Irvine.

Hutton was the front-runner for a while. Lord Lansdowne, the Governor General, favoured his appointment, arguing that an outsider who was free of local prejudices and party politics would be good for the Force.[18] The *Edmonton Bulletin* agreed with him, while expressing regret that it was necessary to go to the "Old Country" to find someone who would be free of political influence.[19] With the assistance of Lansdowne and Lord Melgund, who had returned to England, Macdonald began negotiating the possibility of Hutton accepting the command for a five-year period.[20] Here was one of the difficulties of selecting someone from the Imperial service. No up-and-coming British officer was likely to accept the position as a career. It would simply be a stepping stone to further advancement. Such was the case with Hutton. He was an ambitious and aggressive soldier who had seen active service in Egypt and was considered an expert on mounted infantry. Macdonald, however, changed his mind about the need for a British officer, and Hutton, fortunately, was informed that his services would not be needed.[21] The Government, the Prime Minister explained to him in February 1886, had decided that the job was "more civil than military" and preferred a man who would make it a career.[22]

In early February 1886 a serious "mutiny" broke out among the mounted policemen stationed in Edmonton. This scandalous affront to discipline seems to have been the final straw that broke Irvine. Within days he was summoned to Ottawa.[23] He must have known that a sword had been hanging over his head for months; it was now about to fall.

News of Irvine's departure from Regina touched off another round of applications from office-seekers. One who telegraphed Macdonald to let him know that he was still interested in the position was Lawrence William Herchmer, Inspector of Indian Agencies at Regina.[24] His message prompted Macdonald to wire Edgar Dewdney, Lieutenant-Governor of the Territories, instructing him to send Herchmer to Ottawa.[25] By the time Herchmer arrived in the capital, Irvine had already submitted his resignation, the third Commissioner of the NWMP to be forced from office by his superiors.

There is no record of what passed between Irvine and Macdonald during his visit to Ottawa, but the Commissioner was not to face the ignominy of being shown the door. His departure from the Mounted Police was officially announced as a change of jobs. He was offered and accepted the position of Indian Agent to the Blood Indian Reserve. It would mean a reduction in salary, but Irvine accepted it quietly. He would create no waves for the politicians. There was to be no traditional handing over of command, however. He chose not to face the triumphant glow of his successor. When Herchmer arrived at the Commissioner's office on 1 April 1886, to assume the reins of power, he found that his predecessor had already left for Fort Macleod. In his farewell message Irvine thanked the men for their hearty support.[26] His departure was widely regretted by the rank and file[27] and at Fort Macleod he was feted by the local citizens and members of the Force. In

1892, he was appointed warden of Stony Mountain Penitentiary. A lifelong bachelor, he died in Quebec City in 1916, quietly resentful of the shabby treatment he had received.[28]

Lawrence Herchmer "fills the bill" declared the *Regina Leader*: "He is an officer of the regular army, having been trained at Sandhurst. He knows the country, knows the Indians; is a man of business; with decisions of character; speaks French; is in the prime of life; in a word, fills the bill."[29] Lieutenant-Governor Dewdney, who was also Indian Commissioner for the Territories endorsed his suitability, advising Macdonald that Herchmer's move would be a great loss to his department.[30] There was a good deal of truth in these assessments of the new Commissioner of the NWMP. Lawrence William Herchmer was born at Shipton on Cherwell near Oxford, England on 25 April 1840. His mother was Frances Turner, a niece of the English landscape painter J. M. W. Turner. His father, the Rev. William Macauley Herchmer, was a Canadian from Kingston, Ontario. The elder Herchmer had been educated at Oxford University and for a time was Chaplain to the Bishop of Bristol. After his return to Canada, he was for many years Rector of St. George's Church in Kingston. The place of birth was no accident. Rev. W. M. Herchmer insisted that all his children be born on English soil, necessitating nine such trips for his compliant wife. The Herchmers' roots were firmly Loyalist, Anglican and Tory.[31] Their forebears had come to the American colonies with the Hessian Regiments that the British had brought over in the eighteenth century to fight the French. They eventually settled in the Mohawk Valley in New York State, where Herkimer County is named after them. During the American War of Independence the family was divided, brother fighting against brother. On the American side, General Nicholas Herkimer led a force against the British at the Battle of Oriskany, one of the bloodiest engagements of the War. The loyalist side of the family received land grants in the township of Kingston and, through marriage, soon became connected with some of the leading families of that growing Upper Canadian settlement. The Commissioner's father was a "school fellow and long life friend" of John A. Macdonald, a relationship which certainly had some influence on his sons' appointments to the NWMP. The Herchmers were also members of the same Masonic Lodge in Kingston as the Prime Minister.[32]

The new Commissioner already had one brother in the police, Supt. William Macauley Herchmer. Another brother, George F. Herchmer, had served from 1875-1881 as a staff sergeant.

Lawrence Herchmer had been educated at a preparatory school in England, Trinity College, Toronto and the Royal Military Academy, Woolwich [the *Regina Leader* was in error in saying he went to Sandhurst]. At age 17 he obtained a commission as an ensign in the 46th Regiment of Foot, the South Devonshire Regiment. He served with this unit in India and Ireland. Following the death of his father in 1862, he sold his commission and returned to the Kingston area to take up farming. When Herchmer married Mary Sherwood in 1866, the daughter of Henry Sherwood, a former Attorney General of Upper Canada and leader of the Family Compact, he became closely allied to the upper crust of Ontario society. For reasons unknown, Herchmer decided along with his two brothers, to leave Ontario in the early 1870s and seek their fortunes in the West. In 1872, Macdonald appointed him Commissariat Officer (supply and transport officer) with the British North American Boundary Commission. During the two years that it marked the border between the United States and Canada, Herchmer undoubtedly came into contact with the Mounted Police on their March West. In 1874, he established and operated a brewery in Winnipeg. Two years later he was appointed an Indian agent. For the next decade he remained with the Indian Department, serving at various agencies until he was promoted to Inspector of Indian Agencies in 1885.[33]

The new Commissioner was in many respects ideally suited for his position: he was an experienced westerner; he had been in the country since it was "The Great Lone Land"; he had witnessed the passing of the old order of nomadic Indian nations and the Métis buffalo hunt. The difficulties associated with the transition to settled agricultural communities must have been familiar to him. What better choice than someone who had already spent several years administering to the Indians. He could be expected to work closely with his former department. Nevertheless, his selection was questionable. In spite of his political connections, he had no reputation, not even in the Territories. He was merely an experienced official of the Indian department. The claims made for his military experience were a little hollow considering they dated back over 20 years. In fact, his "military deficiencies" were to be a source of embarrassment and amusement to his subordinates. The likely explanation is that Macdonald saw in him a capable, hard working civil servant who would dutifully take orders from his superiors in Ottawa, and efficiently administer the police, especially in regard to expenditures. In this he was largely correct. What the Prime Minister did not realize, however, was that Herchmer's personal temperament would make his task very difficult.

Herchmer faced one formidable obstacle from the moment he assumed office. He was an outsider and several senior officers resented his appointment in the belief that it should have gone to one of them. From what they knew of him as an Indian agent, they considered him unfit and unqualified to command.[34] Throughout his service Herchmer would never enjoy the full confidence or support of some of them. The *Edmonton Bulletin* objected to his appointment because he had no special qualification, and there were officers already in the Force who were more entitled to the position.[35]

The first to protest was Assistant Commissioner Crozier. As second in command, he naturally felt that he had some right to the succession. "Paddy" Crozier, the proud, spirited Irishman, the man of action who had been instrumental in convincing Sitting Bull to return to the United States, and had figured in many stirring events of the early days, regarded Herchmer's appointment as a slap in the face. His brother wrote to the Prime Minister to complain of the humiliation and injustice of placing a civilian over his head. Macdonald's reply, that the government had done what it thought in the best interests of the public service, only added insult to injury.[36] As if to rub it in, Herchmer seemingly abrogated some of Crozier's responsibility by appointing his brother, Supt. William M. Herchmer, Inspecting Superintendent. That was enough for Crozier. He resigned in June 1886.

Macdonald was glad to see him go. Crozier had been promoted to the vacant office of Assistant Commissioner on the strength of the first reports the government had received about the encounter at Duck Lake. The Prime Minister no doubt regretted his haste when he learned the full facts. The *Regina Leader* also welcomed his departure, agreeing with Macdonald that efficiency should come before seniority.[37] Crozier spent much of the rest of his life engaged in various business enterprises in the United States until his death in Oklahoma in 1901.

Supt. R. B. Deane also resented Herchmer's advancement. Deane was born in India into a family with a long military tradition.[38] He received his education in England and after attending the Royal Military College at Sandhurst, he obtained a commission as lieutenant in the Royal Marines. He saw active service in 1874 on the Gold Coast during the Ashanti War. In 1881, he was promoted to Captain, but the following year the establishment of the Royal Marines was substantially reduced and his career disappeared overnight. Like many of his class, he was forced to start again in the colonies. He brought his family to Canada where, through the influence of T. C. Patteson, a cousin who was well connected to the Conservative Party, he obtained a commission as an Inspector in the NWMP in 1883.[39] Deane was an able and efficient officer; he was well educated, widely read and had the manners and bearing of a gentleman. Unfortunately, as his autobiography attests, he was also very opinionated,

conceited and quick to pour contempt and sarcasm on anyone who disagreed with him. During the fall of 1885, Deane had good reason to believe that he was a leading contender for the Commissioner's position. He had a powerful backer in his cousin who was a close colleague of Macdonald and editor of the party's principal organ, the *Toronto Mail*.

If Herchmer's appointment sparked indignation amongst senior officers, some of his early decisions increased the bitter resentment already felt toward him. Before taking command he convinced Ottawa that a group of officers at Fort Macleod known as the "Macleod clique"[40] (so called because of their independent and self-interested attitudes), should be broken up. The commanding officer at Fort Macleod was Supt. John Cotton, a son-in-law of the Minister of the Interior, Thomas White. Cotton also served as Collector of Customs for the district, and this was reputed to be a very lucrative position. When Herchmer transferred him to Battleford in the summer of 1886, he created another dedicated enemy.

The new Commissioner's overbearing, vindictive and ill-tempered nature soon made itself felt. Deane, who was adjutant in Regina, found that Herchmer lost no opportunity "to vent his spite upon myself", that he was "an impossible man to work with", and complained that he had to dry-nurse him because of the many deficiencies in his "semi-military education".[41] The hatred between the two men even extended to their wives, and eventually led to Deane's transfer to Lethbridge. In order to avoid meeting his superior face to face, Deane developed a little bit of insubordinate subterfuge. Whenever Herchmer visited the post at Lethbridge on official duty, Deane would sign himself off duty, sick, and retire to his quarters, leaving his second in command to meet with the Commissioner. If any communication was necessary between the two men, it was done by hand-written notes carried by an orderly. As soon as Herchmer left, Deane miraculously recovered.

Supt. Sam Steele was another who was piqued over the appointment of Herchmer. Political friends made strenuous efforts to secure the position of Assistant Commissioner vacated by Crozier for him, but it went to the Commissioner's brother instead. When Herchmer accused him of gross negligence, Steele protested to Comptroller White, demanding an official enquiry and stating that the Commissioner had spoken to him in a manner that no officer should be spoken to.[42] Herchmer had certainly started off on the wrong foot with some of his officers. It did not augur well for the future. In fact, his relationship with many of them would get worse, and Macdonald and White must have already started to have some misgivings. In the meantime Herchmer settled in with energy and determination to put the NWMP back in order. To carry this out, announced Davin optimistically in the *Leader*, he has got carte blanche from Ottawa and the assurance that there will be no political interference.[43]

As was often the case with Davin, there was more rhetoric than substance in his claim. Herchmer was energetic and sincere in seeking new cures for old ills, advocating improvements and pushing for sensible changes, but he could introduce little that was new without first getting Ottawa's approval. In fact, the Commissioner's authority had declined since the days of French and Macleod. Macdonald reacted to the independent mindedness of the former and financial mismanagement of the latter by systematically increasing the authority of the bureaucrats in Ottawa over Mounted Police matters. By the time Herchmer took office, the real power, apart from the minister, over administrative and organizational affairs lay in the hands of the Comptroller of the NWMP, Frederick White, one of Ottawa's first civil service mandarins.

White appears to have been a genuine Canadian Horatio Alger, who rose from office boy to deputy minister on the strength of his ability and hard work.[44] He was born in Birmingham, England in 1847, the son of an accountant for the Great Western Railway. While still a teenager he came to Canada, where he worked for a while in the offices of the Grand Trunk Railway in Montreal. Shortly after Confederation be obtained a clerkship in the Department of Justice in Ottawa. His talents attracted the attention of the deputy minister, Hewitt Bernard, Macdonald's brother-in-law, and he was soon making his way up the ladder of bureaucratic success. Under Bernard he assisted with the original organization of the Mounted Police in 1873-74. When control of the Force was transferred to the Secretary of State in 1876, a distinct NWMP Branch was established to handle the work. In 1878, White became head clerk of the branch. The following year Macdonald had the *Mounted Police Act* amended so that the minister's authority over management was more clearly stated.[45] Between 1880 and 1882 he was also the Prime Minister's private secretary, being succeeded by Joseph Pope.[46] As a final measure of Macdonald's trust, White was raised to deputy minister status in 1883. By the time Herchmer appeared, there was little that the Comptroller did not know about the men and the management of the Mounted Police. White was also a member of the Ottawa elite, thereby providing the social status that added to his influence as a senior public servant. He married Clara Cruice, a descendant of two of the area's oldest pioneer families, the Wrights and the Symmes'. One of his daughters married Charles Maclaren, the wealthy lumber merchant. Another helped found the Elmwood School for girls in Rockcliffe and the May Court Club. White himself became a captain in the Governor General's Foot Guards, one of the most prestigious militia regiments in the country. He hob-nobbed with governors general and cabinet ministers and was a part of the social elite of Ottawa society. There would be no one with such stature at the head of the Mounted Police again until Sir James MacBrien in the 1930's.

White's relationship with Macdonald, to whom he owed everything, must have been very close, more akin to master and loyal retainer than ministerial subordinate: White was with the Macdonald family at the Old Chief's bedside during the last days of his life in 1891.[47] Lady Macdonald was fond of White's daughters. Following her husband's death, she arranged for the Macdonald's summer home at Rivière du Loup to be left to them. To what extent White was subservient to Macdonald on Mounted Police matters is difficult to say precisely. Most of their communication in this respect was verbal and as a result few records of it have survived. Macdonald was certainly conscientious and attentive in his ministerial duties. He concerned himself with both the trivial and the significant. His initials can be found on White's memoranda approving everything from minor changes in the uniform to major building expenditures. It is difficult to imagine White forcefully taking a position in opposition to his minister. On the other hand, he sincerely endeavoured to serve what he believed were the best interests of the Mounted Police and in doing so he developed a bit of a Machiavellian touch. He soon became politically very astute. He could chart his way with ease through the labyrinth of government departments and bureaucratic red tape. He developed a keen sense for discerning anything that might bring criticism in parliament. Reports were carefully edited and expenditures drawn up so that they looked like an irresistible bargain. White knew when the time was ripe to push something in front of his minister and when it was wiser to wait for another opportunity. In short, although he was by no means always successful, he became experienced at manipulating bureaucracy in Ottawa to the advantage of his department. As a result, he was a formidable force in Mounted Police affairs for 30 years. Ministers came and went, but White continued on.

White's position was of particular importance to Herchmer. In the early years they interacted like master and apprentice. The Comptroller's correspondence frequently offered advice, corrected, scolded and encouraged greater effort and care. White was a restraining influence when Herchmer got carried away by unrealistic proposals, or was in a fit of temper. "Mr. White" visited the West every summer to inspect facilities at Regina and some of the other main posts. Once or twice a year the Commissioner was summoned to Ottawa to discuss building estimates, recruiting or any other matters that had to be dealt with. White was especially valuable as a buffer against the political realities of commanding the Mounted Police. The appointment and promotion of officers, the large contracts for work or supplies, the establishment of posts went through the Comptroller. To office seekers and those hoping to profit from the police, Herchmer was able to reply that those matters were handled by the Comptroller in Ottawa.

Former Commissioner Irvine had been frequently criticized because the police lacked a system of regulations and procedures to govern both administrative and operational activities. This was largely true. In 1874, the government had introduced a set of "Rules and Regulations" for the guidance of the Mounted Police, but these were very brief and did little more than itemize a number of responsibilities with respect to accounting for expenditures.[48] The *Mounted Police Act* itself was primarily concerned with defining the powers of the police, the qualifications for engagement, pay and discipline. It was silent, for example, on how police duties were to be carried out, authority exercised, kit issued, pay accounted for and men trained. In the absence of anything else the first officers had fallen back on the one system that most of them were well acquainted with, "The Queen's Regulations and Orders for the Army". As a result, the Force developed a more military organization than Macdonald had probably originally intended. Army regulations, of course, did not provide much of a precedent for police duties, but by 1878 the Force was being run like a cavalry regiment.[49] The trouble was that what was adopted from the army sometimes varied from division to division and changed with each new Commissioner. Commanding officers followed their own preferences as to the type of drill given to their men. Headquarters adopted the military practice of making its wishes known by issuing "General" or "Standing" orders. They had never been expanded, however, into a comprehensive system of administration that would provide for the uniform and effective management of the Mounted Police by the Commissioner. To Herchmer's considerable credit, he rectified this deficiency.

When he was appointed adjutant in April 1884, one of the first tasks given Supt. Deane was the compilation of a set of "Standing Orders".[50] He was well aware that a manual of instructions or regulations was urgently needed. On joining the Force a year earlier, he noted that it ran itself in a "go-as-you-please manner". He was no doubt struck by the contrast in this respect between the Mounted Police and his previous experience in the Royal Marines, in which he had also served as an adjutant.

Deane commenced his assignment by sorting out the disorganized clutter of files in the Commissioner's office. The lack of order and the rebellion delayed Deane's work but, under Herchmer, a new impetus was given to the project and the "Revised Standing Orders" were finally issued in 1886.[51]

This was only a beginning, however. The Commissioner also had plans for a constable's manual, a drill manual and a set of administrative regulations. Deane had compiled a "Constable's Manual" in 1883 drawing upon those in use by the Royal Irish Constabulary and the Melbourne City Police.[52] His manuscript, however, was consigned to a "pigeon hole" in Ottawa, probably because of cost. Herchmer felt that a manual with the rules of veterinary practice, drill movements and instructions in police duties should be issued to all constables.[53] It too, however, came to nought.

Although they disliked each other bitterly, the combination of Herchmer's initiative and Deane's expertise finally did succeed in producing the administrative guide that had long been needed. Known as *Regulations and Orders for the Government and Guidance of the North West Mounted Police*, this 127-page booklet was approved by the government and published in 1889.[54] It was a compendium of what had been in practise before under the Standing Orders and the numerous measures introduced by Herchmer since he took office. The Regulations were prefaced with a general admonition to all of the responsibilities placed upon them as members of the Force and peace officers. Prevention of crime, they asserted in the spirit of Robert Peel, the Father of British policing, was of far greater importance than the punishment of criminals. Members were also warned to cultivate the respect of the public by prompt action, impartial discharge of their duties, sober habits and a civil bearing to all classes. They were further cautioned to observe the Sabbath, maintain a spirit of unanimity and good fellowship among themselves, obey all lawful commands and avoid debts. This statement of the ideal characteristics of a policeman was, of course, found in the regulations of many police forces of the time. About half of the regulations were devoted to setting out the duties of all members from the Commissioner down to the lowly constable. A key position to this administrative system was that of the Assistant Commissioner. Following Crozier's resignation, the Commissioner's brother, William Macauley Herchmer, was promoted to this post on 1 July 1886. "Colonel Billy", as he came to be known with some affection by the rank and file, had come to the North-West in 1870 with the Wolseley expedition as a captain with the 1st (Ontario) Battalion of Rifles. He remained with the Provincial Battalion in

Manitoba until he was appointed a Superintendent in the Mounted Police in August 1876.[55] The relationship between the two brothers is not well documented. They do seem to have had somewhat different personalities. William was more level-headed than his elder brother and showed none of the latter's zeal or temper. Nonetheless, Lawrence probably bullied the younger Herchmer as he tried to bully all his officers. The Commissioner certainly lashed out at him for his intemperate drinking habits.[56]

Under the regulations, the Assistant Commissioner became the Commissioner's eyes and ears throughout the Force. It was his task to "minutely inspect" the divisions and detachments and to report on every detail of administration and organization. His monitoring would ensure that the regulations were being uniformly and correctly observed. The message that the Assistant Commissioner was on his way to inspect a post was the signal for frenzied activity to get the books up-to-date, clean, shine and put the best face on everything. Equipment would be examined by the Assistant Commissioner, men drilled, horses checked, accounts audited and supplies scrutinized. Commanding officers knew that the Commissioner would carefully read the inspection report and they would be called to account for any discrepancy.

The regulations also authorized the Assistant Commissioner to enquire into any matter the Commissioner wished to have investigated. In practice this usually involved the holding of a "special enquiry" as provided for by section 17 of the *Mounted Police Act* into public complaints against the Force, or the conduct of commissioned officers.[57] Under this section, witnesses could be compelled to attend the enquiry and give evidence under oath. W. M. Herchmer was well suited for this responsibility. He had practised law in Kingston in the 1860s and had been admitted to the Bar of Manitoba in 1871.

The remainder of the regulations dealt with a variety of organizational and administrative procedures relating to pay, uniform, leave, horses, discipline, forage, transfers, barracks, accounting procedures and reports to be submitted, among other matters. They also listed the books of reference and instruction which would be supplied to assist members in carrying out their police and magisterial duties. These included Clarkes Magistrates and Constable's Manuals as well as copies of federal and territorial statutes. The backbone of the administrative regulations was the reporting system. At the rear of the booklet was a list of 103 forms or reports that had to be submitted to headquarters from the divisions either daily, weekly or monthly. These included patrol reports, defaulters lists, sick reports, muster rolls of horses and men, ration and forage requisitions, and returns on stores and fuel, to mention only a few. It was the beginning of the "paper war" for the Mounted Police. The list of forms would grow longer as the years passed forcing commanding officers and NCOs in charge of detachments to spend more and more of their time filling in returns and writing reports. As time went on, their cries for clerks, typewriters and stenographers would grow louder.

As the recipient of this growing volume of reports and returns, the Commissioner was able to tell at a glance how many bushels of oats were in stores in Battleford, what charges had been laid in Calgary, what settlers were complaining about north of Edmonton, who was sick, which buildings needed repairing and how many prisoners were in custody. In short, it gave him the information he needed to exert greater control over his command and more efficiently use its men and resources. One must hasten to add that Herchmer's administration was dependent upon the growing network of rail lines in the Territories and the frequent and speedier mail services that resulted from them. Herchmer provided the Mounted Police and administrative system that would be followed in the Force for decades with few substantial changes. A lasting and visible legacy of it are the printed annual reports of the Commissioner, which from 1886 to 1916 are an invaluable source on the development of the prairie provinces. These detailed yearly accounts of the activities of the Mounted Police were compiled from the myriad of reports and returns instituted by Herchmer.

The new Commissioner inherited a Force that had just had its strength doubled. The Prime Minister had introduced a motion in the Commons to increase the establishment of the NWMP from 500 to 1,000 men on 10 April 1885, two weeks after the outbreak of the rebellion.[58] He explained to the House that the desired increase did not result from the outbreak of hostilities. The extra men, he continued, were needed to handle the additional civil duties of the police brought about by the completion of the Canadian Pacific Railway and the anticipated influx of population. With justifiable scepticism Edward Blake, the Leader of the Opposition, suggested that Macdonald's argument was merely a smoke screen, and that the real reason behind the increase was a desire to strengthen the defensive forces in the Territories. If this was the government's intention, the liberal leader argued, it could best be accomplished by expanding the militia there rather than the Mounted Police. The increase, Blake pointed out, would raise the expenditure on the NWMP to over $1 million annually. Blake also noted that the government's action was contradictory to what it had repeatedly claimed in the past that as the country became more settled, the Mounted Police would be reduced. When pressed in a later debate for details on the expansion of duties, Macdonald explained that the police now had to patrol the entire border from the Rocky Mountains eastward into Manitoba to protect settlers' livestock from an "organized system of forays from the United States".[59] The Government of Manitoba, he stated, did not have the resources to patrol its portion of the international boundary. He also cited the increased need to keep the Indians on their reserves and protect them from white troublemakers. These were duties, he continued, that could not be accomplished by the militia. Finally, the Prime Minister fell back on an old argument to support his action. If the Opposition felt that 1,000 men was too much, they should look across the border where the Americans had 6,000 troops watching the Indians on their northern frontier. The increase in strength was approved on June 24th.[60]

When he assumed command of the Mounted Police, Herchmer inherited an organization which had been largely shaped by the previous Commissioner. During his visit to Ireland in 1880, Irvine had inspected the facilities and organization of the Royal Irish Constabulary. He was impressed with what he saw, particularly with the Depot of the RIC in Phoenix Park, Dublin where its recruits were trained. Upon his return he proposed the establishment of a similar depot at the headquarters of the Mounted Police.[61] Training in the NWMP had not been very systematic. New recruits were usually posted to Headquarters, but the degree of training they would receive there was determined by the availability of staff and the need for reinforcements in the field. The latter were expected to complete their training, if and when they could. Irvine envisaged a permanent staff of instructors whose sole responsibility would be the operation of a set course of training that would adequately prepare recruits for their duties. The government did not take up his proposal, but with the increase in 1885 Irvine finally achieved his goal. A "Depot" Division was organized at Headquarters in Regina in the fall of that year. With the doubling of strength he was also able to establish four new operational divisions, in addition to the five that already existed. By the end of 1885 the NWMP was distributed as follows:[62]

Strength

"A"	Division	- Maple Creek	102
"B"	Division	- Regina	103
"C"	Division	- Fort Macleod	112
"D"	Division	- Battleford	94
"E"	Division	- Calgary	101
"F"	Division	- Prince Albert	96
"G"	Division	- Edmonton	99
"H"	Division	- Fort Macleod	104
"K"	Division	- Battleford	107
"Depot"	Division	- Regina	121
			1,039

Shortly after taking command, Herchmer obtained White's agreement on the established strength of the operational divisions. Each was to consist of one sergeant major, one quarter-master sergeant, one hospital staff sergeant, six corporals and eighty-five constables, or approximately one hundred men per division.[63] In addition, there were officers, a Superintendent in command, one or two Inspectors to assist him and usually a surgeon. Each division was responsible for policing the district assigned to it. The central post of each district was the divisional headquarters. It commonly consisted of a number of buildings arranged around the sides of an open parade square in the centre of which was a flag pole. The buildings included barracks for the men, mess halls, administrative offices, a guard-room for prisoners, stables, wagon sheds, a small hospital, houses for the married men and officers, as well as facilities for the farrier and other artisans and the stores. Each division also consisted of several detachments of one to a half dozen men, usually under the command of a non-commissioned officer. As a rule they comprised two or three small buildings which supplied accommodation for the men, their horses and their supplies. In addition, many divisions also maintained temporary detachments or "outposts", in which the men were housed in tents for the summer months only. Cpl. John Donkin, who commanded one of these outposts on the Souris River near the international boundary wrote of his experience:

> I had a junior corporal and five constables to bear me company, and one transport wagon. The two tents were pitched close together, facing the river, and properly trenched. In a few days, a cooking stove and some utensils were sent from Carlyle. At first, these were set up in the open air; and when the rain fell, as it always does here, in torrents, it was often hours before we could coax our fire to burn. Some deserted shanties were purchased by our contractor and subsequently removed to this spot, and erected by us. One we very soon put together as a kitchen, and the other we eventually got in order as a barrack-room, to be used when the cold weather commenced in the Fall... There was a deep sleugh [slough] in a depression of the valley, a little to the left of the camp, and, amid the long grass surrounding it, we picketed our horses as long as the feed continued good. Our supply of rations was to be sent monthly from Carlyle, and as we were unable to consume the full government allowance, we exchanged the surplus for delicacies, such as butter, and eggs, and preserves. Eggs were sold at this time at the rate of ten cents (5 d.) per dozen. Our flour we sent to a settler on the plains two miles to the north, whose daughters, two strapping highland lasses, baked our bread.[64]

Comm. Lawrence Herchmer would face 14 difficult years in command of the North-West Mounted Police. The frontier was changing rapidly. The rebellion was over and the Indigenous people of the North-West were subjugated to acceptance of a new order. With the Canadian Pacific Railway in place a trickle of settlers arriving from the East and from Europe would grow to a flood. Maintaining order in these circumstances was a daunting task for the Force and for its Commissioner.

It is interesting, perhaps even surprising, that Herchmer was able to meet the challenges presented to him. Not a pleasant man, he would be constantly plagued with difficulties in dealing with his subordinates. Neither an experienced soldier nor a trained policeman, he was tasked with command of a paramilitary police force. In part, Herchmer succeeded because of his strengths; a penchant for hard work, an orderly administrator and an expectation of high standards from his officers and men. But his success owed much to factors already in place when he took over. Fred White, Comptroller, was an invaluable ally in Ottawa ensuring that the Force received the support it needed from the federal government, and the NWMP itself had already moulded into a cohesive organization with *esprit de corps* and a sense of purpose. Herchmer had the tools in place to do the job required.

Chapter 2

Agents of the National Policy

The preservation of peace and eradication of crime were the primary responsibilities of the Mounted Police in the West, but their duties extended far beyond these traditional police functions. The federal government, under Macdonald's Conservatives, had forged a "National Policy" which aimed in part at the extension of Canada westward through settlement and development. As the first federal agency in place in the North-West Territories the Mounted Police assumed a plethora of responsibilities to ensure implementation of the policy. The effectiveness with which the police expedited orderly development of the West inspired historian, R. C. Macleod, to dub Force members "Agents of the National Policy".[1]

The role of the NWMP in implementing the National Policy evolved during the frontier period. When the Mounted Police first arrived in the West, their goal was to police the process of settling the Indians on reserves. That accomplished, the Force was tasked with patrolling the line of construction of the Canadian Pacific Railway to protect the project from disruption. After the last spike was driven, rapid development of the Canadian West began and the duties of the NWMP became multifarious. In general, these duties can be characterized as fitting into three different categories: protecting incipient communities from natural disaster and human disruption; performing state services normally provided by other agencies in a more mature society; and boosting development through timely reporting to Ottawa of the progress of the West and through the power of the police purse.

The role of the Mounted Police in fostering development in the West is not unique in frontier history. In the United States, the army represented a government presence in the West which was devoted to more than waging campaigns against Indians. In the post-civil war era the U.S. regular army was often engaged in protecting railway construction crews, escorting freight and mail, and

building roads. However, the duties of the Mounted Police were much more extensive than this. Responsibilities ranged from checking on individual settlers to ensuring the protection of lives and property from the sudden menace of prairie fires. In essence the Force's activities represented state intervention to provide for the prosperity and success of settlers and their communities. Historian Carl Betke has concluded that the role played by the Force represented "the first faint stirrings of the Canadian welfare state".[2] Both Betke and Macleod agree that the support services supplied to newcomers in the Territories constituted a significant contribution to the enormous popularity of the Force in that region which has endured to the present.

The most important of the support functions performed by the Force were connected with protecting settlers and communities from natural disasters and human disruptions. Newcomers to the West faced real and often unfamiliar perils. Homesteads had to be established, crops planted, fuel and food stored for long winters. The Métis, long established on the frontier, found it difficult to adjust to the new social and economic conditions that came with settlement. Shelter and sustenance were also threatened by fire, particularly on the prairies where carelessness could result in stubborn blazes which would sweep the countryside, clearing everything before them. Alleviating these conditions usually fell to the Mounted Police. More controversially, the Mounted Police were required to protect the economic development of the West from the worst consequences of labour disputes.

The backbone of all support services provided to communities by the Mounted Police was the extensive patrol system established in 1886. After the rebellion, Commissioner Herchmer organized inter-connecting patrols to link police posts and outposts along the border between the United States and Canada. The system was intended to keep tabs on the Indians, control horse thefts and prevent smuggling across the border.[3] Soon however, members on patrol commenced the practise of calling at the home of each settler in their respective areas and inquiring about the condition of the household.[4] By 1889, the patrol system and the attendant practise of checking on settlers had been extended from the southern area to other divisions in the North-West Territories.[5]

The patrol system created a strong bond between the Mounted Policemen and the settlers.[6] When a patrol area was not within a day's ride of a post or outpost, the police would stay with local families. Particularly in these early years of settlement on the prairies there was considerable identity of interest between Force members and the ranchers in south Alberta. Both groups generally came from the same social and cultural milieu in eastern Canada. Arriving in the West about the same time, they shared common pioneer experiences. Bonds were tied even closer as many policemen left the Force and took up ranching.[7] A Mounted Policeman described his experience with a rancher in the Calgary area while on patrol in the winter of 1887-1888:

> We also patrolled to the Rosebud. This was a very popular patrol and we used to stay with Geo. Hope Johnstone who had a sheep ranch. They were always very kind to us. Mrs. Geo. Hope was an exceptionally sweet woman and very pretty. She used to make us feel so much at home, that you cannot wonder at all the Detachment longing to be sent on Rosebud patrol. We generally stayed two or three days, but I am afraid Geo. Hope's ladies suffered. At the same time, I know we were welcome guests. It was pretty lonely out there, as there were no other dwellers in the country outside a Half-breed family. We used to take the mail out to them, to which they looked forward to very much.[8]

These patrols soon brought to the attention of the Mounted Police the plight of the Métis of the NWT. Cut off from full integration with both the Indian and white societies by their mixed blood, unique customs and French language, the Métis tried to survive as a separate entity although they had been uprooted from their original communities at Red River. By the late 1880s their survival was seriously imperiled by the sweeping economic and social changes occurring on the prairies. The buffalo, the mainstay of Métis existence, had all but disappeared; some Métis found a livelihood in providing freight services for the developing frontier, at first carrying supplies from as far as Winnipeg. Unfortunately, demand for their services declined rapidly as railways were built and white competition developed. Many Métis had little experience with or interest in farming and turned their hands to agricultural pursuits only very reluctantly when they were forced to concede that traditional means like fishing and hunting could not be depended upon to support families.[9]

Inevitably those Métis who could not provide for their own welfare came to the attention of the Mounted Police. As Supt. Perry put it:

> In a thickly populated state charitable societies and institutions of a philanthropic character alleviate suffering by starvation. Here we have nothing of that sort and therefore the Federal authorities must step in.[10]

Perry, however, found himself in a dilemma; he was uneasy about issuing relief to the Métis. In 1888, he observed that for four years the Mounted Police had made help available to destitute Métis and he suspected that they were depending on the aid. The previous growing season several families had not bothered to accept government assistance in the form of seed grain to grow crops and now that winter was upon them they looked to the Force for food.

Based on humanitarian grounds alone, the NWMP and the government did not wish to turn down flat the Métis' evident need for assistance. Mixed in with this altruism, however, was concern that the Métis might be driven by desperation again to rebellion. Commissioner Herchmer did not regard this as a likely eventuality, but nevertheless the Force carefully checked all reports of Métis unrest.[11] Any rumour of an impending uprising influenced government treatment of the Métis because the mere prospect of violence alarmed whites who settled near Métis communities.[12]

Because of these circumstances the Mounted Police offered assistance to destitute Métis throughout this period. Most of the relief occurred in northern communities in the regions of Battleford, Prince Albert and Fort Saskatchewan. The general policy of the Force was to determine where real need existed and then to supply the necessities of life. The Mounted Police tried, whenever possible, to extract a return from the Métis for the welfare provided. Usually able-bodied men were required to perform manual tasks such as cutting and splitting firewood to supply the Force's posts, or building fences.[13] Where there were no able-bodied men in the family or when no useful work could be found for the needy, relief supplies were issued without any return demanded.[14] In order to break the cycle of the same people repeatedly applying for relief supplies, the government authorized the Force to issue seed grain to Métis who wished to try farming. Those who accepted the seed grain were asked to provide harvested crops of the same value to the Force.[15] This program was not as successful as had been hoped because of the reluctance of some Métis to commit themselves to farming and their lingering suspicion that accepting such help might in some way place a mortgage on their land in the hands of the government.[16] Supt. Perry conceded by

1891 that encouraging the Métis to convert to agriculture was no easy task. He envisaged the necessity for a more extensive government program involving loans and education in farm economy.[17]

In some years relief issued to indigent Métis was fairly extensive. For instance, in the winter of 1887-1888, the Mounted Police at Fort Saskatchewan issued food to a total of 663 men, women and children in the Métis community of St. Albert, including 5,334 lbs. of bacon and 20,916 lbs. of flour. Also issued were 50 lbs. of gunpowder, 200 lbs. of shot and 95 boxes of caps, to enable the Métis to hunt. Here no return was asked for welfare provided, as many of those assisted were old or handicapped and no useful work could be found for the able-bodied because of the deep snow that winter. The next year, the Force issued over $3,000 in relief supplies to the Métis of the northern prairies.[18] The almost total failure of Métis crops at Prince Albert in the fall of 1890 brought a winter of what Supt. John Cotton described as "destitution . . . appalling and pitiable".[19] He responded by distributing $1,306.50 worth of clothing, provisions and general stores, most in return for work performed. In Cotton's view: "There is no doubt that the lives of many starving persons principally among the aged and extremely young children were saved by means of Government aid in the shape of work and other assistance".[20]

The government was not particularly happy about the role of providing relief, forced upon it by the plight of the Métis. By 1891, the Department of the Interior, which had been compensating the Mounted Police for the depletion of their stores, decided to take a tougher line. The NWMP alerted the Department in the fall of 1891 that a number of unemployed half-breeds in the Macleod district of southern Alberta were likely to become public charges that winter. An Interior official responded that the Minister had no funds to disburse in relief of such cases. Fred White, Comptroller of the Mounted Police queried the significance of this reply and learned that no relief was to be supplied by the NWMP to destitute Métis because there was no parliamentary appropriation for such a purpose. White duly passed these instructions on to his officers. Such a cut and dried policy could not be maintained by police when they encountered extreme cases of destitution. That winter the NWMP detachment at Duck Lake reported that a Métis widow with four small children was sick and without means. White authorized the issue of relief, observing that while he was violating government policy, "Mrs. LeJour and her children must not be allowed to starve."[21] This fact of life was reluctantly

acknowledged by the Department of the Interior as well as the years passed.

Fighting the numerous fires which swept the prairies in dry weather was a difficult and frustrating job for the Mounted Police. Set usually by settlers clearing land, by careless campers or sparks from railway steam engines, the fires often raged out of control and burned hundreds of square miles of grasslands, often destroying valuable pasturage, fields under cultivation and buildings. The chief defence against these fires in this period of sparse settlement were the men of the NWMP. A prairie fire ordinance of the NWT provided for the appointment of fire guardians charged with the responsibility of fighting the blazes and empowered to require citizens to render assistance. The police also had authority to charge persons who set the fires.[22]

For the Mounted Police, combatting prairie fires was particularly onerous in the years immediately after the rebellion because there were still relatively few settlers to lend a hand. Many settlers in the NWT also felt that the Mounted Police should perform all of this work without calling on them for assistance.[23] Moreover, the work was taxing and dirty. Upon the alarm being raised, all available policemen were rounded up and despatched to the vicinity where, at a furious pace, fireguards were hacked out of the grasslands to cut off the path of the fire while the flames were attacked with wet brooms and sacks. In some cases it was no mean feat just catching the fire. A troop of Mounted Police from Lethbridge in April 1889 made two excursions in pursuit of an elusive fire, spending almost two days in the saddle and covering almost 90 miles before catching and extinguishing it.[24]

Supt. Sam Steele gave a graphic description of his experience fighting prairie fires when he commanded the Mounted Police at Fort Macleod in the late 1880's:

> One morning we had a little example of our share in the prevention of fires spreading. A cowboy rode up to the orderly-room and reported that prairie fires were raging along the northern part of the Porcupine Hills. He looked as if he had ridden hard, and said that the stockmen and their neighbours had been fighting the fires for a couple of days and nights and were exhausted. As there was need of immediate help I sent Sergeant Joyce, a very hard-riding and capable N.C.O., with 50 mounted men to the scene of the fire, some 35 miles distant. They found everyone in a state of exhaustion, but, starting work at once, with the assistance of a few of the ranchers who were able to carry on, they extinguished the fire after 6 hours' of strenuous toil, and were back at Macleod within 24 hours, none the worse for their trip and their 70 mile ride.
>
> In some places where the grass was long and the wind high, nothing could stop it. The fire travelled faster than a horse. On one occasion a rancher was followed by a fire of that sort and had to start another ahead to save himself from being overtaken, resting on

the burnt ground until the pursuing fire had passed on both sides. He followed the flames to his ranch, expecting to find it in ruins, but, to his intense relief, found his stacks and house safe, and the Mounted Policemen of the neighbouring detachment seated on the wood-pile, blackened and panting from their efforts.[25]

While severe prairie fires occurred each year, Joseph Royal, Lieutenant-Governor of the Territories, accurately described 1889 as disastrous despite the zeal of the Mounted Police in combatting the menace. The winter of 1888-1889 had been very dry on the prairies with little or no precipitation. As a result, fires fanned by high winds started in March and burned steadily one after another until November, all over the NWT. In many cases, settlers lost all of their agricultural produce, livestock and their buildings, and at least one life was lost. In northern Alberta, fires raged continuously in all directions throughout the spring. The Mounted Police worked hard to protect settlers. At all times teams were kept harnessed to wagons filled with wet sacks to be despatched to danger points at a moment's notice. Nevertheless, there was a heavy loss in property. On one occasion the town of Edmonton itself was threatened.[26]

From time to time Mounted Police officers vented their frustrations with the prairie fire situation by complaining about the lack of cooperation they received from the general public and the civilian magistracy. Supt. R. B. Deane reported that on one occasion in 1888, his men worked all afternoon in the blazing sun putting out a fire which threatened a property outside Lethbridge, while the employees of the concern would not deign to assist.[27] The police found, too, that it was difficult to bring those who started the fires to justice. Witnesses who could attest to the guilt of parties often refused to give evidence because the accused was a neighbour.[28] Then, in the small number of cases where the NWMP managed to secure conviction, sentences were often ridiculously light. The Territorial Ordinance provided for penalties up to a $200 fine or six months in jail, civilian justices of the peace who heard the cases were levying fines of only a few dollars. On the few occasions when Mounted Police justices conducted the trials and found the accused guilty, they levied fines of between $30 and $75 and twice sent men to jail when they could not pay. This was so infrequent, however, that convictions were no deterrent in a society which believed that accidental, even if careless, kindling of a prairie fire deserved little more punishment than a light slap on the wrist.[29]

Much controversy has been generated over the years concerning the relations of the Mounted Police with labour. In his study of the development of labour organization in Canada, Charles Lipton refers to the "dubious career" of the Mounted Police in labour disputes.[30] This harsh judgement reflects the frustration of this historian, sympathetic as he is to the labour movement, at the obstacles presented by police on many occasions to the successful conclusion of strikes or other industrial actions. Police are, and have always been, responsible for enforcing the laws of a society. During the period under study, Canadian society permitted workers less latitude in organizing to negotiate contracts with employers. The laws placed considerably more emphasis on the rights of employers and of property. As R. C. Macleod has remarked, "Nineteenth-century labour disputes are almost incomprehensible if approached with an assumption that people thought of them then as they do now."[31] The Mounted Police did not regard labour disputes in this era as ideological confrontations demanding a moral commitment to the establishment. Rather, they were occasions fraught with potential disorder and violence which must be carefully watched.[32]

In a sense, the role of the Mounted Police in preserving order in labour relations was an extension of the Force's responsibility as agent of the National Policy. This was most clearly demonstrated during the construction of the main line of the Canadian Pacific Railway when the Mounted Police routinely patrolled construction camps to minimize all influences which might disrupt progress of the track. Liquor and attendant vices were prohibited by law and by the diligence of the Mounted Police. When strikes occurred or employees refused to live up to their obligations under the *Masters and Servants Act*, the Mounted Police responded to the CPR's requests for action. The police did not deny labour any rights allowed under law, but they did block workers' attempts to use disruption as a tactic to win better conditions of service from the company. The NWMP continued to play this role after 1885 in relation to industries in the NWT which employed large bodies of men who represented a threat to order and who organized for collective action. At the same time, the Mounted Police displayed sympathy for workers and acted on their behalf whenever employers took unfair advantage of labour.[33]

Following the completion of the main line of the CPR, branch lines were constructed, extending rail transportation throughout the prairies. As previously, the Mounted Police were assigned to construction camps to preserve order. The police were determined to keep liquor away from the men on the theory that drunkenness was the root of many other disorders. The Force was largely successful containing the problems which arose. In the case of the construction of the Calgary to Edmonton CPR branch there was an incident in 1891 which was dangerous. On July 1st of that year, 1,000 to 1,500 navvies descended on Edmonton to participate in the Dominion Day festivities. The Mounted Police prudently watched the good-natured crowd from a distance and made no attempt to interfere with the flow of liquor on this occasion. As a result, the spree ended with only one arrest for drunk and disorderly conduct.[34] Detachments were also assigned to the Saskatoon-Prince Albert line of the CPR and the Canada and Great Falls Railway. The latter railroad was under construction between Lethbridge and Great Falls, Montana, and Herchmer noted with satisfaction that "while whisky was introduced among the men and outrage and even murder occurred south of the line during the construction, on our side law and order prevailed".[35]

While on duty at railroad construction camps the Mounted Police were called upon from time to time to intervene in labour disputes. Most frequently problems arose in interpreting the responsibilities of the workers and the employers under the terms of the *Masters and Servants Act*. In some circumstances workers who quit their jobs could be prosecuted for violation of their contractual obligations to their company. When this occurred the company called upon the Mounted Police to arrest the deserting workers. Usually charges were dropped if the men returned to work, but refusal to do so led to prosecution. Convictions resulted in fines, nonpayment of which brought a jail term, or a sentence to compensate the company financially. For example, in 1890, the Mounted Police arrested nine workers accused of deserting their employment for Calgary and Edmonton Railway Company. Of the nine, charges against six were dismissed when they agreed to return to work, two were sentenced to pay the company $15 in compensation and one served 14 days hard labour upon failure to pay a $10 fine and costs.[36] In turn too, the Mounted Police attempted to help workers who were victimized by contractors who refused to pay them. Unfortunately, because of a defect in the drafting of the *Masters and Servants Act*, the Force could help only a few workers obtain redress. The police did, however, denounce the unfair practises of the contractors publicly and recommended amendment of the legislation.[37]

The Mounted Police also felt that it was in the public interest to assist private companies operating in the NWT.[38] In the spring of 1887, coal miners employed by the North Western Coal and Navigation Company at Lethbridge went on strike for higher wages. The company had just finished a very slow first year of operations and was anxious to fill orders placed by CPR. Consequently, the company yielded quickly to the demands. Emboldened by their easy success the workers went out again in June. By this time the company's prospects were bleak and it responded by firing the workers and bringing in strike-breakers from eastern Canada and Ohio. Anticipating trouble, the Mounted Police moved men into Lethbridge to protect the strike-breakers. Neither side won in this situation because a few weeks later lack of market forced the company virtually to cease operations.[39]

The federal government used the Mounted Police in the West to perform a variety of services which would gradually spawn their own separate administrations. The most time consuming for the Force was customs work along the U.S. border. Connected to this was the responsibility of protecting the health of western livestock by enforcing quarantine regulations. The health of the people was no less important and Mounted Police hospitals were often the only facilities available in cases of serious injury or illness. Policemen were also used to deliver mail, escort important people and protect game.

Before the arrival of the Force in the West there was no attempt to enforce customs regulations or to collect revenue on goods imported from the United States. From 1874 to the rebellion, members of the Force were virtually the only customs agents in the Territories. The principal collection points up to 1886 were Fort Macleod, Fort Walsh and Maple Creek (after the closure of Walsh in 1882). Settlers and traders crossing the border were stopped by the Mounted Police and assessed duty on goods according to the provisions of the *Customs Act*. For example, the Force collected customs dues to a total of $28,416.61 at Maple Creek for the year 1883 and of $50,501.32 at Fort Macleod up to 30 November 1883. At Fort Macleod this figure represented dues collected on $248,637 worth of articles imported, while $403,907 in goods were admitted free.[40]

After the rebellion, the duties of the Force in customs collection were expanded to meet the expected increase in immigration. In 1886, Herchmer created his outpost patrol system to secure the border more tightly. The interconnecting patrols were deemed successful by the Commissioner in stemming the flow of smuggled goods across the international border from Manitoba to British Columbia.[41] In 1888, the Customs department requested the Force to extend patrols into Manitoba where smuggling was a particularly bad problem along the Dakota border. Moreover, American settlers were compensating for a lack of wood on their side of the line by crossing over and stealing timber from Crown lands.[42] In the winter of 1888-1889, a detachment of one officer and six men was sent into southern Manitoba, but a single detachment proved inadequate to handle the problem. The police, therefore, arranged to open several detachments which would serve as official customs points and increased the strength in the area to 19.[43] In September 1889, the Minister of Customs,

Mackenzie Bowell, was driven the entire length of the border from Gretna, Manitoba, to the Rocky Mountains in police transport to show him the work which the Force was performing for his department.

Duty along the southern border of Manitoba proved to be a difficult and vexatious task. The Officer-in-Charge, Inspector J. A. McGibbon, explained that: "Settlers had forgotten that there was a boundary line, and of course a hue-and-cry was raised against us at first, more particularly in the Sourisford district, as we made a few seizure [sic] there."[44] The Force was successful in stopping much of the smuggling but only by increasing the level of vigilance. In 1890 there were 14 detachments in the province under McGibbon's command manned by 30 ranks including Cpl. Baby, acting collector at Manitou, who had a "particular knack of finding out things, such as smuggling".[45] Both Fred White and Herchmer yearned for the day when the Force would be relieved of responsibility for southern Manitoba; not only was it a heavy drain on the Force, but they also felt that their presence was not fully appreciated by the people of the area. White told Herchmer in 1891: "Mr. Daly, M.P., complains bitterly of the harsh treatment accorded to settlers in connection with Customs matters, and has asked that they may be removed and Customs Officers appointed. I sincerely hope that this will be done, as at present the Police get all the odium and none of the credit."[46] But Customs department officials were generally pleased with the job being done by the Police and made no move to appoint their own personnel.[47]

In the NWT however, the Customs department developed its own administrative apparatus. In May 1886, the Minister of Customs appointed a Collector, W. Cox Allen, for Fort Macleod with the declared intention to relieve the Force of more of this responsibility as soon as possible.[48] By 1891, civilian customs officials were appointed at Lethbridge and at Coutts, assuming duties formerly performed by the NWMP, although the officer-in-charge of the NWMP post at Maple Creek continued to collect customs duties for the department on a commission basis.[49] While the new customs officers provided a starting point for a civilian customs service in the NWT, the Mounted Police continued to do the bulk of the leg work. Police patrols stopped all those encountered crossing the border from the United States and if they carried dutiable goods, referred them to the nearest customs post. Any person suspected of evading customs duties had his outfit seized and turned over to a customs' official.[50]

That the NWMP was the real backbone of the customs service in western Canada was recognized by the Minister of Customs, Mackenzie Bowell.

Recalling his trip across western Canada two years earlier, Bowell in 1891 referred to the NWMP as "an admirable force"[51] for the way they policed the border. He reflected on how futile it would be given the conditions of the frontier to place a dozen customs officers a hundred miles apart in the West and expect them to enforce the Act.

For the most part the transition of the customs service from police to civilian control seems to have been relatively smooth. Hints of acrimony however, were repeated from time to time over the years. In July 1891, for instance, Inspector T. W. Chalmers at Coutts reported to Supt. R. B. Deane at Lethbridge that an American intending to settle in Canada, tried to pass entry at Coutts but got no attention from the Collector, Edwin Allen. As the man was short of rations, Chalmers curtly commented: "I do not suppose that it is necessary to detain people until the Collector of Customs at Coutts sees fit and is sober enough to attend to business."[52] Allen was already suspected by the Mounted Police of selling seized liquor and not long after this incident was reported to Ottawa, Allen was dismissed.[53] Edwin Allen was a former NWMP officer. The son of the long-time mayor of Cornwall, Ontario, he was engaged in the Force as a Sub-Inspector in 1874 and came with "B" Troop under Sub-Inspector E. A. Brisbois on the March West. Most of his four years and four months of service was along the southern border. In 1875, he served under Assistant Commissioner Walsh in the arrest of the defiant Assiniboine Chief Crow's Dance and the first meeting with Sitting Bull.[54] He was evidently a capable officer, if not everyone's idea of the ideal companion. Assistant Surgeon R. B. Nevitt roomed with him at Fort Macleod in the winter of 1874-1875 and later described Allen as: "a broth of a boy, a man without principle and coarse, but he is good humoured and jolly and easy to get along with; does not drink although he swears worse than any trooper".[55] Allen resigned his commission in 1878.

Allen acquired the vice of over-indulgence in alcohol since his days at Fort Macleod perhaps to drown a sorrow. In early 1890, while he was out of town, his wife deserted him in the company of a popular lacrosse player. She sold the house furniture and took all the valuables with her, but left three children behind.[56]

The appointment of civilians to the customs collector posts in the West diminished the incomes of some NWMP officers. The department paid a percentage commission to the police on duties collected and revenues realized from seized goods. For the record, these payments were made to very few officers and sometimes in large sums. For instance, in 1885-1886, Assistant Commissioner L. F. N. Crozier was paid $3,659.46 in commissions, a sum which dwarfed his $1,466.63 in salary as a policeman.[57] Supt. Deane claimed that another unnamed officer earned as much as $25,000 over the years in customs commissions.[58] This changed considerably after 1886 with the appointment of salaried customs officials in the Territories. Some Mounted Police officers continued to receive commissions related to their customs work but on much more modest scales.[59] The detachments in southern Manitoba also received commissions from the Department of the Interior on monies realized from the seizure and sale of illegally cut timber and for the sale of timber permits. These bonuses were divided among the men who performed the work.[60] It is quite possible that Crozier and others in the NWT who received such commissions followed the same practise.

Connected with the problem of customs services was the responsibility assumed by the Mounted Police in protecting the cattle industry in western Canada. In the dozen years since the arrival of the Force in the West a successful cattle industry had developed, mostly in southern Alberta, supported by Eastern Canadian and British financial interests. These ranchers were closely bound to the Mounted Policemen socially and to former members of the Force, many of whom invested in or worked on the ranches. This small group of ranchers were also powerful men with great influence with the Conservative Government in Ottawa. They had little problem extracting from the federal government tariffs and quarantine regulations which shut out imported stock from the States, as well as favourable leaseholds on large tracks of grazing land. From 1885 to 1891, the ranching industry thrived by developing strong markets in Canada and in England.[61]

Once again, the Mounted Police were acting as "agents of the National Policy", responsible for enforcing regulations to protect the new industry. Few problems were encountered during this period. Most cattle brought into Canada arrived as stock belonging to settlers entering the country as immigrants and were not subject to duty.[62] Regulations called for a veterinary examination of these animals to ensure that they were healthy and Mounted Police veterinarians often performed these inspections.[63] Since American border states were regarded by the Department of Agriculture as disease-free, an affidavit from the incoming settler confirming the health of his animals was deemed sufficient.[64] As a consequence, the police were not over-burdened with this duty.

However, this border harmony included some discordant notes which were harbingers of a major problem for the police in the years ahead. There was virtually no method to control the drift of both Canadian and American cattle back and forth across the prairie border. With no barrier to stop them, cattle fleeing a storm or seeking water or feed often moved in entire herds across the boundary, causing inconvenience for both Canadian and American ranchers.[65] The Police usually settled such incidents in cooperation with stock associations on both sides of the line, ensuring that animals were returned across the border to their rightful owners. Occasionally, misunderstandings occurred; in 1887, a customs official at Lethbridge ordered the NWMP to seize some American cattle which were illegally in Canada. The official then sold the cattle. Indignant Montana cattlemen protested that the cattle had accidentally strayed across the border.[67] But these seemingly minor difficulties became major problems in succeeding years when the Canadian government tried to close the border by quarantine to protect British markets at a time when the American cattlemen tried to exploit the undefendable border to drive herds to more lush Canadian pastures. When this occurred, the Force was ordered to divert much of its resources to the impossible task of barring the way.

In addition to enforcing quarantine regulations on livestock crossing the border, the Mounted Police veterinarians were required to carry out federal and territorial regulations aimed at controlling animal contagious diseases. The usual practice was for a Mounted Police veterinarian to investigate reports of diseased animals in his region and recommend a course of action. If destruction or quarantine of livestock was required to stop the spread of the disease, the police veterinarian could obtain an order from a justice of the peace to overcome any reluctance on the part of the owners. For the most part it appears that settlers cooperated with the police, although in an outbreak of glanders among horses in the Maple Creek area in 1891 some owners attempted unsuccessfully to hide the sick animals from NWMP Veterinary Staff Sergeant J. L. Poett.[68] Police veterinarians made a significant contribution to efforts to control animal disease because of the fifteen veterinary surgeons in the Territories in 1891, five were members of the Force.[69]

Circumstances of frontier life meant that the Mounted Police often were obliged to offer medical assistance to the general populace. Principal police posts were equipped with hospital facilities usually manned by a doctor, who was a member of the Force or on contract, or at least by a hospital steward. These facilities were maintained for the treatment of policemen or prisoners in police guardrooms. However, it was a regular occurrence that civilians would be assisted, especially in cases of emergency or epidemic. In theory, this was against

Force policy; as Senior Surgeon Dr. Augustus Jukes wrote in 1890:

> The principal Posts are all situated in the immediate vicinity of the larger and wealthier towns, where competent physicians are always to be found, who, to the credit of their profession, never refuse aid to the destitute or impoverished, where their services are required; and the municipalities should certainly provide accommodation for their own indigent sick, and supply necessary provision for their proper care and attendance.[70]

Most municipalities recognized their responsibilities in this area, but until they could provide adequate medical care facilities, the police continued to offer assistance when necessary.[71]

In the early summers in the North-West, various forms of malarial fever sometimes infected communities, due at least in part to abysmal sanitation practices. In 1896, the fever broke out in the village of Maple Creek and, even though not a single Policeman was infected, the barracks Hospital Steward, J. C. Holme, treated 40 civilians. A recurrence of the fever at Maple Creek in 1889 brought more civilians into the police hospital for treatment.[72]

The Calgary barracks hospital handled eight civilian patients in 1890, but when typhoid fever flared up in the region, civilians had to be turned away for lack of room.[73]

This was not always the situation. In 1887, a NWMP doctor treated a civilian for an accidental gunshot wound.[74] In the winter of 1890, a number of civilians were admitted to hospital by police because of medical emergencies. A young English boy was found in February on the road near Prince Albert with insufficient clothing and a bad case of frostbite. Likewise, a badly frozen man was found near Macleod the same month. Both civilians were admitted to police hospitals despite their inability to pay for their care. Also in February 1890, an elderly man was discovered in a shack near Calgary in extremis from gastritis.[75] The police took care of him until he died the next day. When a patrol discovered an outbreak of smallpox at the Indian school at File Hills in 1890, Commissioner Herchmer immediately ordered the patrol to remain there and establish a quarantine.[76]

The question of who would bear the cost of medical care was a constant worry for the Force which was called upon to perform services outside usual police work. In the case of medical emergencies the Force acted invariably in the interests of the afflicted and only later tried to recover costs from the individual or another agency.[77] In other cases it was possible to anticipate a need for a medical service and the Force could meet a need if its costs were covered. For instance, in 1890 the Mounted Police agreed to allow workers injured on the construction line of the Calgary and Edmonton Railway to be treated, if necessary, at the police hospital at Calgary. The expenses would be borne by the company at the rate of $1.00 per day.[78]

Protection of game in the NWT was also a responsibility which the Mounted Police shared with a few game wardens and fisheries overseers. There were game laws in the Territories which protected wildlife to a limited extent with closed and open seasons. Such laws, however, were weak and very difficult to enforce in such a vast country. Abuses by sportsmen and by the Native peoples were quite possibly within the law and were common. When the NWMP arrived in the West, game was abundant, but, by the late 1880s, some policemen acutely felt the need for increased protection of endangered wildlife. For the time being, however, they were unable to stop a rapid decline in game, fish and fowl all over the prairies.[79]

One initiative, which was taken at an early stage, was the creation of a conservation area in a national park to secure at least a limited haven for wildlife. In 1885, the federal government set aside ten acres of wilderness in Alberta for preservation as a natural habitat, and in hopes that Banff hot springs would become a tourist attraction. In 1887, the area set aside was increased to 260 acres, and elevated to the status of Canada's first national park, officially named Rocky Mountain Park.[80] An outpost of the NWMP was established at Banff in 1886 at the request of the Minister of the Interior who was concerned that the site of the hot springs tourist attraction have a spotless reputation for law and order. When formal park regulations were drawn up in 1890, the Mounted Police were delegated to enforce them. This responsibility entailed much work for the police: "Mounted men have to visit daily all the principal points in the Park, and a dismounted man has to be on duty in the village."[81]

There was, however, an Achilles' heel to conservation regulations in the national park. While most visitors could be forced to conform to regulations banning all hunting within park boundaries, the position of the Indians was unclear.[82] Treaty Seven Indians had been given the right to hunt on Crown land subject to later regulations. The Stoney Indians exercised this right most freely, hunting extensively in the Rocky Mountain foothills. To them, hunting provided a way of life as well as a large part of their diet.[83] Thus the Mounted Police did not feel that they could force these Indians to respect the limits of the park. They were concerned, however, that unscrupulous white traders and trophy collectors were tempting the Stoneys to take even more game than they required for personal needs, in order to sell the meat, hides and heads. So representations were made to the Stoneys through their long-time missionary friend, the Rev. John McDougall, to respect voluntarily the conservation area.[84] This did not settle the matter and the interpretation of

Indian hunting rights under treaty became a long-standing source of contention in the West. In another instance, conservation-minded Herchmer urged government officials in 1893 to pass an order-in-council protecting the buffalo in the Great Slave Lake area, which he described as the last of their kind in the Dominion. The Indians had been killing them in large numbers, he reported, at the behest of white traders who paid them $25 a robe. If the snow was deep during the coming winter, he warned Ottawa, all the buffalo could go.[85]

The Mounted Police were also frequently called upon to escort public figures on tours of the NWT. These trips involved use of police transport, camping equipment and personnel, often for extended periods. In 1889, for instance, the NWMP supported three government officials on extensive western tours: the Minister of Customs was taken the length of the border from Manitoba to British Columbia; the Lieutenant-Governor of the NWT, Edgar Dewdney, was accompanied on a trip to the north; and Deputy Minister A. M. Burgess of the Department of the Interior transported to Prince Albert and Battleford.[86] More elaborate were the arrangements made for the Governor General and his wife, Lord and Lady Stanley, when they visited the West the same year. A guard of honour numbering almost 100 highly polished Mounted Policemen in white helmets and scarlet tunics greeted the vice-regal party upon their arrival in Regina on the 3rd of October. The Mounted Police put on a review for the Governor General consisting of both foot and mounted parades which greatly impressed the *Regina Leader*. "Rarely, perhaps never, has a more splendid event been witnessed in Regina than this review."[87] Proceeding west by train, the Governor General and his party were received by the NWMP in Lethbridge where an escort of 45 officers and men was provided. This guard then conducted the visitors on a week's tour of southern Alberta highlighted by a display of mock Indian warfare at the Blood Reserve and inspections of the large horse and cattle ranches of the region. The Mounted Police arranged for nightly camp sites and entertainment. The party then went on to Calgary where an escort of policemen from that locale met them with the same ceremony and services.[88] As Lady Stanley prepared to leave Calgary with her husband on the 21st of October, she noted in her record of the trip: "Said goodbye to the Mounted Police Force with real regret for they have been so good to us."[89] The military tradition of the Force and its more utilitarian escort duties already were combining naturally to make a Mounted Police guard a Canadian symbol.

Mail delivery in the Territories was frequently handled by the Mounted Police. This practice grew naturally with settlement. The police had established lines of communications and often the policeman was the only government official in contact with settlers. For example, until the CPR brought faster and more reliable mail transportation links with eastern Canada, mail from southern Alberta, civilian and police alike, was channelled through the orderly room at Fort Macleod south to more established American communication routes.[90] After the rebellion, with the CPR main line complete and branch lines being planned, the post office assumed more responsibility for postal operations in the NWT.[91] But delivery of mail by the Mounted Police to more remote settlements was deemed the most practical means as the Force maintained detachments and patrols in these areas. For instance, the mail to the sparsely settled Wood Mountain area was still being carried by the NWMP as late as 1888, entailing an extra burden on men and horses alike.[92]

Safety of the mail was also the concern of the Force. Until 1886, there had been no robbery attempts on the mail in western Canada, but in that year there were two. On 17 July 1886, an armed man held up a stage coach en route to Prince Albert and robbed the mail sack of a sum of money. A little over a month later two masked bandits held up a stage bound for Calgary, cutting open the mail, but this time found no money. The Mounted Police responded quickly to reports of the robberies but in neither case did patrols turn up the perpetrators. However, the robber of the Prince Albert stage was caught a few weeks later and upon conviction received 14 years in prison.[93] Immediately after these incidents, the Force established a system of police escorts for mail carried by stage from the CPR main line to the principal northern communities at Edmonton, Battleford and Prince Albert.[94]

The streams and rivers of the NWT were difficult and sometimes dangerous obstacles to land travel. Bridges and ferries were few and travellers by horseback or wagon were often forced to ford across waterways. This was a constant problem for Mounted Police patrols and prompted the Force, in some cases, to take definite action. At Medicine Hat, the NWMP built their own ferry which was manned by a constable and available to the public at a fee.[95] The police also supported the operation of a private ferry at Saskatchewan Landing with an annual government grant and the town ferry at Prince Albert with the payment of tolls.[96] The Force also built bridges in the NWT, with police labour and material, which were used by the general public. In 1889, bridges were erected across Kipp's Coulee and Middle Coulee on the road from Lethbridge to Milk River Ridge.[97] The previous year the Force had paid $300 to the town of Regina as a police contribution to a bridge for that community.[98] Moreover, police reported routinely and continually to the government on the urgent need for proper crossings in the West if the area was to prosper.[99]

In some ways the NWMP were the eyes and ears of the government in the NWT, particularly after Herchmer became Commissioner. The monthly and annual reports of the Officers Commanding divisional districts included, after 1886, assessments of social, demographic, economic and environmental conditions in the West. This meant that information, often in great detail was eventually relayed to Ottawa on the number of people arriving, where they settled and how they fared. Even for the established settlers, like the ranchers of southern Alberta, the NWMP kept track of the growth of their herds, the effect of annual variances in climate on their success and the development of their markets. Neither were the urban areas ignored; as towns sprang up, the Mounted Police noted the founding of industries, the capital investments, numbers of workers employed, homes constructed and city services initiated. Most of this information was published in the annual reports of the Commissioner of the NWMP, which even today are valuable sources to trace the development of the pioneer west.

These reports did create interest in official Ottawa. The Department of the Interior asked that Mounted Police throughout the NWT fill out monthly forms called "Crop and Weather Bulletins". Properly completed, these forms gave a detailed account of agricultural activity, including types of crops, number of acres under cultivation, average yields and an assessment of weather conditions. The Department of Agriculture also requested more general statements on agriculture in the various districts on a timely basis.[100]

The Mounted Police kept a special watch on settlers from Europe and on group settlements bound together by religious affiliation. When a German Jewish community of 75 families settled south of Dunmore, Alberta in 1889, the Force sent a German-speaking constable to the area to assist them. Copies of prairie game and fire ordinances, printed in German, were posted in conspicuous places. Reports on the progress of the colony were read with great interest at the Department of the Interior.[101] The Mounted Police, on temporary duty in Manitoba, reported on the large Mennonite community in the south of the province. High praise was heaped on the community for its industry, complete absence of crime and its prosperity. However, it was considered deeply regrettable that the elders refused to teach the English language and Canadian ways to their youth. This meant that "so long as they remain so these people will be what they are today – foreigners in language, customs and sentiments".[102] If mild regret was felt for some customs of the Mennonites, stronger sentiments were directed at the Mormons.

In 1887, a group of between 20 and 30 Mormon families emigrated from Utah and established themselves in southern Alberta in the vicinity of Lee's Creek. From the start it was evident that these hardworking people would succeed in creating a successful agricultural base to allow expansion of the community through annual immigration. The Mormons, in fact, led the way in converting the dry lands of the region to agriculture through irrigation techniques which they had developed in Utah.[103] In 1891, the Mounted Police reported favourably on the economic progress of the settlement.[104]

The Mormons, however, did bring with them to Canada a blight on their reputation through the practise of polygamy. This peculiar marriage practice was regarded as alien and abhorrent by most Americans. By the 1880s, the Mormons found themselves under increasing pressure to forsake this custom as their self-imposed isolation in the Utah Territory was drawing to a close because of the growing population in the American West. The Mormon Church finally renounced polygamy in 1896, but before doing so, the Canadian colony was established, perhaps in the hope of finding another refuge in southern Alberta where less notice would be taken of their living arrangements.[105] The Mormon leader in Canada, Charles Ora Card, however, promised the Canadian government that his people would not import the custom to this country.[106] Suspicion, however, is second nature to good policemen and it was turned full measure on the Mormons.

In September 1888, Supt. Sam Steele and Asst. Comm. W. Herchmer spent a night in the new Mormon settlement, and both came to the conclusion that polygamy was being practised. They talked to a number of Mormon men who denied the charge, although they admitted that they hoped for an amendment to Canadian law which would permit them to take more than one wife in the future. The police officers observed, however, that several of the households consisted of one man and several women who were not related. They noticed too that in some instances buxom young women lived in small houses at the rear of the main dwellings. Assistant Commissioner Herchmer recommended that a detective be employed who would infiltrate the colony by pretending to be a convert. He acknowledged that such an operation was expensive but felt it was the only way to get hard evidence of polygamous activity.[107]

Herchmer's report precipitated no undercover action but the Commissioner did place a detachment at Lee's Creek which was instructed to keep an eye on comings and goings in the Mormon settlement. In 1889, Sam Steele continued to report his suspicions of polygamy, providing as evidence that several women had babies whose pretended husbands had been absent from the colony for more than a year. These reports were forwarded to the Department of the Interior, the ministry principally responsible for prairie settlement.[108] The Deputy Minister, A. M. Burgess, found Steele's examples of promiscuity in the community flimsy support for his accusations of polygamy. Burgess commented to his Minister, Edgar Dewdney, "Unfortunately it would not be an extraordinary thing to find in the city of Ottawa a parallel to the case which he has cited in support of the serious charge which he makes against these people."[109] The Department did, however, seek and receive reassurances from Charles Card that the colony was faithful to promises given the government that no polygamy would be practised. Shortly after this, Commissioner Herchmer suggested that, as a check on polygamy, a census be taken of the Mormons and that those leaving or arriving in the settlement be required to report to police. Comptroller White turned down this idea on the grounds that it was unjust to subject Mormons to a form of surveillance not imposed on other settlers in the West.[110] There, the case against the Mormons came to a rest except for an occasional police report, never with substantial evidence. No doubt the government was unwilling to probe too deeply into the private practises of a group which was contributing so substantially to the agricultural development of southern Alberta.[111]

An objective of the National Policy was the protection and stimulation of Canadian industry. As a consequence, the NWMP tried to do its part by making purchases in Canada whenever possible. Moreover, the presence of the police in various locations throughout the West gave it a special responsibility to spread government patronage through the region, encouraging development. Most of the money spent by the Force was committed through contracts for goods or services, entered into after tenders had been invited by advertisement. Some small sums were dispensed for local purchases which would not warrant the trouble or expense of the contract system. There is also evidence that the distribution of patronage by the Force in both the West and the East was guided by the political interests of the Government.[112]

In 1886, the 1,000-man-strong Mounted Police Force was still dependent on sources of supply outside Canada. Since there was military arms manufacturing in the country, the Force was armed entirely with British-made Enfield revolvers and Winchester Carbines from the United States.[113] Ammunition for these firearms also came from British and American sources. Much of the saddlery and most of the wagons used by the Force were imported from the United States because difficulties were experienced in finding Canadian equipment of equal quality. Only in clothing were the police almost entirely supplied by large eastern Canadian manufacturers.[114] But some specialty equipment and officers' dress uniforms were still imported from England. Experiments in the evolution of the uniform also occasioned purchases of coats and Stetson hats from the United States.

There was, however, some significant progress made in changing to Canadian manufacturers over the next several years. In 1886, The Dominion Cartridge Company opened in Brownsburg, Quebec and by 1888 was producing a cartridge for the Winchester Carbine.[115] The Force switched to this company for its source of supply despite continual problems experienced with the uneven quality of its product.[116] Following several bad experiences with Canadian-made imitations of American saddles, the NWMP were reluctant to try new Canadian models. But in 1887, as a result of pressure brought by the Conservative MP from Winnipeg, W. B. Scarth, the Mounted Police tested a saddle made by one of his constituents, E. F. Hutchings.[117] Surprisingly, the saddle turned out to be an excellent article, well designed for prairie work. From this point, the Force bought all its saddles in Canada, with Hutchings enjoying a monopoly on police business for several years without even the formality of submitting tenders.[118] About the same time, the Force reduced its dependence on imported harness and other horse equipment by having it made by artisans in its own employ.[119] No heavy wagons were found in Canada which could equal the durability of American-made equipment. However, McCurdy and Tucker of Moosomin, NWT, made light buckboard wagons which suited some purposes of the police and business was directed to this firm.[120] The purchases from Hutchings and McCurdy and Tucker were motivated at least in part by the desire to stimulate the growth of industry in the West.[121] In the first years on the prairies, the NWMP developed a virtual dependence on western trading companies for goods and foodstuffs. In particular, the Hudson's Bay Company, I. G. Baker and Co. and T. C. Power and Brothers of Fort Benton, Montana sustained the Force. With the arrival of the railway and the influx of settlers in the post-rebellion period, it was assumed that business which had been the almost exclusive concern of the few trading companies would be shared more broadly throughout the community. This, in fact, eventually happened, but the older companies stubbornly retained important shares of police business. This practice was criticized by some opposition members in the House of Commons, but not by the first Conservative MP from Alberta, Donald W. Davis, who was a former manager of I. G. Baker and Co.[122] In the fiscal year 1890-91, the Force purchased from I. G. Baker and Co., now also based in Macleod, $41,999.09 in goods and services, a sum slightly more than was paid out to the Canadian Pacific Railway for an enormous amount of transportation services and several times more than was paid to any other company. The Hudson's Bay Company received $10,765.85 from the NWMP that year and the T. C. Power Company $3,508.11.[123]

Much of the provisions for the men, most of the forage for the horses and fuel and light for the buildings was bought by NWMP locally at division posts. The Officer Commanding usually advertised in a local newspaper, inviting tenders on items needed.[124] An aspiring contractor would then submit a bid offering to supply a certain quantity of the item at a certain price and guaranteeing the seriousness of the tender with a cheque drawn to the sum of five per cent or ten per cent of the value of the contract. After examining the proposals, the Officer Commanding, sometimes with reference to the Commissioner or the Comptroller, would award contracts to one of the tenders, or to several if necessary, to obtain the required quantity of the goods.[125] The Force was not obliged to award contracts to the lowest tenderer; in addition to price, other factors including the reliability or the political stripe of the applicant were considered. Contracts were avidly sought by farmers and businessmen alike and the total money involved was substantial. For instance, in the fiscal year 1890-91, the Force spent $218,274.86 on food, forage, fuel and light for the NWMP posts and detachments in the NWT.[126]

Commissioner Herchmer claimed that this local purchase by contract system was designed to spread Mounted Police business among as many settlers as possible and to encourage enterprise on the Indian reserves.[127] This was probably true, but as these contracts were coveted the awards were closely watched by the applicants and by local newspapers. It is not surprising then that exception was taken on occasion to the decisions made by the Force. Herchmer himself was burned on a hay contract awarded at Battleford shortly after he took over as head of the Force. In 1886, George L. Lytle of Regina tendered successfully on the contract to supply hay to the Mounted Police barracks at Battleford despite tenders submitted by local people, one at a price lower than that of Lytle. Feeling in the district ran very high and when Lytle arrived he concluded that local opposition prevented him from fulfilling his contract despite promises of protection from the police. The bitterness of the Battleford residents was also turned against Herchmer whom they accused of interfering in the contract award on behalf of Lytle.[128] A complicated court case ensued when the government sued the would-be supplier for failing to fulfil his contract. The judicial decision eventually went against the government.[129]

Other issues concerning the settlers related to favour shown to Indians and to large contractors in local purchases. In the spring of 1892, farmers in the Regina area petitioned the government to award all contracts strictly by tender with no special arrangement for Indians and with no contract for a quantity of hay in excess of 25 tons. In previous years, the government had favoured larger contractors who would act as middlemen by buying hay from a number of small farmers and reselling it to the Mounted Police at a profit. Such an arrangement suited the Force if the price was not too high because it was easier to deal with one large contract than several small ones. Moreover, to encourage Indian agriculture on the reserves the Force had been buying hay from different bands without requiring them to submit tenders, setting the price by the lowest tender proposal submitted by the white settlers.[130] In the fiscal year 1890-91, 240 of the almost 650 tons of hay bought by the Force at Regina came from the Indian reserves.[131] Although similar complaints were voiced in other locations in the NWT as well,[132] the Mounted Police continued to show preference for Indian hay for some years for the excellent reason that the quality was the best and the delivery and stacking were carried out efficiently.[133]

The purchase of horses was another source of police patronage for westerners. In 1886, due to the post-rebellion growth of the Mounted Police, 125 horses were purchased in Ontario but proved too delicate for the work of the Force. As a result, Commissioner Herchmer decided that in the future all horses would be bought in the West where they were hardier and less expensive.[134] Obtaining horses was a straightforward procedure. The Commissioner advertised in different newspapers that he, or one of his officers, would be in a certain place on such a date to buy remounts. Those interested would then bring their animals in for inspection.[135] A considerable number of horses were required by the Force each year to replace those worn out by long patrols or rendered unfit by age or disease. For example, the Commissioner reported in 1889 that he had bought 125 horses from ranches across the West. He noted with satisfaction that while 55 of these remounts were obtained from three larger ranches, "many of our best horses were bought from small breeders who only showed two or three horses"[136] and that patronage had been broadly distributed to 29 ranches. Records show that for the fiscal year ending 30 June 1889 the Mounted Police purchased 122 horses at prices ranging from $85 to

$145 and averaging $122.72. The total amount spent for horses was $14,850.00.[137]

For western communities, having a NWMP post or detachment in the vicinity was most desirable, not only for protection but for the stimulus it afforded to the local economy. After the rebellion, the Minister of the Interior, Edgar Dewdney, seriously considered the removal of divisional headquarters at Calgary from the town. Rumour of the plan reached Calgary and residents petitioned Ottawa successfully not to make the change, arguing that the town needed the garrison to protect against Indians and also that the community was growing and deserved the patronage of the Force.[138] Also, in 1886, the *Prince Albert Times* was indignant that its status as a divisional headquarters point had not yet benefitted the town through the construction of a large barracks. The newspaper castigated Ottawa public servants for tardiness in supplying this boost to the local economy.[139] Smaller centres were equally ardent to obtain and keep detachments of police. In 1890, the residents of Pincher Creek, Alberta, attended a meeting to protest the rumoured move of their detachment to the nearby town of Stand Off. At the meeting, chaired by John Herron, an ex-Mounted Policeman and now a successful rancher, a petition opposing this blow to this "thriving village"[140] was drawn up and sent to the Prime Minister. Called upon to explain to Ottawa, Herchmer replied that there was no intention to effect such a transfer but the removal of the Officer living in a house rented from Herron to accommodations closer to the detachment was being contemplated.[141] A personal stake in the location of the police station was shared by Arthur Roberts of Wapella, Assiniboia, who complained to Edgar Dewdney in 1891 about the removal of the constable located there. Herchmer explained to Fred White that there was no longer a need for a constable at Wapella and that, for a year, the complainant had enjoyed the benefit of the constable boarding at his father-in-law's hotel, stabling his horse there and spending his pay at Roberts' store.[142]

Competition between towns for Mounted Police stations and the accompanying patronage advantages was also very common. The Manitoba and Northwestern Railway moved into the NWT, reaching Saltcoats in 1889 and Yorkton in 1890.[143] A police detachment was needed in this region and both towns lobbied the government for the honour. Police opinion favoured Yorkton, but Saltcoats had the support of Sir Charles Tupper.[144] A poor compromise resulted with Saltcoats and Yorkton both getting detachments, although the larger of the two was at Saltcoats which, by 1893, was headquarters for the sub-district which contained Yorkton. A further attempt by Commissioner Herchmer to close the detachment at Yorkton in 1891 as superfluous to police requirements, failed on account of political intervention by the local Member of the Legislative Assembly.[145]

By far the most prolonged and bitter local patronage controversy in this period concerned the Mounted Police canteen at Regina. In late 1889, Herchmer authorized the establishment of a canteen for the other ranks of the Force at Regina. The men were tired of having to go two and a half miles to town and pay exorbitant prices for beer, cigars and good treats. This canteen was set up to provide these items and more at a reasonable price at the barracks. A permit was obtained from the Lieutenant-Governor to allow the canteen to bring in 100 gallons of beer each week.[146] The operation was run by W. F. Buchanan, a caterer from Winnipeg. This event was a rude shock to the Regina merchants and to the journalist MP, Nicholas Flood Davin.

On 28 November 1888, the Regina Board of Trade met and unanimously passed a resolution expressing its displeasure at the establishment of the barracks canteen which was detrimental to the business interest of Regina. Davin was asked to bring this matter to the attention of the Prime Minister and the Comptroller.[147] Not long thereafter, a petition signed by 67 Regina merchants was sent to Herchmer.[148] Davin was quick to attack his avowed foe Herchmer on the theme of unfair competition afforded the merchants by a government subsidized canteen run by an out-of-towner. On 4 December 1888, Davin reported that an order from the barracks placed with a Regina merchant for a lot of turkeys had just been cancelled. It seemed that Buchanan was now to supply the fowls from Winnipeg, no doubt at a better price because with the government-supplied horses and wagons to haul his goods and free accommodation he had little overhead.[149] Davin was quite explicit that the Regina merchants had a right to police patronage:

> Here is a community in Regina on a government town site with three fourths of the town site untaxable; without any benefit from the National Policy; paying their quota of taxes to maintain the police; and then a government body goes into competition with them![150]

The commercial issue at stake here was no doubt important to Davin, but he also used it to slander Herchmer personally. Early in the attack he speculated in an editorial in the *Regina Leader* whether Buchanan was a relative of the Commissioner.[151] He then reported that the two men had a close relationship and that Buchanan had given toys to Herchmer's children.[152] As the struggle wore on, Davin even suggested that Herchmer was taking bribes from the caterer. No foundation for such charges was uncovered later by the Wetmore Commission.[153]

In the end, Davin won the substance of his case. Macdonald bowed to pressure from Davin and from petitioning Regina merchants and he announced in February 1889 the government would terminate its arrangement with Buchanan. However, coming from the garrison city of Kingston, Macdonald was well aware that a canteen was a great convenience to troops and he refused to shut down the NWMP operation altogether. He ordered that management of the canteen be turned over to a committee of Force members who presumably would dispense police patronage locally.[154] Davin kept a close eye on the canteen over the next few months as he was convinced that Herchmer was underhandedly trying to influence Macdonald to reverse his decision.[155] Finally, on 29 October 1889, Davin was able to announce with satisfaction that Buchanan was finally gone from the barracks.[156]

The reality of party politics in Canada has long affected the distribution of patronage. Basically, the party which formed the government used its power to grant offices and fill contracts to reward or gain supporters. There were, however, standards of political morality and devices such as the Auditor-General and the contract tender system to guard against governments squandering the public purse on unworthy employees or contractors. That such safeguards were not always enough was more than proven by the contract abuses uncovered in Macdonald's government by the McGreevy scandal of 1891.[157]

Like other government departments the Mounted Police paid obeisance to politics when making financial commitments. Evidence of this aspect of the administration of the Force is rather sketchy, probably because it was unwise to keep documentation of practices and transactions which would cause embarrassment if they came into the vindictive hands of the government's opponents. It is clear that the government periodically circulated to the departments a printed list of newspapers which, because of the support they gave to the party, were eligible for government advertising. The Mounted Police followed this list when placing "Call for Tenders" and recruiting notices.[158] Some contractors who benefitted the most from Mounted Police patronage were prominent Conservatives,[159] one of whom, James O'Brien, laid claim to police business, partly on the basis of the proven quality of his work and partly on money contributed to the party in the previous election.[160] O'Brien was called to the Senate in 1895[161] as W. E. Sandford had been in 1887, another large contractor for the Mounted Police.[162] Other substantial recipients of police patronage during this period were: Bennett Rosamond of Rosamond Woolen Co. and Conservative MP from North Lanark from 1891;[163] John M. Garland, an Ottawa dry goods merchant, and Hollis Shorey, a Montreal clothier, both described in a contemporary biographical directory as "staunch Conservatives".[164] There is evidence too that the Mounted Police followed the system in vogue, allowing Conservative MPs or heads of constituencies a strong voice in the choice of businesses to be patronized by the Force in miscellaneous purchases, especially when contracts were not required.[165] These small pieces of information taken together lay a basis for conjecture that the Mounted Police conformed to the government's patronage practise of rewarding its political supporters.[166]

The federal government organized and despatched the NWMP to the frontier as an instrument for peaceful settlement. But it was not realized how important and benignly intrusive this instrument would become. In the post-rebellion years, white settlement brought disease and social and economic disruption to the prairies. A strong government presence was needed to minimize the hardships for the inhabitants, new and old alike. The Mounted Police became that presence, performing a multitude of services to foster the development of this incipient society. Credit for the success of this goes to Commissioner L. W. Herchmer for organizing the patrol system which created close communication between the policemen and the people.

Many of the settlers and the Métis came to rely on the Mounted Police to help them in difficult circumstances. This led to the increasing popularity of the Force which, in the future, reached mythic proportions. But in the Herchmer era, there was one duty of the police, the enforcement of morality, which undermined its otherwise positive image. In particular, the people felt almost universally that the police had no place in the bar rooms of the frontier.

Chapter 3

"Curbing Their Appetites": Enforced Morality on the Frontier, 1886-1892

The arrival of large numbers of whites, mostly men, in the NWT coincided with the construction of the Canadian Pacific Railway. With it came the problem of regulating the morality of frontier society to conform to the standards and expectations of more established communities in eastern Canada. The principal appetites of the mostly male populace were for sex and liquor, and satisfaction was stymied by the law. Prostitution was illegal and there were insufficient women for men to seek their pleasures in marriage. Finding solace in drink was difficult too. Alcohol was prohibited in the Territories to protect the Indians from its depredations. However, many, probably most of the men (and some of the women, too), had no sympathy for the moral laws and would transgress them at will or, at least, abide the transgressions of others. The Mounted Police attempted to enforce the laws, thus earning the enmity of much of society. Moreover, the policemen themselves shared and indulged the same physical appetites as their fellow citizens, making their losing battle to enforce the laws appear hypocritical. The inherent contradictions were too powerful to be borne by the society and compromises were reached which brought some regulation but not prohibition, to the consumption of liquor and the purchase of sex.

Prostitution was not the oldest profession practised on the prairies, but it was a part of the vanguard of settlement. Calgary has the dubious honour of having the first brothel closed down by the Mounted Police. In March 1884, Insp. Sam B. Steele in his capacity as a justice of the peace, found Nina Dow and Nellie Swift guilty of keeping a house of ill-fame. Steele allowed them to choose their own sentence – six months imprisonment, or leave town on the next train. They chose the latter.[1] However,

except for very brief periods, it is unlikely that Calgary was ever without a brothel again.

Actually, prostitution had arrived in the Territories about a year or so earlier. Like other criminal activity, it came with the construction of the CPR, advancing westward with each new construction camp from Winnipeg, where it had flourished as early as 1875.[2] By 1886, streetwalkers were plying their trade in Regina, Moose Jaw, Edmonton, Calgary and other prairie settlements. As in the American West, the *demimonde* was part of the retinue of the railway construction crews. From there, the ladies moved into the mining camps that followed the rail lines and finally settled in the red light districts of the new urban communities. Prostitution was one of the prices of development and settlement. In May 1883, the *Regina Leader* reported a number of brothels in the town north of the tracks.[3] For the next three decades, the house of ill-fame would be as much a part of many prairie communities as the schoolhouse, the church and the general store.

Prostitution flourished wherever there was a large body of unattached males. Throughout this period the male population of the Territories considerably outnumbered that of the female. When Nellie Swift was forced out of Calgary, she did what many of her sisters would do. She simply moved on to the next construction camp at Laggan, where four months later she was convicted by Steele again and fined $50.[4]

Under Canadian criminal law, it was an indictable offence to operate a house of ill-fame, or be an inmate or frequenter of one. Upon conviction an offender was liable to a sentence of up to one year in prison.[5] The Mounted Police, however, usually treated these offences as misdemeanours and proceeded against transgressors under the less severe provisions of section 207 of the *Criminal Code* relating to vagrancy.

These provisions included in the definition of vagrant one who:

(i) being a common prostitute or night walker, wanders in the fields, public streets or highways, lanes or places of public meeting or gathering of people, and does not give a satisfactory account of herself;

(j) is a keeper or inmate of a disorderly house, bawdy-house or house of ill-fame, or house for the resort of prostitutes;

(k) is in the habit of frequenting such houses and does not give a satisfactory account of himself or herself; or

(l) having no peaceable profession or calling to maintain himself by, for the most part supports himself by gaming or crime, or by the avails of prostitution

Upon conviction for vagrancy an offender was liable to a fine of up to $50, or imprisonment for up to six months, or both. There was no substantial change in the laws relating to prostitution until the *Criminal Code* was amended just prior to the First World War in an effort to stiffen the penalties, particularly against procuring.

A common bawdy-house or a house of ill-fame was defined as any "house, room, set of rooms or place of any kind kept for the purposes of prostitution or the practise of acts of indecency".[7] To convict keepers and inmates it was not necessary for the police to show that money had changed hands, or that sexual acts had actually taken place. The law only required evidence that the house was resorted to by men and lewd conduct took place.[8] Likewise, the common prostitute, or street walker, was guilty if she was unable to give a satisfactory account of herself.

Whether or not prostitution should be legalized was a hotly debated question from time to time during the latter part of the nineteenth century in both Europe and North America. In most European countries it had already attained legal status, usually under the control of the police. One of the few exceptions was Britain. In 1864, the British Parliament passed a measure which gave it a quasi-legal status, but public reaction to it resulted in repeal of the law in 1886. The British stuck to the double standard. Prostitution may be necessary and it may be impossible to suppress, but it would not be legalized.

Canada and the United States followed the British pattern. There were isolated attempts to legalize prostitution in the United States in the 1870s, but public reaction doomed them to failure. Instead, respectable society and the authorities of both countries turned a blind eye to the presence of the prostitute, leaving it to the police to devise some *modus operandi* for controlling her activities.

The police in North America took a pragmatic approach to the problem. If prostitution was to exist outside the law under their supervision, it would have to do so in an orderly way. The best means to accomplish this was to confine the practice to one area of the community, a place where it would not intrude upon the life of the respectable classes. By segregating it the police could easily maintain surveillance and keep the operators in line by occasional raids and fines. Thus the red light district became a familiar feature of many towns and cities. The problem for the police was that public attitudes were susceptible to change. Most North American communities during this period experienced recurring crusades by reform groups who were bent upon a better moral order. This disrupted the police system of control and often brought charges of corruption down on their heads.

Until the early 1890s, the Mounted Police took little action against prostitutes. In the male-dominated frontier settlements prostitution appears to have been widely tolerated. Indeed, the rank and file of the Force were often some of the women's best customers. With tongue-in-cheek the *Regina Leader* reported that the "red-coat of the Mounted Policeman is seen flashing in and out from these dens at all hours. As no arrests have been made the character of these visits may easily be surmised".[9] The *Leader* went on to report that those in authority in the Force considered the house a necessary evil. The paper did not really quarrel with this view. Nicholas Flood Davin, the editor, would probably have agreed with Kipling that "single men in barracks don't grow into plaster saints".

Sometimes things did go a little too far, however. On the evening of 24 October 1888, three constables arrived in Edmonton from Fort Saskatchewan. They were being transferred to Calgary the next day and wanted to celebrate. On their way into the settlement of some 600 souls one of them dropped off at Nellie Webb's establishment, while the other two set out to paint the town red. Sometime later, quite drunk, they too headed for Nellie's house, but she refused to let them in. According to her testimony later, they threatened to wreck the house and kill her. Drunken customers were one of the hazards of being a prostitute, but Nellie Webb knew how to take care of herself. She got the .38 revolver she kept in the house and warned them that if they tried to break in, she would use it. When they started kicking the door down, she fired through the broken panels, hitting Cst. T. P. Cairney in the thigh and breaking his hip.[10]

Nellie claimed that she had fired in self-defence. Nonetheless, Sgt. Davidson of the town detachment arrested her. She was charged with malicious shooting and released on $2,000 bail. The Mounted Police were not anxious to keep her in the cells since she was also the local midwife and her services were expected to be required at any moment.

The case against her never came to court. The most likely reason was that the constables were too drunk to testify reliably as to what happened. Instead, Nellie was convicted of keeping a house of ill-fame and fined $20 and costs.[11] Edmonton was too hot for her now, and she was forced to move on. She went south to Calgary and re-established her business. Cst. Cairney spent several weeks recovering from his wound in the barracks' hospital at Fort Saskatchewan, then he was dismissed from the Force.

The residents of Edmonton were accustomed to drunkenness and brawling, but the Nellie Webb incident went too far even for frontier standards of behaviour. Frank Oliver, editor of the *Edmonton Bulletin* described it as "one of the most disgraceful affairs that has ever happened in Edmonton, through a set of men that are supposed to protect the citizens and their property".[12] Oliver placed the real fault at the feet of those in charge of the Mounted Police. It was one sign that westerners were beginning to demand better moral standards from those who policed them.

From about 1890, the Mounted Police developed a more systematic approach to the handling of prostitution. Behind the change was pressure from moral reformers, usually Protestant clergy. They were often the same groups or individuals who were in favour of prohibition. Their complaints were much the same. If prostitution was illegal, it should not be allowed to exist. Apart from being immoral, it ruined innocent women and was the cause of disease and crime. The police themselves should set an example and not patronize the houses of ill-fame. Citizens groups, too, objected to their presence, perhaps because they affected property values and were a deterrent to the orderly settlement of the community.

Conditions varied from place to place, but the NWMP evolved a fairly standard procedure for handling the matter. Once a complaint was made, the house was raided and the women charged. They were often given the alternative of a suspended sentence instead of a fine, if they promised to leave town. Should they stay and remain in business, the Mounted Police would raid them again from time to time and impose further fines. Thus the system of licence by fine, which was in common use elsewhere, was from time to time practised in most districts.

In response to public criticism the police also established more control over the running of the houses and the lives of the inmates. The movements of the women were restricted. They were prevented from flaunting their profession in the face of the respectable women of the town. They were also required to undergo periodic medical examinations in some cases. As for the houses, the police usually required that they be segregated in some area where they were out of sight and sound of the rest of the community. Under Herchmer, disciplinary steps were also taken to make it clear that consorting with prostitutes was not acceptable behaviour for a member of the NWMP. In January 1891, Cst. Glenn T. Emigh received 14 days hard labour for walking the streets of Macleod with a prostitute after being repeatedly warned not to do so.[13]

The Mounted Police, however, considered prostitution a necessary evil, and they were able for a time to resist pressures to have the practice completely suppressed. Even when they closed down houses and told the girls to leave, they knew that they would soon be replaced by another party of soiled doves, as they were sometimes called. In July 1889, the Mayor of Regina asked the Mounted Police to remove a house on Lorne Street run by a Mrs. Turner.[14] (The territorial capital still had no police force of its own). The house was closed down. The following year, they gave another group of the *demimonde* 24 hours to leave town. The *Regina Leader* reported that they went bag and baggage[15] but, within a few weeks another contingent had arrived.[16] A group of citizens complained to the Mayor. Once again he called upon the sergeant at the town station. He arrested them but later released them when they promised to leave Regina. No doubt further replacements soon followed.

With a population of almost 4,000 in 1891, Calgary was the largest town in the Territories. It was also rapidly becoming the prostitution capital. Early in that year, the Mounted Police stepped up enforcement against the numerous houses that had been established just outside the town limits. The *Calgary Herald* applauded the Colonel's (Supt. J. H. McIllree) efforts to punish the "strumpets".[17] During that year about 30 convictions were obtained against keepers and inmates.[18] Often they were the same girls being repeatedly charged every few months. For the first offence, the fines were usually $20 for keeping a house of ill-fame and $5 for being an inmate. The alternative was imprisonment for a few days. Everyone convicted in Calgary that year paid their fine. The methods adopted to control prostitution there would be repeated elsewhere many times in the ensuing years.

There was one Calgary madam who was a thorn in the side of the NWMP for a while, undermining morale and proving difficult to dislodge. Her name was Lottie Carkeek, alias Dutch Lottie, alias Lottie Diamond. Prostitutes frequently changed their names and seemed to prefer diminutive first ones that had a ring of familiarity to them, like Tilley,

Trixie, Georgie, Lulu and Allie. Occasionally they adopted a more ribald sobriquet, like the two women who once functioned in the Empress Hotel in Moose Jaw, Knockout Duffy and Pussy Jake.[19] In their tussle with Lottie Diamond, the Mounted Police ran into a problem they would find elsewhere – conflict with the local police.

Lottie first established a house of ill-fame in Calgary in 1888. She soon struck up an affair with Sgt. Sargent, the son of a Church of England missionary and a member of the local NWMP post. The liaison resulted in Sargent being disciplined and reduced to the rank of constable. A short time later he obtained his discharge and married Lottie. The newlyweds moved to Vancouver, but Lottie must have grown tired of respectable life because in 1891 she returned to Calgary and started up a house on the bank of the Elbow River a short walk from the Mounted Police barracks.[20]

In spite of being "old and withered in appearance", Lottie must have had some quality that non-commissioned officers of the Mounted Police could not resist. Within a few months one sergeant major, two staff sergeants and one sergeant had been reduced in rank for being intimately involved with her. In June 1892, Commissioner Herchmer was forced to order her house declared out of bounds to members of the NWMP.[21] The clandestine visits continued, however, and the sergeants' mess became bitterly divided between the "friends" of Lottie and those who wanted to see her closed down.

The personnel problem was solved by transferring a number of men to other districts, but moving Lottie was not so easy. In trying to do so, the Mounted Police trod on the toes of the Chief of the Calgary Police, Thomas English, which in the long run was detrimental to their own interest and that of the public. Lottie's house was within the town limits. It lay, therefore, within the jurisdiction of the town force, although it would not have been illegal for the Mounted Police to have acted.

In June 1892, Insp. A. R. Cuthbert, who had replaced McIllree in command of the Calgary District, wrote to the Mayor asking him to take action against Lottie. The Mayor was sympathetic but Chief of Police English seemed slow to move against her. Cuthbert believed that he was protecting her. The most likely explanation is that English was only tolerating prostitution in the same manner as the Mounted Police did.[22] In any event, Cuthbert threatened to raid her house every night until she was driven out. This brought some action on the part of the town police, but not the results that Cuthbert hoped for. Lottie was simply charged with keeping a house of ill-fame and fined $50. By this time relations between the two police forces had truly soured and Chief English was threatening

a civil suit against Cuthbert for suggesting that he was protecting a prostitute.[23] The futility of Mounted Police attempts to deal with Lottie Diamond was a good example of its ineffectiveness in dealing with prostitution generally.

Unlike prostitution, problems with alcohol did not arrive in the West with the railway. Before the formation of the Mounted Police, western Indians were being poisoned, impoverished and demoralized by whisky traders from the United States. By 1873, the federal government had both enacted legislation to prohibit the use of alcohol in the NWT and provided for the organization of the Mounted Police to enforce the law. When the Force marched west in 1874, it put a quick and effective end to the whisky smuggling and trading, thus winning the confidence and respect of Indian leaders. The Mounties' success in shutting off the whisky traffic was immediately recognized both in Canada and the United States, establishing a reputation for effectiveness which in later years exaggerated the image of the Force to mythic proportions. But the success of the 1870s did not continue in the 1880s when police efforts to enforce prohibition on the burgeoning white populace became ludicrous in face of virtual civil disobedience.

The original prohibition act of 1873 was amended in 1875 and incorporated into the *North-West Territories Act* as follows:

> Intoxicating liquors and other intoxicants are prohibited to be manufactured or made in the said North-West Territories, except by special permission of the Governor in Council, or to be imported or brought into the same from any Province of Canada, or elsewhere, or to be sold, exchanged, traded or bartered, except by special permission in writing of the Lieutenant-Governor of the said Territories.

There were in this prohibitory provision a number of assertions which could be challenged to allow for exceptions to the rule. For instance, at what percentage of alcohol content does a beverage become intoxicating? Under what conditions would the Lieutenant-Governor issue permission in writing allowing the consumption of alcohol? Once admitted to the NWT by special permission, what limitations existed on the use and distribution of the liquor? Constant pressure from the white community for the most liberal interpretation of the section brought an ever increasing flow of alcohol which the Mounted Police proved absolutely unable to stem. In fact, their efforts were so ludicrously in vain that the members were left frustrated and conscious of their unpopularity in the community.[25]

One of the loopholes created by the liquor regulation was the definition of intoxicating liquor. The mere presence of alcohol in a beverage was not considered as proof, at least by the Mounted Police, that it was intoxicating. A rough guideline employed by police, courts and legislators was that an acceptable level of alcoholic content for a drink was 4% by volume. Through this gap in the prohibition defences flowed many the barrel of beer.

In the early 1880s, breweries were established in several towns of the NWT all of which purported to manufacture a non-intoxicating hop beer. The police and other officials were divided and uncertain about how to handle these products. Supt. P. R. Neale, Officer Commanding at Macleod, discovered in November 1886 that a number of his men were getting drunk on hop beer supplied by the local brewer and he ordered sales to cease. However, he decided to check with the local Inland Revenue official who oversaw brewery operations. This gentleman, Mr. Thomas, opined that the beer supplied by the breweries at Macleod and Lethbridge was harmless, saying that he himself consumed 30 to 40 glasses a day without effect. Somewhat dubious, Neale agreed not to interfere.[26]

Supt. R. B. Deane at Lethbridge shared Mr. Thomas' opinion of the local brew even though he, like Neale, had some evidence to the contrary. In 1888, he reported on two incidents involving brawling among drunken Hungarian miners after they had consumed large quantities of Lethbridge manufactured hop beer. He said:

> Taken in moderation, this beer is certainly harmless, and it is puzzling to know how a man can swallow enough to get drunk on. Given, however, a man of the required capacity, who deliberately sits down to consume two or three dozen bottles in an evening, it is to the interest of saloon keepers not to serve him beyond a certain point. Two or three Hungarian miners think nothing of drinking sixty or seventy bottles between them in an evening.[27]

In one of the incidents, the proprietor of the saloon which had served the hop beer, was convicted of selling an intoxicating liquor and fined.[28]

In the meantime, notice was served on the territorial breweries that in the future their operations would be watched more carefully. The Inland Revenue department was responsible for issuing licences to Canadian breweries. In November 1887, the department instructed the Mounted Police to issue circulars to all breweries in the Territories notifying them that they required a licence and that their activities would be monitored. The police reported that this warning resulted in the immediate closing of most of the small breweries which would certainly not have escaped detection for producing intoxicating liquor.[29] Some of the breweries, such as the one at Lethbridge and another at Medicine Hat, continued to operate in defiance of the warning. The real problem for police was the vendors who were selling their brew to the Indians, claiming that it was non-intoxicating, although the Natives were observed in varying states of drunkenness and disorder after its consumption.[30] The first inspection and prosecution of a territorial brewery by Inland Revenue occurred in 1889 at Medicine Hat when an official of the department laid charges against A. R. Tracey for manufacturing beer in contravention of the *Inland Revenue Act*. Mr. Tracey was found guilty and fined $300 and assessed a further $334 in court costs. The minimum sentence was levied since this was first case of someone being charged with this offence in the Territories.[31] Perhaps encouraged by this successful prosecution, Supt. Deane arrested a man in Lethbridge in 1890 who was selling hop beer to the Indians. This time the charge was selling intoxicants to the Indians; the case was won and the convicted, Thomas Farrar, received a $300 fine and six months in prison.[32]

Simultaneous with the federal government's crackdown of the territorial breweries, came a NWT government initiative to induce wider distribution of a "mild" beer in the West. On 4 July 1888, recently appointed Lieutenant-Governor Joseph Royal assumed office in the NWT. Royal was an experienced westerner; lawyer, publisher, cabinet minister in the province of Manitoba from 1872 to 1879, and MP from that province from 1879 to 1888, and had also served on the first NWT council.[33] Moreover, Royal would soon become father-in-law of Supt. Sévère Gagnon and may well have heard stories of the difficulties enforcing prohibition.[34] On 23 July 1888, Royal decided to allow the importation by special permit of light beer, alcoholic content not to exceed 4%, for sale in the NWT.[35] The beer was required to carry the stamp of the Inland Revenue department guaranteeing that it did not exceed the legal alcoholic content. Other conditions were laid down to ensure that the privilege would not be abused: permits to import would be granted only to hotel-keepers of good character, no beer was to be sold between 10 p.m. Saturday and 7 a.m. Monday, and sale was restricted to those 14 years of age or over. Naturally, the Mounted Police were instructed to see that the regulations were observed.[36]

The introduction of the legal sale of near beer in the NWT was welcomed by drinkers as a step in the direction of the end of prohibition. Prime Minister Macdonald assured the House of Commons of the benefits of the brew (though he had admitted 4% was too weak for him)[37] as drinkers would choose it over vile and harmful smuggled potions.[38] Commissioner Herchmer observed that the liberal granting of the beer permits allowed the general availability of the brew, lessening the demand for alcohol and decreasing drunkenness.[39] Among those places where the beer was most welcome included the divisional posts of the Mounted Police. Canteens were quickly established and the officers commanding applied for permits for the 4% beer. On 2 October 1888, Commissioner Herchmer asked the Lieutenant-Governor for a permit to bring from Winnipeg 100 gallons of Drewery's Redwood brew each week for the 170-odd men at Regina. In November, Supt. W. D. Antrobus wanted 512 gallons for his 61 men at Maple Creek, an amount which Herchmer hoped would last the winter. Antrobus also requested 320 gallons for the 25 men at Medicine Hat.[40] The Commissioner anticipated that the canteens would please the men, commenting that members of the Force at Regina were tired of spending 12½ cents for a small glass of hop beer in town.[41]

A seemingly insurmountable problem faced by police in enforcing regulations concerning the sale of 4% beer was ensuring that the beverage did not exceed the authorized strength. Soon after the 4% beer was permitted, Supt. A. B. Perry at Prince Albert pointed out that he did not possess the expertise in his district to make an accurate determination of strength.[42] Apparently the Force did have apparatus which was used to verify the alcoholic content but it appears to have been not often employed.[43] Once, in 1889, Supt. McIllree at Calgary became suspicious of some Drewery's stout although the bottles bore the proper Inland Revenue seal; he sent a sample bottle to Regina for analysis and the 4% beer tested at 11.8% alcohol. Unfortunately, there is no record of any action taken in this instance.[44] On another occasion in 1890, the Mounted Police checked barrels of 4% beer brought into the Territories by the Empire Brewing Company of Winnipeg. In the handling, gas in the barrels was released leading to the beer spoiling. The brewer complained to the Lieutenant-Governor and as a result Herchmer instructed Force members in the future not to check 4% beer unless there was good reason to suspect fraud.[45] Clearly, whatever theoretical responsibility the Mounted Police had to enforce regulation of the 4% beer trade, in practice, the Force was powerless.

A similar, and perhaps even more frustrating, situation existed with regard to the liquor permit system. Under the provisions of the *North-West Territories Act* the importation of liquor required the special permission of the Lieutenant-Governor. Supporters of prohibition argued that this exception from the law was originally intended to allow for alcohol for sacramental and medicinal purposes. The "wets", however, believed that the intent of the Act had been to keep liquor away from the Indians but allow for personal consumption by responsible white persons.[46] Intents and purposes not withstanding, this loophole in prohibition evolved into a system of importing, holding and selling liquor in the NWT.

Again it was the influx of white settlers brought by the railway which created the permit system. Before that, Lieutenant-Governors Alexander Morris and David Laird had exercised personal discretion about granting permissions to import liquor to the small number of whites in the West.[47] When Edgar Dewdney assumed office in 1881, he found the increasing demand for permits required him to devise a system to handle them more efficiently. Accordingly, he began to issue permits which authorized the recipient to import a limited quantity of liquor, wine or strong beer, usually one to five gallons within a certain time frame. There was no longer any pretence to assuage prohibitionists that the liquor was intended only for sacramental or medicinal purposes. Dewdney did, however, try to limit these permits to those of good character who wanted the liquor for personal consumption. Because he could not possibly know all of the newcomers he tried to check the character of strangers through the police or elected representatives.[48]

The permit system was also designed to control the flow of liquor. One part of the form was cancelled by the police on the arrival of the liquor in the NWT, a "coupon" or "stub" was detached from the cancelled permit and returned to the Lieutenant-Governor with any future request for liquor. This coupon bore the information on the person's last liquor importation and so would alert the Lieutenant-Governor if excessive quantity was requested. No doubt the system seemed to the conscientious official to allow control of the flow of liquor to the NWT. However, he had not bargained on the determination of the people to resist such imposed control of their drinking.

First, the permit system allowed for a large importation of liquor into the Territories, supposedly for domestic consumption or for the medical benefit of respectable citizenry. The number of permits issued grew steadily throughout the period from 3,559 in 1886 to 5,973 in 1891. In 1886, the per capita consumption of legally-imported liquor, wine and beer in the NWT was 0.662 gallons. This figure grew during the period peaking at 3.672 gallons each for every man, woman and child in 1889.[49] There are indications that a great deal of the liquor brought into the Territories on permit ended up being sold indiscriminately to the general public.

Every town of any size had saloons and hotels with bar rooms where a man could get a drink as long as a mounted policeman was not around. Before 1888, the proprietor of the establishment usually held a permit allowing him a certain quantity of liquor and/or beer and wine for his own use. This could be obtained by a customer usually on the pretence that he was buying a soft drink or a cigar and the proprietor treated him to a free drink. The amount of liquor allowed on the permit certainly would not allow for the full-time operation of a saloon except that the legal booze was primarily a cover for larger quantities of smuggled liquor which was kept hidden. As long as a proprietor limited the amount of liquor he actually kept at the bar to the quantity listed on his permit, he was safe in case of a police check. There was no way of determining whether the booze at the bar was the actual liquor imported under the permit produced. In a sense, the permit became a licence for a saloon to hold openly and to sell discreetly legal and illegal liquor.[50]

The situation for the town bar owners became even easier in 1888. Judge Rouleau of the Territorial Supreme Court ruled in a case tried before him that liquor and the accompanying permits were transferable from one party to another. This judgement was made despite the fact that the permits were stamped "Not Transferable". So now a private individual could import and consume a quantity of liquor legally with a permit, then give or sell his permit stub to a saloon keeper who would use the document to justify part of his liquor stock in case of a police raid. This greatly increased the amount of stock a saloon could keep immediately on hand and made the police virtually powerless to press charges for possession of liquor without a permit. Now police had to prove the much more difficult case that a bar was selling liquor.[51] One saloon in Macleod was raided in 1890 by Cpl. George A. Greenacre who reported that the proprietor justified his stock with 21 permits, only 2 of which were in his name.[52] Supt. McIllree complained in 1890 that he found 127 permit stubs held by hotel and saloon keepers in Calgary, many of them years old and some made out to men now dead or out of the country.[53] The Lieutenant-Governor tried to counter this abuse in 1890 by stamping on the permit that anyone involved in the transfer of the document would in future be refused further permits. But this was too little too late, because of the thousands of permits already issued allowing the holder to possess liquor indefinitely.[54]

Also in 1888, Judge Rouleau temporarily limited the Force's law enforcement authority when he ruled in an appeal case that police were not allowed to search saloons without a warrant unless they could actually see the liquor for which they were looking. An amendment to the *Mounted Police Act* in 1889 restored the power of discretion to police to determine when circumstances justified a raid.[55] However, in 1888, Rouleau's judicial interpretations of the law which favoured the liquor trade, combined with the decision to allow the legal sale of 4% beer, removed much of the control over drink for the NWMP.

But perhaps the most important aspect of the permit system was that it made legal the widespread presence of alcohol in the NWT, thus masking an ocean of illegal booze. As mentioned above, an individual or a saloon owner in possession of a permit stub stating that he was entitled to hold so many gallons of liquor was in an excellent position to protect himself if caught with bootleg alcohol. He simply produced his permit stub, for which there was no expiry date, and matched it to his stock. As long as he was careful that the kind of liquor he held was the same listed on the permit and the quantity was identical or less, he could not be touched. Another device was to re-use a permit for imported alcohol which had escaped the detection of the Mounted Police. In most cases the permit-holder had one month to bring in liquor. He would place his order with a distiller or brewer outside the NWT with shipping instructions which would make the package look innocuous. Then, if upon arrival in the NWT the Mounted Police failed to identify the shipment at the train station, the man picked up his liquor without producing his permit for cancellation. Then, if time remained on his permit he would place a second order identical to the first. Of course, only one of the two shipments could be openly displayed.[56] This dodge depended upon the acknowledged impossibility of the Mounted Policemen stationed at railway stations checking all freight for liquor. This fact also made smuggling booze by rail a largely successful enterprise.[57]

Large quantities of liquor were smuggled into the NWT during this period and the Mounted Police were able to detect only a small proportion of the traffic. Most of the booze came in by train from points east or west in Canada and often considerable effort was made to disguise the nature of the shipments. Barrels of liquor were sent marked "sugar", "salt" and "4% beer". Crates of liquor in bottles carried innocuous labels like "wallpaper". In one case imitation egg shells were found to contain liquor.[58] Four men were arrested near Langden in 1886 with 300 gallons of whisky buried in a carload of oats.[59] Train passengers brought in liquor in their luggage. One man was found by a Mountie locked in the closet of a CPR Pullman car with a ten gallon keg of whisky.[60]

The cases cited were probably among the minority of shipments intercepted by police. There were too many odds against the police to suppose that they could seriously impair the traffic. There was virtually a public conspiracy to abet the illegal whisky traffic. In many cases the booze was shipped addressed to a false name. If the Mounted Police detected the beverage then it was confiscated and the culprit who ordered it went free. Laying a trap for someone who might turn up to claim it was pointless because railway employees and others always put out the word that a seizure had been made.[61] Even when an individual's real name appeared on a shipment of smuggled liquor, the police were stymied because no charge could be laid unless he took it into his possession.[62] Even the CPR hindered police surveillance by objecting to police disturbing their passengers in sleeping cars with liquor searches. This practice was stopped except for situations where the police had "strong suspicion" of the presence of liquor.[63] Supt. McIllree admitted, by 1891, that much of the liquor flowing into Calgary arrived in railway sleeping cars from which his men were barred except under "extraordinary circumstances".[64] Supt. Neale despaired of enforcing the law effectively, declaring:

> Nearly all classes of the community in this district are antagonistic to the existing liquor laws, and there are very few indeed who will not assist in the smuggling of liquor.[65]

Despite Neale's despair, the Mounted Police still enjoyed some success against liquor smuggling from the United States to the southern NWT. The traditional whisky traders bringing in their kegs by wagon had to run the gauntlet of NWMP outposts and patrols. In July 1889, Cpl. Elliott, on patrol near Milk River Ridge, came across tracks of a heavily laden wagon and decided to track it down. The wagon was being driven by one Edward "Red" McConnell, a notorious whisky smuggler who was indeed bringing in five ten-gallon kegs of whisky from Montana. But before Elliott caught up with the wagon, McConnell, probably aware of police patrols in the area, ditched his precious cargo out of sight by the side of the trail. McConnell then continued on his way until he ran straight into a work party of Mounted Policemen building a bridge over a mud hole. McConnell coolly joined the camp and shared supper. Meanwhile, Elliott had noticed the difference in the depth of the track left by McConnell's wagon after he had removed his load and located the cache of whisky. Elliott waited by the kegs all night and when McConnell returned early the next morning to recover his goods, he was caught red-handed. Unfortunately, because police could not prove that McConnell had originally brought the whisky to that spot, he could not be charged with importing liquor. He was, however, convicted of possession of alcohol and fined $100 and costs. Supt. Deane was delighted at finally nabbing McConnell and discouraging him from pursuing his trade.[66]

The police also recorded the termination of the career of another noted whisky smuggler in this period, Gus Brede. This chronic offender defied authorities on both sides of the line, smuggling illegal Chinese immigrants into Montana from Canada and returning with whisky. Authorities despaired of stopping Brede because he was a daring operator with great knowledge of the country. But fate intervened and, on 11 August 1891 while leading a party of Chinese south, Brede was struck and killed by a lightning bolt. In noting his passing, Supt. Sam Steele reported that recent police patrols had been very successful in sealing the border to the whisky trade.[67]

The NWMP was almost alone in the Territories in its insistence upon enforcing liquor laws. The difficulties encountered by police officers, in their capacity as justices of the peace, with other members of the judiciary have already been explored.[68] One must reiterate, however, that policemen often found the civilian justices of the peace and even the judges in the NWT reluctant to convict those accused of liquor offences. Police complained that offenders were released despite clear evidence of their guilt.[69] Moreover, appeals of convictions were permitted and the judges allowed so much time to elapse before hearing them that the availability of witnesses or the reliability of their memories was questionable.[70] In large part, the reluctance of the judiciary to exercise their full authority in liquor cases can be attributed to the almost universal abhorrence of prohibition. But another factor was a distinct distaste for the police system of investigation and reward which often led to the arrest of suspects. Policemen who made the arrests and presented the evidence at trial were entitled to the "moitie", half the fine in a conviction, leading to their reputation as paid informers whose testimony was questionable.[71] Moreover, these policemen often worked undercover, "spying out" violators of regulations, further enhancing their image as furtive and treacherous.

Perhaps the most public notice taken of the activities of a police liquor undercover operative concerned Cst. Thomas W. Hussey, a young constable from Newfoundland, a former fisherman complete with tattoos of an anchor, a flag and a heart on his arms.[72] In 1891, Herchmer arranged with Calgary Chief of Police Tom English to cooperate with Hussey in an undercover investigation of illicit sale of liquor in city hotels.[73] By April 28th, he had laid charges against eleven Calgary residents for selling liquor and obtained convictions and fines in eight of the cases.[74] The *Calgary Herald* noted "plenty of excitement in liquor circles" over Hussey's activities.[75] Then, as suddenly as Hussey had struck Calgary, so did the town strike back.

On 27 April 1891, Cst. Thomas Hussey underwent preliminary examination in Calgary police court for perjury against one John Mannock, a saloon operator, for laying charges and swearing that Mannock had sold whisky to him. Mannock, in turn, swore that he had sold nothing but 4% beer to Hussey on the night in question and was backed up by Cst. A. C. Ross of the Calgary police force and by a Thomas King, both of whom had been with Hussey that evening. Ross and King testified that Hussey had proposed to them that he pull in Mannock, against whom he bore a personal grudge, and falsely accuse him of selling whisky in order to split the reward of half the fine. The evidence was sufficiently strong for Hussey to be bound over for trial and be placed in the Mounted Police guard-room.[76] The *Calgary Herald* was indignant about the affair and severely critical of Mounted Police methods in liquor cases:

> There can be no impropriety in calling the attention of the M.P. officials who execute judgment in a semi-military fashion, to the unwisdom of future interference with the internal affairs of the Town of Calgary, and especially to the undesirability of encouraging as they have done, the introduction of the spy system into a community where such an outrage upon decency is universally condemned.[77]

Supt. McIllree's view of the case was that it was simply a frame-up designed to put a stop to Hussey's raids. The trial was held before Justice Rouleau on 10 and 11 July 1891 and only Town Policeman Ross appeared to testify. Mr. Mannock had sold his saloon and left town after the preliminary hearing and King had been working on the Calgary and Edmonton Railway construction line and had not been reached in time to serve him with a subpoena. Rouleau dismissed the charge against Hussey and the *Calgary Herald* called "foul" claiming not enough effort had been put into locating King, which was denied by the Mounted Police.[78]

In any case, neither Cst. Hussey nor Cst. Ross remained long out of trouble. Hussey was charged in a Mounted Police service court on 21 July 1891 with attempting to blackmail a restaurant operator and creating a disturbance. Hussey was accused of entering the establishment of one Marriaggi and demanding he provide free whisky or be arrested on a liquor offence. Marriaggi refused to be black-mailed and informed on Hussey. Supt. McIllree sentenced the ace detective to six months in the guard-room and dismissal from the Force. Commissioner Herchmer, however, disagreed with McIllree. He believed that Hussey was innocent; as a result, he reduced the sentence to one month and allowed Hussey to remain in the Force.[79] The *Calgary Herald* was again outraged at Herchmer's action and demanded an investigation into the administration of justice in the NWT.[80] Meanwhile, by now ex-Town Policeman Ross also ran afoul of the law, being arrested and convicted in October 1891 of importing liquor illegally into the Territories. He was fined $50.[81]

Conflicts between the local and Mounted Police forces over prohibition occurred in other communities too. At Prince Albert, one evening in early December 1887, Mounted Police Cst. Archibald Leslie was spotted by Queen's Hotel owner, Thomas Oram, in the vicinity of his stables. Oram sent for the town constable and had Leslie arrested and charged as a "Common night walker".[82] Leslie was tried in a farcical affair before two local justices

of the peace, found guilty and fined $25 and costs. This, despite the fact that Leslie's officer commanding, Supt. A. B. Perry, testified that the constable was on duty searching for liquor and in uniform. Perry explained to Commissioner Herchmer that the evidence at the trial was supplied by witnesses who were whisky traders. Made brazen by this success the liquor interests again tried to defy the police a few days later. Perry sent Leslie in plain-clothes to buy illegal liquor from a local source. When Leslie completed the transaction and revealed his identity, he was again arrested and put on trial, this time for having intoxicating liquor in his possession.[83] This time, however, the local justice of the peace could not swallow the story, dismissing the charge on the grounds that Leslie had seized the liquor in his capacity as a peace officer.[84] Likewise, the original conviction for loitering was overturned on appeal to Judge T. H. McGuire who was astonished at the action of the justice of the peace which he considered a travesty of justice. The citizens of Prince Albert were split over this incident: a public meeting condemned the Mounted Police and resolved to call upon the government to remove Perry, while the Mayor and 50 others signed a petition in support of Perry which was sent to Herchmer.[85]

What goodwill towards the NWMP shown in Prince Albert was, however, largely squandered when Cst. Leslie decided to get a little of his own back a few months later. Leslie was passing some time in the bar room of the Queen's Hotel on 24 September 1888 when a fight broke out between two customers. The same Thomas Oram who had previously had Leslie charged with loitering, now appealed to him for assistance. As Leslie moved in to break up the fight, one Peter Robertson, apparently a newly appointed town constable, arrived on the scene and tried to take charge. Leslie, who later claimed not to have known Robertson, resisted and the fight now was between the two constables which Leslie won with the help of another Mounted Policeman in the bar. Word of the incident spread quickly and as Leslie led Robertson off to the guardroom in handcuffs he was stopped by an angry crowd which included two members of town council. The Mounted Police guard was called out to rescue Leslie and his prisoner from a spontaneous vigilante action. Immediately after, three town councillors went to Insp. A. Ross Cuthbert, who was in temporary command that evening, and expressed their wrath at this challenge to the authority of the town police. Cuthbert wisely chose to bow to the mood of the citizens and ordered Robertson released from custody. Feelings continued to run high for several days. Town Council even had a summons drawn up ready to serve on Leslie notifying him that he was being sued in civil court. It took all of Perry's considerable diplomatic skills to assuage the indignation. He assured the council that the Mounted Police had no desire to interfere with the town police and he produced a copy of a local order which he had prepared instructing his men in the limits of their authority and calling for cooperation with the town constable. This apparently satisfied town council and the threat of civil action was dropped.

As for the Force, internal charges were levelled against Leslie for creating a disturbance and interfering with the duty of the town constable. After hearing the evidence Perry dismissed the charges finding Leslie's contention that he did not know the town constable was credible since the new peace officer did not wear a badge or a uniform.[86] However, Leslie did not long survive in the Force; a series of violations of regulations involving insubordinate behaviour led to a brief period in the guardroom. And finally, dismissal as a penalty for Leslie may well have been influenced by a recent report that when Leslie joined the NWMP almost four years earlier, he had just been released from prison in Ontario after serving a six-month sentence for burglary.[87]

The NWMP was committed by government policy to enforce prohibition longer than it should have been. Although the law was scorned by most in the West, the federal government was slow to end prohibition because of fears about alienating powerful temperance forces in the east. There were prohibitionist organizations in the NWT but these were pale reflections of the more powerful eastern lobby which opposed slipping the bonds of liquor control.[88] But in the Mounted Police commitment to their duty, there was a large element of hypocrisy. The officers and men of the Mounted Police were almost all enthusiastic drinkers. The officers used the permit system to import large amounts of legal liquor while, among the men, it was a common, if forbidden, practise to "spill" confiscated booze down eager throats neat or with a mix if preferred.[89]

Finally in 1891, the federal government gave in to persistent demands from the West and granted permission to the Territorial Assembly to set its own liquor law. This was belated recognition that the prohibition system had already collapsed. The Mounted Police openly admitted that they were unable to control the illegal importation and sale of liquor and that their half-hearted efforts spoiled their relations with local communities. On 6 January 1892, the NWT Council passed the Liquor License Ordinance providing for the granting of wholesale and hotel licences for the sale of alcohol in incorporated towns. The burden of enforcing prohibition was finally removed from the shoulders of the Mounted Police.[90]

Enforcing morality through regulation of prostitution and liquor consumption was not the favourite responsibility of the Mounted Police. In both cases they were forced to tolerate, to some extent, what they could not realistically control. The largely male society demanded a licentious release from the hardships and tedium of the frontier life and it was found in the bars and the brothels. But the community at large paid a price in disorder for this demand. A description of a section of the coal mining town of Lethbridge, about 1890, illustrates the problem:

> On one of the triangular landspits jutting out into the river valley, the saloon keepers, harlots, and gamblers built a little but thriving empire of vice. Bordered by deep coulees on three sides, the promontory, locally known as the Point, became an enclave of vice conveniently isolated from the reputable segment of the settlement. This prominent point of land, topped by practically the only painted house in town, became an ironically, but fittingly, garish landmark second only to the black tipples and smokestacks of the colliery. By 1890 six brightly painted, two and three-storey brothels, a cluster of saloons, and the company's bunk-house huddled together on the Point, catering not only to the local miners and railroaders but enticing men from miles around. Frequently the intemperate carousing erupted into violence, especially so on pay-days when the workers were determined to squander their earnings in one wild drunken week-end. The tensions created by the dangerous underground labour, the boredom of the small isolated town, and the lack of women exploded into frenetic merry-making. A turbulent boisterousness seethed beneath the thin veneer of bourgeois respectability.[91]

As prairie society passed from the frontier stage, however, this disorder would become less acceptable to the populace, increasing demands for police to regulate morality to suit a new community self-image.

Chapter 4

Easing the Transition from Frontier to Prairie Settlement, 1893-1900

As Canada entered the twentieth century, the prairie west began its transformation from frontier to civilization. Between 1891 and 1901, the population of the North-West Territories rose from about 99,000 to about 165,000 with immigration in the later couple of years indicating that more massive growth could be expected.[1] As the rationale for the establishment and maintenance of the North-West Mounted Police was that it would provide order on the frontier until civilization arrived, the status and very existence of the Force were called into question. Numbers of men in the establishment were reduced and a significant proportion were moved north where new frontiers were opening up. Over 250 Mounted Policemen volunteered for service in the Canadian contingents despatched to the South African War and this, too, robbed the Force of trained men. Yet, for all this, the demands made on the Force to foster the development of the West did not diminish. Despite the handicaps, the NWMP responded in a timely and successful manner.

Essentially, the Mounted Police continued to aid the development of the NWT as "Agents of the National Policy". Basically, the Force acted as a convenient agency, already well established in the West, to which the territorial and federal governments could refer the problems of pioneer settlers and ranchers. Services rendered included minimizing the difficulties of settlers from first arrival through economic hardship, distress of illness and protection from prairie fires. The policemen also continued to devote attention to the long international border where maintenance of cattle quarantine grounds and customs work represented a considerable commitment. Labour disputes and conflicts between sheep and cattle owners over grazing land kept the police vigilant for potential violence. And the expenditures made by the Force were vied for by competing firms in the political arena of patronage distribution.

The Mounted Police cooperated with the Department of the Interior as much as possible to smooth the path and to assist the settlement process for newcomers to the West. Often, organized groups of potential immigrants sent delegates from their number to investigate conditions before deciding on a location. Such delegates were usually accorded special treatment by the federal immigration service and by local officials.[2] Because the NWMP divisional headquarters posts were located near several of the centres attracting such delegates, often they were called upon for assistance. The police furnished the land seekers with transport, camping equipment and guides on many occasions. To assist the police with this task, the Department of the Interior provided literature on immigration and land acquisition which was forwarded to every commissioned officer in the Force in 1893, with copies held in all the recreation rooms at divisional headquarters.[3] That year, the persistent demands for services made by Thomas Anderson, the Immigration Agent at Edmonton, prompted Comptroller White to complain to his superior about his attitude:

> He apparently considers that their [*Mounted Policemen*] duty first in importance should be compliance with his demands for transport conveniences for land and immigration purposes.[4]

Once a group decided to move to the West, travel and accommodation arrangements were often made through the Department of the Interior. The NWMP made it quite clear that it could not extend its services to logistic support of this operation.[5] However, upon occasion, emergency situations arose which required police assistance. One such incident occurred in May 1898 as a result of a misunderstanding between the immigration branch and 146 Galician settlers. This group boarded a train in Regina believing they were destined to join other countrymen at established Galician settlements. Instead, an immigration agent led them off the train at Saskatoon and explained that they were to start a new community at Fish Creek north of the town. Neither this prospect nor the lay of the land around Saskatoon appealed to the immigrants, who were so upset that they started en masse to walk back to Regina. The immigration agent, over-reacting to the situation, appealed to Mounted Police S/Sgt. H. C. L. Hooper to bring the people back by force. The Non-Commissioned Officer refused to do so on the grounds that they had not transgressed any law. However, he and his men pursued the walkers, carrying bread to feed them. By the second day, prairie heat, flies and general discomfort disintegrated the resolve of the Galicians and they accepted rides back to Saskatoon in police wagons. There, a new deal was worked out with the immigration service and most of the group proceeded on to join established Galician communities. Thirty-six, however, agreed to accept homesteads at Fish Creek and they were escorted there by the Mounted Police. When the destination was reached, Hooper explained to the group the laws of Canada and led them in an impromptu concert to celebrate the Queen's birthday since it was May 24th. The immigrants called their new community, Bursten, after their hometown in Galicia. Hooper reported to his superiors that the new settlers were hard-working, religious and responsive to the least civility. He blamed the whole incident on the immigration service for not clearly establishing with the Galicians where they were to go.[6]

Once settlers were on the land, the Mounted Police tried to visit them as often as possible to check on conditions and to offer advice. Visits to settlers were included in the regular patrol system and by making special "flying" patrols to more isolated settlements. In the 1890s, each patrol carried a slip of paper for the settlers to sign as proof that they had been visited.[7] The patrols were intended primarily to reassure settlers that the authorities were concerned about their security. However, the police were willing to discuss any problems and even arbitrate disputes if necessary. In the case of colonies of Europeans who had recently arrived, the NWMP tried to station Force members in the area who spoke the language of the group or employed interpreters as required.[8] Throughout the 1890s, the Force struggled to maintain this commitment as an increasing tide of newcomers flooded into the prairies while the total number of policemen was reduced. By the end of the decade, regular patrols in more thickly populated areas were abandoned and the Force responded instead to calls for assistance.[9]

In the course of the patrols, Mounted Police acquired considerable information concerning the progress of settlement and conditions in the Territories which was forwarded to Ottawa. At first, the Department of the Interior welcomed the information but, as time passed, it became more selective about what was needed. The annual reports of the Commissioner of the NWMP contain detailed summaries from various districts including information on settlers' experiences, weather, crops, livestock and the development of industry. For a time in 1892, and perhaps 1893, the Police forwarded to the Department of the Interior special bulletins on crops and weather conditions until, in 1894, it was decided that this amount of detail was not necessary.[10] In 1895, the Commanding Officer of each division was ordered to include in his monthly reports a statement showing the name, size of family and the amount of livestock for all settlers who arrived from the United States.[11] In 1897, Clifford Sifton, Minister of the Interior, instructed the NWMP to record not only the number of immigrants entering the prairies from the States, but also the number leaving by the same route and those bound for British Columbia. The Mounted Police complied as best they could, compiling records on the number of people and stock crossing the line.[12] By the end of 1902, however, the Interior officials asked the police to stop sending such information as they were not using it.[13]

Perhaps the most valuable report made to the Department of the Interior was the census of 1895 which was conducted by the police. All Territorial inhabitants, except Indians, were enumerated, and the results were most encouraging to the government since they indicated an increase of 30 per cent in white settlers since 1891.[14] Some communities, however, were unhappy about the results of the census. The *Calgary Herald*, for instance, questioned the accuracy of the figures because they showed a decrease in the population of Calgary from 3,800 in 1891 to 3,207 in 1895.[15] The NWMP defended the returns by explaining that the 1891 figure had been too high because it included settlers for miles outside the town as well as workers in the Calgary and Edmonton Railway construction camp.[16]

The NWMP were particularly interested in reporting on the various ethnic and religious colonies which were quickly establishing themselves on the prairies. The 1890s witnessed the formation of communities of Mormons, Jews, Mennonites, Doukhobors, Galicians, Hungarians, Finns, Germans, Belgians, French and others. Although individual attitudes varied, most officers who reported on the state of these communities were initially suspicious of the foreign element and alien customs transplanted to the frontier. They generally feared that some of these settlers would be troublesome and would fail economically becoming, in one way or another, public charges. When these fears were not realized, more respect was accorded the newcomers. One indication of the changing attitude can be found in reports prepared by Commissioner Herchmer. He said, in 1896, about settlers:

> About 460 settled in the Edmonton district; 150 were Galicians, who, I consider, are a very undesirable class, as they generally arrive here with very little money, and are very ignorant. Most of them are clothed in sheepskins, and are several centuries behind the age.[17]

However, by 1899, the same man wrote about the Galicians, who had been here several years, "there can be little doubt that these people will eventually make good settlers".[18]

By 1899, when over 7,000 Doukhobors arrived in the Territories, the Mounted Police felt more comfortable in dealing with groups which, while they displayed many unusual customs, were capable of contributing to the agricultural progress of the West. Certainly in early contact there were reservations about their habits. One Cst. J. Clisby reported on their camp at Saskatoon:

> On arrival they [the Doukhobors] have been in the habit of camping on the west side of the railway track close to the station, where the Immigration department had erected two large tents for their accommodation. Whilst camped there numerous complaints were made to me of the manner in which they conducted themselves, indecently exposing themselves, and the filth which they accumulated during their stay. One complaint in writing was strongly worded, that I had to take immediate action in the matter and ordered them to move to the back of the stockyard where their presence was least likely to offend.[19]

Once the Russian immigrants settled in their new villages, they impressed the Mounted Police with their industry and self-reliance. Disapproval was expressed, however, of their communistic ways and the hope was often expressed that these tendencies would soon be abandoned.

Apparently Clifford Sifton too hoped that life in the new land would lead the Doukhobors to adopt the manners and values of Canadian society. Although the Doukhobors had emigrated to Canada to preserve their freedom to live as a religious commune, practically divorced from the civil state, conditions imposed by Sifton himself soon made this difficult. The Minister agreed that the Doukhobors could live collectively, but he insisted that they register their homesteads individually. This created a spirit of restiveness in the Doukhobor community which, in 1902, was combined with the appearance of a messianic fervour induced by leader Peter Veregin that Eden was at hand. The result was a social upheaval within the Doukhobor community which brought the Mounted Police their first experience in dealing with a mass protest demonstration.[20]

In late October 1902, Cpl. Christen Junget reported from Yorkton that several hundred Doukhobor men and women had been wandering among their villages preaching extreme views to their co-religionists. Within a few days an estimated 1,800 people were on the march, some to protest government policy and others searching for an earthly paradise which they felt was nearby. The Mounted Police were concerned because the marchers, including children and invalids, had deliberately not made any preparations for the journey. They carried no food and had made no arrangements for accommodation, trusting God to provide. Because they felt a religious kinship with animals, these extremists did not eat meat or use anything made of leather. So on their feet the marchers wore rubber footwear or nothing at all. The government moved quickly to intervene. On the 28th of October, the marchers arrived at Yorkton where they were met by immigration officials and the NWMP. Assisted by Doukhobors who had not been swept up in the messianic craze, government agents tried to persuade these people to give up their dangerous wanderings. When these pleas failed, the police and volunteer citizens moved on the group and separated the over 1,000 women, children and sick from the men and herded them into an immigration hall and other buildings. This task was accomplished without incident only because the Doukhobors remained largely true to their pacifism and most did not resist. The men, now reduced in number to 600, waited outside the town that night and then continued their march in a southerly direction the next day.[21]

The Doukhobor men endured nine more miserable days and nights before their collective belief that they would stumble into paradise faltered. Trailing behind the trekkers, the Police did not interfere, but were watchful for any incident while they collected clothing and boots that were discarded. In accordance with their interpretation of scripture, the men tried to feed themselves with fruit and vegetable matter found along the way, including grass. This was supplemented in a meager way by handouts from pitying settlers. At night, the men huddled together for warmth.[22] While some marchers became disillusioned and returned home, the majority, aided for several days by unusually clement weather for October, followed the main line of the CPR and crossed into Manitoba looking for the promised land. However, on the 3rd of November the situation deteriorated when snow and cold winds blew across the prairies. The Doukhobors spent three miserable days and nights on the road until they reached Minnedosa. Here, they agreed to take shelter at a skating rink. Once again, immigration agents tried to convince the approximately 450 remaining men to abandon their quixotic quest for paradise and return home. After three days, most were willing to comply, but a contingent of North-West Mounted Policemen and volunteer citizens was needed to steer a good number of the hardliners aboard a special train laid on for the return journey.

The spirit of the march, now much diminished, was left to the NWMP just to wrap up. While the marchers were away, the police had patrolled the abandoned Doukhobor villages to protect them against looters. At Yorkton, the women, children and sick had protested their incarceration by refusing to eat for a couple of days. But this resistance broke down and they preceded the men back to their homes. For the time being, Doukhobor extremism was stifled, but on 23 December 1902, Peter Veregin, regarded as a second coming of Christ by his followers, arrived in Saskatchewan from imprisonment in Siberia. In the next few years he stirred up a fanatical segment in the community to an enduring pattern of social protest and violence which plagued Canada and the Mounted Police for decades.[23]

The provision of material assistance in any emergency was perhaps the most important assistance rendered to new and old settlers alike by the NWMP. Some immigrants arrived with insufficient resources to make a good start at prairie life. For instance, in 1894, it was reported that a group from France who settled near Prince Albert were very badly prepared for their new existence. Some arrived with no money, others tried to borrow funds from established residents. In this case, the Mounted Police looked the other way when necessity forced these newcomers to shoot game out of season.[24] When winter arrived destitution increased and the police supplied rations to at least one family which had no food.[25] In incidents such as this, the Force was compensated for the issue of emergency food by the Department of the Interior, but only very grudgingly so. The department's policy was to limit as much as possible such measures so that no habits of dependence were inculcated into new settlers. In the northern NWT in the winter of 1896, some newly arrived Galician families and others who had lost crops in prairie fires faced serious deprivation. Before issuing relief, Supt. A. H. Griesbach checked with the Department of the Interior; he was sternly reminded that "the largest sum of money that has ever been at the disposal of this Department for purposes of this kind in one year has been $500".[26] Griesbach then went ahead and issued potatoes and flour to the needy in exchange for work such as cutting wood. However, when the Mounted Police proposed further assistance to some of these same settlers in the winter of 1897-98, Interior officials turned the idea down. Following an investigation by the departmental officer, the Interior Department concluded that the Mounted Policemen in the area were too lenient with the Galicians, encouraging them to expect relief instead of providing for themselves. Consequently, Fred White told Herchmer to order his men not visit the Galicians unless requested by the Department of the Interior, and if relief was applied for, the police were to refer the settlers to agents of that department.[27]

However, the most persistent case of deprivation among settlers rested with the half-breeds, many of whom had not adjusted well to the changing West. In the post-rebellion period, the half-breeds tried to accommodate themselves to the new conditions. Still grouped in northern settlements, they tried to subsist through small scale farming combined with hunting, fishing and root gathering. The completion of the railway to Saskatoon eliminated the freighting business and crop failures reduced the living conditions of some to desperation levels.[28] Every winter through the 1890s, the Mounted Police were called upon to issue food, and some clothing to these people, recouping their expenditures later from the Department of the Interior. Whenever possible, the half-breeds exchanged their labour for relief. In March 1899, the police at Battleford were supporting 65 men, women and children on a scale of rations as follows:

	Bacon or	Beef or	Flour[29]
Adult ration	½ lb.	¾ lb.	¾ lb.
Child ration	¼ lb.	⅜ lb.	½ lb.

By June of 1899, police had spent $573 so far that fiscal year on half-breed relief and estimated that the cost would rise to a total of $800.[30] Some half-breed families retreated from the advance of civilization as they had before and moved farther north to Peace River[31] country. Others were more fortunate and achieved individual success as farmers, or established viable communities which needed little help from government such as that at Egg Lake under the leadership of Father Therien.[32]

Another form of relief available to settlers in the NWT was the issue of seed grain in the spring to sow their crops. This was not meant as a gift but was loaned to new settlers, and to those who had suffered a loss of the previous year's crop, and was secured by a lien against the borrower's property until the loan was repaid. The Mounted Police often assisted the Department of the Interior in the distribution of seed grain in years when the demand was great.[33] In the autumn of 1895, prairie fires swept northern Alberta and Saskatchewan destroying crops, stock and buildings. Besides helping the most needy to survive the winter, the Force was responsible for ensuring that settlers were able to plant a new crop in the spring. As winter receded, patrols slogged along muddy roads surveying the needs of all settlers. Based on this information, the Mounted Police purchased large quantities of wheat, oats and barley, spreading their business throughout the southern portion of the NWT and in Manitoba. The grains were then carried by the CPR to a number of distribution centres in the Fort Saskatchewan and Prince Albert districts and apportioned to the settlers by Mounted Policemen in time to plant the spring crop.[34] In the spring of 1896, the Mounted Police issued 59,918 bushels of grain to 1,592 settlers at a cost of $22,484.09.[35]

The prairie fires which caused so much damage in the fall of 1896, were a constant hazard to settlers and a particular headache for the Mounted Police. All members of the Force were also Fire Guardians responsible for the protection of lives and property from fire and for the apprehension of those who may cause the conflagration through carelessness and occasionally by design. Commissioner Herchmer listed the five principal causes of prairie fires: sparks from trains; half-breeds firing the grass deliberately to find buffalo bones more easily; travellers neglecting to extinguish cooking fires; settlers losing control of fires which they set to burn fireguards around their property; and lightning.[36] As districts became more heavily settled, the danger of prairie fire diminished because roads and cleared land provided natural firebreaks and there were more people at hand to fight any blaze in its early stages. The most serious problems were in the sparsely settled areas where a fire could rage unchecked except for the efforts of what few people a policeman could muster. Such volunteer labour was sometimes reluctantly offered, especially when the fire was on Crown land and was not yet an immediate threat to a settler's own homestead.[37]

The reduction of the Mounted Police in settled areas of the Territories during the 1890s necessitated cutbacks in manpower assigned to the suppression of prairie fires. This action led to resentment by many settlers. In the summer of 1894, "B" Division in Saskatchewan established 25 fire stations in addition to its regular outposts. It was a dry summer, and the policemen at these stations fought 85 fires which burned about 7,000 square miles of prairie, most of it unsettled land.[38] Despite these efforts, the police were not able to entirely satisfy the people. That summer, both the Moose Jaw Board of Trade and the town's Agricultural Society petitioned the government to supply more policemen on fire suppression duty. The response of the Force was predictable: that an increase of this kind was impossible given the many responsibilities of the Force and that settlers themselves should be doing more to combat the menace.[39] Commissioner Herchmer complained that settlers were apathetic

and that they waited for police instead of seizing the initiative by extinguishing fires in the early stages. Moreover, settlers often refused to lay information against neighbours who caused fires, and even when they did, the culprits were assessed only light fines by local justices of the peace.

The territorial government took a conciliatory approach to the problem. While on the one hand, the government politely requested increased protection from the Force, on the other, it regularly and publicly praised the work of the police in this regard.[40] As the Force sought ways to reduce its commitment to fire fighting, the NWT government accepted the decision gracefully. In his throne speech of 1895, Lieutenant-Governor Edgar Dewdney announced that:

> in view of the decrease in the Mounted Police force, it will be incumbent upon settlers generally to be more thoughtful than ever in adopting precautions likely to prevent fires. In this connection I am glad to be able to state that the NWMP have for many years tendered great service.[41]

Again in 1896, Dewdney rendered thanks to the police for the "very great service"[42] in battling fires. In reply, the Territorial Assembly addressed the Lieutenant-Governor:

> We gladly recognize the very efficient services rendered the Mounted Police in reducing to a minimum the damage caused by the fires which sweep over different sections of the country periodically.[43]

Newspapers, no doubt reflecting public opinion, took a dim view of the reduction in strength of the NWMP in general and with particular reference to the prairie fire question. The *Edmonton Bulletin* in 1895 contended that the Force was still needed at full strength to assure the orderly development of the West. It argued that since most of the fires were on public lands, it was the responsibility of the federal force and not settlers to suppress them.[44] In 1897, the government announced the end of regular fire patrols by the NWMP in the West, leaving it to civilian fire guardians and settlers to fill the gap.[45] The *Calgary Herald* condemned the decision and a correspondent to that newspaper claimed that "Eastern politicians don't understand or care about the west".[46] The *Battleford Herald* responded to the demise of fire patrols in the same vein:

> This is a long step towards reducing this crack force from a useful to an ornamental footing, and shows how little the government really cares for the people in the Territories.[47]

The Mounted Police was largely successful in divesting itself of the responsibility of providing the vanguard in the protection of property from prairie fires. More civilian fire guardians were appointed and more settlers assumed this duty.[48] However, emergencies continued to arise and Mounted Policemen at outposts and divisional headquarters responded when needed. This occurred in September 1897, when a forest fire threatened to destroy the townsite at Banff. Sgt. Easton, in charge of the detachment, mobilized the residents of the town and the guests and the employees at the Banff Springs Hotel and turned the conflagration away.[49] This response to emergency instead of regular fire patrols and stations became the practice of the Force in settled areas. However, a few men were kept on fire patrols in more frontier areas of the northern NWT.[50]

Preventing the spread of infectious diseases through enforcement of quarantine regulations was another service performed by the Police for settlers in the NWT. Authority for enforcing public health regulations was a shared responsibility depending on circumstances, by local municipalities, the territorial and federal governments. However, any peace officer was empowered to enforce health regulations including the quarantine.[51] In practice, the Mounted Police took charge of all major and many minor quarantine operations in the West during this period and conducted them successfully. Efficiency was maintained because the Force always moved swiftly to contain a problem as soon as it was identified. The methods used, however, were not always supported by the other responsible government agents.

A serious outbreak of smallpox in 1892 in Calgary killed several citizens of the town and instilled fear in many others. From the outset, the Mounted Police took charge of quarantine operations and maintained them under difficult conditions. On 30 June 1892, two Chinese men working at a laundry on Stephen Avenue were discovered to be suffering from smallpox. One of the men had recently arrived from China but his disease had gone unreported to authorities until the second man fell ill. The municipal board of health quickly established a quarantine camp across Nose Creek and obtained the agreement of Insp. A. R. Cuthbert to have the Mounted Police stand guard over the premises to prevent any contact with the outside. Shortly after the camp was established a white customer of the laundry fell ill and he and other white residents of the town joined the quarantine. On the 4th of July, the chief of Calgary's police force, Thomas English, drove a wagon load of supplies past an established delivery point, straight into the camp and visited with the internees. When he tried to leave he was prevented from doing so by Sgt. Dee of the Mounted Police who advised him that because of his exposure to the disease he had to join the quarantine. English was a veteran of past encounters with the Mounted Police over who held sway in Calgary and may have deliberately provoked this incident. In any case he tried to fight his way out and lost. Later the mayor of Calgary personally intervened and obtained the release of the Chief, after promising to be responsible for him.

Following this incident, Cuthbert pressed the town to assume the guard duty but the mayor refused insisting that the disease was imported from British Columbia and, for this reason, it was the responsibility of the federal government. The appearance of three more cases in mid-July and the intervention of the territorial health authorities into the affair ended discussion of Mounted Police withdrawal. Publicity about the disease drove many Calgary citizens out of town, including Chief of Police English, who availed themselves of the opportunity to visit the Winnipeg Industrial Exhibition, then in progress. Of those who stayed, many nursed an anti-Oriental racism which broke into violence during the last three weeks of the quarantine. Attacks on Chinese residents and their property occurred on one occasion by a mob of 200 in full riot. The Mounted Police were forced to step in and protect the Chinese because the town police abrogated responsibility. The quarantine ended on August 17th and, shortly thereafter, tensions eased in the town. Several people had died of the disease including a mother and a recently born infant and another woman and her unborn fetus, but a major outbreak of smallpox had been prevented.[52]

Throughout the decade the Mounted Police handled numerous minor outbreaks of virulent diseases in the NWT. In most cases, the Force cooperated with local officials to isolate infected people, ensure that they were cared for and wait for the disease to run its course. Typical of this was the handling of a smallpox case at Macleod in 1892. In June of that year, a sign painter arrived in town from British Columbia and soon showed symptoms of the disease which he had contracted in an outbreak on the coast. A local board of health was immediately constituted and, at its request, the Mounted Police assisted, organizing a quarantine camp outside town. The patient was housed alone in a tent with another tent for a nurse nearby. A police guard, operating from a tent one-half mile away, was on duty day and night and patrols were sent out to warn settlers and Indians to stay away from the area. The board of health provided the medical care and also purchased the shack in which he was living when taken ill; this was burned down by the Mounted Police. As a precaution, the Police ordered a supply of vaccine from a druggist in Montreal, but the quarantine was effective and no further cases occurred.[53] Where there was no municipality yet incorporated, the Force occasionally was obliged to take the first steps to combat the spread of disease. When diphtheria visited two households in Saskatoon in 1897, the Mounted Police quarantined the homes and, under the guidance of a doctor, two non-commissioned officers provided the patients with basic medical care. Initially the NWT government refused to assist in the operation but soon a health board and a medical officer were appointed. In this case, three children died but the disease was contained.[54]

In the spring of 1901, scattered outbreaks of smallpox occurred all over the Territories, requiring the Mounted Police to maintain quarantines. The largest number of cases were detected in the Edmonton district, beginning in January. On the 13th of February, C. W. Peterson, Deputy Minister of Agriculture for the Territories, arrived in Edmonton to investigate the situation. After several meetings with concerned officials he placed a quarantine on the city and surrounding district allowing no one to leave the region by train without procuring a health certificate. The Mounted Police enforced this rule at the Edmonton and Strathcona railway stations. As for the rest of the quarantine responsibilities, they were divided: the town of Edmonton taking care of the sick and posting notices in the municipality, and the Force doing the same for Strathcona, Rabbit Hills, Wetaskiwin, Lacombe, Stony Plain, Egg Lake, Morinville and St. Albert. In the Mounted Police patrol area, 90 people were stricken by the disease by March. Many of these people and their families were short of food which was issued by the police as relief.[55] In April and May, Dr. James Patterson, an official of the Public Health branch of the federal Department of Agriculture, arrived in Edmonton to help with the quarantine. Patterson marvelled at the work of the Mounted Police in ministering to the afflicted of the region while the disease ran its course late in the spring.

> Allow me to thank, through you, Major Constantine, and the officers and men under him, for their extreme kindness and courtesy. No man has any idea of police life duties and hardships until he associates with the force for a time, what these men accomplished is simply wonderful. I think their numbers ought to be doubled.[56]

In 1902, there were two serious outbreaks of smallpox in the NWT, one around Fort Qu'Appelle and the other in the Prince Albert area. The large number of afflicted or in quarantine taxed the resources of two divisions of the Mounted Police who were primarily responsible for their welfare. The Director-General of Public Health of the federal Department of Agriculture picked up the direct costs incurred by the Force and also supplied some doctors. At Qu'Appelle, by the end of July 1902, the Force reported 118 cases of smallpox and 6 deaths and quantities of relief supplies issued to the needy in quarantine. Much energy was expended patrolling to keep Indians from the File Hills Reserve away from the area of infection. In the Prince Albert area the problem was larger in terms of numbers involved and in complications to polic-

ing because the disease-infested CNR construction camps where living conditions were poor but the work could not be stopped.[57] On the 31st of August Supt. A. Ross Cuthbert at Prince Albert reported to Commissioner Perry that the six-month long epidemic was almost over. He quoted the following figures for his district:

Number quarantined: 587
Number of cases of smallpox: 212
Number receiving relief from government: 432
Number of deaths: 3

Thirty-two of those on relief were Sioux Indians whose expenses were paid by the Department of Indian Affairs. The rest of the direct costs of the Prince Albert quarantine, $1,748.81, was borne by the federal Department of Agriculture. The Mounted Police supplied the services of its regular members without charge to any other department.[58]

In major outbreaks of disease the various government departments usually recognized their responsibility and cooperated with the NWMP in measures necessary to assist the afflicted and prevent spread of the infection. In other minor cases, particularly involving recently arrived immigrants, the police were forced to act quickly on their own and then were left unsupported with the expenses. In May 1902, a group of Ruthenian immigrants arrived by train at Grenfell, Saskatchewan, with one dead child and ten or twelve sick with measles. A local doctor examined the group and instructed the local NWMP Cst. Stouffer that a quarantine should be set up. The constable rented the local agricultural hall, put in stoves and supplied food until the quarantine was lifted. The local doctor billed the Immigration Branch of the Department of the Interior for his services and was paid. When the Force sought reimbursement for $17 in expenses, it was refused not only by the Department of the Interior but also by the federal Department of Agriculture and the North-West Territorial Government.[59] Commissioner Perry and Comptroller White were frustrated and disgusted by this and other occasions when the police, because they were on the scene, deviated from normal duty in the interest of the community and failed to receive support from the responsible government agencies.[60] Perry wrote to White:

> As you are aware, for some years there has been an epidemic throughout the Territories of different contagious and infectious diseases. A very great deal of work has fallen upon our men in this connection. They have been obliged to act on their own responsibility when they felt it was in the interests of the public to do so . . . I should ask you to consider whether it would not be advisable for us to inform the different departments concerned that unless the expenses incurred by us on their behalf are promptly paid that

we have to decline to take any responsibility in assisting the public health ordinance.[61]

Such a drastic step could, of course, be threatened, but never taken.

Another quarantine responsibility which was foisted on the Mounted Police during this period proved difficult and onerous – the protection of Canadian cattle from possible disease-bearing stock from the United States. In theory, there had been for many years a quarantine regulation of cattle crossing the border from the United States into Canada. Supposedly a strip of land along the border two townships wide (12 miles) from the western border of Manitoba to the eastern border of British Columbia constituted quarantine grounds to which cattle from the U.S. could be committed for up to 90 days to prove they did not bear disease. In practice, little attention was paid to the regulation. Settlers entering Canada from the States declared their cattle to customs officers but there was only one quarantine officer in the NWT and he was stationed at Fort Macleod. For a time, the Department of Agriculture was prepared to accept an affidavit from a settler as proof that his cattle came from a disease-free area, but probably even these were not requested at all border points. At the same time, all along the border, Canadian and American cattle ranged back and forth across the line in search of water and food.[62] External circumstances, however, brought change to the laxity in quarantine enforcement.

Until 1892, Canadian beef farmers and ranchers had enjoyed a privileged position in the markets of Great Britain. Canadians were allowed to ship young grass-fed stock to the mother country where local farmers would finish the fattening process and put them on the market. This arrangement was mutually beneficial to farmers on both sides of the Atlantic. The Canadians were able to raise good stock on grass, without incurring the expense of housing cattle in barns and feeding them fodder which is required to finish prime beef. British farmers received a supply of good healthy stock which could be sold in a relatively short time. In 1890, of 123,136 cattle sent from Canada to Great Britain, 90,000 were young grass-fed cattle or stockers which required further fattening before they were ready to be butchered. This privilege of finishing off beef in Britain was not extended to American farmers and ranchers.

As a result, on 20 October 1892, the British government terminated the practice of fattening Canadian cattle in Britain, ordering that this stock be slaughtered within ten days of arrival in port. In the fall of 1892, a veterinary surgeon with the London Board of Agriculture discovered that some imported Canadian cattle were infected with a contagious disease, probably pleuro-pneumonia. The Canadian government vigorously protested this change of policy, vehemently denying that any such contagious disease existed in Canada and therefore could not have been exported to Great Britain.[63] Government spokesmen in the House of Commons argued that the British cooked up the excuse of a contagious disease to institute a policy of protectionism against Canadian cattle which was demanded by Irish and English beef farmers. The opposition Liberals attacked the government for lax enforcement of quarantine regulations for cattle imported to Canada from areas of the United States where disease was suspected. The opposition claimed that the neglect of the quarantine, particularly in the NWT, had forced the British government to take stringent precautions at their ports. Whatever the motive of the British government, all agreed that the embargo had a deleterious effect on eastern Canadian beef farmers whose entry to English markets was now more difficult and less profitable. Western ranchers were less adversely affected because their principal market was local, large customers being the Department of Indian Affairs which supplied beef rations to thousands of reserve Indians and the developing primary industrial centres of British Columbia. Moreover, some western ranchers responded to the British scheduling by keeping their stocks longer on the range producing a leaner animal, and thus actually increased the West's share of the trans-Atlantic market.[64]

The British cattle embargo had immediate and drastic repercussions for several government departments especially the NWMP as more stringent quarantine regulations were drafted for use in the NWT. On 22 March 1893 an order-in-council authorized the establishment of a quarantine system for Manitoba and the NWT. The objective was twofold: to establish a viable quarantine service at government expense for stock coming into Canada from the United States and to do so without discouraging new settlers. Officials noted that in 1892, 513 entries were made for homesteads in Manitoba and the NWT by desirable emigrants from the United States who were bringing livestock, equipment and a wealth of experience in prairie farming conditions. To facilitate a 90-day isolation period for incoming cattle, new quarantine stations were to be established and the frontier patrolled to prevent violation of the regulations. This system was to be mainly the responsibility of the NWMP because

the control of the Mounted Police (a semi-military force) would tend to create greater confidence on the part of the British Government in the enforcement of the Quarantine west of Lake Superior than if it were managed by any purely civil branch of the public service.[65]

The Departments of Agriculture and Interior would pay any extra expenses incurred by the

Police and would provide additional veterinary and inspection personnel as needed.[66]

The NWMP established and operated quarantine stations at Gretna in Manitoba and at Macleod, Lethbridge, Estevan, Wood Mountain and Maple Creek in the NWT. The Department of Agriculture was responsible for another station at Emerson, Manitoba. By the end of the first summer of operation, problems were apparent in the quarantine. For one thing, there was confusion and conflict between the departments supposedly operating the quarantine. As an example, from early in the summer both White and Herchmer had been pointing out difficulties that would be encountered with the quarantine in the winter. Any stock accepted for 90-day isolation after the beginning of August would not be released until November and the Force had no shelter or hay for cattle herds in the winter. J. R. Hall, the Acting Deputy Minister of the Interior, agreed with this assessment and instructed all Canadian immigration agents in the United States to inform prospective settlers that no cattle would be accepted into quarantine after August 31st, unless the settlers themselves were prepared to foot the bill. However, the Deputy Minister of Agriculture, J. Lowe, strongly argued that the government was obliged to provide winter quarantine procedures by the terms of the Order-in-Council of the 22nd of March. Lowe lost the argument and quarantine facilities at government expense were closed to incoming settlers after 30 September 1893.[67]

More confusion ensued when the Mounted Police tried to apply the quarantine regulations during the winter. In October 1893, a prospective settler named John Berry crossed the border into Manitoba with 14 head of cattle and was intercepted by the Mounted Police. Berry told the police that he had the permission of a Veterinary Inspector named Young from the Department of Agriculture to quarantine his animals at his brother's farm four miles north of the boundary. With no knowledge of such an arrangement, the Police gave Berry the choice of continued residence in the States or a sojourn at the quarantine station at his own expense; and he chose the former. Herchmer then queried the Department of Agriculture through Fred White about the identity of the Veterinary Inspector referred to and learned that Young was indeed an official of the department and was empowered to authorize the private quarantine arrangement. Meanwhile, Berry had returned home where straitened circumstances forced him to sell some of his cows. Young was then instructed by this department to make arrangements for Berry's return to Manitoba but the resolution of the situation is unknown.[68] Perhaps partly because of this incident, quarantines at government expense were reinstated for Manitoba and British Columbia on 13 December 1893, but not in the Territories. Then on 22 January 1894, the government met the desire of the NWMP by relieving them of responsibility for the quarantine service in Manitoba and in April the three departments agreed that the NWMP would man the quarantine stations in the NWT under the direction of the Department of Agriculture.[69]

The quarantine service was operated by the Force in the NWT for three years, 1893 to 1896, for domestic cattle imported by prospective settlers. Patrols along the frontier directed incoming settlers to the nearest quarantine station where their cattle were registered, kept in isolation for 90-day periods between the spring and the fall and watched by civilian herders hired by the Force.[70] It was soon found, however, that there was no real need for this service. Never were there more than several hundred domestic animals quarantined in any one year and these were largely disease-free and none had any dangerously contagious infection.[71] Moreover, the continued refusal of the British Government to rescind its order for the immediate slaughter of Canadian cattle upon arrival in Great Britain caused the new Liberal government to review the policy. Maintaining a strict quarantine accomplished nothing and hindered a mutual beneficial trade in cattle between the United States and Canada. As a result, the quarantine requirement for the stock of immigrants from the States was terminated at the end of 1896.[72] However, in operating the quarantine service the government and the Mounted Police were forced to face a much larger frontier problem; a border was no barrier to both Canadian and American range cattle.

Initially, the Mounted Police confronted the problem of range cattle wandering back and forth across the border in connection with the danger of infection. What use was a quarantine for domestic cattle if large herds from ranches on both sides of the border were in contact as they roamed on open range? During the years when the NWMP maintained the quarantine they seized Canadian cattle which had strayed into the States and returned, as well as U.S. stock which had crossed into Canada. These cattle could then be placed in 90-day quarantine with the owners charged for police expenses. At the very least the Mounted Police warned the owners to keep the herds on their side of the line or face prosecution for violation of the quarantine regulations.

The summer of 1895 was particularly dry in the border ranching country and American ranchers drove thousands of cattle to feed and water on better Canadian grazing ground. The Mounted Police did their best to turn back the trespassers but the task was larger than the assigned manpower could handle.[73] Neither did all the American ranchers submit dutifully to reproof from a Mounted Policemen in the matter of where cattle could graze. On 20 August 1895, a patrol in Macleod district seized 495 head of cattle from the U.S. ranch of a Mr. Floweree, grazing on the Canadian side of the border near Milk River. About 2 a.m. on the night following the seizure, a round-up party of American cowboys tried to run the herd off from the Mounted Police guards but were repulsed, one of the cowboys, a J. Holmes, suffering capture.[74] He was arrested, charged with contravention of the *Contagious Diseases Act*. Tried by Mounted Police officers acting as justices of the peace, Holmes was fined and released.[75]

Even after the quarantine on cattle was removed by 1897, ranchers from the U.S. often intruded on grazing areas used by Canadians and evaded customs regulations by herding cattle across the border without paying duty. For several years the Mounted Police forced American ranchers to help them control the border by threatening to seize their cattle for violating the boundary. The U.S. stock owners sometimes reluctantly complied by providing "line riders", cowboys who lived at the Mounted Police detachments and assisted in the task of turning trespassing stock back over the border. However, this was no solution at all because the American ranchers failed to provide cowboys on a consistent basis. Moreover, the line riders were instructed by their employers to hold the welfare of the herds as paramount to the concerns of the Canadians.[76]

The summer of 1900 was another hot one in Montana and prairie fires ravaged grazing areas. A combination of American ranchers drove their herds north to a small strip of good grass adjacent to the Milk River but still in American territory. Over 16,000 cattle invaded this small area which was also occupied by sheep ranchers. The inevitable happened; the cattle could not be contained on the small range and encouraged by exasperated sheepmen, they drifted north into Canada. Complaints to the Mounted Police became frequent from Canadian ranchers. On this occasion their concern was not so much competition for the grass but that trespassing American stock mingled with their cattle and sometimes the mixed herds drifted back across the border. The Mounted Policemen at border outposts, assisted again by American line riders, tried to minimize the situation with limited success. Canadian ranchers responded by driving cattle away from their herds, sometimes in whichever direction was most convenient, including farther north. Frustration among ranchers led to private allegations being made to Clifford Sifton, Minister of the Interior, that Supt. R. B. Deane's friendship with Montana ranchers prevented the Mounted Police in Lethbridge district from pursuing the problem of the cattle invasion with avidity. A sub-sequent investigation proved that these accusations were baseless.[77]

American ranchers discovered that they could ignore the border by running herds in both Canada and the United States. As early as 1886, some American ranchers had moved a segment of their operations into Canada, in an area adjacent to the border; to complicate matters they used the same brand on their stock on both sides.[78] Thus neither Canadian nor American officials could easily detect customs violations if the rancher moved his cattle back and forth at will, wherever grass and water were most plentiful or where the market brought the best price.[79] Canadian officials caught on to this abuse by the 1890s and demanded that ranchers mark their cattle differently north of the border, but this did not resolve the difficulty completely.

In the late 1890s, two brothers, Samuel and John Spencer of Montana, obtained from the Canadian government several townships of prime grazing land along the Milk River on the U.S. boundary line. (Supt. Deane later intimated that Clifford Sifton had dispensed this favour in return for financial reward submitted through legal fees to his former law partner).[80] The Spencers were not allowed to brand their stock in Canada with the same brand that they used in the States, but they had another ingenious angle. They simply imported several hundred head of cattle from the U.S. paying customs dues as required. Now with the American branded stock legally in their Canadian herd, it was very difficult for the police to detect if they brought more stock over to graze without paying duty. However, Supt. Deane at Lethbridge learned of the Spencers' smuggling chiefly because the brothers had alienated their fellow Montana ranchers by, in a remarkably selfish manner, driving back across thin ice on the Milk River other intruding stock from the U.S. in the famine winter of 1900-1901.[81] With the help of a specially appointed Canadian Customs official, J. C. Bourinot,[82] and an experienced crew of cowboys, Deane conducted an extensive roundup of Spencer brothers' cattle conducting a virtual inventory of brands in May 1902. The evidence gathered proved conclusively enough for several subsequent tests in court that the ranchers had imported at least several hundred cattle without paying duty. As a result, the Spencers were required to pay to Customs $6,000, an assessment Deane considered very light in the circumstances.[83] Clifford Sifton took a dim view of Deane's heavy-handed treatment of the Spencers and this, the Superintendent believed, accounted for his transfer from Lethbridge to Maple Creek that same year.[84] On the occasion of his departure from Lethbridge, Deane received a memorial from the executive committee of the Western Stock Growers' Association, a local cattlemen's organization. It read:

> This Committee recognizing the energy and ability shown by Captain Deane N.W.M. Police in the discharge of his duties as Supt. of the Lethbridge District desires to record its appreciation of the services he rendered the Live Stock interests of Southern Alberta.[85]

After Deane's departure, the Canadian Customs Service sent a Special Officer, J. Stunden to western Canada to investigate the question of U.S. stock trespassing in Canada. On September 18th, Stunden requested the assistance of the NWMP at Lethbridge to seize cattle that were being rounded up in Canada by outfits from the Circle and Brown ranches. This action resulted in the discovery of 200 cattle illegally imported into Canada and duty was assessed of $1,600 and paid. One hundred head belonging to smaller American ranches were judged to have drifted over the line without the knowledge of their owners and no duty was levied.[86] Stunden then returned to Ottawa and reported that he believed a Special Officer aided by NWMP patrols could end U.S. cattle incursions into Canada. This method was then tried beginning in 1903.[87]

Related to the duty of the Mounted Police in guarding the line against stock incursions, was the responsibility for animal quarantine within the NWT. There were very few veterinarians in the Territories, only 15 listed in the 1891 census.[88] In 1892, the Mounted Police had 12 veterinary surgeons in its ranks, stationed throughout the West, caring for its horses. All of these men were experienced practitioners, but not all of them had a formal veterinary education. As a matter of course and on a voluntary basis, these men advised ranchers and settlers regarding the health of their animals. And when a contagious disease was discovered, the vet and other members of the Force would act in the interests of the Territorial government or the federal Department of Agriculture to ensure that regulations concerning the destruction of diseased animals and quarantine were observed. John F. Burnett, the Veterinary Surgeon of the Force, described his semi-formal contribution to the protection of private stock in 1893. In June of that year, he investigated a report that glanders, a contagious disease, had broken out among the horses at the Oxarart ranch at Maple Creek:

> After a careful examination I found twelve or fourteen horses affected with glanders. Not having authority to destroy or quarantine any affected animals, I advised Mr. Oxarart to close herd his band until the Lieutenant-Governor could be communicated with and the necessary steps taken to prevent the spread of the disease.
>
> Although but few horses in the force have contracted the above disease, quite a number of cases have been reported from different parts of the country, but with the new *Contagious Disease in Animals Act*

passed by the North-west Legislative Assembly, I hope to see this disease abate in the Territories . . .

> While at Fort Saskatchewan inspecting horses of "G" Division, I received a telegram from Dr. McEachran, [Chief Insp. for the federal Department of Agriculture] requesting me to inspect a flock of sheep, the property of a Belgian settler living near St. Albert; this I did, and found them free from disease.
>
> Although having no authority to make any inspection, as regards disease in animals, outside the force, I have considered it my duty, as police veterinary officer, to report any such case as came under my notice.[89]

The detection of glanders on the Oxarat Ranch prompted the Mounted Police to enforce the Territorial Ordinance concerning contagious disease and 16 horses were shot and the herd of between 1,600 and 1,700 quarantined for several months until it appeared that the spread of the disease had been halted.[90]

In 1896, important changes were made in the legislation concerning the regulation of contagious diseases in the NWT. In that year, parliament amended the federal *Contagious Disease Act* to strengthen the position of the Department of Agriculture and eliminated the need for Territorial ordinances on the subject.[91] Then, at the instigation of the Department of Agriculture, an Order-in-Council dated 22 October 1896 authorized that all veterinary surgeons of the Mounted Police be official Inspectors charged with enforcing the *Contagious Diseases Act*. W. B. Scarth, the Deputy Minister of Agriculture, explained to Fred White that the order was necessary in order to give the veterinarians legal authority, which they had hitherto lacked, to battle contagion in animals.[92] The Commissioner of the NWMP was given responsibility for ensuring that the regulations concerning quarantine and contagious diseases were enforced.[93] As an incentive, the Force veterinarians received an annual fee from the Department of Agriculture for their work. In 1899, remuneration was set at $100 per year and there were subsequent moderate increases. By 1902, Commissioner Perry himself also received a stipend from the Department of Agriculture amounting to the not inconsiderable sum of $400.[94]

According to NWMP annual reports, duties relating to contagious diseases had become quite demanding by the turn of the century. Commissioner Herchmer instructed all detachments and patrols to be on the lookout for disease and Mounted Police parties accompanied at least some roundups to ensure that ranchers did not succumb to the temptation of sheltering afflicted animals.[95] John Burnett felt that this work in connection with the *Contagious Diseases Act* was probably the most important performed by his veterinarians and that increased vigilance had resulted in more cases being uncovered.[96] Shipments of animals originating or terminating in the NWT were inspected by the Mounted Police to ensure all were healthy. Supt. Charles Constantine however, complained that this duty was an onerous burden; he reported in 1899 that in the sub-district of Moosomin alone that year his men had inspected over 8,000 cattle being shipped out of the area.[97] The Mounted Police usually received the cooperation of ranchers, settlers and stock associations in this work because it was in the interests of all to prevent the spread of disease. Occasionally, however, an individual would resist police efforts because of the personal financial loss by enforced destruction of stock. Such was the case at Lethbridge in 1898 when glanders broke out among the horses at W. D. Whitney's livery stables. Assistant Veterinary Surgeon T. A. Wroughton tested and ordered destroyed a number of Whitney's animals and instructed him to close down and renovate his stables. Whitney was quite put out by his ill-fortune and proved obstructive until Wroughton had him charged, convicted and fined $50 and costs for violation of the *Animal Contagious Disease Act*.[98]

In the American West there had been much conflict between cattle and sheep ranchers over grazing land. Cattlemen considered that because they arrived first in the West their stock had prior right to graze even on open range. Sheepmen were inclined to insist on the principle of equal access. The problem arose in Canada in a minor way in the early 1890s and 1900s. The solution arrived at by the Department of the Interior was to designate certain areas in the southern NWT as sheep grazing areas, leaving most of the range to the cattle. The NWMP were responsible for advising sheepmen of the restrictions and ensuring that regulations were obeyed. The system worked well and no major conflicts arose.

The rapid expansion of the Canadian West was not accomplished without social conflict such as the anti-Chinese riots in Calgary cited earlier. The Edmonton land office fracas was another instance of mob violence requiring Mounted Police intervention. The trouble began with the completion of the Calgary-Edmonton branch line of the CPR in 1891. The terminus of the railway was located on the south side of the North Saskatchewan River opposite the then existing municipality of Edmonton. The obvious intention of the CPR was to encourage future development on its side of the river where the company owned land, also saving the cost of the construction of a bridge.[99] This attitude was deplored by the citizens of Edmonton who had no intention of submitting to these heavy-handed tactics. A key to the contest was the location of the public buildings in the area, particularly the land office where newcomers entered land claims. Townspeople on the north side accused vested interests on the other side of pressuring the federal government to move the land office to the south bank of the river. To counter this threat, Edmonton sent a delegation to Ottawa in early 1892 to make the town's views known to the government.[100]

In June 1892, the Minister of the Interior, Edgar Dewdney, took sides on the issue. He cautiously instructed that the land agent in Edmonton should move the records of his office to the south side of the river to conduct business for the rest of the season. The messages, as relayed by the Assistant Secretary of the department, concluded: "If no obstacle is foreseen, do so at once."[101] On June 16th, an Inspector of Land Offices arrived in Edmonton and completed arrangements with the local agent, Thomas Anderson, to move to the south side and establish temporary facilities in a boxcar rented from the CPR. Word leaked out, and on Saturday, June 18th, Anderson began loading a wagon with office records. A hostile crowd quickly assembled numbering between 200 and 300, some drunk, led by prominent citizens including the mayor, Matthew McCawley.

The situation quickly turned ugly. The crowd physically prevented Anderson's departure by removing the wheels from his wagon and repeatedly blocking his attempts to hitch up a team of horses. Meanwhile the mayor conducted a public meeting, filled with threatening rhetoric, to decide on further action. Insp. W. Piercy accompanied by one or two men from the local Mounted Police detachment arrived at the scene. It was later reported that Mayor McCawley turned the crowd into a howling mob with the statement that: "We have been too long dead, we don't want to be called rebels but it has come to this that we must fight for our rights and we will fight for them too."[102] Resolutions were adopted and blistering telegrams sent to Ottawa, including to the Prime Minister, Sir John Abbott, to the effect that a reversal of the decision to move was demanded and that the citizens of the town would physically prevent the move until word was received from the Department of the Interior. Piercy wisely decided to abide by the actions of this informal committee and put the wagon and contents under police guard until a reply to the representations was received from Ottawa. The police guard satisfied a majority of the crowd who soon dispersed with the exception of a few who remained to burn an effigy of the land agent.[103]

On Sunday, June 19th, Insp. Piercy sent Supt. A. H. Griesbach at Fort Saskatchewan a full report on what had transpired. Griesbach gathered a patrol of 30 NCOs and men and proceeded to Edmonton on June 20th. Leaving his men at Rat Creek on the outskirts so as not to provoke a reaction, Griesbach proceeded into the town to assess the situation. He was alarmed to find a sign chalked on a blackboard outside the Town Clerk's office signed by Colin Strang, a Town Councillor, calling out the home guard at 1 p.m. About 80 to 100 men turned out at the appointed hour and were issued with ball cartridges. Griesbach noted that about 30 in the crowd were carrying Snider rifles which the Mounted Police had loaned to Colin Strang for the use of the Edmonton Rifle Association. Others bore arms passed out by the Militia department at the time of the North-West Rebellion. This dangerous situation was defused later in the day when town council received several telegrams from Ottawa explaining that the government intended to operate only a branch office across the river and that the main land office would remain in Edmonton. This compromise placated the leaders of the protest.[104] On Wednesday, June 22nd, Insp. Piercy and four men, with the aid of the mayor and some town councillors, moved across the river only the records needed for a branch office. An alarm was sounded as the wagon moved from the land office and some irate citizens turned out but lacking leadership they made no move to interfere. The next day both the main and the branch offices opened for business and, to test the system, Mayor McCawley accompanied two settlers to the land agency on the Edmonton side and they were dealt with satisfactorily. Almost immediately the government began work on plans to erect a permanent land office building on the north side of the river.

Naturally, there were recriminations over the affair. In a letter to Matthew McCawley, Edgar Dewdney censured the mayor and his officials for their defiance, using force, of a directive issued by a minister of the Crown. The *Edmonton Bulletin*, the organ of the Liberal opponent to the federal government and Member of the Legislative Assembly, Frank Oliver, viewed the situation in a different light. Oliver contended that the citizens had frustrated a nefarious scheme designed to further private interests in which government officials had participated.[105]

Supt. A. H. Griesbach was upset that the government and the police appeared to have been stood off by citizens of Edmonton and worried about the effect of this on restless Indians and half-breeds.[106] Prime Minister Abbott, however, was pleased by the conduct of the police and stated in a letter to Fred White that: "Mr. Griesbach seems to have acted with great discretion and prudence in the whole affair."[107]

There were a few labour disputes in the West during this period which demanded the attention of the NWMP in the interest of preserving order. There were three strikes on the CPR in which the Force played a part. In 1892, the railway conductors and brakemen went on strike. Commissioner Herchmer was initially warned on the 16th of March when the western General Superintendent of the CPR, William Whyte, telegraphed that a strike was imminent and that Mounted Police protection was needed for company property along the line. The strike commenced on March 17th and Assistant Commissioner McIllree ordered men out to protect the company's yards and property, checked on the distribution of handcuffs and leg irons and instructed Officers Commanding that those strikers who broke the law were to be arrested.[108] The strike lasted only a week and was relatively peaceful, marred only by a few threats by excited strikers, and unfounded rumours of acts of violence.[109]

The only untoward aspect of the police response to the emergency was the lengths to which Herchmer went to meet the CPR's plea for protection. The Commissioner ordered, (he later explained at the company's request) Insp. Constantine and eight men to Brandon, Manitoba and Insp. Harper and six men to Field, B.C. to protect company property. Meanwhile, the Lieutenant-Governor of Manitoba, John Schultz, alarmed by exaggerated reports of the violent nature of the confrontation cabled Prime Minister Abbott asking to protect the CPR in Manitoba using the Mounted Police or the military. The Prime Minister replied that the Mounted Police would act in the NWT and that if Manitoba wanted military assistance to preserve order, the province could call upon the militia and assume the expense.[110] When Fred White found out that Herchmer had already ordered the Mounted Police into Manitoba and B.C. he informed the Commissioner that he had exceeded his authority and that his action was in fact illegal because it had not been agreed to by the provincial and federal authorities.

> The strike has raised the old question of the responsibility of the Provinces in such matters and the expenses in connection therewith and your action has, I fear, embarrassed the Govt. here in their negotiations with the provinces.[111]

Two other strikes occurred on the CPR during this period requiring action from the Mounted Police. In 1896, the newly organized Order of Railroad Telegraphers organized a short and successful strike against the Company. Telegraphers and despatchers walked off the job on September 28th bringing chaos to the transportation of goods and passengers and forcing the company to grant a favourable contract ending the strike on the 11th of October.[112] While the strike was in progress, the Mounted Police provided protection for non-union employees who tried to perform the duties of the strikers at several points in the Territories; there were no incidents.[113] In 1901, several thousand track maintenance members belonging to the Brotherhood of Railway Trackmen struck for better wages, working conditions and union recognition. The strike dragged on for 12 weeks, ending in early August on terms which favoured the union men. The company tried unsuccessfully to ride out the strike by hiring non-union workers, mostly unskilled, to replace the strikers.[114] Again Mounted Policemen patrolled the track in the NWT to protect the strike-breakers. Only minor incidents occurred to disturb the peace. For instance, on several occasions Supt. G. E. Sanders at Calgary had to clear strikers trespassing on the railway yard and station and prevent them from boarding trains.[115]

Two serious labour disputes occurred at Lethbridge during this period in which Supt. R. B. Deane, never relishing a passive role, played an important part. Lethbridge was, at this time, a one industry town. Originally called Coal Banks, Lethbridge was a mining community founded and fostered by Sir Alexander and Elliott Galt and named after a British principal investor, Sir William Lethbridge. The town and its inhabitants prospered or suffered according to the fortunes of the Alberta and Railway Coal Company. In 1894, a sudden reduction for demand for coal through closure of a large industrial customer in Montana, left the Elliott Galt's Lethbridge mining company on the brink of bankruptcy. Responding to the emergency Galt, in mid-February, dismissed all of his over 500 men and announced that he would rehire only 130 married workers with an established place in the community, if they would accept a reduction in wages of 17 per cent. The shocked miners decided to resist and all refused to return to work. Recognizing a dangerous confrontation, Deane brought in extra men from Regina to guard the mines and then lent his personal good offices to resolve the situation. Deane met with mine management and with the workers and arranged some improvement in the remuneration offered to the reduced work force. The new terms were acceptable to the workers' negotiating committee but when presented to a general meeting on March 8th, they were rejected at the urging of what Deane described as firebrands. The company then increased the pressure threatening to close up the company houses. This broke the already weakening common cause and, starting on March 10th, men little by little returned to work. For some time the atmosphere remained charged because some former workers remained in town refusing to accept that the match was lost. Finally on the 2nd of April, the last of the unemployed miners and their families departed, transportation by train for the south provided free by Galt upon the virtual demand of Supt. Deane.[116]

Then in 1897, the miners decided that the time was ripe to strike for better wages and working conditions. The labour market was favourable in Alberta because the CPR was pushing the Crow's Nest line through the Rockies and the strikers felt that work they could obtain on that line would see

them through a successful strike. Their hopes were dashed however when Galt's mines obtained CPR's cooperation in refusing to hire the miners. Once again, Deane stepped in to mediate and gained an improved offer from the employer, although not included was the main wage demand. The strikers were not satisfied but returned to work by the end of August without formal acceptance of the new terms.[117] Deane was happy that the threat to order was removed and Elliott Galt later told Prime Minister Wilfrid Laurier that he was well satisfied with Deane's performance at Lethbridge.[118]

In 1897-98, the Mounted Police were once again called upon to maintain the peace along a line of railroad construction. The CPR was then in the process of building the Crow's Nest Pass line, extending the railway 330 miles from Lethbridge into the Rocky Mountains. The railroad company was anxious, as in the past, to ensure the orderly progression of work by using the services of the NWMP. Both the provincial and federal governments were amenable to the suggestion but neither wanted to bear the costs. The result was a compromise in the spirit of the National Policy; the federal government provided an officer and up to 12 policemen, the CPR provided them with food and accommodation, and the province authorized their jurisdiction for magisterial and law enforcement purposes.[119]

For the most part, the NWMP was successful in keeping order along the line of construction. Several murders were committed, however, other serious crimes such as assaults and thefts were not numerous. This is surprising considering that up to 4,500 men were employed, attended by many of the usual camp followers who coveted a share of their wages. Bustling villages sprang up along the line of construction with a temporary population of gamblers, thieves, prostitutes and liquor vendors. As the workers' camps moved with the railhead, so too did the camp followers and, with them, came the Mounted Police. The greatest threat to disorder came with liquor consumption and alcohol was readily available as the provincial authorities granted retail licences to two or three businesses in each of the villages. But the Mounted Police patrolled the make shift villages with particular care after paydays and most of the liquor-related offences were confined to misdemeanours. For instance, in July and August 1898, the Mounted Police laid charges in 82 cases in the Crow's Nest Pass, of which 38 were liquor offences. The most serious charge laid was against one Peter Barry of Moyie City who received six months for theft.[120] Insp. G. E. Sanders spent almost a year in the Crow's Nest Valley in charge of the Mounted Police detachments and he was proud of how the work of the Mounted Police was assessed by the local newspaper, the *Fort Steele Prospector*, in February 1898:

> the crimes along the road, however, are surprisingly small, considering the vicious element which comprises the contingent of camp followers. This happy state of affairs is due to the innate fear of Canadian Justice and the scrupulous surveillance of the efficient Corps of the North-West Mounted Police into whose hands the enforcement of the law is committed.[121]

Sanders also assigned his men responsibility for investigating and, if possible, alleviating any grievances held by the workers and performing small services such as writing letters. In this regard, the policemen had more than their work cut out for them.

The construction of the Crow's Nest Railway line was accomplished despite a whole series of incidents demonstrating the bungling, inefficiency and indifference of the CPR and its subcontractors towards the welfare of the workers. Recruiting agents in eastern Canada frequently hired unsuitable workers from the lumber trade with distorted descriptions of the nature of the work and bound them to labour contracts which gave them small remuneration after paying for transportation, board and medical expenses. When the men arrived at camp sites they were often housed in inadequate, crowded makeshift accommodation. On more than one occasion, reasonable care was not exercised to ensure regular and ample rations were on hand and men went hungry. As a result of such deprivation much sickness occurred and the suffering was aggravated by insufficient medical attention. When men complained of this treatment they were frequently fired summarily and forced out of camp to travel without help from railhead back to settled communities. This did involve some peril, depending on the time of year and the weather.

Workers' grievances were brought to the attention of the Mounted Police at an early date. At Lethbridge, Supt. Deane had little sympathy for men who tried to break their contracts to work on the stretch of line bridging the St. Mary's River in late 1897. A number were charged before him with failing to fulfil their obligations of employment. However, none of these cases required court action and compromises were effected between the parties resulting in the men either returning to work or being released from their contracts.[122] In one instance, seven Galician immigrants were left unemployed and destitute and both the labour contractor and the municipality refused to feed them. Deane was left with no option but to assume this responsibility personally and hope that a way could be found to obtain recompense from the federal government.[123]

More numerous complaints were voiced to the Mounted Police in the Fort Macleod district. Charges were laid by contractors against the workers for failing to live up to conditions of employment. At first the Mounted Police sympathized with the plight of the companies. In August and September 1897, 33 workers were convicted of such offences in Macleod district and, after trials presided over mostly by NWMP J.P.s, were sentenced to short stays in the guardroom or fined. Only five men had such charges dismissed and one was settled out of court. In the same period, 13 workers brought charges against their employers for non-payment of wages, and all were successful in their actions. In seven cases the courts ordered the companies to turn over specific sums to the workers, four actions were settled out of court, and two contractors were fined.

However, by the end September 1897, the Mounted Police were beginning to realize that the labour difficulties in the Crow's Nest Pass were not going to be resolved in the courts. On September 18th, Insp. A. R. Cuthbert at Pincher Creek put six men in the guardroom convicted of deserting their employment on the railway but he was becoming alarmed about the situation. That same day, he reported to Commissioner Herchmer that about 100 French-Canadians had been brought out west under a false impression of working conditions and had signed contracts which they were unable to read. Cuthbert told the contractors that he would not deal with any more charges against such labourers until they settled disagreements with them over conditions of work.[124] In mid-October, the dispute between the CPR and the French-Canadian labourers reached a crisis with charges of desertion of employment countered with charges of non-payment of wages. A settlement was reached whereby the company transported workers back east and paid them $5 cash.[125]

By November, Supt. Sam Steele at Macleod was thoroughly disgusted with the way some of the CPR contractors were treating their men. Workers were being cheated out of their wages and some fired and left without food or money. Only charity from the town of Macleod and the Mounted Police kept men from freezing and starving. Steele reported to the Commissioner that the Immigration officials should investigate the abuse of labour along the line of construction.[126] In October and November, a Mounted Police justice of the peace, Insp. H. S. Casey, heard 74 cases of non-payment of wages brought by workers against CPR contractors. All were settled out of court in favour of the labourers.[127]

As winter approached, the consequences of the abuses by the contractors became more severe. Sickness entered the camps and, on 21 December 1898, Insp. G. Sanders reported from Crow's Nest Lake that the men were not receiving adequate medical care even though they were paying $50 a month for this service. On 26 January 1898, Insp. Cuthbert reported to Supt. Steele the disgraceful circumstances surrounding the deaths of two labourers near Pincher Creek who were employed by CPR contractors Hugh Mann and James Kennedy. These men had died from diphtheria, aggravated by lack of medical attention and exposure to the elements. He attributed their deaths to the complete neglect of all connected to the contractors' company.[128]

Reports on conditions reached Ottawa from the Mounted Police and other sources, sparking some action. On 15 January 1898, the federal government appointed a commission of inquiry "into complaints respecting the treatment of labourers on the Crow's Nest Pass Railway".[129] The Commissioners travelled to the pass at the end of January and in the succeeding two months investigated conditions and took testimony from 282 witnesses. The Mounted Police assisted the Commissioners by providing lodging, transportation, escorts and information.[130] The report to the government dated 30 April 1898 substantiated many of the rumours of ill-treatment. While it was a little late to cure all undesirable work conditions on the Crow's Nest Pass line, the report recommended future government regulations for large public works.

Subsequently, a second commission was appointed to inquire into the January deaths of labourers Charles McDonald and E. Fraser. Again, investigation confirmed reports that the men had been neglected to death. They had lain for several days in unventilated rough bunkhouses without any medical attention. Finally it came to the notice of the contractor of the camp, Hugh Mann that the men were seriously ill, perhaps from diphtheria. Instead of isolating the men and sending for a doctor, Mann packed them off in an unheated wagon on a three-day journey towards medical attention which was finally found near Pincher Creek just hours before the men died. The tale of suffering endured by the men was most poignant. The commission report attributed the death of the men to an inadequate medical system on the line and the poor judgement of those into whose hands their care was thrust. At one point in the journey, the sick men were met by a NWMP corporal who ordered a company agent not to move them any further and himself sent for a doctor. But then in the absence of the policemen the agent ignored the order and sent the men on, fearing that they would die in his hands. Again the report aimed its recommendations at future public works suggesting improved medical and sanitary facilities and government regulation and inspection.[131]

The work of the royal commission convinced the government that legislation was needed to protect workers. In 1900, Parliament passed the *Public Works Health Act* which set standards for accommodation and sanitary facilities for labourers on railways and public works. This was followed in 1902 by an order-in-council allowing for the appointment of an Inspector to enforce the regulations.[132] Somewhat curiously, considering that he had complained about ill-treatment of labourers, Insp. Sanders later regretted that the Crow's Nest Pass railway had earned such a notorious reputation. Sanders was in charge of policing the line for most of the period of construction and he claimed that instances of ill-treatment were the exception and not the rule. Furthermore, he noted that when such complaints were brought to his attention he often obtained redress from the general manager of construction. In making this observation in a published report, Sanders was probably trying to restore some balance to an otherwise distressingly gloomy public record of the project.[133]

The NWMP continued to provide support during this period to a variety of federal and territorial programs in the West. Miscellaneous duties included protection of fish and game, prevention and extinction of prairie fires and provision of policemen as escorts for government officials, distinguished visitors and state occasions. In the case of customs, that fledgling service grew during this period to take over most of the responsibilities in the West. There were several points, however, where the low volume of traffic or the remoteness of the station dictated that the local NWMP detachment should perform customs duties. Throughout this period, Mounted Policemen acted as sub-collectors of customs at Maple Creek and Wood Mountain.[134] However, in 1894, the NWMP removed its detachments from southern Manitoba which had been providing customs services since 1888.[135] Likewise, at Banff, the local officer was assigned the duty of checking the bonded luggage of incoming American tourists in 1894, but was replaced later by a regular customs official.[136] But the major support provided for the customs services was the NWMP patrol system which was a preventive service, the only real barrier in place to deny an open border to smugglers. Reductions in the strength of the police, however, and the increase in other duties did make it difficult for police to be consistently effective along the entire extent of the international boundary.[137]

The Mounted Police were also responsible for enforcing regulations protecting Crown and private timber resources in the West. In many regions, wood was a scarce commodity desired by settlers for construction and for burning as fuel. Removal of timber from both public and CPR owned lands was regulated by a system of permits issued under the authority of Crown Timber Agents of the Department of the Interior. Naturally, it was difficult to enforce such regulations and was quite beyond the control of a small number of forest rangers employed by the department. A particularly bad problem existed in southern Manitoba where Crown timber resources were illegally depleted by settlers from both sides of the border. Continual complaints about this resulted in the recall of the NWMP to southern Manitoba in 1897 and detachments were once again established to issue permits to Canadian settlers and to guard against timber thieves from the U.S.[138] In the Territories, the Force acted on a "when needed" basis for the Department of the Interior. A request for a police investigation of illegal cutting near Scisson's Creek and in the Qu'Appelle Valley in 1897, however, brought a curious response from the officer in charge of the sub-district. Insp. A. C. Macdonell reported that he found thefts had been going on for many years, that most were perpetrated by settlers who were poor and needed firewood.

For this reason he had no intention of charging these people for past misdeeds and if the Department of the Interior wished to enforce regulations in the future, it should appoint a forest ranger to do the job. He continued:

> It is not desirable that this work should be done by Police, whose business it is to ferret out crime. At present the relations between the N.W.M. Police and the farmers of this District are most cordial, and they never fail to assist us in giving all the information they can, but there is no disguising the fact that any enforcing of timber dues is regarded by the great mass of the people of the Territories as more or less grinding the faces of the poor, and would at once destroy our friendly relations.[139]

The records do not show any charges laid by the NWMP for the theft of Crown timber in the area at the time.[140]

The Force continued during this period to wield the power of its purse with consequences for national, local and political patronage.[141] At the national level the NWMP under the Macdonald and Laurier governments pursued a "Buy Canadian" policy. In almost all areas of expenditure, from food to clothing to transport, rarely was a dollar spent outside Canada. Even when a foreign product was preferred by the Force, as in the case with wagons, the government made a determined effort to locate a comparable Canadian model.[142] There were some items, however, which were not made in Canada and had to be imported. A notable example of this were sundry items such as badges, insignia and uniform ornaments which were purchased each year in England.

The most notable exception to the National Policy on purchase was in the area of arms and ammunition. This was a problem shared with the Canadian military; there was no arms industry in Canada and the Dominion was forced to rely on sources beyond its borders. By the mid-1890s, the Force was armed principally with aging Winchester carbines and Enfield revolvers, both purchased from American manufacturers. There were also two machine guns and few field pieces which had been manufactured in England. In 1895, the Force purchased 200 Lee-Metford carbines in England allowing it to replace the worst of the Winchesters. The following year the arsenal was improved again with the purchase of two British-made Maxim machine guns.

In the case of ammunition, the Force was again dependent on British and American sources to meet its needs for its various weapons. One Canadian firm, the Dominion Cartridge Company, produced .45 calibre cartridges suitable for use in the Mounted Police Winchesters. The Force placed orders for a relatively large number of cartridges with this firm over the years and almost always the results were unsatisfactory. A large proportion of the shells were defective, some being mis-sized and others carrying an insufficient charge. The Commissioner and his officers complained both publicly and privately about the Canadian product and several accidents involving misfires engendered fear in those using it on the rifle range. Thus, the Force was able to justify ordering most of the ammunition from the United States. The Winchester Repeating Arms Company of New Haven, Connecticut supplied the Force with .45 calibre cartridges for the rifles and while neither were these shells perfect, far fewer instances of defective manufacture were experienced.[143]

The NWMP continued to dispense large sums of money in the West for food, forage, fuel, horses and miscellaneous items of harness and hardware. Most of these supplies were contracted for by the Force after having invited bids or tenders through newspaper advertisements or posters. About 20 per cent of the money was spent without contract, in part because the Force was widely scattered in small detachments and policemen purchased many necessaries from local merchants at the going price.[144] Naturally then, the presence of the police in any community had an economic appeal.

The reduction in size of the Mounted Police Force in the NWT, begun in 1895 and continued with commitment of men to the Yukon, brought protests from many western communities. In March 1895, a protest meeting was held at Fort Macleod, Alberta in reaction to news that the Force was reducing the number of men stationed in the area. A petition forwarded to the Governor General claimed that the citizens of the town were in dire need of the utmost protection from hostile Indians who were only awaiting the opportunity to pounce on settlers and their livestock. The government learned from a local rancher that those attending the meeting were more concerned about losing the revenue that the Force generated in town and that the chairman of the meeting was the local banker who feared for the security of a loan made to an officer who was being dismissed as a result of the organizational shuffle.[145] The following spring, another petition was received from Macleod asking for the return of two policemen removed from the town detachment. This plea was signed by 84 names, some of them corporate entities like the Hudson's Bay Company.[146] This firm had a very real self-interest in the status quo as the previous year the Force had made official purchases at the Macleod store totalling $11,883.27.[147] In addition, of course, the men themselves made purchases and there were no doubt indirect financial benefits of the general stimulation of the local economy.

Anxiety and protests over Force reductions occurred in other localities as well, including Lethbridge which originated with the Board of Trade.[148] From Saskatoon, the Police received reports that a band of Indians were disturbing cattle in the area in 1897. Supt. Gagnon investigated and concluded that the reports were false and had been circulated possibly to secure police detachments stationed in the area for the economic benefit this would bring.[149] But more intriguing than local patronage is the political dimension of the NWMP patronage. As indicated in a previous chapter, the Conservative government used Mounted Police expenditures and those of other departments in a partisan but hardly irresponsible fashion to reward friends and supporters. Of course, when the Liberals attained power in 1896, patronage favour shifted to the friends of the new government. Herchmer explained how the change in government affected his decisions about expenditures:

> ... if two parties offer the same article at the same price, buy from the conservatives when the conservatives are in power and the liberals when the liberals are in power – if the price is different for the same article buy from the cheapest man no matter what his politics may be – all things being equal, the party in power should get the advantage.[150]

Such pragmatic partisanship would not raise a protest from either party but it is doubtful if patronage could be limited to a decision between articles of equal value. Even where tenders were called for contracts, it was difficult to compare quality of articles or services and measure it against proposed prices, and with a patronage list an additional factor it was unlikely that money would always be best spent. Moreover, a significant amount of purchases were made locally without contract, and there is no evidence that the patronage list was supplemented by any kind of comparative shopping.

Soon after the Liberals came to power, the NWMP Comptroller's Office in Ottawa began to keep a patronage list of manufacturers, merchants and tradesmen recommended by key politicians including the Prime Minister to receive Mounted Police business. It is impossible to trace from remaining records just how direct an impact this list had on fiscal decision making by officers of the Force. However, there are glimpses. One firm listed on 26 September 1896 on the recommendation of Sir Wilfrid Laurier was R. H. Williams of Regina who could supply "groceries, dry goods, lumber, etc".[151] Surviving records also include a memoran-

dum from Commissioner Herchmer to the Officer Commanding "Depot" Division in Regina in September 1897 instructing or perhaps reiterating that R. H. Williams were to be favoured with business for the above articles.[152] It is not clear exactly how discretion was exercised in this case but it is clear that the Williams firm enjoyed much expanded trade with the Force during the first years of the Liberal administration than previously. Between 1892 and 1896, the most that the Williams firm ever sold to the Mounted Police in one year was $968.43. Thereafter, the firm always exceeded that total by a wide margin, its highest volume coming in 1901-02 with a total of $6,865.63. It is also worthy of note that the increased business with R. H. Williams coincided with a considerable decline in expenditures in the NWT, as the Mounted Police reduced strength there to meet the increasing commitment to the Yukon.[153]

An even more blatant example of political favour in dispensing patronage involved purchases of saddlery and harness for the Force. Until the 1896 election, E. F. Hutchings of Winnipeg had an almost exclusive hold on Mounted Police business. However, this changed dramatically following the 1896 Liberal victory. From the fiscal year 1897-98, not one penny of Force patronage went to E. F. Hutchings, the bulk of business going to Adams Brothers of Brandon, a firm which had found no favour with the Conservatives. (See comparative table of NWMP business with the two firms).[154] This change of fortune was directly dictated by the Honourable Clifford Sifton, Minister of the Interior in a letter to Prime Minister Laurier. Sifton requested that future orders for Mounted Police harness and saddlery be placed with Adams Brothers instead of E. F. Hutchings:

> I may explain that the only two wholesale harness, saddlery and leather firms in the Province of Manitoba are E. F. Hutchings of Winnipeg, and Adams Brothers of Brandon. Mr. Hutchings is the most uncompromising and violent opponent of the Government and perhaps the most offensive to our Liberal friends of any Conservative in the City of Winnipeg; one of the firm being a Member of the Legislature.[155]

Apparently the message was passed on to Fred White with some force as, a few days later, he asked Herchmer to substitute Adams for Hutchings on the patronage list and he did not add the usual caveat about this being done with due consideration of the public interest. Instead he warned: "Please send your next order to them [*Adams Brothers*] and do not purchase anything more from Hutchings."[156] This arrangement did not go unnoticed by the Conservatives with Nicholas Flood Davin attacking the government in the House of Commons for allowing Adams to supply the Force without even allowing Hutchings to bid for the contract. Davin revealed that Adams was active on behalf of the Liberal Party in local politics in Brandon.[157]

A similar transfer of patronage occurred after the 1896 election with regard to Mounted Police purchases of hardware. Until 1891, the Force bought most of its hardware not under contract but as required, and much of it was purchased at inflated prices from Miller, Morse and Company of Winnipeg, a staunchly Conservative firm. Then in 1891, the NWMP invited firms to tender for the hardware contract and it was won by J. H. Ashdown of Winnipeg who undercut the prices of his competitors by a wide margin. This evoked protests from Conservatives in Winnipeg that Ashdown was a fervent Liberal. The business then reverted back to Miller, Morse and Company at least partly because the Force was unhappy with the quality of Ashdown's products.[158] In 1896, Ashdown ran for Parliament as a Liberal candidate and was defeated.[159] Following the election Ashdown was placed on the government patronage list and White wrote to Herchmer:

> Do not forget that James Ashdown of Winnipeg is now entitled to Government patronage, provided his prices do not exceed those we have been paying to Miller Morse and Company.
>
> Perhaps it would be well for you to have a list prepared of probable requirements of staple articles during the next two months, and send it to James Ashdown with a request that he will fill in the prices at which he would supply.[160]

Ashdown did very well by NWMP business, supplying for the next few years the bulk of the Force's hardware requirement. (See comparative table of NWMP business with Ashdown and Miller, Morse).[161] This did not go unnoticed by Nicholas Flood Davin who accused the government of letting Ashdown name his own prices for hardware items supplied to the Mounted Police, by awarding him business without allowing other firms to compete through the tendering process.[162] For some reason Ashdown fell from the grace of the Liberal party in 1903 and he was removed from the patronage list.[163]

In defence of his government, Sir Wilfrid Laurier rightly pointed out in the House of Commons that the Mounted Police dispensed 80 per cent of its budget under proper contracts, in most cases involving competition.[164] In the case of kit and clothing contracts, a large item of police expenditure, manufacturing concerns were run by prominent Conservatives such as W. E. Sandford of Hamilton and S. and H. Borbridge of Ottawa. This continuity was necessary because these firms were experienced and equipped to meet the needs of the Force in quantity and quality.[165] However, at the request of politicians, a share of the clothing patronage was given to their supporters, firms also with proven competence. Thus J. B. Laliberte of Quebec and the Guelph Woollen Mills received contracts with the approval of the Prime Minister and in the latter case at the behest of the Minister of the Interior, Clifford Sifton.[166]

There is no doubt that most of the patronage connected with the Mounted Police purse, particularly in Manitoba and the NWT was dictated by Clifford Sifton. Shortly after Joseph Israel Tarte, Minister of Public Works, quit the Liberal cabinet in 1902, he told the Governor General, Lord Minto, that Sifton and his "gang" had controlled all patronage in the West and the Yukon, and then told Lady Minto that they were making personal gain from it and had passed some money on to Laurier.[167] There was, of course, no proof of this supplied by Tarte but Lord Minto was already concerned about Sifton's actions because he had recently learned from Fred White that Sifton was interfering with the Force for patronage purposes to the detriment of its efficiency: "In fact Fred White has to me expressed his utter despondence at the consequences of Sifton's unjustifiable interference."[168] However, when Minto brought this meddling to the attention of Laurier, without quoting White as a source, the Prime Minister denied it all, claiming that he alone ran the Force through the hands of Fred White.[169]

Sifton was not above ordering patronage even at the local level. He was known to take an interest in where detachments were stationed to be sure that they were boarded with Liberals.[170] And when the Force proposed spending $1,200 on oats for divisional headquarters in Calgary, Sifton ordered that his brother, an Alberta judge, be consulted to make sure the order went to Liberals.[171] Also the three Liberal Members of Parliament in the NWT, Frank Oliver, Walter Scott and Rev. James Douglas and local Liberal Associations all had their say on how and where the Mounted Police would direct expenditures.[172] This continual badgering by politicians proved very frustrating for Fred White as is indicated in his reply to Walter Scott after being upbraided for buying wagons in the East instead of telling Commissioner Perry to buy them from the Bain Company representative in Regina:

> Personally, I simply hate the patronage part of the Police work and am only too glad of an opportunity of unloading it upon somebody else. If you will kindly speak to Major Perry I will take care that no more wagons are shipped from the east.[173]

In the 1890s, the NWMP found increasing challenge in overseeing the peaceful transition from frontier to settled community. Migration to the West increased considerably and with it came an expansion of Mounted Police responsibility. The newcomers were met by law enforcement officers whose first concern was that they settle successfully on the land. Where deprivation, adverse conditions or disease occurred, the Mounted Police helped to achieve solutions. Sometimes as in the case of financial hardship or in labour disputes, the solutions were only short-term and sometimes as in the case of political patronage the way of the world prevailed over strict justice. Nevertheless, despite dwindling numbers due to the demands of police in the Yukon, the Force was remarkably successful in its tasks.

Chapter 5

Adjusting to a New Reality: The Mounted Police and the Indians, 1886-1892

The Rebellion of 1885 underscored for the Canadian government the danger posed by large numbers of Indians in the North-West Territories. More than 20,000 Indians lived in the three districts of Assiniboia, Saskatchewan and Alberta[1] and while most of these were treaty Indians living on assigned reserves, some still belonged to nomadic bands who had not yet accepted government policy. The completion of the Canadian Pacific Railway would soon bring masses of newcomers to the West in search of land. It was the responsibility of the Department of Indian Affairs and the NWMP to ensure that the Indians did not interfere with the peaceable settlement of the Territories.[2]

The policy of the Department of Indian Affairs remained unchanged, even in the aftermath of the rebellion. The Department was determined to transform the culture of the Indians by teaching them the same values, mores and ways of earning a living embraced by the white man.[3] Principally responsible for this transformation were the Indian Affairs officials on the reserves who would inculcate in the nomadic Indians the techniques of agriculture and ranching which would lead gradually to a comfortably settled existence. Meanwhile, teachers in Indian schools were educating the more impressionable younger generation in the ways of the white man in the hope that graduates would set an example for others on the reserve.[4] The aim of the policy was to raise the Indians from dependency on the state to self-sufficiency in as short a time as possible. In the interim, they would be wards of the government, sustained by grants of rations and denied the full rights of citizenship by the *Indian Act* of 1876 and by regulations imposed by the Indian Affairs Department.[5]

Perhaps the most onerous regulation placed on the Indians after the rebellion was restriction of movement. No one could leave the reserve unless he or she received a permit from the resident Indian Agent. The intent of the rule was to minimize contact with the growing community of whites which might lead to conflict between the groups or corruption of the Indians.[6] The problems of contact were evident with complaints received from ranchers of Indians killing cattle and with Indian men visiting settlements to procure liquor sometimes by offering their women as prostitutes. However, the Indian Department perceived a drawback to the restriction in that by confining the Indians to reserves they were protected from the assimilative influences of a growing white majority. This the officials tried to offset by forbidding the exercise of some Indian traditions they regarded as particularly barbaric such as dances which involved giving away belongings or the testing of warriors.[7]

For the most part, the Mounted Police were responsible for ensuring that Indians observed both the laws of the country and regulations set by the Indian department. In these first few years after the rebellion the primary concern was that any dissatisfaction felt by the Indians over their radically changed way of life did not result in another outbreak of violence. Beyond this, the police had to investigate and ultimately punish Indians for all infractions of the law, many of which however, did not violate the code of ethics of Native culture. For instance, horse stealing from enemy bands was a threat to order which the police had to terminate even though Indians themselves regarded such raids as courageous assertions of the warrior impulse rather than as antisocial violations of property rights.[8]

Policing the Indians was a most difficult task for the NWMP. Dozens of reserves containing thousands of Indians were scattered over most of western Canada. To meet the sheer immensity of the geographic challenge, an expanded Force of 1,000 men was reorganized to cover the entire area. The new system involved greater de-centralization of the Force within divisional areas into small detachments set up in outposts. Regular patrols from the divisional headquarters as well as from the outposts kept a closer watch on the countryside. As well, special patrols were organized from time to time to visit Indian reserves and report on conditions.[9] The police proved very successful in this period in that the crime rate among Indians was lower than in white communities and that there was no major instance of violent resistance by the Indians to the new order.[10]

Some of the success of the NWMP can be ascribed to their efficiency and determination to maintain law and order, but much of the credit must go to the Indians themselves. Restricting the access of Indians to white communities was a difficult objective of questionable legality.[11] Enforcing a regulation which required the Indians to have permission of the agents before leaving reserves worried police because there was no basis for it in law and furthermore, the practice violated assurances given when the treaties were signed.[12] The only way they could take wandering Natives into custody was to charge them as vagrants. But the pass system did work to a degree in limiting contact between whites and Indians because the latter submitted willingly to these limits upon their freedom of movement. This acquiescence was probably due to respect for police authority and to fear of being cut off from rations for non-compliance.[13] Indian leaders also assisted police by discouraging crime.[14] In some cases they cooperated by turning over band members sought by the NWMP for infractions of the law.[15] Nevertheless, the persistence of Indian culture and the universal weaknesses of human nature kept the Mounted Police busy enough with the western Indians.

Immediately after the rebellion both the government and the Mounted Police were concerned about the possibility of further outbreaks of violence. Some serious consideration was given to establishing a "flying column" of militia troops and Policemen to patrol the West to defend against any large scale uprising.[16] However, the very real danger that such a force might incite reaction from the Natives convinced the government to leave responsibility for law and order in the hands of the Mounted Police.[17]

Similarly, the government rejected proposals to disarm all Indians, but continued to limit the sale of ammunition to the amount that they would need for hunting.[18] In Assiniboia, a number of Indians who refused to remain on their reserves were rounded up by the Mounted Police and transported back. When their leaders balked at the treatment, they were arrested.[19] From this point the only treaty Indians permitted off their reserves were those with passes from their agents. Some anxiety continued in

the NWT over the intentions of the Indians but there had been no indication of any major threat to order.[20]

When trouble erupted, it was in an area not normally policed by the NWMP. In November 1886, the Deputy Superintendent-General of Indian Affairs, Lawrence Vankoughnet informed Fred White, that he was worried about a situation developing in the Kootenay Mountains of British Columbia. Settlers there were complaining of the threatening behaviour of some Indians and they were demanding protection from the government.[21] White decided to send Supt. W. Herchmer, Officer Commanding "E" Division at Calgary, on an unofficial visit to the area to investigate the charges. Herchmer travelled to Victoria in early January and snowshoed into the area through the Moyie Pass. When he returned to Calgary he reported that the situation was serious. The four bands of Indians in the region were unhappy with reserves allotted to them and were particularly aggrieved over the loss of a prized piece of valley land which they regarded as stolen by the local Member of the Provincial Parliament, Lt.-Col. James Baker. The British Columbia authorities were making little attempt to enforce the law and the Indians were contemptuous of the weakness displayed by whites; in one case, no attempt had been made to arrest two Indians who were accused of the murders of two white miners. Herchmer recommended that a force of 150 Mounted Policemen be immediately despatched to the area to restore order.[22]

No action was taken by the government, however, until the crisis developed even further. Early in March 1887, B.C. Provincial Cst. Anderson arrested a Kootenay Indian named Kapula and charged him with the murder of the two miners. Apparently pressured by Kapula's incensed relatives, Chief Isadore led an armed party against the jail and forced the constable to release his prisoner. The Indians then demanded that Anderson and a Provincial Surveyor, F. W. Aylmer, who had worked on the reserve, leave the area. Chief Isadore explained that in the current state of excitement the continued presence of these two men would likely provoke bloodshed. Anderson and Aylmer accordingly departed and the alarmed white residents petitioned the provincial government for help.[23]

Not eager to tackle this volatile problem alone, the British Columbia government tried to shift responsibility to the federal government. On 21 March 1887, just days before his death, Premier William Smithe telegraphed Ottawa asking that the Mounted Police be sent to suppress an "incipient insurrection"[24] by the Kootenay Indians. Anticipating argument over expense Smithe warned the federal government that British Columbia would not pay for the expedition because, from a constitutional perspective, treating with Indians was the responsibility of the central power. Predictably, Prime Minister J. A. Macdonald replied that the Mounted Police would be sent if the provincial government agreed to cover its expenses as provided for in the *Police Act*.[25] There the matter rested for a time while the federal government investigated the background of the turmoil.

The basic problem in the Kootenays was the great dissatisfaction of the Indians with lands allocated to them for reserves. In 1884, an Indian Commissioner, Mr. O'Reilly, was sent to the Kootenay Valley to lay out the reserves and free the rest of the land for settlement. O'Reilly was unable to take a census but nevertheless proceeded to survey five reserves totalling 41,029 acres and his plan was approved by the Department of Indian Affairs. Chief Isadore immediately declared his unhappiness with the lands assigned to his band. Efforts to convince Isadore to accept the reserves as surveyed were unsuccessful. Isadore glibly told government representatives that "it was for him to decide what land he would grant to the Queen, and not for her to dictate to him".[26] The disagreement became more charged when Col. James Baker ordered the Indians off traditional tribal lands to which he now held title.[27] The Commissioner of Indian Affairs for the NWT, Edgar Dewdney, advised the Prime Minister that he considered the Indians to have just cause for complaint about their lands. Further, he was worried because the Stoney Indians in Alberta, close allies of the Kootenays, were very excited about the dispute and he feared an outbreak in British Columbia could lead to Indian war on the prairies.[28] Once more, Supt. Herchmer was sent into the region, this time in company with a local magistrate and the Indian Commissioner for British Columbia, to listen to Indian grievances. They induced Chief Isadore to surrender Kapula when a trial was arranged. Herchmer was impressed by the Indian claim that they had been badly treated and felt that the Mounted Police should be sent to the area:

> Their presence will establish good order and law. There has not been enough of this in the past. I believe the Indians have been very unfairly dealt with both as to their land and also in the way of justice has been misadministered.[29]

He found that the older Indians wanted only peace but that the younger ones were ready for trouble and were well stocked with good guns and ammunition.[30]

In July 1887, Supt. Sam Steele was ordered to proceed from Macleod to the Kootenay Valley with "D" Division of the Mounted Police, numbering 75 officers and men. The expedition proceeded by rail to Golden, B.C. On July 18th, most of the division then started for Kootenay on horseback followed by their supplies as well as some dismounted men who headed for the Columbia Lakes by river steamer. The entire division moved into camp on high ground near the confluence of the Kootenay River and Wild Horse Creek on July 31st. Steele then set his men to the task of constructing what later became known as Fort Steele.[31] Substantial buildings of logs and rough lumber, capable of housing the Force for the winter,[32] were erected in short order. Steele was already communicating to his superiors the necessity of his staying longer than the two months originally envisaged. The Prime Minister agreed that "D" Division should stay the winter upon receiving reports that messengers were travelling between the Kootenay Indians and prairie Indian bands discussing a common uprising in the spring, including the Bloods.[33]

Shortly after the arrival of the Mounted Police, Chief Isadore brought in Kapula and another Indian named Isadore accused of being his accomplice in the murder of the white miners three years previously. Steele conducted a preliminary hearing and discovered there was insufficient evidence against the pair to commit them for trial and dismissed all charges. He then assured Chief Isadore that he was there to bring law and order and promised equal treatment to both whites and Indians.[34] The problem of the Indian land allotment was not solved in the same amicable fashion. A commission, with representatives of the federal and provincial governments, visited the area in September to review the Indian grievances. Unfortunately, most of the Indians were away trading in Montana and were unable to meet with the Commissioners who reached the conclusion that the reserves were fairly allotted and adequate for the needs of the band. The commission then departed, delegating to Steele the unenviable task of communicating the decision to Isadore. Concessions made to the Indians included the allowance of $490 for improvements made to Colonel Baker's land while they occupied it, the digging of an irrigation ditch for the reserve and the opening of an industrial school. The chief was unhappy, but Steele persuaded him to accept the settlement.[35]

The Mounted Police planned to withdraw from the Kootenays the following summer. The outstanding issues with the Indians had been settled and the white population felt reassured by police patrols. Steele's assessment of the Kootenay Indians was most favourable, being particularly impressed with their high moral character and with the discipline that Isadore exercised over the band. Before leaving, Steele held a sports meet and invited the Indians to participate which they did with great success, winning prizes for foot and horse races. At the close of the meet, Isadore led a delegation to the fort to say goodbye. In a farewell speech, Isadore praised the police for bringing to an end the feelings of mistrust which had long existed between whites and Indians in the region.

The planned departure of the Mounted Police was delayed in early July by news that United States authorities were about to launch an expedition against renegade Indians just across the U.S. border. Steele feared that these Indians would seek refuge in Canada and disrupt the friendly relations with the Kootenay Indians. Upon investigation the situation proved not to be as serious as originally reported and "D" Division left their fort on 7 August 1888. Steele withdrew his men from the area by climbing to the summit of the Rocky Mountains and crossing over into the NWT by the Crow's Nest Pass. He arrived in Macleod ten days later, proving that in the event of future trouble with the Kootenays this was a viable route by which to send an expedition.[36]

On the prairies, the NWMP continued to watch for any sign that discontent among Indians and half-breeds would result in an armed uprising. Certainly the cause for discontent among these groups had not been removed. The Indians found the adjustment to agriculture on reserves painful and they resented the careful doling out of rations by the Indian department. Many half-breeds were suffering more than the Indians from economic dislocation and agitation for relief and for favourable settlement of land claims continued. Both the police and government officials were worried that expatriate rebel half-breeds and discontented Indians in the United States were in communication with groups in Canada. Rumours of an impending Native uprising alarmed the police and settlers alike each spring for several years after the rebellion.

There was little the police could do to stave off an uprising other than to watch the situation closely. In the case of the Indians, they tried to enforce the pass system effectively but it was impossible to prevent visiting between bands in Canada and the United States.[37] To a limited extent, intelligence was obtained from agents working for the police among both the Indians and the Métis.[38] The NWMP also took small measures to try to relieve the causes of the Native grievances. In the case of the Indians, they, upon occasion, attempted to mediate between them and the officials of the Indian Affairs Department.[39] Where the destitution was worst among the Métis, the Mounted Police issued relief foodstuffs or employed men for public works.[40] Despite the continuing problems and rumours of trouble, there appeared to be no serious threats to order on the prairie until five years after the rebellion.

In 1889 and 1890, a new religion swept through many of the Indian bands of the western United States. Variously referred to as the "Ghost Dance" or "Messiah Craze" religion, adherents were promised a blissful eternity of Indian society after death. Perverting the message, some of the Teton Sioux of the Dakotas and Nebraska considered that the religion required them to kill all whites to precipitate the heavenly reward. The threats of these hostile Indians led to armed confrontations with the U.S. Army. The unfortunate results of this conflict included the killing of Sitting Bull while resisting arrest by Indian police and the brutal slayings at Wounded Knee in December 1890.[41]

This last violent rejection of the changes which the white men had wrought on the lives of western Indians alarmed Canadians. NWMP patrols from detachments near the U.S. border were normally reduced or suspended during the winter because deep snow and cold reduced border crossings and Indian movements. But during the winter of 1889-1890, the patrols were maintained and even increased. The object of the police was to keep Canadian Indians on the reserves and to turn back American Indians trying to cross the border or to discourage them by stringent enforcement of customs regulations.[42] Police also kept a close check on the amount of ammunition Indians obtained for their repeating rifles. When reports were received that the Indians were crossing the border to buy bullets in the United States, the NWMP sought and obtained assurances from Washington that American authorities would put a stop to such sales.[43] Care was to be exercised by the police when moving armed patrols on reserves to ensure that the Indians were aware of their presence so that they would take no alarm.[44] The Governor General, Lord Stanley, took a personal interest in this police effort and he assured the American government that the Mounted Police was doing its part to ensure that Indian rebellion would not erupt in the West. He did, however, infer that the methods used to secure the Indians were somewhat different than those employed by the U.S. Army:

> Bear in mind that our policy here has always been to trust our Indians, so far as we can, and not to 'dragoon' them – and that this policy has answered up to this time.[45]

There were a number of reports of Indian restiveness throughout the year but fears of a rising proved groundless. In January 1891, the sheriff of Bottineau County, North Dakota, reported to the Mounted Police that Sioux Indians in the Turtle Mountains of Manitoba were holding war dances. The same information was sent to the government from the United States Secretary of State. The police sent out a special patrol to investigate which found the Sioux quiet and peaceful. As a precaution however, the Mounted Police established a detachment at the nearby town of Deloraine to watch if the contagion of the "Ghost Dance" spread to this band of Sioux.[46] The Police learned that two messengers from hostile American Sioux had reached the Peigan Indians immediately south of the

Alberta border but their invitation to establish a common cause was rejected.[47] The provincial government of British Columbia also alerted the federal government that the Kootenay Indians were excited by the example of the U.S. Sioux but the Mounted Police decided to temporize reaction because American troops seemed to have ended the threat in their country.[48] Alarms continued to be received throughout 1891 but, gradually, anxiety receded and no major incident occurred.

The danger of an imminent Indian war caused concern among the whites in the NWT, but little real panic. At Moose Jaw in January 1891, the local justices of the peace requested the government to post more police in their community because they believed that the Indians were about to take the warpath. The NCO in charge of the detachment refuted the argument, stating that unfounded rumours of trouble had been flying about town for days, spread principally by the local hotel owner who hoped for police board at his nearby empty establishment. The Indian Department received a similar report which also claimed that mischievous whites were feeding the alarm at night by prowling on the outskirts of town hooting and screaming in imitation of Indians.[49] Prairie newspapers carried much news about Indian activities on both sides of the border and tended to be critical of heavy-handed treatment of Indians in the United States which fuelled resentments.[50] By contrast, newspapers reflected confidence in Canadian policy and in measures taken by the Mounted Police to respond to any trouble.[51]

Although much of the rationale for segregating Indians from white society on reserves was to prevent conflict, the government also sought to protect the Indians from corruption. Liquor held a great attraction for many Indians and unrestricted access to it had proven disastrous for individuals and had threatened the very existence of tribal society before the arrival of the Mounted Police. To diminish the temptation, the government instituted prohibition on the importation of liquor into the NWT, its sale to Indians and their consumption of it.[52] But the attraction of intoxication remained strong and many Indians would sacrifice much, even on occasion the prostitution of their wives, to obtain alcohol. The responsibility for policing prohibition of Indian access to alcohol lay with the NWMP. Most resistance to prohibition was met from the Indians of southwestern Alberta and the problem grew throughout this period probably as white settlement brought more intrusion into Indian society.

Opportunities for drink and prostitution brought Indians to the white communities where they often ran into trouble with the Mounted Police who preferred to have them back on the reserve. In August 1886, a group of Sarcees camped in a ravine near Calgary for the purposes of prostitution; they resisted police attempts to remove them and gunfire was exchanged. The police thought they wounded some in the party but all escaped.[53] The following June, Blackfoot Indians moved into the Calgary area and prostitution resumed. The Indians resisted the efforts of Chief Crowfoot, their Indian Agent and the Mounted Police to move them back to the reserve.[54] In the Battleford area some Indian women fell into the practice of visiting town to prostitute themselves. Police responded by checking them for passes and turning them back to the reserves. In addition, they charged and convicted a man for keeping Indian women for the purposes of prostitution. He was imprisoned for three months at hard labour.[55] When an Indian named Two Horns, from Piapot's Reserve in Regina, touted his wife as a prostitute in 1887, the police treated him as a vagrant and steered him back to his reserve.[56]

Part of the difficulty in enforcing prohibition of liquor with the Indians was that it was becoming increasingly more available in the NWT. Widespread abuse of the liquor permit system was impossible for police to control. Moreover, the government, after much internal conflict, decided in 1888 to allow the brewing and sale of beer containing up to 4% alcohol.[57] In reality the government was only recognizing the practice of the previous several years during which western breweries produced "light" beer which they contended was non-intoxicating. The police pointed out the danger that widespread availability of beer posed for Indians only to be instructed to keep it away from them.[58]

In southwestern Alberta, the towns where beer was brewed became special problems for police. On 11 September 1887, Sgt. Williams and three Mounted Policemen came upon a party of 11 drunken Blood Indians on the reserve, one of whom was "Big Rib", an escaped convict. The Indians resisted arrest and disappeared into the bush. Attempts by the police to prosecute Macleod brewers who were selling beer to the Indians, which was tested at up to 9.2% alcohol, failed when a medical witness refused to say the beer was intoxicating. At Lethbridge in 1887 and 1888, Blood and Peigan Indians gathered on several occasions to buy beer or to barter for it by prostitution.[59] Once when refused beer by a local brewery two Indians retaliated by smashing windows.[60] In December 1888, two Indian women were arrested for drunkenness by the Mounted Police in the river bottom at Lethbridge. The women, one of whom was 14 years old, had traded sexual favours to white men in return for ten bottles of beer.[61] Supt. R. B. Deane dealt with this problem by allowing visiting Indians only one night in town to conduct business and then requiring them to move on.[62] This was a useful method of control but Deane found that he could not eliminate the problem altogether.[63]

Indians had access not only to the generally available beer but also to liquor imported into the Territories either legally or illegally. Liquor was often acquired through the permit system from the Lieutenant-Governor for personal use and was then surreptitiously sold to Indians. Many of the traffickers were men close to the Indians, such as half-breeds and white men living with Indian women. Supt. McIllree described this trade as continuous in Calgary particularly among the Sarcees who lived close to town.[64] Supt. Steele hired Indian detectives and secured the cooperation of various chiefs to try to stamp out this commerce among the Bloods.[65] He managed to discourage some of the sellers but could not claim any overall decrease in the availability of liquor to Indians.[66] One night in January 1891, a gang bringing bootleg liquor into the NWT provided a windfall for a camp of non-treaty Cree Indians near Medicine Hat. The gang tossed considerable quantities of illegally imported liquor off a train onto the prairie before it reached Medicine Hat station where it could be searched by the Mounted Police. The bootleggers intended to retrieve the alcohol later but the Indians beat them to it.[67] The result was considerable revelry in the Indian camp. Again working with Indian scouts the Mounted Police began patrolling the area, particularly vigilant for trouble because of the Sioux uprising in the United States.[68] The police arrested 13 Indians for drunkenness and convicted 9 of these which resulted in fines or jail terms. About 30 gallons of liquor was seized from the camp.

The problem for the Mounted Police of trying to control Indians' access to liquor grew in the first few years after the rebellion as more whites and more alcohol arrived in the West. Indicative of this was the rise in the number of Indian-related alcohol offences in these years.[69] From 1886 to 1891, the number of persons charged and convicted for both supplying liquor to Indians and for Indian drunkenness or possession rose considerably. For those convicted of supplying liquor to the Indians punishments imposed ranged from a minimum fine of $50 and costs to a maximum fine of $300 and costs and six months in prison at hard labour. By far the majority of the offences were committed by or connected with the Indians on Treaty No. Seven Reserves in Alberta. For instance, from 1 December 1889 to 30 November 1890, 17 of the 18 convictions for supplying liquor to Indians were in the Treaty No. Seven area as were 12 of the 16 convictions for Indian drunkenness.[70] Of course, the numbers convicted still represent a very small proportion of the Indians in the Treaty No. Seven, let alone the NWT. Nevertheless, these statistics indicate increasing police attention to the growing problem of Indian alcohol abuse. It was also a foreshadowing of how the situation would deteriorate after 1891 when prohibition in the Territories was lifted.

For the most part, the NWMP were responsible for investigating the criminal activities of Indians involved in cattle and horse stealing. The Indians were attempting to follow traditional ways of life in the altered setting of the white-dominated West. Frustrated by the mysteries of agriculture and the parsimony of the rations system, Indians would sometimes hunt the cattle which had displaced the buffalo on the prairies. Similarly, young warriors sought to prove their mettle by raiding rival bands for horses. These activities took place primarily in southern Alberta where ranches were numerous and where the cross-border tribal antagonisms were the strongest. The Mounted Police found these crimes frustrating because of the stealth, defiance and occasional violence of the perpetrators and the sympathy for their actions felt by many fellow band members. Moreover, stock owners continually complained about the disappearance of animals, which they blamed on Indians with little or no justification. Such frustration led one Mounted Police officer, Supt. J. H. McIllree, to comment in 1886 that Indian stock thieves infesting the Cypress Hills were probably from the United States:

> It is a great pity that we cannot shoot a few of these Indians, they are continually infesting these hills, and knowing as they do that we are not allowed to shoot them on sight, they are very bold and impertinent and give a great deal of trouble and annoyance to the detachments.[71]

This proposal met swift rebuke from the Prime Minister, John A. Macdonald, who instructed that McIllree be cautioned that "supposed thieves cannot be shot down on sight".[72]

Not long after McIllree complained about armed American Indians wandering into Canada, a serious clash between bands occurred in southern Alberta. In September 1886, a small party of Canadian Indians, five Blood and one Blackfoot, were on foot near Writing-On-Stone looking for lost horses. Only two of the Indians were armed adults, the other four were just boys. Unexpectedly the group encountered 24 Gros Ventres Indians from the United States who were searching for some Bloods they suspected of stealing their horses. Escape was impossible and the Canadian Indians were surrounded and quickly slain. When news of the killings drifted back to the Blood Reserve the predictable reaction occurred with young warriors vowing to raid the Gros Ventres seeking revenge. Only the onset of winter delayed the launching of a war party. Hostilities were aggravated by considerable stealing of horses which had been occurring between the Canadian Bloods and the American Ventres and Assiniboines.[73]

When spring arrived in 1887, the Bloods prepared for war. The head chief of the tribe, Red Crow, vigorously opposed retaliation and with the help of visiting Chief Crowfoot of the Blackfoot tribe, managed to persuade the older Bloods to stay the hand. Supt. P. R. Neale of the Mounted Police and the Indian Agent, W. Pocklington, calmed the waters more by promising an investigation.[74] Some younger warriors, however, would not listen and began an exodus from the reserve. To stave off war, Edgar Dewdney, the Lieutenant-Governor of the NWT, met with the Bloods in May and arranged to seek a settlement with the American bands. On 1 June 1887, Insp. G. E. Sanders and a unit of Mounted Police escorted Pocklington, Red Crow and several of his advisors to Fort Assiniboine, Montana. On the way out the party passed the spot where the six Indians had been killed the previous May and there found the bloody evidence of the massacre.[75] On crossing the border, the police were met by a patrol of U.S. Cavalry who asked them to store their weapons out of sight in a wagon while on American soil.

Arriving at Fort Assiniboine the Canadians began negotiating with the chiefs of the Gros Ventres and the Assiniboines. Before talks actually began a Gros Ventres' chief admitted that he had led the party which fought the Canadian Indians but claimed they had killed only one Blood. Because of the sensitivity of the issue all parties agreed not to mention the incident during negotiations. At the meeting after speeches were made by both whites and Indians, an agreement was reached to cease raids and return stolen horses to each other. The treaty was sealed by the passing of a peace pipe. The Bloods picked up 35 horses stolen from them by the Assiniboines and returned to Canada.[76] Keeping their part of the bargain, Red Crow, later in June, turned over to police three horses stolen from the Assiniboines and surrendered the Blood Indian, Star Child, who had committed the deed.[77] The peace agreement defused a volatile situation which threatened to turn into serious warfare, even if it did not entirely eliminate horse-stealing raids across the border in succeeding years.

Chief Crowfoot is said to have sensed an "air of wild freedom"[78] among the Blood Indians in the spring of 1887. Several reports were received at Mounted Police posts in southern Alberta of cattle being killed and horses stolen during the winter of 1886-1887. Patrols were despatched to search for the depredators but the police had little luck following trails through snow.[79] Then, in April 1887, a four man patrol under S/Sgt. Spicer was sent out from "A" Division Headquarters at Maple Creek to locate Indians reported killing cattle in the vicinity.

The Indians, believed to be Bloods, were found on the 27th of April but had no intention of meekly surrendering. The party fired on the patrol and then scattered. Initial pursuit was unsuccessful and subsequent patrols fared no better. The incident was regarded as serious because of the violent defiance displayed by the Indians. Lieutenant-Governor Dewdney rather shrewdly observed, however, the Indians probably only intended to intimidate the police because if they had wished to hit them, they would have done so.[80]

Soon after this incident, Indian Agent Pocklington on the Blood Reserve reported to Fort Macleod that two Indians, The Dog and Big Rib, had ridden onto the reserve singing the war song and driving horses resembling those reported stolen at Medicine Hat recently. Pocklington also believed that this pair had been in the party which had fired on S/Sgt. Spicer. On May 6th, Supt. Neale sent into the reserve Insp. Gilbert Sanders with 30 men to bring in the suspects but they slipped away. The patrol did recover one of the stolen horses. Sanders then took 15 men on a flying patrol south of the Blood Reserve and on May 13th arrested The Dog and Big Rib. The two were charged and convicted of horse theft before Judge Macleod and sentenced to five years in penitentiary at Stony Mountain, Manitoba. The charge that the two fired on the police patrol could not be proven because S/Sgt. Spicer was not able to identify them.[81]

Unfortunately for the NWMP, the saga of Big Rib and The Dog did not end with their sentencing. The Indians were turned over to the custody of Sheriff Campbell along with two constables to help escort the prisoners to Stony Mountain. En route, the party stopped over for the night in a hotel at Dunsmore. Sheriff Campbell ordered the Indians secured for the night by shackling their legs together and having the two constables sleep in the same room with their mattress against the door. Campbell told the policemen to go to sleep as the 20-foot drop to the ground precluded escape by the window. The next morning the Indians were found to have exited through the window.

The successful escape of the rogue Bloods heartened other Indians who wished to defy police and made law enforcement more difficult. Big Rib turned up a few months later in a group of Indians found drinking in the bush on the Blood Reserve. Aided by his friends, Big Rib again escaped. One of the party, Eagle Rib, received three months hard labour in Macleod guardroom for his part in obstructing justice. Some Bloods were now openly contemptuous of the impotence of the Mounted Police. To counter this, Supt. Neale ordered a coordinated raid on the reserve from "H" Division at Macleod and "K" Division at Lethbridge to pick up the two wanted Indians. The combined force of about 40 men travelled by night and arrived at the reserve early on 8 November 1887, where it arrested Good Rider for cattle-killing and Calf Shirt for possession of alcohol. Both received jail terms and some wariness of the Police was restored in the Bloods.[82] As for Big Rib and The Dog, they remained at large until March 1890 when, finally tired of the fugitive life, they surrendered themselves to police using the good offices of Chief Red Crow. The two expressed their regret for past actions and in view of the fact that they had surrendered voluntarily, served reduced prison terms of about one year.[83] The *Macleod Gazette* which had been complaining about Indian cattle thefts commented facetiously that the pair emerged from their prison sojourn well dressed and bragging about the good life at Stony Mountain.[84]

Complaints about Indian cattle killing in southern Alberta continued throughout this period. As would be expected, the principal complainants were the ranchers and the stock associations who were upset that armed Indians were allowed to roam away from reserves on passes.[85] The Mounted Police always investigated reports of Indian cattle killing but were of the opinion that the problem was exaggerated by the ranchers who were reacting to mere suspicions and who tended to blame natural stock losses due to weather or disease on the Indians.[86] Moreover, the Indians did not share white men's inhibitions about eating meat of cattle found already dead on the prairies during a severe winter.[87] On the other hand Indians vehemently protested throughout the period that their rations were insufficient and it seems likely that some would take the opportunity occasionally to appropriate this new game.[88] The Mounted Police found evidence of this difficult to uncover and as a result prosecuted only a few cases of cattle killing in this six-year span. However, several which they did pursue led to troubled relations with the Indians.

In March 1890, two Indian scouts employed by the Mounted Police arrested a Blood Indian, Medicine White Horse, for cattle killing. Another Blood named Good Young Man assaulted the police scouts as they were taking their prisoner in and so facilitated his escape. Both men were later taken by police and received jail sentences, Medicine White Horse for cattle killing and Good Young Man for assault. The incarceration of the latter caused particular distress on the Blood Reserve because he was an important figure in the celebration of the Bloods' Sun Dance. Indian representations to secure his early release were unavailing.[89]

A temporary rupture in relations between the Bloods and Mounted Police occurred over cattle killing in 1891. Two Mounted Police constables, Ryan and Alexander, were on patrol from Stand Off detachment looking for whisky smugglers, when they accidentally encountered a party of Bloods carrying a load of freshly killed beef. As they galloped up to take the Indians in custody, one of them, Steals Fire, threw up his rifle and fired, grazing Alexander on the neck. Ryan then drew his revolver and exchanged shots with the Indian, finally bringing him down with a bullet through the back. Alexander (who was not seriously wounded) and Ryan then tried to help the wounded man who was still trying to resist capture, weakly waving a knife. However, the policemen were forced to adopt a strategic withdrawal by the approach of a number of potentially hostile Indians.[90] This party took the badly wounded Steals Fire back to the Blood Reserve where considerable indignation soon built up about the actions of the police. Young warriors muttered threats of retaliation and Red Crow claimed compensation for the family if Steals Fire died.[91] Commissioner Herchmer strengthened the division by 20 men and alerted outposts to be prepared for trouble. But the excitement subsided as most Indians accepted the police explanation that Steals Fire had received his just desserts for resisting arrest with gunfire. Steals Fire hired a Medicine Man to cure him, paying ten horses for his ministration. Within two weeks, Steals Fire was once again able to ride a horse, although a Mounted Police surgeon predicted a mortal relapse within months.[92]

Despite the agreement of 1887 between the Bloods in Canada and the American Assiniboines and Gros Ventres, intertribal horse-stealing did not stop. The pact broke down the next year with the Indians from the U.S. raiding the Bloods and vice versa. In May 1888, a number of horses were reported stolen from the Blood Reserve and the Mounted Police wired the U.S. cavalry at Fort Assiniboine to watch for them. Col. Otis, the American commander, very quickly recovered these horses in the hands of U.S. Indians and returned them to Canada.[93] The Mounted Police were anxious to return the favour because they estimated that about 100 stolen horses were on the Blood Reserve. However, Supt. Neale at Fort Macleod could do little about it unless he actually caught the Indians bringing the horses into Canada. Commissioner Herchmer feared that the chiefs had no control over the younger warriors and feared that as many as 50 Bloods were in Montana in May 1888 to steal horses.[94] On 27 May 1888, a Mounted Police patrol sent out at night to search for horse thieves who had raided Gros Ventres in Montana rounded up four Bloods returning from the U.S. with several of these animals. In the course of the subsequent investigation, more horses were recovered and arrests made. Chief Red Crow adhered to his part of the bargain struck in Montana by even turning over his own son who had taken part in the raid. In the end, three Blood Indians were convicted of bringing stolen property into Canada and were sentenced to three months hard labour.[95]

These occasional forays finally led to violence. On 22 April 1889, an Indian scout, Star Child, employed by the Mounted Police, informed Supt. R. B. Deane at Lethbridge that a party of Bloods had left the reserve bound for a horse-stealing raid on American Indians. Deane informed Col. Otis, Commander of the U.S. cavalry at Fort Assiniboine, and Mounted Police patrols were warned to be on alert for the party. Five Bloods and one North Peigan Indian successfully raided the Crow Reserve south of the line and ran off about 100 horses. However, while returning to Canada they ran into a large party of Gros Ventres who gave chase. Gunfire was exchanged and the Bloods later claimed they saw several of their enemies fall. While still in flight, the party ran into two Assiniboine Indians on the trail, killed one of them and took his scalp, gun and horse. At this moment a U.S. cavalry patrol galloped onto the scene and the Canadian Indians were forced to flee again, abandoning most of the stolen horses. Crossing the border into Canada, one of the raiders and several of the horses were picked up by the Mounted Police. Within a few days, three others in the party surrendered themselves to the authorities and the recovered horses were sent back to the United States.

The four Indians were held for several weeks in the guardroom at Fort Macleod. But since no charges were forthcoming from injured parties on the American side, the police and Indian Affairs officials decided upon the release of the prisoners with a severe reprimand. The arrest of the remaining two raiders sparked a confrontation on the Blood Reserve between police and Indians in July. This pair, like the others, was soon let go by police.[96]

Both Supts. Steele and Deane, whose divisions patrolled near the Blood Reserve, were frustrated by the arrogant flaunting of the law displayed by some of the younger Bloods. Deane felt that this attitude stemmed from the belief of the Bloods that they were "the cream of creation".[97] He also found that their criminal methods were becoming somewhat more sophisticated. On 30 September 1889, eight horses were stolen from Cree Indians living near Medicine Hat. The Mounted Police tracked the horses to the Blood Reserve and recovered them in short order. Much to their surprise, the police discovered that the horses had already been marked with the Blood brand which should have been under the control of the Indian agents. When Deane captured one of the horse thieves, Come Singing, the man admitted that an accomplice had forged the brand with a piece of iron.[98]

Aside from the liquor offences and the stock thefts which occurred mostly in southern Alberta,

the police had very little Indian crime with which to deal. Annual returns of criminal statistics kept by police were a short litany of minor offences from creating a disturbance to maiming an ox. Only two of these offences ever appeared even a few times each year, that is assault and petty theft.[99] The former was not a great concern for the Mounted Police because they stemmed usually from the simple disputes between Indians and offered no danger of turning into a larger disturbance. The problem of petty theft, however, was some worry to police because it was sometimes perpetrated on white communities and could lead to quite serious consequences. Such was the case with the acrimony which developed between the Mounted Police and the Blackfoot Indians in the 1880s.[100]

On 22 August 1887, William Thompson, a rancher at High River, had his house ransacked, he believed, by Indians. He and a neighbour, Tucker Peach, went to the nearby Blackfoot camp and there found and began removing his goods. This precipitated an exchange of gunfire, Thompson shot one of the Indians, Trembling Man, in the chest while Tucker Peach was wounded in the arm by another Blackfoot, The Meat.[101] The Mounted Police investigated and took both Thompson and The Meat, into custody, the former charged with assault with intent to kill and the latter with wounding. Thompson, however, was granted bail while The Meat awaited trial in the Mounted Police guardroom in Calgary. The Blackfoot Indians were considerably agitated over these events. Not only had one of their band been grievously wounded but the man who committed the offence walked about apparently free while another Blackfoot languished in jail. The Mounted Police explained the law of bail to Crowfoot, the Blackfoot chief, who was satisfied, but evidently many of his warriors were not similarly appeased. Their ire increased considerably on the 4th of September when Trembling Man died and the Blackfoot reportedly demanded that Thompson be turned over to them for hanging.[102]

By unfortunate coincidence, another conflict with the Blackfoot followed hard on the heels of the shootings. On 24 August 1887, a settler east of Calgary complained to the Mounted Police that Indians had broken into his house and stolen some articles. Corporal Racey and a small police party, including the Blackfoot interpreter William Gladstone, were sent out to investigate. The first Indian caught was Deerfoot, also known as Scabby Dried Meat, who was a professional runner well known in Alberta. Some police, however, regarded him as "a very hot-headed young man, as a matter of fact, he was looked at as not being properly balanced".[103] After his arrest, Deerfoot found an opportunity, before being hauled off to the guardroom, to seize an axe and, swinging it in the air, defied the Mounted Police to try to take him. When the Police fired a couple of warning shots into the ground, Deerfoot laughed at the tactic perhaps knowing that with the Blackfoot in their present mood he would come to no harm. The party was forced to allow him to escape.[104]

Fate again dictated bad timing. The day that Asst. Comm. W. Herchmer visited the Blackfoot Reserve to convince the Indians to give up Deerfoot, Trembling Man died. Failing to secure Deerfoot's surrender, Herchmer took a party of 50 Mounted Policemen on the reserve and spent several days on a futile search. Prudently, the police did not press the matter further but kept alert for sign of the fugitive. Meanwhile both William Thompson and The Meat were acquitted of charges against them.[105]

The situation took a more serious, if farcical, turn over the prairie Indian practice of employing more than one name. In January 1888, a civilian employed by the Mounted Police as a scout, William Giveen, stopped at a roadhouse north of the North Peigan Reserve in Alberta. There he encountered an Indian whom he thought might be Deerfoot. When called upon to identify himself, the Indian produced a certificate for running naming him as Bad Dried Meat. Giveen immediately concluded this was indeed Deerfoot who, as a runner, was also known as Scabby Dried Meat. In fact, this man was a North Peigan Indian also called Runs Backwards and Forwards, and he too was a professional runner. Giveen arrested the Indian and attempted to take him into custody. Runs Backwards and Forwards, unsure of Giveen's identity and his status as a policeman, broke away, got hold of a rifle, and pointed it at Giveen. The scout responded with his revolver wounding his suspect in the thigh. After Runs Backwards and Forwards arrived at police hospital at Macleod, Giveen's error was discovered.[106]

This time the Blood and North Peigan Indians were upset about treatment meted out to a band member. Supt. Neale at Fort Macleod worried about reports that the Blackfoot, Bloods and Peigans were holding meetings to discuss the shooting. He advised that Bad Dried Meat be given immediate and generous compensation for injury suffered, advice with which the Department of Indian Affairs concurred.[107] On 2 February 1888, the chiefs of the Bloods and the Peigans met with the Mounted Police and Indian Affairs officials at Fort Macleod to discuss various grievances. The chiefs expressed grave concern about recent shootings of Indians by whites and particularly wanted compensation for Bad Dried Meat.[108] The suggestion was favourably received and compensation was arranged for the injured man. However, following an investigation Giveen was absolved of all blame,

the police judging that his suspicions were sufficiently reasonable to justify the arrest and that the shooting was strictly in self-defence.[109]

Meanwhile, Deerfoot (Scabby Dried Meat) had been reportedly residing in Montana, out of reach of the NWMP.[110] But by the spring of 1889, however, Deerfoot was back in hiding on the Blackfoot Reserve; tired of the fugitive life, at his behest, Crowfoot began to bargain with the government for the price of his surrender. An accommodation was arrived at and Deerfoot surrendered to the Blackfoot Indian Agent, Magnus Begg, on 6 April 1889.[111] He pleaded guilty as charged to larceny and assault and received the relatively light sentences of one month imprisonment at hard labour and 14 days hard labour respectively, sentences to be served in the Calgary guardroom.[112] This ended an episode which had created uneasy relations between the Mounted Police and the Indians. Deerfoot, however, continued to be a thorn in the side of the police for some years to come. The Mounted Police arrested Deerfoot after a chase and a fight in July 1891 for assaulting a settler named Allen in a robbery attempt. Deerfoot was released, however, when Allen decided not to press charges. Then in 1897 Deerfoot was convicted of assault and sentenced to two months in the Calgary guardroom. On admission to the jail, he was found to be ill and despite care by the police doctor he died before completing his term of imprisonment.[113]

The acculturation of the western Indian to the manners and mores of white North American society was the avowed objective of the Department of Indian Affairs. At the heart of this program action was taken to convert the Indians from the nomadic hunter-gatherer lifestyle to the rooted existence of the agriculturalist. For this aim some assistance was provided by the Mounted Police in enforcing the pass system. Encouraging Indians to forget so-called savage festivals and to allow their children to attend schools were other elements of the plan. The Mounted Police were expected to render assistance in these efforts too.

In 1884, the Department of Indian Affairs amended the *Indian Act* to forbid potlatch and Sun Dances among Indians in western Canada. This ban was imposed because Indian Affairs officials abhorred pagan ceremonies and because of the potential of an emotional celebration of the traditional rites to lead to a violent rejection of the new order. In particular the Sun Dance practised by several western bands was regarded as dangerous.[114] The Sun Dance was a highly ceremonial religious gathering lasting about eight days which included what the police regarded as inflammatory recitation of brave deeds of war and accounts of horse raids.[115] A highlight of the celebration was a self-torture ceremony performed by warriors who had made vows in return for special favours received from the sun deity. The self-torture took place inside the central Medicine Lodge and involved the insertion of two skewers in the flesh of the warrior's chest and one in his back. The skewers in the chest were attached to ropes suspended from the ceiling of the lodge and the skewer in the back to a shield. Once attached to these devices the young man would offer silent prayer, tear the shield and skin from his back and dance about the lodge suspending his weight on the skewers and ropes until the skin and flesh pulled away from his body. This frenzied ritual horrified and frightened most white men especially missionaries who were contributing to the acculturation of western Indians.[116]

Although the legislation which banned the Sun Dance had specified penalties for participants, some discretion had been left to police in serving warnings instead of laying charges. During this period, a number of Sun Dances were staged by the Bloods, Blackfoot and Peigans and the Mounted Police were unusually careful and circumspect about how they handled them.[117] For instance, in 1888 when the Bloods held their Sun Dance, the Police acted at the request of Red Crow to stop the sale of beer to the Indians. Supt. Neale sent out a party headed by Insp. Piercy to camp near the site of the Sun Dance to turn back beer vendors coming out from Macleod. As a result there was no drunkenness and the ceremonies were unmarred by any incident.[118]

There was, however, a problem at the 1889 dance when the Mounted Police appeared at a Blood Sun Dance to arrest some band members suspected of crimes. Sgt. Chris Hilliard and two constables were searching for Calf Robe, a Blood Indian who was accused of threatening a Mounted Police constable with a rifle. The police entered the sacred Medicine Lodge and, spotting Calf Robe among the assembled, placed him under arrest. When the party attempted to remove their prisoner they met the resistance of 200 incensed warriors, a fight broke out with Hilliard and his men trying to force their way through the crowd. Calf Robe was torn from the grasp of the police and they were compelled to leave empty-handed. When Supt. Sam Steele learned of this occurrence, he ordered Insp. Z. T. Wood to the Blood camp to arrange the surrender of Calf Robe and the leaders of the resistance through Chief Red Crow. The Blood Chief, a consistent voice of moderation, agreed and five Indians were taken into custody.[119]

Calf Robe stood charged with assault and the four other Bloods for obstructing police. All five accused appeared before two police officers acting as justices of the peace for preliminary hearings and grounds were found to commit them for trial.[120] The case was heard at the next sitting of the Supreme Court of the NWT by Judge J. F. Macleod, former

Commissioner of the NWMP. The Blood Indian agent, W. Pocklington, also a former member of the Force, was unhappy about the police handling of the case. Judge Macleod agreed with him that the Mounted Police had intruded on what was essentially a religious ceremony and that they got no more than they deserved when the Indians reacted violently. He also ruled that when police entered an Indian reserve to make an arrest they should carry a warrant. He dismissed all charges in connection with this case deciding that since no warrant had been issued no legal arrest had taken place.

The Mounted Police strongly disagreed with Judge Macleod's interpretation of the law. Supt. Steele noted that since the Indians learned from Macleod that a warrant was needed for their arrest they were becoming increasingly insolent.[121] Commissioner Herchmer commented that Macleod himself had arrested Indians without warrants on scores of occasions. Moreover, since this incident, the Indian Affairs Commissioner, Hayter Reed, was insisting that the Mounted Police swear out a warrant before arresting a Blood Indian, although he felt that such a procedure was not "required for the weaker bands of Indians".[122] Comptroller Fred White, in referring the question to the Department of Justice for clarification, pointed out that Macleod's dictum might, in fact, mark an important departure from the firm but paternal authority the NWMP had exercised over the Indians since their first days in the West. He wrote:

> The Indians have hitherto been advised to respect the authority of the police at all times, being assured that they would be fairly dealt with. If it is now decided that in future no arrest can be made without a warrant having been first issued, I fear the administration of justice, as far as the Indians are concerned, will be extremely hampered.[123]

On the whole, the opinion preferred by the Deputy-Minister of Justice, R. Sedgewick, favoured the position taken by the Mounted Police. Sedgewick dismissed entirely the suggestion that there was any privilege attached to the Sun Dance. The questions of whether to arrest someone in the ceremony was a matter of policy not of law. Moreover, the procedure for arresting anyone, including an Indian, with or without a warrant, was clearly laid down in the *Criminal Procedure Act*. A peace officer who reasonably suspects any person of being guilty of a felony may arrest him without warrant and then initiate an investigation.[124] Such an opinion did not necessarily vindicate Mounted Police actions in the Calf Robe case, but it left the Force with more options in similar situations in the future than Judge Macleod and the Indian Affairs Department wanted the police to have. However, a warning had been served on the Force that in a changing West, it might not exercise the same authority over the Indians as it had previously done.

By 1878, the Department of Indian Affairs decided to use residential schools in the West to immerse Indian children in white culture. The idea was simple enough: turn Indian youth, particularly boys, into model white men who would act as examples for the rest of their band. Religious missionaries, both Protestant and Catholic, had already opened up orphanages, boarding schools and day schools on reserves to Christianize the children and train them in the ways of the whites. The government decided to extend this effort in 1883 by building three Industrial schools, one in each of the Treaty areas. These schools would provide older boys not only with cultural education but training in practical skills which would facilitate their adaptation to the white economy. The industrial schools were turned over to the missionaries to manage. The system continued to grow from these modest beginnings.[125]

Children sent to residential school experienced a radical change of environment and lifestyles. Mike Mountain Horse, a Blood Indian, describes his initiations to St. Paul's residential school on the Blood Reserve in 1893:

> My father brought me to the school one cold winter morning. After the entry of my name in the school books by Harry Swainson, the boys' overseer, my brother Fred, then a pupil at the school, took me in charge. My Indian clothes, consisting of blanket, breech cloth, leggings, shirt and moccasins, were removed. Then my brother took me into another room where I was placed in a steaming brown fibre paper tub full of water. Yelling blue murder, I started to jump out, but my brother held on to me and I was well scrubbed and placed before a heater to dry. Next came Mr. Swainson with a pair of shears. I was again placed in a chair. Zip went one of my long braids to the floor: the same with the other side. A trim was given as a finish to my haircut. My brother again took me in charge. 'Don't cry any more', he said. 'You are going to get nice clothes'. Mr. Swainson then came into the room with a bundle of clothes for me: knee pants, blouse to match with wide lace collar, a wee cap with an emblem sewn in front, and shoes. Thus attired I strutted about like a young peacock before the other pupils.[126]

Many pupils did not take as naturally to such a wrenching change in their lives as Mike Mountain Horse claimed to have done. And many parents grew lonely for their children and sceptical of a system which exposed their youth to white diseases, including tuberculosis.[127] Indian Affairs officials soon turned to the Mounted Police for assistance in returning pupils who ran away from schools or had been removed by their parents.

Under the terms of a Territorial ordinance in 1886, Indian parents who admitted their children to industrial schools temporarily transferred their guardianship to officials of the Indian Affairs Department. By this regulation, runaways could be compelled to return to the schools and peace officers were given the authority to apprehend them.[128] Soon thereafter, the NWMP received requests from the principals of industrial schools to round up and to return recalcitrant pupils who had left on their own accord or been induced away from the classroom by their family or friends.[129]

The problem was common enough at the High River Industrial School near Calgary that the Mounted Police stationed a man at the school year-round, beginning in 1889.[130] In Battleford in 1890, a number of Indians from Poundmaker's band in town to spend their treaty money, induced three boys to quit the industrial school there and return to the reserve. The Mounted Police went after them and one so stubbornly refused to return to the school that the officer was required to arrest him on the charge of unlawfully absenting himself from Indian school. The case was tried by Mounted Police Justice of the Peace Supt. Antrobus, and the convicted boy was sentenced to return to his school.[131]

Since the arrival of the Mounted Police in the West, the Force had employed Métis as guides and interpreters. The most famous Native western assistant employed by the NWMP was Jerry Potts, who had guided the police unerringly in the latter stages of the trying March West in 1874. Potts had been a great help to the police in establishing rapport with the Indians not only because of his knowledge of Indian languages but because of the personal influence he had with the bands of the Blackfoot Confederacy to whom he was related. Potts still served the Force during this period although his health was poor.[132] Perhaps in reaction to the Rebellion the Prime Minister, John A. Macdonald was unhappy about the dependence which the police had developed on the services of these guides. He considered it "discreditable that it should be necessary to employ Interpreters in 1886 for a Force which was organized in 1873".[133] Macdonald wanted future promotions with the Force to be based in part on the ability to speak Blackfoot and Cree. The plan had merit but despite its apparent favourable reception by Comptroller White and Commissioner Herchmer it never was implemented.[134]

Rather than terminating dependence on Native personnel after the rebellion, the Mounted Police increased it by hiring full-blooded Indians for the first time in the history of the Force. The practice began as an experiment in 1887 at Macleod, four Indians being hired as special constables. Initial judgements about the work of these scouts were good. They were remarkable trackers and could cover great distances on horseback very quickly. A bonus was that scouts provided an important intelligence pipeline to the reserves. For instance, Calf

Shirt, a Blood Indian scout, kept the Mounted Police apprised of the mood on the reserve during the Sioux uprising in the United States.[135] The scouts even proved willing to arrest members of their own band. They were, however, restricted from exercising any authority over whites. The pay was good, $25 per month plus rations with the Force supplying arms and saddles and the Indians providing their own horses.[136] No uniform was supplied at first but the scouts began to sport old stable jackets and breeches which they picked up, which led to police condoning their wear by supplying these items.[137]

The Mounted Police did discover that the scouts needed special handling. Any hint of harshness would cause them to quit.[138] Also, most did not regard this police work as a career and would quit after earning a little money.[139] The Indians especially did not like to work in the winter because it was too hard on their horses.[140] The police also agonized about training and supplying these scouts with ammunition. Their concern was that some day the skill and weaponry would be turned against their employer and the white settlers.[141] The services of these men were appreciated on the whole and the practice of hiring them spread to all the other divisions, the Indian agents being consulted on appointments. But the turnover in personnel limited the effectiveness of the system.[142] Given these drawbacks, proposals did not succeed that an Indian police force be formed, auxiliary to the NWMP, similar to one which existed in the United States.[143]

The years immediately following the rebellion were relatively pacific for Indians in the NWT. Most stayed on their reserves trying to adjust to the unfamiliar demands of a life of agriculture. Little serious crime was committed by Indians and the Mounted Police were required mostly to see that increased contact between white settlers and Indians did not bring conflict or corruption. The most prevalent form of the latter was abuse of alcohol to which Indians seemed particularly prone. Only in southern Alberta was there a continuous pattern of serious crime. There, the several bands of the Blackfoot Confederacy particularly the Bloods, continued to chafe at the restrictions brought by their altered status in western Canada. Some young warriors refused to accept that they could not demonstrate their prowess by horse-stealing raids nor supplement their rations by killing a few of the multitude of cattle found on the prairies. The Mounted Police found dealing with these problems delicate and frustrating and learned primarily by trial and error.

Chapter 6

A Pragmatic Approach to Law Enforcement: The Police and the Western Indians, 1892-1900

It is only the presence of large numbers of police in the country which keep [*sic*] the Indians in order. It is absurd to lull ourselves into the belief that the Indians have become reconciled to the new order of things, or that their feelings towards the whites are any kindlier than they were 25 or more years ago. They remain submissive simply because they have sense enough to know that in the presence of a large armed force, any other attitude would be disastrous to them.[1]

Reacting to the news that Almighty Voice, a rebellious Cree Indian, had killed and wounded several whites in a dramatic shoot-out, the *Macleod Gazette* rather crudely over-simplified the role of the Mounted Police in the government's Indian policy. During the closing decade of the nineteenth century, the federal government, under both Conservative and then Liberal administrations, continued efforts to turn Indians into white men. The Western bands were trained by Indian Affairs officials in new skills to take advantage of the natural resources of their reserves. For the most part, the Indians learned farming and ranching but some also learned to exploit the potential of coal and timber resources on their lands. In hope of encouraging self-sufficiency, the Indian Affairs department gradually reduced the amount of rations being issued. At the same time, the government and the Christian churches prepared new generations of Indians for white civilization through education in schools.[2] There was, however, an element of danger in the policy. Naturally, some Indians resisted such a radical alteration of habits and mores, and resistance always carried the potential of violence. The Mounted Police were to ensure that any violence was contained.

As it turned out, the transition of the Indians from hunter to agriculturalist during this period was modestly successful and remarkably peaceful. To be sure, western Indians were neither accultur-ized nor assimilated by the turn of the century. However, the government was encouraged by signs of progress. Each year Indian agents reported advances towards self-sufficiency on the reserves. The Mounted Police confirmed the reports and were very pleased with the conduct of the Indians.[3] The traditional horse thieving and war parties became a thing of the past and serious crime was rare. It appeared that the Indians were responding to the benevolent paternalism of the government. However, problems remained which required a police solution. Sporadic acts of violence by individual Indians demonstrated that the warrior impulse was not dead. A continued predilection for alcohol abuse threatened to undermine the sense of purpose which the Indian department sought to instill in the native people. And despite the efforts at assimilation many bands stubbornly refused to abandon traditional rites and practices.

A generation of Indians experienced a transition from being masters of the prairies and their own destinies to become semi-dependent wards of a remote and unfamiliar government. Starvation and hardship brought on by the disappearance of the buffalo had forced the Indians to accept restrictions on their freedom which came with life on the reserves. In return for their cooperative behaviour the Indians received food without which they could not survive. But the government had no intention of creating a permanent dependency of the Indians on free issues of rations. The welfare system was in place only to support the bands while they learned new skills which would make them financially self-sufficient in white society. In the 1890s, the government reduced the amount of rations issued to levels considered by Indian Affairs officials as more appropriate to the growing prosperity of the Indians.[4] This decision did not sit well with some of the Indians, settlers and Mounted Policemen because an empty stomach could provoke crime.

In 1892, a number of complaints were made to the NWMP in the central and southern NWT that Indians were killing cattle belonging to ranchers and settlers. Some of the settlers, however, were not interested in pressing charges against the Indians for their offences, fearing reprisals from the band. Instead they wanted increased Mounted Police patrols to prevent the killings. One prominent rancher in southern Alberta, W. F. Cochrane, informed the Minister of the Interior that his cattle were being killed by Blood Indians because the Indian department had reduced their rations. Supt. Steele at Macleod believed that Cochrane was correct that the rations had been reduced and observed:

> I think it is a great pity, for there are so many cattle along the borders and none on the Reserve that the temptation to starving men to help themselves will be very great.[5]

The problem grew worse during the hard winter of 1893, principally in Alberta. Many reports were received by the police that Blackfoot and Blood Indians were off the reserves and living on range cattle. Severe weather had killed many of the steers and the Indians were slaughtering the carcasses, sometimes with the permission of the ranchers. But there was suspicion that some Indians were ensuring a plentiful supply of beef by having their dogs chase cattle over cut banks and into snowdrifts. And, of course, because the Indians had permission from some settlers to take dead cows, they always had an explanation for fresh beef in their possession if they encountered a police patrol. The police had to catch the culprits in the act of actually killing a steer or slaughtering a carcass without the permission of the owner in order to lay a charge. Again the reason for the trouble with the Indians was that the rations were too short on the reserve.[6] A. B. Macdonald, owner of the "44" ranch in southern Alberta, informed the Mounted Police that in January and February 1893, a number of Blackfoot had camped near him in very cold weather. He suspected that the Indians were after stray cattle and when he spoke to them, they complained that they were being starved on the reserve; Macdonald was sympathetic but wanted more police patrols to protect the ranchers' stock.[7]

Restlessness on account of the rations system affected other bands besides the Blood and the Blackfeet. On 8 February 1893, three Peigan men broke into the ration house on their reserve in southern Alberta and stole a quantity of beef. The acting Indian Agent, H. Nash, stopped the issue of rations until the guilty parties surrendered themselves. Three men were taken into custody. On the 4th of March the three convicted felons were sentenced by Judge J. F. Macleod to one year hard labour in prison. The following night, Agent Nash

was attacked by several Indians, presumed by police to be relatives of the prisoners, and received minor gunshot and stab wounds. His assailants were not caught.[8] On the Sarcee Reserve, Agent Sam Lucas made the Indians cut down trees to earn their rations, a task hated by the men. One Wolf Coat, whom the Indians claimed was required to work even though he was ill, was struck by a falling tree and killed. Much excitement followed with the Sarcees quitting work and threatening violence.[9] Near Battleford, the Indians at Red Pheasant's Reserve threatened to kill their own breeding stock of cattle because they had not been getting a regular meat ration. When local Mounted Police referred the matter to the Indian department, little sympathy was evinced. Hayter Reed, then Indian Commissioner for the NWT, explained that a contractor had indeed failed to supply meat for the reserve:

> But considering how we attend to their wants in this respect, I think they have little to complain of. Not only in such seasons but in a great part of the year one may travel through the country and find White settlers without a mouthful of meat and in other respects not nearly so well supplied as our Indians are. Rest assured that with all the cattle upon the Reserve our Indians will not starve. Had our own cattle been fat we would have killed them, but the Agent thought it better for the Indians to go without the meat ration than for poor animals to be killed.[10]

Conflict between the Natives and the Indian Department over rations worsened in 1894, and the Mounted Police generally sided with the Indians. Asst. Comm. McIllree visited the reserves in the Battleford area in the spring of 1894 and found very unsettled conditions due to starvation. The officer commanding in the area, Supt. J. Howe, told McIllree that neither flour nor bacon had been issued to the Indians for nearly two months.[11] He warned of trouble brewing. Closer investigation showed that on Red Pheasant's Reserve each Indian got 4 lbs. of flour and 11 lbs. of beef, about one week's rations, for the entire month of April. In May, members of this band and the Indians on the Stoney Reserve were each given 10 lbs. of flour and no beef at all. Moreover, seed grain and potatoes for planting were in short supply that spring resulting in insufficient crop yields in the fall. The Indians were unhappy and local white settlers were worried about an uprising.[12]

In the south, short rations again led to more cattle killing. The Blood Indians complained to the Mounted Police that some members of the band were forced to kill settlers' steers to compensate for the inadequate rations. Food was issued to the Bloods twice a week, three days' rations on the first occasion and four days' on the second. One Indian showed Sgt. Chris Hilliard what he had received to feed a family of seven for three days. The issue was calculated to be 5 lbs. of flour and 11 lbs. of beef.

However, the piece of beef was a shank of a hind quarter which was mostly bone with less than 4 lbs. of meat adhering to it.[13] Given these circumstances, the Indians felt no qualms about sneaking off the reserve on the night that rations were issued and killing a steer on the range. Fresh meat would not attract undue attention on the reserve so close to the time of the ration issue.[14]

The standard issue of rations at the Blood Reserve was 1 lb. of beef and ½ lb. of flour per day for every man, woman and child. Flour in fact represented a problem because the Bloods were not familiar with its use and would have been better served if pupils at the reserve school had been taught to make bread. Then the fact that rations were issued on a twice-weekly basis brought spoilage of the beef in hot weather because of lack of refrigeration. Single or recently married men were hardest hit by the scarcity of food because those with families might supplement the intake of the adults with some of the rations not consumed by small children. Unfortunately, it was these young men who were most likely to sneak off the reserve in search of a steer.

Complaints from the Indians received little attention from the Indian Department and so the Natives naturally turned to the Mounted Police for help. Frustrated by crimes which were seemingly incited by government administration, the Mounted Police supported the Indian complaints to the Indian Department. An Inspector, a Mr. Wadsworth, was sent to the Blood Reserve in July 1894 where he met with Supt. Steele and the Indian leaders and attended several rations issues. As a result, he increased slightly the amount of flour issued but in general showed little sympathy for the Indians. He concluded that Indians killed cattle "out of pure devilishness, and young Indians who wish to gain a reputation of being brave among their fellows".[15]

The results of this investigation confirmed the belief within the Indian Department that the complaints they had received were just groundless grumbling. Hayter Reed accused the Mounted Police of sympathizing too readily with the Indians and so interfering with his department's policy of encouraging them to be self-reliant. Fred White vehemently denied this charge saying that the insufficiency of rations was evident to the police who issued four lbs. of rations per day to each policeman compared to the 1½ lbs. given the Indian. He dismissed also the accusation that the police were too soft on the Indians pointing out that in August 1894 alone, 15 Bloods had been convicted of cattle killing. White wryly commented to his minister that the Indian Department was so suspicious of the Mounted Police representations on the part of the Indians that "at present it appears to be considered an offence for a policeman to speak to an Indian, or set foot on an Indian reserve".[16]

The fear voiced by the Mounted Police was that the Indians' dissatisfaction over their meager rations might lead to wide-spread crime and general disorder. This, however, did not come to pass. After 1894, the lot of most Indians in the NWT showed improvement. Contracts to supply hay to Mounted Police posts and larger ranches brought in money for bands throughout the Territories. So too, the raising of cattle, the mining of coal and the provision of freight services all began to pay dividends. The high level of cattle killing and theft which occurred in 1894 dropped off sharply thereafter, much to the relief of the police. Hayter Reed of the Indian Department attributed the successful curbing of cattle killing to the energetic action of his officials and the NWMP.[17] This is not to say that Indian hunger and discontent disappeared overnight but rather that in its diminished form there was not the degree of concern for police about the violence which it might spawn. There were, however, between 1895 and 1897 a series of acts of violence by individual Indian men which gave police plenty to handle.

Two violent episodes occurred among the Blackfeet over the issue of rations. The first incident occurred in April 1895 after the young son of Blackfoot Indian, Scrapping High, was returned home from the residential school on the reserve suffering from an advanced state of tuberculosis. The father was reported to have approached the rations issuer Frank Skynner for some beef for the child and was refused. When the child died, the distraught parent went to Skynner's home and shot him dead. Scrapping High then took up a position in the Indian burial ground and held off with gunfire a pursuing party of police for two days until he was finally killed by return fire from Cst. Magnus Rogers.[18] The incident caused unrest on the reserve, sparking demands by the Blackfeet for changes in the administration of the school and the rations system. Blood Indian chiefs, Red Crow and Day Chief, perhaps hoping to exploit the unrest for a general improvement, told the Mounted Police that the root cause of dissatisfaction on the reserve was poor and short rations.[19] The Minister of the Interior responsible for Indian Affairs, T. M. Daly, answered the Blackfoot protest in the House of Commons saying they had no grounds for complaint:

> There are greedy Indians who will grumble, but we must give them the bone with the flesh and no matter how much meat or flour you give them they would continue to grumble. You can never satisfy an Indian in that respect.[20]

The second episode also concerned a Blackfoot attack on a rations issuer. It appears that at this time Indian scouts in the employ of the Force were assigned to attend each rations issue on the

Blackfoot Reserve to protect Indian officials from any of their dissatisfied charges. The necessity of this was demonstrated in August 1896 when a Blackfoot, Man-Who-Carries-the-News, attacked the rations issuer, Thomas Lander. The Indian scouts arrested the man who was tried and convicted of assault and sentenced to six months in the Calgary guardroom.[21]

One of the most dramatic incidents in Mounted Police-Indian relations in this period involved the brief criminal career and the death of a Cree Indian, Almighty Voice. A young Indian man, raised in poverty, stole, was arrested, killed a policeman in a flight to freedom, was relentlessly pursued and fought to the death rather than be captured. The stuff is there for the story of a hero who made a last stand for a doomed Indian culture against the genocide of the white men. Numerous journalists, writers, poets and film makers have indeed seized the opportunity presented, adding romantic if false embellishments such as: the cow which Almighty Voice killed really belonged to his father, or in a variation, to the band; the young Indian in jail on a minor charge was goaded to escape by the threat of hanging made by a sadistic policeman; and, the unjust imprisonment of the innocent father of the unfortunate fugitive. But even after rejecting these myths one scholar has found in the Almighty Voice story a symbolism of the futile defiance of a proud culture being crushed by a repressive government:

> Almighty Voice, in his last moments, does become a symbol for his people, a symbol of a once proud race hurling defiances at the Government's attempts to recycle them into wards of the state. It is hard to endow Almighty Voice with nobility, but he did, at the end, epitomize the Indian protest against the inevitability of the new era, against the coercion of the police and the Indian Department against the systematic destruction of Indian culture. He embodied the Indian longing, before the old memories were snuffed, 'to rage against the dying of the light'.[22]

Such powerful imagery clouds rather than clarifies the facts concerning Almighty Voice, who bore individual moral responsibility for his actions rather than acting as a mystical representative of a dying culture.

Almighty Voice was born and raised in difficult times. In 1876 when he was only two years old, his band of Crees led by his grandfather, One Arrow, signed Treaty No. Six and retreated to a reserve measuring sixteen square miles about four miles northeast of Batoche. The disappearance of the buffalo forced the Indians to seek survival in an altered way of life with many of its terms dictated by white men. The adjustment was difficult and when Louis Riel led a rebellion against the dictates of a remote government, One Arrow and part of his band followed the Métis leader. For this crime, One Arrow was sentenced to three years in prison but was released after seven months when he fell ill. He died two weeks later. Meanwhile, in the aftermath of the rebellion, One Arrow's band suffered. A Mounted Police Officer, Insp. A. Ross Cuthbert, investigated reports of destitution on the reserve and found people starving and almost naked. He wrote to his superior, Supt. A. B. Perry: "I was prepared for a sight of poverty but I must state that the condition of these miserable wretches was even worse than I had been led to believe".[23] Cuthbert distributed a little tea, tobacco and sugar, and more substantial assistance followed after his report was forwarded to the Indian department. The situation on the reserve improved thereafter until, by the early 1890s, the over 100 band members on the reserve can be said to have been adequately fed, clad and housed.[24] These Indians shared the same hardships as most in the NWT, and there is no indication that Almighty Voice suffered any more pain and alienation than any other western Indian youth.

There are indications, however, that Almighty Voice was a headstrong, selfish adolescent who caused trouble in his own band. There are reports that Almighty Voice was a wild young man, feared by many of the other Indians. He was reputed to have taken and abandoned three teenage wives in succession, deserting the last a few weeks before she gave birth to their son. At a Sun Dance in 1895, he had a violent quarrel with an Indian from the Battleford Agency who accused him of molesting his wife. The Indian agent, R. S. McKenzie, regarded Almighty Voice as dangerous and had his own life threatened by the young man. Almighty Voice also demonstrated his independence by choosing to make his living as a hunter rather than as a farmer like his father and most of the Indians on the reserve.[25]

Finally, in October 1895, Almighty Voice's independent nature brought him into an ultimately fatal conflict with the law. Things went awry on the 19th of October, when Almighty Voice's father, John Sounding Sky was arrested, charged with stealing a pea jacket from a settler. He was tried and convicted the same day and sentenced to six months hard labour in the NWMP guardroom at Prince Albert.[26] Then, on October 22nd, Sgt. C. C. Colebrook and a constable of the Batoche detachment proceeded to the One Arrow Reserve at the request of the Indian Agent, R. S. McKenzie, who was there making treaty payments. Acting for the agent, Colebrook arrested Almighty Voice for killing a cow which did not belong to him, a second man as his accomplice and a third woman for an unrelated theft. Colebrook then returned to Batoche and sent his prisoners over to Duck Lake to be held at the NWMP detachment there for trial by Mr. McKenzie, the Indian agent, on the following day.[27]

What transpired that night of October 22nd was the result of the combination of the slackness of the

NWMP custody and the restlessness of Almighty Voice. Sgt. H. Keenan was the NCO in charge of the detachment and he issued orders for the guarding of the three Indians. Although the prisoners had been delivered to the detachment secured in irons, Sgt. Keenan ordered them removed. The detachment had no cells so the NCO instructed the five men to take two-hour shifts through the night watching the prisoners. Both guard and prisoners were locked in the office with the guard in possession of the key. Beds were set up for the prisoners. When it was time for a shift change or if a prisoner wished to go outside to relieve himself, the guard was to signal for a constable sleeping in an upstairs room by rapping on the ceiling with a broom handle.

No doubt Almighty Voice lay in his makeshift bed aware that there was opportunity for escape in this arrangement. He had reason to fear what awaited him in the morning. His grandfather had died probably as a result of, but at least immediately after, his seven months in jail. His own father had just been sentenced to six months for a lesser crime than that of which he was accused. The man who would judge him the next day was the Indian Agent McKenzie whom he had once threatened to kill. Even before his arrest, Almighty Voice had tried to stave off this fate by offering to make restitution to the man from whom he had stolen the cow with the gift of one of his own horses.[28] Now it must have seemed that the only way remaining to avoid jail was to escape.

Cst. Robert Casmir Dickson provided Almighty Voice with the opportunity. On guard duty from midnight to two a.m. Dickson told a later inquiry that all was well until the end of the shift. Instead of signalling with the broomstick, Dickson, leaving the key to the door on the desk, proceeded upstairs and notified the next man that he was on duty. When the constable descended to assume his post, the detachment door was open and Almighty Voice, alone of the three prisoners, was gone. Dickson's story was not believed by the OC of "F" Division who investigated the incident. He considered it more likely that Dickson fell asleep and Almighty Voice slipped out giving himself enough head start to evade pursuit.[29]

After leaving the detachment, Almighty Voice struck out on foot for the One Arrow Reserve and was forced to swim across the freezing South Saskatchewan River. Sgt. Colin Colebrook at Batoche learned of his presence there and on the 23rd of October swept the reserve with a patrol but did not find his man. He did, however, speak to relatives of Almighty Voice's newly spurned third wife, who promised Colebrook that they would tell when they learned something. On Friday, October 25th, Colebrook was informed that Almighty Voice

had left the reserve. He set off after him, accompanied by Francois Dumont, a Métis guide. Dumont picked up Almighty Voice's trail heading northeast towards Fort la Corne and the nearby James Smith Indian Reserve.[30] Almighty Voice had with him his latest love, Small Face, a 13-year-old Cree girl from that reserve. By Monday evening, Dumont was able to tell Colebrook that they were getting close and that from the signs of the camps left by Almighty Voice that they would catch him the next day. Colebrook warned Dumont that when they encountered the fugitive, he was to draw his revolver but not fire and to tell him to stop.

The showdown the next day must have begun much as Colebrook had anticipated. The pursuers spotted Almighty Voice from a distance at about 10 a.m. The Indian was on his feet, having just shot a prairie chicken, and tied it to his one horse on which Small Face was mounted. Colebrook instructed Dumont to tell Almighty Voice in Cree not to run, and set the pace to close the gap, then about 150 yards, at a regular trot. Almighty Voice replied "I want to shoot the Sergeant",[31] and began to ready his muzzle-loading shotgun. Small Face began to cry and asked her lover not to shoot. Colebrook approached Almighty Voice carefully, still on horseback, repeating, "Come on boy" in a persuasive manner. Almighty Voice retreated before the advance, loading his gun. When the gun was armed, Almighty Voice continued to retreat but several times knelt, aimed at Colebrook and warned him to go away. Finally, the Indian was backed into the edge of small wooded bluff with Colebrook still coming, now only 25 feet away, his right hand held up in the air and his left hand in his pocket on a small calibre revolver.[32] Almighty Voice fired a single shot knocking the sergeant off his horse and killing him as the bullet splintered his collar bone and severed the carotid artery.

The scene of the crime was vacated quickly by all save Colebrook and his horse. Small Face's view of the incident had been obstructed by the bushes of the bluff and after the shot was fired she rode over to see what had happened. She found Colebrook lying on the ground and Almighty Voice already fleeing the scene on foot. Almighty Voice turned and waved Small Face to join him and they continued together, he running and she riding. When Almighty Voice got tired he too climbed on the horse and rode. Suddenly he stopped the horse and left Small Face to continue her journey on foot, explaining that now the police would not leave him alone; he then rode off.[33]

Meanwhile, Francois Dumont was escaping in the other direction to fetch help. He did not even stop to check to see if Colebrook was dead for fear that the Indian would shoot him too. As he rode away, he played with the unfamiliar service revolver which Colebrook had loaned to him. Suddenly the gun went off startling both Dumont and Small Face who was still within earshot. Dumont went to the home of the nearest settler and told his story. The closest policeman was Cst. Tennant stationed on prairie fire duty about six miles away at Flett Springs and one of the settlers went to fetch him. By the time he arrived at the murder scene it was late in the day. Tennant notified Prince Albert and arranged for the body to be brought back; then he and Dumont went after Almighty Voice but without success. Two more patrols followed but they also failed.

Thus ended another phase in the Almighty Voice affair. Initial pursuit failed and the fugitive had disappeared to the north where he was believed to be sheltered by other Cree bands. There were some details to clear up. Small Face was picked up by a police patrol and, testifying at the inquest, she and Dumont were able to give a detailed account of the tragic encounter. Dickson and Keenan were punished for their negligence; the former was sentenced to two months in the guardroom and dismissal from the Force, and the latter was demoted from sergeant to constable. Colebrook's funeral was at Duck Lake on November 3rd and he was buried in the cemetery with the volunteers and police who had fought and died at the Duck Lake fight in the North-West Rebellion. He was accompanied to his resting place by a contingent of Mounties consisting of twelve in a firing party and six pallbearers. Cst. Dickson was one of a gang of prisoners who dug his grave. Colebrook's widow was allowed to continue as cook for the Batoche detachment until a government pension was arranged for herself and her four-year-old son.[34]

There was speculation among Mounted Policemen about Colebrook's method of approach when he encountered Almighty Voice. Some felt that he counted too heavily on his air of authority to convince the Indian to surrender. Having caught him on foot, Colebrook should have bore down on him and disarmed him before he could finish loading his shotgun. But Commissioner Herchmer had probably a better insight into the sergeant's conduct. He says that the muddled state of the legal authorities dealing with the right of a policeman to shoot a prisoner "always will cause our men to risk their lives in making arrests even in the case of notorious criminals rather than run the risk of being tried for manslaughter".[35]

Almighty Voice proved to be a very elusive fugitive. The police surmised, partly on information given by Small Face, that Almighty Voice would continue north in his flight, contact the Indians on the reserve near Fort la Corne and then pass on to live with the Indians hunting in the area of Nut Lake. This later turned out to be true and the nomadic hunting practices of the band of Crees proved suitable for Almighty Voice's purpose. He was always on the move in rugged, sparsely populated country where no policeman could venture without alerting the Indians of his coming. The Mounted Police persisted in their efforts, stationing a detachment near Nut Lake and sending patrols into the area but Almighty Voice got the better of the game.[36]

The police also decided to watch One Arrow's Reserve closely on the assumption that their man would inevitably return to visit his family. Frequently, the reserve was swept and houses searched but each time nothing turned up. The Indians on the reserve refused to cooperate with the police. Indian officials contended that the Indians would not give information because they were afraid of Almighty Voice. However, the police believed and feared that the young man was becoming a hero to his people.[37] Sympathy among his band members was compounded when the rumour circulated that the Indian agent, Mr. McKenzie, had no real grounds for originally charging Almighty Voice with killing the cow.[38] This story was refuted by McKenzie who cited witnesses and an indirect admission of guilt by Almighty Voice.[39] As it turned out, members of the band were sheltering Almighty Voice on his occasional visits to the reserve. There was a tunnel under his parents' house where the fugitive hid when the police were searching.[40] Even the government's offer of a reward of $500 did not break the conspiracy of silence among the Crees.[41]

But justice finally caught up to Almighty Voice late in May 1897. On May 26th, Indians from the One Arrow band, including Almighty Voice's father John Sounding Sky, were off the reserve to the east digging seneca root to sell to traders. Two Métis brothers, David and Napoleon Venne, spotted three Indians, presumably from this group, running after some of the Venne cattle. Giving chase they caught one of the three after his pony tripped and threw him. The Indian turned out to be Going-up-to-the-Sky, a 13-year-old cousin of Almighty Voice from the Nut Lake band. The young man named one of his companions as Tupean or Dublin but refused to identify the other. Drawing a possible conclusion, Napoleon Venne rode to Batoche and reported to Cpl. W. J. Bowdridge that Almighty Voice might be in the area. The next day Bowdridge and Venne, now appointed a police scout, rode to the Indian camp to investigate. There they learned the disquieting news that on the previous night Going-up-to-the-Sky had traded his horse for a rifle. As they stood discoursing, Bowdridge noticed two Indians running into a bluff just outside the camp. He sent Venne around to the right of the bluff and he took the left, and they would see what was going on. Venne quickly discovered the price of curiosity receiving a bullet in the shoulder. Bowdridge packed Venne off to receive medical attention and sent word of events to Duck Lake. Skirmish two went to Almighty Voice.[42]

The Mounted Police wasted no time responding to Almighty Voice's challenge. Insp. J. O. Wilson came north with a small party from Duck Lake. The other One Arrow Indians had retreated to the confines of their reserve. The whereabouts of Almighty Voice was unknown until reinforcements coming up from Prince Albert blundered into him on the morning of May 28th, about three miles east of the One Arrow Reserve. Insp. Jack Allan, two guides and a dozen men were riding to the scene of the Venne shooting when some miles shy of their objective they saw three figures which could have been Indians flit into a bluff near their path. Thinking this might possibly be Almighty Voice, Allan led his patrol over to investigate. The Police surrounded the bluff and Insp. Allan started across on horseback while Sgt. C. C. Raven came in from the opposite side on foot. Raven ran into the Indians first and, in the exchange of gunfire, was shot through the thigh. Allan then met the fleeing Indians and in an attempt to ride them down was shot off his horse, his right arm shattered. He was then on the ground at Almighty Voice's mercy, which is just what he received. Almighty Voice did not attempt to finish the job but instead motioned for Allan to surrender his ammunition which the Inspector refused to do. Just then, the wounded Raven and Cst. Hume arrived and their fire caused Almighty Voice to disappear back into the bush. *Hors de combat*, Insp. Allan and his senior NCO, Sgt. Raven, were forced to go back south for medical attention.[43]

After Allan departed the scene, Cpl. Charles Hockin assumed command of the police patrol. The 36-year-old Hockin was new to police work, having only engaged in the Force in October 1894, but he was accustomed to the burden of command. The son of a British Admiral, Hockin had spent 12 years in the British Army as a commissioned officer. Reinforcements had been sent for but as the day wore on, only a few civilian volunteers had turned up to augment his small force. Hockin was concerned that if he did not take action before nightfall, the Indians would slip away in the dark. Therefore, in the early evening, Hockin led a seven-man party of police and civilians in an attack upon the bluff. They found the Indians dug into a pit and holding fire until proper targets were presented. In this the attackers obliged them, and Cpl. Hockin, Cst. John R. Kerr and Mr. Ernest Gundy, the Postmaster from Duck Lake, all fell with mortal wounds. As some life still remained in Hockin, he was dragged to safety by Cst. Hume. Ironically, Supt. Sévère Gagnon soon arrived with more reinforcements,

but too late to overrule or amend the plan of attack. Despite medical attention, Hockin died at 1:30 a.m. on the 29th of May. Supt. Gagnon commented in a letter to Admiral Hockin that: "His last moments were those of a true British soldier and his last words were 'tell my mother I die like a soldier'".[44] Even if apocryphal, this account of Hockin's demise was in the best tradition of British imperial service.

So far Almighty Voice had successfully defied police but forces now gathered which would inevitably destroy him since he refused to surrender. At midnight on the 28th of May Insp. Wilson brought in his small patrol to augment the siege force around the bluff. Supt. Gagnon wired to Regina requesting more men and a 9 pounder gun. The message arrived at Regina, dramatically being delivered to Commissioner Herchmer late in the evening of Friday, May 28th at a police ball. The full dress concert and dance was being held in honour of the NWMP contingent under Supt. Perry which was to leave the next day to take in the mammoth celebration in London of the Diamond Jubilee of Queen Victoria's reign. The waltz was halted and the announcement made of the events unfolding to the north. The ball was quickly terminated and rumours flew through town that Almighty Voice would inspire a general uprising of western Indians. Commissioner Herchmer worked through the night organizing a troop to render assistance.[45] Assistant Commissioner McIllree, 25 men and horses and the requested artillery piece were put on a train specially hired from the CPR which pulled out of Regina by 10:30 a.m. on the 29th of May.

As the train from Regina headed north, preparations were also being made by those already on the scene for the final confrontation. Supt. Gagnon returned to Prince Albert on May 29th and picked up an old brass 7 pounder cannon with which he hoped to flush the Indians from their cover. On his arrival, Gagnon was handed a message from Commissioner Herchmer instructing him to swear in civilian volunteers as special constables to serve for the duration of the crisis. With the help of James MacKay, Q.C., a prominent local Conservative leader, 30 volunteers were quickly sworn and sent forward. When Gagnon himself returned to the scene of action that evening he found that during the day Insp. Wilson had tried to smoke the Indians out by setting fire to the bluff but the brush had failed to ignite. Gagnon then ordered his men to train the 7 pounder on the bluff at the spot where the Indians were dug in and open fire. After the first shell exploded, one of the Indians ran forward to the edge of the wood to see what was happening and quickly returned to cover. The Indians responded with a few shots directed towards the gunners.

Asst. Comm. McIllree's train pulled into Duck Lake about 4:50 p.m. on May 29th and as soon as the horses were watered and fed, the reinforcements set out to cover 17 miles to join Gagnon.[46] About 10 p.m. McIllree arrived at the scene in advance of his party which straggled in over the next hour having been delayed by the small size of the ferry at the Batoche river crossing. Command was turned over to McIllree but for the besiegers little transpired that night except for the odd exchange of rifle fire. In fact, that night was the beginning of the end of the Indians. Cold, the men covered themselves in clothing removed from the bodies of Cst. Kerr and Mr. Gundy which still lay in the bluff. To slake their thirst the Indians stripped bark off trees to capture the moisture underneath. A shell fragment had smashed one of Almighty Voice's legs. He apparently bandaged his wound and then fashioned a rudimentary crutch. The Indians then probably tried to escape but could not get through the ring of police and volunteers; Almighty Voice abandoned his crutch near their line off the bluff and returned to his pit. At some point during the night, if not before, Almighty Voice's brother-in-law, Tupean, was killed when hit by a stray bullet from the besiegers.[47]

At dawn, police and volunteers alike, now numbering about 100 in all, were anxious to decide the issue. Early in the morning the force opened up on the bluff with both of its guns. Joseph Walton, a volunteer who operated the 7 pounder was a veteran of both the NWMP and the Royal Canadian Artillery. He charged the shells with powder and inserted a nine second time fuse. This allowed Walton to elevate the barrel of his cannon and to lob the shells into the bush in the expectation of dropping them in or around the pit where the Indians hid. The bombardment continued intermittently for several hours with no response from the bluff. By noon the civilians were impatient for action but McIllree was opposed to risking lives in an attack on the Indians' position when cannon and a short siege could achieve the same end. But the civilians insisted and, to avoid a split which would see the volunteers charging alone, McIllree ordered a general attack. As it turned out there was no danger. The still warm but quite dead bodies of Going-up-to-the-Sky and Almighty Voice lay in their pit, both the victims of the cannon fire. Tupean was found further down the bluff, cold and rigid with a bullet through his forehead.[48]

It is difficult to read much significance into the Almighty Voice affair. Despite some concern by the police and the white populace, the defiance of this young man was no prelude to a general uprising nor even a sign of the repressed rebelliousness of the other Indians. Even the Indians of the One Arrow and Nut Lake bands told officials that they were not upset about the violent deaths of the band members.[49] The real victims in this story were the four white men killed, the three whites wounded and the two young Indian companions dead because they so foolishly emulated Almighty Voice's example.[50] Despite the absence of a wider significance, this story deserves to be fully treated in this history because of the loss of so many lives and because of the unique nature of the final showdown. No particular credit can be accorded the Mounted Police for its handling of this case. Lax security had allowed Almighty Voice to escape and his crimes to escalate from cattle killing to multiple murder. Nevertheless, the police were forced to doggedly pursue the fugitive, concerned not only that a criminal be brought to justice but that the authority of the police not be weakened in the eyes of the Indians.

Coincidentally, in 1896, while Almighty Voice mocked the efforts of police to capture him in the north, another Indian in the south became a rather spectacular fugitive. Charcoal, or Si'k-okskitsis, a 40-year-old Blood Indian came to the notice of police through the killing of his wife's lover. Then, after abortive attempts to take the lives of two Indian officials and his own chief, Red Crow, Charcoal fled his reserve and eluded capture by the Mounted Police, members of his band and volunteer settlers, for a month. Unwillingly accompanied by members of his family, Charcoal desperately resisted capture, to the point of shooting and killing Sgt. W. B. Wilde. When Charcoal was finally captured it was by two of his own brothers who were coerced to act by Supt. Sam Steele.

Until recently, most writers have characterized Charcoal's actions as those of an unfortunate victim who killed out of passion and then ignorant that the circumstances might temper justice, irretrievably threw away his own life in his violent flight from authority. Mike Mountain Horse, a Blood Indian and former NWMP scout added a Native cultural dimension to Charcoal, arguing that he had been forced by a sense of honour to kill his wife's lover and describing his flight as an assertion of an earlier freedom enjoyed by his band.[51] However, Hugh Dempsey in his biography of Charcoal, has created an original psycho-historical portrait of his subject. He too relates Charcoal's behaviour to culture but in a very specific way. Basing his case mostly on tribal oral tradition and on conjecture, Dempsey asserts that Charcoal acted in conformity with his perception of the code of his Native religion. Before white law put an end to tribal warfare, if a Blood warrior knew he was soon to die of some illness, he would rather seek death in a suicidal assault on an enemy band. If he succeeded in slaying enemy men in the attack, they would precede him into the spirit world and alert the denizens there that a great warrior was coming. In Dempsey's view, Charcoal was a very religious man and thinking that his life would be forfeited ingloriously at the end of a rope, he sought a warrior's death. Lacking enemies in other bands Charcoal chose his own chief, Indian Affairs Department officials and policemen as acceptable substitutes, important enough to raise the expectations of the spirits when they learned Charcoal had performed the executions.[52] Dempsey's approach is novel and interesting but not convincing. It is difficult to reconcile Charcoal's sneak approaches to Red Crow and McNeil and his cruel second mortal shot into the body of the wounded Wilde, with the image of a brave warrior winning a place in the hereafter through great feats in war. Certainly, other members of his band could not have been impressed by the religious motivation of Charcoal, whose battle plan included the murder of their revered chief. In fact, they demonstrated this with wholehearted cooperation to effect his capture.

Charcoal was a member of his brother Left Hand's sub-tribe within the Blood tribe.[53] He and his relatives had a reputation among their fellow band members as being quarrelsome and lazy. Charcoal had been convicted of cattle killing in April 1883 and spent a year in jail as a result.[54] Despite his brush with the law, Supt. Sam Steele admired Charcoal's ability as a warrior which he believed was recognized within the Blood tribe.[55] By 1890, Charcoal had been married three times: one wife had died, another had left him while he was in jail and the third had returned to her parents disgusted at the troublesome traits displayed by Charcoal's family. In 1891, Charcoal married 26-year-old Pretty Wolverine Woman, a widow who had already been married four times. Although in the beginning this liaison may have been satisfactory, in the end it proved Charcoal's undoing.[56]

Perhaps alienated by Charcoal's taking a comely 18-year-old girl, Sleeping Woman, as a second wife, Pretty Wolverine Woman, by the summer of 1896, had become the lover of Medicine Pipe Stem. This young man was regarded as a Lothario on the reserve with a reputation for his adulterous affairs. When Charcoal found out about the affair, he was particularly embarrassed because the relationship was incestuous, the two being cousins. Although he had confronted the lovers and demanded an end to the infidelity, he was ignored. The two became so bold that on 30 September 1896, while at a temporary hay cutting camp off the reserve, they brazenly defied Charcoal to his face and went together into a nearby cattle shed. Charcoal had had enough. He made his way to the shed, rifle in hand, and discovering his wife and her lover in the act of inter-

course, shot the latter dead through his open left eye. He then led his wife away.

It was almost two weeks before Medicine Pipe Stem's body was discovered and the police became aware that they had a murder on their hands. Medicine Pipe Stem's relatives were worried about his disappearance and had been looking for him, but without success. On October 11th, some women from the reserve gathering wood near the shed spotted what appeared to be a corpse inside but they were afraid to enter. Learning of this, Medicine Pipe Stem's relatives investigated the next day. The Indian Agent and police were quickly informed that Medicine Pipe Stem had been found. Initially, there was some confusion about the cause of death because the point of entry of the bullet was hidden by the man's closed eyelid, and the bullet had fragmented in the skull without exiting. The coroner and the police surgeon sent to the scene of the crime suspected violence because of blood on the body but did not confirm the fatal gunshot until an autopsy was performed on 14 October.

Meanwhile Charcoal, learning on the night of the 12th of October that the evidence of his crime had been uncovered, proceeded to compound his misdeed. He rode to the home of Red Crow, head chief of the band and Medicine Pipe Stem's brother-in-law, with the intention of killing him. There he was frightened away by dogs but not before Red Crow and his wife observed his approach and sensed danger. Charcoal next went to visit Indian Agent, James Wilson, and found nobody home. About 8 p.m. the frustrated Charcoal spotted a light at the home of the reserve's farm instructor, Edward McNeil, and availed himself of this target of opportunity. He crept up to the window of the room where McNeil was doing some paperwork and fired through the window, hitting and wounding the white man in the back.

Events were breaking fast for the police, first a murder then a wounding on the Blood Reserve. Learning of Medicine Pipe Stem's affair, the police suspected Charcoal of the first crime and on the 14th of October came word linking him with the wounding as well. Little Pine, a brother of Pretty Wolverine Woman, brought the news that Charcoal had visited him the previous night and told him that he was responsible for both shootings and that he also had intended to kill Red Crow and Wilson. Meanwhile Charcoal had escaped the reserve, forcing six members of his family to go with him – his two wives, a mother-in-law, his teenage daughter and two step-children.

Sam Steele reacted quickly to the discovery of Charcoal's departure. On October 15th after a coroner's jury recommended that Charcoal be charged with murder, a warrant was sworn out for his arrest. Steele surmised correctly that Charcoal would head south for the forested area near the Rocky Mountains where it was easier to hide. Insp. A. M. Jarvis, in charge of the detachment at Big Bend, had already arranged for parties of Indians and Mounted Police to patrol to the south and the west. Steele also ordered Insp. H. J. A. Davidson at Lee's Creek detachment to track west in the direction of the mountains. On the night of October 16th, when Steele was at Big Bend planning with Jarvis the next day's patrols, a local settler named Henderson rode into the detachment to report the theft of his overcoat by an unknown Indian. Henderson had shed his coat to load timber on his wagon at a spot about 15 miles south-west of Big Bend when the incident occurred. It was an excellent clue since the description of the thief matched that of Charcoal. Jarvis and his men and Indian scouts, accompanied by Henderson who volunteered to help, started for the scene of the crime at once. Charcoal's camp was located in a valley crowded with trees and thick undergrowth. To make as little noise as possible the policemen removed their boots and hats and crept through the bush until they spotted Charcoal's teepee. Unfortunately, the approach of the patrol was heralded by a loud crack when somebody stepped on a dried branch. Charcoal was out of the teepee in a flash. Versions differ of what happened next. Insp. Jarvis and Henderson later reported that Charcoal fired on the police first and drew return fire. Indian scouts present testified at Charcoal's trial that they never saw the fugitive fire and that one of their number, Green Grass, shot first. When consulted later, Green Grass agreed with the scouts' story.[57] In any case, someone's bullet creased the skull of Insp. Jarvis and a fusillade from the patrol caused Charcoal's party to scatter. Charcoal and his two wives and a stepson disappeared into the woods. Rushing the camp the patrol grabbed his mother-in-law, daughter and another stepchild. The police took possession of Charcoal's teepee, his horses, and provisions enough for two months including meat from a steer which Charcoal had recently killed. But the man himself had got away, still armed and still accompanied by three hostages who had been unlucky enough to flee from police bullets in the same direction as Charcoal.

At first it seemed that Charcoal's escape would be only a brief reprieve for him. Insp. Jarvis strung out his men to surround the woods and by good fortune, Insp. Davidson arrived with his small party to help block the south end of the valley. Charcoal was expected to try to break out of the woods that night and Davidson and one of his men, Cst. Basil Nettleship, stabled their tired horses at a nearby unoccupied ranch and, on the evening of October 17th, posted themselves in the woods to await developments. About midnight the pair returned to the ranch to see if reinforcements which had been summoned had arrived. There they discovered to their shame that the horses and saddles had been stolen. Davidson surmised that Charcoal had been watching the movements of the policemen and after spotting where the horses were stabled, slipped past the watchers in the woods and continued on his way, his party mounted two to a horse. Steele was furious that his quarry had escaped, especially in a manner so acutely embarrassing to the Mounted Police.

Charcoal reappeared about 35 miles to the north in the vicinity of the Peigan Indian Reserve. On the 18th of October he entered the home of Mose Legrandeur who ran a stopping house for stagecoach travellers on the Macleod-Pincher Creek trail and stole some food. Legrandeur was not at home and his wife and children were in hiding, having spotted Charcoal's approach and guessed his intent. A few minutes later Cst. Michael Kerrigan reined in at the stopping house on his way to Macleod from Pincher Creek. Learning what had just transpired Kerrigan sent word to Insp. A. R. Cuthbert, conducted a brief search and then went on to Macleod where he notified Insp. G. E. Sanders of Charcoal's presence in the area. Mounted Policemen began to converge on the scene. First to arrive was Insp. Cuthbert who was followed shortly thereafter by two policemen from Pincher Creek and two more from the Peigan Reserve detachment. The two played-out police horses abandoned by Charcoal were quickly found but there was no sign of the elusive Indian. About 1 a.m. on the 19th, Insp. P. C. H. Primrose arrived with six more men having been sent down from Macleod by Insp. Sanders. Just after dawn the search resumed and Charcoal's saddles and some tracks were found. That afternoon Supt. Steele arrived from Big Bend bringing 16 policemen and 16 Indians from the Blood Reserve. Patrols were sent out night and day and everyone in the vicinity warned to secure their horses and property.

Charcoal, meanwhile, continued a step ahead of his pursuers. On the night of October 18th he stole two Indian ponies he found grazing on the prairie and proceeded northwest and went into hiding at the edge of the Porcupine Hills. Then on the night of October 19th he and his stepson set out again, this time headed for the Peigan Reserve in search of food and more horses. His wives were left at the camp securely tied up to prevent their escape. Charcoal tried twice to steal horses but had no luck, being forced in one attempt to shoot at the owner, a Peigan Indian called Commodore, who had been awakened by his horse. In the confusion of this confrontation, Charcoal's stepson ran off and could not be found. But Charcoal had a brother on the reserve, Running Crow, (called Long Mane by police) and his visit to his home was more successful. Running Crow had been expecting Charcoal and had prepared clothing and food for him to bring back to camp.

The next morning the police learned of the incident at Commodore's house. Then came news that Charcoal's stepson had been taken to the Indian agent by a Peigan Indian who had sheltered him overnight. The boy agreed to show the police his stepfather's last camping spot. A party was sent out to investigate but the camp had been abandoned. A group of white volunteers from Pincher Creek under ex-North-West Mounted Policeman, John Herron, joined the hunt for two days, and served on other occasions during this long chase when requested by police. Patrols continued but Charcoal had slipped away again. Steele ordered the arrest of Running Crow and other members of his family whom he suspected of helping the fugitive so that assistance would cease. Steele returned to headquarters at Macleod on October 21st, leaving Insp. Sanders in charge on the reserve to continue searching with his 3 officers, 24 NCOs and men, and some Indians hired as scouts at the rate of 50 cents per day. On October 24th, Steele ordered Sanders and his men further south where sightings and thefts indicated that Charcoal was now returning to the area nearer the Blood Reserve.

Charcoal led the various police and Indian patrols a merry chase for another week before there was any break in the case. He killed a cow, stole provisions from a white rancher and a racehorse from an Indian on the Blood Reserve. His trailers were tantalized from time to time with the discovery of his tracks but they always petered out as fresh snow fell or as Charcoal found well-trampled ground. Charcoal had been receiving valuable help from his relatives on the Blood Reserve but, on one of his visits he lost his hostages. On October 30th, Charcoal tied up his two wives at his camp site and headed once more for the Blood Reserve. This time he was a little careless with his knots and the women were able to struggle free and, once safely back on the reserve, were placed in protective custody in the Macleod guardroom.

Frustrated by the inability of dozens of policemen, Indian scouts and white volunteers to track down one lone Indian, Steele decided to take drastic action. By the end of October, Steele had Charcoal's 2 brothers, Bear Back Bone and Left Hand, arrested, along with 23 members of their families, including wives and children, for giving assistance to a fugitive. Steele let them sit in the guardroom for a few days and then, with the assistance of Indian agent Wilson, proposed a deal. Steele would release Bear Back Bone, Left Hand and their families if the brothers would agree to cooperate with police in the capture of Charcoal by informing them of Charcoal's movements and detaining him if possible. Included in the deal was freedom for Bear Back Bone's son Crane Chief, then awaiting trial for cattle theft. Fooled by Steele's bluff that the entire family could receive prison sentences for aiding a fugitive, the brothers agreed to help. They returned to their houses on the reserve and awaited an inevitable visit from Charcoal.

Charcoal continued to leave behind a trail of violence and larceny. On the night of November 1st, Cpl. William Armer at the Cardston police detachment was headed for the stables, lantern in hand when without warning he was hit by a shot fired from behind a nearby water trough. Evidently gauging his aim in the dark by the position of the light held by the policeman, Charcoal directed his bullet between Armer's body and arm, wounding him only slightly in the side. After the attack Cpl. Armer found a makeshift rawhide bit in front of the stable door and concluded that Charcoal was after a horse. That same night, a Mrs. Lamb, alone in her house at Lee's Creek heard someone break into her storeroom and later determined that Charcoal had made off with some foodstuffs. Charcoal also replaced his worn-out horse with a pony stolen from near the Blood Reserve and headed north, back to the vicinity of the Peigan Reserve.

On 10 November 1896, the police finally caught up with Charcoal. Cst. James Hatfield in charge of the detachment on the Peigan Reserve found Charcoal's camp and, accompanied by several Indian scouts, was on his trail. Hatfield notified Sgt. W. B. Wilde at nearby Pincher Creek of the direction of Charcoal's movement. Wilde joined the chase along with Interpreter Charles Holloway and Indian scouts. Wilde warned his party that if they found Charcoal not to take foolish risks. They were to tell him to stop and if he ignored this, Wilde said to shoot him. Wilde's group headed south from Pincher Creek, travelling about 20 miles through harsh cold and hindered by the 6 inches of snow on the ground. Charcoal was sighted at a place called Dry Forks; Wilde and his men gave hot pursuit, followed by some scouts from Hatfield's patrol which had just arrived on the scene. Charcoal had two racehorses with him stolen from the Peigan Reserve and, though they had been ridden a long way, the one upon which Charcoal was mounted still had strength. Most of the pursuing horses were played out. Holloway and a Peigan named The Sword, after warning the fleeing man to stop, both tried to shoot him without success, their guns either misfiring or the aim off the mark.

It was now up to Sgt. Wilde to take on Charcoal. Formerly of the British Army, Wilde was a 14-year veteran of the NWMP with a good reputation. He was mounted on a big strong horse and he gained on Charcoal. As Wilde passed Blood Indian scout

Tail Feathers, he grabbed this man's revolver, a handier weapon at close range on horseback than the Lee Metford rifle which lay across the sergeant's saddle. Wilde then did a strange thing. Just like Colebrook the year before, he ignored his own warning to his men not to take chances closing in on Charcoal. Wilde rode right up to within a few feet of the Indian, apparently with the intention of seizing hold of him. Like Almighty Voice, Charcoal refused to be taken. He turned in his saddle drawing a carbine from his belt and shot the policeman in the side. Riding on a short distance, Charcoal turned his head in time to see Wilde fall from his horse. Charcoal then rode back, dismounted beside the then dying sergeant, who raised his head only to receive a second bullet in the abdomen. Charcoal then mounted Wilde's horse and continued his escape.

The other horses in the police parties were not capable of further pursuit. However police scout, Tail Feathers, after getting off a chance shot, had the presence of mind to take the horse that Charcoal had abandoned which had superior stamina. Tail Feathers continued to trail Charcoal until the evening of November 11th, being joined that morning by several civilian volunteers from Pincher Creek, led by John Herron. According to Herron, Tail Feathers "showed great coolness, ability as a tracker, and also, especially in searching the brush in the dusk, and until dark, considerable courage".[58] As a result the party found Charcoal late in the day on the 11th in the mountains near the north fork of the Kootenay River. Shots were fired at Charcoal but did not find the mark and he was able to slip away as night fell.

Harried now, not only by Tail Feather's party but by several patrols of Mounted Police and Blood Indians sent out after Wilde's murder, Charcoal left the mountains and rode about 70 miles to the Blood Reserve. There early in the morning of November 12th he called upon his brothers Left Hand and Bear's Back Bone. Charcoal was invited into the house but either because he was suspicious or hearing a strange noise he retreated towards his horse. His brothers followed, tackled him and wrestled away his rifle and his knife. He was then bundled into the house and the police sent for. At some point shortly after his capture, evidently due to the inattention of his guards, Charcoal was able to put to desperate use an awl, a pointed tool he carried to mend his moccasins. He opened up blood vessels in both arms but the ensuing profuse bleeding was stopped by his captors' application of tourniquets to the arms and flour to the wounds.

Charcoal was weak from loss of blood and so was not conveyed directly to the guardroom at Macleod. Instead he rested for a time at the Roman Catholic mission and then moved to the detachment at Stand Off where he was attended to on the 12th of November by a NWMP hospital steward. A police doctor, C. S. Haultain, examined him the next day and declared him fit to travel. At Macleod, Charcoal's confinement was especially secure; he was chained to the floor and watched by a guard 24 hours a day. His food was cut for him and he was allowed no utensils. When permitted out of his cell to visit the privy the prisoner had hands shackled, feet encumbered with a ball and chain and was escorted by two guards. At first Charcoal refused to take food and the police, concerned about his weakened condition, resorted to force-feeding. He soon agreed to eat.

Charcoal was tried in January for the murder of Medicine Pipe Stem and Sgt. Wilde. He pleaded guilty to the first offence and not guilty to the second. Charcoal contended that he acted in self-defence against Wilde who fired at him first and whom he did not recognize as a policeman. The evidence clearly showed such a defence was preposterous. Unbelievable also, were Charcoal's statements that he had not fired at McNeil, that his family had gone with him willingly, and that he had not robbed the Legrandeur home. He was convicted of the murders and sentenced to die by hanging on 16 March 1897.

There is confusion about Charcoal's state of mind at the end of his life and about the disposition of his remains. Police and newspaper reports at the time said that Rev. Father Emil Legal, the Roman Catholic missionary on the Blood Reserve, converted Charcoal to Christianity in the few weeks before his death. Then the *Macleod Gazette* reported on the 19th of March that Charcoal spent his last evening smoking, eating and singing hymns in the company of Fr. Legal. Citing no historical evidence, Hugh Dempsey, rejects these observations by white men who did not know Charcoal's true state of mind. Dempsey contends that Charcoal was far too deeply committed to his Native religion for any facile conversion. In any case, Charcoal went quietly to his death on 16 March 1897, except for briefly beginning an Indian song as he left the guardroom until silenced by Fr. Legal. Afterwards Fr. Legal took the body to the Roman Catholic cemetery, showed it to a group of about 20 Indians, who wanted to be sure it was Charcoal, and conducted a quiet burial about 5 p.m. that evening. Dr. Dempsey claims Charcoal was buried in spite of the opposition of his family, in direct violation of Charcoal's wish. He treats this as a vile irony for the deceased whose entire will had been bent to arrive gloriously as a spirit in the Indian afterlife and now was trapped forever with lesser spirits underground. Again Dempsey cites no direct historical evidence for his contention which appears to be based on an oral tradition among some members of the Blood tribe concerning Charcoal's religious zeal.

For the police the most significant aspect of the Charcoal affair was the strong assistance given to the Force by the Peigan and Blood tribes. Many Indians assisted the police in the search although not more than 30 were under arms at any one time. The police paid out about $200 to Indian scouts at the per diem rate of 50 cents each. Moreover, rewards were given out. Most substantial perhaps was the granting of a suspended sentence to Crane Chief and his two accomplices on their cattle stealing charge. Left Hand and Bear Back Bone were given $75 each by the government and four other Indians who helped in the capture of Charcoal received $10 a piece. Tail Feathers was also given $75 as a reward for his persistent pursuit of Charcoal which helped drive him out of the mountains back to the reserve. A sum of $35 was given to Blood Agent Robert Wilson to buy provisions for Indians who had served as volunteers without pay in the chase. The police were very gratified for the support given them by the Blood and Peigans, contrasting their attitude to that displayed by the Crees in the Almighty Voice case.[59] Herchmer felt that if the Bloods had helped Charcoal instead of the Force, the police would have been powerless.[60]

A more pedestrian concern of the Mounted Police was preventing the use of alcohol by Indians. This became more difficult after 1892 when the ending of prohibition made alcohol more freely available. The statistics suggest that as the Force declined in size over the period and was assigned a host of new duties, Mounted Policemen concerned themselves less with charging Indians with illegal use of alcohol. Probably this responsibility fell more and more to the Indian agents. The police did, however, continue conscientiously to arrest and prosecute those who supplied alcohol to the Indians. The control which the police exerted over this illegal liquor trade apparently had a deterrent effect as well. As A. J. McNeill, the agent at the Sarcee Reserve explained it in 1898:

> These Indians are passionately fond of strong drink, and will, when an opportunity occurs, indulge freely. They are looked after very closely and their great dread of the North-West Mounted Police guard-room has more to do with their sobriety than anything else.[61]

As in white society, the inordinate consumption of alcohol by Indians sometimes led to the perpetration of more serious offences. Drinking sprees led on occasion to incidents of assault[62] and even murder. In 1896, a quarrel over liquor on the Lac Ste. Anne Reserve north of Edmonton resulted in two of the band members killing a third. The pair was convicted of manslaughter and sentenced to ten years in prison. The case had been difficult for the police to investigate because the family of the murdered man had been promised compensation in money and gifts by the wrongdoers, as was the Indian custom.[63] Then in 1900 near Calgary, two intoxicated Saulteaux Indians fired at two passing Mounted Policemen. After apprehension, one of the culprits confessed that he was seeking revenge for his son who was himself serving a sentence in the NWMP guardroom for drunkenness. Insp. J. O. Wilson toyed with the notion of charging the Indians with attempted murder but settled for their certain conviction for drunkenness.[64]

One of the most prolonged fugitive cases of this period also began with a drunken quarrel resulting in murder. The police surmised that on 15 September 1894, Tom Lamac, an Indian on the File Hills Reserve near Fort Qu'Appelle, bought $2 worth of liquor in town. Returning to the reserve he took up with another band member, Josieh Matorna. At one point during the day people passing a bluff about two miles from the agency heard the pair singing in an intoxicated manner. At the end of the day some of the reserve heard two shots but put it down to hunters. The next day Matorna was found mortally wounded but not yet dead. Before he expired, Matorna accused Lamac of shooting him. The motive for the crime was unusual. Lamac bore his companion a grudge, blaming him for the death of his favourite sister. Matorna was a Native doctor who had treated the girl and Lamac suspected that the medicine administered had been gopher poison.

Although the identity of the murderer was known, police suspected from the first that his apprehension would be difficult. Lamac was intelligent, spoke several languages and had a thorough knowledge of the country.[65] As in many cases of well-publicized manhunts, conflicting reports of Lamac's whereabouts came in from many sources and were conscientiously and futilely investigated. Finally in 1896, Lamac was located in Montana and the police sought the advice of the Department of Justice on the advisability of seeking his extradition from the U.S. The opinion of the Deputy-Minister was that such an action would not succeed because the case against the accused rested principally upon a dying declaration taken in a too informal fashion. On this advice the police let the matter drop and then closed the file in 1897 when the Indian killed with Almighty Voice using the name "Tupean" was tentatively identified as Tom Lamac.

The case was resurrected in 1901 when information was received that Lamac was alive and still in Montana. Again the Department of Justice was asked to reconsider the question of extradition and this time the police received a more favourable response.[66] Lamac was arrested and returned to Canada to face trial. It came out in court that he had confessed to the shooting to his sister.[67] Lamac was found guilty and Judge Hugh Richardson sentenced him to death by hanging on 27 June 1902. The sentence was afterwards commuted to life imprisonment.[68]

Less serious disorder occurred on the Indian reserves on account of the holding of Sun Dances and give-away dances, forbidden by the *Indian Act*. The Indian department tried to eradicate the ceremonies because they interfered with the "civilizing" process and because the Indians tended to neglect their day-to-day duties to participate in the festivities. Basically, it was the responsibility of the Indian agent to enforce the ban and individual officials took various means to achieve this end; at some reserves the agents restrained their objections to Sun Dances on the conditions that there was no interference with work and that there were no self-torture ceremonies performed. At least one agent attempted to persuade the Indians to replace these Native religious demonstrations with a more strictly social event like a horse race. However, when all efforts failed the agents called in the Mounted Police to lay down the law.

Requests for assistance of this kind put the police in a real dilemma. Simply put, there was no way a Mounted Police patrol could prevent hundreds of Indians who were absolutely determined to perform their dance from having their way. Insp. W. B. Scarth prudently observed this dictum in 1894 when he patrolled to Piapot's Reserve north of Regina. There, on the border of the neighbouring Muscowpetung's Reserve, Piapot's band had erected a Sun Dance camp comprised of 150 teepees housing over 1,000 Indians. On this occasion Scarth chose to observe the activities rather than attempt to interfere. The dance lasted several days with seven or eight young men proving themselves and the Indians then quietly dispersed, returning to their reserves.[69]

On other occasions the Mounted Police were more successful at banning the dances when they acted forcefully. In 1897, the Indian agent responsible for treaty Indians in the Battleford area requested Mounted Police assistance to punish Indians who had held a give-away dance on Thunderchild's Reserve. The agent had been trying to stop these dances himself for several years but without success. He was particularly concerned because the Indians had allowed the rites to interfere with their work to such an extent that their cattle were left to starve. The Mounted Police arrested four of the participants, including Chief Thunderchild, and charged them with taking part in a dance forbidden by the *Indian Act*. Supt. Cotton and Insp. Bégin heard the case and convicted all four. Two were released on suspended sentences but Thunderchild and Wapath were given the minimum sentence allowed under the law, two months without hard labour. Having demonstrated the intention of police to enforce the law, Supt. Cotton interceded for the prisoners as they were old men and had them released by the clemency of the Governor General. About a week later, Bégin had three more prominent Crees arrested and convicted of participation in a give-away dance. Again two were released on suspended sentence and one served three weeks of a two-month sentence.[70] When released from the guardroom the Cree leaders promised not to allow give-away dances again.[71]

The Indians of Treaty No. Seven bands in Alberta proved most difficult to dissuade from performing the Sun Dance. The Blackfoot and Peigan tribes persisted in holding their annual Sun Dance ceremonies most years with only the occasional success by the police in preventing gatherings.[72] Referring specifically to the Blackfeet in 1896, Supt. J. Howe advised that attempts to stop their sun dances would be "ill-judged". He based his opinion on the sentiments expressed by the Indians at a meeting with A. E. Forget, the Indian Commissioner, at the agency in June of that year. Howe was impressed by the Blackfoot "determination to adhere to this ancient custom in spite of all opposition".[73] What made these dances more easily acceptable was the agreement by the Indians to give up the "self-torture" ceremonies. But what was grudgingly acquiesced to by officials on the Blackfoot and Peigan Reserves met a more forceful reaction at the Blood Agency.

Blood Indian agent James Wilson was an avowed foe of Indian dances which he believed promoted immorality, indolence and savage practises. In 1895, he managed to prevent the Bloods holding a Sun Dance by the simple but effective device of denying them the whole cattle tongues required as a vital part of the ceremony. Temporarily stymied by the tactic, most of the Indians were persuaded to give up the dances and accept in return an annual sports day featuring horse races and a steer from the Indian department to consume at a feast. Then in 1898, Wilson served warning on the Bloods that he disapproved of all pagan ritual gatherings by arresting three band members for putting on a medicine pipe dance. This was a ceremony occasionally performed by members of a secret religious society within the band. Wilson did not proceed with judicial action beyond the initial charges, but his action presaged a confrontation with the Indians and the Mounted Police later the same year.

On 8 June 1898, Calf Shirt, the former police scout, led a delegation of Blood Indians to Macleod to visit Supt. R. B. Deane, now Officer Commanding in the district. Calf Shirt had complaints about Wilson's treatment of the band including his opposition to all dances. Deane explained to the Indians that all dances were not forbidden by law but only those involving giving away property or held on Sundays. Then on June 29th, Deane was visited by Red Crow at the head of a group of Bloods of both sexes.

Red Crow spent a hot afternoon airing his complaint to Deane that Wilson had threatened to arrest the chief if he proceeded to arrange a dance for the Medicine Pipe Society. It seemed that Red Crow was the head of the society and was obliged to hold a sacred gathering to initiate a new member. This initiation was special because it involved the purchase of one of the group's 15 revered pipes, by the new member, the wife of Heavy Shield, who was fulfilling a vow made when seeking recovery from a serious illness. Deane was caught in a dilemma. He understood that the agent was annoyed at the intention of the Indians to spend 11 days dancing just when they should have been cutting hay. But as he interpreted the *Indian Act*, the ceremony which the chief proposed was not illegal. Therefore, he told Red Crow that he would ask Wilson to allow the dance, and slyly extracted a promise that the Bloods would forego agitation for a Sun Dance that year. Deane's support was all the encouragement Red Crow needed and despite the continued opposition of the agent, the Indians put on their dance. And encouraged by this success they could not again be deterred by Indian officials. The Bloods held another religious festival in 1899 and resumed the Sun Dance in 1900, continuing it on an annual basis.[74]

Evidently Wilson blamed Deane's interference for the eventual breakdown of the interdiction he had attempted to place on Indian dances. Early in 1901, the Deputy Minister of Indian Affairs, James Smart, brought Wilson's complaint to the attention of Comptroller Fred White. Smart said that internal management of the Indian reserves was entirely the affair of the agents and the Mounted Police were not to interfere.[75] In reply, White argued the propriety of Deane's actions in this instance but, more importantly, stressed the need for cooperation between policeman and Indian agent.[76]

During this period the Mounted Police did cooperate successfully with the principals of the three industrial schools in the North-West at Fort Qu'Appelle, High River and Battleford, as well the school at Elkhorn, Manitoba. Police patrols visited these residential institutions for Indians and received requests for aid in returning runaways who had gone back to their families. Such a duty was fraught with danger because Indian families were very close and parents were not always convinced of the value of the education being received by their children. But the Mounted Police were sensitive to the situation and usually managed to arrange the return of the students with little difficulty.[77]

In 1894, Parliament approved a new set of regulations governing the education of Indian children.

Authority was given to the Department of Indian Affairs to compel any child whose education was being neglected by his parents, to reside at an industrial or boarding school.[78] Responsibility for the enforcement of this regulation was extended to the Mounted Police along with the authority to obtain warrants to search for and effect the removal of such children. Mounted Police officials were not happy about the new rules because they would undoubtedly antagonize the Indians. Commissioner Herchmer felt that indiscrete application of the regulations could lead to a serious breach of peace and security in the NWT.[79]

Almost immediately after the regulations were passed, events proved that they were ill-advised. In December 1894, Standing Buffalo, chief of a band of Sioux on a reserve about four miles from Fort Qu'Appelle, visited the nearby industrial school where his son Dominic resided. He found the boy suffering from consumption and insisted on bringing him home to cure him by traditional Indian medical treatment. The principal of the school, Reverend Father Hugonnard, called upon the constable at the local detachment to return the boy, citing the new regulations as authority. The constable had never heard of any new regulations but visited the reserve anyway. His interview with Standing Buffalo was terminated by retreat in face of the upset father's threats on his person. Insp. Constantine investigated and reported that, in any case, the boy was too ill to move. Commissioner Herchmer sent word to the Indian Department that he refused to act in this case unless ordered to by the Prime Minister. The department agreed that Dominic could stay with his father but instructed that the regulations were to be followed, albeit with discretion, in other cases.

Soon, however, it was evident that the regulations had gone too far. The Indians of Star Blanket's Reserve in the File Hills told their agent that they would defy the regulations. Their children would not go to school or be taken from them. The agent reported that a strong body of police would be needed for any confrontation.[80] On the Blackfoot Reserve, the Indians were restless and unhappy with the white schools in the wake of the Scrapping High incident which was triggered by the death of a child returned home from the boarding school with tuberculosis. The principal of the school, the Reverend J. Tims, was subsequently shot at by an unknown party and, for his own safety, was transferred from the reserve. By mid 1895, Hayter Reed, Deputy Superintendent-General of Indian Affairs, instructed his officials not to enforce the regulations governing compulsory education, and even to relax enforcement of longer-standing rules against capricious removal of children from the schools by their parents.[81] The next year when Clifford Sifton became Superintendent-General of Indian Affairs and James Smart his Deputy, compulsory attendance became a dead issue. Neither man had confidence in the industrial school system and did not want to waste money on Indian children who did not want to learn.[82] This change in policy removed a very dangerous responsibility from the shoulders of the Mounted Police.

To control the movements of Indians and reduce possible friction with white settlers, the Indian department and the Mounted Police continued to insist in this period that Indians carry a pass from their agent while off their reserve. Supt. A. B. Perry fretted in 1892 that an incident was bound to occur because the pass system had no basis in law and that when the Indians learned their rights they would refuse to obey.[83] In 1893, Commissioner Herchmer issued a circular memorandum to his Officers Commanding warning them that they had no power to compel Indians without passes to return to their reserves. He suggested that using an authoritative manner of persuasion the policemen would induce the Indians to return to their reserves.[84]

For most of this period this system seemed to work, probably because the Indians caused few problems and because, in most cases, the police were judicious in their recourse to this form of control. Indians apparently abroad on legitimate purpose such as shopping in town would not be bothered. But Indian women in Lethbridge for purposes of prostitution or men wandering aimlessly across the prairie near Macleod were advised to return to their reserves and usually complied without question.[85] Occasionally it was necessary to be very strict about the pass system as in Calgary in 1892 when there was an outbreak of smallpox. Agents on the reserves nearby warned their charges to stay at home.[86] Special patrols of Mounted Police enforced the interdiction and when "a couple" of Indians managed to reach town anyway, they were arrested as vagrants and given "a few hours of hard labour in the barracks" to warn others not to follow their example.[87] But this system, a pragmatic preventative policing measure clearly depended on keeping the Indians ignorant of their right to freedom of movement. This being explicitly recognized by Insp. J. O. Wilson at Calgary in 1899 when he had a half-breed named Johnson Lone-Man arrested, tried for vagrancy and run out of town after a couple of days in the guardroom. The real reason Lone-Man had been nabbed was that he had been discovered telling Indians that the NWMP had no right to order them back to the reserves.[88]

To assist in patrolling reserves the Mounted Police continued to hire Indians as scouts and interpreters. Employed as special constables these Indians were sworn-in members of the Force with powers of arrest. As the number of regular members of the Force diminished during the period due to reduction and reorganization, more scouts were hired. In 1896, Herchmer reported he had 50 scouts on strength.[89] In addition, when the Charcoal emergency arose many Bloods and Peigans were employed as scouts on a daily basis to assist with the chase. Herchmer occasionally suggested that a separate Indian police, modelled on the U.S. example would be useful for the reserves but the idea was not taken up.[90] It is worthy of note that the Force's earliest and most illustrious scout, guide and interpreter, Jerry Potts, died of consumption during this period on 13 July 1896.[91]

The Mounted Police also helped in the resolution by the U.S. and Canada of the question of refugee Indians in each other's country. In Canada were the remnants of Sitting Bull's Sioux who had crossed the border in 1876-1877. These Indians were not numerous but being non-treaty were poor and caused minor annoyances by killing off wild game and allowing their ponies to trample settlers' crops.[92] In the U.S. were several hundred refugee Crees who had fled from Canada as rebels after the uprising in 1885. An exchange was arranged between the two governments and the Mounted Police provided escorts. The Crees were brought to the Canadian border in groups in the summer of 1896, each escorted by troops of the U.S. Army. Each group was met in turn by one NCO and one constable of the NWMP. Such a contrast enhanced the reputation of the Force for its quiet authority over the Indians.[93] The exchange was only partially successful. Probably only a minority of the Sioux returned to the U.S. in 1894 and even some of these filtered back across the border to Canada.[94] So in 1900, the 125 non-treaty Sioux still in southern Saskatchewan were incorporated into the Assiniboine Indian agency.[95] Also, some of the Crees found it difficult to adjust to the return to Canada and crossed back over to the U.S.[96]

The police had remarkably little trouble with the Indians during this period. Despite the continual hardship of trying to adjust their lives to a foreign culture, the Indians evidently were determined to make the effort. Episodes like pursuits of Almighty Voice and Charcoal were in dramatic contrast to the behaviour of most western Indians. Ironically, a major concern of the Mounted Police was that the impatience of the Indian Department to make their charges self-sufficient would provoke a major incident by hungry Indians. This did not happen, at least partly because the Mounted Police maintained

good relations with the Indians and were pragmatic
in approaching problems as they arose.

Chapter 7

Mountie Justice on the Canadian Frontier, 1886-1891

Two contrasting myths have emerged concerning law enforcement in the frontier Wests of the United States and Canada. In the American West violence was the hallmark of pioneer society. Pistol-toting gunfighters were supposed to have both plagued and titillated early communities. Slow in developing regular police forces, these communities were imagined to have met violence with violence by hiring gunslingers as peace officers or by forming bands of vigilantes to impose lynch law. In Canada, the exact opposite myth evolved. In the popular mind, the redcoated Mounted Policemen ruled the West with paternal firmness which precluded violence. Woe to the malefactor who broke the law in western Canada, because the NWMP 'always got their man'. Scholarly research has considerably modified these myths while admittedly making little impact on the image held by the majority of the public. Somewhat surprisingly, however, the essential thrust of the myths has been sustained by research.

The frontier period of American western history was not thickly populated with deadly gunslingers daily duelling in dusty streets. Robert Dykstra, an American historian, has written a fascinating study of five Kansas towns, Abilene, Dodge, Ellsworth, Wichita and Caldwell, which became markets and shipping points for the Texas cattle trade in the post-civil war period. In these famous frontier communities, Dykstra discovered all the roots of the wild west myth. Cowboys descended on the towns after long cattle drives with a thirst for drink, women and excitement, to the profit of saloons, brothels and gamblers. The sudden growth of these towns was not accompanied by a parallel development in municipal institutions particularly law enforcement. As a result, in the early days order was sometimes imposed injudiciously through vigilante lynch gangs and criminals hired as peace officers. But Dykstra found incidents of this kind were far fewer than is popularly believed. The towns were indeed visited by infamous outlaws such as

Clay Allison, Doc Holliday, Ben Thompson and John Wesley Hardin. But of these men, only Hardin killed anybody, firing through a hotel wall to silence a man snoring in the next room. While Wild Bill Hickok was city marshal at Abilene he killed only two men, one a policeman by mistake. In all, there were 45 homicides in these towns during their development period in the 1870s. Of these, 39 did indeed involve lawmen, cowboys, drovers or gamblers. But only in one-third of the cases did the incidents involve an exchange of fire of the stereotypical gunfight. Dykstra's work sustains the picture of cattle towns as catering to the baser appetites of western cowboys. However, despite the weakness of early law enforcement, the violence spawned by lusty excesses was far less than portrayed by novelists and film-makers.[1]

Most historians of the American West agree with Dykstra that the government and the people failed to develop adequate law enforcement agencies to police the frontier. The principal failure was in not organizing a central authority with the resources and jurisdiction to ensure efficient pursuit of criminals. The United States Army was available to quell major disorders such as conflicts between Indians and whites or labour disputes, but rarely stepped in to combat crime.[2] Federal marshals and their deputies were concerned mostly with civil cases and conducted criminal investigations only when federal laws were violated as in a mail robbery. Some states tried to develop their own police agencies but only Texas succeeded in organizing a force which endured and was effective. The brunt of law enforcement fell upon local marshals usually appointed by town councils or sheriffs elected to police districts. The quality of such men was uneven and the resources and jurisdiction provided them was limited.

Into the gaps left between these different levels of law enforcement fell several kinds of unofficial or semi-official agencies. When no peace officers were available, frontier communities sometimes formed vigilance committees to punish malefactors. The justice meted out by vigilantes was often harsh with scant regard for anything resembling due process. Private police forces were also formed by railroads and stage lines, or for hire, like the Pinkertons. It was Union Pacific's ranger force of elite riders and trackers which, equipped with a special train, broke up several bandit gangs in the 1890s, including Butch Cassidy's. Ranchers formed stock associations, hiring detectives to protect their herds from rustlers. These men sometimes were commissioned by the state as stock Inspectors giving them powers of arrest. Most of these detectives performed useful and legal services, but some abused their authority, performing as little better than assassins, hence the legend of the bounty hunter.[3] The most notorious abuse by ranchers of employing killers with powers of arrest took place in Johnson County, Wyoming, in 1892. There, 22 gunmen were sent out to kill 70 suspected rustlers on the pretext of resisting arrest. They managed to kill 2 men on the list before 250 enraged homesteaders besieged the gang in a ranch house. Only the intervention of the U.S. Sixth cavalry staved off a blood-bath.[4]

The failure to achieve, or even to seek, a central and effective law enforcement agency for the frontier West can be attributed to the American character with its admiration of rugged individualism and antagonism towards central authority. Frederick Jackson Turner fingered the frontier experience itself as forging a society made up of self-reliant egalitarians who broke with customs and traditions to develop their own institutions of order.[5] Others consider that the American revolutionary experience embedded in the national psyche an abiding mistrust of regulation by a central authority.[6] In the absence of strong law enforcement agencies, more acts of violence were required to impose order on the American frontier. Almost immediately these acts were exaggerated and glorified to a form of folk heroism which became the myth of the wild west. It has been cogently argued that this experience has conditioned Americans of subsequent generations to find violence a readily acceptable means to an end.[7]

The experience of the Canadian West was markedly different from that of the American. When the Canadian government assumed control of the vast NWT from the Hudson's Bay Company in 1870, Prime Minister Macdonald was determined that its settlement by whites would not result in the violence which accompanied that process in the U.S. He created the North-West Mounted Police in 1873 to impose order in advance of the railroad and the flow of immigration to a West then dominated by American whisky traders.[8] While the American disdain for central authority sprang from the revolutionary tradition, Macdonald's decision to impose

control on the Canadian West derived from the paternalism of British Toryism. The Canadian West would not be a freely evolving frontier but was to be a Crown colony whose principal affairs were directed by the federal government in Ottawa. The presence of a paramilitary police force in the area ensured that the desired development would be peaceful and orderly.[9]

From the beginning and for several decades, the NWMP controlled the West. The Force garrisoned the region through headquarters posts and outposts linked by horse and rider. As railroads and settlement grew, the police turned their attention from Indian affairs to the prevention and punishment of white lawlessness. In the frontier days the Force members were the principal peace officers in the NWT, although other law enforcement agencies slowly developed to support, and finally by 1917, to replace the Mounted Police. Towns became incorporated and established police forces. After 1905, the Provinces of Saskatchewan and Alberta commissioned provincial police officers. The railroads, too, organized police forces to protect their property and the safety of passengers and freight.

Moreover, the Force's mandate to maintain order was not limited to these police powers. Commissioned Mounted Police officers were appointed justices of the peace and in the frontier period were responsible for much of the judicial work, handling preliminary hearings for indictable offences and the entire case for summary offences.[10] A majority of the lawbreakers convicted of lesser offences in the territorial period served their terms in Mounted Police guardrooms, while serious criminals were despatched to the federal penitentiary at Stony Mountain, Manitoba, usually with Mounted Police escorts.

This chapter deals with the manner in which the Mounted Police handled more serious offences in the period 1886 to 1891. Excluded from purview are apparently victimless violations of laws meant to control moral conduct such as liquor consumption, prostitution and gambling. Police responsibility for enforcement of these laws was, in fact, a major preoccupation during this period and has been treated in a separate chapter. Also crimes committed by Indians have been dealt with in the chapter devoted to the Force's relations with these people. What will be considered are those crimes which appeared to the police and contemporary society to have been significant violations of peace and order committed by the white populace of the West. In this way the validity of the legend of the success of the red-coats in combatting crime can be examined.[11]

The precise origin of the shibboleth that "the Mounties always get their man" is unknown. A variation of the phrase appeared in the *Fort Benton Record* as early as 1877 when the newspaper concluded an account of the NWMP's arrest of three whisky smugglers with the remark "the M.P.'s are worse than bloodhounds when they scent the track of a smuggler, and they fetch their men every time".[12] This image appealed to the public and was transformed into an exaggerated false notion, which was widely believed, that the Mounted Police literally caught every criminal they went after. The legend is, however, an accurate reflection of the perseverance often shown by the NWMP in its work.

The Mounted Police had only infrequently to deal with crimes of serious violence in the frontier west. Perhaps this stemmed from the fact that few Canadians carried firearms or used them as ultimate arbiters of disputes which might arise. In an 1885 debate in the House of Commons concerning limiting the availability of firearms in the NWT for fear of a second rebellion, several members of Parliament were adamant in defence of the right of settlers to bear arms. The argument made was that Canadians had a constitutional right to weapons to defend themselves against wild beasts and hostile Indians.[13] There were, however, already several laws on the books which limited the right of Canadians to carry weapons in certain circumstances, such as in the vicinity of public works or at public meetings. Moreover, the police had broad authority to charge those carrying arms if the evidence suggested criminal intent.[14] On a few occasions, during this period, persons were convicted of such offences. For instance in 1891, in Moosomin, a vagrant, G. Garraity, was convicted of carrying a loaded revolver and received three months hard labour.[15] Supt. Sam Steele at Macleod believed that the lack of serious violent crime in the West was due to the close supervision of the Mounted Police which drove the "tough element" over the border where they would be less closely watched.[16]

There were, however, seven cases of apparent murder in the Territories during this period and only three of these were resolved convincingly by the police.[17] Inexplicably, a rash of murders occurred at the end of May and in early June 1887, in four locations in Assiniboia. Mounted Police patrols were despatched to investigate the homicides of Messrs. McLeish, McLean, Poole and Smith, at Wolseley, Whitewood, Sumner and Salt Plains respectively. In the case of the first two incidents, Métis horse thieves were suspected of having perpetrated both crimes. Extensive search parties were despatched to the scene, however, the suspected murderers, James Gaddy and Moise Racette, slipped away from the Mounted Police and entered the United States. Their trail was followed by Sgt. Macpherson and two constables into Dakota where, with the cooperation of U.S. authorities, the pair was arrested and extradited back to Canada. At a trial in Wolseley the following year both Gaddy and Racette were found guilty of the murder of McLeish and sentenced to be hanged. The penalty was carried out at Regina in June.[18] In the case of Smith, two Indians who were suspected of the murder were arrested but sufficient evidence could not be garnered to bring the case to trial and they were released.[19] In the murders of McLean and Poole the Mounted Police made no arrests.

Some individuals and organs of the territorial press were critical of the NWMP's lack of success in solving what was indeed a high level of homicide for the NWT.[20] The response of the Mounted Police was somewhat defensive:

> Considerable discredit was endeavoured to be attached to the police for the failure to arrest in these cases, but the enormous tract of country, the sparse settlement, the time that elapsed before the victims were found, and the facility with which the murderers could travel for several days without being seen by a human being, are sufficient reasons for our bad luck.[21]

Armed robberies in 1886 also challenged the Mounted Police. On July 17th, a lone unmasked bandit held up a party of five travellers near Humboldt. The men were caught asleep in their tent by the robber who fired warning shots to show his serious intent. Three of the victims were tied up, searched and relieved of their money. Evidently the robber was disappointed by the takings, especially by the small amount given up by a wealthy area resident, a Mr. Swanston. About 1 p.m. that day, the same man held up the regular stagecoach which carried mail and passengers between Prince Albert and Humboldt. Again the bandit tied up most of his prisoners, allowing only one free to tend the horses. He then cut open the mail sacks, stole the registered letters and left the scene. It was estimated that he got away with about $1,300 from the mail.

The first report of the robbery to reach Regina was an exaggerated account claiming six masked bandits were responsible. The Mounted Police immediately concluded that this was the first incursion into Canada of notorious outlaws from Missouri. Comm. Herchmer ordered Supt. A. B. Perry, then at Regina with his division, to deploy patrols east and west and then move his men northwards cutting off escape routes to the American border. Over 60 men were committed to the chase but they failed to turn up the culprit because of the false premise on which it was based, that the criminal(s) would be fleeing south to the United States. In fact the bandit was one George T. Garnett, a ferry operator at Hudson Bay Crossing on the South Saskatchewan River who was seen and recognized in Prince Albert the next month by the stage driver whom he had robbed. The Mounted Police promptly arrested him, his conviction was secured and he was sentenced to 14 years in prison. Garnett's guilt was confirmed for police when his cell mate at Regina, a man named Smith, repaired to

Garnett's ferry crossing on release from jail, suddenly displayed new found wealth and departed for the United States. Police concluded that Garnett had confided the whereabouts of his cache to the wrong man.[22]

The Prince Albert mail robbery, as it became known, was the first such occurrence in the NWT, but it was soon followed by another in what seemed to police to be a crime wave. On 5 August 1886, masked men held up two brothers named de Rainbouville who were camped on the bank of the Elbow River near Calgary and took from them $372. A newspaper reported that the brothers had recently arrived from France to take up ranching and were fooled by the bandits who passed themselves off as Mounted Policemen searching for illegal whisky. The Mounted Police were not informed of the crime until August 14th and initial investigation made Supt. W. D. Antrobus at Calgary suspicious of one William Mitchell. A week later the police arrested Mitchell along with T. Behan and J. Patton who were suspected as accomplices. No charges were brought against the latter two, and in September, Mitchell was tried and acquitted of the robbery.

Just after noon on the same day that the police arrested Mitchell, Behan and Patton, two men (both masked, one with a shred of cloth torn from a Union Jack) robbed the stagecoach travelling between Edmonton and Calgary. They ripped open the mail bags, evidently found nothing worth taking, and had to content themselves with the money from the pockets of the three passengers. Supt. Antrobus at Calgary learned of the theft at 5:30 p.m. and by 6:15 p.m. was on the trail with a party of 17 policemen. They tracked the robbers for about two miles until all trace of them disappeared on hard ground. This was long enough however, to discover two sets of overalls and the Union Jack mask which had been used in the robbery. One of the overall sets was identified by police as belonging to one J. Young, a whisky trader who had just been released from Calgary guardroom where he had served six months for a liquor offence. Two days later, word came of the murder of Scott Krenger at his shanty near Calgary. Police now believed that the de Rainbouville and the stagecoach robberies as well as the Krenger murder were the work of the same gang, of which Young was a member. Antrobus speculated that Krenger may have known of the gang's activities and was killed to ensure his silence. The police at Calgary carefully searched the district and warned other Mounted Police posts and American law enforcement officials by telegram to watch for the suspects, but nothing turned up.[23]

The *Calgary Herald* was alarmed at the outbreak of wanton violence in the area. After the de Rainbouville robbery the newspaper felt that it would be difficult for the police to track down and apprehend disguised thieves, concluding that "it is evident that revolvers must be the order of the day when our citizens travel in the country now".[24] After the Calgary stagecoach robbery, the newspaper, which was usually complimentary of the Force's record for law and order, suggested that new initiative was needed to improve the NWMP. The Mounted Police, the paper said, was essentially a military force which could not be expected "to be expert in hunting and tracing criminals".[25] To better respond to crime a corps of detectives should be formed, its personnel picked from eastern police forces, and attached to the NWMP.

Similar sentiments were expressed by the *Calgary Tribune* and the *Regina Leader* within the year.[26] These astute observations recognized that crime in an increasingly more settled frontier was becoming more devious, requiring a more sophisticated response than a police patrol sent out to round up known culprits. Coincidentally with the appeals from the newspapers for trained detectives, the Mounted Police were arriving at the conclusion that this expertise was required. In fact, Supt. Antrobus assigned three men as detectives to track the Calgary stagecoach robbers. He also hired a civilian as a special constable to trace the bandits. All were equally unsuccessful in bringing in the criminals. In these cases what was meant by detectives were policemen or experienced prairie men assigned to a particular investigation to be carried out in plain clothes. These men would try to track down suspects by asking questions and following leads and they might or might not identify themselves as policemen as it served their purposes. The model for these detectives was found in eastern cities or in private forces like the Pinkertons in the United States. It was a distinct departure from the military mould of the Mounted Police enforcement of law and order.

In the post-rebellion period, the Force even experimented with the idea of creating a distinctive detective branch. Comm. Herchmer recommended such a step shortly after assuming command of the Force.[27] In October 1886, Charles Constantine, Chief of the Manitoba Provincial Police since 1880, was commissioned to be an Inspector in the Mounted Police to organize a detective branch.[28] No action was taken on this plan until 1887 when the murders and robberies lent impetus to the project. Comptroller Fred White was worried that the Force seemed incapable of handling these cases and demanded the immediate attention of the Commissioner to select men from the ranks of the Force for training as detectives.[29] Herchmer then solicited the advice of Constantine on the approach to organization. The former police chief recommended the selection of "old young men, men who have a knowledge of the world and of men, able to control themselves, ever secret and watchful, able to go in, without giving information and above all to hide their calling".[30] Citing the Pinkertons as an example, Constantine said that the initiative in solving a case must be left to the individual agent in the field who would work independently of the regular Mounted Police organization in whatever area he worked. Financial flexibility was also required so that a detective always had sufficient money to run his own operation without close accounting to his superiors. Herchmer forwarded Constantine's report to White recommending organization of a four-man detective corps. He worried about expenses, however, claiming that it was almost impossible to keep a close eye on money spent by detectives.[31]

The organization proposed by Constantine amounted to a kind of criminal secret service branch of the Force. White agreed with the approach and recommended to Prime Minister Macdonald in August 1887 that a detective corps of ten men be formed under Insp. Constantine. Dubbed "Old Tomorrow" for his procrastination, Macdonald did not get around to sanctioning the project until April 1888.[32]

By June 1888, Constantine filed his first report on the fledgling detective branch. He had four men working in this service, three regular members of the Force and one civilian. The men were stationed at points along the Canadian Pacific Railway at Regina, Moosomin, Dinsmore and Lethbridge. They rode the trains and gathered information on liquor law infringements and on criminal operations. Constantine anticipated gaining enough evidence to break up a gang of cattle and horse thieves whose work had previously been blamed on Indians. One of the detectives was about to begin work on the Poole murder case:

> I find that assistance and information is readily given by the public in all matters of a purely criminal nature. When it comes to being connected with the suppression of the liquor trade, everyone is against us, and do everything possible to impede and obstruct.[33]

Despite this encouraging report, the NWMP detective branch did not last long and, by the next year, the Force members were returned to their regular duties and the civilian was dismissed.

The swift demise of the detective branch is probably due to several factors. The expense was heavy, $55 per man the first month, not including train fares. Herchmer approached the CPR for free passes for his detectives, but was turned down by the company.[34] Then a conflict arose between the established Mounted Police command structure and the independently operating detectives. In ordering the dismissal of the civilian detective Alex McGowan in March 1889, Herchmer made it clear that he was disappointed in the return he had

received for his investment: "The amount of information received from him since his appointment is quite inadequate to the costs".[35] On 19 July 1888, Supt. Antrobus at Maple Creek forwarded a complaint from Insp. Moodie at Medicine Hat. Recently, Cst. Paddy Doyle dressed in civilian clothes had approached Insp. Moodie to lay charges in two liquor cases. Moodie was slightly acquainted with Doyle but knew nothing of his detective work and demanded papers to substantiate his story. Doyle could produce nothing and Moodie was left wondering whether Doyle was a member of an elite service or a deserter boldly trying to pick up a quick reward for a liquor conviction.[36] Finally, White and Herchmer probably considered that they may have over-reacted to the events of 1886 and 1887 in deciding a separate detective branch with undercover operatives was needed. The unsolved murders and armed robberies did not presage a wave of violent crime in the Canadian West. Moreover, individual Force members were proving themselves quite capable of conducting successful investigations without the special trappings of the independent detective service. In succeeding years the undercover operatives and special detectives were used only occasionally on cases which seemed to defy solution by conventional investigative methods.[37]

A law enforcement problem which plagued the Canadian frontier west was horse and cattle stealing. Loose supervision of stock by ranchers made such thefts relatively easy to commit and considerably more difficult to detect. The presence of the border further complicated matters, hindering pursuit and arrest even when the culprits were identified. In the past, such difficulties in the United States had spawned lynch laws where vigilante groups sometimes cut through the red tape of due process by throwing a rope over the limb of a tree. However, in Canada, policing the range was left to the NWMP with whom the ranchers enjoyed a close relationship.[38]

Stock thefts were only occasional occurrences in the northern NWT where there were few ranches and no convenient border to assist escape. There was, however, a unique case of cattle stealing in 1886 which featured popular support for the perpetrators and a slight to justice. In December 1885, police discovered a quantity of beef on the prairie near Prince Albert which appeared to have been cut from a stolen cow. Boot prints in the vicinity suggested that a white man had committed the offence. Further investigation led the Mounted Police to a local settler who, when presented with the evidence gathered, broke down and confessed his guilt and gave the names of others involved in the crime. His story was that a gang had been formed to round up cattle which had strayed during the turmoil of the rebellion. The conspirators knew that no report would be made to police of the thefts because the owners had already claimed compensation from the government. Three persons were charged in the affair and when brought before magistrates in preliminary hearing were bound over for trial, two being refused bail. However, Supt. A. B. Perry later claimed that when the cases came to trial the strong evidence of guilt produced, did not secure any convictions. He attributed this failure to a widespread sympathy for the offenders in the district in what, because of the unusual circumstances, were victimless crimes.[39]

In the southern region of the NWT, stock theft, particularly horse stealing, was a more common complaint during this period. This was ranching country where cattle roamed the prairies and horses were numerous and often not securely corralled. Such a situation created opportunities for stock thieves, often requiring the Mounted Policemen to perform as cowboys. Insp. Constantine at Moosomin complained in 1891 that settlers in the area expected police in all circumstances to round up missing stock for them:

> In many cases where horses or cattle strayed from their owners they at once went for the police station, and without being able to give any grounds of suspicions or reason, except that the horses or cattle could not be found, at once concluded that they had been stolen and expected the police to turn out and hunt for them. In some cases this has been done, and the stock reported stolen has been found in bluffs within a short distance of the owner's place.[40]

Supt. Deane at Lethbridge was frustrated by the same experience in his district and he took the trouble to break down statistically the occurrences of missing horses for the year 1891. In the 12 months preceding 1 December 1891, 24 horses were reported missing of which 22 were found and proved to be strays. One of the horses, indeed, turned out to have been stolen and the thief was caught, convicted and sentenced to three months in prison. The lost horse reported missing was a suspected fraudulent attempt by a man to claim a stray which police had found but which he could not accurately describe.[41]

Although a large proportion of alarms over missing stock were false, there were thefts during this period. American horse thieves sometimes stole horses in the border states and ran them into Canada where they hoped to dispose of them in communities where their ownership was not known. The Mounted Police watched for this illegal commerce. For instance in February 1886, a Montana horse thief named Peter Osler was nabbed by Insp. McGibbon near Wood Mountain with a band of 45 horses stolen in the States. Osler received two years in penitentiary for his crime. One member of Osler's gang who was not caught was the notorious "Dutch" Albert Koerner, a deserter from the Mounted Police.[42] The border

offered complications in dishing out justice to American malefactors because for crimes committed in the U.S. it was generally necessary to return the suspect to that country for trial. In the case of theft, however, Canadian law provided for the charge of bringing stolen property into Canada. The Mounted Police found this most useful in guarding the line against horse thieves.[43] The success of the NWMP in this regard was recognized by American ranchers who had suffered stock losses. In 1888, the president of the Montana Territorial Board of Stock Commissioners relayed to Comm. Herchmer the gratitude of these ranchers for the work of the police in a letter which read:

> At the August meeting of the Montana Stock Growers' Association and also of the Territorial Board of Stock Comms., a resolution was passed giving a vote of thanks to the officers and men of the NWMP, and also the Canadian authorities generally, for assistance given to many of the citizens of Montana in recovering horses stolen from our Territory.
> Please accept the assurance of our appreciation of courtesies received at your hands, which we hope to be able to reciprocate in the future.[44]

The specific incident which had inspired the note of appreciation from the ranchers was a good example of how the complications of law enforcement along an international border could be reduced by cooperation from both sides. In May 1888, the Mounted Police received circulars from the Montana Stock Growers' Association alerting them to the possible presence in Canada of two horse thieves, "Slim Jim" McIntyre and Bruno Azuare, who had stolen 41 head in Montana. Supt. Antrobus sent out a patrol to search and the men were arrested in a few days. McIntyre had already served four years in a Montana prison for horse theft and this time he and his companion were sentenced to five years in the Manitoba Penitentiary at Stony Mountain for bringing stolen property into Canada. The Montana ranchers' association also expressed their gratitude to the police in a form more tangible than the above letter to the Commissioner. A $200 reward was sent to Supt. Antrobus who divided it, $50 to each of the three men who brought in the suspects, and $50 to purchase goods for the messes at Maple Creek.[45]

Reciprocity of justice was extended to the Mounted Police by Americans in cases where thieves from Canada sought refuge in the United States. In 1888, an American, Edward Austin, alias "The Kid", stole a horse and other articles at Lethbridge and crossed the border to Montana. The stolen horse got away from Austin on the prairie but he was found by cowboys and given hospitality at a ranch. Unfortunately for Austin, the horse's owner showed up and told his tale. Austin revealed his guilt by trying an escape in which he planned to steal another horse from the ranch. The cowboys were not pleased and after considering dealing with "The Kid" vigilante style, agreed to let him return to Canada where he was turned over to the NWMP and shortly thereafter was tried and sentenced to two months in prison.[46]

In 1889, cross border cooperation resulted in prison for a man who stole on both sides of the line. A man named Lambert appropriated another man's horse at Lethbridge, crossed the border and sold the animal at Conrad, Montana. Supt. Deane sent word to American authorities to watch for Lambert. Perhaps in response to the interest being shown by the American peace officers, Lambert suddenly returned to Lethbridge on the back of a horse he had acquired in the U.S. Warned by a confederate that the police wanted him, Lambert headed with speed for Dinsmore following the railroad. An unusual chase ensued when Sgt. Charlie Ross and three of his men took a handcar and gave pursuit. They caught him 15 miles down the track. A witness was brought from Montana for Lambert's trial and he got six months for stealing the horse and another six months for importing a horse into Canada without paying the duty.[47]

Such a system was not foolproof and on more than one occasion a horse thief disappeared across the border without a trace. Such was the case with Al Dowser in 1890 who rather boldly stole four horses from a prairie campsite, three of which belonged to the Mounties. In July, several Mounted Policemen provided escort for contractors preparing the grade for the railway track to run south from Lethbridge to the border. One night about 11 p.m. a lone rider approached the night herder at the camp, saying that he was searching for missing horses. At the stranger's request the helpful herder identified according to owner the band of horses picketted near the camp. The next morning the four horses were missing, picket ropes neatly cut with a sharp knife. The Mounted Police were convinced that the nocturnal visit was the work of Al Dowser who was avenging a police seizure of an illegal whisky shipment in which he had an interest. The police notified American officials but no record has been discovered of his capture.[48]

Of course the problem of law enforcement along the Canadian and U.S. border in the NWT was broader than that of chasing horse thieves. Refuge from justice was sought by all manner of suspected criminals and the border was a convenient barrier. For most classes of serious crimes the legal process by which the two governments arranged the return of wanted persons from each other's territory was extradition.

The principle behind extradition is a dual one: balancing the assertion of state sovereignty against international concern for effective law enforcement. Canada, like the United States and most nations, will not allow another state to claim legal jurisdiction over persons within her borders. However, Canada will accept requests from other nations for return for trial of suspected criminals who have taken residence in Canada. Such arrangements are reciprocal and are formalized by treaties which include schedules specifying crimes eligible for extradition. These treaty obligations to extradite criminals are implemented in Canadian courts under the authority of the *Canadian Extradition Act*. Over the years the regulations governing procedures to be followed in extradition cases have become formalized. The state requesting extradition must satisfy Canadian law enforcement and judicial officials at several stages from arrest to extradition hearing through appeal. Even when the individual sought is surrendered to the foreign country, it is on condition that he may be tried only for the offence specified in that country's extradition request. Likewise, Canada must employ similar methods when seeking extradition from a state with which it has a treaty. These formalities can be simplified, however, if the accused agrees to waive extradition and return voluntarily to the other country to face trial. Even here the Canadian judiciary must ensure that the suspect understands the rights of legal recourse which he is giving up.[49]

This extradition process existed in Canada in an incipient form in the 1880s and 1890s and was used by the Mounted Police. The Dominion of Canada did not then exercise the full authority of the modern nation state. Britain retained the responsibility for foreign relations for all components of the Empire including Canada. Consequently, the mother country made all treaties and conventions governing Canada's external relations. The first of such extradition agreements with the United States came in 1842 when that country and Britain signed the Webster-Ashburton Treaty settling a number of outstanding issues. The crimes listed in the treaty as extraditable offences were major: murder, piracy, arson, robbery, forgery and uttering forged papers. In time these provisions proved inadequate as persons committing other serious offences were finding safe haven across the border. After lengthy negotiations between Britain and the United States, with some pressure from Canada, a convention was ratified by the two countries in 1889 to expand the list of extraditable crimes by ten more categories including manslaughter, perjury, embezzlement, rape and abduction. Canada had, already in 1877, passed its own *Extradition Act* which as amended in 1882 consolidated in a single general statute the legal definition of extradition as practised in the country.[50]

Extradition was used as a method of resolving the difficulty of the border by the Mounted Police and law enforcement officers in the western United

States. In the cases of the murderers Gaddy and Racette examined above, U.S. peace officers arrested them upon application of the Mounted Police in 1887 and extradited them back to Canada. Similarly, in 1888, one Max Hoppie, wanted in Montana for murder, was arrested by the Mounted Police in southern Alberta and, after extradition proceedings, turned over to American authorities.[51] Often, however, the threat of extradition proceedings was enough to convince a wanted man to waive his rights. This was the method preferred by both the Mounted Police and U.S. peace officers to avoid the legal complexities and extra work involved in an international transaction. In most cases, the wanted men themselves preferred to avoid more time spent in jail and the extra legal expenses of extradition hearing and appeal. To illustrate, in August 1889, a Deputy Sheriff from Montana turned up in southern Assiniboia in pursuit of an Albert "Brick" Brazier wanted for murder. Reporting to the police post at Wood Mountain, the lawman was provided with a fresh horse and an escort and went on to Moose Jaw where Brazier was located and arrested. After being held for four days, Brazier decided to sign a document waiving his extradition rights. He was then escorted by the NWMP to the border and turned over to U.S. authorities. A reward which came to $50 had been offered for the capture of Brazier and it was shared by the Mounted Policemen who effected the arrest.[52] In 1889, the NWMP welcomed the news that Britain and the United States had agreed to a new convention in which the list of crimes eligible for extradition was expanded. Supt. Sam Steele observed in 1890 that with this convention came the opportunity to deny Canada as a refuge to more American criminals.[53] Nevertheless extradition continued to be a complicated process and a drain on law enforcement resources.

When the Force marched west in 1874, it was responsible not only for law enforcement in the NWT, but also for all judicial work. By virtue of the *NWMP Act*, the Commissioner had the power of a magistrate and the other officers were authorized to act as justices of the peace.[54] As the apparatus of territorial government was established in the West, so too was a civilian judicial system. By 1886, five civilians performed as stipendiary magistrates in the superior courts operating in the five judicial districts of the Territories. These judges were based in the major centres; Battleford, Calgary, Edmonton, Fort Macleod and Regina. Together *en banc* the judges would form a Supreme Court for the NWT.[55] Moreover, civilian justices of the peace had been appointed in great numbers to exercise local authority in minor judicial matters in return for small fees for each service rendered.[56]

Despite the development of the civilian justice system, the Mounted Police justices remained the backbone of the magistracy in the NWT. In contrast to most of their civilian counterparts, police justices of the peace possessed legal knowledge, experience and the time to devote to their duties. An historian who studied the North-West Territorial judiciary observed that in 1890, over one-half of the fines reported to the Lieutenant-Governor were imposed by Mounted Police officers.[57] The brunt of the work performed by the justices of the peace involved minor offences subject to summary conviction, that is, by a justice of the peace with few trial formalities. Breaches of law or ordinance such as illegal possession of liquor, setting prairie fires and keeping brothels fell into the category of summary offences and were punishable by fine or relatively short periods of imprisonment. Police justices also acted in cases of the more serious indictable crimes by holding preliminary hearings to establish if sufficient evidence existed to proceed to trial by jury and/or judge.[58] Usually the five superior court judges sat on trials involving indictable crimes, but occasionally two justices of the peace, together bearing the authority of a single magistrate, would handle these cases.

There was some dissatisfaction among the people of the West concerning the role of judges being played by a policeman. Most of the criticism came about because of police insistence upon enforcing the unpopular law prohibiting the importation of liquor into the NWT except by special permit. Abuse of the law was widespread, amounting almost to deliberate civil disobedience. Newspapers decried NWMP officers convicting offenders and attempted to elevate the cause of the "wets" to a virtual violation of the *Magna Carta*. In March 1890, the *Calgary Herald* editorialized that while the Mounted Police was a splendid law enforcement agency, its officers should not be allowed to adjudicate too harshly in liquor cases:

> In short the officers of the police should not be compelled to perform magisterial duties, for this lays the responsibility for the prosecution and the judgment upon the same person. The very idea of making the public prosecutor act as judge is repugnant to every idea of British justice.[59]

The other side of the coin was that Mounted Police justices had complaints about the judicial responsibilities thrust upon them by circumstances in the NWT. Civilian justices of the peace were usually selected by the Lieutenant-Governor upon the recommendation of politicians or officers of the NWMP because they were prominent, respected men in a community or they had the right political connections. Such men were almost always untrained in law but were constrained to accept the appointments as recognition of their place in society.[60] The problem was that these men were often very reluctant to sit in judgement upon their friends and neighbours, particularly over violations of unpopular laws. In 1887, Mounted Police officers at Macleod, Maple Creek and Moosomin all reported to the Commissioner that civilian justices refused to sit on cases involving violations of the liquor laws which were abhorred by most members of the community.[61] In 1889, Supt. Deane reported that on one occasion he had persuaded a reluctant civilian J.P. to do his duty and try a liquor case in Lethbridge district. The result was that the magistrate thereafter suffered from the disapproval and mistrust of his neighbours.[62] Similarly, civilian justices were reluctant to penalize their friends for the careless, if unwitting, setting of fires which often raged out of control and set ablaze the prairie. Mounted Police reported their discouragement at spending long hours to bring guilty parties to trial which ended in punishments of no deterrent value. For instance, those convicted of setting prairie fires by civilian justices in Saskatchewan in 1891 received fines ranging from 50 cents to $3.[63] Many NWMP officers felt that they were forced to perform their judicial duties by the absence of a professional magistracy.[64]

Another related source of controversy during the period was the question of Herchmer's authority over his officers when they were acting as justices of the peace. The *Regina Leader*, the instrument of N. F. Davin's vendetta against Lawrence Herchmer, accused the Commissioner of interfering in the judicial duties of his officers to the point of forcing them to act contrarily to their consciences.[65] This concern had also been voiced by C. E. D. Wood, the editor of the *Macleod Gazette* and a former policeman, who claimed that Herchmer had dictated the magisterial decisions of his officers.[66] Herchmer denied these charges and sought vindication by ordering all of his officers serving as justices of the peace to attest to his rectitude in this matter. Most of his officers complied, reporting no interference from the Commissioner, but not all. Supts. Antrobus and Steele and Insp. Constantine all recalled isolated incidents when Herchmer attempted to influence their decisions on the guilt of parties or the most appropriate punishment.[67] It is clear that Herchmer did not draw a line of distinction between his authority as chief of a police force and the independence of his officers as magistrates. In June 1889, for example, Herchmer requested Lieutenant-Governor Dewdney to instruct all justices of the peace on the railway line to punish more harshly the increasing number of tramps travelling in the Territories. Dewdney refused, reminding the Commissioner that determining "the extent of punishment is within the discretion of a Magistrate".[68]

The Wetmore Commission investigated charges of Herchmer's interference in judicial matters and found his misconduct to have been of a minor nature.[69]

The guardrooms of the Mounted Police divisional headquarters provided the only jail facilities in the NWT. Here policemen undergoing punishment for breaches of discipline were incarcerated with accused persons awaiting trial, the convicted serving short sentences, serious offenders awaiting escort to the Manitoba Penitentiary or the insane awaiting transport to the Selkirk asylum near Winnipeg.[70] Often there were large numbers of prisoners in police cells, thus throwing considerable responsibility on the police to care for and guard them. For instance, Supt. J. H. McIllree reported from Calgary in 1890 that 74 prisoners had been confined to that post's guardroom in the past year. Of this total, 34 had served terms of imprisonment there, 5 went to the Manitoba Penitentiary at Stony Mountain and 1 was sent to Selkirk asylum.[71] The construction of a territorial jail at Regina, opened by 1891, relieved some of the pressure on police guardrooms in the NWT, especially for incarceration of short-term prisoners.[72] However, the Mounted Police did derive one benefit from maintaining prisoners: those sentenced to hard labour could be assigned to work details to keep the posts in good repair.[73]

Reorganization of law enforcement and judicial systems after the rebellion created new demands for better jail facilities on the prairies. The Mounted Police opened detachments in more communities across the NWT, and the superior court judges travelled to these outposts to conduct trials.[74] Very soon a problem arose concerning lack of proper accommodation for prisoners. In June 1887, Judge Wetmore complained to the Lieutenant-Governor that the Mounted Police at Moosomin had chained two men accused of theft to the wall of the detachment shanty for several days while they awaited his arrival to conduct their trial. Then, after the judge had found both of them guilty, they remained so fettered while awaiting transportation to the Manitoba penitentiary. The judge was concerned that such a primitive method of confinement was used on the men before the trial when they stood accused of crime but legally innocent. Wetmore pointed out that the situation in Moosomin was not unusual and could have happened at any of the police detachments in his judicial district, adding that "of course, there are Mounted Police here and there through it and there are small houses where they eat and sleep, but they are not Police Guard houses or Guardrooms".[75] This matter was referred to the Mounted Police who confirmed the accuracy of the Wetmore's observations concerning this particular incident and the jail situation in the NWT generally.[76]

Prime Minister Macdonald decided that a federal initiative was required to provide the police with suitable jail facilities, at least on a temporary basis, until county jails were built in the West. At Macdonald's request, Lieutenant-Governor Dewdney solicited opinions from the Supreme Court judges and from Comm. Herchmer on the locations and nature of the required buildings. Using this information Dewdney drew up a list of locations requiring small facilities combining courthouse, lock-up and public quarters in one building. This list was submitted in April 1888 to the federal Department of Public Works with recommendations concerning the priority of sites. Public Works acted with reasonable despatch, beginning work in the next fiscal year on the Moosomin courthouse and lock-up. Work on a similar building at Moose Jaw began in 1890 and, in the next fiscal year, funds were set aside to convert the immigrant shed at Medicine Hat in to a jail and courthouse. This construction program continued through the territorial period as local situations required.[77] In addition, Public Works built a more elaborate courthouse at Calgary in 1888-89 to serve as the seat of the judicial district of Alberta. This two-storey sandstone building was the largest structure erected by the federal government in Alberta during the territorial period.[78] Prisoners awaiting trial at Calgary, however, continued to be lodged in the Mounted Police guardroom or in the local police cells at the town hall.[79]

The Mounted Police regulations of 1889 were stringent about custody of prisoners in the guardrooms. The routine of the jail was the responsibility of the Provost NCO. He organized the prisoners for work, searched their cells for unauthorized articles and ensured that prison buildings were kept in good repair. In addition, the orderly officer visited all cells each day and night to ensure all was in order. If a prisoner had to be moved outside the guardroom, the armed escort was expected to inspect frequently handcuffs and manacles and be constantly on guard for an attempted escape. Should a policeman, through connivance or negligence, allow a prisoner to escape he was liable for various punishments up to and including imprisonment with hard labour and dismissal from the Force.[80] Despite all this theoretical order, there were several escapes in this short period, attributable to poorly equipped guardrooms, prisoner ingenuity or police carelessness. A frustrated Herchmer complained after an escape in 1887 that "the carelessness of the NWMP in the matter of the safekeeping of prisoners is becoming a byeword".[81]

One of the more colourful and successful escapes in this period was pulled off by William Jones, alias "Crackerbox Johnson", and A. "Danny" Gallagher. "Crackerbox" was described by police as "an old jail bird"[82] and he was reputed to have received his nickname when he won so much money in a poker game that he was forced to carry it away in a crackerbox. Three Mounted Policemen arrested the armed "Crackerbox" in an Edmonton pool room after he had boasted that the Mounted Police could never take him in.[83] On 28 April 1886, Jones was convicted of vagrancy and being drunk and disorderly and was sentenced to six months in the police guardroom.[84] He shared accommodation with Danny Gallagher, a Mounted Policeman, who was also serving six months for leading a police mutiny at Edmonton in February 1886. The confinement of the guardroom proved no real challenge to these enterprising gentlemen. On 8 May 1886, Jones released himself from ball and chain, probably by picking a lock, and he and Gallagher worked loose a bar in a window and took what a newspaper described as "leg-bail" from the prison.[85]

This pair of escapees proved to be a match for the Mounted Police, eluding a series of patrols and an extensive dragnet for 12 days. Finally, on Thursday, May 20th, Sgt. Gordon and Cst. Baker surprised and arrested the two who were travelling south to Calgary with a freighter. Apparently with their prisoners safely in custody, securely handcuffed, the policemen headed back for Edmonton. On Saturday, May 22nd, the party stopped for dinner at a roadhouse run by ex-Mountie Ed Barnett. Lowering their guard somewhat, the police removed the prisoners' handcuffs to allow them to eat. As Cst. Baker had broken his holster he was carrying his revolver tucked into his boot. After dinner, Jones, who had a reputation as a cardsharp, spotted a deck of cards on the table and offered to show his escorts a trick they had not seen before. The trick turned out to be on the police officers because, as they approached, Gallagher snatched the gun from Baker's boot and turned it on his former comrades. Ignoring a warning to raise his hands, Gordon tried to draw his own gun, causing Gallagher to fire two shots which narrowly missed the sergeant. Duly chastened, the policemen submitted. The fugitives then placed their handcuffs on their captors and resumed their journey southward, this time armed, equipped and mounted courtesy of the NWMP. Despite an intensive police manhunt, the two escapees disappeared, presumably over the border.[86] The last heard of either was a newspaper report eight months later that "Crackerbox Johnson" was running a saloon in Ellensburg, Washington Territory. As for the policemen, following an investigation Sgt. Gordon was reduced in rank to a corporal and Cst. Baker was sentenced to four months in the guardroom.[87]

96

Less spectacular but more typical of escapes in this period was that of Fred Shoultz. In September 1891, Shoultz and an accomplice were charged with burglary of a jewelry store and were incarcerated in the NWMP guardroom at Regina awaiting trial. As in the case of Jones and Gallagher, Shoultz took advantage of a technologically unsophisticated "cage" and inattentive guards. Reaching out from his cell, Shoultz was able to remove the screws from the hinges of the cell door and, in the early morning hours, he slipped out of the guardroom either through an open exit door or a window with widely spaced bars.[88] The sentries on duty were later found to have neglected their duties and as a consequence ended up serving time in the same facility.[89] Shoultz was recaptured a few days later hiding in a privy behind a Calgary restaurant.[90] He was tried and convicted of burglary and sentenced to ten years in penitentiary.[91]

There was uncertainty among the Mounted Police as to how much force should be used to stop an escape. On several occasions during this period, policemen shot at the fugitives but in only one case did they hit anyone. The question of the right to fire was raised in particular regarding the escape of Deerfoot from NWMP custody at Calgary in 1887. Deerfoot had broken from restraint, ignored warning shots and defied his captors, daring them to shoot him. His guards were intimidated because they were unsure of their authority to fire in this situation, especially as such an act might inflame members of Deerfoot's band.[92] On 30 May 1887, Cst. C. A. Fisher attempted to escape from Calgary guardroom where he was serving a sentence for desertion. The guard fired a warning shot which did not slow the prisoner and then fired again bringing him down with a slight wound. An investigation assessed no blame on the guard and the prisoner recovered from his wound.[93]

Comm. Herchmer issued instructions in 1888 which clarified the authority question. He said that a policeman could not shoot at an escaping prisoner under arrest for a misdemeanour but could shoot at someone under arrest for a felony when all other means had been tried to prevent the escape. He added that "it is most desirable to shoot only when absolutely necessary"[94] and in such a case an investigation was to follow immediately. These instructions still left the policemen considerable discretion as to when to fire, and controversy could, and did, occur later when that judgement was exercised.

In the immediate post-rebellion years, the NWMP were faced by a new priority in law enforcement. The completion of the Canadian Pacific Railway brought an increase of white settlement and also of crime in white communities. In the absence of other law enforcement agencies, the NWMP bore the exclusive responsibility of pursuing and averting these criminals. Due to its unique role on the Canadian frontier, the Mounted Police also were responsible for the trial and incarceration of many of the people who they apprehended. Research largely supports the conventional judgement that the NWMP were more successful in law enforcement than were their American counterparts.

Chapter 8

"An Iron Fist in a Velvet Glove": The Mounted Police and Crime, 1892-1900

When A. Bowen Perry took over as Commissioner of the North-West Mounted Police on 1 August 1900, he took stock of the Force and its duties in the Territories. Perry had been absent from the prairies for almost three years, on duty mainly in the Yukon. He was most surprised by the changes he encountered:

> I noticed everywhere a great increase in settlement, activity in business and a general buoyancy which was not too apparent when I left three years ago. New towns had sprung up, old towns grown and settled localities appeared where scarcely a farm house had then existed.[1]

In contrast, the previous few years had been hard on the Force. The Klondike Gold Rush and the South African War had badly depleted the Force of its best men and horses. The strength of the Force in the West had fallen from 914 in 1892 to 682 in 1900. Yet Perry concluded that the police had been doing a good job through energy and ability – the problem of crime was well in hand.[2]

Perry did not paint a full picture of the status of the Force in the West on this occasion. In fact, the decrease in numbers and the despatch of men to the north were a direct consequence of considerable political pressure to remove the Force entirely from the North-West Territories. The frontier was rapidly disappearing, the Indians had been pacified and westerners were trumpeting their ability to handle their own destiny. Both Conservative and Liberal governments favoured removal of the Force from the prairies and handing over responsibilities for law enforcement to local authorities. The NWT was granted responsible government in 1897 and, throughout the 1890s, villages, towns and even a city (Calgary) were incorporated and assumed control of local affairs.

But the Mounted Police did not disappear from the NWT for two principal reasons. First, as the major federal agency in the West, the Force rendered public services of all kinds; this was heartily appreciated by westerners, a fact which did not escape the notice of politicians. Second, throughout this period the federal government was responsible for the administration of criminal matters in the Territories. It soon found that any discussion of settlers assuming responsibility for law enforcement was purely theoretical and did not quickly translate into action. Incorporated municipalities reluctantly organized police forces which were costly and less efficient than the Mounties. Some did so, however, motivated by the necessity to see municipal bylaws enforced and fines levied. By 1905, there were only 47 municipal policemen in the NWT, the largest police department being at Calgary and consisting of 6 men.[3] Crime fighting and criminal investigation were left largely to the Mounted Police.

Overall crime statistics for the Territories in this period are generally unreliable. However, Mounted Police figures support the unstartling conclusion that crime, measured by charges laid and convictions obtained, grew relative to the numbers of incoming settlers.[4] The passing of the frontier, of course, allowed the Force to devote more energy to increased criminal work. The railway, the telegraph and the telephone improved the efficiency of police communications. The menace of a widespread Indian uprising had diminished significantly; this relieved the Force of its military garrison role and the necessity of much of the time-consuming patrols on horseback. Similarly, regular patrols to assess the security of settlers and to guard against prairie fires were phased out. Increasingly, the Mounted Police turned its attention to crime and better methods of its detection.

Besides the main task of law enforcement, the Mounted Police continued to perform other functions in the criminal justice system. In spite of the construction of three territorial jails, the Mounted Police were still responsible for the custody of many prisoners in the NWT. Likewise, Mounted Police officers, serving as justices of the peace, continued to adjudicate at trials, although the significance of this contribution was reduced as the growing volume of judicial work was assigned to territorial judges, police magistrates and civilian justices of the peace.

Increased immigration to the NWT brought with it undesirable elements on which the Mounties kept close scrutiny lest they perpetrate serious crimes. The police were particularly worried about tramps, single men on the move with little money and a propensity to steal rides on CPR trains. Another group inspiring justifiable anxiety was the American outlaw, a second generation of that class of criminal spawned by the Civil War and cattle drives, who had stymied the efforts of U.S. law enforcement agencies. Immigrants from Europe, particularly east Europeans, were initially regarded with some apprehension because they lacked a knowledge of the British system of justice. Finally, serious crime occurred more frequently even among the native-born as passion and greed led some to deprive others of life, health or property.

The problem of tramps and vagabonds was apparently a North American phenomenon in which men without means were able to traverse great distances by stealthily boarding poorly guarded trains. At conventions in the 1890s and early 1900s, the International Association of Chiefs of Police, a largely American organization with some Canadian participation, discussed the tramp problem. It was recognized that in difficult economic times, itinerant labourers in search of work would move about the country by the least expensive means available. But authorities had little sympathy for unemployed men who stole rides on the railroad, denying the company a just return for services rendered. Moreover, senior police officers were well aware that indistinguishable from the disadvantaged in the ranks of the hobo were professional tramps who had no intention of working and who survived by begging and stealing. In 1900 and again in 1904, William Pinkerton described to the Association how a new breed had emerged from the professional tramp fraternity known among themselves as "Yeggmen". These men often started as tramps but, through association with criminals on the road or in prisons, picked up specialized knowledge of burglary including the use of nitroglycerine and dynamite to break open and plunder safes in stores, post offices and banks. Yeggmen usually worked in bands of five or six and since their explosions often attracted attention they were armed and prepared to use violence to accomplish their aim. Pinkerton

supplied statistics indicating that hundreds of such burglaries in past years had been the work of Yeggmen.[5]

The prospect of crime committed by tramps concerned the Mounted Police very much during this period. Police vigilance increased because of the example of the United States where burglaries and holdups were regularly attributed to tramps. There was anxiety too about the possibility of violence directed against women and children left alone in homes if hobos were allowed to wander at will. There were several ways in which vagabondage could be discouraged by police. If someone was caught availing himself of rail services without a ticket, he could be charged with stealing a ride. Suspicious characters without money could be jailed as vagrants. If a dangerous weapon was found on either of the above categories of tramps, a more serious charge could be brought under firearms control provisions of the *1892 Criminal Code.* Several incidents of serious crime in this period gave the Mounted Police grounds for concern over footloose strangers.

The Ole Mickelson affair was one of the more bizarre criminal cases in early western Canadian history. Early in the morning of 11 May 1892, a settler named P. O. Skallent was murdered on the trail between the railroad station on the south bank of the North Saskatchewan river and the landing for the ferry that served Edmonton on the opposite bank. The murder was particularly cold-blooded. The victim had been struck from behind, then shot in the head and a considerable sum of money removed from his person. The Mounted Police investigated and suspicion quickly fell on an apparently impecunious stranger, Ole Mickelson, who had been seen with Skallent on the train which arrived at the south Edmonton station shortly before the murder. Insp. William Piercy of the Edmonton detachment received several conflicting reports on the direction of flight taken by the suspected murderer and he obtained the permission of his Commanding Officer, Supt. A. H. Griesbach, 20 miles distant at Fort Saskatchewan, to have posters printed and distributed describing Mickelson and asking the public for information of his whereabouts. While arranging to have this bill printed at the *Edmonton Bulletin* newspaper office, Piercy discussed with Frank Oliver (the paper's publisher and Member of the Legislative Assembly for the NWT) the possibility of tacking on a $200 reward for assistance in the capture of Mickelson. Oliver and another MLA, Antonio Prince, wholeheartedly supported the idea and the reward offer was added to the poster before the necessary authority of the Lieutenant-Governor was obtained.[6]

The reward very probably brought the swift demise of Ole Mickelson, who headed south on foot after the murder following the railway line. On November 13th he got hold of a railway handcart which aided his progress to a point north of Red Deer by the next day. But Mickelson's rather conspicuous route was his downfall; he was sighted and identified and a number of armed citizens from Red Deer went hunting for him. When he encountered his pursuers, Mickelson fired upon them and continued to flee. Eight men gave chase for about four miles, exchanging gunfire with him. Then, just before the fugitive was about to enter a house occupied by two women, he was shot dead, apparently by one William Bell. This incident touched off a bitter controversy over law and order in the Territories.[7]

Many citizens held a rather sanguinary view of the outcome of this affair. According to the *Edmonton Bulletin*, the murderer was "ten times more dangerous than a mad dog" and his fate was most deserved. The paper also saw an important deterrent factor in this case:

> And there is not a man disposed to commit a crime but will now count in the cost the fact that he not only has to reckon with the regular officer of the law, but that justice is at his heels in the person of every law abiding citizen.[8]

This sentiment was echoed by the *Calgary Herald* with the single reservation that it would have been more seemly for this sudden rendering of justice to have come at the hands of accredited peace officers.[9]

However, the vigilante nature of these proceedings horrified Mounted Police authorities and Lieutenant-Governor Joseph Royal alike. Comm. Herchmer was very dissatisfied about the manner in which Piercy had handled the case. He believed that the murderer should have been caught at once by police and attributed the failure to do so to a lack of energy and judgement on Piercy's part.[10] Compounding the problem was the $200 reward which had been offered without proper authority and now Royal was refusing to honour it. He blamed Griesbach for not having in place carefully laid down procedures which had to be followed before a reward was offered. The Lieutenant-Governor felt that the offer of a reward encouraged a number of armed settlers who were a serious menace to anyone resembling the suspected murderer. As for Bell killing Mickelson, Royal had serious doubt that this could be judged justifiable homicide.[11]

The doubts of the authorities led to legal action. Bell was charged with manslaughter and tried in the Supreme Court of the NWT in May 1893. Witnesses described the running gun battle and testified that Mickelson had been given several opportunities to surrender. They also claimed that they could not be certain whose bullet had finally felled Mickelson. The judge instructed the jury that this incident was a good case for justifiable homicide. He remarked that "in this country the machinery provided for enforcing the law was considered sufficient for its enforcement. There was no lynch law here nor would it be countenanced. It is only right, when a man killed another, no matter how fully the killing might be justified, that he who did the killing should be called upon to show justification before a proper tribunal".[12]

The jury brought in a verdict of not guilty after deliberating for only one minute and drew applause from those in the courtroom for its work. Despite the objections of the Lieutenant-Governor, the Legislative Assembly of the NWT granted William Bell his $200 reward and another $100 towards his legal expenses.[13]

Another victim of this tragic affair may have been Insp. William Piercy. On 13 March 1893, this officer called on a doctor at the Hotel Edmonton, complaining of feeling unwell. The doctor ordered Piercy to lay down while he went down to the kitchen to fetch some refreshments. While the doctor was out of the room Piercy got hold of a shotgun and discharged it into his mouth resulting in death instantly.[14] Comm. Herchmer was left wondering whether his criticism of Piercy's handling of the murder case had contributed to his decision to commit suicide.[15]

In June 1893, the body of an itinerant Italian knife-grinder named Battaralla, was found in a railway ditch east of Grenfell. The man was not immediately recognized but, when identified, local residents remembered that he had been travelling by foot through the area in the company of two itinerant musicians, also of Italian extraction. An alert was sent out to watch for these men and they were arrested in Winnipeg by the city police. Returned to Grenfell the two men, Luciano and Dejendo, were tried, found guilty of murder and sentenced to death, although the latter's sentence was commuted to life imprisonment. Again, the motive for murder was robbery.[16]

The growing number of men without means travelling in the NWT, often illegally on trains, was of great concern to Comm. Herchmer. By the spring of 1895, he had decided on a crackdown to discourage tramps lest they become as bold as those in the States and band together to rob a train. Herchmer enlisted the support of the CPR in his effort, explaining to General Manager William Whyte that train crews were refusing to assist his men because if they did they would miss work by being forced to stay around to give evidence at a trial.[17] Whyte agreed to help and on 5 May 1895, he telegraphed Herchmer that a train crew had detained three men stealing a ride on a train and he asked the NWMP to arrest them.[18] This was done but because the men had money and good clothes in suitcases they could not be charged with vagrancy. Herchmer had them brought to Regina and charged with stealing a ride on a train, an offence under the *Railway Act*. On 12 May 1895, they appeared before Insp. Cortlandt Starnes and were found guilty. The maximum penalty for this offence was ten days in jail without hard labour, but Herchmer later explained that the police made them work anyway because they believed the punishment should have been more severe.[19]

A few days after this trial, Herchmer issued instructions to all Mounted Police posts to crack down on tramps and itinerants stealing rides on trains. All tramps, men with no employment and no visible means of maintaining themselves, were to be charged under a provision of the *Criminal Code* which allowed a maximum penalty of a $50 fine and term of up to six months in prison without hard labour. If the accused was also carrying a pistol he was to be charged under other provisions of the *Criminal Code* which allowed for a further term of imprisonment with hard labour. In bringing such vagrants before a justice of the peace, the arresting officers were to point out what a nuisance this class of offenders was becoming and the danger they afforded women and children in isolated farm houses. Also, police at posts along the railway were to attend the arrival and departure of all trains and arrest those stealing rides. The full cooperation of the CPR train crews was assured.[20]

It appears from police reports that Herchmer's instructions had some effect on control of tramps and itinerants in the NWT. In 1895, as a direct result of the new policy, Supt. A. B. Perry at Regina reported that in his district alone, 25 persons were charged for stealing rides on trains. All were convicted and most received the maximum sentence of ten days imprisonment with the additional (and illegal) penalty of hard labour tacked on. In the previous two years no one had been charged with this offence in Regina district although Perry pointed to the increase in the number of those convicted of vagrancy to 34 in 1895, from a total of 17 in the previous two years. Indeed, two men convicted of vagrancy in Perry's district in 1896 were also wanted for murder in North Dakota. They were returned to the American side where they were tried for murder, convicted and sentenced to life imprisonment.[21]

The crackdown on tramps was generally effective. Both the police and CPR reported that it caused some of the travellers not to repeat their offence. Enforcement problems continued however. In some cases, the itinerants found a short stay in jail a welcome break in a long journey, with wholesome food and plenty of rest. In another case, police discovered that CPR train men were paid by tramps to secure their places on a freight train. Putting prisoners to work and arranging the dismissal of the train men were tried as a means to fill these holes in the system.[22]

Occasionally, newspapers criticized the Mounted Police treatment of the unemployed as tramps,[23] although most western communities appreciated a police watch on strangers. Particularly attractive to petty criminals were events such as fairs and circuses, held occasionally at prairie towns; the Mounted Police usually detailed men to patrol these events, sometimes working undercover. Thus, at the Territorial Exhibition at Regina in 1895, S/Sgt. A. F. M. Brooke supplemented the uniformed NWMP patrol with his plainclothes activity. He met every train and identified several criminals from Winnipeg. He kept an eye on these characters and eventually arrested two for minor thefts.[24] But probably the principal contribution of the Mounted Police at these events was the dissuasion of those tempted to crime by their conspicuous presence in uniform. So it was noted in the *Calgary Herald* when the circus visited nearby Wetaskiwin:

> It may not be out of place in these columns to say a word in praise of the tactful manner in which the NWMP perform their duties on occasions of this kind, when the fears of the public on the score of an invasion of dangerous thoughts are but too well grounded. Moving about in an unobtrusive way, chatting with friends, laughing when there is something to laugh at, putting on no bogus airs, hunting no trouble, they are ready, should trouble arise, to attend to it on the instant in a very thorough-going manner. The iron hand in the glove of velvet should make a good crest for the NWMP.[25]

The iron hand of the Mountie did not rest easily in the velvet glove, however, while the American West suffered from the criminal activities perpetrated by gangs of outlaws. From 1891 to 1894, the Dalton brothers and their gang held up banks, express companies and trains in Missouri, Arkansas, Indian territory, Oklahoma and California. Then from 1895 to 1902, Butch Cassidy and his Wild Bunch gang committed a string of robberies from Wyoming to Texas, hiding out between jobs in their Hole-in-the-Wall canyon retreat in Wyoming.[26] The notorious exploits of these bandits created unease among Mounted Policemen who worried that similar depredations would be performed in Canada.

Several minor episodes seemed to confirm the danger. In August 1895, an unarmed Mounted Policeman was shot and wounded by a mining camp bully in an unprovoked attack just across the border from Writing-on-Stone, Alberta.[27] Gangs of stock thieves organized and disbanded almost continuously in American border towns making incursions into Canada. But there was one episode in 1895 which led police to jump to the conclusion that Canada was becoming a new territory for American "stick-up" men.

In January 1895, two men known as Elliott and Laird and a feeble-minded boy named Tommy Roswell entered Canada from Minnesota at Emerson, Manitoba. Declaring themselves settlers bound for Calgary, their effects were placed in bond until they arrived at their destination. However, when the train stopped at Medicine Hat, the men asked permission to remove their property from bond and explore the vicinity with a view to finding homesteads. Authority was given without a second thought in spite of the fact that the men's effects consisted of nine horses, three saddles, a tent, a stove, a little food, five rifles, three shot guns, three revolvers and a large amount of ammunition. The men travelled on the prairie for about two weeks acquiring through trade in the course of their journey a rough sleigh called a "jumper", and selling one of their horses. After the first few days, one of them returned to Medicine Hat and stated to CPR authorities that they were still looking over the area. But by this time the railwaymen were suspicious that the equipment and actions of these three did not conform with the usual profile of settlers entering Canada and they alerted the NWMP.

To the minds of the policemen such a report gave reason to believe that the three were American outlaws and that they were at large preparing to rob a train or commit some other major crime. The response was immediate. At Maple Creek, headquarters of "A" Division, the Mounted Police swore out a warrant for the arrest of the trio for violation of customs regulations concerning bonded goods. Starting on February 7th, patrols were sent out from divisional headquarters at Lethbridge and Maple Creek as well as from area outposts. However, progress was slow because of deep snow near the border and cold weather. On the 11th of February, Sgt. Sparrow of Pendant d'Oreille located the men on the U.S. side of the border at Kennedy's Crossing, 25 miles east of Coutts. Insp. A. C. Macdonell, carrying the warrant, took a patrol to the ranch where they were staying to pay them a visit. Meanwhile, Supt. R. B. Deane at Lethbridge had telegraphed a Mr. Ringwald, a U.S. federal deputy marshal, requesting him to assist Macdonell with his investigation.

Macdonell characterized Laird and Elliott "as hard men, especially the former the latter blusters a bit".[28] But they had been ill-clothed and unprepared for the severity of the prairie winter and Laird had frozen both feet. A settler had taken them in, although with some misgivings. The men had bragged to the man's wife how easy it was to do counterfeit money and pass it in small towns. Questioned by Ringwald and Macdonell, Laird and Elliott claimed to have travelled all over the U.S. on horse and cattle business but they declined to account for their time in Canada. The boy had been picked up in Minnesota, and they gave him a job when he expressed a desire to see the country. Elliott gave a little demonstration of his prowess with a rifle and impressed the Mounted Policemen, although Cpl. Dickson beat him in a contest of marksmanship. Deane telegraphed authorities in Minnesota trying to trace these men but received no replies. The three declined to recross the boundary and be arrested and, since their offence was non-extraditable, Macdonell and his party reluctantly left them after two days and returned to Canada.

The police were convinced that Laird and Elliott were desperadoes who had intended to rob something, probably a train. Herchmer surmised that they had not realized when they started out how far the CPR line was from the border and they had been worried by the strong police presence in Canada. Then, the severe weather had finished hopes of any ill-gotten gains. In a sense, this was an exercise in crime prevention for the NWMP, and they tightened communications procedures with customs officers and railway authorities so that in the future the alarm would be sounded as early as possible when suspicious characters entered Canada.[29] The incident also served to remind Mounted Policemen that American outlaws could any day descend on the Canadian frontier. For example, in November 1896, reports were received from a sheriff in Kolispelle, Montana, that three desperate men had escaped from his jail; soon afterward, the NWMP detachment at Anthracite, Alberta, reported that strangers acting suspiciously had been seen in the area. The police were nervous because large shipments of gold were being shipped east on the CPR through Anthracite from new gold fields in British Columbia. Police escorts were assigned to these shipments and the Anthracite detachment reinforced. When no attack materialized, CPR Vice-President Thomas Shaughnessy attributed the security of the line "entirely to the vigilance of the Mounted Police".[30] Small alarms of this nature were occasionally sounded over the next few years, but not until 1902-1904 did an almost stereotypical American outlaw, Ernest Cashel, operate in Canada, bedeviling the pursuit efforts of the Mounted Police.[31]

Despite the best efforts of police, murders were a growing problem in the NWT. During this period 15 deaths occurred which the Mounted Police characterized as murders committed by white men.[32] Examining the circumstances of the deaths it is apparent that they can be divided into two separate categories. Numerically, the most significant type of murder occurred within the family or was a result of a fit of passion. The other category of murder was apparently committed in the course of another crime, usually robbery. Domestic violence leading to murder was usually a simple crime for police to solve but the latter category was much more difficult.[33]

There were ten deaths in this period which were the result of family violence or passion. In all cases the Mounted Police believed that they had successfully identified the perpetrators and all were charged with their crimes and tried, except for one who committed suicide. Six of those tried were convicted by judge and jury while three won acquittals. One acquittal was won on the grounds of insufficient evidence; another incident was judged to have been accidental; in another three cases, suspects pleaded self-defence; and in the third case, the perpetrator was too young to judge the consequences of her act.

Of the six convictions involving death by domestic violence, in only one case was the death penalty imposed. John Morrison was hung for his shockingly brutal murder of five members of a family near Welwyn close to Moosomin in present day Saskatchewan. Morrison was obsessed with lust for the 15-year-old daughter of the family of Alexander McArthur, a respectable farmer and local postmaster. Thus driven, Morrison entered the McArthur home early in the morning of 9 June 1900 and attacked every member of the family, save the girl, with an axe as they lay sleeping in their beds. When he was finished, he had killed the mother and father, a two-week-old infant and two boys, aged five and eleven. Another brother was attacked also with the axe but later recovered from his injuries. Morrison then turned his attention to the teenage girl and as Supt. C. Constantine rather awkwardly reported, "attempted to ravish"[34] her. He then proceeded to the stable and tried unsuccessfully to end his own life by shooting himself with a shotgun.

Morrison was arrested and nursed back to health at Moosomin. He was then sent to Regina for trial, pleaded guilty and was sentenced to death by Judge Wetmore. He was examined by a doctor appointed by the Dominion government, but no evidence of insanity was found. Neither the police nor the public seemed as interested then as they are now in probing the sociological origins of a man like Morrison and so little is known of him. He was illiterate and found the months in jail waiting for his execution quite boring. He ate and slept well and became quite stout. He was not a talkative man, but he did admit the circumstances of his crime and the uncontrolled passion for the young girl which had caused it. He was visited by the Salvation Army occasionally and he expressed remorse for his deeds, wept and prayed. As the execution date, 17 January 1901, approached preparations were made. The scaffold erected in the yard at the Regina jail had a platform completely boxed in so that the

spectacle of the drop would be concealed from those assembled as official witnesses to his death. Radcliffe, the hangman, was in Regina for several days before the execution, "making free with whomsoever sought his acquaintance" and bragging about past deeds.[35] On the day of the execution Morrison prayed with his spiritual counsellor, Captain Gillan of the Salvation Army and then walked quietly to the scaffold. Just before his execution Morrison was granted his request to make a statement. He acknowledged his sinful life but felt assured that God in his mercy had forgiven him. He hoped that his fate would serve as a warning to others not to take the path that he had chosen. The drop was clean and Morrison's life was quickly over. A black flag was raised over the jail roof to announce to those outside that the execution had been carried out. John Morrison was buried in the jail yard near the grave of Luciano, executed in 1894 for the murder of the knife-grinder Battaralla.

Other than Morrison, the most serious penalty for premeditated homicide committed in a fit of passion was life imprisonment given to Thomas Ellsworth Shephard for the murder of May Buchanan in Fort Saskatchewan in 1893. Buchanan, a long-time prostitute and brothel-keeper, was well known to the Mounted Police in the NWT. She had been fined several times in 1891 by the Mounted Police in Calgary and Canmore on various charges related to the operation of a disorderly house.[36] Perhaps discouraged by this attention, she moved to Edmonton, no doubt aware that only one prostitute had ever been fined there by the Mounted Police. That single exception occurred in 1888 when one Nellie Webb called too much attention to her activities by shooting and wounding a drunken Mounted Policeman who was breaking into her house.[37] In any case, May Buchanan was practising her trade unhindered in a house about one mile from the Mounted Police barracks when, on the night of 7 December 1893, she got into a drunken brawl with her live-in lover, Shephard, who killed her by striking her over the head with an axe.[38]

Shephard pleaded not guilty to murder claiming that his life had been ruined by his association with Buchanan. The trial lasted a bare two days, the 16th and 17th of May, and the jury deliberated a scant 20 minutes before returning a verdict of guilty of manslaughter. In sentencing Shephard, Judge C. B. Rouleau referred to May Buchanan as Shephard's partner in crime and infamy, adding, "You have lived a life of debauchery. You have defied all the laws of morality. I don't think I would be doing my duty if I gave you less considering the circumstances of the case, so you will go to the

Manitoba penitentiary for the remainder of your life."[39]

In three of the cases of death as a result of passion or domestic quarrel, the original charges of murder laid by the Crown were reduced to manslaughter upon conviction by judge and jury. In two cases, the sentences were ten years in prison, in the third, three years. In two of the cases the reduction of the charges seems to have been related to the deaths occurring as a result of the escalating violence or fights. But the remaining case was a heart-rending story of family life gone wrong which must have had a devastating affect on the jury.

The first tragic case was one of patricide. One day in August 1897, a dispute over the ownership of a shared flock of chickens broke out between Andrea Grega and his son Adam on a farm near Whitewood, in present day Saskatchewan. The father, who had a reputation as an ill-tempered man, struck his son in the face. The son then invited his father to strike him again and then again, the father complying each time. The successive blows apparently worked the young man up to what police termed "a fit of ungovernable passion".[40] He picked up an axe lying nearby and struck his father on the head. The first swing of the axe was probably enough to kill the father but his son added several more. Adam Grega then broke down in tears and walked 27 miles to the Mounted Police outpost at Whitewood to surrender himself. There was great popular sympathy for the young man who was liked and respected as a hard-working and orderly person. A jury found him guilty of manslaughter and recommended mercy. He was sentenced to ten years in Stony Mountain Penitentiary.

The killing of a friend resulted in a manslaughter conviction for Lee Purcel at Lethbridge in 1893. Purcel was a well known frontier character who had been involved in the illegal whisky trade since the days of Fort Whoop-Up. As recently as 1890, he had been sentenced to six months in jail for whisky smuggling. The man he shot, Dave Akers, was also a veteran frontiersman who in fact had been in charge of Fort Whoop-Up when the NWMP arrived in 1874. Akers later bought the fort and lived in it until his death.[41] Purcel and Akers were friends and sometimes partners in legitimate business deals. However, a dispute over a cattle deal brought a sudden end to the friendship. On 3 December 1893, Akers rode from Fort Whoop-Up to Purcel's ranch at Pothole Creek, south of Lethbridge. Akers was on horseback when he confronted Purcel, who was on foot, over their business deal. Akers goaded Purcel by crowding him with his horse and hitting him with a whip. After a warning, the angry Purcel shot Akers to death with his rifle and then turned himself over to the authorities. Purcel was tried for murder but the jury brought in a verdict of guilty of manslaughter, probably because of the provocation, and recommended mercy because of his advanced age. The judge responded with a light sentence of three years in prison.[42]

One of the most bizarre murder cases of this era was a suspected family affair, but no conviction for homicide could be reached because of the wholesale perjury of family members. On 21 October 1895, a woman named Sarah Jane Thompson was found dead in bed, in her home just outside Moosomin. The police had been suspicious for some time that the family was not entirely law-abiding and an inquest established that the cause of death was poison. The NWMP arrested the girl's father and her two brothers, Charles Albert and Samuel and charged them with homicide. Charles Albert then pointed the finger at his sister Nancy Smith and her husband Silvester. Apparently the circumstances fitted this couple and they were charged for murder in place of the father and brothers. However, Samuel Thompson remained in custody charged with perjury for this testimony at the coroner's inquest. When the trial of the Smiths opened at Moosomin on January 6th, the chief witness against his sister and her husband was Charles Albert Thompson. His testimony was a transparent tissue of contradictions and lies and resulted in the withdrawal of the charges against Silvester Smith and the acquittal of Nancy Smith. Instead Charles Albert Thompson was tried for perjury, found guilty and sentenced to 14 years in prison. His brother Samuel received six months in jail for his earlier perjury. The father's testimony had also been steeped in contradictions but outright perjury could not be proven, so both the Mounted Police and the Crown were left with what they were certain was murder, a whole family of possible culprits and no way of singling out one due to the untruthfulness of nearly all.[43]

There were five murders between 1892 and 1900 which were committed in the course of robbery. These deaths proved more difficult for police to solve. In only one of the five cases did the police obtain a conviction and in another, the man charged was acquitted. In two more cases the crimes were unsolved by the Mounted Police. The fifth case was that of Ole Mickelson, where the suspect was shot and killed before he could be charged. Evidently the police failure to solve these violent crimes confirms that they did not always "get their man". However, the grim determination with which the NWMP tracked the perpetrators is an explanation of why the myth of complete success became such a part of the public perception of the Force.

One of these murders was motivated by robbery and while the Mounted Police believed that they had their man, they failed to win their case in court. On Christmas Eve 1891, a Montana man,

Frank Ford, brought the dead body of a travelling companion named Mathieu to the NWMP detachment at St. Mary's saying that he had died of a fit. Ford was a known whisky smuggler and, suspicious of the circumstances of the death, the police invited him to remain until the coroner could hold an inquest. Instead, Ford took the first opportunity to bolt back across the border. Indeed, the inquest concluded that Mathieu's death was a result of a fracture of the skull caused by a severe beating. A warrant was issued for Ford's arrest and with help from American authorities, he was taken into custody in Montana and charged with murder. The accused refused to admit his guilt and, at a hearing in the U.S., the Extradition Commissioner held that police evidence was insufficient and Ford was freed.[44]

There were two instances in this period where murders, probably motivated by desire for personal gain by the perpetrators, were unsolved by the Mounted Police. Louis King, a recent arrival in the West, was murdered north of St. Albert in 1897 while investigating the possibility of taking up a homestead. One arrest was made in the case, but the evidence was not strong enough and the suspect was not even required to appear at a preliminary hearing before his release.[45] Similarly, on 25 November 1899, Joseph Deffee, a store-keeper at Canmore was found murdered, the back of his head caved in by a blunt instrument. Robbery was almost certainly the motive and three men were arrested, but with insufficient evidence they were discharged.[46] In neither case was the perpetrator ever found.

Abortion and infanticide were crimes related to murder in the *Criminal Code* and investigated by the Mounted Police. A recent history of women on the Alberta frontier states that women in western Canada used abortion as a birth control method despite its illegality and the consequent danger presumably from back room butchers. The author made this statement based on conversations with several pioneer women and no sense was conveyed of how widespread the practice of abortion was in the frontier west.[47] Certainly from Mounted Police records, it appears that this crime rarely came to the attention of the Force. In all of this period there were only four cases of abortion investigated by the Mounted Police, only one of which resulted in a conviction.

Somewhat revealing concerning the illegal practice of abortion in a prairie community were the cases involving one Professor Andrew Campbell, alias Dr. Lovingheart of Calgary. This unsavoury character was not a medical doctor despite his self-bestowed title and, although a man of property, he was held in low regard by the community. In 1892, he was arrested by the Mounted Police for neglect-

ing to provide for the welfare of a young employee who had run into bad weather on his way to purchase coal at Knee Hill mine, 50 miles from Calgary and died from starvation and exposure. Lovingheart was acquitted by Mounted Police Insp. J. P. Cuthbert since the evidence indicated that the employee was irresponsible. A few months later Lovingheart was in trouble again, this time charged with procuring an abortion.[48]

Lovingheart was suspected by Calgary town police of illegal activities and, early in 1893, he was placed under surveillance. On April 15th, the Calgary police arrested the bogus physician for obtaining the abortion by administering a noxious substance to a woman named Maggie Stevenson. Lovingheart was overwhelmed by his situation and wept incessantly in his cell for several hours while begging to see and kiss his wife. Such privileges were refused. He was arraigned before Justice of the Peace James Walker later that day and bail was denied, but permission was granted to transfer the prisoner to the Mounted Police guardroom because the town police cells were unsanitary. The Calgary police bungled the case by allowing Maggie Stevenson to slip undetected out of town. Lovingheart was brought into court again on April 19th, the Crown being forced to seek an adjournment which was granted and the prisoner was released on bail. Five days later, the Crown dropped its charge against Lovingheart since Stevenson could not be found. The Mounted Police resumed the search and on the 2nd of May located the missing witness at Langden apparently having driven there in a carriage by a round-about route with the intention of continuing her journey by train.[49] Lovingheart was re-arrested but the whole case fell through when Maggie Stevenson steadfastly refused to identify Lovingheart as the abortionist. No charges appear to have been laid against Stevenson herself.[50]

Again in 1894, Lovingheart's name cropped up at an abortion trial. In May, one Fred Gibbs was arrested by S/Sgt. A. F. M. Brooke and charged with administering a noxious drug to a young girl named Ida Morton in an attempt to procure a miscarriage. At the trial in July, a sordid story unfolded of Gibbs' family life. His common-law wife, Alice Morton, had many years before left her legal husband and arranged that her daughter be raised by relatives in a respectable manner. Alice then led what was described in the press as a wild life under assumed names before taking up with Gibbs. Having achieved a degree of stability, Alice brought her daughter Ida to Calgary in 1890 to live in her house where Gibbs posed as a boarder. Not long after, the girl who was 16 years old, was seduced by her mother's lover. Gibbs forced the girl into a continuing sexual relationship, apparently through fear and guilt, which was kept secret from her mother. Finally, early in 1894, the girl became pregnant. Gibbs then obtained a bottle of noxious liquid which he said he got from Dr. Lovingheart to precipitate an abortion. He poured out the first dose and forced Ida to take the potion on a daily basis. He told her that if a miscarriage did not occur, Dr. Lovingheart had agreed to perform an abortion by operation for $50. However, Ida's mother became suspicious and the daughter confessed. The Mounted Police were called in and S/Sgt. Brooke ordered a chemical analysis of the contents of the bottle. It was found to contain in part "cantharides" which was believed to cause miscarriages. Gibbs was arrested.

Gibbs was represented by a well-known lawyer, J. P. Nolan, but curiously little defence was offered at his trial. No witnesses were called by the defence attorney, and Judge Rouleau, in addressing the jury, made much of the fact that Dr. Lovingheart was not called to the stand to deny that he supplied the noxious potion. The jury took less than an hour to find Gibbs guilty. Before sentencing, Gibbs made a long rambling statement claiming that the girl had wanted the abortion and that he had supplied her with what he thought was a harmless substance to prevent her from achieving her end through more drastic means. In sentencing Gibbs, Rouleau referred to the case as one of the most unpleasant he had presided over in 17 years on the bench. He commented that he had heard that abortion had become too common in Calgary and he intended to make an example of every case which came before him. Gibbs received nine years and six months in a penitentiary for the abortion charge and an additional six months for stealing a watch.[51]

As for Dr. Lovingheart, he managed to stay one step ahead of serious trouble with the law. On 4 May 1894, he was charged with practising medicine without a licence, appeared before Insp. Frank Harper the next day and was fined $25 and costs. He appealed the decision but lost. Later that fall he was again charged with attempting to procure an abortion and appeared before Judge Scott on the 23rd of November and won an acquittal.[52] Dr. Lovingheart/Professor Campbell left Calgary in a malodorous fashion in 1895. He apparently persuaded the parents of 14-year-old Anna Sterzinger to allow her to accompany him and his wife on a trip to the United States. When the trip was extended beyond the anticipated period, the parents contacted Calgary police. The girl had been allowed to write to her parents so she was known to be in Washington, D.C. Chief English contacted the police in that city who found the party in the back room of an isolated tenement. The girl told a lurid tale of Lovingheart's alternate threats to skin her alive and promises to buy her expensive presents,

accompanied by frequent attempts to kiss her. She was returned to her parents but there is no record of charges laid against Lovingheart. The *Calgary Herald* commented obliquely "the doings of the 'Professor' while a resident here are well-known to the citizens of Calgary".[53]

There were also several cases investigated where presumably unwanted infants died not long after birth. Of course, today's standard of obstetrical care was not available to frontier women. Isolated on farms and ranches, births unattended by a doctor or an experienced midwife were often risky affairs. Infanticide would be very difficult to prove if a newborn babe succumbed even under suspicious circumstances. If fact, during this entire period the Mounted Police only laid one charge of infanticide and they did not obtain a conviction. To cover this weakness in the justice system, the legislators had placed in the *Criminal Code* of 1892, section 240 which made suspicious circumstances of an infant death itself a crime. If a person disposed of a dead body of a child in a manner which intended to conceal that the birth had ever taken place, he or she was liable upon conviction to a sentence of up to two years in prison.[54] During this period, six charges were laid by the police for concealing the birth of a child and in all these instances convictions were obtained. Two other cases resulted in acquittals and dismissals and in one, the outcome is unknown. Examination of three of these six cases shows, however, that these convictions were not easily obtained.

In 1897, an unmarried woman in a farming community south of Regina gave birth to a child which died and was buried without the authorities being notified. However, the Mounted Police learned of the birth and investigated the circumstances. First, the body was exhumed and a coroner's inquest convened. The jury found that the baby had died due to the negligence of the infant's aunt who had attended the birth and that she had furthermore buried the child to conceal the fact that it had been born. The accused woman stoutly denied her involvement insisting that she had not even known that her sister was pregnant, a claim seemingly so preposterous that she was also charged with perjury. However, when the case came to trial a jury judged that neither charge was proven and she was acquitted.[55]

In 1897, a farmer near Moose Jaw was living in a sexual relationship with his step-daughter. Sgt. Hefferman of the Mounted Police suspected that a child had been born to the couple. He inquired and the woman admitted giving birth to a male child whose grave was then located. A coroner's inquest was convened and the medical evidence suggested that the child had been given a corrosive substance immediately after birth. Further, analysis of the corpse in a Winnipeg laboratory produced a noncommittal report to the effect that the child may or may not have been so poisoned. The child's mother and father were then charged with concealing the death of a child but, at a preliminary hearing, the charge against the father was dropped and the mother was committed to trial which was held on the 21st of June before Judge Hugh Richardson. In a surprising turnaround, the evidence at the trial incriminated the father rather than the mother. Accordingly, the charge against the latter was dropped and the father was subsequently charged, tried and convicted the same day. He was sentenced to one day in jail and fined $200.[56]

The third case was straightforward. The body of an infant was discovered at the bottom of a well in the Swedish community of Oblen near Whitewood in September 1900. The well was located on a farm last occupied by an Anna Palenguist whose husband had been away for five years. Sgt. McGinnis of the Mounted Police arrested Mrs. Palenguist and a coroner's inquest was held. At the hearing, medical evidence led to the conclusion that the child had died after being dropped into the well partly from the impact and partly from drowning. At a subsequent trial, Mrs. Palenguist was found guilty by Judge Wetmore of concealing the birth of her illegitimate child by throwing it into the well and sentenced to 23 months hard labour in Regina jail.[57]

In October 1897, Supt. J. Howe of Regina District commented in a report to the Commissioner that he was pleased that although two charges of rape had been made that month, neither had been proven. He observed:

> This Headquarters District being for some time free of this heinous crime it is to be hoped that as civilization advances in the North West this crime will grow less, as it only occurs when the brute nature of man predominates over his finer feelings.[58]

The circumstances of the two crimes to which Howe refers are unknown, but it is curious that he was so entirely satisfied that justice was served by the charges not being proven. It might be expected that a policeman's bias would be that if evidence was sufficient to warrant a charge he would be disappointed by the failure to convict. An explanation may lie with the very nature of the sexual offence. A woman may charge that she had been sexually assaulted but even if it was clear that a sexual act had taken place, a court had to be satisfied that she did not consent to it. In fact, one of the cases to which Howe may have been referring illustrates why policemen and courts at times were dubious about claims by women that they had been sexually assaulted. In 1897, at Oxbow, an unmarried woman whose obvious pregnancy provoked comment complained that she had been raped by a showman from a circus which had performed there earlier in the year. As the complaint was rather dilatory and as the circus grounds had been well patrolled by Mounted Policemen, her story was not believed. In fact, Sgt. J. Hynes in charge of the sub-district commented, "It was, of course, a story to cloak her real seducer."[59]

Between 1892 and 1900, there were about 62 cases of rape, attempted rape, or indecent assault which went to trial and which involved the Mounted Police at some stage in the legal process. Only about 30 per cent of these cases resulted in convictions;[60] not an impressive showing and well below the overall success rate for criminal proceedings involving the Force. Unfortunately, only incomplete data is available on a small number of these cases. This is not enough to draw any definitive conclusion about the low rate of convictions. However, what does exist tends to support the point made by other students of legal history that for conviction, the criminal justice system demanded strong incontrovertible evidence in addition to the word of a woman or a child that a sexual offence had occurred.[61]

In some cases the perpetrator was caught in the act and this made conviction easier to obtain. On 24 May 1899, a nine-year-old girl attending holiday festivities at the Calgary race track was indecently assaulted by a man. Her screams attracted the attention of her father and others who chased and caught the suspect. The case was open and shut and the man was sent to the Regina jail for two years.[62] Similarly, in 1901, a man named Whalen attacked a young woman riding a bicycle in broad daylight on a trail outside of Qu'Appelle. The lady strenuously resisted her attacker until he was forced to flee by the arrival of more travellers. The man was identified by the witnesses and was arrested the next day by the Mounted Police. Whalen was tried, convicted and sentenced to one year at hard labour in Regina jail and fined $300.[63]

However, in other cases where the outcome of the case rested on the evidence provided by the alleged victim, prosecutions were less successful. Consider the case of a Hungarian girl near Irvine, Alberta, who complained to police at Maple Creek in 1896 that she had been indecently attacked by a railway worker named Locklin Bruce. Insp. White-Fraser had little confidence in winning a conviction:

> As evidence in such a case, and especially from that nationality, would require corroboration, and it is always difficult to ascertain what encouragement has been given to the assaulter when the woman is the only witness.[64]

The Mounted Police overcame the difficulty in this case with a compromise. The man was offered the opportunity of a less formal summary trial before two police justices in return for a guilty plea. Bruce agreed, was convicted and paid a fine of $25 and costs.[65]

Where corroborative evidence did exist in cases of this nature it was the duty of the court to weigh it and this was far from an exact process. Sometimes examining the corroborator also involved probing the character of the accused, the alleged victim and even of witnesses. The previous chaste character of the woman complainant was considered particularly pertinent. Such was the case in Regina in 1895 when Katherine Legg, a young woman married only one month, accused Town Inspector Thomas Hiscox of indecent assault. Hiscox delivered a municipal notice to the home of Mrs. Legg and found her in bed. Legg contended that she was then assaulted by Hiscox who denied the charge saying he simply explained the notice and then left, the visit lasting about two minutes. The trial was before Judge Hugh Richardson in June.

The prosecutors produced a woman who testified that in similar circumstances the accused had made improper advances towards her. A man named Nixon said that he had been working near the Legg residence at the time of Hiscox's visit and had seen the window blind being drawn. Later this was discredited when Nixon admitted to having a grudge against Hiscox. The defence launched a telling blow against Legg's character by bringing to the stand a harness maker with a wooden leg who swore that he had had sexual relations with the woman before she was married and that she was an unreliable character. The mayor of Regina, Mr. Darke, came forward and testified as to the good character of the Inspector. Judge Richardson found for the accused and dismissed the charge.[66]

There was a tragic case in Lethbridge in 1901, the attempted rape of an eight-year-old girl, where again the corroborative evidence was judged too weak. The police were outraged at the decision because they were sure of their culprit. The little girl had been walking home from school on the 16th of January when she was viciously assaulted by a man near a brick yard. She gave a description to the Mounted Police that evening and a man newly arrived in town was quickly arrested. Four other witnesses were found who saw the accused in the area of the assault that day. Judge Rouleau ruled that this did not constitute corroboration.[67] It was very difficult to obtain a successful prosecution when the victim of a sexual assault was a child. Testimony and statements by children could be accepted as admissible by the court even if a child was too young to understand the nature of an oath. But to obtain a conviction, very strong corroborative evidence was required.[68]

Homosexual practices were banned by law and it appears that such behaviour remained very much in the closet. In this entire period, the Mounted Police were involved in the prosecution of only two cases where men were charged with homosexual offences. A very controversial case occurred in Regina in 1895 when Frank Hoskins, proprietor of the town's largest dry goods, grocery and liquor store was charged with "gross indecency with another male".[69] Also charged with the same offence were Basil Hume, a boy of 14 or 15 years from a respectable local family and William Macpherson, described as an unmarried man from Toronto. At the trials, evidence was presented in the form of the testimony of two boys who had watched the homosexual acts of the three through a basement window.[70] Curiously, though found guilty, the three were only bound over to keep the peace for six months and received fines: Hoskins – $200; Macpherson – $50; and, Hume – $20. Supt. Perry, then in charge of "Depot" Division reported that:

> This case caused a great deal of excitement in the town owing to the prominence of one of the defendants. The light sentences inflicted are attributed to a petition for leniency signed by the Mayor of Regina and a large number of leading citizens.[71]

The other case involved a man charged with sodomy in Edmonton in 1900. The man was found not of sound mind by Judge B. Rouleau and committed to Brandon Asylum.[72]

Another crime which received attention during this period was assault on a wife or child. As the magistrate's manual of the day pointed out, "An assault is none the less a breach of the peace because it is committed by a husband upon the person of his wife, and the wife is a competent person to make the complaint."[73] Records were found for eight cases involving the Mounted Police proceeding against a man for beating his wife.[74] In all of the cases the man was found guilty and six resulted in jail terms for periods ranging from eight days hard labour to twelve months hard labour. In the two other convictions, fines of $1 and $10 plus costs were levied.

In one case of child abuse, the North-West Mounted Policemen acted on an anonymous tip. Cpl. Hamilton at Saltcoats in 1900, arrested a man who had tried to persuade his daughter to work by hitting her across the shoulders with a stick and heaving a pitchfork at her. Brought before a civilian justice of the peace the man was found guilty (presumably of assault although the source did not specify) and fined $10 and costs.[75]

Commenting upon the chronic problem of theft of cattle and horses, Insp. McGinnis reported that ". . . it ought to be remembered that opportunity often suggests the crime".[76] Ranchers turned their cattle out to graze on the open prairie and would often only do an inventory once a year in an annual round-up. Similarly, horses were often allowed to roam in search of grass. Owners branded their animals and this offered some protection against many thieves, but bold ones took their chances and some more devious ones altered markings. Calves and colts born on the open prairie were prime candidates for theft if they could be taken before a rancher branded them. There was also a curious acceptance, almost complicity, in the thefts by the normally law-abiding populace of the western frontier. Many ranchers felt that it was wiser to accept the loss of a steer or horse now and again than to make formidable enemies by insisting that the police intervene. Even when caught, a thief would often escape punishment by offering financial compensation to his victim in return for dropping the charges. Similarly, juries were often more sympathetic to an accused who perhaps stole a head or two of cattle than to a wealthy rancher who had only a rough idea of how many cattle he had in his herd. These were problems that the Mounted Police faced and never really overcame in trying to police the ranching frontier. Where offenders were flagrant and persistent, as in organized gangs of stock thieves, they were energetically and often successfully opposed by the NWMP.

Understandably, stock thefts were a more pressing problem in areas where there were large concentrations of cattle and horses. In southern Alberta and the Calgary cattle ranching districts, cattle rustling was a common problem. Such crimes were usually carried out on a small scale but sometimes, particularly later in this period, organized gangs tried to make rustling a paying business. Southern Saskatchewan, particularly the Wood Mountain and Willow Bunch area, was invaded by gangs of horse thieves from Montana on a basis frequent enough to require increased Mounted Police attention to the district. The number of stock theft cases investigated in the NWT did not increase significantly until after the turn of the century, presumably due to the pressures of rising population.[77]

Marking cattle by burning a distinctive brand on the hides was practised by the larger ranchers throughout the Territories. It was an effective, but far from foolproof, means of identification. In the early years of the ranching frontier there were few problems because the larger ranchers were willing to respect each other's brands and to cooperate in the disposal of "maverick" unbranded offspring of range cattle whose ownership was not immediately apparent. However, this system of cooperative control began to break down in the mid-1890s when small ranchers and settlers with a few head of cattle began to turn their animals loose to share the range. It was soon apparent that some of these small proprietors were not above increasing their herds at the expense of the large ranchers and vice versa.

In 1897, Supt. R. B. Deane complained that the branding system had done him very little good in rendering justice to small time cattle rustlers in his district.[78] He cited the case of one William Morgan, who two years previously had come from Montana to the Milk River area, south of Lethbridge to start a ranch with 40 head of cattle. He attracted the attention of the Mounted Police because he was quarrelsome with his neighbours and because his herd increased too quickly. In little over one year, Morgan had eighty-nine cattle bearing his brand even though he had bought no new stock, apparently defying natural laws governing the rate of increase. Neighbours informed the police that Morgan's prosperity was due to his poaching unbranded stock off the range and adding them to his herd. The Mounted Police raided the ranch and found a supply of freshly cut beef. As he was required to do under a North-West Territorial Ordinance, Morgan produced the hide of the newly killed calf which bore his brand. However, under questioning, his hired man admitted that he had helped Morgan take the unbranded calf away from its mother which bore brand "W". Morgan's mark had not been applied to the calf's hide until after it was slaughtered. Inspecting Morgan's herd more closely, the police discovered an unbranded bull which proved to be the property of the Benton and St. Louis Cattle Company.

The trial heard by Judge B. Rouleau was most disheartening for the police. On the first charge of cattle killing, Rouleau put little faith in the testimony of the Crown's witnesses about the origins of the calf. According to Deane, Rouleau implied that the witnesses were as likely as Morgan to have rustled stock. Moreover, the judge was not impressed by the story of the calf's mother bearing the brand "W", especially when the police could not identify a ranch using such a brand. The case against Morgan was dismissed. On the other charge of stealing the unbranded bull, Rouleau found Morgan guilty but let him off on a suspended sentence. Deane observed that this lenient treatment would encourage others to imitate Morgan and indeed one local had already done so.[79] Comptroller White complained to E. J. Newcombe, Deputy Minister of Justice, that Morgan had been let go free.[80]

Until 1898, the fact that a brand was not accepted by the courts as *prima facie* evidence of ownership of the animal was a complication for both the police and the Crown in preparing a stock theft case for trial. In that year, the NWT enacted an ordinance accepting a brand as the basis of identifying ownership. That same year the brand gained legal status in the courts in the interesting case of *Regina v. Forsythe*.

Harry R. Forsythe was a NWMP constable and a cattle thief. In 1899, Forsythe applied to join the Mounted Police giving as relevant experience 13 months service in the U.S. Army in the war with Spain and 4 years on a cattle ranch in Arizona. His credentials also included recommendations from his Member of Parliament, Dr. Haley of Windsor, Nova Scotia and the cabinet member from Nova Scotia, Dr. F. W. Borden, Minister of Militia and

Defence. As a result, Clifford Sifton, the Minister of the Interior, who controlled much of NWMP patronage, instructed Fred White to engage Forsythe who was sworn in as a special constable at Regina on 24 April 1899; following two weeks of probation, he was converted to a constable for a five-year term of service.

In short order, Cst. Forsythe demonstrated that his experience as a cowboy in Arizona might not be all to the benefit of the Force. In November 1899, Forsythe was on town patrol in Maple Creek where part of his duty was to report on stock transactions so that irregularities could be spotted. Instead, on the 6th of November, he sold a cow bearing an indistinct brand to a local butcher for $32 when the market price would probably have brought $35. Naturally, this transaction was not recorded in Forsythe's report for this period. Then on November 17th by accident, as he claimed, or for some unknown purpose, Forsythe discharged his .38 calibre Smith & Wesson service revolver into the fleshy part of the calf of his right leg, grazing the large bone. He was treated and admitted to hospital at Maple Creek.

About December 6th, Special Constable D. Paterson reported Forsythe's sale of the cow to Insp. Frank Harper. Forsythe claimed that he had purchased the cow from a sheep rancher named Wallace, who had subsequently gone east. Insp. Harper reached Wallace by telegram and received in reply a denial that any transaction had taken place. Harper then obtained the hide from the butcher and hired an Indian woman to scrape it carefully on the inside, opposite where the brand had been applied on the outside. This method succeeded in bringing up clearly the brand "J" which was registered to John Lawrence, a prosperous rancher from Fish Creek. Moreover, Lawrence stated categorically that all his steers were shipped east when sold, so that any found in the western range belonged to him. Forsythe was now charged with cattle stealing.

The judicial system was slow in dealing with Forsythe because of his medical condition. What was considered a minor wound was slow to respond to treatment. Continued festering forced doctors to re-open the wound on five separate occasions, thus necessitating a longer stay in hospital. A guard was assigned to his room each night to ensure he did not escape. However, because Forsythe was in such a poor state of health the guards fell into the habit of sleeping the night through in a bed in the ward where the prisoner was kept. Each night the ward was visited several times by the night guard but he took little notice of Forsythe, being principally concerned that the fire in the stove was kept burning. On the night of 12 March 1900, Special Constable Mat Sandquist reported to the hospital about 9:35 p.m. to guard Forsythe and shortly after 10 p.m. was asleep. He was awakened about 6:10 a.m. by the night guard on his last round at which time it was discovered that Forsythe had disappeared.

Forsythe's escape was easy enough. At about 12:30 a.m. on the 13th, he walked out of the ward past his sleeping guard and headed for a small room under the stairway where he conveniently found a pair of police breeches and a cloak. After donning this apparel he left the hospital and walked the short distance to the building housing the Division "A" Office. Once more, he conveniently found it open and a bunch of keys laying on the table. Taking the proper key he opened the adjacent storage room from which he removed his personal clothing and lifted a Mounted Police fur hat and ripped off the badge. Thus clothed, Forsythe left the Mounted Police grounds and walked painfully into town, his progress slow on account of his injury. He hid out most of the day in a stable belonging to Jean Claustre and begged a box of crackers from Claustre's 14-year-old daughter. About 8 p.m. the girl warned him to move on. He walked out to the road and begged a ride from two half-breeds in a passing wagon which took him east along the railway line and dropped him during the day of March 15th near Colley, a section point on the CPR. Forsythe spent the rest of the day and the night near the track and early the next day he walked over to the CPR section house where he bought himself dinner and supper. That night he obtained a bed at a nearby ranch. In the morning, he walked to the railway track and hitched a ride further east with a passing hand car manned by railway workers who spoke little English. They let him off near a water tank at Bear Creek. In the early hours of the next morning two trains stopped for water but Forsythe did not attempt to steal a ride either because the train men knew he was there or because his leg was causing him a lot of pain. In any case, about 5 a.m. on March 17th, Special Constable Paterson, acting on instructions from the officer commanding at Maple Creek to watch for him at this likely boarding point, arrested Forsythe and returned him to Maple Creek.[81]

Forsythe was tried before Judge J. Scott at Maple Creek on the 25th and 26th of April 1900, and was found guilty of stealing cattle and sentenced to two years and eight months in prison.[82] The case was appealed to the Supreme Court of the NWT to decide the principal point at the initial trial, the judge's acceptance that the brand and ear marks were those of Lawrence and that he had not sold the steer. The majority of the Supreme Court upheld the original conviction, deciding that the brand system was reasonable evidence of ownership if the trial judge was satisfied with the circumstances attendant to the case. However, Judge

J. Rouleau dissented from this verdict, contending that it was common practice in the West for some men to put their brands on cattle which belonged to others but had not yet been branded. He said it was, thus, a dangerous precedent to declare that because a man's brand was found on a steer that the steer belonged to that man. Nevertheless, in 1901, Parliament passed an amendment to the *Criminal Code of Canada* making the brand a *prima facie* proof of ownership and throwing upon the accused in a cattle theft trial the burden of proving that he came into lawful possession of an animal bearing another man's brand.[83]

The precedent established in the Forsythe case which worried Rouleau was cause for concern. For many years the big western ranchers cooperated through regional stock associations. One of their principal annual activities was the common round-up in which the big ranchers collected their cattle each year from winter grazing grounds, branding new-born calves. Any unbranded cow or calf whose ownership was not obvious was sold by the round-up crew and proceeds went to pay their expenses. This system worked well in the early days when all the ranchers belonged to the associations and participated in the round-ups. However, the arrival of small ranchers and settlers with a few head of cattle, often unbranded, who did not join the associations complicated matters. Unfortunately, the big ranchers refused at first to acknowledge that the situation had changed.

As early as 1895, Judge Rouleau had warned the stock associations about their branding practices. Evidence was presented in a case, *Rex vs. McHugh*, that the High River Stock Association routinely took and sold all unbranded cattle found west of the Blackfoot trail and south of the Bow River. Rouleau warned that the ranchers could not create laws to suit themselves and that he would severely punish such a practice if a complaint was placed before him. This was the one aspect of the Forsythe case that worried Rouleau and, in fact, it was tested soon thereafter. During the 1903 spring round-ups, the Medicine Hat Stock Association collected a herd of unbranded cattle, one of which was claimed by one Sam Herman, a non-member of the association. The captain of the round-up, a Mr. Crawford, paid no attention to Herman and sold his steer with the others and used the money to pay round-up expenses. Herman laid a complaint with the Mounted Police and a charge was brought against Crawford for theft. The case was tried before Chief Justice A. L. Sifton at Medicine Hat on the 20th of November. The defence admitted that taking the steer was wrong, but argued that no felony was intended because Crawford simply followed the round-up practice which had been in place for 30 years. The lawyer even stated that unbranded cattle should not be allowed to roam on the prairie. Sifton disagreed. Crawford was found guilty but received only a suspended sentence because he was clearly a pawn in an illegal system which he did not create. Herman's steer was ordered to be recovered and returned to him. Judge Sifton answered at least part of Rouleau's objection in the Forsythe case that the brand would be the pre-eminent means of identifying ownership. Unbranded cattle were free to roam the prairies and their owners would be protected by the law.[84]

The petty pilfering of Forsythe and the disdainful larceny of the big ranchers does not fit the popular conception of cattle rustling on the western frontier. Surprisingly, however, there were tough, dangerous men, at home on the range, who singly or in gangs led criminal lives based on stock theft. These men were feared by law-abiding settlers and respected by the police as worthy opponents.[85] Such men were successful for a time because it was so difficult to guard against stock theft on the open range and because they were not afraid to threaten or employ violence when the occasion demanded it. In fact, some of these men became minor legends in their own time, making it difficult for an historian to separate fact from fiction even in normally coldly factual police reports. Hyperbole was commonplace in describing the exploits of these outlaws.

Perhaps the most notorious gang of stock thieves in this era was the Nelson-Jones gang. This so-called "gang" was a loose alliance of about a half-dozen men with cowboy experience who seized opportunities to profit from theft of cattle or horses. These men operated mainly in Montana and North Dakota where they frustrated the efforts of individual lawmen to bring them to justice. They also used the Canadian border to advantage, seeking refuge across the line from pursuit and committing the odd crime in this country as well. The region they chose to operate in was conducive to their efforts. The topography was irregular with hills, ridges and ravines affording excellent concealment. The population on the Canadian side around Willow Bunch (of then Assiniboia, later Saskatchewan) was mostly mixed blood, originally from the Red River settlement who moved into the area subsequent to the events of 1870. The community was close-knit and given to communicating to police as much misinformation as information about the activities of the American outlaws whose depredations it feared. Evidently this anxiety at one point communicated itself to the Mounted Police, temporarily paralysing their efforts to effectively police the area.

The first time Dutch Henry Leuch (aka Teuch and Geuch) appeared in NWMP records was in a notice from a Montana lawman, George Dunnell, that Dutch Henry, under arrest for cattle theft, had escaped from custody in Culbertson, Montana and was believed headed across the border for Willow Bunch. His description was given as standing 5'6", 150 lbs., blue eyes, small moustache, 26 years old, a cowboy but well-dressed, several gold-filled teeth and speaking English with a strong German accent.[86] Sgt. John Foster Stewart of the Wood Mountain detachment met Stock Insp. George Dunnell of the Montana Stock Association and together with a local rancher, Pascal Bonneau, set out to track down Dutch Henry. After two days, on 30 January 1898, the trio came upon Dutch Henry six miles south of the border.[87] The man described by the *Regina Leader* as "one of the most daring cow thieves Montana has ever known" was called upon to surrender. He was reported as having said: "All right boys two days ago my tent caught fire and I lost my outfit, gun and all, or you would not have taken me so easily."[88] Dutch Henry was taken into custody by Dunnell, but American authorities failed to obtain a conviction at a subsequent trial.[89]

By 1902, the Mounted Police were thoroughly alarmed by reports of wholesale stock theft and smuggling in the Big Muddy district. Patrols were despatched to investigate and a detachment was established at Big Muddy. This increased police activity resulted in the capture of John and William Martin, a father and son team of thieves in possession of stolen horses; on conviction they received seven and four years respectively in prison. Also netted at Willow Bunch were a pair of Canadian horse thieves, François Gosselin and Joseph-Napoleon Hamelin, who received prison terms of eighteen and twenty months respectively after conviction on four charges of stock theft.[90] However, the principal object of police concern continued to elude capture. This was a gang of American thieves consisting of Dutch Henry, Frank Carlyle, a former member of the NWMP, two men actively sought by U.S. lawmen named Nelson and Jones and several others. Reports were received throughout the year that these men were stealing cattle and horses in the United States and disposing of them in Canada. Those who encountered these men on the prairie were warned away at gunpoint. Some residents of Big Muddy were suspected of collusion by purchasing this stolen stock.[91] In September 1902, three masked men held up Alexander McGillis near Willow Bunch taking his horse and his money; suspicion pointed to members of the Dutch Henry-Jones gang. These events created great unrest among residents of Big Muddy and Willow Bunch who lived in fear of further depredations from these desperadoes. This anxiety escalated considerably after 24 November 1902, due to a desperate deed of

a morose Mounted Policeman, Cst. L. P. Lachapelle.[92]

A little after 9 p.m. on 24 November 1902, a 24-year-old constable named Leon Lachapelle with less than one year's service in the Force, staggered into the detachment at Willow Bunch with gunshot wounds in his left arm and his left thigh. His cry for help brought forth S/Sgt. M. Hayne from the detachment building. Putting his rudimentary knowledge of medicine to good use Hayne dressed the wounds with strips from bed sheets and placed the constable in bed. In answer to his questions, Lachapelle stated that he had been returning from a visit at the Bonneau ranch when he was accosted by two strangers on the trail who gunned him down without warning. Lachapelle lay still on the ground where he fell and escaped further injury by feigning death. Shortly after the men left, he heard the sound of horses galloping in the vicinity of the detachment. S/Sgt. Hayne checked the stable and found that the two police horses had been turned loose and driven away and their equipment damaged, presumably to impede pursuit. Later, it was found that the descriptions given by Lachapelle of his assailants matched those being circulated of two of the men implicated in the McGillis hold-up who were believed to be Dutch Henry and Frank Carlyle.

Word of this incident spread quickly in the Big Muddy area and a mood of excitement, verging on hysteria, spread throughout the community. The first intimation of this came to Hayne when he tried to summon a neighbour to help treat Lachapelle and the man, aware of the commotion, refused to answer the door. The next day Hayne tried to hire a man to deliver a message to Wood Mountain concerning the attack, but was refused by many who were afraid to leave their homes while outlaws were at large. He finally convinced a man named Massi to go if Hayne provided the horse, the saddle and $5 a day. Massi reached Wood Mountain without incident, bringing the alarm to Insp. Henri LaRocque who notified Headquarters in Regina of the incident. The next morning, November 26th, LaRocque set off with a small party of men for Willow Bunch. Upon his arrival there in the late afternoon, reports were received that the desperadoes were still threatening the community. A Mr. Heaton claimed that he had been fired upon by an unseen person in a nearby coulee late in the afternoon of the 25th. Another resident, Louis Gaudry, said that on the night of the 25th, three men had been lurking near his corral and that he had driven them off with rifle shots. Thoroughly alarmed, LaRocque sent word of this outbreak of lawlessness back to Regina.

Comm. Perry was not impressed by the excitable reports he was receiving from LaRocque, an officer who had graduated from RMC, but was virtually untrained in police work, and who had served to-date only one year in the Mounted Police. He sent Insp. Moodie and another small party out to Willow Bunch, and they arrived there on the 30th of November. Moodie soon discovered that the only imminent danger in Big Muddy country was the hysterical state of the populace which also infected LaRocque and his men. He reported to Regina:

> When I arrived here the place might have been in a state of siege. Insp. LaRocque [sic] was here with his men and everyone turned out to meet us and all armed. Even in the house revolvers were not laid aside. The whole country appeared to be in a state of panic . . . Insp. LaRocque [sic] firmly believes that his life is in danger on account of his being mixed-up with the sending in of the seized horses. He has been told by the breeds here, many of whom appear to think that it is fact . . . there has been such an amount of talking done about the dangerous men in the country that no deed is considered too desperate for these men.[93]

LaRocque returned to Wood Mountain and Moodie methodically began to investigate the alleged incidents. He quickly discovered that no attempted ambush had occurred involving Heaton. This man now said that he had told Insp. LaRocque that he had heard shots fired in the coulee on the 25th, and his son had joked that perhaps he ought to look for bullet holes in his clothing. Heaton had never intended to report an attempt on his life, in fact, he believed the shots emanated from a .22 calibre rifle in the hands of someone hunting rabbits or prairie chickens. Likewise, Louis Gaudry's story became more vague and when questioned more closely he was not entirely sure what he saw that night at his corral. On checking further Moodie found that:

> Gaudry's brother says he would not be surprised if he fired at his own horses and never saw a man at all. All the breeds around Willow Bunch were in a state of panic and this man Gaudry has the reputation of even in ordinary times, seeing all sorts of ghosts and goblins in the dark.[94]

Moodie then turned a critical eye on Cst. Lachapelle and his story. There was no doubt that the constable was a very unhappy young man. Lachapelle joined the NWMP at his home city of Montreal on 11 November 1901 and shortly thereafter, was sent to Regina. This was a time when there was considerable pressure of work on the Force with the demands of the Klondike, South Africa as well as the rapid settlement of the prairies. Some policemen were assigned to duty with little training and Cst. Lachapelle appears to have been one of them. In March 1902, while attending to a prisoner in Regina he, under great provocation, struck the man. Brought up before Supt. W. S. Morris for this offence, he was fined a token $1 because, while he had to be reminded not to take the law into his own hands, he had also never

received a lecture on police duties. Shortly thereafter, Lachapelle was granted compassionate leave because of the serious illness of his mother who subsequently died. Lachapelle sought and was granted extensions of his leave for a period of over two months until it became very clear that he did not want to return to the Force. On his behalf, his father appealed to Prime Minister Laurier, a personal friend, for a free discharge. Laurier replied that this was not permitted and regulations required discharge by purchase, in Lachapelle's case at a cost of $165. Lachapelle reluctantly returned to Regina on 24 May 1902, only after being warned that failure to do so would result in one year imprisonment at hard labour in a Montreal jail.

Lachapelle was posted to Willow Bunch in June 1902, but things did not improve for him. He confessed to acquaintances there that he was very lonely and that he felt like shooting himself. On the 13th of November the local priest laid a complaint against Lachapelle for misconduct and neglect of duty and the constable knew that this incident was about to be investigated. After the shooting, Lachapelle remarked to S/Sgt. Hayne to the effect that his "father had refused to let him go home, but supposed he would take him home now".[95]

Studying the actual circumstances of the shooting, Moodie was not satisfied that Lachapelle was telling the truth. For one thing, the wounds he bore were made by a light calibre revolver, probably a .32. Lachapelle had such a weapon which had been recently discharged and five bullets were missing from his cartridge box. The idea that Dutch Henry or Carlyle would use such a weapon was almost ludicrous: "Men such as those first suspected do not carry such toys". Moreover, the paths of the two bullets through Lachapelle's body were completely at odds with the alleged positions of the assailants. The wound in the arm could have been inflicted by another person only if the man reached over Lachapelle's shoulder and fired down into his arm. It was also strange that Lachapelle's cries for help were clearly heard by a neighbour, Louis Dumais, but the sounds of the horses galloping away were not. Moodie also found it hard to believe that experienced men bent on murder would botch the job so completely. Yet, Lachapelle vehemently denied that he had shot himself and stuck to his basic story, though the details sometimes changed in retelling.

A curious tangent to this story was the reaction of Frank Carlyle to the rumours that he and his friends were sought by the Mounties for shooting Lachapelle. Carlyle rode to the detachment at Big Muddy and asked the constable there, Pitt Waller, to write a letter to Insp. LaRocque attesting that he, Waller, could account for the whereabouts of Carlyle and his friends at the time of the shooting of Lachapelle. Waller complied and alibis were duly established. However, Carlyle picked a weak reed to support his case. Waller was drinking heavily and suffering from paranoia. He believed that Carlyle's request was a threat on his life and he wrote the letter under delusion of compulsion, not even reasoning whether the information he imparted was true. When Moodie brought him to Willow Bunch for questioning a few days later, Waller fell apart, confessing his fear for his life and his involuntary support for the alibis. This temporarily clouded the issue for Moodie until further investigation revealed that the alibis did indeed stand up and that Carlyle and his friends were not near Willow Bunch when Lachapelle was shot.

The Lachapelle incident was an example of a sort of local community hysteria flowing from an exaggerated anxiety concerning the danger from a few criminals. Instead of dealing with the problem, a few misfit policemen actually fuelled fear, both by accident and design. These men were soon out of the NWMP. Lachapelle, although he steadfastly denied it, most likely shot himself in a desperate attempt to escape his unhappy situation. Unfortunately, he paid a high price for his release from the Mounted Police since the gunshot wound in his leg led to partial paralysis and disability. On 28 April 1903, he was discharged from the Force on medical grounds. The troubled Pitt Waller ended his mostly commendable 18-year career in the Mounted Police in an inglorious fashion at Big Muddy. On 23 February 1903, he rode to the ranch of ex-Mounted Policeman Jim Marshall where Dutch Henry and his friends sometimes stayed, left his service shotgun and continued on across the border. Explaining his desertion later in a letter to S/Sgt. Hilliard, Waller said that "he was sick of the outfit".[96] However, a fellow constable reported that Waller had been abusing drugs of late. Insp. LaRocque did not develop into an effective police officer and resigned his commission as of 1 April 1904.[97] Although the problem of stock thefts in this area of southern Saskatchewan continued for a number of years, better policemen never again allowed the situation to get out of hand.

The days of the Dutch Henry-Jones gang were numbered by 1903 as their notorious actions attracted more attention from police on both sides of the border. In late September 1903, Insp. Strickland, now Officer Commanding Wood Mountain subdistrict, received a report that Jones, Nelson, Carlyle and Dutch Henry had kidnapped a rancher on the United States side of the border because he had informed local police of a theft of his effects by members of the gang. Strickland sent out a patrol in case the party tried to cross the border but they did not do so. The gang members held the rancher, a man named King, for 12 days. He was apparently forced to perform chores for the gang

and was threatened with death. After his release he reported his ordeal to the authorities and the State of Montana offered a reward of $400 each for the capture of the outlaws. In October 1903, Insp. Strickland received a report that another American settler had been shot and killed about one mile south of the line and that Nelson was being sought for the crime.[98]

The gang began to break up in 1904. The most spectacular incident involved a showdown with Fred Jones. In February 1904, Sheriff Harry Casner of Glasgow, Montana reported to the Mounted Police in Regina that two of his deputies had shot Fred Jones dead. His men surprised Jones on the trail from Wood Mountain about 20 miles south of the border. Casner said that "when he was called on to throw up his hands and surrender, he jumped to his feet and tried to get his gun, but was not quick enough".[99] The sheriff was determined to round up the remaining members of the gang against whom he had clear cases of grand larceny. After Jones was killed, Nelson surrendered to American authorities and another gang member named Reid was captured by Cpl. Bird of Big Muddy Detachment and turned over to the Americans. Both of these men were acquitted and thereafter apparently gave up the life of crime.[100] In 1905, Frank Carlyle was reported in Montana state prison for trying to pass counterfeit coins.[101]

The last episode of this gang's activities in Canada involved Dutch Henry Leuch and Edward Shufelt. In 1903, Joe and Pascal Bonneau, Willow Bunch ranchers, hired Dutch Henry to buy horses for them in Montana, giving him $5,500 for this purpose. The Bonneau brothers trust was seriously misplaced. Dutch Henry bought the horses, about 100 head, but cut the Bonneau's out of the deal. Instead, a fellow gang member, Edward Shufelt, ran them into Canada through Big Muddy and offered them for sale. The Mounties picked up Shufelt in October 1904 and he came to trial in Regina in June 1905. The trial was complicated by the problem of sorting out who was acting for whom in the deal, to which was added the difficulty of securing witnesses from both sides of the border. A mistrial occurred when the jury could not agree on a verdict. However, at a second proceeding the jury convicted Shufelt of bringing stolen property into Canada, and he was sentenced to five years in prison.[102]

Dutch Henry was not brought to justice with Shufelt but the fates soon caught up with him. In 1905, Dutch Henry was shot and killed by a friend, Alexander McKenzie, in Roseau County, Minnesota.[103] McKenzie, the son of a former member of the legislature of Prince Edward Island, was convicted of murder and sentenced to life in prison. There was a flurry of excitement in 1910 over an erroneous press report that Dutch Henry had been killed in a gun battle with a Mounted Policeman south of Moose Jaw. The Lieutenant-Governor of P.E.I. petitioned the federal Minister of Justice to investigate with a view to securing a pardon for Alexander McKenzie if it turned out that Dutch Henry had indeed been alive the past several years. However, Asst. Comm. J. H. McIllrcc quickly squashed these hopes with a telegram to the Comptroller which read "no foundation whatever for report about Dutch Henry".[104]

There were a number of other stock thieves operating along the border in this period who were able to use the international divide to their, at least temporary, advantage. Although American law enforcement officials usually cooperated with the NWMP in rounding up suspects, a Mounted Policeman in pursuit of a criminal across the border faced many difficulties. These are illustrated by a case in March 1899 when Sgt. G. W. Byrne tracked a cattle thief Frank Webber to Culbertson, Montana. Byrne tried to keep his identity secret, posing as a cattle merchant, because he had been warned not to trust the local sheriff and his deputy. However, the guise did not work, perhaps because of his association with State Stock Inspector Harry Lund, and Byrne soon had cause to believe Webber was part of a gang which was determined to protect him. Byrne described the situation which he and Lund met in Culbertson as follows:

> The Town of Culbertson consists of two stores, two gambling saloons, one boarding house and a couple of houses of ill fame. There are about 20 cowboys or horse thieves and gamblers who take turns to watch our every movement and immediately when one of us leaves the town scouts are sent in all directions to give the alarm.[105]

Byrne also suspected the postmaster of opening mail. The leader of the local gang operated the only boarding house, and Byrne stayed there despite his suspicions that gang members were trying to manoeuvre him into a room either to assault or murder him.

Even if Byrne exaggerated the danger, his account of the complications which arose when his suspect was finally cornered rings true. Frank Webber was apprehended by the sheriff at Fort Benton who took him to Glasgow where he was advised by a learned magistrate on extradition procedure. This gentleman, after consulting his books for three hours, took the strict interpretation that Webber should not even have been arrested until a formal approach had been made to the U.S. government through the British government. The prisoner simplified matters by readily agreeing to waive his rights under the treaty. However, another problem immediately arose because the American peace officers were unwilling to escort Webber to the border and Sgt. Byrne had no authority to take the prison-

er in custody on U.S. soil. This was resolved when ex-Stock Inspector George Dunnell persuaded the sheriff to appoint him a deputy for the occasion to act as escort. Dunnell volunteered because he wished to repay the Mounted Police for similar assistance that they had provided in the past, probably referring to the capture of Dutch Henry Leuch the previous year. Dunnell, Byrne and Webber took an express train for the border to avoid a stop in Culbertson where Webber's gang lurked. Byrne claimed that this was a wise decision because the gang did meet the local train with the intention of freeing the prisoner.[106]

Webber was tried in Moosomin, NWT and convicted on two charges of cattle theft. He was sentenced to five years in penitentiary on each count, the sentences to run concurrently. The Mounted Police claimed Webber's imprisonment "taught a great lesson to the rest of the gang 'across' the line".[107]

Perhaps Webber's gang took the message of Mounted Police persistence to heart, but others did not, including one Sam Larson. Larson lived for several years near the border spending time in Medicine Hat, NWT and Fort Benton, Montana. He usually employed the surname Larson but was known at various times as Sam, Fred and George and bore the nickname the "Buckskin Kid".[108] He was convicted of theft in Medicine Hat in December 1897 and spent one month hard labour in the Mounted Police guardroom. Soon after his release, rumours suggested that he was involved in stock thefts and opium smuggling, but no charges were brought against him.[109] Not until the fall of 1901 did the Mounted Police manage to corral Larson.

In September 1901, S/Sgt. Charles Allen discovered that Larson had, in the several weeks previously, been importing bunches of horses into Canada from Montana without paying customs duty. Moreover, Allen suspected that the horses had been stolen in the U.S. An investigation revealed that the horses were left with Sam's brother Henry who operated a ranch on the Canadian side and with another rancher who appeared to be in league with the Larson boys. The horses were seized and Allen formed a patrol to search for Larson. The division was shorthanded because a number of men were serving as an escort for their Royal Highnesses the Duke and Duchess of Cornwall and York, on a tour of western Canada. Allen collected a constable and supplemented his force with the customs officer, a Mr. Walters, and several scouts in his employ who were sworn in as special constables. Keeping an eye on the two ranchers he frequented, the patrol spotted Larson twice on October 1st but he eluded capture on both occasions. At one a.m. on October 2nd, Cst. Baker and one of the customs scouts ran into Larson about seven miles west of Medicine Hat and were fired upon, the suspect again making his escape. Later that morning relief came in the form of Insp. Montague Baker with a party of eight men from Calgary. Insp. Baker did not have long to wait to close in on Larson. On October 3rd one of the scouts reported that a heavily armed Larson was held up at his brother's ranch and refused to surrender. That night Insp. Baker went to the house where some very frightened women begged him not to fire on the building. The house being in darkness, Baker searched it with the aid of his portable electric light and found Larson hiding under a bed armed with a rifle, a bowie knife and an axe. Baker shoved the brilliant light in Larson's eyes temporarily blinding him and, closely covering him with his revolver, forced him to surrender.

When Larson was in custody, the Mounted Police could initially only charge him with evading customs, but went to work on finding a more serious charge to lay. The sheriff at Fort Benton, Montana, was contacted and he held a warrant for Larson's arrest for shooting with intent to kill. When Larson went to trial on October 9th, a lawman, Mr. Crawford, from Fort Benton sat in court awaiting an opportunity to execute his warrant. Sam Larson was convicted of evading customs and sentenced to forfeit his horses and pay a $50 fine or serve 30 days hard labour in the Maple Creek guardroom. Fearful of the American warrant, Larson chose jail.

At first, the Mounted Police were pleased by Larson's incarceration. They were sure that his horses were stolen and wanted the chance to prove it by extending their investigation to the United States. Their efforts proved successful but before they could bring Larson to justice on the new charges, he foiled the police by escaping from jail. At 6 p.m. on the 20th of October, Larson was assigned to empty buckets kept in the cells for toilet purposes. Taking advantage of an inattentive guard, Cst. Bleakney, Larson took off into the cold evening in stockinged feet and no coat. Bleakney fired several shots into the air to induce the prisoner to stop but to no effect. The shots gave the alarm but the initial pursuit proved futile. It was later learned that Larson had crossed a nearby creek and stowed away on a train which had stopped to take on coal. Search parties picked up his trail from a sheep herder who complained that someone had stolen his boots and blankets and from a settler who had lost a horse on October 25th. By this time Larson was over the border. His guard, Cst. Bleakney, was soon in his own cell serving one month hard labour for ignoring specific instructions from Supt. Moffatt that Larson be attached to a ball chain when not locked up. Larson turned out to be just running into the arms of more serious

trouble in Montana. On 15 April 1902, Moffatt, at Maple Creek, received a letter from the undersheriff Crawford at Fort Benton, to the effect Sam Larson had been shot and killed by Deputy Sheriff Martin of Gilt Edge, Montana on January 23rd. Larson had been using the alias Bud Tyler but Crawford and another man, A. P. Gill who knew Larson well, viewed the body and affirmed his correct identity.[110]

Another notorious stock thief who, for several years, bedeviled the police on both sides of the border was one Percy De Wolfe, originally from Kentville, Nova Scotia. However, in 1901, the Mounted Police and Montana authorities cooperated to ensure that De Wolfe's thievery was finally stopped. In October 1900, Percy De Wolfe, assisted by Frank Smith, stole about 40 horses from a Mr. Lindquist in southern Alberta and drove them into Montana. The thieves were detected by a U.S. Customs agent who informed the Mounted Police. Supt. R. B. Deane arranged to have the suspects apprehended through the Montana Stock Growers' Association and the Cascade County Attorney. This time, instead of being returned to Canada, both men were tried in Great Falls, Montana on charges of importing stolen horses into the United States. Deane played a large part in building the case against the accused, ensuring the presence of witnesses from Canada and attending the trials himself. The two men were convicted; Smith was given a lighter sentence of one year in penitentiary while De Wolfe received ten years. On hearing his sentence De Wolfe made a dramatic suicide attempt by swallowing potassium cyanide, but was thwarted by a stomach pump.[111] The Mounted Police were very grateful that Montana officials had secured the conviction of these men.

The prosecution of these cases threw considerable expense upon the State of Montana, but the United States authorities generally expressed their pleasure in being able to contribute so materially to the maintenance of law and order along the International Boundary Line.[112]

Deane noted later in his memoirs that De Wolfe escaped the full brunt of punishment due to the efforts of a wealthy foster father who successfully campaigned to have him released from prison after serving only four years.[113]

Farther into the interior of the NWT, the border was not available to the prospective cattle rustler or horse thief as a convenient escape hatch. Hence, the only option for the thief was to either dispose of the stolen goods quickly and covertly in Canada or to try to hide them in some manner. Caught in the act of stock theft were both ambitious criminals trying to grab a herd and petty larcenists content with taking one at a time.

One of the cleverest cattle stealing operations was run by a Calgary area man, Adam Dagleish. In the fall of 1894, he shipped two carloads of horses to Prince Albert to a local man named Edward McBeth. McBeth then traded these horses for cattle in the district. This legitimate business was, however, only a cover for the theft of cattle and local ranchers began missing stock. Suspicion fell on McBeth when a local settler found one of his missing cows among stock being shipped to Calgary. The Mounted Police in Calgary were alerted and the connection made between Dagleish and McBeth. In the subsequent investigation, S/Sgt. A. F. M. Brooke discovered that Dagleish had been selling the stolen stock locally for a very good profit. However, Dagleish got wind of the investigation and financed McBeth's rapid departure from the scene. Undeterred, Brooke tracked McBeth to his hiding place at Kildonan near Winnipeg and had him arrested by Chief McCrea of the Winnipeg police and returned to Prince Albert. This accomplished, Brooke rounded up Dagleish, a suspected accomplice and 22 of the 30 stolen cattle. Luckily, the evidence against them was bolstered by two incriminating letters found in McBeth's possession. Judge McGuire and a Prince Albert jury convicted the pair after a trial in April 1895 which lasted 11 days and heard 26 witnesses. McBeth was sentenced to three years in prison for cattle theft and Dagleish received one year for receiving stolen goods. There was insufficient evidence to convict the suspected accomplice.[114]

A most brazen case of cattle theft in the Calgary area involved a colourful character named Carl Schultz who arrived in the district about 1898 via the U.S. and Argentina. Shultz was a self-proclaimed expert on cattle raising and demonstrated his knowledge with articles of advice to ranchers in Calgary newspapers. He successfully solicited financial support for a ranch near Calgary and sought investment in a meat-packing establishment he hoped to build. For his cattle, he spurned the open range and instead, erected fences to keep them from wandering. However, when in 1902 two steers bearing another brand were found on Shultz's land bearing his brand as well, suspicion was aroused that his fences may have been intended to keep strangers out rather than cattle in. Cpl. Zachariah McIlmoyle of the Mounted Police investigated and discovered that Shultz's success in managing his herd was aided considerably by increases due to theft. Charges were laid and after a preliminary hearing Shultz was committed to trial and freed on bail of $2,000. He promptly skipped town and was believed to have returned to Argentina much to the dismay of a portion of the Calgary populace who

had refused to believe the accusations against this guru of the range.[115]

Also in the interior was practised the act of theft referred to as "here a steer, there a steer". It was not difficult to pinch a cow from the open range and one can reasonably surmise most thefts went undetected. Some information about the process is available from those who were caught either because they were unlucky or they failed to exercise a modicum of discretion. A favourite procedure was to pinch a cow, slaughter and quickly destroy the hide bearing the owner's brand, and consume the beef or dispose of it for profit. Sometimes, however, there was a hitch in the proceedings. In 1900, in Battleford District, David Whitford and William Ducharme grabbed and slaughtered someone else's calf. To dispose of the evidence of their crime they buried the hide under water in a creek bed. Unfortunately for them, their operation was observed by a witness who notified police. Upon conviction, one received one year in prison at hard labour and the other nine months.[116] They were unlucky and possibly indiscreet. As has been emphasized here stock thefts were frequent because opportunities abounded in the West. Moreover, even otherwise law-abiding people were tempted by what was widely held to be not a serious matter on a small scale. Police found such investigations difficult and they frequently ended in failure.

Aside from incidents of violence already discussed in terms of activities of tramps and murderers, thefts other than of stock were mostly petty affairs in the NWT during this period. Crimes categorized as offences against property included frauds, burglaries and receiving stolen goods. But, always a high percentage of these offences were simple thefts. Instances of these increased considerably as population grew. In 1892, there were 67 offences against property brought to trial by the NWMP with a conviction rate of 47.76 per cent. By 1895, the number of offences had almost doubled with the conviction rate remaining close at 45.9 per cent. Little change occurred in the number of cases or convictions thereafter until the first years of the twentieth century when a rapidly increasing population was accompanied by a considerable increase in petty thefts.[117] There were, however, no banks or trains or stagecoaches robbed during these years.

Some of the easiest larcenies occurred at commercial establishments or post offices where security was lax. In October 1892, two men broke into the Queen's Hotel in Edmonton by simply scraping away the putty from around the glass in a window and removing the pane. They then lifted two valises containing a total of 500 cigars. Sgt. Dunning of the Mounted Police nabbed them with the goods while they were waiting for a train at the station. They were committed for trial but the outcome is unknown.[118] In September 1901, someone forced the back door of the post office at Strathcona and helped himself to $800, a simple matter since there was no safe in the office. No record was found to indicate that the culprit was ever tracked down by police.[119] Greed tripped up another thief at Whitewood in 1901. The manager of the Hudson's Bay Company store reported to the NWMP that someone had, on several occasions, removed small sums of money from the till during the night. Cpl. Quinn laid in wait several nights in succession until he caught the thief in the act, a local man named Fisher. He was tried and convicted of the theft and sentenced to one year hard labour in Regina jail.[120]

A number of theft cases involved a betrayal of public trust. One of the most sensational cases was the defalcation of Percy Neale, the federal sub-collector of customs at St. Mary's, Alberta and a former Superintendent in the NWMP. At the end of August 1894, Neale misappropriated $6,000 in customs fees and crossed the border. When the Customs Services discovered his departure, an official notified the NWMP and S/Sgt. A. F. M. Brooke crossed over into the U.S. in pursuit on September 13th. Brooke tried to follow Neale's trail through Fort Benton, Montana to Chicago, Illinois but to no avail. Meanwhile, the police in Neale's native England were alerted and this led to his arrest in London. Neale was returned to Regina where he was tried for theft in November 1894, convicted and sentenced to seven years in Stony Mountain prison.[121] The *Edmonton Bulletin* in reporting on the trial, reflected on some of the ironical circumstances of Neale's position. He was tried and sentenced by an old friend, Judge Hugh Richardson. The warden of Stony Mountain prison, A. G. Irvine, had been a fellow officer in the NWMP. On his way to prison Neale lodged overnight at the Leland Hotel in Winnipeg and he and his police escort were registered as "Sgt. Green and friend".[122] After his release from prison, Neale moved to Winnipeg and took a part-time job with the city engineer's department. On the night of 31 January 1906, Neale was talking to friends in the same Leland Hotel when he suddenly took a fit. He died the next day in hospital of a brain haemorrhage.[123]

In another no less spectacular case of breach of public trust, the Mounted Police successfully pursued Daniel Campbell, a Member of the Legislative Assembly for Whitewood, NWT. In 1893, Campbell, who was also the local post-master, absconded across the line with funds not belonging to him. He was charged with embezzling money from the Whitewood Agricultural Society and with forging a money order, all to the sum of about $2,500. Insp. C. Constantine followed him into the United States on the suspicion that Campbell would go to Chicago where his brother-in-law,

John McTafferty lived. The Inspector interviewed McTafferty but failed to locate his man. As a precaution, Constantine swore out a warrant in Chicago for the arrest of Campbell which the local police promised to execute if he showed up. This action eventually paid off as the Chicago police arrested the fugitive in September 1894. He was returned to Whitewood where he was tried by judge and jury on 25 February 1895 and convicted on the forgery charge. He was sentenced to three years in Stony Mountain penitentiary.[124] Meanwhile a by-election had been held on 16 February 1894, and a successor selected for Campbell's seat in the assembly.[125]

Perhaps the most professional crime committed during this period was the gold brick swindle pulled on the Molson's Bank in Calgary in 1897. This classic "sting" operation was the work of three con men who encountered a most gullible pair of western bankers. Late in July 1897, a man calling himself Sam Fowler and claiming the colourful nickname "Trail Sam" visited the Molson's Bank in Calgary and told the manager, a Mr. McGregor, that he was a mining prospector with gold bars to sell. Fowler told the banker he had discovered gold in northern British Columbia, which he had stashed in the bush near Revelstoke, B.C. He was reluctant to bring the bars to Calgary because he feared robbery en route and because his partner, a mountain Indian, would not descend to the prairies. Intrigued, the manager assigned a representative, a Mr. Young to accompany "Trail Sam" to the site of the gold stash. Samples were taken by the bank's representative and together with Sam Fowler, he returned to Revelstoke where by chance he met a mining assayer at the local hotel. The man examined the samples and declared that they were pure gold worth $20 an ounce. The manager in Calgary was wired the good news and he promptly proceeded to Revelstoke where he exchanged $11,200 for the gold bars. Several days later while the gold was being crated for shipment to Montreal, a piece was cut off a bar to make it fit. To the horror of the bankers, the interior of the bars was a different colour from the exterior. A bona fide assayer soon confirmed that the bars were copper with a thin veneer coating of gold.

By the time the Mounted Police were alerted, the trail of the bogus prospector, the Indian and the assayer was cold. S/Sgt. A. F. M. Brooke set off, nevertheless, on August 8th, his expenses paid by Molson's Bank. Evidence led him to Seattle, Washington where he found that a private bank there had exchanged $6,000 of the Molson's bank notes for its own issue on the 2nd of August. Brooke continued his investigation on the Pacific coast for a month, visiting Spokane, Portland, San Francisco and Los Angeles and enlisting the co-operation of the local police in each place. In the end, the effort was futile; the three men disappeared without a trace.[126]

The Mounted Police assisted in solving an important criminal case originating in London, England during this period. Two men, P. G. Somers and H. B. Christie, stole Buenos Aires bonds with a face value of £23,000 in London and managed to convert them into £8,000 in gold and cash. £6,000 was deposited at railway station cloak rooms around London and the pair departed with the rest for Canada, Somers travelling under the pseudonym W. H. Crick. Christie had a brother living north of Qu'Appelle and they arrived at his farm early in June, stayed a few days and then proceeded to British Columbia. Apparently the London Metropolitan Police learned of Christie's connection with Qu'Appelle and Detective-Inspector Abbott was sent to Canada to follow the lead. He enlisted the help of the Mounted Police and S/Sgt. J. H. Hefferman was sent to Qu'Appelle. He questioned the brother and with the cooperation of the postmaster opened some mail addressed to Christie. From these sources, Hefferman and Abbott learned that Crick and Christie had gone to Donald, B.C. to organize a prospecting expedition to search for gold in the northern part of the province. Christie was not equal to the rigours of prospecting however, and soon injured his knee. As a result, he had returned to England passing through Qu'Appelle in the middle of July. Hefferman and Abbott then went after Crick. Luck was with them; only a few days after their arrival in Donald, Crick returned with his party and was arrested. The subsequent investigation discovered Christie's new address in England and he was then also arrested. Insp. Abbott returned Somers (Crick) to London and he and Christie were tried for theft. Upon conviction, Somers received four years and Christie three years in prison. The money deposited at the railway stations was recovered.[127]

There were a number of instances during this period in which citizens of the NWT were responsible for law and order. Two serious examples of this have already been explored, the Edmonton land office affair and the Ole Mickelson killing. There were two other more minor incidents of vigilante justice which made the NWMP uneasy. The first case in 1893 and 1894 was attributable to a detachment not exercising proper control in a community. The other two were more classic cases of vigilante justice with which the Force took pains to deal.

In the small village[128] of Red Deer, Alberta in the period 1893 and 1894, there was some social friction which had led to threats and violence. A small faction of prominent citizens in Red Deer led by the Rev. Leonard Gaetz, one of the original founders of Red Deer, offended their fellow citizens by some of their actions, leading to the trouble. In the summer of 1893, Gaetz castigated the local school teacher, a Miss Duncan, for being inefficient and displaying favouritism in the classroom. In response, on July 28th about 15 to 20 people demonstrated in front of Gaetz's house, hanging and burning his effigy. The Mounted Police knew of the affair but did not interfere since no violence had taken place. A Mr. Green, a local lawyer, and a Gaetz sympathizer, warned Comm. Herchmer that a repetition of this type of action might lead to bloodshed. S/Sgt. William E. Diamond, who was in charge of the Mounted Police detachment, was instructed by his superior, Inspector A. E. Snyder, of his duty to disperse unlawful assemblies, a responsibility of which the NCO was quite ignorant. Insp. Snyder explained this lack of knowledge of the law pointing out that none of the detachments under his command had been supplied with a copy of the *Criminal Code*. It was also considered wise to move S/Sgt. Diamond out of Red Deer at that time.[129]

Another ugly incident at Red Deer produced more strife in the community. A veterinarian, a Mr. Pardue, reputedly a member of the Gaetz faction, castrated three pigs on 29 August 1894. As a practical joke, he wrapped up the testicles and had them delivered to a Mrs. Ellis at her home. The Mounted Police were called in and, after an investigation, the new NCO in charge of the detachment, Sgt. Sidney Dunning, reported to Mr. Ellis the name of the perpetrator. Ellis, quite understandably, avenged this indignity to his wife by horsewhipping Pardue. Outraged by this attack, Pardue had his lawyer friend Green prepare information concerning the assault which he presented to a justice of the peace, thus obtaining a warrant for the arrest of Ellis for attempted murder. That day Pardue was accompanied by another friend, Cst. John Brown of the Mounted Police, and the pair celebrated the issuance of the warrant until they were quite drunk, resulting in Brown's arrest on his return to barracks. Ellis appeared before three justices of the peace on August 30th and all charges against him were dismissed. This turn of events sparked Rev. Gaetz to organize a protest meeting at which complaints were aired about the conduct of the Mounted Police. A local merchant, a Mr. Brampton accused Sgt. Dunning of advising Ellis to whip Pardue. Dunning was incensed by the charges and wanted to sue for libel. Another Mounted Police investigation revealed that Cst. Brown was indiscreetly allied with the Gaetz party, otherwise Mounted Police conduct had been above reproach.[130]

Supt. R. B. Deane encountered two incidences of vigilante behaviour in Lethbridge in the 1890s which offended his sense of order. On 13 February 1895, a local man, Charles Gillies, committed suicide by shooting himself in the head. The man was a habitual drunkard who was humiliated by the fact that his wife indiscreetly dabbled with a lodger in their home named James Donaldson. The respectable citizens of Lethbridge were upset by the supposed connection between the marital discord and the suicide and were doubly offended when Donaldson appeared at the funeral acting like a chief mourner. On the night of February 15th, a gang of eight armed men wearing masks broke into a house occupied by Donaldson and his brother Maxwell. The former was hauled out of bed, tarred and feathered. He was then led with a rope around his neck to the principal hotel in town, the Lethbridge House, pushed in the door which was then fastened from the outside. His humiliation accomplished, the gang dispersed allowing Donaldson to proceed home on foot through a snowstorm.

Deane faced a number of problems in his investigation of this vigilante action. Donaldson was reluctant to press charges and left town for a time, returning only at the insistence of his family to face the situation. All the men were masked and only the leader of the gang had spoken. Then, to Deane's horror, he received a report that Sgt. Thomas Hare, in charge of the NWMP detachment in Lethbridge, had been seen that night with a mask and carrying his Winchester carbine to which clung tar and feathers. Moreover, the respectable citizenry almost unanimously approved of what had happened. The Presbyterian minister remarked to Deane one day that while he did not agree with mob rule neither did he like to see wrongdoing unpunished.

Deane got a break when Maxwell Donaldson heard a voice in the street one day which he recognized as belonging to the leader of the gang. The man turned out to be Charles Warren, a recent arrival from the United States, who was supposed to have had vigilante experience south of the border. Deane also struck a deal with Sgt. Hare not to punish him for his behaviour under the *North-West Mounted Police Act* if he would testify against Warren. Because of the sentiment in favour of the accused in Lethbridge, the venue of the trial for riot and burglary was moved to Fort Macleod. Warren's trial was held on July 6th and, while the evidence suggested a conviction could be obtained, members of the jury refused to convict Warren resulting in no verdict and a new trial. Proceedings fell apart shortly thereafter when Sgt. Hare deserted and fled to the U.S., apparently financed by the other gang members. Released on bail, Warren decided that it would be more prudent to return to his native country. Deane was left with only a pious hope that his pursuit of the investigation would cause citizens to hesitate before participating in similar actions in the future.[131] This confidence he did not test too severely, as a year later his advice for a man who intended to run off with the wife of another was that the Mounted Police could not guarantee his protection from an irate gang. The man left town alone.[132]

A land dispute between a long-time resident of St. Albert and a new settler sparked a large vigilante action in 1896. Since the 1860s, Octave Majeau had held title to land bounded on one side by a body of water known as Big Lake. However, over the years the water had receded considerably, creating a hay meadow along the former shore line. Over Majeau's objection, the government land office sub-divided his claim and granted the hay meadow as a homestead to a new settler, Louis Camo. Majeau referred his case to the Dominion Land Commission office in Winnipeg but was not satisfied with the lack of progress. As a consequence, on August 6th, Octave Majeau and about 60 of his friends, white, Métis and Indian alike, descended on a shack built by Camo, tore it to the ground and threw the material in a nearby creek. All his farming implements were then removed from the property and placed on a public road. Learning of the incident, Insp. A. E. Snyder and a small party rode out to St. Albert and arrested 56 men, charging them with riot and destroying a house and committing them for trial. The outcome of the case has not been discovered.[133]

The regulation of moral behaviour was one category of law which the Mounted Police were not eager to enforce. Drinking, frequenting prostitutes and gambling were part of the frontier scene, where men out-numbered women, base appetites sought release and crude recreation flourished. Generally, western communities tolerated a certain level of moral transgression as long as the crimes were victimless. Certainly, the Mounted Police which consisted mostly of young single men with a lust for life, had no natural inclination to scrupulously enforce the law in this area. The only faint voice of protest came from some Protestant clergy and a fledgling temperance movement, however, this had no impact on law enforcement during this period.[134]

In January 1892, the Territorial Assembly passed the Liquor License Ordinance which established a system for wholesale and retail sale of liquor similar to systems in the eastern provinces. Hotels could apply for licences to open bars to sell liquor and beer by the glass. In exchange for this privilege, the hotel had to pay an annual fee and follow strict regulations regarding the bar which was to be segregated from the rest of the hotel premises. All forms of entertainment associated with a saloon, such as card playing or billiards were strictly forbidden. Likewise, in incorporated towns and cities, stores could apply for licences to sell wholesale liquor and restaurants for the privilege to sell liquor with meals. In all cases, the number of licences for any area was restricted and subject to revocation for breach of regulations.

The new ordinance provided for the establishment of several regional boards of Commissioners which administered the granting of licences and supervised the operation of licensed establishments within defined local areas. Each board could appoint one or more licence inspectors who in turn reported to a Chief Inspector under the Attorney-General of the Territories. The inspectors visited licence-holders and if they discovered violations of the regulations, they were prosecuted before a justice of the peace. Two convictions would result in loss of licence. All police officers in the NWT, municipal as well as NWMP, had the same authority under the ordinance as the licence inspectors.[135]

The end of prohibition and the beginning of liquor licensing did not end liquor problems in the frontier west. In some larger centres, hotel and bars fostered considerable drunkenness, particularly on pay days for hired workers and at harvest times for farmers and their work crews.[136] There were only a few district Inspectors to enforce regulations during this period and they were not inclined to be strict. As for the Mounted Police, they tried to wash their hands of the enforcement of liquor laws.[137] In 1892, the Force was involved in only thirteen cases of violation of the liquor ordinances, eight resulting in convictions. In 1896, there were 25 cases with 16 convictions and in 1900, 34 cases with 24 convictions.[138] For the most part, the Police considered liquor laws the responsibility of the liquor Inspectors and referred violations to these officials whenever possible. Occasionally, such referrals resulted in a fine, but all too often the liquor Inspector did not take action. An illustration of the lack of interest in dynamic enforcement of the ordinance came from Insp. M. H. White-Fraser of the Mounted Police who reported in 1896 from Maple Creek:

> I received a letter on the 20th September, 1896, informing me that liquor was being sold at Gull Lake and asking that a policeman might be sent down to investigate. I accordingly sent a man down in plain clothes who, however, failed to get any evidence.
>
> The matter was then reported to the local license Inspector. Since then I have heard nothing more of the matter, probably 'filed'.[139]

However, when over-indulgence led to drunkenness and disorder the Mounted Police did step in to keep the peace. In 1892, the NWMP handled 136 cases relating to public drunkenness and disorder and won 115 convictions. By 1900, these totals had risen to 304 cases with 276 convictions.[140]

After several years of operation, it was abundantly clear that the enforcement of the liquor ordinance was not effective and some amendments were needed. In July 1899, S/Sgt. J. H. Hefferman complained to the Commissioner that hotel-keepers in Regina were ignoring regulations concerning closing hours for their bars. The problem, it seems, was the liquor Inspector who was too old for his job and seldom ventured out at night. Herchmer brought this matter to the attention of Regina town council who apparently referred it to the Territorial government. On 24 October 1899, Premier F. W. G. Haultain instructed Herchmer that the Territorial licence Inspectors would enforce the liquor ordinance but needed the cooperation of the Mounted Police who should notify them of any infractions. Herchmer concurred and issued orders to this effect the next day.[141] However, the next year when the estimates for the administration of the liquor ordinance was being debated in the assembly, Haultain voiced an altered view of the enforcement question. He acknowledged that the inspection system was not working and he wanted the Mounted Police to enforce the law. He also said that he had discussed this with the Commissioner the previous year and that Herchmer had ordered his men to enforce the law.[142] Herchmer was then in South Africa and could not comment. Pressure on the police to take a larger role in enforcement of the ordinance was to continue after Perry was appointed Commissioner.

The Mounted Police also demonstrated little inclination to enforce laws against prostitution in this period. Most towns had brothels usually at a discreet distance from respectable neighbourhoods. Usually, these establishments were tolerated for what was believed to be the necessary service performed for this predominantly male society. Seldom were prostitutes charged directly for their crime. In 1892, in the entire NWT, only two women were charged in cases involving the NWMP with keeping, and six for being inmates of, a house of ill-fame; all were convicted. In 1896, four women were charged as keepers, six as inmates and all were found guilty. In 1900, six were charged as keepers, fifteen as inmates and all were convicted. In all three years there were no charges laid against men for frequenting these places.[143] These figures cannot be considered as conclusive proof that prostitutes were seldom prosecuted because charges of vagrancy or of creating a disturbance were sometimes laid against ladies of the night to put a check on their activities. From the limited information available on criminal cases it is impossible to calculate accurately how often other statutes were used to control prostitution.

Prostitution flourished in Lethbridge during the 1890s, largely because of the hundreds of men who worked in the nearby coal mines. On Saturday nights they flocked into town to enjoy themselves. The town was incorporated in 1891 and its first council quickly passed a bylaw aimed at closing the brothels. It was an abortive attempt, however. The newly appointed town constable proved to be ineffective and the bylaw was considered *ultra vires*.[144] Nevertheless, two dedicated guardians of the town's morals kept prodding away at the local authorities to do something. Getting no response, one of them, the Rev. Charles McKillop, a Presbyterian minister, finally wrote to Herchmer asking him to remove the houses from the town.[145] McKillop, who was known locally as the "Fighting Parson", claimed that there had been 26 prostitutes in the community since he moved there in 1886.

He received no satisfaction from the Mounted Police either, who had returned to police the town under an arrangement with the council. Deane, the commanding officer in Lethbridge, told Herchmer that McKillop and the Methodist minister, a Rev. Bates, had publicly addressed the town council on the matter but had "retired covered with ridicule".[146] Deane had no sympathy with their cause either. He was a strong believer in tolerating prostitution under the strict control of the police.[147] According to Deane, the two clergymen would have done better to pay more attention to the juvenile depravity among their own congregations as two of their respectable young ladies had recently been involved in love affairs with married men. The "professional ladies", said Deane, are "orderly, clean, and on the whole not bad looking".[148]

While at Macleod a few years later, Deane successfully thwarted another attempt to disturb the control of the police over houses of ill-fame. The Macleod town council asked him to close down the establishments in the municipality. He knew that this would result in the houses scattering throughout the district, which would make supervision more difficult. Deane artfully responded, therefore, by telling the town fathers that if they were closed in Macleod, they would not be allowed to open elsewhere. He gave them a choice, in other words, of prostitution in the town under the eye of the police or no prostitution at all. Under this threat, another council meeting was quickly called and it was decided to leave the matter to the discretion of the Mounted Police.[149]

The discretion of the police was exercised against prostitutes who unduly angered them or the community. For instance, one Laura Clifton operated a house of ill-fame in Macleod in 1891 and 1892. She appeared before police justices of the peace on six occasions charged with offences such as selling liquor, creating a disturbance and stealing garden produce. On two of these occasions she was convicted and fined. Laura Clifton also came to Mounted Police attention when one of their constables was picked up in Macleod improperly dressed in her company and that of another convicted and syphilitic prostitute, Maude Hall. The constable served one month hard labour in the guardroom for his breach of regulations. Then in October 1892, she again appeared before police justices Supt. Sam Steele and Insp. G. E. Sanders charged with vagrancy. The police had had enough by this point and, upon conviction, Laura Clifton was sentenced to one month hard labour if not out of town in three days. She apparently chose the latter as she ceased her court appearances.[150]

Similarly, annoying the community at large invited recrimination from the Mounted Police. In May 1900, the Calgary City Solicitor complained to the commanding officer of "E" Division, Insp. J. O. Wilson, that prostitutes from north of the Bow River were frequently coming into town in a drunken state. Wilson had these ladies arrested and, in his capacity as J.P. convicted them of prostitution, fining the keepers $10 each and the inmates $5 each. At their appearance in court, Wilson made it plain that his action was to discourage them from causing trouble in town. He warned that if he heard any more complaints he would jail them and on release require them to leave the area. In explaining his action to the Commissioner he hoped that they would take his caution to heart because he had no accommodation in the guardroom for so many female prisoners.[151]

Scant attention was paid to gambling in the NWT although the NWMP were bound to enforce relevant ordinances. In 1892 and 1900 there were no charges laid by NWMP for gambling and, in 1896, ten such charges were laid but all were dismissed or acquitted.[152] In other years there were occasional cases involving gambling which led to conviction. Fines seemed to range from about $20 for gambling to about $100 for allowing gambling on the premises.[153] Odd offences such as selling Louisiana State Lottery tickets[154] and operating a wheel of fortune at the Regina races also resulted in convictions.[155]

Occasional complaints were also heard about violations of the NWT "Ordinance to Prevent the Profanation of the Lord's Day".[156] This statute forbade all commerce and all public games on Sunday,[157] the maximum penalty being a fine of $100. References to such cases are rare in Mounted Police reports. There were none recorded in 1892 and one in 1896 leading to three convictions. Seven people were charged in 1900 and six convicted although it is evident that the NWMP did not actively seek violators but rather acted on complaints. In 1895, a Calgary rod and gun club complained to authorities in Ottawa that some residents of that town were shooting firearms for sport on Sunday. The Mounted Police were ordered to stop this and several men were arrested and appeared in court on October 1st. It turned out that four were preeminent members of the rod and gun club. They were dismissed with a caution not to repeat the offence.[158] Sgt. Aston of the Banff detachment found himself under figurative fire from two sources in 1897 when he tried to enforce the Sunday observance. A local clergyman, a Mr. Michener, complained that a party was playing hockey with sticks and pucks near the bridge. Sgt. Aston went out and stopped the game warning the players they risked arrest. One of the participants, John Folson complained to Aston's commanding officer in Calgary, Supt. Perry, that outdoor sports had always been played at Banff without interference from the police. Perry instructed Aston that in the future he was not to stop the hockey playing which consisted of just skating around and passing a ball or puck. To constitute an offence the participants had to choose up sides and formally contest a game.[159] Interpreting such moral nuances did not usually appeal to Mounted Policemen.

During the years of Herchmer's term as Commissioner, there were few innovations made in criminal detection methods. No formal detective service was instituted although some experienced NCOs were continuously employed solving crimes, especially stock thefts. Some police methods such as intercepting mail and inducing prisoners to confess to crimes were called into question. Methods of identifying criminals through photographs or physical measurement were discussed during the period but not employed by the NWMP. But perhaps the biggest impact on police work were the technological advances of the telegraph and, to a lesser degree, the telephone.

Through the initiative of the federal government and the Canadian Pacific Railway, a telegraph system was built in the frontier stage of western development. By 1891, all major towns and cities in the NWT were linked by telegraph. For the Mounted Police, the advent of modern communications was a great improvement in the battle against crime. A fugitive criminal did not have to be chased to effect an arrest. The usual procedure became for the Mounted Police to telegraph in the expected destination of the suspect and the NWMP post would be on the look-out for him. Even if the criminal fled the Territories, police in the other provinces or in the United States would receive a telegram and often cooperated in the arrest, holding the suspect until a Mounted Policeman arrived to take him back to the proper jurisdiction for trial. This process was simplified sometimes when the fugitive chose the train for transportation. Then it was often simply a matter of telegraphing to a policeman down the line to meet the train at the local station and take the malefactor into custody. In some cases the long arm of the telegraph extended overseas as in the case cited earlier of the arrest of Percy Neale in London.

Telephone service was installed in western communities at this time and became for police a rudimentary communications facility, often an extension of the telegraph. As a result, divisional Headquarters posts were linked to outposts with a great saving of men and horses previously used to maintain communications. However, there were many drawbacks. The telephonic equipment was unreliable and frequently broke down. Even when the telephones did work, the facility was often shared with others in the community to the possible detriment of police work. Insp. E. G. O. Hopkins in Cardston, Alberta, complained to his divisional headquarters that the only phone available to him was in the general store meaning that all the police business he transacted by this device was known to the entire Mormon community.[160] Whatever slight economy or improvement in communication that the telephone brought to the Force in this period, there is no evidence that it became a significant instrument for combatting crime.

Occasionally, the Mounted Police checked the movements of suspected criminals by intercepting and opening mail. This was usually done with the cooperation of postal officials without any fuss about the propriety of such actions. For example, as pointed out earlier, the trail of English thieves P. G. Somers and H. B. Christie was picked up by the Mounted Police by opening mail addressed to the latter at the Qu'Appelle post office.

Similarly, since the early days of the Force, mail to and from prisoners in Mounted Police guardrooms was opened to check for any references to plans for escape. The legality of this practice was challenged by ex-Constable Robert Casmir Dickson who was serving two months in the police guardroom at Prince Albert for allowing Almighty Voice to escape custody. According to the *Post Office Act*, nothing was to interfere with the security of the mail. Dickson had Supt. G. B. Moffatt, officer commanding at Prince Albert, charged with violation of this Act. Moffatt's lawyer prepared a defence based on the fact that wardens of penitentiaries were excepted from the security provisions of the *Post Office Act* and so those in charge of police guardrooms had the same rights. Comptroller White felt that this was a flimsy contention, but the Department of Justice decided it was strong enough to enter a *nobli prosequi* in this case when it came to trial on 15 April 1896 and the prosecution was dropped.[161] Now unsure of his ground, Comm. Herchmer issued a general order on 17 March 1896 that all prisoner's mail was to be held by police until the termination of their sentences unless the prisoners authorized the police in writing to open and read their letters. This was intended as a temporary measure until the Department of Justice rendered an authoritative opinion on the right of police to open prisoners' mail.[162] Such an opinion was never offered in this period and there is evidence that routine mail opening soon resumed at police guardrooms.[163]

An interesting development during this period was the realization by the police that it was advisable to caution a suspect being questioned that what he may say may be held against him in court. It was a principle of common law that any confession to a crime made by someone must have been made freely and voluntarily to be admissible in court. In Canada, any person charged with an indictable offence was required to appear at a preliminary hearing where the evidence against him was presented and weighed by a magistrate. If the magistrate decided to commit the accused for trial he usually cautioned him in a manner suggested by a section of the *1892 Criminal Code*:

> Having heard the evidence, do you wish to say anything in answer to the charge? You are not bound to say anything, but whatever you do say will be taken down in writing and may be given in evidence against you at your trial.
>
> You must clearly understand that you have nothing to hope from any promise of favour and nothing to fear from any threat which may have been held out to you to induce you to make any admission or confession of guilt, but whatever you now say may be given in evidence against you upon your trial notwithstanding such promise or threat.[164]

There were, however, precedents occurring in common law which made it advisable for police officers who were interrogating suspects to issue a similar caution to protect the admissibility of a confession as evidence at a trial. An English case of 1893, *Regina v. Thompson*, held that the Crown must prove that no person of authority offered threat or inducement to procure a confession.[165] Then, in a case that directly affected the Mounted Police, the confession of the Indian murderer, Charcoal, was quashed by the court because the policeman had not issued a caution to the prisoner.[166] In 1898, Supt. R. B. Deane reported on a case at Lethbridge which he considered the culmination of the common law precedents of Thompson and Charcoal affecting the admissibility of confessions made to the Mounted Police. Two policemen, Cpl. Callahan and Cst. Taft had arrested a man named Rose for stealing a cheque. While in custody, the man confessed his crime to the two officers. However, when the prosecutor attempted to have this confession admitted as evidence at the trial the judge refused. The judge was not satisfied that the confession had been given voluntarily because the prisoner had not been cautioned that anything he might say might be used against him. Deane predicted that in the future confessions made to police would rarely be admissible in courts.[167]

Certainly, the experience of the Mounted Police in the 1890s underscored the advisability of issuing a caution to prisoners, but it is unclear when this practice became routine. There is evidence that other police forces instituted the practice of issuing cautions at about this time. In 1905, Chief Benjamin Murphy told the International Association of Chiefs of Police meeting that his police department in Jersey City, New Jersey, had adopted a rights warning in 1895. Upon the arrest of a suspect in any serious crime, a caution was read to him that if he chose to make a statement it would be used at his trial. Chief Murphy said the caution had provided much assistance in establishing the voluntariness of such statements at the subsequent trials. William Stark, an official with the Toronto Police, addressed the same body of police chiefs in 1909 and reported that his men also issued cautions to suspects before they were questioned and statements taken. However, when a question was voluntary and unsolicited the caution was not given.[168] Evidently some time after the period dealt with here, the Mounted Police also began to give cautions but exactly when is not known.

In the 1890s, police throughout the world were on the threshold of a new era in police work based on methods of criminal identification. A long-standing limitation in combatting crime had been in properly identifying wanted and habitual criminals. If a person was arrested on suspicion of a crime in one police jurisdiction, there was no way of knowing if he was an habitual criminal from another jurisdiction or if he had escaped from incarceration elsewhere. If he identified himself as "John Smith, itinerant labourer", the matter rested. But in France, an anthropologist named Alphonse Bertillion devised a system which promised to provide a basis for identification. Bertillion's idea was to record a full physical description of each criminal to which information concerning his activities could be attached making identification communicable between police forces. He devised a set of instruments to measure body parts, such as the dimension of the head, the length of arms and fingers, legs and feet. To this data Bertillion added observations such as complexion and colour of hair and eyes and shape of nose. Any oddities such as a mole or tattoo were also recorded. Finally, appended to the record were full-face and profile photographs. The system did not depend on a certitude that no two individuals could have the same physical features but rather provided enough basis of comparison to proceed to certain identification. Bertillion developed this system while serving as the head of the identification bureau at police headquarters in Paris, France. When he published a book detailing the results of his operation and an explanation of his methods in 1893, it was well received in some police quarters.

The city police in Chicago, Illinois had already created an identification bureau based on Bertillion's system of measurement. In 1893, Chief Robert McClaughry of that force demonstrated the work of his bureau to representatives of a number of American police departments participating in the founding convention of the National Chiefs of Police Union (which evolved in 1902 into the

International Association of Chiefs of Police). The enthusiasm of several chiefs of police was such that, by 1897, the association had succeeded in setting up the National Bureau of Criminal Identification with a view to creating a records centre on criminals which could support the identification efforts of individual police departments.[169]

In Canada, Parliament passed the *Identification of Criminals Act* in 1898 which provided that anyone charged with or convicted of an indictable offence could be subjected to Bertillion measurement. To lay the basis for such a system, the Dominion Police in Ottawa was to open a central records bureau to which other police departments and the federal penitentiaries would contribute data and draw on its resources.[170] On 8 June 1898, Parliament authorized the Dominion Police to spend $1,000 to purchase Bertillion measuring instruments and cameras.[171]

During Herchmer's Commissionership, there is no record of the Mounted Police taking interest in instituting a scheme of criminal identification. This changed after the turn of the century. In the Yukon, for instance, the Mounted Police experimented with photographing prisoners and the Bertillion system.[172] In 1903, Comptroller Fred White investigated participating with the Dominion Police in the development of the Bertillion records system.[173] Also that year, Comm. Perry wrote to Chief of Police Henry J. Grassett in Toronto inquiring about the possible benefits of joining the International Association of Chiefs of Police. Grassett replied that not only was he a member but that he was on the Board of Governors of its National Bureau of Identification and thought membership well worthwhile for the identification services alone.[174] However, the Mounted Police did not participate in either the American or Canadian Bertillion identification bureaus, possibly because they were aware that fingerprint identification was about to make the complicated Bertillion system obsolete. Research into the use of fingerprints as a means of identification was proceeding in several parts of the world in the 1890s.

In England, Scotland Yard had been experimenting since 1895 with a method devised by Sir Francis Galton of keeping track of criminals by means of their fingerprints which were found in unique form in every individual. In 1901, Asst. Comm. Edward Henry committed Scotland Yard to a system of fingerprint identification which he had designed, and advanced the credibility of the scientific nature of this form of identification considerably for the rest of the law enforcement world.[175] Comm. Perry wrote to the Commissioner of Scotland Yard in 1904 for information on his system of criminal identification.[176] That same year, Cst. Edward Foster of the Dominion Police met

Detective J. K. Ferrier of Scotland Yard at the World's Fair at St. Louis, Missouri. Ferrier was a fingerprint expert and he convinced Foster of the efficacy of the system. Foster became the fervent apostle of fingerprinting in Canada, aided considerably by the fact that, at the founding meeting of Chief Constables Association of Canada in 1905, a resolution was passed unanimously supporting the creation of a national fingerprint bureau. By 1908, the *Criminal Identification Act* was amended to allow fingerprinting as a basis for identification. In 1911, Edward Foster, now a commissioned Inspector, opened the Canadian Criminal Identification Bureau in Ottawa which was the central repository run by the Dominion Police for fingerprints submitted by other Canadian police forces and penal institutions.[177] That same year, Foster began instructing the Mounted Police in the fingerprint system.[178]

In the United States, some municipal police departments turned to fingerprint identification just after the turn of the century causing the International Chiefs of Police to agree to maintain fingerprint files as well as Bertillion records at the National Bureau of Criminal Identification in Washington. For almost two decades, a dual system was maintained before the superiority of fingerprint identification won over vested interest in the Bertillion system and the latter was dropped.[179]

There was little change in the Mounted Police role in the judicial system in the later years of Herchmer's term as Commissioner. Commissioned officers of the NWMP still acted as justices of the peace in preliminary hearings and minor criminal cases. Most of the important criminal cases were heard by the five superior court judges in the NWT. The Mounted Police continued to complain that its officers spent too much time on judicial duties which should have been performed by civilians appointed as part-time J.P.s.[180] A partial solution proposed by Comm. Herchmer, for Calgary at least, was to have a salaried police magistrate appointed who could handle the bulk of the city's judicial business.[181] This idea was seconded by the *Calgary Herald* in 1895[182] and such an appointment was made.[183] Other municipalities followed the lead but not until several years later.

It is difficult to measure how important the police J.P.s were to the western judicial system. However, one scholar who judges the police the backbone of the Territorial Magistracy quantified their contribution by the amount of fines assessed by police and civilian J.P.s for contravention of territorial ordinances and concluded that their contribution had declined somewhat in 1901 from the position 11 years previously.[184] A rough survey of J.P. files of the Attorney-General's Department from the period 1896-1906 shows records for 33

NWMP officers acting as justices and 735 civilian J.P.s. The files may be incomplete, so no firm conclusions can be drawn. However, from the evidence available at least eight of the NWMP justices were busy with J.P. duties at times during this ten-year period.[185] One of these, Supt. R. B. Deane, was occupied on the bench at Lethbridge and then at Maple Creek throughout the period. A busy quarter (the three-month reporting period for J.P.s) for Deane was about twenty criminal cases. Most of these cases were minor offences against the *Criminal Code*, Territorial Ordinances and the *Indian Act*. Occasionally, Deane sat with another J.P. to try a slightly more serious offence such as theft. In any truly serious crime from stock theft to murder, Deane did no more than conduct a preliminary examination to discover if there was enough evidence to commit the accused for trial by a superior court judge. Any fines collected were sent to the Attorney-General, except occasionally when part of the fine was kept to pay an informant. The court costs were kept to pay the J.P.s fees and the expenses of the witnesses.[186]

Only two civilian justices were found in the Herchmer period who were as busy as Deane. One was William Trant at Regina who served as a J.P. from about 1891 to 1904, then resigned to practise law and in 1907 returned to the bench as a salaried police magistrate.[187] The other was W. C. Sanders of Moose Jaw who served from 1897 until his death in 1907.[188] Both of these men were kept occupied mainly hearing violations of municipal by-laws and petty offences against the *Criminal Code* committed in the town. There was almost certainly an understanding that Mounted Policemen, town constables and other prosecutors would refer offences committed within the boundaries of Regina and Moose Jaw to Trant and Sanders respectively.

Mounted Police officers continued to work as J.P.s because they were sufficiently trained in law to be counted on to do a professional job. Sir John Thompson, the Prime Minister and Minister of Justice, told the House of Commons in 1894 that NWMP justices were the equivalent for the West to the salaried police magistrates who performed the ordinary judicial functions in the eastern provinces:

> If we leave the administration of the criminal law to the ordinary justices of the peace of the Territories, we shall have no trained organized or official body of men to administer that law. Whether they shall take a case or decline to take it is a matter purely for themselves.[189]

Speaking on the same question, W. B. Ives, the Minister responsible for the Mounted Police, underscored the value of police justices by demeaning the efforts of the volunteer civilian J.P.s. He said that the law would not be effectively enforced:

> if it were entrusted to a magistracy composed of busy men – men who devote their time to their own affairs of money-making and are not willing to spend it in disposing of cases, when there is neither honour nor glory nor emolument to be gained. Our experience in the North-West Territories is that the people are very ready to do what they are paid for doing, but will not give their time for nothing.[190]

Ives was no doubt indulging in rhetoric in his condemnation of civilian J.P.s in the NWT, but there were problems with the system. The Lieutenant-Governor was responsible for the appointment of J.P.s who were to be respectable, prominent men with lawyers excluded because of the possibility of conflict of interest. Advice was given on suitable candidates to the Lieutenant-Governor by the judges of the NWT Supreme Court, members of the Legislative Assembly and by the NWMP Commissioner.[191] In 1894, the federal government amended the *NWT Act* requiring the Lieutenant-Governor to limit appointment of J.P.s to those men possessing property valued at $300 or more. This proved a hindrance to the appointment of good and willing men and drew complaints from the NWMP. The requirement was removed in 1897.[192]

Lack of training in law was perhaps the greatest problem with these volunteer civilian justices. Naturally, the government which appointed them anticipated this problem and compensated in various ways. The federal government supplied J.P.s with copies of the *Criminal Code* and the North-West Territorial government distributed copies of its ordinances, although in both cases there were frequent complaints about delays in this process. Manuals were available to explain judicial matters in a simplified manner and one such manual was distributed free to J.P.s in the NWT in the 1890s.[193] More trained government officials such as North-West Mounted Policemen, Crown Prosecutors and employees of the Attorney-General's department supported the J.P.s with advice on the law and procedures.[194] But even with this help there were protests that the ignorance of some J.P.s was a scandal. One such situation existed at Cardston in 1899 where the local justice was elderly, infirm and reportedly incapable of drawing up basic court documents such as information, summons and subpoenas. The local Mounted Police NCO, Cpl. John T. Bolderson, complained that the light sentences meted out by this particular J.P., such as $1 for setting a prairie fire and $10 for illegal cattle branding, made a mockery of justice. His conduct in court was also irregular. The illegal cattle branding was cited by Cpl. Bolderson as a case in point. A man was charged by the NWMP with this offence which involved putting his brand on an unmarked steer belonging to someone else.[195] When brought to court the J.P., instead of letting the prosecution present its case, began sorting out the story with the defendant whom he addressed as "Brother" and in turn was addressed as "Uncle Henry". After the case was heard, the J.P. found the man guilty, pronounced his sentence and provoked this exchange:

"Well Johnny you shouldn't do it!"

"But Uncle Henry it was my hired man!"

"I know you wouldn't do a thing like that but it's your hand and I'll have to fine you $10!"

"All right Uncle Henry!"

"Would it be agreeable to you Johnny to pay in two weeks or I could give you longer if you say so!"[196]

A scandalous situation among the civilian J.P.s in Calgary in 1895 led to the creation of a salaried police magistrate for the city. The *Calgary Herald* reported that court proceedings in the city had been reduced to a farce. J.P.s were repeatedly appearing on the bench drunk. Fines were not accounted for and in some cases were deposited by the convicted directly into the bank account of the J.P. who had presided at the trial. At least one justice had charges laid against him for misappropriating police court fines. The charges were later dropped but public accusations continued that the J.P.s were most tardy in turning in fines.[197]

In other parts of the Territories, Mounted Policemen complained about the conduct of the civilian J.P.s. In 1892, S/Sgt. Fyffe at Moosomin reported that a railway conductor had put a drunken man off the train and he was arrested. The constable asked three civilian justices to hear the case and all said they were too busy. The man had to be discharged.[198] In 1894, the NWMP at both Fort Pelly and Fort Saskatchewan complained that they were very short of J.P.s because while several men accepted the post they had so little interest in the duties that they have not troubled themselves to take the obligatory oath.[199] Sgt. Forrester at High River was incensed about what he called "Justice tempered with scotch whisky". Forrester brought a young man charged with theft before two civilian J.P.s and upon conviction suggested a light sentence as he was young and because it was a first offence. One agreed and proposed two weeks in jail. The other who was drunk and whose language was "borrowed from a bar-room lexicon" wanted the maximum sentence of three months. Finally a compromise was reached of one month hard labour. Even then, the drunken justice instructed Forrester to make sure that the labour was hard and not to let the young man off with kitchen duties.[200]

A related difficulty of a non-professional extra-legal system existed in southern Alberta in the 1890s. In 1897, Insp. Davidson reported that he believed that the Mormons in that area were holding their own courts instead of complaining to the proper authorities. He learned that Bishop Ora Card had warned his congregation that some members were stealing and killing cattle and that if they did not confess they would be "handled".[201] In 1899, Insp. Irwin claimed that at Cardston the Mormons held court for minor offences and had their own

system of punishment. For instance, a man found guilty of petty theft was required to pay his victim three times the value of the stolen items. As far as can be found no action was taken on these reports.[202]

Despite the flaws, the judicial system of the NWT worked without giving rise to major injustice. When difficulties arose with civilian J.P.s not acting responsibly, they were isolated instances and probably were duly reported to the Attorney-General. Frequent major overhauls of appointments in this period probably sorted out the lazy and the incompetent.

Throughout this period the NWMP continued to be the principal jailers in the Territories. Transgressors of the law, along with policemen who breached discipline, shared accommodation in police guardrooms with lunatics awaiting transportation to asylums. Conditions in the jails were often poor including chronic problems such as overcrowding and inadequate sanitation. Men, women and sometimes children were forced to share facilities in a manner which allowed little privacy. For the Mounted Police it was a struggle to make the system work, considering the many other demands on their over-stretched personnel and financial resources. There were occasional escapes from these primitive jails. However, the only incident which arose related to the unresolved question of how much force could be used to detain a prisoner came with the killing of a man who resisted arrest.

Serious offenders sentenced to more than two years in prison were sent to the Manitoba Penitentiary at Stony Mountain or sometimes to the Territorial Jail at Regina. However, the guardrooms of the NWMP were the principal detention centres for short-term prisoners. Some municipalities built lock-ups which could be used for a prisoner awaiting a court appearance or someone who violated a local by-law and did not pay the fine. The detention of anyone who violated the *Criminal Code* was the responsibility of the NWMP even if the arrest was made by a town policeman. Also those who violated the ordinances of the NWT and were sentenced to a jail term could be incarcerated in a Mounted Police guardroom.

Until 1893, the only compensation that the Mounted Police received for being the jailers of the frontier was 60 cents per day per prisoner from the Department of Justice for prisoners serving terms for violations of the *Criminal Code*. They were also annoyed that they were required to give care and custody without compensation to violators of municipal by-laws and territorial ordinances. Complaints were voiced that the towns, at least, took advantage of this loophole sending prisoners to the NWMP whom they could well incarcerate themselves. On 30 June 1893, a federal Order-in-Council was passed which required the NWT Government and municipalities to pay the Mounted Police 75 cents per day for the maintenance of prisoners sent to guardrooms for offences against the ordinances or by-laws. The information is incomplete on how strictly this requirement was enforced but the records do indicate that the satisfactory arrangements for compensation were achieved.

An exact quantitative analysis of the importance of the Mounted Police guardrooms in the West is impossible due to missing data. However, from what is available, it is apparent that the guardrooms were the principal repositories for short-term prisoners. For instance, the daily average number of prisoners held in Mounted Police guardrooms for violations of the *Criminal Code* in 1897-98 was 45.04.[203] For that same year, the Regina Jail incarcerated a daily average of 21 prisoners. The Prince Albert Jail, opened in 1898, was probably not much of a factor in this equation. The unknown quantity of prisoners held in Mounted Police guardrooms for municipal or territorial offences would probably offset the numbers of prisoners held in local lockups. Moreover, the guardrooms also held policemen convicted of breaches of discipline and lunatics destined for asylums. A rough guess would be that the guardrooms held a factor of two to one in numbers of short-term prisoners over other places of detention.[204] Not mentioned here by the provost guard, however, were the four policemen imprisoned at Calgary that year for violations of police regulations.[205]

There was some debate in Calgary in July 1895 about how pleasant a place the Mounted Police guardroom was for the incarcerated. One released prisoner complained to the *Calgary Herald* of the brutal and inhumane treatment meted out there by the Mounted Police saying he "would sooner be at the mercy of the savages of Africa" and signed his letter "A Sufferer".[206] This prompted the newspaper to send out a reporter to investigate conditions. Based on the premise that "when a man breaks the laws of his country he cannot expect to be lodged in a prison parlour with plush furnishings", the reporter found conditions "tolerable and comfortable". The reporter interviewed discharged prisoners and elicited no complaints. The food was plain, but there was plenty of it. They were not overworked and spent lots of time outdoors, shovelling, cutting grass and washing wagons. The guards treated their prisoners with consideration but maintained discipline. One prisoner who used abusive language to a guard was rewarded with an extra three days added to his sentence. In short, the

Herald could find nothing to support the anonymous complaint of ill-treatment.[207]

Perhaps it was because the *Herald* reporter investigated the guardrooms in the summer that he did not uncover all its shortcomings. Later that year, Supt. J. Howe, the Officer Commanding at Calgary, reported that he was far from satisfied with conditions in the guardroom.

> The prison accommodation here is hardly adequate at times to contain all the prisoners confined. There are only fourteen cells and sometimes as many as thirty prisoners have to be crowded into them, during the summer months it is not so bad as the windows can be kept open, but during the cold weather when these have to be hermetically closed the aroma arising from the cells is anything but pleasant.
>
> Sometimes two and even three prisoners have to be placed in one cell owing to the presence of female or lunatic prisoners, and if a common jail is not to be erected here, the accommodation of the guardroom should be increased.[208]

An accompanying report from R. D. Sanson, the medical officer at Calgary, stated that due to almost constant overcrowding the state of sanitation in the guardroom was not good. The themes touched on by Howe and Sanson, chronic overcrowding, poor sanitation and the incapacity to segregate sexes and classes of offenders, were common to most Mounted Police guardrooms in this period.

Overcrowding was worst at Calgary and Fort Saskatchewan guardrooms and it was not unusual that three men would share a cell designed for one. Consequently, there was no room for amenities in these cells. Ideally, the Mounted Police wanted to supply each man with a bedstead and a straw mattress as prescribed by the regulations governing the operation of common jails. However, there was no room for these when three men shared a cell and so the issue was at times restricted to a towel, blanket and night pail for each man.[209] Occasionally, the Mounted Police moved prisoners from an overcrowded guardroom to another with empty cells. This practice was frowned upon by the Department of Justice, as of dubious legality, and so did not occur often.[210] At Maple Creek in 1895, Supt. Sévère Gagnon was forced by overcrowding to take prisoners out of guardrooms and put them in tents. Obviously the only solution was expanded facilities either in the form of larger guardrooms or the new territorial or federal jails. However, governments were reluctant to assume these expenses and Calgary and Fort Saskatchewan guardrooms received little attention during this period. In the latter case, Supt. A. H. Griesbach converted an old saddle and harness room to more cell space in 1893, but this local improvement was no long-term solution.[211] Only at Fort Macleod in 1894 was substantial improvement made with the building of an extra wing to the guardroom, adding eight cells and a bath and store room.[212]

The new wing for the Fort Macleod guardroom was necessitated in part because previously female prisoners were being kept in the same corridor as men.[213] Unfortunately, most of the Mounted Police guardrooms were not totally segregated by sex, meaning that women were kept in separate cells, but they did not enjoy complete privacy from male prisoners. This situation, in the view of the officers of the Force, was positively indecent. Another difficulty was that the guards were all males leaving them "liable to be maligned" should any female prisoner complain of mistreatment.[214] In 1896, the Women's Christian Temperance Union (WCTU) chapter in Edmonton complained to the federal Justice Department concerning conditions in the jails of the NWT. On the advice of the Comptroller of the NWMP, the Justice Department obtained an Order-in-Council authorizing the Mounted Police to hire women jailers at the rate of $2 per day plus rations. Comm. Herchmer thus ordered the Commanding Officers of all divisions in February 1897: "if possible to establish a separate corridor for women, install enclosed chemical toilets and hire female guards, preferably wives of members of the Force".[215] Some progress was made in the next few years, at least in the area of hiring female wardens.[216] Also, whenever possible, female prisoners were sent to Prince Albert and Regina jails where separate accommodation and female guards were available.[217]

Despite scrupulous attempts by the police, using prisoner labour, to keep guardrooms clean, it appears that these premises were often unhealthy places to spend any time. Indian prisoners frequently reacted to confinement by falling ill and serious cases usually had their sentences remitted.[218] However, the famed Indian runner Deerfoot died in the Calgary guardroom on 24 February 1897 after serving 50 days of a 2-month sentence for assault. He had been ill from the time he entered the guardroom and deteriorated despite the care of the post's assistant surgeon.[219] On several occasions, the Mounted Police were anxious to rid themselves of prisoners who suffered from contagious or repulsive illnesses. The police magistrate in Calgary in 1896 sentenced a vagrant to three months hard labour in the NWMP guardroom. This man was described as horribly diseased with syphilis and the police appealed to the Calgary General Hospital to admit him but the hospital refused to accept patients with venereal disease. It appears that the Mounted Police, on the advice of the Justice Department, released the man on the grounds of ill-health and fumigated the guardroom.[220] Release was also the solution for a woman sentenced to Calgary guardroom for vagrancy in 1897, who was described as crippled, utterly depraved and having

filthy habits.[221] In 1894, typhoid fever broke out in the Prince Albert guardroom infecting four prisoners and spread to the barracks where nine policemen were stricken. Most of these were very serious cases and, in fact, one of the prisoners died. The Assistant Surgeon, Dr. Hugh M. Bain, attended to the patients and he was somewhat baffled at the source of the outbreak, but he felt that the overcrowded condition of the guardroom was "a predisposing cause".[222]

Dr. Aylen at Fort Saskatchewan was particularly irate in 1901 about conditions at the guardroom at that post. Not only did he communicate his concern to the management of the Force but also to his political masters through his Member of Parliament, Frank Oliver. Aylen complained that the guardroom was chronically overcrowded, insufficiently ventilated and crawling with vermin. He regarded the situation as dangerous to the health of both prisoners and guards, all of whom experienced headaches and languid feelings. A minor outbreak of five cases of smallpox had recently occurred and Aylen warned that worse could come.[223] There was no question of upgrading the facilities; they must be replaced. Probably as a result of Aylen's strong message, the new guardroom was built at Fort Saskatchewan the next year, in 1902.[224]

The Mounted Police during this period were also temporary custodians for what nineteenth century society called "lunatics". These were people apparently so mentally deranged as to be adjudged insane necessitating commitment in jail or a lunatic asylum. The way the process worked was that information was laid before a justice of the peace to the effect that someone was believed to be insane. The J.P. would order a Mounted Policeman to take the person into custody and an inquiry would be launched into the person's mental condition. If satisfied as to the insanity, the J.P. would be empowered to commit the person to custody indefinitely at the pleasure of the Lieutenant-Governor until his condition was cured.[225] Most lunatics from the NWT were sent under Mounted Police escort to Brandon Asylum in Manitoba where they were kept at the expense of the federal government. To give some idea of volume, in 1900 there was an average daily number of 135 lunatics from the NWT in custody at the Brandon Asylum.[226]

In most cases, insane persons were in the custody of the Mounted Police for periods as brief as a few days or a few hours even while their fate was decided by a J.P.. Then, if found insane, they were escorted by Mounted Policemen on the train to commitment at Brandon.[227] Even in such a short period of responsibility for these unfortunate people, the Mounted Police experienced difficulties. A man was taken into custody by the Mounted Police in the Edmonton vicinity in 1896, judged insane and committed to Brandon Asylum. This man was extremely violent and in the several days after his arrest, refused all food and would not sleep. He became very weak on the train to Brandon, was taken off at Calgary and died in the "E" Division guardroom, despite the care of the post doctor.[228] Another insane man, who believed at times that he was Jesse James, was on his way to Brandon in charge of Cst. Hetherington in 1895 when he suddenly attacked an innocent bystander at the Red Deer railway station. Hetherington wrestled him to the ground and placed him in shackles for the rest of the trip.[229] In 1898, an alleged lunatic, incarcerated temporarily at the guardroom at Lethbridge, evaded the vigilance of the provost guard and hanged himself to death from a bar on his cell door.[230]

Occasionally, the NWMP were responsible for someone who was not mentally capable of caring for himself but was not insane. One such person was Abraham Shattock, found by a CPR crew in December 1896 living in a ditch adjacent to the railway line near Grassy Lake, east of Lethbridge. The man was starving and had no protection against the weather, so the police took him into custody. With some care and food the man's health improved. Thereupon the police discovered that the man was not insane but an "imbecile" which presumably means mentally challenged. He could not, therefore, be sent to Brandon Asylum but neither was he able to earn a living and take care of himself. Furthermore, he was an American citizen who had recently arrived in Canada from Great Falls, Montana but was originally from Indianapolis, Indiana. Abraham was bound to be somebody's ward and by default he became that of the Mounted Police. The municipality of Lethbridge would not care for him because he was not a local man, and likewise the NWT government and federal Department of the Interior refused to acknowledge any responsibility. So the man lived in the Mounted Police guardroom for about one year, doing odd jobs around the post. The police gave him a plug of chewing tobacco occasionally and he seemed reasonably content. The Commanding Officer at Lethbridge, Supt. Deane, elicited information from Shattock concerning relatives in Indianapolis and he wrote to these people as well as the Chief of Police there but received no replies. Deane also communicated with the Chief of Police at Great Falls, Montana and received acknowledgement that the man was more properly a public charge in the United States and if he was sent there he would be cared for. Accordingly, the NWT government provided $20, $15 for a train ticket to Great Falls and $5 for Abraham Shattock's pocket, and he returned to the United States.[231]

A minor problem for the Mounted Police was what to do with some prisoners when they were released. Some persons had no money to support themselves or even to return to their homes. The municipal governments in Regina and Calgary complained to the NWMP that released prisoners were hanging around their cities and they feared increased crime. Therefore, the Force instituted a policy of providing released prisoners without means with transportation and money for meals so that they could return to the place where they were arrested. This policy was applied to Regina in 1893 and extended to the rest of the NWT in 1894. It, however, did not apply to those who served terms for vagrancy on the assumption that it was immaterial where they were released because they had no fixed destination.[232] The vagrancy exception and the lack of a reformatory in the NWT left the NWMP in a dilemma with regards to a juvenile released from the Moosomin guardroom in February 1897. The youth, "Boy" Clune, was a notorious vagrant whom the Commissioner said had been arrested in every town from Toronto to Vancouver. He had no money and no clothes and the winter weather was severe. To resolve this, the Mounted Police took up a collection in barracks and gathered enough to send him back to Toronto in the company of an NCO who was to arrange to place him in a reformatory in that city.[233]

The vast majority of law breakers taken into custody by the NWMP offered little resistance to arrest and incarceration. There were, however, occasional attempts to escape. On 10 July 1894, W. J. Jones was convicted of theft at Canmore, Alberta and sentenced to three years in prison. Before he was transferred to the Regina Jail to serve his sentence, he broke out of confinement. He managed to evade capture for two days but was finally picked up on the CPR line under the axle of a passenger train heading west.[234] Another prisoner escaped from the Regina guardroom in 1895 and was not recaptured.[235]

The Mounted Police officers worried about the problem of how much force they could employ in arrest and detainment. In 1893, Comptroller White learned that Supt. Griesbach at Fort Saskatchewan had ordered his guards to deliver two verbal warnings to an escaping prisoner and then fire three shots over his head. If these actions did not halt the fugitive the guards were authorized to fire at his legs to stop him. White told Herchmer to drop those instructions because it was by no means clear in law when a policeman might fire at fleeing prisoners and Griesbach was leaving himself open to prosecution in case of an accident.[236]

On one occasion during this period, a Mounted Policeman shot and killed a man and invoked public censure for his action. On the evening of 27 September 1898, Csts. Robert Lock and Cecil Hamilton of Yorkton detachment went to the farm of Robert Moore, five miles north of town. Moore had failed to answer a summons issued to him for allegedly killing a bull belonging to a neighbour and Lock and Hamilton carried a warrant for his arrest. Moore had a reputation as a dangerous man; four years earlier, he had shot and wounded a man with whom he had been quarrelling, subsequently being acquitted on grounds that he had acted in self-defence.[237] When the constables arrived at the farm it was after dark and they were met outside the house by Moore armed with a shotgun. The Mounted Policemen explained their mission and Moore agreed to go with them, only asking that he be allowed to pick up some things in his house. The constables agreed and Lock accompanied Moore into the house. On the way out Lock preceded Moore through the door and had it slammed behind him. Moore then told the Mounted Policemen to get off his property. This left an armed Moore inside the house and the two constables standing outside the house in the bright moonlight. In this circumstance the policemen chose discretion and left the premises.

The following afternoon, Lock and Hamilton returned to Moore's place and encountered the same standoff. Moore stayed in his house and refused to heed the arguments made by the policemen that he should surrender himself. Frustrated, the constables decided to force the issue. Lock picked up a log and charged the door succeeding in breaking it open. Hamilton followed in to be met by a shotgun blast from Moore, which missed. Before Moore could fire a second time, Lock got off a shot striking Moore. The two constables quickly transported Moore to a doctor but he was beyond help and died a few hours later.

A public inquest into the shooting was held the following day in Yorkton. The jury censured the two constables for having missed the opportunity for a peaceable arrest on the evening of September 27th when Moore initially agreed to go with them. The coroner, however, strongly disagreed with this censure and, in his verdict, found Lock fully justified in firing at Moore. The coroner maintained that there was no reason to suppose that Moore would not have opened fire on the 27th, as he did on the 28th, had the policemen forced the issue. It was the feeling of the coroner that the jury's censure came from a desire to draw attention to the tragedy of this affair.

The NWMP conducted its own investigation of the shooting. Insp. A. C. Macdonell reported to Comm. Herchmer that Lock had acted correctly throughout this affair. He and Hamilton had dealt very patiently with Moore to secure his surrender before they broke down his door. Moreover, Lock's firing at Moore very likely saved Hamilton's life. Macdonell believed that the public in Yorkton also agreed that Lock's actions were justified.[238]

Despite the vindications, this was not quite the end of the affair for Lock. Fearing civil action from Moore's relatives, he retained a lawyer at his own expense but he does not seem to have been sued. Then, just when it seemed his troubles were over, came lightning from an unexpected source. Clifford Sifton, Minister of the Interior and cabinet member in charge of western patronage, abruptly and without explanation ordered Cst. Lock transferred out of Yorkton. One can only speculate that Sifton was responding to pressure from a political supporter. In an unofficial letter to the Comptroller, Asst. Comm. J. H. McIllree reported that he had regretfully complied with the order:

> I had to give him [*Lock*] a few days, as he was only married a short time ago and has fixed up a house etc., and it appears rather hard lines on him as he has always done his work well.[239]

Lock took his discharge from the Force in Regina five weeks later.

Chapter 9

The Herchmer Scandals

By the 1890s, the NWMP had established an international reputation for efficiency, daring and integrity. Young men came from Europe seeking adventure in its ranks. Visiting journalists from the great newspapers of the world heaped praise upon the Force. It was applauded in Parliament. Canadians took pride in it as a truly Canadian institution that was one of the best police forces in the world. But its *esprit de corps* was not as high as it might have been. In fact, there was a good deal of internal discontent, which like a festering sore would soon extrude itself before the public eye in what the press labelled the "Herchmer Scandals".

A small group of officers still resented Herchmer's appointment. The Commissioner's overbearing nature and hasty temper, meanwhile, increased their bitterness and alienated others who ran afoul of him. Their sense of injustice was so strong that they were prepared to accuse him openly, to wash the Force's dirty linen in public in the hope of having him removed. A few were prepared to use deceit to blacken his name by spreading false stories about him or writing anonymous letters regarding his conduct.[1] All they needed was someone with sufficient influence and position to take up their cause.

The disaffected group found its champion in the person of Nicholas Flood Davin or, more accurately, they found each other, for Davin had his own axe to grind. In 1887, representation in the House of Commons was extended to the North-West Territories for the first time. Four seats were allocated to the three provisional districts, one for Alberta, one for Saskatchewan and two for Assiniboia. In the subsequent election, the riding of Assiniboia West, which included Regina and NWMP Headquarters was won by Davin, an Irish-born journalist who was editor and proprietor of

the influential *Regina Leader*. Sitting in the Commons as a Conservative, his superb eloquence and his journalistic skill soon established him as one of the foremost proponents of territorial self-government. Davin also had a significant part in improving the working conditions of the members of the Mounted Police. Supt. R. B. Deane referred to him, with some disdain, as the "silver-tongued orator of the Western prairie".[2] Under Davin's leadership the campaign to oust Herchmer eventually succeeded in forcing the government to appoint a judicial commission to investigate the Commissioner's conduct.

Davin's conflict with the Herchmers, for it also involved the Commissioner's brother William, had begun several years earlier. In 1883, while returning by train from Ottawa, Davin, much the worse for drink, had wandered through the first class coaches without any trousers on. Such shenanigans were probably not unusual, but on this occasion the wife of the Lieutenant-Governor as well as Supt. W. M. Herchmer and his wife were also on the train. The ladies were not amused by the sight of the Regina newspaper man parading about in his underwear, and the Superintendent was forced to take action. Davin was charged with illegally bringing liquor into the NWT and subsequently fined $50 and costs.[3] He protested to the Prime Minister that it was all a mistake, that he had accidentally fallen out of his sleeping berth, but no one believed him.[4] Although his subsequent attack upon the Herchmers was not entirely motivated by personal vengeance, there is little doubt that Davin blamed Supt. Herchmer for this stain upon his character and was only waiting for an opportunity to even the score.

At first the *Regina Leader* had nothing but praise for Lawrence Herchmer's appointment as

Commissioner. In fact, Davin claimed to have had a part in getting him the job, and the paper commended him for the administrative progress he made.[5] A change in attitude started to take place in the summer of 1888 when, in an anonymous letter signed "Justitia", the *Leader* accused Comm. Herchmer of interfering with the civil rights of local citizens.[6] It was just the beginning of a venomous flood of personal abuse, ridicule and distortion which appeared in almost every issue of the paper. With consummate skill Davin used his considerable abilities as a newspaperman to destroy Herchmer's character and undermine his credibility as Commissioner. It was nineteenth century journalism in its most scurrilous and dishonest form. By 1889, it had acquired the intensity of a crusade whose sole objective was the removal of Herchmer from office.

At the start Davin's charges focused on two main issues: the tyrannical misuse of the authority of the Commissioner's office, particularly as it related to discipline, and the operation of the canteen in the barracks at Regina. His campaign attracted all those both inside and outside the Force who had some grievance, or who believed that they had been a victim of Herchmer's tyranny. They could tittle-tattle to Davin knowing that he would protect their identity. Their accusations would appear in the newspaper anonymously signed "One of the Oppressed", or "A voice from the Barracks". Meanwhile, in his editorials, Davin maligned Herchmer at every opportunity, suggesting that the canteen's suppliers were Herchmer's relatives, that they ran it as a private business and that he and they conspired to make thousands of dollars in profits for themselves.[7] The canteen was also cited as the cause of drunkenness among the men.[8] The Commissioner was called a "czar" who had "the instincts and practices of a tyrant, the manners of a boor and the insolence of an up-start".[9] He was accused of fraudulently converting government funds to his own use, of imprisoning men who had committed no crime and of causing one member to commit suicide. "Should such a 'low, violent and half crazy malignant', continue to command?" asked the *Leader*.[10]

Davin was supported in the cause by a former Constable, C. E. D. Wood, editor and owner of the *Macleod Gazette*. Other western newspapers followed the controversy, but none entered so fully into the crusade to get rid of Herchmer as Wood's publication. Charles Edward Dudley Wood was born in Washington, D.C. in 1856, a member of a southern family that moved to Canada as a result of the American Civil War. Educated at Trinity College, Port Hope, he enlisted in the NWMP in 1880. Two years later, he suffered a serious injury when a horse fell and rolled over him. Invalided

from the Force, he settled in Macleod where he founded the local newspaper. In later life, Wood became a lawyer, a deputy attorney general of the NWT and a district court judge in Saskatchewan. Like the *Regina Leader*, the Macleod paper began to carry a litany of petitions against Herchmer's tyranny. The Commissioner complained bitterly to White that Wood was related to the wife of one Inspector at Macleod, and was the cousin of another Inspector there (Insp. Z. T. Wood), and that every time he had difficulty with them the *Gazette* abused him.[11]

Davin, meanwhile, had taken his case against Herchmer to the House of Commons. He must have had mixed motives for doing so. Although there was his personal vendetta to settle, he honestly saw himself as a defender of the underdog. There were also important political considerations. In the election of 1887, Davin had won comfortably, defeating his Liberal opponent by 726 votes to 423. Some 150-200 voters in the constituency, however, were Mounted Policemen. It was a group whose interests he could hardly ignore. He took a leading part in seeking pensions and other benefits for them. Then there was the Regina Board of Trade which was smarting because of the business its members were losing to the canteen at the Barracks. Whatever the reason for pursuing the campaign against the Herchmers, it created difficulties for him within his own political party. As a Conservative member he was embarrassing his party and its leader, who was also the minister responsible for the NWMP.

In the House, Davin centered his criticism upon what he felt were the "enormous powers" given to the Commissioner by section 18 of the *NWMP Act* to enforce discipline.[12] It was to be a recurring theme in Mounted Police history. The section listed 22 offences for which a member, other than a commissioned officer, could be summarily tried by the Commissioner or an officer delegated by him. Upon conviction, the member was liable to imprisonment for up to one year with hard labour and/or a fine of up to one month's pay. There was no provision for appeal. What Davin objected to was that the legislation did not distinguish between serious and minor offences. He believed that each offence should have a specific penalty attached to it, as in military regulations, that was commensurate with the degree of misconduct. As the Act stood, the Commissioner could sentence a man to a year in prison for a minor infraction. Davin claimed that Herchmer was using this power unjustly and with increased severity, that sentences of one year were being handed out for offences which in the civil courts would only bring three months. He called upon the government to amend the Act so that the sentences handed down by the Commissioner could be subjected to an appeal.[13]

Replying for the government, Macdonald, the Prime Minister, promised to look into the individual cases Davin had brought up, but he rejected any idea of changing the disciplinary system. As the principal architect of the Mounted Police, he defended the principles upon which it had been founded. Offences committed by members of a constabulary, he argued, were more serious than those perpetrated by ordinary citizens. Policemen were guardians of the peace and enforcers of the law. They could not be allowed to be indiscreet in their conduct. If they were, their punishment should be instant and firm. As officers whose duty was the administration of justice their "sentence should be more severe".[14] Davin expressed himself satisfied with Macdonald's promise to look into the cases he had raised. The debate concluded, but not before one member accused the owner of the *Regina Leader* of being motivated in his attack upon Herchmer by personal animosity. Davin of course firmly denied this.

The crusade against the Commissioner continued, however, in the two western newspapers throughout 1889. They found their ammunition in a number of new "revelations" that they attributed to Herchmer's tyranny and incompetence. Most of these charges would later be investigated by a judicial commission. There certainly was cause for complaint in the case of Cst. Thomas Craig. The *Leader* accused the Commissioner of imprisoning him although he had not been charged or convicted of any offence.[15]

The Craig incident started as a result of some bureaucratic bungling in the Comptroller's office in Ottawa.[16] Thomas Craig joined the Mounted Police in 1882. He signed his name to the necessary testimonials (or perhaps someone did it for him), but apart from that he was completely illiterate and unable to make simple mathematical calculations. Shortly after enlisting, he asked to have an amount deducted regularly from his pay and placed to his credit in the Dominion Savings Bank. In 1887, he closed the account and received a cheque for $538.57. The money was used to acquire ranching property in the Pincher Creek area. Two years went by. In July 1889, another constable with the surname Craig, who had also been contributing to the savings scheme, asked for the balance in his account. It was at this point the clerks in Ottawa discovered that some of the second constable's contributions had been erroneously credited to his namesake Thomas Craig, who had as a result been overpaid in 1887 by $377.

It was here that things went wrong for Herchmer. When Craig was confronted with the error by his commanding officer at Macleod and

asked to repay the amount he refused. Being illiterate and unable to keep track of his financial affairs, he genuinely did not know how much he was entitled to and was therefore suspicious about the request. Perhaps he believed that banks never made mistakes, certainly not involving sums as large as this. On hearing of his refusal, Herchmer ordered his arrest. He later explained that considering the size of the amount, he feared Craig would desert. On August 12th he was placed in the Macleod guardroom. Because of a misunderstanding between the Commissioner and his officers at that post, Craig remained in the jail for nine days without any charge being brought against him. Finally, on the 21st of August none other than F. W. Haultain, one of the leading lawyers in the Territories and member of the Assembly for Macleod, obtained a writ of *habeas corpus* from Judge J. F. Macleod (former Commissioner of the NWMP) ordering his release.

The constable's freedom was short-lived. He was arrested again a day or two later on a criminal charge of fraud. This, however, did not improve matters. Herchmer soon realized that it would be difficult to get a conviction. Public sentiment would be strongly in favour of Craig; an impartial jury would be difficult to find. As the Commissioner pointed out to White, "Stealing from the government is not considered criminal in the West."[17] The situation worsened when it was learned that Craig would call Supt. Sam Steele, his commanding officer, to testify in his defence. When the local Crown prosecutor learned that Steele would swear that Craig was an ignorant but honest man who really did not know how much he should have received, he decided to withdraw the charge. Herchmer was now concerned about the effect upon discipline that would result from a constable apparently defrauding the government of over $300. Fortunately, Craig was an honourable man, and when he finally realized that he had been overpaid, he agreed to pay the excess back in instalments.

Even Herchmer recognized that Craig had been improperly treated. His incarceration, however, had not been a deliberate act. It resulted from an oversight on the part of himself and the responsible officers at Macleod. Had the Commissioner realized what was going on, he could have had Craig charged, at least with an offence under the *Mounted Police Act*. Nevertheless, Herchmer had to accept responsibility for the constable's treatment. Davin, of course, portrayed the incident as the calculated act of a vicious and ruthless tyrant.

In the case of S/Sgt. Bagley, which was also a prominent subject of the *Leader's* exposé, Herchmer's bad temper and impulsive nature did get the better of him. Frederick Bagley joined the Mounted Police as a bugler in 1874 at the age of 15.

He was an avid musician, and had a role in the organization of numerous bands, both inside and outside the Force. In later life he would be widely known and respected for his musical accomplishments throughout the prairies.

One day while acting as Bandmaster at Regina, Herchmer gave him an order regarding the attendance of the band members at the Church of England choir practice. The exact nature of that order would later be debated at great length. When several members failed to appear at the time appointed for practice, the Commissioner flew into a rage. Bagley was arrested and brought before him charged with disobeying an order. He was found guilty and reduced in rank from staff sergeant to sergeant. This was a considerable loss of pay for a married man with children. Three bandsmen who also missed the practice were each fined $5. The *Leader* sensationalized the incident as "sing or be dismissed".[18] It was soon clear that Bagley and Herchmer had different understandings of the meaning of the order. The former claimed that since he was a Roman Catholic he could not be ordered to sing in an Anglican choir. The Commissioner explained to White that it was not his intention that Bagley should attend, but only that he see that the Church of England members of the band participated.[19] In response, the Deputy Minister chided him for his thoughtlessness. Church services could not be considered a part of a member's duties, he told the Commissioner, and the cut of 50 cents a day in Bagley's pay was a harsh punishment not in keeping with his good record.[20] It was too late, however. Davin and others could make hay with the case as an example of harsh punishment and interference in religious freedom.

Another "victim" of Herchmer's tyranny that Davin defended in the press and parliament was Cst. J. D. Somerville. In reality this was much more a case of influence in high places, than any wrong doing on the part of the Commissioner.

Somerville was one of the hastily chosen recruits of 1886. By 1889, he had acquired a lengthy list of defaults to his discredit for drunkenness or breaking out of barracks. At Macleod in August of that year, he tallied up another conviction for intoxication. Supt. Sam Steele warned him that if he came before him again, he would recommend his dismissal. Both Steele and Supt. A. C. Macdonell had reported him to be an habitual drunkard. Somerville was transferred to Regina, where he could be more closely supervised. One night in October his bed was found empty, again. He had slipped out of barracks without a pass in search of a little stimulation. This time he was brought before

Herchmer, who sentenced him to one month's hard labour followed by dismissal from the Force.[21]

Somerville's latest escapade resulted in Prime Minister Macdonald tampering with the disciplinary system. Davin brought the case up in the Commons at the first opportunity, charging that the punishment far exceeded the crime, and that Somerville had not been given a chance to defend himself.[22] Davin was only seeking publicity however. By the time he spoke, the matter had long since been resolved, as he well knew. Young Somerville's father was a Hamilton businessman, who was an associate of Sen. William E. Sandford, one of the largest clothing suppliers in the country and a close friend of the Prime Minister. As soon as the constable's family heard of his plight, Sandford, members of the Commons and other influential friends petitioned Macdonald to give the boy another chance. White, who clearly agreed with the sentence, explained to the Prime Minister that the dismissal resulted from his incorrigible behaviour in the past, not just the latest offence. Macdonald, however, gave in to the pleas of his supporters. Herchmer was informed that the sentence was "extremely severe", and he was instructed to cancel the dismissal. A few days later he was also notified that in future all disciplinary offences involving dismissal would have to be forwarded to the Minister for his approval.[23] This in itself was a surprising turn of events since there was no provision for interference of this nature into the authority of the Commissioner, either in the *Mounted Police Act* or the Force's regulations. It was the kind of meddling that neither French nor Macleod would ever have tolerated. Herchmer, on the other hand, although overbearing to his subordinates, was by contrast dutifully subservient to his masters. As for Macdonald, his interference was indefensible. Many constables had been dismissed for what Somerville had done. The Prime Minister's political manipulation can hardly have helped morale. The message was clear: anyone who had enough influence in Ottawa need not worry about the disciplinary code. The Father of Confederation was not always an honourable or wise Minister of the Crown. Unfortunately, for Herchmer it was his conduct that would be investigated not that of the Prime Minister.

Eventually, even Somerville's ability to have strings pulled on his behalf in Ottawa came to an end. He continued to drink to excess and while he was quite unsuitable for service, he was dealt with leniently as long as Sen. Sandford and others had Macdonald's ear. In June 1891, after another bout of drinking at Maple Creek, Herchmer recommended his dismissal. Somerville's friends once again called on the Prime Minister, but with Macdonald on his death bed, White was finally able to tell Sandford that this was "the drunk that broke the camel's back", and the young reprobate was discharged.[24]

During the fall of 1889, the newspaper campaign against Herchmer reached a peak. Each new edition of the *Regina Leader* and *Macleod Gazette* carried another story of his wrongdoing, another insult, another slur upon his character. Other western newspapers began to follow the controversy more closely.[25] Herchmer must have felt the strain. Davin's "yarns" could no longer be ignored. The *Grip* in Toronto carried a satirical cartoon showing four mounted policemen tossing him in a blanket. An anonymous barrack room ballad with an unmistakable Davin touch appeared in the *Leader* entitled "The Night before Larry was Stretched":

> The night before Larry was stretched,
> The boys they all paid him a visit,
> And his Lariat so far was she fetched,
> She cried out, "Boys you may, kiss it,
> kiss it, kiss it".[26]

A suicide at the Barracks in Regina was attributed to his severity under the heading "Death or Herchmer? Give me death, cried the unhappy boy".[27] He was further accused of transferring an Inspector and his family in bad weather knowing full well the wife was in the last days of her pregnancy.

The Governor General's visit to the Territories in October 1889, exacerbated the Commissioner's troubles. At Regina, a lavish reception was organized at the Barracks in honour of Lord Stanley of Preston. Among the scheduled events, was a mounted demonstration of skirmishing. Shortly after it ended, stories began to circulate that it had not been performed with the proper military precision. There were whispers that the Commissioner's knowledge of military drill was inadequate. It was said that he had to write the orders of command on a slip of paper and hold it in his hand in case he got mixed-up. The *Leader* reported that he bungled the review because he was unable to handle 200 men without getting muddled.[28]

Further notoriety awaited him as he accompanied the vice-regal party on its tour. In Calgary, a large crowd waited at the railway station to greet the visitors. Herchmer alighted from the train and began to assist the police already there in trying to control the enthusiastic citizens. In doing so he got into an argument with one Thomas Ede who objected to his abrupt command to move back. Ede charged him with assault and brought a civil action against him for $2,000. The Commissioner was eventually cleared of both charges,[29] but the incident provided further fodder for the newspaper crusade against his tyranny. Further incidents occurred when the Governor General reached Fort Macleod. The *Gazette* charged that Supt. W. M. Herchmer, who was also accompanying the party, had made discriminatory remarks about French-Canadian officers, comments allegedly uttered by his brother while in a state of intoxication.[30]

Davin now had plenty of ammunition to renew the campaign for the Commissioner's removal once Parliament reopened. The latest accusation of racial prejudice was a serious one which would have much to do with the eventual appointment of the judicial commission. In a major editorial indictment, the member for Assiniboia West listed his principal charges:

1. Tyranny towards his officers and men
2. Insufficient knowledge of drill
3. Racial prejudice
4. Causing men to drink their pay away in the Canteen
5. Using the force as a private company for his own financial gain
6. Interfering with the medical treatment prescribed by the surgeons
7. Interfering with the decisions of officers in their capacity as justice of the peace
8. Unjustly treating defaulters
9. Awarding illegal punishments.[26]

To top it off, the Territorial Assembly also passed a resolution in the fall of 1889 calling for a federal enquiry into the Commissioner's conduct.

This latest series of attacks was too much for Herchmer. He decided that the controversy had gone on for long enough and should be settled. In December, he wrote to White stating that the newspaper campaign was demoralizing the Force, that there was no truth in the charges, and that he himself wanted the Minister to have them investigated under oath to clear his reputation.[32] Macdonald, however, for his own reasons was not ready to open the doors to such an enquiry, and Herchmer remained the subject of the vicious persecution undefended.

The resolution of the Territorial Assembly was Davin's pretext for raising the subject in Parliament in the spring of 1890. When the Prime Minister replied that the government intended taking no action upon the demand for an enquiry by the elected representatives in the Territories, Davin moved for the appointment of a select committee of the House of Commons to enquire into the management and conduct of a man who treated his subordinates like "dirt" and was "utterly unfit" for his position.[33] When the debate on the Mounted Police resumed a few days later he repeated at length the numerous allegations his paper had been carrying for months: the "fiasco" at Regina during the Governor General's visit; the "Draconian" nature of the *Mounted Police Act*; the cases of Somerville and Craig; the choir practice; the management of the canteen; the prejudice against French-Canadians. He also used his Commons immunity to accuse Herchmer of adding $1,500 to $2,000 to his pay by fraudulent means.[34]

In reply, the Prime Minister rejected outright any suggestion of a public enquiry by select committee. He accused Davin of carrying on a personal feud, and declared that his accusations were based upon nothing but hearsay. He launched into a stout defence of Herchmer's management, but he agreed that the Commissioner had faults of character. He was bad-tempered, and at times he had been too severe, but the Force had become lax and needed disciplining.

Nonetheless, Herchmer had transformed the Mounted Police into an efficient and reputable body of men. There was no question of dishonesty in the operation of the Regina Canteen. It was operated by the men themselves for their own benefit, and was a great success. Macdonald was prepared to make some concession, however. He was willing to agree to an internal departmental enquiry, but not a public one. If something was amiss in Regina, the Prime Minister was determined to ensure that he knew about it first. The Opposition was divided on the issue. Wilfrid Laurier, the young new Liberal leader, supported Davin, but his predecessor, Edward Blake, sided with Macdonald. When the vote was finally taken on Davin's call for a select committee, it was defeated.[35] It was now up to Fred White to conduct the internal investigation that his minister had promised.

As expected, the member for Assiniboia West claimed the credit for Macdonald's concession. In July and August, White visited the western posts to hear complaints about the Commissioner. The local newspapers carried notices calling upon everyone who felt aggrieved to come forward and see the Deputy Minister.[36] Davin expressed his confidence in the Comptroller's honesty and ability to carry out a thorough investigation. It was soon apparent, however, that his efforts would not satisfy the malcontents. White had no authority to subpoena witnesses, or to take evidence in public under oath. He was entirely dependent upon information that was volunteered. The *Macleod Gazette* was the first to label the departmental enquiry a "farce" and a "whitewash" held "in camera".[37] Davin agreed that under the circumstances White would not be able to overturn every stone. Nevertheless, he believed that once the Comptroller had an opportunity to examine the official records, Herchmer would be found guilty on some of the charges. He was prepared to wait, therefore, until the report of the Deputy Minister was tabled in the Commons.[38]

Following White's return to Ottawa, the anti-Herchmer anecdotes all but disappeared from the press, but the campaign against him started again with increased fervour shortly after federal election writs were issued on 5 March 1891. Canada was in the midst of a severe depression. The Liberals blamed the government's National Policy and called for commercial union with the United States to solve the country's economic problems. Macdonald countered by raising the spectre of annexation by the Americans. Under the rallying cry of "a British subject I was born. A British subject I will die!", he led the Conservatives to his last electoral victory. Within a few weeks the 76-year-old prime minister was dead. In Assiniboia West, Davin was returned again with an increased majority, yet he renewed the attack on Herchmer in his newspaper shortly after the election. In spite of his comfortable victory, he accused the Commissioner of electoral interference by ordering mounted policemen in Assiniboia West to vote against Davin. It was reported that those who disobeyed were punished.[39]

The latest indictment and the renewal of the newspaper campaign brought matters to a crisis again for Herchmer. In exasperation he wrote to White asserting, with some justification, that Ottawa was not supporting him. The serious charge that he was racially prejudiced against French-Canadians still went unanswered. He attributed it to lies spread by Supt. Sam Steele and Insp. Wood. The department had conducted an investigation and he demanded to know why the results had not been made public and his name cleared.[40] The delay only encouraged the belief that he was guilty, undermined his authority and demoralized the Force further. It was imperative now, he told the Comptroller later, that a Royal Commission of three judges be appointed to investigate all the charges, once and for all.[41]

What action Macdonald would have taken upon this request will never be known. On 6 June 1891, he died. Herchmer would get his way however. In the disarray within the government that followed Macdonald's death, his successors soon caved in to Davin's demands. As soon as Parliament reconvened, the member for Assiniboia West called upon the government to table White's report.[42] Macdonald's heir as minister responsible for the NWMP was the new Prime Minister, Sir John Abbott. Because the latter sat in the Senate, the discussion of Mounted Police affairs in the Commons devolved upon the Minister of Justice, John Thompson.

Davin demanded again and again that the report of the departmental investigation be made public.[43] Each time, the government side made an excuse for its non-appearance. Tiring of this, Davin once again moved for the appointment of a select committee to enquire into Herchmer's conduct. To all of his earlier charges, he now accused the Commissioner of using his office in an effort to prevent him from being elected.[44] To Davin's surprise, Thompson capitulated. Although the Minister of Justice admitted that he had not read White's report, he announced that the Commissioner had requested a full public enquiry under oath and the government had decided to comply with his wishes.[45]

If the truth were known, the real reason for the government's change of heart was that Thompson already knew what the next speaker in the debate that day was about to say.

Lt. Col. Guillaume Amyot had commanded the Quebec Rifles, the 9th Voltigeurs, during the North-West Rebellion. As a Liberal member from Quebec, he was sensitive to French-Canadian issues. He read into Hansard a damning extract from a Montreal newspaper, L'Etendard. First of all, the paper denounced Herchmer for giving orders that no French-Canadian officers be allowed to participate prominently in any official function during the Governor General's visit to the West in 1889. It then went on to state that his brother, Asst. Comm. W. H. Herchmer, had publicly stated at a social gathering during the tour that "all French-Canadians were b——ds, sons of b——-s and sons of w——-s".[46] It concluded by reporting the case of Bagley who, it claimed, had been punished for being a Roman Catholic. Amyot called for an immediate investigation into these charges of bigotry. The Justice Minister had to agree that no one who could be shown to be responsible for such actions could remain in the Force for a moment.

The question of the Herchmer's conduct was no longer just a squabble between a newspaper editor, some disaffected officers and a government official in a remote part of the country. It had now become a part of the most sensitive and divisive national political issue of the day. Since Riel's execution in November 1885, there had been bitter racial and religious controversy over such questions as French language rights in Manitoba and compensation for the property of the Society of Jesus, a Roman Catholic order, that had been confiscated by the British after the capture of New France. White's report was finally made public, but it was too late.[47] The Comptroller concluded what Macdonald had claimed all along: the charges against Herchmer were founded upon the malice of Davin and Wood, and there was no substance in them. The only fault, he reported, was the Commissioner's bad temper and tactless manner. The Leader and the Macleod Gazette immediately labelled it a "whitewash", but their condemnation was now unnecessary.[48] In the light of the latest charges, the results of the internal enquiry were irrelevant.

Shortly after its release, Amyot renewed his attack in the Commons. He produced a letter from C. E. D. Wood in which the latter asserted that the language Amyot had attributed to Asst. Comm. Herchmer regarding French-Canadians was accurate. The owner of the Gazette went on to assert that he could produce five witnesses who would attest to the truth of the matter.[49] The government, meanwhile, had asked William Herchmer for his explanation of the incident. His response, made public in the Commons by Thompson, was not very reassuring. He admitted that he was involved in a heated exchange of words with some militia officers from Quebec in which he had used strong language in response to insults from them. He flatly denied, however, that he had said anything derogatory regarding the French-Canadian race.[50] His explanation did not satisfy the critics. The government, Thompson announced, had decided that the forthcoming commission would investigate the conduct of both Herchmers.

To carry out the enquiry, Ottawa established a one-man judicial commission.[51] Chosen for the task was Mr. Justice Edward Ludlow Wetmore, Q. C., a former mayor of Fredericton, who had been appointed a judge of the Supreme Court of the NWT in 1887. Wetmore was empowered to consider and enquire into all accusations relating to the conduct of the Commissioner and his brother. The learned judge was undoubtedly an acquaintance of all the main participants in the coming hearing, but no party ever questioned his impartiality. He commenced his task by placing notices in the western newspapers calling upon all who had any complaint against the two men to forward it to him in writing, stating the facts of the case and the names of any witnesses. By the time the deadline for submitting complaints was reached, 19 December 1891, Wetmore had received 137 charges against the Commissioner: 89 were laid by C. E. D. Wood, 4 by Davin, 38 by members and ex-members of the Force and 6 by other citizens.

Several accusations were also levelled at his brother, notably among them were those of racial prejudice. These, however, were never considered by the Commissioner. On New Year's Day 1892, Asst. Comm. W. M. Herchmer died suddenly from heart failure in Calgary at the age of 47. How far his health may have been affected by anxiety over the coming enquiry will never be known. There could have been little doubt about his future in the Force had it been shown that there was any truth in his alleged racial comments. There would have been few in Calgary that would have felt concerned about anti-French attitudes, but the effect in the East would have ruined his career. In Calgary, the younger Herchmer had been a popular and respected figure. Cheering crowds had greeted him there as a hero on his return from the rebellion in 1885.[52] Now they lined the streets to pay their final respects as he was buried with full military honours. At that time, it was the largest funeral the town had ever seen. The body was carried on a gun carriage preceded by an escort of 36 Mounted Policemen. Behind the coffin came the colonel's charger with his boots reversed in the stirrups in the traditional way. It was followed by a long procession of mourners moving slowly to the beat of Handel's "Death March" played by the Fire Brigade Brass Band.

The "Herchmer Scandals", as the press tagged the enquiry, opened its proceedings in the Regina Court House on 19 January 1892. The first day was taken up with procedural arguments. Herchmer's accusers agreed to drop some of the charges because they were vague or imprecise. Wetmore refused to consider others because they had no factual foundation. This left him with 116 charges to investigate. Hearings, he decided, would be held in Macleod as well as Regina. Each side employed counsel, and witnesses would be subject to cross-examination. Some of the best legal minds in the Territories would be involved. Wood was represented by F. W. G. Haultain, the member of the Territorial Assembly for Macleod and the leader in the struggle for provincial status. Wood and Haultain would later enter into a long and successful legal partnership. Davin and Supt. Cotton retained T. C. Johnstone, another prominent local lawyer. To defend himself, Herchmer obtained the services of E. P. Davis of Calgary. With legal fees at $20 to $30 a day, he was concerned about the crippling bill he would face, if the enquiry became protracted.

The Commissioner soon found that he was as much on trial as if he were in a criminal court. The counsel on both sides adopted hostile positions, and witnesses found themselves closely cross-examined. Herchmer himself spent many hours in the witness box. The dirty underwear of the NWMP was hung up for the whole world to scrutinize. The newspapers had a field day with the revelations. Officers testified against their commanding officer. Others gave contradictory evidence. To the amusement of the public, some developed sudden lapses of memory when being closely questioned about an incident. The contents of private letters were read in court revealing off-the-cuff comments by some officers about Herchmer. The Commissioner had to publicly admit that he made a mistake in giving the commands during the Governor General's visit, that he did call Supt. Cotton a liar, and had lost his temper on numerous occasions. At the end of the enquiry, one opposing lawyer claimed that there must be something wrong with Herchmer's command when 25 per cent of his subordinates had testified against him.[53]

Although Davin made the best use of his wit and eloquence in reporting the scene, it soon became apparent to others that while there was great sport to be had at the expense of Herchmer very little of substance was being uncovered against him. The first few days were devoted to Davin's principal allegation that Herchmer had used his position to influence the recent federal election in Assiniboia West, that men had been threatened with dismissal, demotion or punishment, if they voted for Davin. As soon as the evidence showed that there was no truth in the charge, some who had earlier supported the demand for a public hearing began to have doubts. The *Calgary Herald* reported that the enquiry was working out badly for its promoters.[54] Many of the complaints had already been satisfactorily explained by White, and the investigation was going to cost the public thousands of dollars. The excitement had subsided, it continued, and there was a "general feeling that the famous charges have not been sustained".[55] Even the *Macleod Gazette* had to admit that "very little interest is taken in the enquiry now the election charges are through. A great many of the remaining charges are trivial, though, as the judge remarked at the opening, they might if proved in bulk amount to a serious matter".[56] After listening to the evidence for a month, the Calgary paper opined that the farce had gone on long enough as it had become clear that it was nothing more than the washing of foul linen between Herchmer and his officers.[57] Nevertheless, the "Herchmer Scandals" dragged on for another month, finally concluding on 16 March 1892. Davis' final speech in defence of Herchmer was a tour de force lasting seven hours.[58] Eventually the Commissioner received a bill from his counsel for almost $1,500, an amount equal to more than half his annual salary.[59] Much to his relief, the government agreed to pay it.

Shortly after the hearing concluded, Thompson announced in the Commons that the judge's report would be ready in five or six weeks.[60] Actually it took Wetmore a good deal longer than that, and almost a year would pass, a long one for Herchmer, before his conclusion was made public. In February 1893, rumours began circulating that the results of the enquiry would exonerate Herchmer and he would not have to resign.[61] Under pressure from Davin, Wetmore's findings were finally tabled by the government on 3 March 1893. The report, which was 60 pages in length and accompanied by 13 volumes of evidence, was never published.[62] In it, the learned judge made it quite clear that he had found no evidence whatsoever to substantiate any of the serious charges against the Commissioner of the NWMP. On occasion, he had overstepped his authority to discipline his men. At times he had not given individuals an opportunity to defend themselves. He had been wrong to put offenders on a diet of bread and water. He did use "unjustifiable" language towards his officers when admonishing them. He was bad-tempered and overzealous, but nothing more. He had not misappropriated any public funds, interfered in elections or meddled with the justice system. The report concluded:

> It will be seen that some of the matters of complaint brought home to the Commissioner were the outcome of too much zeal on his part: some arose from mistakes of the law or from misapprehension of his power. These mistakes and misapprehensions are such as any person in his position might be likely to make, and do not strike my mind as being of such a character as to amount to misconduct in office. The most learned and experienced of judges make mistakes at times and misconceive the extent of their powers, and it is not a matter of surprise that the Commissioner has sometimes done so. As to the remainder of the charges brought against him I have nothing to add beyond this: that a very large proportion of them are attributable to infirmity of temper, brusqueness of manner or hasty conduct.[63]

The government accepted Wetmore's findings unequivocally. By now Thompson had succeeded Abbott as prime minister and responsibility for the Mounted Police had passed to the president of the privy council, W. B. Ives, a railroad entrepreneur and lawyer from Sherbrooke. In the Commons, Davin asked him how many charges had been proven against Herchmer and what the government intended to do.[64] Ives replied that, of the 137 charges originally made, 14 had been proven and 23 proven in part. He assured Davin, however, that he agreed with Wetmore that none of the things of which he had been found guilty touched upon his honesty, his business capacity or the efficiency of the police. His only faults were his temperamental nature, and his overzealous use of his authority in trying to achieve perfection. It was not enough to dismiss him on, or to use him as a scapegoat. As to what action the government would take, Ives replied that it had not decided.

Ottawa's indecision left Herchmer hanging on a limb. He, of course, had no intention of resigning. In his view, the enquiry had vindicated him, cleared him of the injustices that had been heaped upon his head. Under the circumstances there was little the government could do, unless he failed to mend his ways. The commission did have one positive effect however. Within the Mounted Police itself, it had cleared the air. It had given those who felt the need a chance to get things off their chest, vent their spleen and have their day in court. As Deane said:

> I said what I had to say without fear or favour, and as a result, my Commissioner treated me thereafter with respect, although we had no greater affection for each other than before . . . . It was a pitiable exposé, but it had the effect of clearing the air.[65]

In Insp. Charles Constantine's opinion, it brought a sense of relief and a desire for renewal. "It appears to me," he wrote in his annual report, "that we must trust more to men and less to regulation."[66]

Ives sensed the change when he made his inspection tour in the summer of 1893. After his return to Ottawa, he wrote a memorandum to all officers informing them that he was so impressed by the efficiency of the Force and the improvement in relations between the Commissioner and themselves that the government had decided to take no action on Wetmore's report.[67] Unfortunately for the future of the Mounted Police, the effect of the enquiry on many outside the Force had not been so beneficial. Its image had been seriously tarnished. The "Herchmer Scandals" provided ammunition to those in Parliament in the years ahead who argued that the usefulness of the Force was over, and its strength and its budget should be reduced.

Chapter 10

Herchmer, The Final Years

During the last years of Herchmer's command the most frequent and time-consuming topic of debate in the House of Commons concerning the NWMP was the question of its reduction and eventual disbandment. In May 1892 James McMullen, the Liberal member for Wellington in southern Ontario, placed the following resolution before his parliamentary colleagues:

> That, in the opinion of this House, the corps known as the North-West Mounted Police should be annually reduced in numbers.[1]

A long time critic of federal spending for policing the NWT, McMullen repeated the arguments for reduction that had been made before. He agreed that at the outset the presence of the Mounted Police had been necessary to establish peaceful relations between Canada and the Indian nations, but a military force was no longer required to overawe the indigenous inhabitants. "The West is settling up fast," he argued. "It has towns, railways and the telegraph system. There is no indication that the peace of the country will be disturbed again by the Métis or the Indians." During the previous eight years, he charged, the government had unnecessarily spent six million dollars to provide security for a territory that no longer needed protecting. If there were cattle to inspect, they should be inspected by employees of the Department of Agriculture. If there were customs to collect, they should be collected by the Department of Customs. The frontier police had served its purpose and the government should commit itself to its systematic reduction.

Few disagreed with the notion that the organization of the NWMP was only a temporary measure designed to oversee the transition of the Canadian prairies from a lawless frontier to a settled and orderly community. The Force's founder, Sir John A. Macdonald, had affirmed this on numerous occasions. It was assumed that eventually the "Great Lone Land" would be replaced by incorporated municipalities that would provide for their own law enforcement as was done in the older provinces. Opinions diverged, however, over the date when this point of transition would be reached and the police could be withdrawn.

The government's official response to the resolution was handled by Edgar Dewdney, the Minister of the Interior and former Lieutenant-Governor of the NWT, the most knowledgeable and experienced member of the cabinet on the affairs of the region. His statement included a clear message of alarm and fear at the prospect of withdrawing the police. The government was committed to a policy of retrenchment in police expenditures, he informed the House, but only in so far as it was compatible with the safety of the country. He agreed that the Indians had given no trouble since the rebellion. The NWMP, however, was an important deterrent. Remove the police and who knows what might happen. Dewdney compared the situation on the Canadian prairies with that south of the border, where the "Messiah Craze" had recently spread unrest among the Sioux, resulting in a tragic confrontation with U.S. troops at Wounded Knee. He repeated an argument used again and again by Macdonald. It was cheaper in the long run to spend $700 per Mounted Policeman per year to ensure peace, than to face the huge expenditures encountered by the Americans in sending thousands of soldiers to suppress recurring outbreaks of violence. The actual strength of the Force at the present, Dewdney continued, was only 1,015 and the government hoped to reduce this number to 650 at sometime in the future. He concluded, however, that at the moment, any reduction would be unwise until the Indians were sufficiently "civilized".[2]

Dewdney's warning of the unpredictable nature of Indian society and the possibility of further violence were views widely held in eastern Canada. Reason should have told them that the frontier era was over, but Easterners, both in Canada and the United States, continued to be fascinated by the prospect of the "Wild West". Newspapers frequently carried stories in both countries of the savagery of Indian uprisings. There was a morbid interest in the exaggerated and usually false accounts of scalping, raping and murder by Indians in both countries. Their ill-informed interest in the lawlessness of the West and their stereotypical image of the uncivilized nature of the Indians clouded the judgement of Easterners in dealing with affairs on the prairies. One might have expected Dewdney, however, to be more enlightened.

McMullen's position, nevertheless, was strongly supported by other Liberals in the ensuing debate. One suggested that the question of security could easily be solved by replacing the NWMP with volunteer militia companies of 40-50 settlers organized at strategic points. The militia system of part-time soldiers had not so far been extended to the Territories. If each settler, he argued, supplied his own rifle and horse, there would be a saving to the public purse of thousands of dollars annually. In response to the criticism, Thompson, the Minister of Justice and soon to be Prime Minister, made it quite clear that the government was committed in principle to reducing the police as soon as it was possible. Having exacted this pledge from the Conservative leader in the House of Commons, McMullen agreed to withdraw his motion.[3]

With the country in the grip of an economic depression, both parties had good reason to favour cutting Mounted Police expenditures. They differed only in their perception of how fast this could be completed. What few in Ottawa fully appreciated, however, was that the police did not just sit around on horseback all day waiting for an Indian uprising, but rather they were occupied in carrying out a multiplicity of duties, either on behalf of other government departments, or simply because there was no one else to do them. McMullen's comment that "the corps is largely made up of English dudes who are paid large salaries for travelling around the country" was a misconception that many Easterners had of the NWMP at the time.

The reduction issue was the biggest challenge to Herchmer's administration in the remaining years of his command. On the one hand, settlement on the prairies would rapidly increase, bringing with it additional responsibilities. On the other, Herchmer would have fewer men with which to meet the demands for police service.

In 1892, the NWT had been given a measure of self-government. The new territorial government, however, showed no interest in taking over authority for law enforcement.[4] Nevertheless, Ottawa politicians of both parties assumed that law enforcement on the prairies would develop at the local level as kind of a natural progression as it had done in the older provinces with a system of magistrates and constables based upon British traditions. When Herchmer complained of a lack of men, his political masters suggested that he withdraw personnel from more settled areas leaving the latter to provide for their own policing. Organized settlements and municipalities, however, showed little interest in forming their own police forces and when they did, the forces were small and often inefficient. Their members were usually occupied issuing licences, impounding stray animals, maintaining streets and acting as sanitation inspectors and part-time firemen. If a serious crime occurred, the Mounted Police were expected to take over. A vacuum in law enforcement existed into which the Mounted Police were inextricably drawn because there was no one else to do the job. Politicians in Ottawa talked of the police withdrawing from settled areas, when in fact the Force was becoming more and more committed to policing them. Ministers either did not understand what was happening, or were unable to find a solution.

In the cabinet shuffle of December 1892, responsibility for the NWMP was assigned to W. B. Ives, a lawyer and business man from Sherbrooke, who seemed determined to not only reduce the police but to get more work out of it by more efficient management. When he tabled the Mounted Police estimates in the House in the spring of 1893, provision was made for only 850 men for the coming year, a reduction of about 200 over the previous establishment.[5] News of the government's intentions was welcomed by McMullen, but his eye was also caught by a new allocation for capital expenditure. If the government was committed to further reduction, why was it spending money on a building program. Ives explained that it had been decided that the Mounted Police should take over the administration of the quarantine regulations along the border and this required the construction of a number of quarantine stations. In view of this added responsibility, the Minister explained, any further reduction in the Force in the near future was unlikely.

Ottawa's latest plans came as a surprise to Comm. Herchmer. He immediately wrote to Fred White, anxiously asking how, when he was already understaffed, he was to meet present and now new commitments with even fewer men. He was already having difficulty keeping liquor out of the Athabaska District, he complained, and another lot of immigrants would soon arrive to open up new areas of settlement. On top of this, he was now expected to operate a series of quarantine stations for American cattle from Gretna, Manitoba to the British Columbia boundary. He also warned White that the reduction was hardly likely to induce good men to join the Force, and those already in it would start to look for their future elsewhere.[6]

The Commissioner sought permission to come to Ottawa to discuss the future distribution of his men. Ives, however, had already determined his own priorities for redeployment. White forwarded these to Regina within a few days of receiving Herchmer's letter. In addition to taking charge of the quarantine stations, the Minister wanted an effective patrol system maintained along the international frontier. Reserves of men would also be maintained at Regina, Macleod and Calgary in the event of any Indian uprising. The additional men required to carry out these duties were to be obtained, Ives instructed, by reducing the strength of the detachments in the settled districts, particularly those in incorporated communities.[7]

Herchmer was no doubt chafed to receive these orders without any consultation or warning from a new Minister who obviously knew little about the Territories. Later that year, however, Ives sent him a confidential questionnaire that sought his opinion on many issues essential to future policing on the prairies. The answers revealed much about Herchmer's understanding of the role of the Force and the problems it faced.

The first question was the key one. It asked him how much longer he believed the Mounted Police would he needed. His answer left no doubt as to what the Commissioner saw as the two principal tasks facing the Force. First and foremost, in his mind, was the Indian threat. The West was a tinder box. All that was needed was one spark to touch off another rebellion. As a result, some kind of military force would be needed for many years to come. Secondly, he informed his superior, the U.S. territory just south of the Canadian border was seething with horse thieves and desperadoes. Unless the boundary was constantly watched, they would flood into Canada. It would be years before a municipal police system could ensure the safety of the country. The municipalities were too few and too far apart. Furthermore, as evidenced by the recent smallpox riots in Calgary and disturbances over the land office in Edmonton, the public did not put much confidence in local police forces and justices of the peace. The only alternative was to maintain a force of militia in the country or the Mounted Police. The latter was preferable because as well as being a military force it could perform useful police duties.[8]

Just how much of this Herchmer really believed is difficult to say. Publicly, he paid lip service to government policy by assuring readers of his published annual reports that reduction would not seriously affect efficiency. In expressing alarm at the possibility of Indian attack, he was not alone. This garrison mentality was shared to some degree by some of his officers, reiterated by newspapers, and expressed by numerous westerners. Yet the police never uncovered any reliable evidence of a plan by the Indians to rise as a body against the white population. Likewise, his fear of the tide of crime spreading north was based upon a widespread understanding by Canadians of the nature of American society. Again, keep the "gunslingers" out of Canada was a common theme in the reports of his subordinates. Herchmer by nature tended to see issues in distinctly defined terms. It is hard to believe, however, that in responding to the questionnaire he was not being defensive in some degree by putting forward such alarming views. After all the government was asking him to commit a sort of administrative hari-kiri. He was not about to preside over the dissolution of the Force he had worked so hard to promote and of which he was unquestionably very proud.

In a further question, Ives asked for his recommendations on the distribution of men in the future. The Commissioner's response was predicated on the view that containing the Indian threat was his primary objective. He proposed to do this, however, without deploying men from detachment duty in settled areas, as the Minister suggested. There were only three municipalities in Assiniboia with their own police forces, he informed Ottawa, and the largest of these consisted of only two men. He recommended the following distribution:

"B" Division	Regina	120 men
"C" Division	Battleford	65 men
"D" and "H" Division	Fort Macleod	200 men
"E" and "Depot" Division	Calgary	160 men
"F" Division	Prince Albert	60 men
"G" Division	Ft. Saskatchewan	80 men
"K" Division	Lethbridge	90 men
		775 men

The principal change in this proposal over the existing distribution was the transfer of "Depot" Division and the Headquarters of the Force to Calgary. Herchmer suggested that the latter place was centrally located as far as rail routes were concerned, and its climate, unlike that of Regina, would permit drill to be carried out year round. It was also close to the horse breeding country, but most important of all, the concentration of a larger force at Calgary would provide a strong reserve garrison in the Alberta District where it was most needed. The Commissioner considered the Blackfoot and the Bloods the biggest potential threat to peace.

His plan retained a large division at Regina to maintain the policing of the District of Assiniboia at the same level. Maple Creek was eliminated as a divisional post. This would create a small surplus of men who could be distributed elsewhere. The Commissioner's proposal called for a total strength of 775. He was careful to point out in his response, however, that more men would be needed, if the

143

Athabaska and Peace River regions continued to attract settlers.[9]

In October 1893, Ives with his Deputy Minister, Fred White, toured the West to see things for themselves. They met with Herchmer and visited most of the divisional posts. Judging by press reports, the Minister from Ottawa made a good impression upon westerners. Even the Liberal-backed *Edmonton Bulletin* agreed that he seemed just the man to run the Mounted Police.[10] His reception, however, may have had something to do with the fact that he avoided any discussion of further reductions. It was a subject about which many in the West were greatly concerned; after all, with several hundred thousand dollars spent in the Territories maintaining the police every year, any reduction would be at their economic expense. The Territorial Assembly had already passed a resolution calling on Ottawa to desist from any further cuts in strength.[11] Ives' reply to the Lieutenant-Governor assured the Assembly that the reductions so far had been done without "endangering the maintenance of order or the protection of life and property". He promised to ensure this in the future and gave no hint of any further cuts.[12] Herchmer's annual report at the end of 1893 confirmed his Minister's position. Although reduced in strength, he wrote, with the support of all ranks the Force had been able to meet its various responsibilities.[13] Whether the Commissioner's earlier recommendations had had any effect is not clear, but it does appear as if the government had relaxed its determination for further reduction.

Inevitably, however, McMullen would be waiting to question the Minister on the matter as soon as the opportunity presented itself in Parliament. "What is the present strength of the force, and what are the government's plans for continued reduction?" he asked Ives during the debate on police expenditures in June 1894.[14] In reply, the Minister informed the House that it had been decided to withdraw the Mounted Police from quarantine duties in Manitoba, a saving of about 12 men. He had to admit with obvious embarrassment, however, that the present strength was about 900, or some 50 more than the target of 850 that the government had pledged itself to reach a year before.[15] With this admission, the Liberal member launched into a bitter attack on the failure of the government to keep its promises, deriding its effectiveness and repeating his now familiar arguments for the withdrawal of the police. When Ives reported that during his visit to the Territories he had received no demonstrations for reduction from the inhabitants, McMullen retorted that they were hardly likely to want to diminish an organization that put $600,000 annually into their pockets.

The criticism must have stung. Its effect was felt almost immediately, perhaps another indication of the general malaise of the post-Macdonald Conservative government. On the day following this exchange in the House, White informed the Commissioner that the Minister had decided to reduce the strength of the Force to 750 by 1 April 1895.[16] It was an ultimatum. There would be no discussion of the matter. Henceforth, no new recruits would be engaged except in very special circumstances. The number of special constables was to be reduced by amalgamating the two divisions at Fort Macleod into one, and the same with the two in Regina. For obvious reasons, the Comptroller warned Herchmer, these decisions should not be made public, the Indians particularly should not find out.[17]

Confronted by more demands for men, Herchmer probably wondered whether his Minister would stick to his ultimatum. Although warned not to make the government's intentions public, his annual report for 1894 made it clear that a further reduction was in progress.[18] He assured the public that with the return of the men from quarantine duty in Manitoba the Force would be able to meet its present responsibilities, but, he warned, it would no longer be able to look after prairie fires in the settled districts in the future.

The report, which was made public in January 1895, no doubt gave credibility to persistent rumours of cutbacks, and helped stir up opposition. On January 15th, the *Calgary Herald* reported that the Force had already been reduced to 900 men and that Ottawa intended to remove another 100. In order to achieve this, the Commissioner was said to have been given orders to "weed out" inefficient members.[19] In February, the same newspaper, in an angry editorial, announced its opposition to reduction by a single man.[20] A few weeks later, at a public meeting in Fort Macleod, a resolution was passed calling upon Ottawa to increase the strength to 1,000 men so that a sufficient force could be maintained in the area to protect settlers from the thousands of Indians who were just waiting for an opportunity to pounce on them and their livestock.[21]

Not everyone in the West opposed government policy. Oddly enough, it was the government's own supporters who were most vocal in denouncing the policy. Liberals tended to approve of the action. The *Edmonton Bulletin*, an influential Liberal organ, took the view that efficiency was the true test. If the Force could be reduced and yet maintain its efficiency, all well and good.[22] While on a horse buying trip in Calgary in March 1895, the Commissioner, in an interview with the local press, confirmed that this was indeed the government's intention. "Instead of having 950 good, bad and indifferent men," he assured the public, "we will have say 800 first-class men . . . we are not discharging any of our good men . . . the force is stronger today than it ever was."[23] Three days later, the Calgary City Council passed a resolution opposing further reduction until there was a sufficient population in the country for a volunteer militia to be organized.[24]

It is reasonable to conclude that most westerners were against decreasing the strength of the NWMP. The government, however, remained determined to stick to its parliamentary commitment. In April 1895, the Comptroller informed Herchmer of the Cabinet's latest decision. It had been intended, he wrote, to reduce the estimates for the coming year for the Force from the $655,000 of the previous year to $580,000, but at a recent meeting it had been decided to reduce even further to $500,000:

> You have authority to purchase 30 horses. Can you get along with less? Please go over your list of detachments in settlements and see where you can reduce. We must keep up our strength in the Macleod country, the frontier patrols and a few men along the line of Railway, but the well settled up Districts will have to rely more upon themselves in future.[25]

"I don't know how we are going to keep the force doing its duties," White noted with resignation, "but we must try." In odd comments like this the Deputy Minister seems to have sympathized with Herchmer. Surviving records do not reveal very much, however, about White's position on the reduction question during this period. What advice he gave his Ministers, if any, is unknown.

The Commissioner responded by pointing out once again to Ottawa that most of the incorporated towns were still dragging their heels when it came to expanding or organizing their own police departments. As a result, the Mounted Police had to come to some temporary arrangement to assist, or fill the void where they defaulted. He had just reached an agreement with the Regina authorities, he informed White. The town's own constables were unable to provide sufficient protection for the community at night. It had agreed, therefore, to provide board and extra pay for two Mounted Policemen to patrol the streets after dark. If anything serious happened, like the recent fire at the courthouse, the Mounted Police were still expected, however, to take action. The situation, he reported, was much worse in Lethbridge, Fort Macleod and Edmonton. At the first two places he had a total of six men policing the communities and was paying rent for the buildings out of which they operated. In Edmonton, meanwhile, he had one officer and six other ranks in a rented building costing $40 per month. He suggested that, in future, the detachments in Lethbridge and Fort Macleod be reduced to one man each, who would only patrol at night, and that all town duty in Edmonton be curtailed.[26] Ottawa's response is not known. A reduction was made at Lethbridge,

which evidently forced the community to hire its own "Town Inspector", but a large detachment continued to function in Edmonton.[27] A notable exception to the reluctance among western communities to provide for their own police protection was Calgary. Where others were only too happy to have the Mounted Police come in and take charge, Calgarians were sensitive about their rights and tended to disagree with the Mounted Police on questions of jurisdiction.

The cutbacks became more clearly visible to westerners when the Commissioner proceeded with the reorganization of the divisions that Ives had ordered for the Spring of 1895. "D" and "H", the two divisions located in Fort Macleod as a strong force to discourage any incursion by the Blackfoot or Bloods, were to be amalgamated into one, as were "Depot" Division and "B" Division in Regina. The unification would create a surplus of men who held divisional appointments. There would in future, for example, only be a need for two rather than four division sergeants major. The surplus NCOs and constables could be transferred to operational duties elsewhere, or not re-engaged when their time expired. In some cases, those who were incorrigible disciplinary problems were summarily dismissed.[28]

It was not quite so easy to re-assign the redundant officers. Reducing four divisions to two would leave five commanding officers, Superintendents, where there was now only an establishment for two. The fifth was Supt. Sam Steele who had been in overall command of the two divisions in Fort Macleod. There was only one vacancy for a commanding officer. It was at "E" Division in Calgary where Supt. E. W. Jarvis, the commander of the Winnipeg Field Battery during the rebellion, had recently died suddenly from cellulitis.[29] This would leave two Superintendents and, as it turned out, two Inspectors with nowhere to go. It was left to Comm. Herchmer to recommend whose services should be dispensed with. It was an opportunity for him to get even with those officers who had tried to unseat him in 1891-92, or others for whom he had a deep personal dislike. It was one measure of his ability to command, however, that his decision did not take into account these considerations. His recommendations to the Minister were based upon identifying the least qualified and suitable officers to carry out their duties.[30] Those he named, of course, considered themselves sacrificial victims for one reason or another. In the case of one Inspector, the son of a senator, Herchmer put his convictions up against some powerful political influence. The government, nevertheless, acted upon his recommendations and two Superintendents were retired to pension, and two Inspectors, not having enough service for a pension, were retired with gratuity.

Comptroller White later tried to obtain appointments for these with the Customs Service.

The untimely death of Prime Minister Thompson in December 1894 had resulted in a cabinet shuffle and the new Prime Minister, Sir Mackenzie Bowell, assumed responsibility for NWMP affairs from Ives. Since Bowell was a senator, police matters in the House of Commons devolved upon George Foster, the long time Finance Minister for the Conservatives. In July 1895, Foster brought down the government's new budget proposals for the coming year of $500,000, a reduction of $155,000 over the previous one.[31] He was also able to confirm with satisfaction that the administration had met its target for cutting the establishment. The present strength of the Force, he reported, was 853, with about 750 NCOs and constables, as planned. He then announced that it was proposed to get this latter figure down to 700 by the end of three years. The security of the country would be maintained, he assured the House. The cutbacks had not impaired the efficiency of the police. They had been made possible by more stringent management, lower food prices in the Territories and greater use of new railway branch lines.[32]

These statements left the opposition with little room for criticism. McMullen continued to demand the abolition of the Force, but he appeared to have little encouragement or support in this view from his Liberal colleagues. At least one expressed concern that the government not reduce the Force too quickly lest it discourage future settlement.

During the remaining months of 1895 Ottawa pushed on with reduction. Recruiting was almost at a standstill. Men whose term of service expired were not re-engaged. In addition, Herchmer lost 20 first-class men when they left under the command of Insp. Charles Constantine to extend Canada's authority in the Yukon. No one realized at the time that this was but a small vanguard soon followed by many more.

By November, the Commissioner had become increasingly anxious about the extent of the reduction. He told White that he was now down to 680, excluding officers and special constables. Worst of all, some of his best men were not re-engaging because of the uncertain future of the Force. The response from Ottawa was for more cuts. White informed Herchmer that the Minister wanted to reduce the Force to a total figure of 750, including NCOs, constables, officers and special constables. This could only be done, Herchmer replied, by discharging more of the special constables employed as scouts, interpreters and artisans, leaving the regular constables to cook their own meals in future.[33]

The annual report compiled at the end of 1895 indicates that the Commissioner almost achieved the government's target. It listed 675 NCOs and constables, 46 officers and 53 special constables, a grand total of 774 as compared to the 750 Ottawa had asked for.[34] The significant decrease, however, was not in the number of special constables, as Herchmer had warned, but in NCOs and constables. The report assured the public that in spite of the considerable cuts and the reduction in the number of divisions the patrol system had been maintained and all serious police business attended to.[35]

In April 1896, Canada's seventh Parliament was dissolved. After five years of governing the country the Conservatives, unable to find a suitable successor to Macdonald, rocked by scandal and divided internally over religious and language issues, had to face the country. Opposing them was a rejuvenated Liberal Party ably led by its new leader, Wilfrid Laurier.

There could be little doubt that the future of the Mounted Police would be an election issue in the four territorial constituencies. While it was true that both parties had favoured a policy of reduction, the prospect of a Liberal victory must have appeared as the least attractive result for those westerners who felt that the cuts had gone far enough, or should be reversed. As for the police themselves as individual voters, a ballot cast for Laurier would be like cutting their own throats.

During the campaign, the reduction issue became a political football in the press with charges and countercharges from both sides. The Conservatives attempted to play upon the fears of the electorate. As one correspondent to the *Macleod Gazette* observed, the "NWMP bring a larger percentage of criminals to justice than any other force in the world; take away the police and the country will have a regular hot bed of criminals, as bad as Texas".[36] Local Liberals, on the other hand, disassociated themselves from strident calls for disbanding the Force and stressed a policy of smaller but more efficient.

At dissolution, the four federal territorial seats were all held by Conservatives. The police vote was an important factor in at least two ridings. With the large number of men attached to the headquarters in Regina, police affairs usually had a prominent place in local politics. This campaign was no exception. The incumbent for Assiniboia West, N. F. Davin, found himself in a bitter contest in which reduction was an important issue.[37] The other seat was the District of Alberta with a large number of police in Fort Macleod and divisional posts at Calgary and Fort Saskatchewan. It was here that the future of the Mounted Police was most hotly debated. The Liberal candidate was Frank Oliver, publisher of the *Edmonton Bulletin* and local member of the territorial assembly. Oliver had long taken a leading position in favour of reduction, provided of course that the efficiency of the Force was not impaired.[38] His opponent was T. B. Cochrane, a representative of the local ranching community, who announced publicly that if elected he would endeavour to see that the Force was returned to its old strength of 1,000.[39] He was supported by the *Calgary Herald* which warned its readers that a vote for the Liberals was a vote for the abolition of the NWMP.[40]

To the surprise of most Canadians, Laurier and the Liberals won a majority in the 1896 election. A new era in Canadian history was about to unfold. The tally of the votes on June 23rd indicated that a major realignment of voting patterns had occurred. The election issues on the prairies were complex, but at least one thing stood out. The party that had consistently favoured a more rapid reduction of the Mounted Police and its eventual disbandment had won three of the four seats. In Alberta, Frank Oliver had easily defeated Cochrane. Laurier himself had captured the riding of Saskatchewan. Canada's first French-Canadian Prime Minister had also been elected in a Quebec constituency, however. When he opted to represent the latter, a by-election in Saskatchewan later in 1896 returned another Liberal. Only in Assiniboia had the Conservatives hung on, and even there only by the skin of their teeth. After all the votes had been counted, Davin, who had strenuously opposed reduction, and his opponent were tied. This impasse was broken when the returning officer, Mr. Dixie Watson, cast his deciding vote for the incumbent. Davin was with some derision henceforth known as "the hon. member for Dixie".[41]

The election results seem to indicate that old fears of an Indian uprising were no longer a serious concern to westerners. It had in fact become a bit of a red herring. They were still anxious to retain something of a police presence, but this was no longer because they feared that they would be scalped in their beds. Clearly Comm. Herchmer's advice and the reasons for his opposition to reduction were undermined by this conclusion. This would not have enhanced his credibility with the new government which already had reason to distrust him.

The Commissioner and his subordinates must have been very anxious about their future as they waited during the summer of 1896 for some indication of what the Liberals would do. The new Minister responsible for the NWMP was the Prime Minister himself, Laurier. They received some reassurance from the *Regina Leader* which claimed that since Laurier's recent trip across the prairies he had become convinced of the necessity of retaining the police.[42] The paper had become an influential Liberal organ following its sale by Davin to Walter Scott some months earlier. What they did not know

was that J. M. Walsh, a former Assistant Commissioner who had attained considerable publicity as "Sitting Bulls Boss" some years before, had strenuously advised Laurier that anything above a strength of 500 was a waste of money.[43]

Parliament re-opened in August 1896, but it was not until September that Mounted Police affairs came before the House when Laurier tabled its estimates for the coming year. The amount was $530,000 or $30,000 more than the Conservatives had spent the previous year. On being asked about a possible reduction in strength, the Prime Minister stated that the government had no plans for further cuts at the moment. The duties of the Force, Laurier observed, were expanding in the North. If there was any reduction in the settled areas of the prairies, it would be to move men to the Athabaska District and the Yukon.[44]

There must have been many a sigh of relief in the mess rooms of the police posts. The axe was not to fall abruptly. The Liberals did not look so bad after all. Even if there was reduction later, the new government seemed committed to an expanded role for the Mounted Police on the northern frontiers that were rapidly opening. Of course, no one realized in September 1896 just how explosive the need for the police would be in the Yukon in just a few months once the news of the discovery of gold on a tributary of the Klondike River by George Carmacks and his companions just a month earlier was flashed around the world.

Any optimism that was generated about the future of the Force soon received a stunning setback. By the spring of 1897, Laurier re-affirmed the Liberal's former position and a new target was set of 500 men on the prairies, with the eventual disbandment of the police to follow.[45] Surviving records suggest that the Commissioner played little or no part in the decision. This policy was vigorously pursued by the new Minister of the Interior, Clifford Sifton, who the busy Prime Minister allowed to run police affairs on the prairies pretty much as he saw fit. The government was determined to proceed with the plan despite continuing fears of an Indian uprising and the increasing demands for police service.[46] Settlers would have to provide for their own law enforcement in the future. In the event of any possible emergency, Ottawa toyed with the idea of establishing a "Police Reserve" as a replacement for the NWMP.

Two violent incidents briefly provided grist to those who continued to argue for the maintenance of the police as a military garrison. In October 1896, a Blood Indian named Charcoal shot and killed Sgt. W. B. Wilde near Pincher Creek. Six months later, the hunt for a Cree named Almighty Voice, who had murdered Sgt. C. C. Colebrook in 1895, ended in a violent confrontation near Duck

Lake that left three Indians, two more Mounted Policemen and one civilian dead. Both events rekindled fears of an Indian uprising. The *Calgary Herald* regarded the Charcoal incident as evidence that the Indians were by no means yet civilized. It attacked the advocates of reduction for not truly understanding the state of affairs in the Territories.[47] Comm. Herchmer also saw possible danger in Wilde's murder. He suggested to Ottawa that any plans for cutting the Force should be reconsidered, especially in view of the fact that if the Bloods had rushed to Charcoal's side, Steele would not have had enough men in the area to overawe them, and he could not have been adequately reinforced.[48]

The government, however, was not deterred by these alarms. Speaking in the House of Commons in May 1897, Sifton confirmed that it was still the intention of the government to reduce the police to 500 men.[49] A few days later, Almighty Voice and his two Cree companions were surrounded by the police in a bluff at Duck Lake. Rumours began to circulate of young Indians rushing from the reserves to join them. Even Frank Oliver was momentarily agitated. He suggested in the House that the government should reconsider its position on reduction of the Force. Davin, on the other hand, claimed that events clearly demonstrated the need for a return to full strength of 1,000 men.[50]

The fears of the alarmists turned out to be hollow. There may have been sympathy for Almighty Voice among his people, but no thought of organized resistance on his behalf. His war cries were the last to be heard on the Canadian prairies. Fear of the Indians threatening the security of the West was about to be put to rest. The curtain was coming down on Canada's western frontier. Soon the Indians would be pushed aside, neglected and forgotten as the great period of settlement began under Sifton's vigorous immigration policy. As for the police, within a few days of the shoot-out at Duck Lake, Herchmer had no hesitation in despatching over 30 men to London for several weeks to participate in Queen Victoria's Diamond Jubilee. In his annual report for 1897, the Commissioner confirmed that the recent acts of violence were those of isolated individuals. "With the exception of the Almighty Voice trouble, the Indians have been unusually quiet during the last year, and have generally made very great progress."[51]

As an alternative to the NWMP, Ottawa briefly considered the formation of an auxiliary force of former Mounted Policemen. Ex-members themselves were responsible for this scheme when, in 1886, a number of them held meetings in Calgary and Fort Macleod for the purposes of establishing a NWMP veterans' association. One of the declared objectives of the new organization was a willingness to volunteer the services of its members to the government in the event of an emergency.[52]

In December 1896, White wrote to the Commissioner asking for his comments on devising a practical scheme for a "Police Reserve". The deputy Minister's first consideration was the usefulness of such a force in the event of an emergency, but he also suggested that its members might provide rudimentary police service in the settlements where they lived by acting like the "County Constables" did in Eastern Canada. As White perceived it, the reserve policemen would need some training from time to time and would have to be governed by some authority. The most attractive thing about the scheme, however, was that the men would only be paid when actually called out on police duty. Thus, the reserve might replace the Mounted Police at a considerable saving to the taxpayers.[53]

The Commissioner responded by canvassing his commanding officers for their views on the organization, equipment, pay, duties and discipline of a reserve force of ex-policemen. He received a variety of answers. Some were favourable to the concept, suggesting that the reserve policemen be attached to the regular force in the division in which they lived, be appointed peace officers, receive two weeks annual training, be issued firearms and a uniform different from that of the regulars, and be paid at a rate of $0.75 to $1.50 when on duty. Other officers disagreed. Supt. Sam Steele observed that a local resident acting as a constable would be of little use because settlers as a general rule would not arrest their neighbours, or give information against them. As for the use of a reserve force in time of emergency, he expressed the view that that possibility could best be met by extending the militia system to the prairies. Supt. R. B. Deane advised that he saw no need for such a force at all. In Edmonton, meanwhile, a group of police veterans on hearing of the proposal held a meeting to express their own views on the subject. These they forwarded directly to Laurier. Like Steele, they opposed the formation of a police reserve and agreed with him that the militia should be organized on the prairies, with grants of land going to its members as an incentive.[54]

When the results of the Commissioner's survey reached Ottawa, they must have dampened any real enthusiasm to form a police reserve. It was not a serious setback, however, since it was only a half-hearted attempt to find a solution to the future of policing in the Territories. In truth the government did not really know what to do about these "colonial" dependents who steadfastly refused to take the administration of justice into their own hands. Elsewhere in the country local authorities usually jealously guarded their responsibilities in such matters.

The government was certain about one thing though. It would stick to the promise Sifton had made in the Commons to reduce the Mounted Police to 500 men on the prairies, regardless of what the settlers did. The *de facto* Minister in charge of the Force asked his deputy for advice upon where duties could be reduced. White suggested discontinuing patrols through settled districts, closing some more remote posts and reducing the prairie fire service and the work for other departments. He also thought that the police might abandon some of their military practices. The Comptroller had in mind such things as the training and maintaining of artillery gun crews. The field guns located at strategic posts were considered one of the principal deterrents against an Indian attack. As to the Indian threat, he advised moving the Force's headquarters to Calgary, and replacing it in Regina with the Mounted Infantry from Winnipeg, which could be utilized in the event of an emergency.[55] Calgarians would have welcomed such a move, but one could hardly imagine Winnipeggers cheering at the thought of the large militia establishment being removed from their city. These were the kind of political considerations to be faced in any major reorganization.

Herchmer was asked once again for his recommendations for implementing the latest reduction. Like his deputy Minister, his response was calculated on the understanding that it was still one of the Force's primary functions to maintain a military garrison in the event of an Indian uprising. "Macleod is our most important post," he informed White, "because of its proximity to the Blood, Piegan and Blackfoot Reserves." As a result, he recommended concentrating almost 200 men at that point, closing Lethbridge as a divisional post in the process. A further 200 men should be located at Regina, he advised, which would remain the site for headquarters. This could be achieved by reducing Maple Creek to a detachment and amalgamating the divisions at Prince Albert and Battleford into one with headquarters at the latter location. Calgary and Fort Saskatchewan would remain unchanged. Finally, as a means of maintaining the Force at its fullest fighting potential, he suggested that as many special constables as possible who were not trained soldiers should be discharged and replaced by regular members. The work done by these specials, who were mostly artisans, would be taken over by enlisted men, and if necessary, they would remain on duty longer hours to complete tasks. This could be accomplished, he thought, by making only every other Saturday a half day holiday, and that only when all required work had been completed.[56]

No major reorganization occurred as the result of these recommendations, but the government was determined to reduce the number of men on the prairies. This it proceeded to do by transferring more and more personnel to the Yukon. By November 1897, there were 100 men on duty in the gold rush country. One year later, the Yukon Force there had been organized into two divisions with a total compliment of 285 men, leaving only 563 in the older Territories. This emasculation of his command was made all the harder for Herchmer because the men transferred to the Yukon were removed from his control and administered directly from Ottawa on orders from Clifford Sifton.

The removal of men from the prairies ignited another round of protests. In September 1897 the *Regina Leader* denounced the government's action as deplorable and dangerous, leaving the country open to be ravaged by prairie fires.[57] A few weeks later the Territorial Assembly passed another resolution calling upon Ottawa to increase rather than decrease the police.[58] Early in 1898, the East Assiniboia Liberal Association forwarded a petition to Laurier opposing its own party's policy on the matter.[59] The *Calgary Herald* responded angrily to news that the government was to recruit men for service in the Yukon but not for duty on the prairies.[60] In Parliament, Davin called upon the administration to ensure that the ranching country would continue to be protected, if men were to be transferred from there to the Yukon.[61]

Ottawa gave not the slightest attention to this agitation. As news of the discovery of gold became general knowledge throughout Canada and the world, and the great stampede for the Klondike began, the focus of Mounted Police work was transferred to the new frontier in the north. As praise for the exploits of the police on the Chilcoot Pass and at Dawson increased, attention to their duties on the prairies diminished. In June 1899, Laurier was able to announce with satisfaction in the Commons that the strength of the police in the older Territories had been reduced to 550 men. The government's target of 500 would shortly be met, he promised, when another 50 men were transferred to the Yukon. This reduction, he assured the House, had been carried out without any loss of efficiency, and he anticipated even further decreases as the rapid settlement of the country continued.[62]

As the century drew to a close it must have looked to Comm. Herchmer and many in his command that the days of the NWMP were decidedly numbered, on the Canadian prairies, at least. Uncertainty about the future may partly explain why many members were eager to volunteer for service in the Yukon. Others took their discharge to seek their fortunes elsewhere. Some with a soldierly frame of mind were watching developments in South Africa with interest. The Prime Minister's stated views on the future of the Force did not bring forth an outburst of criticism. The wrangling over reduction had petered out for the time being. During the final months of 1899, it was the possibility of war against the Boers that pre-occupied the hearts and minds of mounted policemen.

In his annual reports for the period 1897 to 1899, Herchmer took pains to make it clear that despite fewer and fewer men on the prairies, the police had been able to investigate all serious crime, and had maintained a satisfactory although less extensive patrol system. To meet these commitments, he explained that he had to all but eliminate drill, except for recruits, and target practice. "All ranks are generally doing the best they can for the credit of the force," he reported in 1897, "but in the case of emergency it would be impossible now to collect 20 men in the whole force in the Territories without interfering with some duty."[63]

Herchmer did not enlarge on the overall effects of reduced numbers, but in fact, a fundamental shift had occurred in the organization of the NWMP in the 13 years since he took command. This becomes only too clear from a comparison of the distribution of men and detachments in the first year of his Commissionership with those of the last.[64] In 1886, with a total strength of just over 1,000 men, the police operated some 40-odd detachments and 10 divisional headquarters. These detachments were manned by about 16 per cent of the total strength. The remainder were concentrated in the divisions, drilling and training like soldiers. Thirteen years later, in 1899, with a strength of just over 500, or only half of that of 1886, the Mounted Police had over 90 detachments on the prairies, or more than twice as many as in the immediate post-rebellion period. Furthermore, the proportion of the total strength committed to detachment duty doubled from 16 per cent in 1886 to 33 per cent in 1899.

Faced by increased settlement, the policy of reduction had forced Herchmer to withdraw men from the garrisons concentrated at divisional posts in the event of an Indian uprising to meet the growing demands for police service in the new farming communities. In 1886, 63 men were stationed at Prince Albert; in 1899 this had been reduced to 20. Calgary had been reduced from 99 to 41. The same was true at other command headquarters to one degree or another. The proportion of men on detachment duty not only substantially increased, but their new posts were no longer concentrated near Indian reserves. Instead, they were located in new settlements such as Yorkton, which had just experienced a large influx of Doukhobors and Ukrainians attracted to western Canada by Sifton's immigration policy. Many of the detachments now operated year-round, and were manned by one, two, three or four men whose time was devoted almost entirely to providing police services of one kind or another. No longer did a division close its detachments in winter and return men to headquarters for military drill. Gone, too, were the summer camps for training and maneuvres. In their dress uniforms, the NWMP still looked every bit like soldiers, but in reality they had all but ceased to be a viable military force on the prairies.

Under Herchmer's administration the energies of the Mounted Police were now centered upon providing a police service to the new inhabitants of the West, and performing a variety of duties on behalf of other federal government departments. There was some lingering discussion that settlers should provide for their own law enforcement and that the usefulness of the NWMP was coming to an end. Herchmer and many others may have been pessimistic about the future of the Force in 1899, yet in reality, a new set of circumstances were evolving not only in the North, but also on the prairies that would provide a new role for the police in the twentieth century.

Conclusion

The decade and a half after the North-West Rebellion was an important period of transition for the Canadian West. The railway transported increasing numbers of newcomers intent on earning livelihoods and perhaps establishing roots on the frontier. The Aboriginal people struggled to adjust to the changing environment and the new way of life thrust upon them. The NWMP were cast for the role of the regulatory force ensuring that order was maintained in an unstable situation. For the most part, the NWMP successfully coped with the responsibilities they bore.

The Indians had a very difficult time adjusting to their diminution in status from masters of the prairies to semi-dependent wards of the state. Government policy effecting the transition was administered by the Indian Department but the Mounted Police were an important agent of control. The principal concern was that another violent uprising would occur like that in 1885. Indeed there were signs that this might happen like the dangerous situation in the Kootenays in 1887 and conflicts across the border that might have spread. The NWMP maintained a readiness to respond and in the case of the threat in the Kootenays deployed a significant segment of the Force to the area. But diplomacy and negotiation eased the tensions without either side having to resort to violence.

There was less crime among the Aboriginal population than among white settlers. In the first few years after the rebellion there were a number of cases of horse stealing and cattle killing, particularly in the Blackfoot Confederacy, but this dropped off over time. More common were offences like drunkenness and prostitution, the unfortunate effects of contacts with the settlers. Then, of course, there were the spectacular aberrations of the Almighty Voice and Charcoal cases. These are in the category of dramatic criminal sprees without much significance in the area of Aboriginal/settler relations.

Another vital role for the NWMP on the frontier was assisting in the settlement of the prairies by newcomers from eastern Canada, the United States and Europe. In the case of transient workers on railways and in coal mines, the Force was involved in labour relations. This was a delicate balancing act between protecting the property of employers and preventing the abuse of the workers. Settlers coming to the new land often needed help in the form of advice or assistance to survive before they could prosper. Again the Mounted Policeman was the individual on hand to meet the need. The government, too, depended on the Force to ensure that regulations about agriculture, immigration and customs were observed. This role has caused the NWMP to be aptly described as 'Agents of the National Policy'.

And a growing role for the Force throughout this period was to act as police in the emerging new settlements. In the early years the predominantly male population exercised illegal appetites for liquor and sex. Mounted Police attempts to enforce laws in this respect were energetic but futile. But as the frontier began to pass, settlements became more conventional and crime grew in variety and in numbers. The Mounted Police adjusted to these changes displaying a capability to investigate crimes and apprehend the perpetrators. Again, because the Mounted Police were the unique presence on the frontier, their role in the system of justice was more extensive than was usual for police forces. Acting as justices of the peace and magistrates, the commissioned officers of the Force judged and sentenced offenders. Then, as principal jailers for the NWT the Mounted Police incarcerated criminals in their guardrooms.

On the whole, the NWMP handled their multifarious responsibilities in a remarkably efficient manner. But the process of doing so was neither easy nor neat. There were serious conflicts within the command of the Force which caused continuous turmoil. And while the NWMP services were appreciated by most in the NWT, there were many in the federal government who were anxious to truncate or even terminate their services. The feeling was that the West must now assume responsibility for its own policing.

By 1900, an important era in Mounted Police history had passed. Lawrence W. Herchmer had commanded the Force as Commissioner from 1886 to 1900. He had seen the police through a unique period of transition of the Canadian West from frontier to settlement. Now, Aylesworth Bowen Perry would take the helm with a new set of challenges as Commissioner. Instead of diminishing as forecast by many, the Force would flourish under Perry, expanding into northern frontiers, participating in military expeditions overseas, and extending its police services throughout Canada. At the end of the next period the modern Royal Canadian Mounted Police emerged.

Part II:
All Sorts and Conditions of Men

Introduction

When Lawrence Herchmer was named Commissioner of the North-West Mounted Police in 1886, he faced a daunting task. The Force had just been through the difficult period of the North-West Rebellion. Subsequently, in response to the perceived continued threat from the Indians, its number had been doubled from 500 to 1,000 members. The majority of the officers in the Force were new and unfamiliar with their duties. Many of the men had been hastily recruited and would prove unsuitable for police work.

On top of all these problems, there was considerable reason to criticize the choice of Herchmer as Commissioner. He had military education and experience in the British Army, but that had ended 24 years previously. Since then, all his service for the Canadian government had been in civil capacities. Also, he was known for his intolerant and quarrelsome nature. He was inheriting a Force whose senior officers bitterly resented that Herchmer had been brought in from the outside, thus blocking the opportunity for advancement of one of their number. Herchmer immediately gave further cause for resentment by promoting his own brother, William Herchmer, from Superintendent to Assistant Commissioner.

But there were positive aspects to Herchmer which ultimately led to his qualified success in command of the NWMP. He had spent a long time on the western frontier, in fact, he had been there two years before the arrival of the Mounted Police. He had spent ten years as an Indian agent and an Inspector of Indian agencies and so was familiar with the problem of relating to the Aboriginal people. Moreover, he was an extraordinarily determined individual. He tenaciously dealt with the problems besetting the Force and often achieved improvement. Despite bitter disputes with his sub-

ordinate officers, politicians and the press, he refused to bow to pressures to resign. He stayed and prevailed over most of his critics, even enduring a judicial enquiry which many hoped would pillory him, but in the end awarded him virtual vindication.

The successes that Herchmer achieved were not reached on his own. Much credit is due to the Comptroller, Deputy Minister in Ottawa, Fred White. Comptroller White was an experienced and capable bureaucrat who had climbed to the pinnacle of the civil service. He directed and supported Herchmer when necessary and represented the needs of the NWMP most ably to the minister responsible and to Parliament. The ministers too, especially Sir John A. Macdonald, responded when possible to the needs of the Force with required resources and supported Herchmer's methods of operation.

It would not do to overstate Herchmer's degree of success as Commissioner. He had no great vision of how he would transform the Force from its troubled post-rebellion state. Instead he had the ability to cope with the many problems he saw and to seek solutions. He did this the hard way, by relentless work and without the benefit of charismatic leadership qualities which draw the support of subordinates. As the following chapters demonstrate, he achieved improvements in most areas of the conditions of service in the Mounted Police before leaving for overseas military service in 1900.

Chapter 11

The Officers' Life in the North-West Mounted Police

The shock of the North-West Rebellion and the anticipated demands of increased settlement pointed to the need to increase the strength of the Mounted Police. In 1885, the size of the Force was doubled from 500 members to 1,000. The increase in strength also doubled the officer complement of the Force from 25 to 50, including half a dozen medical or veterinary surgeons, or approximately one officer to every 20 men.

By October 1886, of the 49 officers in the Mounted Police, 29, including Herchmer, had been appointed to the Force in the previous ten months. During the same period, only four officers left, among them Crozier, Irvine and Insp. Francis Dickens, a sad figure who had found it difficult to live within the shadow cast by the fame of his father, the English novelist, Charles Dickens. Growing increasingly deaf and in poor health, he was invalided from the Force on 1 March 1886. Never very prudent where money was concerned, he accepted an opportunity to improve his finances by making a speaking tour of the United States. His father had made similar tours many years before with considerable success. On the eve of his first engagement, however, he suffered a severe heart attack and died suddenly at Moline, Illinois, in June 1886.

Of the twenty-nine new officers, only seven had served in the Force before. This must have had some impact on the efficiency of the organization, for a time at least. Four of the new Inspectors, Z. T. Wood, P. C. H. Primrose, T. W. Chalmers and V. A. S. Williams had attended the Royal Military College, Kingston. The latter was the son of Lt. Col. A. T. H. Williams, MP, of the Midland Battalion, who had died of typhoid a few days after leading the charge against the rebels at Batoche. His appointment probably stemmed from the military tradition that the son of an officer who dies on active service becomes entitled to a commission. Williams, who was only 19 years old, would have to command men more than twice his age and a lifetime ahead of him in experience. Eleven of the new appointees had served with the Canadian militia at one time or another. Of these, five had participated in the recent rebellion. They included Supt. E. W. Jarvis who had commanded the Winnipeg Field Battery; Jarvis, a native of Prince Edward Island, had first gone west as a surveyor with the Boundary Commission in 1871.

The new officers were selected through the system of political patronage and geographical representation which was the established practice for filling government positions at the time. Sir Richard Cartwright queried the government in the Commons on its policy for selecting officers, asking that places be found for RMC graduates. Macdonald replied that it had been his practice to choose men from three sources – experienced non-commissioned officers, likely officers of the Active Militia and graduates of the military college in Kingston. He cited Supt. A. B. Perry as a fine example of the way in which the Mounted Police was benefitting from RMC.[1] Herchmer could recommend men from the ranks, but the Minister made the final selection. Five did come from the ranks, but even they needed political support as well. The *Regina Leader* vigorously argued that all officers should come from the ranks.[2] Napoleon's army was invincible, proclaimed Nicholas Flood Davin, because every man carried a marshal's baton in his knapsack. Herchmer no doubt agreed with him, but pork barrel politics were firmly entrenched. It was a system that did not always work to the best interests of the Force. Many experienced NCOs, with little political influence, had to watch while others were commissioned who had neither the ability, training nor motivation. It was difficult, however, for the government to ignore outstanding efforts of one kind or another by NCOs and Macdonald and later ministers sincerely endeavoured to select the best possible candidates that they could, under the circumstances. All provinces were represented among those chosen from outside the Force except British Columbia. There were six from Quebec, eight from Ontario, three from Manitoba, two from Nova Scotia and one each from New Brunswick and Prince Edward Island. Support from a cabinet minister or member of parliament from the province was behind almost every appointment. Tupper advanced the claims for those from Nova Scotia, Tilley for New Brunswick and Langevin or Caron for Quebec. They went to the privileged and the powerful, to those whose appointment would advance the governing party's position.

The new subalterns had a varied background.[3] Insp. H. S. Casey was an insurance broker and school trustee from Port Colborne, Ontario. Mills was a pay clerk from Hamilton. Casey told Macdonald, "Thank you from the bottom of my heart for my appointment. I look forward to seeing our government returned on the 22nd. I enclose a clipping from our local paper to show how well my Appt. was received in East Northumberland."[4] Casey referred to the general election that was set for 22 February 1887. Whether his appointment was a part of the election campaign is unknown. If it was, it did not tip the scales in favour of the government, the Liberals took the riding by 12 votes. Insp. J. B. (Captain Jack) Allan was an elected member of the Manitoba Legislature. Premier John Norquay pleaded for a commission on his behalf, on the grounds that he was going to lose his seat in the coming redistribution.[5] Born in Armagh, Ireland, Allan certainly had the military experience. He fought for the North in the American Civil War and served in the Canadian Militia during the Fenian Raids, the Red River Expedition and the North-West Rebellion.

The only candidate selected because of his practical police experience was Insp. Charles Constantine. A Yorkshireman by birth, son of a Church of England priest, he first went west, like Allan, with the Red River Expedition in 1870. His subsequent career made him a very useful addition to the Mounted Police. From 1880 to 1886, he was the Chief of the Manitoba Provincial Police. White had deliberately recommended Constantine to Macdonald with the intention of using his experience to organize the detective service he planned for the NWMP.[6] Four of the officers were French-Canadians. They included Insp. Cortlandt Starnes, a future Commissioner, and Insp. J. V. Bégin who had been a steamboat captain on the St. Lawrence River. He was a cousin of Cardinal Bégin of Québec. Insp. A. R. Cuthbert's father, Edward O. Cuthbert, was a Conservative member of parliament for Berthier. Twenty-four-year-old Insp. A. E. Snyder obtained his appointment through the influence of his uncle, George Hilliard, Conservative member for Peterborough, Ontario.

A familiar cry in the press and parliament was that too many appointments in the Mounted Police went to Englishmen. Several were British by birth, Herchmer for example, but with one exception, they had all lived in Canada for many years. The exception was Insp. W. G. Matthews, a former riding master of the 3rd Hussars, an imperial regiment with which he had served for ten years in India as a lieutenant. Matthews' appointment was intended to improve the riding instruction for recruits in the new "Depot" Division. He was, in fact, to become the organizer of the first musical rides.

Some of them had illustrious forebears. Insp. Zachary Taylor Wood was named after his great-grandfather, Zachary Taylor, 12th President of the United States. He was also a nephew of Jefferson Davis, President of the Confederate States of America. Wood was born at the Annapolis Naval Academy, Maryland, where his father was an instructor. The Woods were southerners and upon the outbreak of the Civil War, the elder Wood became a captain in the Confederate Navy. He had a distinguished career, commanding the TALLA-HASEE when it broke through the blockade by federal cruisers of Halifax Harbour, and taking part in the famous fight between the MERRIMAC and the MONITOR at Hampton Roads. With the end of the war, Capt. Wood escaped to Cuba and made his way to Halifax where the family settled.[7]

Two of the new surgeons had antecedents that had been closely associated together at one time as members of the Legislative Assembly of Upper Canada and had left their mark on the political development of the province. Surgeon H. Y. Baldwin was the grandson of Robert Baldwin, the political reformer, who with Louis H. Lafontaine, was credited with bringing responsible government to Canada. Surgeon J. W. Rolph, on the other hand, was the son of Dr. John Rolph who had been implicated with William Lyon Mackenzie in the 1837 plot to overthrow the Government of Upper Canada.

Both Herchmer and his successors subscribed to the nineteenth century idea that commissioned officers should also be gentlemen. It was an ideal for which they strove, but were never able to fully achieve. Many officers did come from middle and upper class families, and had acquired the acceptable manners and courtesies required for social relationships and public behaviour. The system of political appointments, however, had a levelling effect on a candidate's ability to handle a knife and fork. Political patronage opened the doors to the churlish, but upwardly mobile lower classes. On the other hand, the impoverished gentry did on occasion join the ranks beneath them. There were many constables who would have been more at ease in polite society than a few of their officers. Of Insp. Casey, Supt. A. H. Griesbach wrote:

> He has no control over men, being at one time too familiar and at other times indiscreetly and unreasonably severe, and it is quite impossible to expect men of education in the ranks to respect him, as he is ignorant and without the manners of a gentleman.[8]

C. P. Dwight, a constable from a well-to-do Toronto family, noted that the Commanding Officer of "A" Division (E. W. Jarvis) was a thorough gentleman and his treatment of men at all times considerate and impartial, but the qualities of a number of officers "would recommend them but little in any respectable society".[9]

The large infusion of new blood in the commissioned ranks placed a greater responsibility on the older officers, the ten Superintendents and Asst. Comm. Herchmer, to provide leadership. As it happened, between them they represented a considerable amount of experience with western conditions and police duties. With the exception of Deane and Perry, they had all been in the Territories for over a decade. Four of them, Steele, Griesbach, Cotton and Herchmer had originally arrived on the prairies with the 1870 Red River Expedition. McIllree, Steele, Neale, Antrobus and Griesbach had been with the Mounted Police since its formation in 1873-1874. All of them had military service of one kind or another. Herchmer and Gagnon, who was the only French-Canadian, were qualified barristers. They included at least seven Anglicans and one Roman Catholic, Gagnon. Four were British in origin. These were Deane, Neale, McIllree ("old John Henry", the only officer educated at Sandhurst Military College) and Griesbach, who had served with the Cape Mounted Rifles in South Africa. The other seven were native Canadians. Cotton, who spoke fluent French and Blackfoot, was also a son-in-law of the Minister of the Interior, Thomas White. Sam Steele, "Smoothbore" to the rank and file, was the son of a Royal Navy Captain who had settled in Simcoe county, Ontario. Two with unimpeachable Loyalist backgrounds were Perry and Herchmer, the former would succeed to the Commissionership in 1900. Aylesworth Bowen Perry was born in Lennox county, Ontario. In 1880, he graduated at the top of the first class of cadets at Royal Military College, Kingston, winning the Governor General's Medal.[10] After a short period of service with the Royal Engineers, Perry was appointed an Inspector in the NWMP in 1882.[11]

Officers of the NWMP were appointed to their positions of trust by Her Majesty, or Her Representative, under the Great Seal, like those of the regular military service. As with the army officers, they considered themselves a part of a distinctly privileged social class, which was called upon to serve society and follow an accepted code of behaviour. So often in the nineteenth century, however, an appointment to such office did not always bring with it sufficient financial resources for the holder to live up to the standards and obligations expected of him. An Inspector's salary in 1886 was $1,000 per annum, exactly the same as it was when the Force had been established. It was a good deal more than a school teacher or skilled tradesman could expect, about twice as much as a staff sergeant, and four times that of a constable. An Inspector earned the same amount as a captain in the Active Permanent Militia, but less than that received by customs, post office and inland revenue Inspectors in the civil service.[12]

There were numerous positions at the time, both in the federal government and elsewhere, to which the titles "Inspector" or "Superintendent" were attached. It was to avoid being identified with the undistinguished and civilian connotation attached to these terms that Mounted Police officers preferred to use military ranks. A Superintendent received $1,400 a year for the added responsibility of commanding a division. The Commissioner's pay was $2,600, which put him one step down on the Civil Service salary scales from White who earned $3,200 as a deputy minister. It was considerably less than the judges of the Supreme Court of the NWT who received $4,000.

Most officers without other means of support found it difficult to live on their pay, especially if they had a wife and several children. As gentlemen they were expected to buy and maintain their own uniform. As a result, they faced a crippling expenditure on appointment of about $500, or half of the first year's pay, to outfit themselves.[13] Also at the outset, they had to spend $15 for their parchment commissions and pay an annual fee to an insurance company in order to be bonded against any loss of public funds under their control. In addition, there were pension deductions and mess bills. The most worrying burden, however, was the social obligations expected of him and his wife. This necessitated the employment of domestic help, at least part-time. Because of its clubs and its "high society", Calgary was notorious as the most expensive posting for an officer of the NWMP. When Herchmer wanted to move Supt. Perry there, he threatened to resign, declaring that he could not live there on his pay.[14] On the other hand, he had no trouble sending Insp. D. H. Macpherson, the son of Sir David

Macpherson, the railway magnate, because "he is well off and would suit Calgary well".[15]

Officers of the NWMP had a great deal of social status in nascent western society, but they paid for it through their pocket books. As a result, many of them had to seek additional income and to economize in every way possible. Some obtained appointments as customs or preventative officers, which at certain posts could bring them in several hundred dollars extra. Supt. Cotton's commission for collecting customs at Fort Macleod amounted to over $700 one year.[16] Supt. Perry profited from his background in civil engineering by acting as a surveyor from time to time. Insp. Drayner received $50 a month while employed as private secretary to the Lieutenant-Governor. Deane was enabled to live in conspicuous style by the $900 a year he received as clerk to the territorial council. The surgeons usually maintained a private practice for local settlers, in addition to their police duties. Even Herchmer cultivated a vegetable garden at Headquarters to supplement the rations issued. At Lethbridge, Deane kept several cows for milk as well as chickens.[17] The wives of officers could not take in sewing or washing like those of the other ranks, but they had an important role in the family economy. In 1886, Lily McIllree, wife of the commanding officer at Maple Creek, raised Plymouth Rock chickens, kept a large vegetable garden and caught fish for dinner in a nearby creek.[18] In spite of their efforts, debt was the lot of a number of officers, particularly the younger ones, with tradesmen complaining to the Commissioner about their tardiness in paying their bills.

In addition to pay, officers received other material benefits, notably free rations, housing and medical care, for themselves and their families, as well as a pension. In 1886, the *Mounted Police Act* was amended so as to bring officers under the provisions of the *Civil Service Superannuation Act*;[19] another indication that the government saw the Force less and less as a temporary arrangement. Under the plan, an officer could retire at age 60 with a pension for life, provided he had a minimum of ten years of service. He could retire earlier, if he was in some way incapacitated. It was a contributory scheme into which they paid two per cent of their annual pay. The pension was calculated on the principle of one-50th of the average pay for the 3 years prior to retirement for each year of service to a maximum of 35 years. As an example, an Inspector who retired with 30 years service at an average salary of $1,000 a year would receive a pension of $600 for life. There were no carry over provisions for his wife, however, in the event of his death. Once he died, his pension died with him. Interestingly enough, there was no compulsory age of retirement. An officer could serve until he was 95, provided he

was still capable of carrying out his duties. Insp. George Stevens, who retired at age 75, was probably the oldest person ever to serve the Force.[20] The officers' pension plan was quite separate from that provided for the other ranks in 1889. This was to be a problem for NCOs promoted to commissioned rank.

The officers were treated generously as far as leave was concerned. Under the regulations, the Commissioner could grant up to 30 days a year for each officer, provided the leave was spent in the Territories.[21] Sick leave was granted liberally upon the recommendation of the surgeon. For periods of leave beyond 30 days, or for permission to leave the Territories, application had to be made to Ottawa. Macdonald usually complied with requests providing they were not for leave during the busy summer months. In 1887, Supt. W. D. Antrobus was given two weeks leave to go to Banff for treatment for rheumatism, followed by a further two months to convalesce in eastern Canada. In the winter of 1890, Steele obtained four months leave in order to get married. His bride was Marie Elizabeth Harwood, daughter of Robert Harwood, MP, a seigneur of Vaudreuil county, Quebec, and a descendant of the Marquises of Lotbinière. The newlyweds spent their honeymoon in the United States and returned to Fort Macleod in May after spending a "very pleasant time in the east".[22]

Drunkenness and marriage were the *bêtes noires* of the Mounted Police for Herchmer and White. Married men were more of a drain on the public purse than single ones. They also became concerned about the welfare of their families which distracted them from their duties. Worst of all, they were inclined to seek the comforts of hearth and home rather than patrolling their districts on horseback in bad weather. Herchmer would no doubt have preferred that his officers came from a professed order of celibates. Unfortunately, they turned out to have a natural human desire for female companionship. Reflecting upon this fact, White concluded that in spite of the great inconvenience to the service, it was better for them to be married than single.[23] After all, unmarried officers were likely to get involved in some scandal that would damage the Force's reputation and ruin their careers. It was safer to have them caught up with the concerns of marital domesticity than foot loose and fancy free.

Married officers, nevertheless, would create many problems for the Force in the years ahead. The quarters at some posts were insufficient to accommodate them. As a result, they were forced to rent houses in town at government expense which removed them from the site of their duties. White was angry when an NCO who had just been commissioned announced he intended to get married. Had he known this beforehand, White told him, he would not have recommended his promotion.[24] At one time, the Commissioner suggested that only half of the Inspectors should be allowed to be married, but nothing came of it. He was angered by situations such as existed at Calgary where both Inspectors were married, lived over a mile from the barracks and were not available, as a result, to see that discipline was maintained at night.[25] When Insp. W. S. Morris was transferred from Fort Macleod to Pincher Creek, he left his wife and family behind. The result, complained Herchmer, was that he regularly visited Fort Macleod, "killing horses in the process". At Maple Creek, he continued, Insp. Gilbert Sanders, who was married, had slept every night that year in his own bed, leaving Insp. Jarvis, who was unmarried, to make all the patrols.[26] The efficiency of the Force was undermined, he believed, because wives and children prevented him from moving some officers to where they would be most useful.

Being a married officer did bring some material benefits. In 1887, Macdonald approved an issue of double rations for them.[27] The Commissioner was also authorized to grant them free issues of coal. Those forced to live out of barracks because of a lack of government quarters could expect a reasonable cash allowance to cover the rent. Certain unwritten privileges also accompanied rank. Officers obtained manure from the stables for their gardens, prisoners were often available to do gardening and household chores, and artisans could be inveigled into repairing windows, fixing chimneys and doing other maintenance jobs. They could also expect to find a spare constable to drive their wives into town to do their shopping, although the Commissioner would not have approved of the latter.

When the Mounted Police arrived on the prairies in the 1870s, they had mixed socially with the Métis, particularly the English-speaking group, even married them. A decade later, an officer with a wife of mixed Indian and white ancestry was unthinkable. Officers' wives were expected to be educated young ladies from the respectable classes. In the late 1880s, such eligible womenfolk were still not plentiful in the Territories. Single officers had to do their courting while on leave in the East or in the Old Country.

In 1884, Lily McIllree left her home in Ireland to travel alone all the way to Maple Creek to marry her fiancé, Supt. J. H. McIllree. A year later, Insp. Frank Harper's intended came from Suffolk in England for the same reason. Lily McIllree struggled to make a new life in a strange environment to bring some gentility to the prairie landscape, often under primitive circumstances. She played the organ in church, participated in local charities, entertained and, although she had a servant, spent many hours cooking, sewing and cleaning to make a home for her family. For most women of her time there was the ever present danger associated with childbirth and children's diseases. Periodically, diphtheria and scarlet fever appeared among the young inhabitants of the Mounted Police posts and took their toll. She was fortunate to have a doctor present for her first child, but it almost died when she was unable to breast feed it. The Harpers were not so lucky. Their first child did die. There were sadder cases however. In 1890, Supt. Cotton's wife died giving birth to twins. They also died shortly after.[28] Three years later, Supt. J. Howe and his wife lost two infant sons in Calgary.[29]

Some wives found the move to the prairies a traumatic experience. Insp. William G. Matthews' wife detested Regina. She finally left her husband, refusing to live in the Territories any longer. Left with a four-year-old son to care for, he eventually resigned his commission to take up a more sedentary occupation.[30]

For a period of time, Lily McIllree kept a daily diary. In February 1885, she and her husband spent a few days in Regina staying with Comm. Irvine. It was a social visit that indicates the close camaraderie of the officers and their families, but the proper formalities were observed:

Feb. 15 Left M.C. [Maple Creek] for Regina - met by Col. Irvine who drove us to his house.

Feb. 16 Tea next door with Mr. [Insp.] White-Fraser at 5 p.m. Dined at the Colonel's – the Colonel is one of the nicest men I ever met.

Feb. 20 Went to Dr. Jukes [the Senior Surgeon] after dinner and played whist.

Feb. 21 The White-Frasers dined with us.

Feb. 22 Mrs. Deane, the Adj's [Adjutant] wife called on me. She would have called before but her mother had only been dead a week.

A few entries from her diary in the spring of 1886 while in Maple Creek give us a glimpse in to the hopes, anxieties, joys and activities that filled her daily life:

Mar. 17 A white world. We went in sleighs to a dance given by our men in the Commercial Hotel in account of S. M. [sergeant major] Douglas' wedding. They gave him a tea service, electric plate and tray and illuminated address. Everybody was there.

Mar. 21 I went to a social of the ladies Aid Society.

Apr. 7 Mrs. Harper spent the day and she and her husband [Insp. Harper] dined. I made a pudding for lunch and cooked dinner. Servant off.

Apr. 15 2nd anniversary of our wedding day - was so sorry J. [her husband]161 was away.

May 1 Nearly made a pink gingham dress for baby.

May 3 I painted again at my plaque of Canadian flowers.

May 9 Mr. Tudor [Church of England minister] held service and Holy Communion here. Baby cut her 2nd tooth.

May 17 I drove down town in the morning with baby – then sowed potatoes, onions – cooked dinner in the afternoon then planted cucumbers, water melons and flowers.

June 4 Mrs. H. [she was attending Mrs. Hooper who had just given birth] fainting in night - very, very ill - delirious - baby bad. Dr. came.

All newly appointed officers were required to report to the Commissioner in Regina for instruction in their duties.[31] They remained at Headquarters under his exacting eye until such time as he was satisfied that they were sufficiently qualified in foot and mounted drill and the regulations of the Force. He made it clear to them that efficiency in drill was a necessary criteria for his recommendations for future promotion.[32] They were also supplied with the necessary legal manuals and statutes to prepare themselves for their magisterial duties. As a rule, all officers were appointed justices of the peace and would be required to hear both civil and criminal cases. Instruction did not end when they left Regina. Their commanding officers were required to maintain their competence at drill and to see that they were thoroughly instructed regarding all aspects of their duties. With his customary vigour, Steele at Fort Macleod organized spring drills at which he personally put his subordinate officers through their paces. By 1891, he was setting written exams for them that covered a wide range of duties, including horse shoeing, criminal court procedure, accounting and management.[33] Nevertheless, in spite of the attention given to training, by far the biggest teacher was still experience, and it took several years of this to produce a proficient officer.

Promotion within the commissioned ranks was very slow, and would remain so for decades to come. Without an increase in establishment, officers had to wait for their seniors to die or retire before there was a chance of advancement. Of the 20 men appointed Inspectors between 1886 and 1891, only 5 were ever raised to Superintendent rank, and they waited an average of 18 years for the promotion. The worst case of lack of advancement was Insp. D. M. Howard, a graduate of the University of Toronto and a member of the bar of Upper Canada. Commissioned an Inspector in 1890, he retired 35 years later in the same rank.

Promotion could be based upon merit, seniority in rank or a delicate combination of both. Seniority was the rule observed in most cases, partly because it was easier and less contentious to show who had the most service than who was the better man, and partly because it was traditional. Outstanding ability could, however, result in an officer being promoted over his seniors. In all cases, of course, the additional political influence was also necessary. In 1886, Macdonald abruptly issued a new qualification for advancement.[34] Angrily criticizing the older officers for not having learned the Indian languages, he ruled that in future officers who did would be given preference in promotion. The Prime Minister's motive here was unclear. On the one hand, he seemed concerned to improve communications between police and Indians. On the other, in his usual penny-pinching manner he was counting the money he could save by no longer having to pay interpreters. Perhaps it was a combination of both. In any event, his anxiety over the matter did not last very long. There is no evidence that ability to speak an Indian language was ever considered in any future promotion, which was probably another sign of the declining importance of the Native threat in his mind. Actually, there was always a small number of officers who were fluent in one Indian language or another.[35]

The sudden death of a senior officer, or rumour that one was considering retirement, was the signal for those who thought they had a chance to get their friends lobbying on their behalf for the vacancy. It could be a bitter scramble that engendered a good deal of resentment amongst those who were unsuccessful. In January 1892, Asst. Comm. W. H. Herchmer died suddenly as a result of heart failure. The three senior Superintendents were Cotton, McIllree and Gagnon, in that order. They were clearly the eligible contenders, but the ambitious Supt. Sam Steele set out to challenge their claim. He put his case in a letter to his father-in-law, a former Conservative Member of Parliament, who was to proceed to Ottawa to use his influence on Sam's behalf.[36] Steele's argument rested upon extending the matter of seniority to include service in the ranks as well. Thus, as they had all entered the Force after him, they were his juniors, he argued. Steele also thought that his service record merited the step-up. He had some justification here. None of the other three had seen active service in the recent rebellion. He, on the other hand, had been conspicuous for his dash and initiative in the hunt for Big Bear, had creditably policed the construction of the CPR and the trouble with the Kootenays in 1887. Regarding his opponents, Cotton was the son-in-law of a federal cabinet minister, McIllree appears to have had no notable political friends, but Gagnon was the son-in-law of Edgar Dewdney, Lieutenant-Governor of the NWT.

As Deputy Minister, it was White's job to listen to the representations on behalf of the candidates and draw up his recommendation for the approval of the Minister. Following Macdonald's death in 1891, responsibility for Mounted Police officers had been taken over by John Thompson, who became Prime Minister late in 1892. White told Thompson that Cotton was the senior man, thus rejecting Steele's interpretation of seniority, but that he could not recommend him.[37] The Comptroller did not have to expand on his unsuitability. His Minister knew exactly to what he referred. In the preceding months, Cotton had been a leading figure in a campaign to have Comm. Herchmer removed from office for mismanagement. To have promoted him as Herchmer's assistant would have been disastrous. White, therefore, came down in favour of the second Superintendent in order of seniority, J. H. McIllree. "His record has always been satisfactory," he told Thompson. "He is not a brilliant man but he is exceedingly reliable."[38] The Minister approved his choice. It was a judicious one, as the future would show. The Jamaican-born son of a surgeon-general of the British Army, McIllree was a gentlemanly, hard-working, conscientious administrator. Without burning ambition or an over-inflated ego, he was just the man to work under Herchmer.

The increase in the officer establishment in 1886 brought about a more permanent and fuller development of the institution of the officers' mess. In military tradition, the officers' mess was more than just separate living quarters from the other ranks. It was a community within itself whose function was to mould the social and occupational behaviour of its members. Being an officer was a way of life. The mess sought to inculcate acceptable gentlemanly conduct, to reinforce the identity of the officers as members of a morally and socially elite class in society and to regulate their relationship with the other ranks. Promoting esprit de corps amongst themselves was an important part of the process. "Officers are to cultivate that spirit of unanimity and good fellowship among themselves," stated the 1889 regulations, for which every force should be distinguished.[39] The officers of the NWMP inherited the mess tradition from the British Army and the Canadian Militia, in one of which most of them had previously served. They never established the same social exclusiveness that the military sometimes did, but Herchmer and his successors fully subscribed to the ideals of the mess tradition.

There had been messes for officers at Headquarters and in some divisions since the Force's inception, but they were for the most part temporary or short-lived establishments. Although they had occupied government quarters, they received no grants from public funds and the furnishings and other comforts had come largely from members. As there were usually no more than two or three officers in each division, the messes there had consisted of little more than a combined dining and living room. There had simply not been enough officers in one place, even at Headquarters, to support anything very pretentious.

After the increase in 1885 and the reorganization in Regina, the officer strength there reached 18, several of them being single. In addition, other officers began to visit Headquarters for short periods of training and other purposes. In April 1886, Herchmer informed Ottawa that the officers had taken over Irvine's house on the Barrack square and were about to establish a mess in it.[40] He argued that one was badly needed as some of the officers now had to be put up in the hotels in town. He submitted an estimate of $400 for furniture and furnishings to get it in working order and asked that it be met from public funds. White agreed and recommended to Macdonald that it be approved.[41] He further suggested that it should receive an annual allowance of $200, similar to that granted to military messes. The Prime Minister gave his approval to this also.

Situated in the territorial capital, the officers' mess in Regina came to play an important role in the social life of that community. It became involved in the various official functions observed by the local government, and was host to many dignitaries from Ottawa and elsewhere who visited the city. Because of the prohibitory laws there was no bar in the early days, although alcohol was obtained by the necessary permit for certain special occasions. In 1889, a billiard table was acquired at a cost of $315. That same year, the officers had the honour of having the Governor General, Lord Stanley, for lunch.[42] The following year, a steward was hired to do the catering.[43]

As there were two divisions headquartered in Fort Macleod, it was another location with an unusually high number of officers. They held a meeting in October 1888 and also decided to establish a formal mess.[44] Herchmer supported the decision, telling White that officers visiting there were forced to put up at the "wretched hotels", and no hospitality could be given to the many officials who passed through the town.[45] He requested an additional grant for its maintenance, but nothing came of it.

The fact was the $200 allowance for the Regina mess had been criticized in the House of Commons. A member who noticed it in the estimates had suggested that it would have been better spent on library books for the rank and file rather than comforts and conveniences for the officers.[46] It was agreed in 1892, however, that Fort Macleod could have $50 of the annual grant to Regina at the Commissioner's discretion.[47] In the meantime, they had already gone ahead at their own expense to get a mess established in style. In 1888, they purchased a quality dinner service, silver plated cutlery and dishes inscribed with the "MP" monogram, a large dining table, carpets, glasses for all formal occasions and four nickel plated spittoons.[48] Meanwhile, officers' messes of sorts continued at other posts from time to time dependent upon whatever resources were available.

As members of an elite group in the community, the officers moved in the highest social circles. They counted among their friends the senior officials of government, the large ranchers, executives

2. *Lawrence Herchmer, Commissioner,
North-West Mounted Police, 1886-1900.*

1. *Sergeant of the North-West Mounted
Police in full dress uniform, 1898
(Ralph-Clark-Stone Ltd., painting by
Tom McNeely).*

3. *Mounted Escort for the Governor General and
Countess of Aberdeen on their visit to Calgary
in October 1894.*

Complete photograph captions start on page x.

4. *Church Parade, Regina, 1890. Once around the square led by the band and into the chapel.*

5. *Winter travel in Regina, 1895. A four-in-hand cutter with sleigh bells.*

6. *Clowning about in the pharmacy at Regina in the 1880s. The surgeon seems to be prescribing something that might put some life back into the skeleton.*

7. *9 pounder gun drill at Fort Macleod, 1894.*
Both guns and the two mortars between them were taken west by the police in 1874.

8. *Almighty Voice,
Kah-kee-say-mane-too-wayo,
the Cree Indian who shot
and killed Sgt. Colin
Colebrook
in October 1895.*

9. *$500 reward notice for the
capture of the Almighty Voice,
Kah-kee-say-mane-too-wayo.
(facing page)*

PROCLAMATION.

ABERDEEN.
(L.S.)

CANADA.

VICTORIA, by the Grace of God, of the United Kingdom of Great Britain and Ireland, *Queen*, Defender of the Faith, &c., &c.

To all to whom these presents shall come, or whom the same may in anywise concern,—GREETING:

A PROCLAMATION.

E. L. NEWCOMBE,
Deputy of the Minister of Justice, Canada.

WHEREAS, on the twenty-ninth day of October, one thousand eight hundred and ninety-five, **COLIN CAMPBELL COLEBROOK,** a Sergeant of the North-West Mounted Police, was murdered about eight miles east of Kinistino, or about forty miles south-east of Prince Albert, in the North-West Territories, by an Indian known as "Jean-Baptiste," or "Almighty Voice," who escaped from the police guard-room at Duck Lake;

And Whereas, it is highly important for the peace and safety of Our subjects that such a crime should not remain unpunished, but that the offenders should be apprehended and brought to justice;

Now Know Ye that a reward of **FIVE HUNDRED DOLLARS** will be paid to any person or persons who will give such information as will lead to the apprehension and conviction of the said party.

In Testimony Whereof, We have caused these Our Letters to be made Patent and the Great Seal of Canada to be hereunto affixed.

Witness, Our Right Trusty and Right Well-beloved Cousin and Councillor the Right Honourable Sir JOHN CAMPBELL HAMILTON-GORDON, Earl of Aberdeen; Viscount Formartine, Baron Haddo, Methlic, Tarves and Kellie, in the Peerage of Scotland; Viscount Gordon of Aberdeen, County of Aberdeen, in the Peerage of the United Kingdom; Baronet of Nova Scotia, Knight Grand Cross of Our Most Distinguished Order of Saint Michael and Saint George, &c., Governor General of Canada.

At Our Government House, in Our City of Ottawa, this Twentieth day of April, in the year of Our Lord one thousand eight hundred and ninety-six, and in the Fifty-ninth year of Our Reign.
By command,

CHARLES TUPPER,
Secretary of State.

DESCRIPTION OF THE AFORESAID INDIAN "JEAN-BAPTISTE" OR "ALMIGHTY VOICE":

About twenty-two years old, five feet ten inches in height, weight eleven stone, slightly built and erect, neat small feet and hands; complexion inclined to be fair, wavey dark hair to shoulders, large dark eyes, broad forehead, sharp features and parrot nose with flat tip, scar on left cheek running from mouth towards ear, feminine appearance.

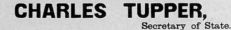

10. *Sgt. Colin Colebrook, a former shop clerk from London, England, endeavored to apprehend Almighty Voice without resorting to violence.*

11. *Ida Colebrook, the widow of the slain Sergeant, was one of the first women to be employed by the Mounted Police as a matron.*

12. *Mounted Police field guns shelling the bluff where Almighty Voice and his companions were trapped in May 1897.*

13. *In 1891, teams from Winnipeg, Moosomin and the NWMP played off against each other for the Hamilton Cup in the first challenge for the rugby football championship of Manitoba and the North-West Territories.*

14. *The NWMP rugby football club, 1891, known locally as the "Rough Riders".*

15. *Group of NWMP commissioned officers, ca. 1894.*

16. *NWMP detachment teams leaving Regina for Wood Mountain in May 1895.*

17. *Members of the NWMP Sergeants' Mess, Regina, 1896.*

18. *Headquarters NWMP band playing outside Commissioner Herchmer's house on the barrack square at Regina, 1890.*

19. *"D" Division under Supt. Sam Steele, wearing white helmet, on the march from Fort Steele to Fort Macleod, August 1888.*

20. *Supt. Samuel Benfield Steele.*

21. *Supt. Joseph Howe's funeral at Macleod in 1902. The firing party at the slow march with rifles reversed leads the gun carriage carrying the body to the grave site.*

22. *"The Tampered Brand" by Canadian artist Arthur Heming. Stealing cattle by changing their brands was a common offence.*

23. *"Home Sweet Home". A barrack room at Battleford, 1898.*

24. *A montage of police photographs put together by Steele & Co. of Winnipeg to be sold as a greeting card for Christmas and New Years.*

25. *NWMP mounted band at Regina, 1890, under Sgt. Harry Walker (left foreground).*

SKETCHES OF THE CANADIAN MOUNTED POLICE.—DRAWN BY FREDERIC REMINGTON.—[SEE PAGE 782.]

26. *Sketches of the Canadian Mounted Police by the American artist Frederic Remington.*

27. Remington's drawing of the charge of the NWMP Musical Ride which appeared in Harper's Weekly on 24 December 1887.

28. S/Sgt. Pat Mahoney "was a wonderful foot drill instructor" recalled a recruit. "One of the old school" who used a "little rough talk".

29. *A social afternoon for the officer class at Macleod, 1899.*

30. *Members of the Stand Off detachment on the Blood Reserve, 1890.*

31. *Group of constables at Battleford in 1895 in typical everyday working attire.*

32. *NWMP cricket team, "E" Division, Calgary, 1890s.*

33. *The imposing riding school in Regina. In this building the first NWMP musical rides were performed in the winter of 1887.*

34. *NWMP town station, Regina, 1895. Once described as having holes in the floor, a cracked stove, no storm door and no toilet.*

35.

36. *Fred White, Comptroller in charge of the Mounted Police, 1878-1913.*

37. *Ten Mile detachment in the Cypress Hills, 1891. The police kept lots of dogs, especially large ones, that went with them on patrol.*

38. *Writing on Stone detachment. A lonely and isolated post close to the American border from which desertions sometimes occurred.*

39. *Boundary Creek detachment, 1887. Log walls chinked with mud and sod roof. Hospital S/Sgt. J.F. Foster, mounted.*

40. *Graburn detachment in the Cypress Hills about 1890 was named after Cst. Marmaduke Graburn who was murdered nearby in 1879 by a person or persons unknown.*

41. *Winchester model 1876 .45/75 calibre carbine in service with the police from 1878 to 1914.*

42. *Lee-Metford bolt action .303 calibre carbine in service from 1895 to 1914.*

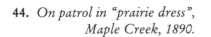

43. *Mark II Enfield .476 calibre revolver in service with the police 1882 to 1905.*

44. *On patrol in "prairie dress", Maple Creek, 1890.*

45. *Aylesworth Bowen Perry who succeeded Herchmer as Commissioner of the NWMP in 1900.*

46. *Blood Indian Charcoal, or Si'k-Okskitis, who was hanged at Macleod in 1897 for the murder of Sgt. W. B. Wilde (Glenbow-Alberta Institute).*

47. *S/Sgt. C. Hilliard and Blood Indian scouts at Fort Macleod in 1894. Some of these had an outstanding and courageous role in the pursuit of Charcoal two years later.*

48. *With their "prairie suits", "cowboy hats", bandoliers, Winchester carbines and revolvers at the cross draw, members of the NWMP at the Queen's Diamond Jubilee looked like just the kind of resourceful, mobile men of action that were needed to keep the peace on the far flung corners of the Empire.*

49. *Members of the Jubilee contingent in London, 1897.*

50. *The "E" Division band under S/Sgt. Fred Bagley (seated centre in front of the bass drum) at Banff in 1888 to play at the newly opened Banff Springs Hotel.*

51. *NWMP contingent at Queen Victoria's Diamond Jubilee in London, 1897. Their proud bearing and workman-like dress caught the imagination of the crowds in the capital of the British Empire.*

NORTH-WEST MOUNTED POLICE.

Ottawa, 12th February, 1897.

Memorandum for the Information of Applicants for Engagement in the North-West Mounted Police Force.

———•◦•◦•———

1. Applicants must be between the ages of Twenty-two and Forty, active, able-bodied men of thoroughly sound constitution, and must produce *certificates of exemplary character.*

2. They must be able to read or write either the English or French language, must understand the care and management of horses, and be able to ride well.

3. The term of engagement is five years.

4. The rates of pay are as follows :—

Staff Sergeants..................... $1.00 to $1.50 per day.

Other Non-Commissioned Officers........85c. to $1.00 "

	Pay.	Good Conduct Pay.	Total.
Constable—1st year's service..	50c.	—	50c. per day.
2nd "	50	5c.	55 "
3rd "	50	10	60 "
4th "	50	15	65 "
5th "	50	20	70 "

Extra pay is allowed to a limited number of blacksmiths, carpenters and other artisans.

5. Members of the Force are supplied with free rations, a free kit on joining and periodical issues during the term of service.

6. Married men will not be engaged.

7. The minimum height is 5 feet 8 inches, the minimum chest measurement 35 inches, and the maximum weight 175 lbs.

8. *No engagements are made in Eastern Canada.*

9. Application to join the Force must be made personally at the Head Quarters, Regina. If there are vacancies and an applicant possesses the necessary qualifications, he is employed on probation for two months, at the end of which period he is either engaged for five years or discharged as being unsuited for the service.

10. No expenses, travelling or otherwise, of applicants can be paid from public funds.

500—24-2-'97.

52. *Information for applicants for engagement in the NWMP, 1897.*

ORIGINAL.

Form No. 71

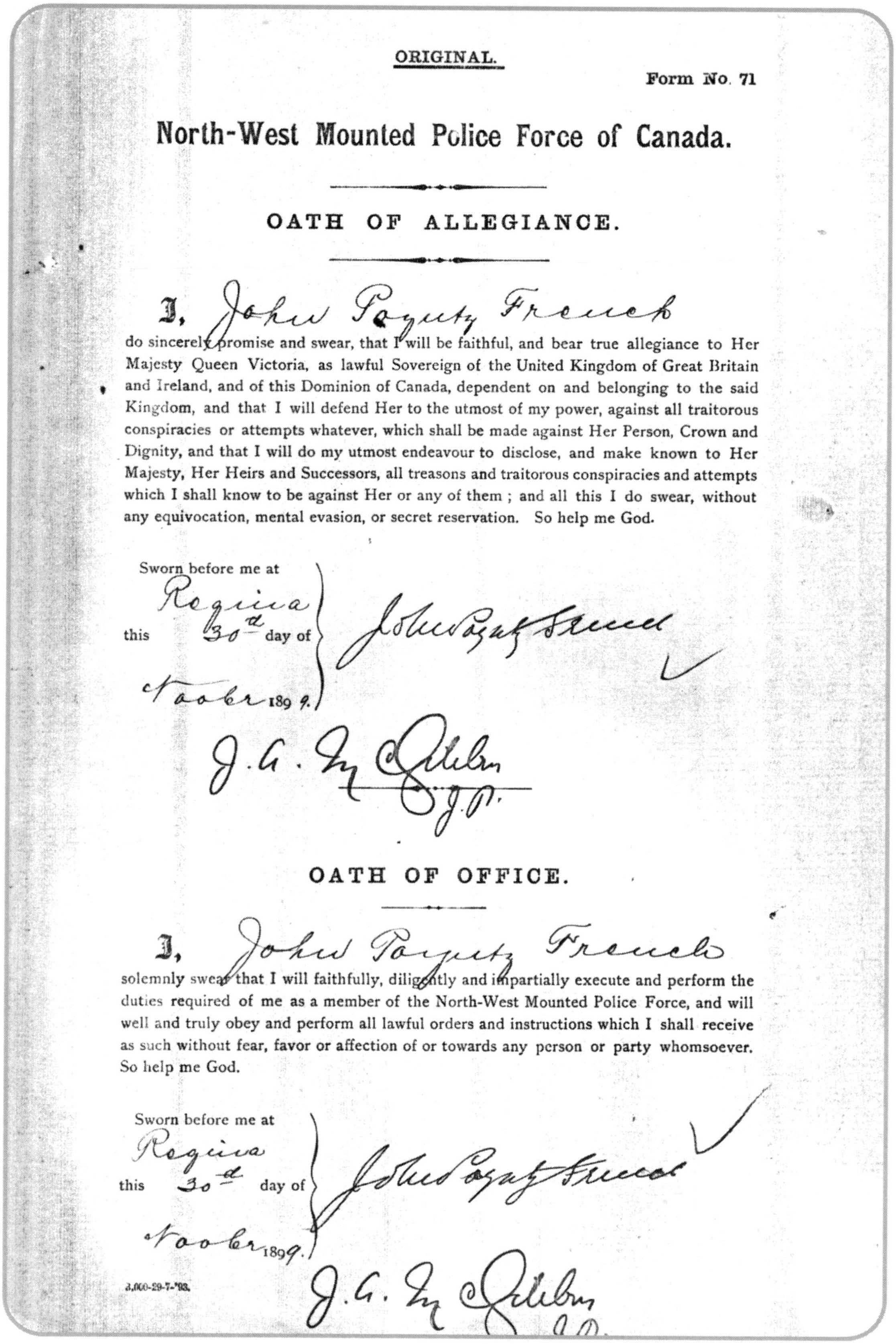

North-West Mounted Police Force of Canada.

OATH OF ALLEGIANCE.

I, John Poyntz French

do sincerely promise and swear, that I will be faithful, and bear true allegiance to Her Majesty Queen Victoria, as lawful Sovereign of the United Kingdom of Great Britain and Ireland, and of this Dominion of Canada, dependent on and belonging to the said Kingdom, and that I will defend Her to the utmost of my power, against all traitorous conspiracies or attempts whatever, which shall be made against Her Person, Crown and Dignity, and that I will do my utmost endeavour to disclose, and make known to Her Majesty, Her Heirs and Successors, all treasons and traitorous conspiracies and attempts which I shall know to be against Her or any of them ; and all this I do swear, without any equivocation, mental evasion, or secret reservation. So help me God.

Sworn before me at Regina this 30th day of Novbr 1899. } John Poyntz French

J. G. McGibbon J.P.

OATH OF OFFICE.

I, John Poyntz French

solemnly swear that I will faithfully, diligently and impartially execute and perform the duties required of me as a member of the North-West Mounted Police Force, and will well and truly obey and perform all lawful orders and instructions which I shall receive as such without fear, favor or affection of or towards any person or party whomsoever. So help me God.

Sworn before me at Regina this 30th day of Novbr 1899. } John Poyntz French

3,000-29-7-'93.

J. G. McGibbon J.P.

53. *The oath of office and the oath of allegiance required to be attested to by all recruits since the organization of the Force in 1873.*

N.W.M.P.

XMAS 1888.

F. **MENU.** F.

Soup.
Oyster Soup.

Fish.
Lake Trout, Red Deer Sauce.

Roast.
Turkey, Chickens, Bread Sauce

Boiled.
Ham.

Sweets.
Plum Pudding, Mince Pies
Blanc Mange.

Dessert. *Coffee.*

54. *Menu card for Christmas dinner at "F" Division, Prince Albert, 1888.*

North West Mounted Police Force, Canada.

Form No. 84a.

DISCHARGE.

This is to Certify that J. G. Donkin

served as Constable and Corporal

in the above Force from 30 September 1884 to 12th March 1888

and is now discharged in consequence of his having been permitted

to purchase his discharge

Dated at Regina, N.W.

13th March 1888

Commissioner N. W. M. P.

Conduct during Service   Good

Commissioner N. W. M. P.

This Discharge does not entitle the Grantee thereto to a Free Grant of Land.

55. _The discharge certificate issued to all members._
This one is for Cpl. J. G. Donkin, the author of "Trooper and Redskin".

North West Territories.

No. 2026

LIQUOR PERMIT
NORTH WEST TERRITORIES

NOT TRANSFERABLE

LIQUOR PERMIT.

56. _An example of the notorious liquor permits required to import alcohol into the NWT._

SCHEDULE of Free Kit issued to Constables.

Articles issued on joining, to be kept in serviceable condition at the Constable's expense during his whole term of service.—

Buffalo Robe	1
Blankets	2 pair.
Waterproof Sheet	1
Buffalo Coat	1
Cloth Overcoat	1
Helmet	1
Fur Cap	1
Gauntlets, Buckskin	1 pair.
Drawers, Woollen	2 "
Undershirts, Woollen	2
Overshirts, Flannel	2
Socks, Woollen	4 pair.
Stockings, Woollen	2 "
Mitts, Woollen	1 "
Spurs	1 "
Towels	2
Kit Bag	1
Haversack	1
Moccasins	1 pair.
Holdall	1
Knife	1
Fork	1
Spoon	1
Razor and Case	1
Comb	1
Shaving Brush	1
Blacking "	1
Polishing "	1
Cloth "	1
Button "	1
" Brass	1
Sponge	1
Burnisher	1
Cup	1
Saucer	1
Plate	1

Articles issued annually, to be kept in serviceable condition at the Constable's expense:—

Forage Cap	1
Tunic, Serge	1
Jacket, Stable	1
Breeches, Cloth	2 pair.
Trousers, Stable	1 "
Boots, Long	1 "
" Short	1 "

One Scarlet Cloth Tunic will be issued to each Constable on joining, and another during his third year of service.

57. Schedule of free kit issued to new recruits.

LAYING OUT KIT

For Inspection.

—DRESS.

Summer :—Serges, Breeches, Boots & Spurs, Side Arms, Carbines, Forage Caps.

Winter:—Serges, Breeches, Fur Caps, Moccasins & Stockings no spurs, Side Arms, Carbines.

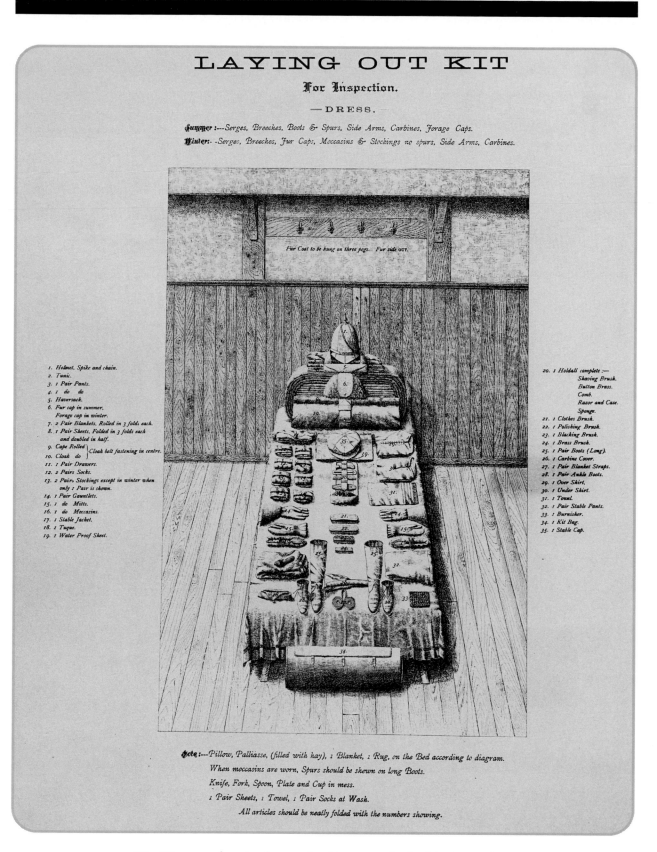

Fur Coat to be hung on three pegs.   Fur side out.

1. Helmet, Spike and chain.
2. Tunic.
3. 1 Pair Pants.
4. 1 do do
5. Haversack.
6. Fur cap in summer.
   Forage cap in winter.
7. 2 Pair Blankets, Rolled in 3 folds each.
8. 1 Pair Sheets, Folded in 3 folds each and doubled in half.
9. Cape Rolled } Cloak belt fastening in centre.
10. Cloak do
11. 1 Pair Drawers.
12. 2 Pairs Socks.
13. 2 Pairs Stockings except in winter when only 1 Pair is shown.
14. 1 Pair Gauntlets.
15. 1 do Mitts.
16. 1 do Moccasins.
17. 1 Stable Jacket.
18. 1 Tuque.
19. 1 Water Proof Sheet.

20. 1 Holdall complete :—
    Shaving Brush.
    Button Brass.
    Comb.
    Razor and Case.
    Sponge.
21. 1 Clothes Brush.
22. 1 Polishing Brush.
23. 1 Blacking Brush.
24. 1 Brass Brush.
25. 1 Pair Boots (Long).
26. 1 Carbine Cover.
27. 1 Pair Blanket Straps.
28. 1 Pair Ankle Boots.
29. 1 Over Shirt.
30. 1 Under Shirt.
31. 1 Towel.
32. 1 Pair Stable Pants.
33. 1 Burnisher.
34. 1 Kit Bag.
35. 1 Stable Cap.

Note :—Pillow, Palliasse, (filled with hay), 1 Blanket, 1 Rug, on the Bed according to diagram.

When moccasins are worn, Spurs should be shewn on long Boots.

Knife, Fork, Spoon, Plate and Cup in mess.

1 Pair Sheets, 1 Towel, 1 Pair Socks at Wash.

All articles should be neatly folded with the numbers showing.

58. *Diagram showing how to lay kit out on the bed for inspection.*

Northwest Mounted Police

RECRUITS WANTED.

APPLICANTS must be between the ages of twenty-two and forty, active, able-bodied men of thoroughly sound constitution, and must produce certificates of exemplary character and sobriety.

They must understand the care and management of horses; and be able to ride well.

The term of engagement is five years.

Members of the force are supplied free with rations, a free kit on joining, and periodical issues during the term of service.

Applications to be made to

RECRUITING OFFICER, N. W. M. Police.

At 677 Main Street, Winnipeg, between the hours of 9 a.m. and 6 p.m. 830

59. *Recruiting poster for the NWMP, 1893.*

N. W. Mounted Police.

PATROL REPORT.

"F" DIVISION 29th October 1895

Reg. No. 1118 Const. Thompson H.J.

FROM	TO	SIGNATURES OF SETTLERS VISITED.
Snake Plain	Muskeg Lake	A. Brown
		A. Marcelin
		H. Vachon. Sec

NOTE.—Settlers are requested to sign this report when visited by Patrolman who is instructed to ask if there are any complaints and to call at every ranch on his line of patrol.

Harry J Thompson
Commanding
In charge of Detachment

8.000-21-7-'22.

60. *Constables on patrol were required to visit every settler on their route and ask them if they had any complaints. This patrol slip indicated the settler had been visited and asked the question. The settler was then asked to sign this patrol slip indicating that he had been visited and asked the question.*

61. *NWMP detachment, Pincher Creek, 1895 with Sgt. W.B. Wilde,
who was murdered by Charcoal a year later, seated centre
(Glenbow – Alberta Institute).*

of the Hudson's Bay Company, the CPR and the judiciary. Deane was frequently a guest of Lt.-Gov. Dewdney.[49] At Macleod, Steele and his wife were entertained by the ranching aristocracy.[50] As befitted their station they were permitted to employ a volunteer from the ranks as their personal servant for $5 per month.[51] They travelled first class on the trains. Their red tunics added colour and dignity to the continuous round of official dinners and balls that were held in most large centres. In Regina, they became an essential element in numerous state occasions like the opening of the legislature, the Lieutenant-Governor's New Year's levee and the spectacular Jubilee Ball, held to celebrate the 50th anniversary of Queen Victoria's reign in 1887.[52] After the completion of the riding school in 1886, the officers were able to return the hospitality by organizing balls, concerts and smokers for the "leading citizens" of the territorial capital.[53]

The officers also accepted that it was their duty to participate in numerous cultural activities that added to the stability and enrichment of prairie society. In Regina, Supt. Percy Neale was Master of the local Masonic Lodge.[54] Deane occupied a similar position in Lethbridge. Steele was a founding member of the Calgary Branch of the Independent Order of Foresters.[55] Earlier at Macleod, he had encouraged sporting and social activities that brought the police and local citizens together.

At Macleod and throughout the district, although life was strenuous, there was no lack of amusements or sports. During the summer quadrille and tennis parties, polo and golf were frequent, and, when transport could be spared, the guests to the barrack dances with their visiting friends in town were driven to and from them. There were few halls in the town to accommodate a large ball or party, and to help the people, a wing of the barracks was thrown open to the St. George's, St. Andrew's and St. Patrick's Societies for their annual balls.[56]

Many officers were keen sportsmen. Inspectors Baker and White-Fraser were active members of the polo club in Fort Macleod. Insp. Gilbert Sanders was secretary of Calgary's first skating club.[57] The club used an open air rink provided by the police. The Calgary officers were also members of the local curling club.[58] In Regina, Comm. Herchmer was a leading spirit in organizing the local Hunt Club; whether it ever chased a fox is not very clear. Deane, meanwhile, was an enthusiastic actor who organized theatrical troupes in both Regina and Lethbridge in which he performed himself.[59]

Like most of their class, Mounted Police officers were strong believers in the moral benefits to be derived from religious worship. As individuals they set an example. Deane was a warden of the Church of England parish in Lethbridge and when there was no minister available, he led the worship himself. They also used their influence as officers. The 1889 regulations made it incumbent upon all members of the Force "to attend divine service at their respective places of worship", and "to show an example of due respect for . . . the Sabbath day".[60] Under Herchmer church parades were held every Sunday in Regina, the non-Conformists and Roman Catholics were excused so that they could go to their own churches in the town. Later, one of the buildings at Headquarters would be converted in to a permanent chapel.

At Battleford there were no formal church parades, but the men were expected to attend the church of their choice on Sunday morning. Shortly after taking over command, Steele noticed that there were only five Mounted Policemen at divine service in the Church of England, when there should have been at least a hundred. Such indifference to religious duty would not be allowed to continue. So that there could be no excuses, he cancelled the noon stable parade on the following Sunday. To his disappointment this did not bring a large turn-out. The five faithful worshippers were only increased by two. The men obviously preferred sleeping to praying. Orders were given, and on the next day of worship all hands were paraded and marched to their respective churches. This filled one-half of the Anglican church, but the men showed their resentment at losing their Sunday morning lie-in by refusing to put any money in the collection plate. This continued for several weeks until the rector's warden, Mr. Robert Wilde, an ex-member of the Force, decided to put a stop to it:

> When the time came, he proceeded with the plate in his left hand to take up the collection. On approaching the first of the obstinate troopers he made the motion of pointing a revolver at him with his right hand as if to hold him up! This ended the boycott . . . and the civilians were almost convulsed as the men groped in their pockets for silver.[61]

Herchmer put a lot of energy into disciplining the conduct of his officers. As representatives of the respectable class, the leaders in the community, he expected them to set an example in their social and moral behaviour for the other ranks and the public at large. He strongly believed that if the men were to be raised from their dissolute and ignorant habits, their superiors would have to show them the way, providing them with an acceptable role model. The cardinal sins in his view were drunkenness, insubordination, moral turpitude and debt. A drunken officer encouraged drunkenness among his men, thereby reducing his effectiveness to command and discrediting the reputation of the Force in the eyes of the public. The trouble-makers were few, but the scandals they caused from time to time created much dissension, drove Herchmer to distraction, and seriously affected morale. In order to enforce his will upon them, he spied upon them, humiliated them, threatened them and wrote angry notes to Ottawa to have transgressors severely punished. He was only partly successful, however, in recasting them into the mould he desired. There were several reasons for this. First, Herchmer had no say in the appointments from outside the Force. He simply had to make do with any unsuitable character that the patronage system forced upon him. Second, he did not have complete control over the disciplinary procedures. Ottawa was the final judge of their misdeeds. On top of this, his own ill-tempered and vindictive nature did not help to calm things down. Instead, it bred resentment which in turn fostered insubordination. Finally, Herchmer expected too much from mere mortals. It was a time when drunkenness was common. In this respect, the habits of officers of the Mounted Police only reflected what were widely practised in the society from which they sprang. They were not paragons of virtue.

When a military system of discipline had been introduced into the Mounted Police in 1874-75, the commissioned officers had been excluded from its provisions.[62] As befitted their station, they were subject to quite different disciplinary procedures from those of the men. In dealing with their misconduct, the Commissioner could only suspend them from duty, order an inquiry into their behaviour and forward the results along with his recommendations to Ottawa for a decision. The Minister decided upon their punishment. As they could not be imprisoned like the other ranks, this usually consisted of a loss of seniority, a reprimand, a demand for their resignation and, in a few cases, demotion or dismissal. This loss of power over their subordinates should not have been a serious problem for future Commissioners. From Macdonald on, the responsible ministers also supported the idea that they should act like officers and gentlemen. With odd exceptions, they were able to keep political influence from affecting their judgement. At times, they even meted out punishment harsher than that recommended by the Commissioner. They could, however, vacillate in coming to a decision, which tended to extend personal tensions unnecessarily. In Herchmer's case, this added to the difficulties. His demands could be so unreasonable, his superiors were unable to support him. This further undermined his authority and contributed to the growing controversy over his command.

The dislike between Herchmer and his adjutant, R. B. Deane, finally exploded into the open at Regina in 1887. The latter strongly objected to the Commissioner's order to have the flag at Headquarters lowered whenever he left the post, just like the Queen. Deane claimed that the Commissioner "vented his spite upon him". Later,

after a "row" between the two of them, Deane put "his side of the story" to White who was visiting the headquarters. According to Deane, the Comptroller agreed that Herchmer had been unreasonable and sympathized with the difficulty of having to serve under him.[63] To avoid any further unpleasantness, Deane was sent east on a recruiting trip. Such action only encouraged Deane's perverse nature. A year later, Herchmer complained to Ottawa that matters had deteriorated to the point where Deane ignored his requests and acted as if he had no authority over him which was having a bad effect on the other officers under his command.[64] This was true. Eventually, Deane was punished for his insubordination by being reduced two places in the order of seniority for Superintendent.[65] It was a light penalty. He did not lose any salary and there was no prospect of promotion in any case.

Another incident occurred at Fort Macleod in 1891. What happened appears so comic on the surface, it could have been mistaken for a typical drawing room farce of the period. In command was Supt. A. R. Macdonell, popularly known in the ranks as "Paper Collar Johnnie" or "Nose Bag Johnnie". The former sobriquet had its origin in his reputed habit of economizing by wearing paper collars, the latter because on one occasion he put a horse's feed bag on his head to protect himself during wet weather.[66] Herchmer arrived at the post one evening in October on an official visit. Normal etiquette would require that the post commander, on learning of his superior's arrival, would report to him and pay his respects. The Commissioner made his way to the officers' mess, where he waited in anticipation of receiving the recognized courtesies. When Macdonell failed to appear, he became angrier and angrier. Finally, he retired to bed. The next morning he was in a furious rage. Stomping into the Orderly Room, he shouted at Macdonell, demanding an explanation. He became even more excited when the latter failed to salute him and appeared to be improperly dressed (Herchmer claimed that his underwear was sticking out from under his tunic). He attempted to bring Macdonell to attention in order that he might bring the offending undergarment to the notice of two other officers in the room, his brother, Asst. Comm. William Herchmer and Supt. Sam Steele (both testified later that they had not seen the offending garment). Macdonell refused to be treated in such an ignominious manner and after a heated exchange of words, he turned his back on his superior and marched from the room.

In his explanation to White, Herchmer accused Macdonell of acting in a "most insubordinate" manner towards him, which was true. In his defence, Macdonell claimed that the Commissioner "seemed to lose control of himself" and spoke to him "in a manner and tone of voice that would not be used by a drill sergeant addressing a recruit", which was also true. Macdonell had been undoubtedly insubordinate, but Herchmer's conduct was hardly calculated to inspire respect or warrant obedience. It was, in fact, subversive of the authority of his office. Ottawa would support him in genuine cases of misbehaviour, but there was little that White could do in disputes of this kind, except to try to smooth things over again.[67]

Most serious disciplinary cases had their origin in a bottle. In 1927, in a book entitled *The Silent Force*, T. Morris Longstreth asserted that the "Mounted Police were suckled on whisky". He went on to describe a well-known officer whose capacity to drink was "the height of regimental envy".[68] By the time that Longstreth wrote these words attitudes had changed and there were many who preferred that this aspect of the Force's past was forgotten. A protest was made and in subsequent editions of the book, the offending sentences were removed.[69] Unfortunately, Longstreth was close to the truth.

As in Canadian society at large during the latter part of the nineteenth century, the misuse of alcohol was a serious problem among both officers and men of the NWMP. The country was led in this respect by its Prime Minister, Sir John A. Macdonald, whose predilection for the bottle was well known. At least 25 per cent of commissioned officers of the Mounted Police were addicted to heavy drinking. Comm. Perry, who saw it ruin the career of many an officer, described it as the "bane of the Force".[70] Drinking in itself was not a sin. It was the inability to hold one's liquor that brought the Commissioner's wrath down upon one's head. In masculine society of the time, he who could imbibe large quantities of liquor without outwardly being affected by it was much admired. Correct attitudes are revealed in an apocryphal story repeated by Deane concerning Comm. J. F. Macleod. As the legend goes, Macleod was visiting a U.S. Army post in Montana. The American officers decided to get him drunk. As they were well aware of his reputation for holding his liquor, they arranged to have relays of sober officers held in reserve in case the first party should fail to obtain its objective. The plan was to no avail; Macleod drinks them all under the table and puts the last of them to bed.[71] The point of the story is that Macleod's heroic capacity to drink is able to uphold national honour, regimental pride and the superiority of Canadian manhood, or perhaps in this case, Scottish-Canadian manhood. The disciplinary problems were those who became stupefied and incapacitated by the excessive use of alcohol and disgraced the Force by their actions in public.

It is evident too that there were those in the community at large who expected officers to set high moral standards. On hearing that a former Inspector whose services had been dispensed with for improper conduct was working as a bartender in Minneapolis, the *Regina Leader* remarked that he found his true vocation.[72] There were plenty of outsiders who were quick to tattle to the Commissioner about officers' drinking. In 1887, the Lieutenant-Governor himself brought reports to Herchmer about Supt. Neale's drinking at Fort Macleod being responsible for the demoralization of the men there under his command. An inquiry was ordered immediately to look into the charges. A few weeks later, a Protestant minister in Calgary accused two officers of being the worse for liquor in a hotel at Banff.[73] An investigation exonerated them, but Herchmer warned them to confine their social gathering to private houses in future.

In the meantime, the Commissioner had become more preoccupied with the inebriated activities of two young Inspectors. Both had been promoted from the ranks a year earlier. One was reported drinking with his men whilst on duty searching for the murderers of a Métis near Fort Ellis. Deane was despatched to conduct a "thorough but quiet investigation so as not to attract comment from the press".[74] In justifying his action, Herchmer pointed out the impossibility of expecting constables to do their duty or refrain from drinking when officers set this example.

> I have lately had to imprison for a year several men charged with drunkenness who publically disgraced themselves, but if officers are guilty of the same offence, it will be impossible for me to inflict severe punishment in the future. Insp. Brooks has been warned on several occasions but it has no effect on his conduct.[75]

Deane's report confirmed the worst. Herchmer called for his removal, saying it would be impossible to maintain discipline if he remains.[76]

To his dismay, Ottawa decided to give Brooks another chance. Macdonald, however, did act with despatch in the case of Insp. Mills who was drunk in company with a staff sergeant in Maple Creek. Herchmer was told to give him the opportunity of resigning or being dismissed. He chose the former.[77] Poor Brooks soon followed him. The Commissioner suspended him after he was found to be incapacitated by drinking for several days. A medical examination revealed that he was suffering from rheumatism of a syphilitic origin, made worse by his consumption of alcohol.[78] This time Ottawa supported the demand for his removal, and he was forced to resign. The unfortunate Brooks was given a one-way ticket out of the Territories so that he would not continue to embarrass the police.[79]

Instances like these quickly convinced Herchmer that more drastic action was needed to stop the excessive fondness for the bottle. The answer he decided was to establish his own system of prohibition. Like other citizens in the Territories, Mounted Policemen could only obtain liquor legally by submitting an application to the Lieutenant-Governor for a permit to import a quantity from Manitoba for their own use. Herchmer saw that if he issued an order requiring all such applications to be sent to him first for approval, he would be able to control which officers drank and how much. He outlined the plan to Dewdney who expressed his willingness to cooperate. Early in 1887, the new regulation was put into effect.[80]

The arrangement might have had some success, but Herchmer went at it in his usual heavy-handed manner. Instead of just trying to regulate those who over-indulged, he insisted upon applying it to all, even their families, regardless of their drinking habits. There was soon another uproar followed by embittered feelings and damaged egos. As might be expected, Deane was in the forefront, denouncing the regulation as an infringement on his civil liberties and an insult to him as an officer and a gentleman.[81]

The squabble broke into the open in May 1888 when Herchmer discovered that at least two officers, Deane and Insp. White-Fraser, had found a loop hole in his scheme. They were obtaining liquor by getting their wives to apply directly to the Lieutenant-Governor for permits.[82] Mrs. Deane had two permits for ten gallons of rye whisky each, and Mrs. White-Fraser one for two gallons of rye. Such quantities were commonly imported at one time. It was cheaper that way, and reduced the frequency of going through the bother of getting permits. Herchmer fired off a note to Deane, who was still adjutant at headquarters, warning him that as he had not recommended his wife's permit, the liquor could not be brought into the barracks. Actually, of course, Deane was only a few feet away in his office, but the two men were still not on speaking terms as a result of their last disagreement.

Things really heated-up the next day when Herchmer discussed the matter with Dewdney at Government House. He discovered that the Lieutenant-Governor had knowingly issued these permits and others to some officers or their wives. It was soon apparent that the two men had quite a different understanding of the arrangement they had agreed to for regulating the drinking of officers. Dewdney considered that it only applied to the younger ones who were known to be intemperate, not the respectable families of the Force.[83] He accused Herchmer of being unreasonable in applying the order, stating that he refused Supt. Moffat's wife a permit for port when she was quite ill. The Commissioner had, however, shown compassion in the case of Surgeon Paré whose wife was dying of consumption. The conversation between the two men became angrier and angrier. Herchmer said

that he would arrest Deane if his wife brought the liquor into barracks. The Lieutenant-Governor then unwisely told him that such action would result in a public scandal as it was widely rumoured that he, Herchmer, had received more permits than any two men in the Territories. He offered to meet with his officers and try to mediate in the matter, but Herchmer, now beside himself with rage, refused the suggestion. Returning to his office, he wrote two angry letters to Dewdney, their tone displaying a streak of paranoia. He accused the Lieutenant-Governor of betraying his trust, his officers of deceit, led by the "contemptible" Deane, and began threatening civil and criminal proceedings against those responsible for the conspiracy of lies regarding his own conduct.[84]

A few days later, Dewdney summoned the Commissioner to Government House in an effort to mollify his injured pride and settle any unpleasantness between them. He told him that the reports of his drinking were just gossip and he put no credence in them. This seemed to put an end to the threat of legal suits, but it did not dislodge the deep sense of injustice buried within Herchmer. The Lieutenant-Governor, he told White, "has behaved badly to me in this matter."[85] Dewdney also told him that he would no longer be a party to any internal disciplinary procedure. Henceforth, he would treat the officers exactly like other citizens. If he wished to regulate their drinking habits, he would have to find another means of doing it. This Herchmer was quick to do. He sought the advice of Supt. Sévère Gagnon, who was a qualified lawyer. Gagnon informed him that in his opinion he did not have the power to prevent families of members from obtaining liquor, but, if they lived on a police post, he could regulate what they could bring into their quarters and what they could not.[86] As a result, General Order 2270 was cancelled and replaced by a new provision which forbad the possession of liquor on Mounted Police property without his written permission.[87]

Like the prohibition laws in the Territories, Herchmer's attempts to regulate drinking had little effect upon those determined to satisfy their desires. In February 1889, it was reported directly to the Prime Minister that a senior officer had made an exhibition of himself in uniform at a public banquet in Fort Macleod. According to Macdonald's informant, the officer in question had become intoxicated and persisted in making a speech, against the orders of the chairman; that he tried to sing 'Scots wha hae', broke down, and tried again; and that he then commenced a war dance which he kept up for some minutes.[88]

The Prime Minister wanted an explanation. The subsequent inquiry confirmed the report of his informant.[89] Later that year, Herchmer was complaining about the "disgraceful conduct" of a young Inspector, a graduate of RMC. He is "socially a pleasant fellow," he told White, "but is too fond of staying out at night."[90] A few months later, the same officer was drunk on parade on the parade square in Regina at 10 o'clock in the morning. Herchmer gave him a warning but he staggered into the officers' mess that night still drunk. Another Inspector became so sozzled whilst watching a match at the Regina Cricket Club, he had to be taken back to barracks.[91] He would die a little over a year later in the Kingston Asylum for the Insane, leaving a wife and two young daughters.

The worst public exhibition of drunkenness of the period occurred in Winnipeg in September 1890. A group of officers descended upon the city for a few days relaxation with their wives. One Inspector, the scion of a famous Nova Scotian family, was well under the influence before he arrived. Herchmer, who was with the group, warned him, but to no avail. On the final night they attended a performance of "The Miller and His Men" at the Winnipeg Opera House. Also present were the Lieutenant-Governor of Manitoba and Lady Macdonald. The Inspector turned up in uniform in "a very advanced state of intoxication". During the play he went to sleep and then fell out of his chair into the lap of a lady sitting next to him, disturbing the entire proceedings in "a shameful exhibition of himself".[92] Herchmer was furious. He had recommended him for promotion, but now wrote to Ottawa asking that he be dropped ten places on the seniority list for Inspectors instead. The department promptly supported him. Everyone in the Opera House had seen him, including the Prime Minister's wife. "Sir John has decided that you must lose the promotion," White told the Inspector. "I trust that it will be a lesson to you. The part which cannot be got over is your condition, while in uniform, during the performance." The penitent offender promised never to drink again. It was a vow he was unable to keep. Like others he faced a life-long battle with alcohol.[93]

Drinking was also responsible for dragging down the commanding officer of "C" division at Battleford. Upon hearing rumours of "glaring irregularities" in the stores at that post, Herchmer ordered his brother to hold an enquiry under section 20 of the *Mounted Police Act* into the conduct of Supt. W. Antrobus.[94] The investigation concluded that Antrobus had been drinking heavily, had misappropriated money from his official contingency fund and had falsified the accounts of his stores.[95] These were serious revelations. Instead of sending the results of the enquiry to Ottawa with his recommendations, the Commissioner formally charged Antrobus under the disciplinary provisions of the Act, a procedure seldom followed for offi-

cers, with being drunk in public, drinking with his NCOs and using public funds for his own purposes.[96] Upon being found guilty, he received unusual punishment. He was reduced in rank from Superintendent to Inspector. Six months later, his services were concluded. The government probably used that time to recoup its losses from his pay. Antrobus' defence contained a heart-rending confession of his problem. "My great fault and weakness has been liquor. I have given it up for a couple of years at a time, but one glass taken and I am done for."[97] It was a time when many others could have said "me too" to that.

Debt was another target for Herchmer's censure. Unpaid bills brought the Force into disrepute. He also worried that indebtedness would tempt officers to convert the public funds entrusted to them to their own use. It took only a note from a creditor to bring a sharp rebuke from the Commissioner, whether the sum was large or small. "The Hudson's Bay Company tells me that you owe it $7.06," he wrote to Insp. Draynor, "you will settle without delay, or you will bring 'Discredit on the Force'."[98] When his debts continued to mount, Herchmer reported the matter to the Minister and threatened Draynor that he must turn over a new leaf or his days in the Force were numbered.[99]

One serious case of indebtedness did lead exactly to what the Commissioner feared. Supt. Neale was constantly being hounded by creditors. The cause seems to have been his wife's extravagance. In 1887, he was forced to start selling his household furniture, including an $800 piano that Mrs. Neale cherished in order to meet a shortage in his contingency fund. Matters did not improve, however. Finally, Herchmer relieved him of his command at Fort Macleod, and started an investigation into reports of deficiencies in the division stores. "Neale is up to his ears in debt," the Commissioner told White. He suggested that Neale find a solution to his liabilities, or look for other employment.[100] Ottawa procrastinated and several months went by. Herchmer complained again that Neale was making no effort to pay his debts, and could no longer be trusted with public funds.[101] He was finally forced to retire and soon found employment as collector of customs at Fort Macleod. Once again, temptation got the better of him. Still in debt, he began converting government money to his own use. This time he was charged with embezzlement and, upon conviction, sentenced to a term in Stony Mountain penitentiary.[102]

When it came to the question of improper behaviour with the fair sex, Herchmer could count on obtaining support and decisions from Ottawa promptly. Victorian middle class moral standards were strictly adhered to by the Commissioner and his superiors. The rank and file might visit brothels, but such action by an officer would result in his summary departure from the Force. Single officers had to remain chaste. In all his dealings with women, an officer's conduct had to be beyond the slightest suspicion. There was always someone in the community who would feel it was his or her duty to see that this was so. In 1888, Herchmer was notified by a self-appointed guardian of public morality that the Inspector at Battleford was paying "assiduous attention" to a young married lady. The Commissioner quickly warned him privately to

> Drop it or it is certain to cause you trouble. I don't want to have to write officially on the matter. I know Battleford is dull but we are police officers and there are things we cannot do that others can.[103]

A similar report of another Inspector becoming the talk of a settlement by carrying on with a married woman resulted in a terse note to his commanding officer ordering him to put a stop to it immediately.[104]

At the most these were only flirtatious incidents. Outright sexual misconduct called for much more drastic action. In 1887, the assistant surgeon in Regina was one of the few officers of the period to suffer the ignominy of being summarily dismissed. Without much ado, a rail ticket was purchased for him and he was hastily bundled on to a train heading for the west coast. The nature of his offence can be discerned from a letter written by the Commissioner to the Attorney General of British Columbia. Comm. Herchmer warned him not to allow the former officer to practise medicine in any capacity that would bring him into contact with women and children.[105] As was often the practice, the actual details of his offence never appear to have been committed to paper. They were probably considered too shocking to be recorded. There was a tendency to sweep such immorality under the carpet, to only refer to it in whispers. This was done not only to avoid the disgrace that would accompany publicity, but also to protect society from the knowledge of such unseemly things.

By the spring of 1891, Herchmer's frustration over the difficulty of disciplining some of his officers reached the boiling point. Even if he was ill-tempered and tyrannical, Ottawa should have acted decisively and with despatch, either supported Herchmer or replaced him. To allow Deane, for example, to the full knowledge of everyone, to be insubordinate with impunity could only exacerbate relations between the Commissioner and those under him. As in other matters, Macdonald was slow to make decisions regarding Mounted Police discipline. A well-known tippler himself, perhaps he found it hard to punish others for the same behaviour. As his health worsened, one must also question whether as Prime Minister he was not carrying too large a responsibility to administer the Mounted Police properly. After waiting several months for action from Ottawa regarding the misconduct of four officers, Herchmer became desperate. He wrote to White pointing out that the delay only encouraged the recalcitrant officers to think that they would get off scot free, which further undermined his authority. One officer had been reported drunk on several occasions but nothing was done.

In another case of drunkenness, he had ordered the offender transferred, only to have his decision countermanded when the officer in question had gone over his head and used his influence in Ottawa. "I have done my best to make this an efficient force," he told the Deputy Minister, but without support from the department, "I am losing my ability to command." He concluded by calling for an investigation into his own conduct as Commissioner. This, however, also related to the growing public controversy over his management of the Force, of which disciplining his officers was only a part.[106]

A major item of expense for all officers was their uniform. The uniform was the outward and visible sign of their authority and their social position. Members of the NWMP did not see themselves as descendants of Peel's "Bobbies", dressed in blue with their distinctive blue helmets dutifully plodding their urban beats. They looked down upon the municipal policemen and disparagingly referred to them as "Civil Police". They saw themselves as part of an auxiliary military force with certain police duties which was called to keep the peace on an unsettled frontier. It is not surprising, therefore, that when the officers' dress regulations were revised in 1886, the uniform remained essentially a military one. It consisted of almost nothing that identified its wearer as a policeman. To the casual observer, a Mounted Police officer was attired like many other cavalry officers in regiments throughout the British Empire. Only a close scrutiny of his buttons and badges would reveal that his unit was the NWMP. Had he walked down a street in London, Capetown, Bombay or Melbourne, he would have been easily recognizable as an officer and a gentleman of one of Her Majesty's military forces. The only things distinctively Canadian were the maple leaves and the buffalo head on his badge. The adoption of the familiar broad-brimmed felt hat was still in the future.

The uniform brought with it considerable social prestige, but the officers paid dearly for this elevated status. As gentlemen they were expected to provide their uniforms at their own expense. The "uniform" in fact was more than just one set of clothing. It was an entire wardrobe designed to provide him with a completely different outfit depending on whether he was attending a social gathering, was mounted or on foot, on parade or in the office, out in summer or winter, or attending upon the dignitaries of state. A newly commissioned officer with no other source of income but his pay could be financially strapped for years by the cost. He would have to obtain credit from a military tailor and usually repay the amount in monthly installments from his pay. He could economize by borrowing items which were frequently used, or buying secondhand articles from officers leaving the Force. Even after he had outfitted himself, there would be additional expenses in order to keep up with the frequent changes in the regulations. Military fashions in the nineteenth century changed almost as often as the dress lines of the couturiers of Paris. As in most clothing of the time, the appearance of uniforms was a more important factor in their design than comfort.

The original uniform worn by NWMP officers had been plain and undistinguished, differing very little from that of the other ranks. In 1876, the government approved a distinctive set of new dress regulations for officers which were patterned after those of the 13th Hussars of the British Army.[107] These elaborate and very expensive uniforms were obtained from Maynard, Harris and Grice, well-known military tailors of Leadenhall Street, London, England. The complete outfit for an Inspector cost $500 to $600, or about half his annual pay.[108] Apart from their cost, it was soon realized that they were not very practical for use on the Canadian prairies. During the 1880s, therefore, there was some thought and discussion on the need for more sensible and lower priced replacements.

The influx of new officers in 1885-86 accelerated the need for change. Irvine had drafted new dress regulations in January 1885, but the rebellion had delayed their adoption. These were modelled on the style of the British Dragoon regiments rather than the Hussars. They would display considerably less gold braid, and were expected to be half the price of the previous type. The new officers, however, were reluctant to buy anything until the matter was settled. As a result, White asked Herchmer shortly after he took command to review Irvine's proposals and send his recommendations to the department. With only minor changes, Macdonald approved the new dragoon-style wardrobe in May 1886. Later that August, the new dress regulations were officially sanctioned by privy council order. The latter procedure was necessary for two reasons. First, unless they were authorized by the government, the officers would have to pay duty on any article they imported. Second, without the official stamp of approval, the Commissioner would be unable to force the officers to abide by them, and thus ensure uniformity.

Unfortunately, the adoption of these new regulations did not settle the matter of officers' uniforms. It would take another four years of discussion and revision before that was accomplished. In the first place, Maynard, Harris and Company (Grice had left the partnership) found the wording of the regulations too imprecise to proceed with the manufacture of some articles. This resulted in further revision and a protracted correspondence between Regina, Ottawa and London.[109] In the summer of 1887, a representative of the tailors visited Canada taking orders for articles and making arrangements for the officers to meet the cost by monthly deductions from their pay.[110] Maynard and Harris remained the principal supplier of uniforms, although individual officers did have them tailored elsewhere.[111]

In June 1887, Supt. E. W. Jarvis, the Commanding Officer of "Depot" Division, was given the task of reviewing the regulations in order to remove any confusion as to the specifications. A new draft was forwarded to Ottawa later that year, but White raised doubts about the type of lace to be used and the delay continued.[112] In February 1888, yet another revision was sent to White. It included modifications of the dress code as it related to veterinary and medical officers.[113] Herchmer urged prompt approval as he wanted every officer in the same style of tunic for the coming Dominion Day festivities. When he did not get it, he went ahead on his own and issued the revised regulations as a General Order in April 1888.[114]

The matter was far from settled, however. Over another year of delay and discussion would pass before new regulations would be approved. The Commissioner did not get everyone uniformly outfitted for the coming national celebration. Senior officers, who had invested considerable money in the old style of uniform, objected to having to equip themselves again.[115] From the photographs of the period, it is apparent that the officers were still a mixed bag as far as appearance in their regimentals was concerned. Some were still wearing the Hussar pattern, some the new dragoon style, some a combination of both and a few no uniform at all.

It was not until 1889 that White placed an agreed set of new regulations in front of Macdonald for his approval. The Comptroller told him that changes had been made with a view to reducing the expense. "An officer's complete outfit under the proposed Regulations," he informed him, "will cost about $350 to $500 according to rank."[116] The Prime Minister expressed concern that officers and men should look alike when on active service, "otherwise the officers will be spotted and knocked off by sharp shooters". Macdonald was no doubt aware of the controversy in military circles in Britain over the adoption of khaki uniforms following the recent campaigns in Egypt and the Sudan.[117] He also obviously considered that an outbreak of organized violence on the prairies was still a possibility.

The latest uniform regulations for officers were finally authorized by privy council order on 24 January 1890. A provision was included permitting officers to wear khaki jackets and breeches while on patrol. Actually, some of them had been doing this unofficially for several years. The new regulations did not substantially change those of 1886. A bit more gold lace was added here and there in keeping with the general trend in military uniforms. They were still modelled on the dragoon style. What they did do was clarify the uncertainty of the previous years as to what was the authorized order of dress. Once the order-in-council was printed and a copy circulated to all officers, Herchmer was able to insist on the uniformity he desired. To assist him, James Inch and Company of London, England, who took over the business of Maynard and Harris, prepared a detailed catalogue of uniforms and other accoutrements for officers of the NWMP.

Chapter 12

All Sorts and Conditions of Men

After having been about two months in the corps, I was able to form some idea of the class of comrades among whom my lot was cast. I discovered there were truly "all sorts and conditions of men." Many I found, in various troops, were related to English families in good position. There were three men at Regina who had held commissions in the British service. There was also an ex-officer of militia, and one of volunteers. There was an ex-midshipman, son of the Governor of one of our small Colonial dependencies. A son of a major-general, an ex-cadet of the Canadian Royal Military College at Kingston, a medical student from Dublin, two ex-troopers of the Scots Greys, a son of a captain in the line, an Oxford B.A., and several of the ubiquitous natives of Scotland comprised the mixture. In addition there were many Canadians belonging to families of influence, as well as several from the backwoods, who had never seen the light till their fathers had hewed a way through the bush to a concession road. They were none the worse fellows on that account, though. There were none of the questionable characters then, who crept in after the Rebellion, when recruiting parties went through the slums of Ontario towns. Several of our men sported medals won in South Africa, Egypt and Afghanistan.[1]

John Donkin wrote this description of his troop mates not long after he was discharged in 1888. A similar analysis of the background of the men appeared in a contemporary American journal. "The rank and file are not surpassed by any picked corps in any service," wrote J. A. G. Creighton in *Scribner's Magazine* in October 1893. "A significant proportion of the men are of good family and education," he continued. "There are lots of Englishmen who come out to try their hand at farming in Manitoba and 'drift' into the Mounted Police. One also finds well-connected young Canadians, farmers' sons from Ontario, clerks tired of city life, immigrants who have not found their 'El Dorado', and waifs and strays from everywhere." There were men of aristocratic lineage, he informed his readers, university-educated men and former British officers who were at home in the fashionable London clubs and the great country houses of England.[2] Donkin and Creighton did not exaggerate. All of these elements were represented in the NWMP. What they failed to make clear, however,

was that the overwhelming majority of the rank and file were native Canadians. It was not as "British" as was popularly believed then and later, nor quite as representative in its composition of the Empire and its colonies as was often thought. In fact, there was a significant and growing number of members not of British origin. These authors were also too close to their subject to reveal that among these well-bred, well-connected and well-educated men were impoverished failures and misfits seeking a new start, husbands escaping from unhappy marriages, alcoholics, old sweats, adventurous ne'er-do-wells and former criminals.

The British upper classes had several representatives. One of them was a young man who presented himself at the barracks in Regina for engagement in September 1891. The surgeon noted upon examining him that "he is evidently a gentleman by birth and education, though now, for reasons known only to himself, is dead broke".[3] The new recruit gave his name as John Temple. In reality he was Sir Granville Louis John Temple, 12th Baronet of Stowe, a former officer of the Lancashire Fusiliers. This scion of an ancient and illustrious family, who counted the Dukes of Buckingham and Chandos in his lineage on his father's side and the Austrian aristocracy on his mother's, would end his Mounted Police service in 1919 as the night watchman at the Prince Albert barracks.

The sons of at least three other baronets were also rankers during this period. Cst. Ralph Coote, who served 1896-99, was the son and heir of Sir Algernon Charles Coote of Wicklow, the Premier Baronet of Ireland. He succeeded to the title in 1920. Cst. Malcolm Blomefield was the son of the Rev. Sir Thomas Blomefield, 3rd Baronet of Yorkshire. The father of another Yorkshireman, Cst. Lionel Palmer, was the son of Sir Charles Palmer, Bart., of Grinkle Park in that county.[4] Another ranker with aristocratic blood was Cst. Arthur Onslow, a nephew of the Earl of Onslow. To name just one more, there was also a young Scot of 17 years, Cst. Robert Baillie, a cousin of the Earl of Aberdeen, the Governor General from 1893-98, who deserted in 1898.

The willingness of upper and middle class Britons to serve in the ranks of the NWMP was evidence of the high reputation that the Force was acquiring. Many of them would never have thought of lowering their status by enlisting in the British Army. In April 1886, Reginald Gwynne, Esq. of Folkington Manor, Sussex wrote to enquire about joining the Mounted Police. He had been educated at Eton and Oxford, he told the Commissioner, and would prefer to be an officer but was prepared to join the ranks providing "gentlemen" were accepted in the ranks.[5] Having been assured that such was the case, he eventually turned up in Ottawa. The police found, however, that his gentlemanly upbringing made him a poor acquisition. Like others of his class, he had no practical work experience. He had never had to groom a horse, wash his clothes or cook anything in his life. These things had all been done by servants. One English gentlewoman saw the NWMP as a means of reforming the character of one of her wayward offspring. She wrote to ask the Commissioner if he would take her 18-year-old son as he had got a bit out of control and needed some discipline.[6]

John Mackie was a well-educated Scot of respectable origins from Stirlingshire. He had already led an adventurous life by the time he joined the Force in 1888. Before that he had been a South Sea Island trader and a boundary rider and gold prospector in Australia. After his discharge in 1893, he became a popular writer of adventure stories like *The Devil's Playground* and *Sinner's Twain*. Cst. J. R. Warren was the son of Sir Charles Warren, a controversial Commissioner of the Metropolitan London Police, whose resignation from that force in 1888 was partly due to its failure to capture the notorious Jack the Ripper.[7]

Cst. Albert Byron, who committed suicide in Calgary in 1891, was the son of H. J. Byron, a well-known English writer of melodramatic plays. Byron had previously served in the Cape Mounted Rifles. Following his death, it was revealed that he left behind a wife and two children in England.[8] Another member of the British upper classes was Cst. Walter Osbourn who had earlier served with the prestigious Life Guards and may have had legal training.[9] Cst. Reginald Macdonald had been an officer in the British Army in India before engaging in the Mounted Police in 1886. The son of a major general, he had lost his commission after making a spectacle of himself in the Officers' Mess in Delhi. Although the Governor General and other people in very high places in Britain and Canada tried to

get him a commission in the NWMP, he had to settle with service in the ranks.

Cpl. John George Donkin was typical in many ways of the British who joined the Force. Born in the north of England, the son of a doctor, he intended to follow his father's profession, but failed to complete his medical studies. He next tried his hand at journalism. This was followed by two years in the 17th Lancers, the regiment famous for its part in the charge of the Light Brigade, as an enlisted man. In 1884, with little money and no plans, he set out for Canada to start afresh. He tried farm work in Manitoba, but quickly found like many other middle class Englishmen, that his origins had not prepared him for the monotony and hard manual labour of a prairie homestead. Hard up and unable to find a civilian job, as a last resort, he decided to re-enlist in the military. To Donkin the organization and appearance of the NWMP resembled just another army regiment. Following his discharge from the police in 1888, he returned to England where he wrote an unembellished, perceptive and highly literate account of life in the Force entitled *Trooper and Redskin*. Addicted to alcohol, a condition that probably had something to do with the instability of his career, he died in the Alnwick workhouse in 1890 from the effects of excessive drinking at the age of 37.[10]

By the 1890s, the reputation of the NWMP had spread throughout the western world. During these years dozens of letters were received annually in Regina from young men in the United States and Great Britain, from members of police forces like the Royal Irish Constabulary, the Natal Mounted Police and the Mashonaland Mounted Police, enquiring about the possibility of joining the Force.[11] Popular literature seems to have had something to do with this. One Irish applicant stated that he had first read about the NWMP in an article in the *Boy's Own Paper*, a British magazine for young lads.[12]

News of its renown had also begun to spread beyond the British Empire and Europeans started arriving in Winnipeg and Regina to serve in the famous Force. Two of them, William Van Pittius and John Von Hemert, were from Amsterdam, where they had previously been in the Dutch Army. The former deserted when it was discovered that he was wanted for fraud in Holland. Cst. Hans Kjosterud was a member of the Norwegian Army before coming to Canada. In 1895, a group of men in the Swedish Cavalry enquired about engagement. From Paris came Cst. Leon Monjeau, a one time officer in a French regiment of dragoons. Vincent Miniszowsky was a Pole who had already served for five years as a scout with the U.S. Cavalry when he enlisted in 1885. Cst. Paul Wolters had earned an

Iron Cross whilst fighting with a German hussar regiment in the Franco-Prussian War of 1870.[13]

Many of these men perceived of the Mounted Police as a kind of Canadian Foreign Legion, a place to which they could escape, start a new life and find excitement and adventure. Some of them had language skills that the Force found useful as immigrants from central and eastern Europe arrived on the prairies. Cst. Emil Tryhaft spoke German, Polish and Russian. Following his training, he was placed on a detachment where he could put his linguistic abilities to good use as an interpreter among the new settlers. Christen Junget had been a lieutenant in the Danish army. When he arrived in Regina in 1899 he did not speak English sufficiently well enough to make himself understood. He did have a knowledge of several other languages, however. This knowledge became a vital asset in dealing with the Doukhobors who arrived in the Yorkton area. Thirty-five years later he retired with the rank of Assistant Commissioner.[14]

Most of these men, of course, were not British subjects when they presented themselves at the barracks in Regina for engagement. The recruiting posters did not, in fact, specify that they had to be. The police had been accepting European and American recruits since the Force's formation in the belief that when they took the Oath of Allegiance to Her Majesty Queen Victoria, which was a necessary part of the engagement process, they became British subjects. In 1902, the Deputy Minister explained it this way:

> Every effort is made to employ British Subjects but it often happens that a good man speaking French, German or other languages, so essential to the successful handling of the foreign elements in the new settlements, is engaged without first taking out naturalization papers.

They were however, he continued, required to take the Oath of Office and the Oath of Allegiance.[15] This relaxed approach to the national origins of recruits came to an end with the outbreak of war in 1914.

The basic conditions of engagement in 1886 had changed little since the beginnings of the Force. An applicant had to be single, between 22 and 40 years of age, an "active able-bodied" man of "thoroughly sound constitution" who must produce "certificates of exemplary character". In addition, he was required to read and write either the English or French language. The minimum height was set at 5 feet 6 inches and weight at a maximum 175 lbs. The term of enlistment was for five years.

If it was one thing to formulate a set of qualifications for enlistment, it was quite another to see that they were observed. In the first place, the recruiting officers who were sent to eastern Canada often found that it was expedient from time to time to overlook some of the requirements. Secondly, they were too easily circumvented. In an age when few had birth certificates or other documentary forms of identification, it was only necessary to look 22 years old to satisfy the recruiter. Likewise, a false surname could hide a debtor from his creditors, a deserter from his former regiment, a wayward husband from his wife and an ex-convict from his past.

Another problem was the eastern doctors, paid $2 for each examination, who, to do a favour for a friend or a politician, certified chronically ill or infirm applicants as "fit for service". In 1887, Herchmer complained that a number of recruits passed by such practitioners arrived in Regina with defective eyesight. They included several who wore glasses and could not recognize a man at 100 yards.[16] He reported that he found it necessary to invalid "a good many men" that year, all but one or two of them suffering from conditions they had when they joined the Force.[17] Local members of Parliament, meanwhile, in search of votes, were quite capable of describing an incorrigible relative of one of their constituents as sober, honest and reliable.

Upon taking command, Herchmer found that, in addition to half of his officers being inexperienced, almost two-thirds of the men were little more than recruits. During 1885, 608 men had joined the Force, the majority of them in the latter part of that year following the increase in strength from 500 to 1,000. To the Commissioner's dismay, a large proportion of these were unable to ride and were unfamiliar with horses.[18] He described some of them as idle townsmen who did not like the discipline and deserted, and others as quite unsuitable either by character or ability to perform their duties.

A typical sample of these recruits was the group of 40 men engaged in New Brunswick and Nova Scotia in December 1885.[19] At least 24 of them had previous military service, 21 with the Canadian Militia, 2 with the British Army and 1 at Royal Military College, Kingston. Men with some military training were preferred. It was one of the questions asked on the application form. All but four of them were native Canadians. Their average age was just under 24. The oldest was 34, the youngest 19. They came from a variety of occupational backgrounds, which may have reflected a lack of employment in those areas of work. The largest group was five store clerks, followed by four labourers, two hostlers and two fishermen. The remainder included a carpenter, a butcher, a barber, a teamster, a tinsmith, a soap maker and a pipe fitter. Only one had previously been a farmer. At least a dozen of them had been recommended by prominent local leaders of the ruling federal Tory party, Charles Tupper, Charles Daly or T. E. Kenny.

The progress of these recruits gives some idea of the difficulty of securing suitable men during this period. Of the 40 that originally signed up for 5 years service, only 17 actually completed the term. Of the 23 that did not, 2 were dismissed for bad behaviour, 11 deserted and 7 had to be discharged for health reasons. One of those invalided was Cst. Robert Smith. The doctor who had examined him in Saint John for $2 had pronounced him hale and hearty. When the police surgeon checked him upon his arrival in Regina, he was found to have had several attacks of rheumatism and was suffering from heart disease. Two others passed by local medical men were discharged when it was discovered that they had gonorrhoea.

Like the English woman earlier referred to, some people saw service in the NWMP as a means for reforming the wayward habits of young men. A Halifax judge caused a brief uproar of indignation in the West in 1896 when he sentenced two criminals to service in the Force if their behaviour did not improve. The two young men in question had been convicted by Judge Johnston of burglary. In sending them to jail, he gave them a choice, change their ways, or he would see that they got on the Mounted Police. Upon seeing his remarks in a Halifax newspaper, the western media was incensed and rushed to defend its famous Force. Under the heading "The Force Insulted", the *Regina Leader* stated: "The North West Mounted Police force has from time to time had to put up with a great deal of injustice and misrepresentation at the hands of eastern newspapers. Probably nothing that has been said can compare for blackguardly impudence and gross and insulting indecency" than that which was reported in Halifax.[20] In the House of Commons Davin described the judge's remarks as an "insult", and called upon the government to investigate the matter and remove him from the bench if they were true.[21] Comm. Herchmer informed the Deputy Minister that the incident had caused "great discontent among the men", and expressed the hope that action would be taken against the magistrate.[22] The Department of Justice promised to investigate, but nothing came of it and the affair soon blew over. It did show, however, how sensitive westerners could be about the reputation of their Force.

With his usual determination, Herchmer pushed hard to improve the standards of recruits. His aim was to reverse earlier tendencies and make the Force "very hard to enter and very easy to get out of".[23] Like his predecessors, he saw the native sons of farmers as the backbone of the Mounted Police. Led by a few experienced NCOs from the British Army who could pass on the right values and tradi-tions of the old country, the uncorrupted scions of Canada's backwoods would make ideal policemen.

> The men we want are farmers' sons, with good common school educations, and a proportion of the better class of discharged short service men from the Imperial service . . . .[I]t is to the farmers' sons, raised in the Dominion, that I should like to look for the majority of our recruits; this class of recruits all understand the care of horses, and are accustomed to hard outdoor work.[24]

The Mounted Police had an understanding with the federal Immigration Agent in Winnipeg by which the latter would keep an eye open for any likely looking man who presented himself at his office looking for employment. For each prospective recruit he sent on to Regina, he was paid $2. Herchmer preferred this method of recruiting. It was first of all cheaper. Their fares only had to be paid from Winnipeg to Regina, rather than from eastern Canada. Secondly, they were examined by the police surgeon before being engaged. It gave him more control over the selection process. In 1886, however, the number of men obtained in this manner was quite insufficient. The trickle would grow as settlement increased, but in the meantime, the police had to rely largely upon the annual recruiting drives made by officers in eastern Canada.

In May 1886, Insp. Moodie was sent to Ontario. He advertised in the newspapers and travelled through the larger towns contacting local politicians and militia officers. Before he left, Herchmer instructed him to avoid "rough" or "low class" men and take on only those of respectable appearance and antecedents.[25] As it turned out, Moodie found it difficult to find "first class prospects" who were 22 or older. He asked for permission to reduce the minimum age limit to 20. The Commissioner was in favour of getting them younger. He also wanted to increase the minimum height, but Comptroller Fred White would only agree to these changes in exceptional cases.[26]

Recruiting in 1887 was extended to Quebec as well as Ontario. The minimum height was raised to 5 feet 8 inches, and Supt. R. B. Deane, who visited Ottawa, London and Toronto, was told to use his discretion as far as age was concerned. White also warned him to be very wary of former members of the Royal Irish Constabulary (RIC), as he had seen many of them, but few good ones.[27] Deane examined 183 applicants out of which 63 were accepted and sent to Regina. One deserted on the way. Most of those that were not engaged were rejected for medical reasons. Two could not read or write. Once in a while, however, men were taken on who signed their name with an X.[28] In Montreal, meanwhile, a former corporal, Avila Poitevin, was hired to assist Deane in locating suitable French-Canadians. The Deputy Minister instructed him to reduce the standards, if necessary, as the Force needed more French-Canadians.[29]

The 1887 recruiting campaign caused a bit of public controversy. On August 3rd the *Toronto Mail* printed a letter which criticized the standards for recruits as being too high, and accused Herchmer of favouring old countrymen for promotion, thereby discouraging Canadians from applying. Even Deane had expressed the view that the increase in height was an "unusually high" standard. A survey of the Force in 1891 showed that the average height of its members was 5 feet 9½ inches.[30] Herchmer admitted that the increase in height and the greater care given to medical exams had made it more difficult to obtain recruits, but he took umbrage at the assertion that he gave preference to old soldiers from Britain in making promotions. To refute his critics he produced the following statistics on the national origins of the members.[31] Unfortunately, he lumped English- and French-Canadians into one group. He was also at pains to point out that many of those of British origin had earned their promotion as a result of their long service and experience:

NCOs NWMP 8 August 1887

Rank	Eng.	Irish	Scot.	Can.	French	Ger.
S/M	3	2	-	5	-	-
S/Sgt.	10	5	3	18	1	-
Sgt.	12	5	2	39	1	2
Cpl.	25	6	-	42	-	-
Total	50	18	5	104	2	2

Origin of all Members of the NWMP
24 July 1887

Canadian	532
English	227
Irish	76
American	45
Scottish	39
German	9
Welsh	6
French	5
Misc.	12

Total 951

In spite of the change in qualifications and the care taken with physical examinations, the 1887 recruiting campaign still picked up a considerable number of "bad characters, deserters" and "drunkards".[32] The background of the applicants still could not be checked thoroughly enough. The present system, Herchmer told the Deputy Minister, was unsatisfactory.

> The recruiting officer must be given more opportunity to enquire into the character of all intending recruits, and to travel through the country places where most of our best men come from. No one should be engaged until the officer is completely convinced that he is "honest, sober and industrious". The proportion of town-bred men, is getting much too large. They miss the pleasures of town life, and are bound to procure liquor, and not only desert but induce others to do so as well.

Just how difficult it was at the time to verify the background of people can be appreciated by the fact that a few ex-convicts managed to slip through the recruiting screen. Law enforcement agencies in Europe and the United States had been photographing criminals for many years, but their rogues galleries were not assembled together in national collections that were accessible to all police forces. Even if they had been, it was well known that felons could easily change their appearance, by growing a beard or moustache, or shaving them off, for example. In the 1880s and 1890s, the scientific identification of criminals was still in its infancy. The Frenchman, Alphonse Bertillon, did not publish his system of identification based upon body measurements, physical description, body marks and photographs until 1893. It was not until three years later that Edward Henry (later Commissioner of the Metropolitan Police in London) perfected his method of classifying fingerprints. In 1898, the Canadian Parliament passed the *Identification of Criminals Act*, which provided for the examination under the Bertillon Signaletic System, as it was known, of anyone charged with or convicted of an indictable offence. Few Canadian police forces, however, had the necessary equipment. By the time many of them acquired it, the Bertillon System was being superseded by fingerprinting as the most scientific method of identification.

Cst. Albert David was engaged in his home town of Kingston in October 1886. He had come into the Force with the usual assurances of good character from local citizens. His previous occupation was listed as "tailor". There was always a shortage of tailors in the Force, and eventually David became the division tailor at Lethbridge. In 1891, Supt. Deane received information that suggested that Cst. David had served a term in Kingston Penitentiary. Deane wrote to the warden of that institution in an effort to get at the truth of the matter. The reply verified his suspicions. A young lad by the name of Albert David had indeed been confined there for three years for larceny. Were the convict and the constable one and the same person? The only way at the time to be certain would be to bring someone from Kingston who could personally identify the convict. Inmates of Canadian prisons were not routinely photographed. Bearing in mind the cost of this, Deane decided that he would first of all confront David with the information. When the constable admitted that he did have a prison record, he was discharged.

Insp. Primrose described Cst. Bill Humphries as a "desperate character". After he was imprisoned in the guardroom for insubordination, a search of his kit revealed a well-used set of burglary tools. Just what his criminal past was, was never discovered, because as soon as he was released, he deserted. The case of Cst. Joseph Jacobs, meanwhile, was to illustrate more clearly the inadequacy of the existing means of identification, and just how profound a change the adoption of fingerprinting would make to law enforcement.

Jacobs was engaged in Toronto in April 1900. With regards to his character, he produced two letters from former employers which attested to his hard working and honest nature. Several months later, a visitor to Macleod thought he recognized him as someone he had known in Toronto with a criminal record, and so informed Insp. Moodie at that post. The Commissioner wrote to the Chief of the Toronto Police Department. The latter responded by sending the criminal record of one Joseph Jacobs. He was listed has having nine convictions; the most serious being horse stealing, for which he had received five years in prison, and the most recent being breaking and entering in 1897, for which he had gotten six months. The Toronto authorities also sent a copy of a photograph they had taken of Jacobs and a physical description of him. The Commissioner and others in Regina studied this information. There clearly was a resemblance, but they were still not 100 per cent certain that it was one and the same person. Appearances could be misleading. Once again, as in the David case, Moodie was instructed to confront Jacobs with the information in the hope that he would confess. Once again, much to the relief of the police, Jacobs readily admitted to his record and was duly discharged. The incident illustrates how easy it was at the time for anyone to conceal his past and fool even the police themselves. Few probably realized that, with fingerprinting, they were about to acquire a scientific tool that would for all practical purposes remove any doubt as to the identity of every individual.[33]

To return to recruiting, during 1888 and 1889, the police continued to send officers to eastern Canada. Unemployment was increasing and they had no trouble finding the numbers they required, although the old selection problems remained. In 1888, Insp. Sanders was deluged with applicants during a recruiting drive in Ontario.[34] Herchmer had cautioned him to take careful notice of their hands. "If men are workers, their hands will show it," he instructed Sanders.[35] Sanders examined 227 applicants. Out of these he selected 82, many of them farmers' sons. S/Sgt. Bremner was detailed to look out for suitable men in Nova Scotia while enjoying a few days leave there. The Deputy Minister told him to call upon T. E. Kenny, one of the Tory members of the House of Commons for Halifax, to arrange the selection.[36] In 1889, the Commissioner reported that the 163 recruits

obtained that year were generally "very fine men and well adapted for our service".[37]

The Mounted Police was having little trouble obtaining men, but it was still having problems retaining them, a circumstance that effected its efficiency. In 1887, Macdonald complained that the Force was made up of too many recruits. The Mounted Police were "pretty well paid", he told the House of Commons, but they were unwilling to remain in the service. No sooner did a man become fully trained and familiar with the duties than he took his discharge. The Prime Minister claimed 300 such men out of a total strength of 1,000 would leave the Force in 1887.[38] His estimate is perhaps a bit high, and cannot be accurately checked for that year. Reliable data is available, however, for the three years 1889-1891.[39] During that period, 536 new men enlisted for a term of five years. As a consequence, out of the total strength of 1,000, in 1892 slightly over half of the entire Force would have had three years service or less. In other words, the NWMP was largely composed of young single men who were either recruits, or had, at the most, a year or two of experience. The pension plan and other improved benefits were designed to improve this situation. In fact during the 1890s, more and more recruits did decide to re-engage.

In 1890, the source of recruiting underwent a significant change. All of the 153 men who were taken on that year had either applied at the office of the immigration agent in Winnipeg, or presented themselves in person at the Barracks in Regina.[40] The westward flow of migrants and settlers was starting to increase. Herchmer was delighted. No longer would he be stuck with the unsuitable products of pork barrel politics and unprincipled doctors in the East. There would still be a certain amount of patronage in high places, but the selection process was largely in his hands. He could bring into play his avowed desire to make the Force hard to get into and easy to get out. Ottawa was happy with the new trend too. It would save a considerable amount of money by not having to transport recruits to Regina from Ontario, Quebec and the Maritimes. By 1892, the Deputy Minister was telling applicants that they would have to make their own way to Winnipeg, if they wished to join the Force, as it was no longer recruiting in eastern Canada.[41]

Following the government's decision in 1894 to reduce the strength of the Force, the intake of recruits was drastically cut. During that year 130 men were engaged, but in 1895 only 5 were taken on and in 1896 and 1897 only 49 and 39 respectively. There were no shortage of applicants, however, which prompted the Commissioner to try and improve the selection process even further, and thereby increase overall efficiency. In 1895, he informed Ottawa that he proposed henceforth to give all recruits a two-month trial before engaging them.[42] "With our greatly reduced strength," he reported, "we cannot afford to take on poor men." During the test period they would serve as special constables. As he further explained, it was impossible to tell what a man is at first. While fairly intelligent, he may have no head for drill or turn out a poor horseman. In a couple of months they could size a man up, and determine if he was suitable.

After a year of experimenting with the probationary period of service, Herchmer reported that it was working well.[43] A selection process that allowed the Force to weed out those unsuitable was in effect for the first time. Out of 191 probationers taken on in 1898, only 138 were finally accepted. The following year it was 98 out of 163.[44] Unfortunately, Herchmer's innovative experiment was abandoned in 1900 while he was absent in South Africa. This was in part because of an urgent need to replace the men going off to war, but it was also due to some faults in the probationary system which, in the opinion of the officer commanding "Depot" Division, the training division, made it unworkable.

Supt. Charles Constantine found that there were too many "snowbirds", men who joined in the winter seeking only food and shelter, and had no intention of engaging when their two months were up. He further reported that some of the probationers get so discouraged by the training, which is the worst period of a "policeman's career", that they decide not to continue in the service. In addition, he complained that the keeping of separate records on pay, stores and clothing for probationary recruits overly complicated the accounting system. After communication between Asst. Comm. McIllree, who was temporarily in command of the Force, and Deputy Minister White, it was resolved to end the probationary system and "swear each man in when he first enters the service".[45] Had Herchmer been present, the decision would likely have been different.

Although for several years the Force had managed to secure almost all of the recruits it needed in the West, the number of applicants arriving at Headquarters fluctuated and Herchmer suggested in 1896 that it might be necessary, once again, to send recruiting officers to the eastern provinces. White balked at the idea. Ottawa, he told the Commissioner, would not return to the earlier practice of subsidizing train fares to Regina. If recruits were to be obtained in the east again, they would have to pay their own way.[46] As far as the department was concerned, the Force should make every effort to keep its strength up from local sources. Herchmer actually preferred westerners. They usually had the advantage of being acclimatized, as well as being familiar with the landscape and how to survive on it. The *Regina Leader* agreed with him. Western recruits were far superior to eastern tenderfoots, who were useless for several months until they became use to the ways of the country.[47]

Nevertheless, with the Force expanding its duties in the Yukon and more and more men being transferred there, the need for recruits started to rise once again. Whereas only 39 men had been engaged in 1897, the numbers rose in 1898 to 138 and in 1899 to 115. There were still men from eastern Canada and Europe who made their own way to Regina to join the police, but in order to get the numbers they wanted they had to adopt new strategies. In 1898, the members on detachment were instructed to keep an eye open for likely candidates. They were promised a fee of $2 for every one they referred to Headquarters who was taken on.[48] In 1899, the NWMP for the first time placed recruiting notices in western newspapers.[49]

The South African War, however, put a drain on manpower that could not be halted simply by recruiting on the prairies. In January 1900, in addition to several officers, 134 constables and NCOs left Regina with the Canadian Mounted Rifles. They were followed shortly after by another group of volunteers with Lord Strathcona's Horse. The Yukon, meanwhile, continued to absorb men. During 1900, the police engaged 319 new recruits, a third of its total establishment. To do this, it had to once again send officers on recruiting drives in eastern Canada. "The Mounted Police is to be recruited to full strength," announced the *Regina Leader*. "Insp. Primrose is being sent to the Maritimes where he hopes to get 125 men."[50] As in the past, political patronage and irresponsible doctors would have a role in the selection process. The result was another influx of unsuitable candidates, similar to that of 1885-86, that could not be culled out by Herchmer's probationary system. For the future, the Force was left yet again with a high proportion of inexperienced men, and a resurgence of desertion and disciplinary problems.

With a few exceptions, new recruits were kept at Regina for a period of training before being transferred to divisions. For most of them, the months spent there would be a memorable experience, although perhaps not a happy one, during which they would develop some pride in their regiment and establish lifelong friendships with their fellow recruits. In spite of its pretensions, the territorial capital in the late 1880s was still a rough frontier settlement of about 1,000 souls. It did not always offer a heartening appearance to those arriving at the station after the long journey from the East.

John Donkin left a vivid description of his first impressions:

> Any homesick youth would have fairly broken down at the dismal scene; all around outside lay a great muddy expanse, with pools of water, while a soaking rain fell from a leaden sky. A few unpainted wooden houses opposite, bearing dingy sign-boards, formed Broad Street, as it is known now. A few more erections of the band-box style of architecture, at right angles to the former comprised present South Railway Street. These houses all stood in open order, with dismal spaces of clay, and puddles intervening. The great prairie stretched away, far as the eye could reach, flat and cheerless like a ghostly sea, the railway lines and telegraph poles running to a vanishing point, far, far in the distance. A Cree squaw, with painted vermilion cheeks, gaudy blanket drawn over her unkempt head, and bedraggled leggings, was standing at the corner of the Pacific Hotel, looking utterly forlorn. Her tepee was visible across the railway track.[51]

Another recruit of this period, Cst. E. A. Braithwaite, who was a former medical student, wrote: "I was sent on to Regina, a most desolate city, once called Pile of Bones, the Cree name for the site." The bones in this case were the skeletal remains of the herds of buffalo that had once grazed in the area. Upon arrival in Regina those seeking to join the Force made their way to the small police detachment in the town, which was connected by telephone to the Barracks about two and a half miles to the west. A wagon was sent and they were driven out to start a new life in the NWMP, if they were accepted.

The "Barracks", as the citizens of Regina commonly called the NWMP establishment on their doorstep, was almost as big as the town itself in the early years. In the late 1880s and 1890s there were seldom fewer than 200 mounted policemen stationed there. To this figure must be added their wives and children, as well as a complement of civilian employees. The police presence made a significant economic and social contribution to the life of Regina. Actually, the Barracks consisted in those days of three distinct organizations. It was first and foremost the Headquarters, or central command post for the administrative and operational control of the NWMP. Led by the Commissioner and his clerks, the Headquarters staff also consisted of the Adjutant, Paymaster, Supply Officer, Senior Surgeon and hospital, guardroom or jail, which included civilian as well as police prisoners, armourers, saddlers, tailors and other such artisans. Secondly, it was the headquarters of "B" Division, which was responsible for policing the southeast portion of the District of Assiniboia. In the spring, "B" Division moved out to Wood Mountain, returning to Regina before the winter set in. Lastly it was the site of "Depot" Division, the training unit to which recruits were first assigned. "Depot" Division was established on 1 November 1885. It was the brainchild of Comm. A. G. Irvine. During a visit to Dublin in 1880, he had been impressed by the Depot of the Royal Irish Constabulary in Phoenix Park, where all recruits were posted for a regular period of training, and advanced courses were provided for senior ranks. When he returned home, he strongly recommended the establishment of a "depot of instruction" for the NWMP, but nothing was done until the post-rebellion reorganization in 1885. Irvine put himself in charge of the new division, and he was succeeded for a while by Herchmer when he took over in April 1886, the only division in the Force ever to be commanded by a Commissioner.

The creation of "Depot" enabled the Commissioner to revive the position of senior NCO of the Force. By a General Order of April 1886, the sergeant major of "Depot" Division became ex-officio regimental sergeant major (RSM). The first to hold the office was RSM Robert "Bobbie" Belcher who had served in the 9th Lancers before coming to Canada and joining the Force as an "original" in 1873. The RSM was to be a key figure in the maintenance of discipline and the smooth running of the training program. Of this august personage, one recruit of the time wrote: "He carried a world of weight about the place."[52]

The original instructors at "Depot" were a notable group. S/Sgt. George Kempster, the senior riding instructor, had served in the 11th Hussars and the 2nd Life Guards. The Riding Master, Insp. W. G. Matthews, had held the same position in the 3rd Hussars, serving in India and West Africa. It was Kempster and Matthews who were the principals in producing the first musical rides in 1887.

The senior drill instructor must surely be the only one the Force had ever had who had a Master of Arts degree, and was a classicist to boot. S/Sgt. Charlie Connon, one time head boy at Upper Canada College, had graduated from the University of Toronto with an MA in Latin and Greek. He was assisted by a Scotsman, Sergeant Joe White, who was a pensioner of the 12th Lancers. He had emigrated to Montreal, and when the rebellion broke out in 1885, had gone west with a militia unit. One day Comm. Irvine happened to see him drilling soldiers in Regina, and was so impressed that he persuaded him to join the police. Lectures on police duties were given by a French-Canadian Officer, Supt. Sévère Gagnon, who had qualified as a lawyer in his home province of Quebec before he entered the Force.

Having passed the doctor and satisfied the other requirements, a recruit then took the Oath of Allegiance and the Oath of Office. These were usually administered by the Commissioner himself as stipulated by the legislation with the recruit holding a Bible, or placing his hand upon one. Upon completing his articles of engagement for five years, he was then marched away by an NCO to begin his initiation into the ways of the NWMP. His first uniform was a pair of brown pants and a tunic made from heavy cotton, or "duck" as it was called. This he soon found out constituted "fatigue dress", and was to be worn in carrying out the many chores required of him to keep "Depot" spick-and-span. He was also issued with a palliasse or mattress cover, two blankets, two wooden trestles and a supply of boards to stretch between them. On these he placed his palliasse filled with straw from the stables, and made himself as comfortable as possible in the barrack room he had been assigned to.

New arrivals were kept at fatigues until there were enough of them to form a drill squad. One frustrated new arrival complained to his mother that it is nothing but fatigues "all kinds of work is called fatigue, snow fatigue is what we hear most of, then there is general fatigue on Saturday morning".[53] As soon as there were 12 to 15 of them, they were then formed into a squad and commenced training. Recruits soon learned to look sharp and move on the double when spoken to by an NCO. Under the critical eye of the riding staff, they were taught with exact precision how a horse should be groomed and a stable mucked out. They quickly learned how to polish boots and buttons, and clean a rifle to the satisfaction of a very fastidious drill instructor.

From the moment that they were awakened by the bugle sounding Reveillé in the morning until Lights Out, they were kept busy. As one recruit later wrote: "We had Foot Drill, Mounted Drill, Stable Duty, Fatigue Duty, Stable Picket, Guard Duty, Dress Parades, Gymnasium Work, Mess Fatigue, Room Orderly and so many other duties squeezed in, you didn't even have time to get homesick".[54] He did not dislike the experience, however. "I rather enjoyed it," he continued, "with plain food, lots of exercise, and regular hours I was growing and getting as strong as an ox." Cst. Vernon Shaver also found the regimen of recruit life to be beneficial. "I am in good health," he assured the folks back home. With beef, pork, beans or potatoes and "all the bread we can eat", he had put on "seven pounds in three weeks".[55]

Playing jokes on new recruits soon became a well-established tradition at "Depot". In the 1880s, easterners still believed that the West was a wild and savage frontier inhabited by murderous Indians. It was not hard to frighten the wits out of new arrivals about to undergo their first assignment as Night Guard with stories of Indians creeping up on sentries in the dark and scalping them. It was one way of making sure that they would not fall asleep on duty. Another favourite ruse was to tell them that they had to go to the carpenter's shop to be measured for their own sentry box. The carpenter, who went along with these larks, took the necessary measurements and reminded the recruit to be sure and pick up his box before he went on duty.

As the *Regina Leader* said, one of the Force's biggest weaknesses in the past had been the lack of systematic training.[56] Raw recruits had often been transferred to divisions without any grounding in their duties whatsoever. Sir John A. Macdonald acknowledged the earlier deficiencies, and was on record as stating that the Mounted Police should be thoroughly trained not only in a military sense but in constabulary duties as well.[57] It was the responsibility of the new "Depot" to see to this task. According to the 1889 regulations, the "course of instruction" there was to include "mounted and dismounted drill, as adapted to the Mounted Infantry Regulations; manual and firing exercise for the Winchester carbine and Enfield revolver; musketry instruction; and the duties of a constable, as laid down in the Constable's Manual".[58]

Quite apart from the needs of parades and fighting formations, drill was stressed in training because it was believed to instill in men self-discipline and obedience to authority, qualities considered essential for a policeman. A textbook of the time put it this way:

> [Just read policeman for soldier]: Drill is the discipline of the body, but tends also materially to discipline the mind, and, as the discipline of the mind is a hundred-fold more important to the efficiency of the soldier, the constant practice of drill, in which all ranks have to render spontaneous and silent obedience to the commands of their superiors, is absolutely necessary.[59]

There was no fixed period of training in these years. This was because, unlike later, recruits progressed through the course of instruction as individuals rather than as a group. A man, for example, who had served in a mounted force before engaging would likely move quickly up to No. 1 drill squad, and having completed the other requirements, could find himself transferred long before a recruit who joined at the same time but had no military experience. Three to six months was the usual time spent at "Depot" by most recruits. "At the end of three months setting up drill, by some of the hardest boiled drill sergeants who were ever allowed to live," wrote Cst. James Tinsley, "we were deemed capable and transferred to different divisions."[60] Some men, of course, who lacked the right co-ordination found drill difficult. Cst. Leo Dalton seems to have been one of these. He was sentenced to one month in the guardroom for being "inattentive while at drill, and stubbornly persisting in performing the extension motions awkwardly and contrary to the directions of the instructor".[61]

In the spring of 1886, orders came from Ottawa that the Mounted Police should henceforth adopt the new mounted infantry drill which had recently been introduced in the Department of the Militia. The Cavalry School in Winnipeg was one of several such militia units involved in this tactical transformation. Shortly after the Rebellion it had been renamed the School of Mounted Infantry. When in action, the cavalryman's horse was used as a fighting arm. For the mounted infantry the horse was merely the means of transportation to the scene of the fighting. Once there the riders dismounted and fought like infantry on foot. The change, as far as the police were concerned, was to enable them to act in uniformity with the militia in any future armed confrontation.

The decision was not a popular one with many of the police officers, although some modifications were made to the instructions to suit the requirements of the Force. Supt. Sam Steele described mounted infantry drill as a "wretched substitute for our first-class single rank drill, which was good enough for Stuart and Sheridan", two well-known cavalry officers of the American Civil War.[62] The change also involved the introduction of new and unwelcome terminology to the Force for drill purposes. Basic cavalry units like the squadron and the troop became mounted infantry divisions and subdivisions. A division consisted of four sub-divisions of 16 men each. Sub-divisions were broken down into sections and half sections. In 1892, Commissioner Herchmer expressed his dissatisfaction with the mounted infantry drill and recommended that the Force return to its former practices. After some consideration Ottawa agreed.[63]

In 1888, Herchmer purchased a small printing press. Its acquisition enabled him to produce publications for internal dissemination that would promote uniformity and increase his administrative control. One of the first of these was *Drill Regulations For the North-West Mounted Police*, which appeared in 1889.[64] It was printed and bound by Cst. John Harvey, apparently the Force's first printer. Three years earlier, the Commissioner had arranged for the printing in Ottawa of a 16-page booklet on firearms drill entitled *Manual and Firing Exercise for the Winchester Carbine and the Enfield Revolver*.[65] These two publications were distributed to all divisions and became the standard textbooks for training. In addition to instructions on recruit and division drill, the 228-page *Drill Regulations* contained sections on stable management, target practice, sword drill, swimming horses across rivers and orders of dress for officers, NCOs and constables.

Yet another innovative improvement of Comm.

Lawrence Herchmer was the *Handbook and Guide for the use of Constables* by Cst. Walter Brook Osbourn. The need for a constables' manual which would be available to all members as a guide to their police duties had been suggested on several occasions.[66] Osbourn was a former member of the 1st Life Guards who seems to have had some legal training. In 1887, his leg was badly injured as a result of being thrown from a horse at Wolseley Detachment. Unable to perform regular duties, he was given clerical work. With Herchmer's approval, he began the handbook in 1890 in his spare time. It was completed in the spring of the following year. The Commissioner was delighted with the result, and thought that it would be of great assistance to members. He recommended Osbourn for $50 from the Fine Fund as a reward. Before printing and distributing the manual he had its accuracy verified by Supt. Sévère Gagnon, who was a lawyer.[67]

A more authoritative guide to police powers and duties appeared in 1893 when Carswell, the publishers of law books in Toronto, put out a new edition of the *County Constable's Manual* by J. T. Jones, the High Constable for the County of York. Commonly referred to as "Jones' Constables Manual", it was based upon the new *Criminal Code* of 1892, and soon became the standard textbook for police officers throughout Canada. Herchmer wanted every member of the Force to be issued with a copy, but at 50 cents a piece Ottawa does not seem to have agreed.[68] It did agree, however, to the purchase of 100 copies which were distributed throughout the Force. It was not until 1907 that a modified version of Jones' book was published for the Force under the title of the *Royal Northwest Mounted Police Constable's Manual* and issued to all members.[69]

In addition to drill and the care and treatment of horses, recruits also received lectures on what were described at the time as their "police duties". There were no textbooks or manuals for these but it is possible by reading the notes that recruits took on these occasions to get a good idea of what they were taught. William Somerville Clarke was the son of a Church of England clergyman, who joined the police in February 1894. In a notebook, which has survived, he kept a record with pen and ink in a clear fine hand of the substance of what he was taught in the seven or eight lectures he seems to have attended.[70] The first session dealt with the provisions of the *NWMP Act*. The second set out some "Maxims for the Guidance of Constables" which he noted down in point form. Among these were:

"Constables are placed in authority to protect not oppress the public"

"Be impartial in the discharge of duties and discard all political & sectarian prejudices"

"Never strike but in self-defence. Never treat a prisoner with more rigour than may be necessary to prevent escape"

"Treat with utmost civility in words, manner & tone of voice all classes of the public. Cheerfully render assistance to all in need of it"

Other lectures covered the "Legal Principles & Definitions of Canadian Law", the "Preservation of Peace" and the "Prevention of Crime". In the latter, Sir Robert Peel's dictum was clearly drummed into recruits' heads, "The prevention of crime is of far more importance than the detection & punishment of it". As to making an arrest, they were taught to "touch the person of the prisoner saying I am a Constable & arrest you for so & so". Immediately after doing so they were instructed to "warn the prisoner that he is in custody & not bound to say anything but that anything he may say will be brought in evidence against him".

"Depot" Division did not of course turn out a finished product, a fully qualified Mounted Policeman. One officer wrote:

> The efficient training of a recruit requires twelve months. He must be drilled, set up, taught to ride, learn to shoot with carbine and revolver, acquire a knowledge of his duties and powers as a peace officer, be instructed in simple veterinary knowledge, understand how a horse ought to be shod, and become an efficient prairie man.
>
> The latter means a smattering of cooking, a judge of a horse's work, able to find his way about, and to look after the comfort of himself and horse.[71]

Their experiences at Regina took the rough edges off of the recruits. It was up to the officers commanding the divisions to which they were transferred to round them off.

The winter of 1886 was so cold, reported Sam Steele, it was not possible to drill outside. He kept his men busy in their barrack rooms, however, going through the manual on firing exercises and taking instruction in horse shoeing. Once spring came he commenced mounted and dismounted drills using the new mounted infantry regulations. These were kept up until July when, with the temperatures reaching 105°F in the shade, it became too hot to continue.[72] In 1894, Steele arranged a "course of lectures on Police Duties" under the supervision of Insps. Sanders and Davidson, assisted by Sgts. Maj. Spicer and Barker. All available NCOs and constables were required to attend and examinations were set at the end of the course. The subjects covered included: Regulations and Orders, Drill, Constable's Manual, Territorial Ordinances, *Indian Act, Criminal Code* and the Proper Mode of Framing Charges. The examination consisted of 12 questions on each subject covered. The top students were:

Reg. No. 1754	Cst. Cunningham	75.6 %
Reg. No. 2802	Cst. Brankley	74.6 %
Reg. No. 1026	Sgt. Watson	74.5 %
Reg. No. 1572	Cpl. Camies	71.6 %
Reg. No. 626	Sgt. Birtles	71.5 %

In the thorough manner that was characteristic of everything Steele did, all candidates who failed to obtain a pass mark were re-examined ten days later. Fortunately they all passed on the second try, otherwise Steele would undoubtedly have kept them at it until they did.[73]

"Depot" Division was not established solely for the training of recruits. According to Regulations and Orders it also had a mandate to provide instruction for officers and NCOs. As a rule, all newly commissioned officers were posted there for a period. They were placed under the tutelage of the regimental sergeant major and other officers until the Commissioner was satisfied they were ready to be transferred to divisions. In keeping with his desire to create a more professional Force, in 1887 Herchmer started instruction courses for sergeants at "Depot". The subjects included horsemanship, drill, signalling, cipher reading and camping. The results of the examinations at the end of the course were taken into account in making future promotions. Sgt. Lewis Hooper who finished in first place with 140 marks was shortly thereafter raised to the rank of sergeant major.[74]

Another sign of the increasing professionalism and emphasis on training was the growing use encouraged by the Commissioner of instruction books and reference manuals. In 1895, he convinced Ottawa to supply over 200 such volumes both for use in courses at "Depot" and for sale to members in the Canteen. These works included the *Criminal Code, Statutes of Canada, Clarkes Magistrates' Manual, Jones Constable's Manual, NWMP Act* and *Red Cross Ambulance Lectures*.[75]

By the 1890s "Depot" Division, in the words of its commanding officer, had a "very efficient staff" turning out "well-trained men".[76]

In 1895, however, as a result of the government's policy of reduction, it ceased to function as a training facility. Only five recruits were taken on that year. With fewer men and an increasing demand for services, the training staff were returned to regular duty. "Depot" Division itself did not disappear. As a part of the reorganization that year it absorbed "B" Division and thus became an operational unit. The recruits that were taken on during the next two or three years were either transferred directly to divisions, or kept at Regina for whatever training was available when NCOs could be spared. Eighteen-year-old Vernon Shaver, for example, spent only three weeks there before being sent to the Yukon. Comm. Herchmer complained bitterly that such circumstances were undermining the Force's efficiency. With recruiting once again picking up to meet the demand for more and more men to police the Gold Rush, he finally received Laurier's approval in 1899 to re-establish a "School of Instruction" at Headquarters in Regina.[77]

Chapter 13

Health and Happiness:
The Benefits of Service

The federal government made a reasonable effort to compensate members of the North-West Mounted Police for their service. Provisions for pay, leave and pensions were sufficient to attract men to join the Force. And the health care provided was the best available in the frontier west. While the NWMP was primarily a corps of bachelors, some provision was made to accommodate married members.

The amount spent on pay for the police grew from approximately 35 per cent of the total Force expenditure in 1886 to approximately 48 per cent by the turn of the century.[1] The increase in the proportion was largely due to the graded pay scales for constables. At the beginning of his five-year term of engagement a recruit received 50 cents a day. If at the end of his first and each subsequent year his conduct had been good, he would receive an additional five cents a day until in his final year he reached a maximum of seventy cents per day. As an incentive to encourage well-behaved, experienced men to stay in the Force, he would receive a further five cents, if he agreed to re-engage for another five years when his time was up. On the other hand, if he took his discharge, he would be replaced by a new recruit at 50 cents, a saving to the government of 25 cents a day, or $91.25 a year. Put in larger terms, 100 men who re-engaged could cost $27,375 a year in pay. Their replacement by recruits only amounted to $18,250. What happened during this period was that more and more men decided to re-engage rather than take their discharge. Hence, the total pay bill gradually rose. The two principal reasons for this were the scarcity of job prospects outside the police and the gradually improving benefits inside.

Basic per diem pay rates for constables and NCOs had not changed since 1882:

Sergeants Major/ Staff Sergeants	$1.50
Sergeants	$1.00
Corporals	.85
Constables	.50 to .75

These rates were revised slightly when the *NWMP Act* was amended in 1894. The Commissioner had long pushed for higher pay for certain senior NCOs occupying positions of increased responsibility, particularly division sergeants major. One amendment permitted him to pay up to four sergeants major or staff sergeants $2 per day. Another regularized the existing practice of engaging boys under 18 years as buglers at 40 cents a day. The pay scales for NCOs and constables were not revised again until 1905.

Pay parades occurred once a month. At division the men marched forward one at a time from the ranks to receive their due amount from the officer who acted as paymaster. Halting in front of him, they saluted, stepped forward, picked up the money, signed the pay ledger in acknowledgement, stepped back, saluted once again and then returned to their place. The pay for detachment men was taken out to them by an officer on patrol or some other duty. The important thing on these occasions was to make sure that the pay ledger was signed. As the men were considered to be on duty everyday, they were paid for every day. A month's pay consisted of the number of days in the month multiplied by the daily rate. All payments were made in cash. Many federal government employees of the time were paid by cheque. Such a system avoided the necessity of handling large quantities of cash. Comptroller Fred White refused to extend it to the police, however, because the men would have to take their cheques to a bank and the bank would charge them a fee for cashing it.[2]

There were opportunities for NCOs and constables to earn extra income. Conspicuous examples of police investigation could be rewarded by cash grants from the Fine Fund. In 1894 Sgt. Charles Brown was promoted to staff sergeant and awarded $50 from the fund for his outstanding detective work in securing the conviction of two men for the murder of an Italian knife-grinder near Grenfell.[3] They were also paid small amounts when acting as officers of the courts. There was an authorized scale of "Constables' Fees", as they were known. The most frequent of these were serving a summons: 25 cents; executing a warrant to arrest: $1; and serving as court orderly: 25 cents an hour. They were permitted to collect and retain these fees themselves.[4]

The commonest way of obtaining additional remuneration, however, was through working pay. The legislation provided that men could be paid up to 50 cents per day "working pay". This was taken to mean performing tasks that required the skill of an artisan or tradesman and were not strictly police in nature. From its earliest days, the Force had been required to be as self-sufficient as possible. The government also learned that it was much cheaper to pay a qualified constable extra money to repair saddles, for example, than it was to send them out to a civilian saddler. As one commanding officer put it:

> It is very desirable that we should have as good men as it is possible to get to fill the important position of artisans in different trades, to enable us to have our own work performed in a thoroughly efficient manner, I refer particularly to blacksmiths, shoeing-smiths, carpenters, saddlers and tailors. All skilled workmen, particularly shoeing-smiths and carpenters, command high wages in this country.[5]

Experienced tradesmen who joined the Force could add "working" pay of between 15 and 50 cents to their basic rate of pay.

How well-off were the rank and file of the NWMP on their pay? In the House of Commons Sir John A. Macdonald is on record as having said that "they are pretty well paid, but they have exceedingly hard work to perform".[6] Herchmer believed that their pay was "liberal" and compared "favorably with the earnings of citizens".[7] He later expressed the view that with their free clothing, free pension and opportunities for extra pay they should be able to save for a "comfortable old age".[8] As previously noted, a constable started at 50 cents a day or $182.50 a year. If he re-engaged he would get 75 cents a day or $273.75 a year. With working pay he could make well over $300 a year. His board, uniform and medical care were included. Like most other employed persons of the time, there were no deductions for income tax, insurance premiums or pension contributions. The closest comparison would be with the Canadian Militia. Upon enlistment a private soldier received the same as the con-

stable, 50 cents a day. In the army, however, there was no provision for increases beyond that. NWMP NCOs were also better paid. Militia corporals got 60 cents a day, sergeants 75 and staff sergeants $1.[9] Their police counterparts received 85 cents, $1 and $1.50 respectively.

The pay rates also compared favourably with those of other occupational groups in the depressed economic circumstances of the 1880s and early 1890s. On the Hamilton Police Department, a constable was paid $1.60 per day in 1887. His more affluent Toronto counterpart received $2.[10] In both cases of course board and medical care were not included. At $300 a year a constable was on about the same income level as a school teacher. In eastern Canada, unskilled labourers were commonly paid $1 for each actual day of work, again without board. In the West, their wages were higher at $1.25 to $1.50, but so were prices, and in both cases the work tended to be seasonal.[11] Skilled tradesmen in Winnipeg could earn 25 cents an hour, but few would be fortunate to work 12 months of the year.

Not everyone agreed with the Commissioner. Cst. P. W. Pennefather claimed that by the time he purchased boot polish, brasso, pipe clay, tobacco, and paid 10 cents a day for extra messing and 25 cents for a haircut there was very little left of the $15 he received a month.[12] Of course when he finally did get some working pay, he found that with drinks at 10 cents each he could "cut quite a swath" on a day's pay. There were other temptations besides alcohol that would drain away a man's capital. Playing cards for money was a common amusement on lonely detachments or in barrack rooms during cold winter nights. Cpl. Donkin recalled that at one detachment the men played poker every evening to pass the time, one constable losing $100, over six month's pay, at a sitting.[13]

For this and other reasons, some men were forced to borrow money from their comrades. Usury was strictly forbidden by the regulations, but it seems to have thrived for those whose expenditures exceeded their income.[14] Cst. Alfred Coulson was accidentally shot and killed whilst out hunting. This resulted in an inventory being made of his personal effects in the trunk under his bed. Upon joining the Force he had given his name as Alfred Coulson son of D. Coulson of Stroud, Gloucester, England. The first surprise that was discovered was that he was actually Samuel J. Earl, son of Daniel Earl of London, England. The second was a list of IOUs in Coulson's favour signed by 11 members of the Force totalling $644.50. Upon investigation, the Commissioner found that Coulson was in fact well known as a money lender who charged "very high rates" of interest, $1 per month on every $5 borrowed.[15] Neither White nor Herchmer liked the idea of acting as a debt collector. The Deputy Minister informed his "rich relatives" in London that the Force would try to collect what was due, but that he did not believe that resorting to legal process would be any good.

In spite of the moneylending, gambling, drinking and the complaints, there is good reason for accepting Herchmer's view that indeed a sober and industrious young constable could get ahead in life on his pay. Those who wished to could have money deducted from their pay each month and have it deposited for them in the Dominion Savings Bank. Many of the men took advantage of this scheme. In 1886, the CO "E" Division reported that he had 22 regular depositors on his payroll.[16] His counterpart in "B" Division revealed that a total of $3,209 had been saved by his men for that year.[17] In 1888, the Commissioner reported that many men put all of their pay in the bank during the summer months when they are out on patrol.[18] It was not unusual for men to withdraw amounts totalling several hundred dollars, when taking their discharge.[19] For 1889, Herchmer stated $32,929.47 was deducted on behalf of the NCOs and constables. With what some of the men also sent home to their families, bought stocks with and invested in ranching, he estimated they saved over $40,000 that year.[20] The total pay for NCOs and constables for fiscal year 1889-90 was $247,014.[21] If Herchmer was right, as a group they were saving approximately 17 per cent of their income.

A Mounted Policeman's free time was subject to paramilitary regulations. His working day, Monday to Saturday, ended once evening stables, which normally commenced at 4:30 p.m., had been completed. In theory, the rest of the day was his own. In practice, however, he had to take his turn at a variety of duties around the post. He might find himself detailed for night piquet, guard duty or stable orderly. While performing such duties, he could find himself confined to barracks for 24 hours or even a week at a time. If he managed to escape from being assigned to these unpleasant tasks, he was free to leave the post. Before he could do so, however, he had to obtain a pass signed by the officer on duty which specified precisely at what hour he was to return. This pass, Form 33, was his ticket to freedom. He had to carry it with him at all times, and surrender it at the guardroom on his return. There the time of his arrival would be noted. If he had overstayed his pass, he would be paraded by the sergeant major before the orderly officer the next morning and punished. Naturally enough, young Mounted Policemen thought up all kinds of excuses and came up with all kinds of tricks to beat the system. Sometimes they were successful, and sometimes they were not. An old ruse on being late was to sneak past the sentries and then claim the next day that you had, in fact come in so early, that you

had forgotten to hand your pass in. Comm. Herchmer decided to put some restrictions on these passes. If men were allowed to stay out night after night until all hours, they would inevitably get into trouble. It was ruled, therefore, that once a week a member would be permitted to remain out until midnight. All other passes granted to him that week would require him to be back in barracks by 10:30 p.m.[22]

Everyone looked forward to Sunday. Once morning stables were over and the obligatory church service attended, the men were free for the remainder of the day, unless detailed for some duty. Of course they still needed a pass if they wished to leave the post. For many, Sunday was a time for resting up after Saturday night, or engaging in a favourite pastime. They had to be careful about the latter. In nineteenth-century Canada, Sunday was still the Lord's Day. One guardian of Christian morality once complained because he spied what he thought was an organized game of hockey one Sunday on the Wascana Creek at the barracks in Regina.

"Sunday Routine" as it was known, was also followed on public holidays. Those observed by the NWMP in the NWT were New Year's Day, Good Friday, Arbor Day in May, Queen Victoria's Birthday on May 24, Dominion Day, Thanksgiving Day in November, at the same time as the Americans, and Christmas Day.[23] Arbor Day was also an observance from south of the border. On this day Americans traditionally planted trees and gardens. On Queen Victoria's Birthday and Dominion Day a special parade was usually held at which those posts having artillery pieces fired a salute.

The regulations also provided for longer absences from duty than an evening out on the town. The Commissioner could grant up to 10 days leave (extended to 21 in 1892) at one time, but not exceeding 30 days per annum to any officer providing the leave was spent in the NWT or Manitoba.[24] Commanding officers were authorized to give constables and NCOs up to ten days leave a year providing it was taken in the Territories.

Longer periods of absence than this were referred to as "furloughs". When on furlough, a member could travel anywhere. To obtain one of these, an officer had to apply to the Deputy Minister in Ottawa. In 1890, for example, Supt. Sam Steele received a four-month furlough in order to get married. The wedding took place in Vaudreuil, Quebec. The bride was Miss Marie Elizabeth Harwood, the daughter of Mr. Robert Harwood, MP (a principal source of Steele's political influence), a seigneur of the county and a descendant of the last Marquis de Lotbinière. After their marriage, the newlyweds enjoyed a honeymoon in New York and eastern

Canada before making their home in Fort Macleod.[25]

Furloughs for NCOs and constables could be authorized by the Commissioner for up to 30 days. Applications for longer than this also had to be sent to Ottawa. In addition there was a special provision for men whose term of engagement was about to expire. If they agreed to re-engage, they were eligible for a two month furlough, as a reward for past service and an incentive to stay on. Sick leave was also granted to both officers and men, the length and need being certified by one of the surgeons. All leave was granted with pay. Of course it was granted as a privilege, not a right. It could be denied or cancelled as the Commissioner felt was in the best interests of the Force. As to who should get it and how much they should be allowed, it was left to the judgement of the authorizing officer to make a decision based upon the conduct of the applicant, the length of his service and the time that had elapsed since he last had leave.

In practice, leave was more generously handed out to the men than the regulations might suggest. By November, many detachments and outposts were closed and the men on them recalled to division headquarters until the spring. They spent much of the winter months simply doing routine drills and fatigues. The Comptroller gave Herchmer the authority to grant up to three months leave during the winter to anyone that requested it, providing the ability of the Force to meet any emergency was not endangered. By doing so, the department would save money; the men had to be paid while on leave, but they did not have to be fed.[26]

Comm. Herchmer believed that one of the principal reasons good men did not stay in the Mounted Police was that it did not offer them a career. This would change, he argued, if a pension scheme was to be introduced. Within days of taking office, he was urging Ottawa to provide one.[27] To Herchmer a pension plan was a vital step in building an efficient and professional police force. Not everyone agreed with him. The idea that the state should superannuate its employees was too progressive for some. Members of Parliament claimed that pension plans undermined the Victorian values of self-reliance, thrift and hard work. Fortunately, Macdonald also favoured a retirement scheme for the police.

The issue was first brought before the House of Commons by Nicholas Flood Davin, the member from Regina, who raised his voice in support of such a measure in April 1887. Many of Davin's constituents, of course, were Mounted Policemen. Speaking for the government, Macdonald replied that a pension plan was in fact already under consideration.[28] The Mounted Police Pension Act did not appear in Parliament, however, until 7 March 1889. The Prime Minister explained that it was closely modelled on the Royal Irish Constabulary retirement plan, although not quite as generous in its benefits. Its purpose, he continued, was to increase both the efficiency and economy of the Force by inducing trained men to stay in it.[29] Davin supported him, arguing that under the existing circumstances the best men left after five years because they had to get out while they were still young enough to find civilian jobs.

The Opposition did not agree with Macdonald's rationale for the bill, nor with the principles upon which it was based. Although the federal civil service had had one for several years, government run superannuation plans were still something of an innovation. The civil service plan was a contributory one financed by salary deductions. What irritated the opponents of the police measure was that it was non-contributory and would be a direct burden on the public purse. One member charged that it was undemocratic to pension one group at the expense of others. Where would it lead? he asked. If Mounted Policemen were to be superannuated at public cost, why not farmers, labourers and mechanics as well? Others argued vigorously that it would motivate the lazy and the shiftless to remain in the Force, and have exactly the opposite effect to that claimed by the Prime Minister. Another pointed out the inconsistency of providing a pension plan for a force that all parties agreed was only temporary in nature and would be eventually disbanded.[30] The government's majority secured the passage of the bill, which received royal assent on 2 May 1889.[31]

The Commissioner had hoped that the officers would be included in the measure, but this was not to be. They were already participating in the civil service superannuation plan and would continue to do so until 1902, when a separate bill was passed to regulate their pensions. One attractive feature of the plan, apart from the fact the men did not have to pay contributions, was that it was made retroactive to the organization of the Force in 1873. Overnight some of them found that they had 15 or 16 years pensionable service. Under the terms of the measure NCOs and constables were entitled to a lifetime pension after a minimum of 25 years of service. The amount was determined by dividing the individual's average pay for the previous 3 years by 50 and multiplying the result by 30. For example, a constable with 25 years service who had been receiving the maximum rate for his rank of 75 cents a day for the previous 3 years would get a pension of 45 cents a day for the rest of his life, whether it lasted 40 minutes or 40 years. If he wished to serve beyond 25 years, he could do so. For each year that he did, a further one-fiftieth of his average pay would be added to his pension until he reached the maximum allowable which was two-thirds of his pay. All ranks would reach this in their twenty-ninth year of service. Thus, the maximum possible pension for a constable of the time was 50 cents a day, a sergeant 66 cents and a staff sergeant $1. Once he died, of course, the pension died with him, and his dependents, if any, received nothing. There was also a provision for stopping the annuity, if the recipient was convicted of an indictable offence or consorted with criminals.

The bill also authorized the payment of medical pensions for those who became unfit to carry out their duties and had between 15 and 25 years service. Their disability had to be certified by a medical board. The scale of benefits was not quite as generous as for those who retired with over 25 years. Between 15 and 20 years of service their pension was calculated on the basis of one-fiftieth for each year of service. For each year between 20 and 25 it was two-fiftieths a year. Thus a man receiving a disability pension after 23 years, would get an amount based upon 26-fiftieths of his average pay over the previous 3 years. Men who recovered from their incapacity to work, could be recalled to duty and forfeit their annuity. Almost as soon as the bill was passed, Davin began lobbying in parliament to have the minimum term of service required to retire reduced from 25 to 20 years. This he finally succeeded in doing in an amendment to the legislation in 1898.[32]

The first member of the Force to retire to pension under the Act was a Prince Edward Islander, S/Sgt. John Martin. He had been sworn in as a member of the Force at Lower Fort Garry on 3 November 1873. He was struck off strength exactly 25 years later on 3 November 1898. As a staff sergeant for several years, his average pay for the last three was $1.50. Thirty-fiftieths of this amounted to a pension of ninety cents a day. Martin spent the remaining 35 years of his life back on his native island, where for reasons he never disclosed, he was known as Malcolm MacIntosh. The first member to be pensioned for medical reasons under the legislation was Sgt. Bill Perrin, an Irishman. He joined the NWMP on 22 January 1884, and was invalided to pension just over 15 years later on 30 June 1899, when confined to a wheelchair with locomotor ataxia. As a sergeant his average daily pay was $1. With 15 years service he got 15-fiftieths of that, 30 cents a day pension. When he died in 1906, however, leaving a wife and three children, his pension died with him.[33]

The department's interpretation of the medical provisions of the legislation was that the physical or mental disability had to be due to hardship or exposure in the performance of one's duties. It was the task of the medical board to verify this. It was made up of three officers, including a surgeon. As such, it was not an independent body. In 1900, Cst. Phillipe

Casault launched an interesting challenge against the administration's interpretation. Casault's term of service ended in April of that year. He was not re-engaged because in the opinion of the surgeon he was in ill-health due to his alcoholic habits. At the time of his discharge he was just a few days short of completing 15 years service. The former constable claimed that he had been unjustly treated and was entitled to a pension. Deputy Minister White responded that the cause of his disability was due to his own overindulgence and not the result of any duty he had performed. Casault's supporters countered that the conditions under which the men lived in the early days were so bad that they were forced to drink heavily and that for this the government was "responsible". They had some powerful political influences on their side, but the department stuck to its view that alcoholism was a matter of individual choice and the claim was eventually dropped.[34]

The police also provided compensation to the dependents of those members who were killed on duty, and to those members who were injured or crippled as a direct result of their duties, but did not have the necessary 15 years service to qualify for a pension. There was no statutory authority for these benefits in the *Police Act*. It had long been the practice, however, with respect to militiamen being killed or wounded for the government of the day to accept its responsibility in such circumstances. The amount of the compensation was included in the annual expenditure of the Force which was put before Parliament for approval. Once passed, payment was then authorized by Order-in-Council.

Cst. Sam Hayes died as a result of injuries received at Fort Calgary in 1876. His mother, who was dependent upon him, was eventually awarded the sum of $200. A similar amount was granted to the father of Cst. Marmaduke Graburn who was shot and killed by a person or persons unknown near Fort Walsh in 1879.[35] Graburn was the first member of the NWMP to be murdered on duty. Similar awards were made from time to time to the dependents of other members during the early years of the Force.

The question of compensation came very much to the fore in 1885 following the rebellion. During the hostilities, eight members of the NWMP were killed and eleven wounded. Many of these or their dependents subsequently received annuities or cash payments as redress. As an example, Cst. Patrick Burke died at Battleford on 3 May 1885 as a result of wounds inflicted the day before during the engagement with the Indians at Cut Knife Hill. He left a widow, five sons and one daughter. After due bureaucratic delay, Mrs. Burke eventually was awarded a lump sum gratuity of $273.75, which was equal to one month's pay for each year her husband had served in the Force, and a pension of 37½ cents per day. The children were also provided with an annuity. Each received 7½ cents a day, the daughter until she reached age 21 and the boys until they became 18.[36] All of the sons later served in the Mounted Police at one time or another. To further assist the widow to maintain herself and her family, work was found for her as cook at the Battleford post for many years.

Another sad and shocking case of widowhood during this period was that of Ida Colebrook. Her husband, Sgt. Colin Colebrook, was shot and murdered by Almighty Voice, or Kah-kee-say-mane-too-wayo, meaning Voice of the Great Spirit, near Kinistino in October 1895. Mrs. Colebrook was one of the first women to be employed by the police as a matron. As early as 1890, she had escorted female prisoners to Stony Mountain Penitentiary. Shortly after the killing, Comm. Herchmer wrote to her expressing his sympathy on behalf of the Force and promising to do everything he could to expedite a pension for her. A few weeks later he informed her of the compensation that was being recommended for her and her four-year-old son, George. She was to receive a cash gratuity of $565.50, which was based upon the number of years her husband had served, and a pension of $182.50 per annum, or 50 cents a day, which was exactly the same amount as that paid to a recruit, and half of what her husband had earned as a sergeant. Her son was awarded $121.66 in cash and a pension of $35.50 per annum.[37]

As in other cases of widows, her pension would be forfeited, if she became wealthy, re-married or became unworthy of it, that is to say no longer lived a respectable life according to the standards of the time. Her son's annuity would be paid until he reached 18 years of age, as was the rule with the Burkes.[38] Precisely how Ottawa determined these amounts is unclear, but an unofficial assessment of Mrs. Colebrook's means seems to have been taken into account. Herchmer asked the local commanding officer discreetly to find out how much insurance she would get, and what other financial resources she might have.[39] There was no entitlement to these gratuities and pensions. They were handed out as the government in its generosity saw fit. On the other hand, of course, there were no premiums to pay. Ida Colebrook's pension was discontinued in 1904, following her re-marriage in the United States.

As in the case of those killed on duty, there was no statutory provision for paying compensation to members who were disabled as a result of their duties, but did not have sufficient service to qualify for a pension. Once again it was a question of following what had been customary practice in the militia.[40] After 1885, the police used the compensa-tion schedule formulated by the government to recompense those injured during the rebellion. This set out a scale of payments determined by the degree of disability and the rank of the individual. A medical board of three officers decided the degree of disability. The department in Ottawa then determined the amount of compensation, which had to be put before parliament each year in the police estimates. Should a member recover or partly recover from his injuries, his pension was reduced accordingly.

Four degrees of disability were recognized by the schedule. The most serious was for men who had lost two limbs, or both eyes, or were so badly incapacitated that they were unable to earn a living and needed someone to permanently assist or care for them. In those circumstances, their pensions would be approximately 90 per cent of their pay. The second level applied to men who while unable to earn a living did not require the care of another person. The third was for those who although disabled were able to contribute to a small degree to their livelihood. Lastly, the men who received the lowest rate of compensation were those who, although still able to materially support themselves, remained unfit for further police duties.

The most common causes of disablement were accidents involving horses or injuries caused by firearms. As examples, Cst. J. W. Boyd was left permanently lame in one leg after he was kicked by a horse. He was awarded compensation of 30 cents a day. Cpl. Avila Poitevin received 60 cents a day for a deformed arm caused by being bucked off a horse. A shoulder of Special Cst. Napoleon Venne was maimed when hit by a bullet during a skirmish with Almighty Voice. His injury was valued at 23 cents a day. Cst. Seymour Farquharson had to have one arm amputated four inches below the shoulder after he accidentally shot himself. His compensation was set at 30 cents a day. The 22-year-old Prince Edward Islander remained on disability pension until he died in 1964, a total of 64 years. His compensation was increased to 72 cents a day in 1925 and 93 cents in 1945, after further examinations by medical boards determined that his degree of disability increased as he became older.[41] By 1901, 16 members of the NWMP were in receipt of annual disability pensions in amounts ranging from $73 to $356.[42]

In the Order-in-Council which brought the NWMP into existence in 1873, every member was promised, in addition to pay, rations and accommodation, "medical attendance free".[43] To oversee this health care, Sir John A. Macdonald had included two provisions in the earlier legislation which had been passed to authorize the Force's establishment. The first provided for the appointment by commission of one Surgeon whose pay was not to exceed

$1,400 per annum, nor be less than $1,000 per annum. The second authorized the government to pay local civilian medical practitioners for providing the service.[44] When recruiting began in the fall of 1873, Macdonald favoured the second option, and he did not appoint anyone to the position of Surgeon. The Prime Minister optimistically believed that the men would eventually be stationed in locations where civilian doctors would be available. In the meantime, medical attention for the first contingent of men that was sent out to Lower Fort Garry was provided by Dr. Alfred Codd, who was Surgeon to the Provisional Battalion of Militia in Winnipeg.

By the spring of 1874, it had become evident to Macdonald's successors, however, that some of the Mounted Police at least might end up in places where there was a complete absence of medical men. As a result, when the Act was amended that year, the provision for appointing one Surgeon was changed to read "Surgeons".[45] The first men to be commissioned under this provision were Dr. John Kittson, M.D., a graduate of McGill University Medical School, who was appointed Surgeon in April 1874, and Mr. Richard Nevitt, B.M., a graduate of the Trinity University Medical School in Toronto, who was appointed Assistant Surgeon in June 1874. The latter was a Southerner by birth who had come to Canada as a refugee with his family to escape the dangers of the American Civil War. After he left the NWMP in 1878, he returned to Toronto, obtained an M.D., became a successful obstetrician and gynaecologist, and was one of the founders of the Women's Medical College in that city.[46]

Both Kittson and Nevitt took part in the March West. It was while at Fort Dufferin in June 1874 preparing for its departure, that they were confronted with the first cases of serious illness in the Force. A deadly epidemic of typhoid broke out in Manitoba that summer, which claimed many lives. Four of the recruits contracted the disease. Typhoid was the principal cause of natural death among the police. The four sick men had to be left behind and missed the great expedition. To care for them, it was arranged that Capt. Clark, the U.S. army surgeon just across the border at Fort Pembina, would attend them daily. In between his visits, they were nursed constantly without any concern for her own safety by the Force's own Florence Nightingale, Mrs. Cotton Almon, the wife of the Farming Superintendent for the Boundary Commission at Fort Dufferin. Surgeon Kittson described her as "an excellent Lady, braving all dangers, administering to their wants personally, and every day adding to their comfort by many acts of kindness".[47] Sub-Cst. William Parker credited the spoonfuls of sherry she fed to him with having "saved my life".[48]

Unfortunately, two of the men, Sub-Csts. Brown and McIntosh, died from the fever.

As the number of police posts increased, further appointments of Assistant Surgeons were made. At the larger ones, hospitals were constructed to provide care for the sick and isolate them from the healthy. Among the early posts to have hospitals were Fort Macleod and Swan River (1874), Fort Walsh (1875), Calgary (1882), Regina (1883), Maple Creek (1883), Battleford and Prince Albert (1884). Very often the surgeons were assisted at these medical centres by men in the ranks who had some formal medical training or, in some cases, were qualified physicians. According to their ability, they were appointed hospital sergeants, or hospital staff sergeants. Their duties included acting as dressers, nursing, dispensing and administering drugs, and assisting with surgery. Occasionally such men were placed in charge of the medical care at a post, thereby saving the government the expense of appointing a surgeon. At smaller detachments private practitioners were engaged, usually on a monthly fee, to visit the post daily and attend to those reporting sick. These became known as Acting Assistant Surgeons, a title which led later to their being mistakenly identified as members of the NWMP, which they were not.

When Dr. Kittson resigned in 1882 as the Senior Medical Officer, he was replaced by Dr. Augustus Jukes, who had formerly had a family practice in St. Catharines, Ontario. His political appointment as Senior Surgeon did not sit too well with some of the Assistant Surgeons, who felt that they had better qualifications and better right to the position. However, Supt. R. B. Deane described him as a "very fine old gentleman", and a competent practitioner.[49] In 1885, Jukes established a permanent place for himself in the history books of Canada when, at the trial of Louis Riel, he had to testify as to the sanity or otherwise of the rebel leader. Riel, he told the court, was suffering from illusions on matters of politics and religion, but was otherwise a normal human being. In a private letter to Macdonald, Jukes expressed the hope that Riel would not be executed.[50]

The duties of the Senior Surgeon and his staff were set out in detail for the first time in the 1889 Regulations. As the principal medical officer at headquarters, Jukes was responsible to the Commissioner for the operation of all hospitals and the supervision of the medical staff throughout the Force. He was required at least once each year to visit all large posts for the purpose of inspecting the hospitals, medical records and the pharmaceutical supplies. Surgeons were forbidden to use the hospitals or their dispensaries to interview or treat their civilian patients. Many of the doctors had also established private practices among the local population in addition to their official responsibilities. The administration had found that if they did not permit them to add to their income in this way, they would have had a hard time retaining their services. They were expected, therefore, to see their private patients in their own time, after their official duties had been attended to, off government property. The only exception to this was the families of the policemen, who the government later permitted to also receive free health care. Some of the surgeons, however, found these regulations too restrictive, and the prospect of additional income so attractive that they did not stay with the police very long.

The Senior Surgeon was responsible for purchasing all medical stores. All prescribed drugs had to be recorded in the "Day Book" in the dispensary at each post showing the date, name of patient and quantity administered. A "Medical History Book" also had to be kept at each post. In it the name of each patient was entered, the date admitted to hospital or placed under care, the nature of the complaint, the treatment ordered and the date of discharge. When a man was injured as a result of his duties, an inquiry was to be held to determine the circumstances under which he had sustained his injuries. The latter procedure was necessary in the event that there were later claims for compensation.

Members of the medical staff were required to examine all men presenting themselves for engagement in the Force, and to attend the daily Sick Parade at their posts to examine all constables and NCOs who reported themselves as sick. Such parades were normally held each morning at 8:30 a.m. Every malingerer was familiar with the procedures at Sick Parade. After the surgeon or hospital sergeant had determined the nature and seriousness of the illness, he would place the member on M&D (Medicine and Duty), LD (Light Duty) or ODS (Off Duty Sick). For those trying to avoid work the latter was the most desirable decision. When Off Duty Sick, one returned to one's barrack room and was excused all duties. Whereas on Light Duty, drills and parades were escaped, but one was deemed well enough to perform fatigues. Every post had one or two chronic malingerers. Jukes cited one, in 1886, who had tried every dodge he could think of to escape duty since he entered the Force, and was quite capable of artificially inducing one condition or another to get himself on Sick Parade.[51]

Surgeons were also responsible for the health of the prisoners in the guardroom. They were required to visit the cells daily and examine anyone who had reported himself ill to the provost. These too could be excused "Hard Labour", if, in his judgement, it was necessary. They were also expected to be available during firearms practice in the event of any accidents. Another of their tasks was to ensure that the sanitation system at the barracks was properly cleansed and disinfected and not a threat to the well-being of the command.

In addition to Senior Surgeon Jukes, the medical staff in 1886 consisted of five assistant surgeons, all of whom were well-qualified medical practitioners. They were Dr. George Kennedy, at Fort Macleod, Dr. Robert Miller, at Prince Albert, Dr. Henry Baldwin, at Battleford, Dr. John Rolph, at Regina, and Dr. Peter Aylen, at Fort Saskatchewan. Kennedy and Baldwin had obtained their degrees at the University of Toronto. Aylen was a graduate of McGill University. Rolph, meanwhile, had received his qualifications from the Royal College of Physicians in London, England. The source of Miller's degree is unknown. Dr. Kennedy had the distinction of presenting a paper entitled "The Climate of Southern Alberta, and Its Relationship to Health and Disease" at the annual meeting of the Canadian Medical Association in Banff in 1889.[52]

All the physicians were native Canadians, some descended from families that had left their mark on the country's earlier history. Robert Baldwin was the grandson of the Upper Canadian political reformer and proponent of responsible government of the same name. John Rolph's father, Dr. John Rolph, pioneered medical education in Toronto, was associated with Robert Baldwin in the reform movement, and joined with William Lyon Mackenzie in the ill-fated rebellion of 1837. Dr. Peter Aylen's antecedents were even more colourful. His grandfather had been Peter Aylen, the "King of the Shiners", the lumber baron who with his Irish supporters used intimidation and violence to gain control of the lumber trade on the Ottawa and Gatineau Rivers in the 1830s.

At Calgary and Lethbridge in 1886, the police employed local doctors to provide the medical care, respectively Drs. Andrew Henderson and F. H. Mewburn. Dr. Hugh Bain was also employed temporarily at Prince Albert. The only two major posts without surgeons were Maple Creek and Wood Mountain which was the headquarters of "B" Division during the summer months. At the former location, health services were carried out by Hospital S/Sgt. John Holme, who had a doctor of medicine degree and had been working as a medical attendant at various posts since 1879. Hospital S/Sgt. Robert Hazelton, whose qualifications are unknown, was in charge at Wood Mountain.

The number of local doctors who were employed from time to time at various posts for fees ranging from $30 to $60 per month as Acting Assistant Surgeons during the term of Herchmer's command is too numerous to record. Among the Assistant Surgeons there were a few changes as some of them died, resigned or retired. One was actually dismissed for sexual improprieties involving his female and child patients. Among the replacements to the rank of Assistant Surgeon during the period were the following: Dr. Henry Dodd, a Member of the Royal College of Physicians (Edinburgh); Dr. Louis Paré, formerly Surgeon Major of the 65th Mount Royal Rifles, who served with the regiment during the North-West Rebellion; Dr. Charles Haultain, educated at the University of Toronto Medical School, a nephew of F. W. G. Haultain, the "Premier" of the NWT; Dr. Samuel Fraser, a graduate of the University of Western Ontario Medical School; and Dr. George Bell, a member of the Royal College of Surgeons, who had served as a surgeon with one of the large steamship lines before his nomination to the NWMP. As with all commissioned ranks, an appointment to the position of Assistant Surgeon required political support.

There were a number of men during the period who served as hospital sergeants and hospital staff sergeants. The following are just a few of them. S/Sgts. Richards and Graydon were employed at different times as pharmacists in the hospital at headquarters in Regina. Both men were graduates of the Ontario College of Pharmacy. Another qualified pharmacist was Hospital S/Sgt. Charlie Wallace. When he left the Force in 1891, he opened a drug store in Calgary. Edward Braithwaite studied medicine at King's College in London, England. After he failed his final exams, he was advised to go to Canada for his health. He engaged as a hospital sergeant in 1884. The following year found him in charge of the wounded following the Battle of Batoche. In 1889, he was granted four months leave to go to Winnipeg to study for the medical exams at the University of Manitoba. Herchmer agreed to let him have the leave, if he promised to engage for an additional three years service. Over half a century later, educational leave would be introduced into the Force as a new and enlightened procedure that had never existed before. This time around, Braithwaite duly passed the tests, received his degree and became a qualified practitioner. He returned to his duties and was placed in charge of the health of a division still as an NCO. When his time was up in 1892, however, the prospect of greater remuneration for his services lured him into private practice in Edmonton. The Force immediately retained him as an Acting Assistant Surgeon to care for the men at the local detachment, a position he held until 1931. Dr. Braithwaite later became Edmonton's first Medical Officer of Health and Chief Coroner of Alberta. In 1911, he received the unusual distinction of being appointed an "Honorary Surgeon" with permission to wear the uniform of that rank, in recognition of his long association with the Force as a medical doctor.[53]

Two hospital staff sergeants made the transition from medical assistant to regular police duties. Christopher West failed to complete his medical studies at Guy's Hospital in London. He joined the Force in 1888 as a hospital staff sergeant. In 1898 he finally obtained his M.D. Two years later he was appointed an Inspector. He was promoted to Superintendent in 1913 and commanded a division until his retirement in 1922. Murray Hayne was the son of Fleet Surgeon Leonard Hayne, Royal Navy. As with other hospital staff sergeants, he failed his medical examinations and headed for the colonies. In 1895, he accompanied Supt. Charles Constantine's party to the Yukon as aide to Assistant Surgeon Wills. In 1898, he published an account of his sojourn in those northerly climes under the title of *The Pioneers of the Klondyke*. During the South African War, he was captured and imprisoned by the Boers while serving with the Canadian Mounted Rifles. In 1903, he went off to another northerly outpost with Supt. J. D. Moodie's expedition to the west coast of Hudson's Bay. Hayne received his appointment to the rank of Inspector posthumously. At 45 years of age, he died of uraemia in April 1906. He was buried in a lonely grave at Fullerton. Four months later, the supply ship, which was the party's only contact with the outside world, brought the news of his promotion.

NWMP surgeons had to be jack of all trades as far as their medical duties were concerned. In the absence of specialists and clinics, they were forced to act as coroners, public health officers, hospital administrators, surgeons, urologists, cardiologists, dermatologists, dentists, ear, nose, eye and throat experts and the like, as well as gynaecologists and obstetricians where their civilian patients were concerned. To assist them, they had the benefits of the revolutionary advances that had been made in the practice of medicine earlier in the century. To mention a few, an Englishman, Dr. Edward Jenner, in his struggle to eliminate smallpox had shown that some diseases could be prevented by vaccination. The use of ether and later chloroform in the 1840s in the United States to render patients unconscious during operations not only made surgery possible for a greater number of conditions than ever before, but also vastly improved the survival rate. Louis Pasteur, meanwhile, had all but invented the science of bacteriology when he demonstrated that diseases could be spread by invisible germs, or bacteria. The result was the introduction of antiseptic methods in surgery and hospital care. At home, a Canadian, Sir William Osler, who had established an international reputation as a physician and medical teacher, had published in 1892 an authoritative text book that would be on the surgery shelf of almost every doctor in the English-speaking world entitled *The Principles and Practice of Medicine.*

Each year, the annual reports of the Senior Surgeon and the Assistant Surgeons were published in the Commissioner's Annual Report. Jukes' report of 1886 was typical of later ones in explaining his duties and exposing the difficulties he encountered in caring for the health of the Force. During the spring, he made his annual trip east to buy supplies and attend to other matters. In Ottawa he examined discharged men who were claiming compensation for injuries received while serving. From there he continued on to Montreal to purchase drugs and other equipment for the year ahead from Messrs. Kenneth Campbell & Co. In Toronto, he recruited three recent graduates from the Ontario College of Pharmacy to fill vacancies for hospital staff sergeants.

Shortly after his return to Regina, he left with the Commissioner on a tour of all major posts to inspect hospitals and sanitary conditions generally. At Fort Saskatchewan, he found the hospital too small for the number of men posted there. In Calgary, he noted the hospital was still located in an old condemned log building. The one in Fort Macleod he identified as the best in the Force. The Maple Creek hospital he declared was very small with an insufficient number of beds. He also remarked on the poor state of the water at that point. The supply in both wells was so impregnated with alkali and other corrosive deposits, he reported, that it rapidly destroyed all metal cooking utensils, used up stove implements in a few weeks, even decomposed wood, and was a constant source of diarrhoea for the men.[54] He further noted that at two posts the health care was provided by local doctors. Jukes did not approve of this practice of the government. He believed that the men would receive better treatment from full-time uniformed assistant surgeons. It was an opinion he was to express again, but Ottawa found it cheaper to employ acting assistant surgeons. The practice also conveniently gave the Minister an opportunity to reward his friends and supporters.

Another frequent complaint of the Senior Surgeon was that men were still being recruited through political influence who were not physically fit. One of his tasks in Regina was to examine those sent in from divisions who were unable for one medical reason or another to carry out their duties. Those found permanently unfit were discharged as invalids. In 1886, he approved the removal of 33 such men. As he pointed out, however, only nine of these had obtained their disability during their service. The other 24 had been allowed into the Force with a medical condition which had got progressively worse. Most of them were seriously ill with either phthisis (consumption of the lungs), rheumatism or syphilis.[55] Jukes urged that measures be taken to ensure that eastern doctors examining recruits, at $2 each, were more thorough, but once again, such a change in the system lay in the future. Some doctors, in fact, recommended men for engagement because they believed that the dry prairie air and an active life in the Force would cure them of their ailments.

Medical officers frequently had to deal with serious accidents. Shortly after his return to Regina the Senior Surgeon was urgently called back to Maple Creek by S/Sgt. Holme, the hospital steward there. Sgt. David Paterson had gone out on to the prairie to practise firing from the saddle by shooting at jackrabbits with his pistol. The horse he rode was a new one unaccustomed to the noise of firearms discharging. At the sound of the explosion, the animal plunged violently forward. Paterson grabbed for the saddle horn with the hand holding the weapon in order to prevent himself from being thrown. As he did so, the .45 Deane & Adams revolver accidentally went off, the ball striking his left thigh close to the groin and shattering the thigh bone.

Jukes knew from his reading on the treatment of wounds in the U.S. Civil War that such a gunshot injury usually required the leg to be amputated and that few patients survived the procedure. The Senior Surgeon took the next available train from Regina to Maple Creek. After examining Paterson's wound, Jukes realized that he had a choice. He could either amputate or remove the broken pieces of bone, repair the tissue, and try to knit the thigh together again. As he found that the main artery and principal nerves had escaped damage, he decided to try and save the leg.

The operation was to take place in a hospital he had earlier described as very small and badly constructed. He had chloroform to render the patient unconscious and painkillers like morphine, but there was no electricity, no antibiotics, the operating table was likely a wooden one scrubbed down with disinfectant for the purpose, and his instruments were probably sterilized by being boiled in a pot. In spite of these conditions, the treatment was successful. Following the surgery, Jukes had a fracture bed constructed so that the patient's leg could not be moved for several weeks. Two and a half months later Paterson was back on his feet. The injured leg was two and a quarter inches shorter than before, but he was able to walk without difficulty and resume his duties as quartermaster.[56]

The surviving data for the period is not sufficient enough to produce a complex statistical analysis of the degree of illness and its effect upon the efficiency of police work. Some of the medical officers submitted far more detailed reports than others. In 1900, however, Dr. Bell, who eventually succeeded Jukes as senior surgeon, calculated some Force-wide figures (excluding the Yukon) for the first time on the total number of cases treated that year, and the average number of men who daily were off duty sick.[57] The total number of cases was 1,058. The average number reported sick each day he broke down by divisions as they then existed on the prairies:

"A" Division	.857	"F" Division	.350
"C" Division	.657	"G" Division	1.449
"D" Division	1.561	"K" Division	1.315
"E" Division	2.164	"Depot"	6.334

Bell explained the larger number at Regina by the fact that it was the training depot for recruits. These, he claimed, tended to have more ailments because of the change of environment they were exposed to and the fact that most of them had previously led a more sedentary life. Another medical officer at Regina had earlier accounted for the difference in a similar fashion by saying that until recruits became hardened they got more bruises, chafes and blisters than the other men.[58] With a total strength on the prairies in 1900 of something over 500 men, the 1,058 cases means that, on average, every man was ill approximately twice a year. Bell's calculation did not distinguish between serious cases such as typhoid and those not so serious such as a bad cold. In reality, of course some men were not sick at all, whilst others sought medical treatment on numerous occasions. As Jukes had stated many men appeared at the daily sick parades for trifling ailments such as constipation or its opposite a "trivial relaxation of the bowels".[59]

The daily average number of men for the entire Force on the prairies off duty receiving medical treatment Bell calculated as 2.63. It would appear from this, that what the surgeons claimed year after year in their reports that the health of the men was generally good would appear to be true, but perhaps this was only to be expected given that, as most of them were between 18 and 25 years of age, they were in the prime of life.

As a sample of the types of medical problems that existed in the police and had to be treated by the surgeons take the cases reported for Regina, which had a complement of approximately 170 men, for 1895. There were 465 cases of sickness or injury reported for that year. The biggest group consisted of 141 cases (30%) requiring minor surgery, that is bruises, wounds, cuts, fractures, sprains and teeth extracted, 103 cases (22%) of colds and coughs, 34 cases (7%) of diarrhoea, 30 cases (6%) of biliousness, 26 cases (5%) of rheumatism, and 22 cases (4%) of neuralgia. In the second largest group, there were twelve cases of headaches, nine of colic, eight of influenza, eight of conjunctivitis, seven of tonsillitis and seven of frostbite. Lastly, among the ailments that occurred less than five times, were pneumonia, bronchitis, syphilis, diabetes, lumbago, gonorrhoea, snow blindness and varicocele (varicose veins of the spermatic cord). Five

men were invalided as a result of their condition and one died from consumption of the lungs.[60]

As to the general principles of treatment followed by the police medical officers, there was a great insistence on cleanliness, fresh air, proper ventilation and sunshine. "Sunlight and pure air are the best and cheapest disinfectants and they are at our doors and windows in all their purity," wrote Assistant Surgeon Paré, "why not take advantage of them and admit them as freely as possible. No chemical substances, skillfully used as they may be can equal sunlight, ventilation and cleanliness as antiseptics."[61] Latrines were routinely disinfected with lime once a week, twice in hot weather, at all posts. The surgeons also placed considerable emphasis upon good wholesome food for their patients. By this they meant a daily diet that included meat, green vegetables, potatoes, bread and milk. Hospitals were permitted to purchase extra supplies of the latter. To provide fresh vegetables, some posts started hospital gardens. They also had confidence in the restorative benefits of giving their patients beef tea or a regular glass of heavy beer or fortified wine. Hence, the Auditor General's reports show annually the purchase of large quantities of Guinness, Bass, Port and Sherry.[62]

As to the specific use of drugs, an analysis of one assistant surgeon's records shows that to reduce pain he prescribed colchicum, iodine of potassium, calomel, opiates, belladonna or prussic acid. With nervous disorders such as neuralgia, lumbago and gastralgia, he used quinine, iron tonics, arsenic and valerian. For syphilis or syphilis-related cases, nitrate ammonia was used, and for skin diseases, boils, eczema and erysipelas, mercury was applied. Expectorants and rubefacients were ordered to treat respiratory ailments such as coughs, colds and pleurisy. He also made use of leeches and poultices on some patients. Like most of his colleagues, he freely issued alcohol in the form of whisky or brandy, often referred to at the time as hospital comforts, as a stimulant.[63]

The medical profession in the last quarter of the nineteenth century was still largely ignorant of the causes of two serious diseases with which the NWMP surgeons were frequently confronted.

Malaria was an ancient malady. It had been very common in Ontario during the early decades of the century. Outbreaks had reached epidemic proportions during the construction of the Rideau Canal in the 1830s. Fortunately, it was seldom fatal because it was known that it could be treated successfully with Peruvian bark or conchina which contained quinine. What was not understood until the end of the century was that the disease was transmitted to humans by the bite of a mosquito.

Typhoid was the biggest natural threat to the lives of Mounted Policemen during this period. The disease was spread by Salmonella Typhosa, a bacterium that entered the bloodstream as a result of drinking water or food which had been contaminated by the urine or stool of a carrier. In cases of typhoid, the surgeons were careful to isolate the patients, disinfect everything that they came into contact with, and see that latrines were sanitized. Considering, however, that the water supply at most posts came from a nearby well or creek, they took no steps to purify it with something like chlorine, for example. What is more, they did not understand that another very likely source of the disease could have been a cook in the division mess who did not wash his hands. There was, of course, no vaccine at the time that might have provided immunity.

The most popular explanation for the spread of malaria and typhoid was the poisonous smells theory. Jukes referred to them as "noxious emanations".[64] According to this theory, decomposing vegetable matter on low lying land which was subject to a combination of hot days followed by cold nights generated the foul air that carried the germs. In 1887, Assistant Surgeon Paré described such a location across the river from Fort Steele as the source of the "deleterious exhalations" to which he attributed the outbreak of typhoid at the Kootenay post.[65] The poisonous smells theory explains the emphasis of the medical officers on fresh air and ventilation.

Not everyone agreed with this explanation. In fact, Jukes and Assistant Surgeon Kennedy bitterly disagreed on the subject, and openly quarrelled about it in their annual reports for 1886. Kennedy agreed that bad air was important in spreading the disease, but he asserted that it was not typhoid at all. He saw it as a condition peculiar to the western United States and Canada which was essentially malarial in nature and varied in its symptoms and effects according to altitude and location.[66] He preferred to call the disease Mountain Fever, a fact that would later confuse researchers into thinking it had something to do with the bite of a tick.

Between 1886 and 1900, 23 members of the NWMP died of the typhoid, the biggest single killing disease. This number included five who expired from an outbreak at Battleford in 1886 and four under similar circumstances at Fort Steele in 1887. The Battleford occurrence was by far the worst. According to Assistant Surgeon Miller, who was in charge of the hospital at the post there, the epidemic erupted in July after a long spell of extremely hot weather had dried up the low lying swamps in the area.[67] The disease quickly spread among the townspeople and the police. Miller prescribed judicious amounts of quinine, medical comforts and beef tea. He did not spare himself in doing all that he could for his patients. As a result, he also contracted the disease. By the end of August, 24 men, about a quarter of the strength at the location, including Miller were seriously ill with typhoid,

and Assistant Surgeon Rolph had to hurry from Regina to take over the medical care of the post.

Altogether 96 members of the Force died between 1886-1900, the largest number (23) were a result of typhoid. The other principle causes of death were: accidents, most involving horses or drowning, 16; suicide, 12; heart diseases, 7; murdered, 4; pneumonia, 4; kidney failure, 3; peritonitis, 3; and cancer, 2. The deaths included three of the medical staff: Assistant Surgeon Dodd, who died of unknown natural causes at the age of 62; Hospital S/Sgt. Holme who succumbed to pneumonia; and Assistant Surgeon Miller, the hero of the Battleford typhoid epidemic, who according to the coroner's inquest, blew his brains out with a rifle whilst temporarily insane.[68]

It was the usual practice of the time, as far as individual circumstances would permit, to give all members who died in service, including suicides and special constables such as interpreter Jerry Potts, a military funeral. In 1891, in a bid to keep a ceiling on such expenses, the Deputy Minister restricted the expenditure of public funds to a sum not exceeding $10 to pay for the funeral of a member. The amount in question was obtained from the regulations governing funerals in the Canadian Militia.[69] The *Macleod Gazette* considered this a mean and miserly policy which, given the price of coffins, caused it to remark that the men would have to die in pairs in order to get a decent burial.[70] Actually, it was quite common for the former comrades of the deceased to pass the hat around to meet any outstanding accounts.

Funerals were another custom that the Mounted Police copied from the military. The procedure for such an event, which was overlaid with ancient symbolism and superstition, had its origin in the mists of time. One notable element of a military funeral was that almost everything was done backwards. The members of the funeral procession advanced at a slow march in order to show their reluctance to be parted from their fallen comrade. The firing party, which led, reversed its rifles as a sign of shame upon the weapons of war which brought death. The body, in the flag-draped coffin on the gun carriage, was placed with its head facing to the rear so that the deceased might symbolically take a last look at his friends and loved ones. His horse, which came next, had a black shroud over the saddle, and the boots of the dead man were reversed in the stirrups, once again acknowledging the reluctance to part and the desire to gaze one last time upon old comrades. The order of the mourners who then followed was also reversed. The most junior ranks were placed to the front, the senior to the rear. This change in order symbolized the equality of all men in death. The volleys fired by the firing party at the graveside were to frighten away any evil spirits that might intercept the soul of the deceased and prevent it from passing safely into the next world. Finally, the flag at the deceased's post was flown at half mast until a respectable time after the funeral.

As might be expected, Jukes had his problems with Herchmer and the administration from time to time. Being the senior medical officer, it was his task to bring to the attention of his superiors any matter which in the opinion of himself and his professional colleagues conflicted with their ability to provide the best possible care for their patients. A persistent problem, in their view, was the admission of civilians into their tiny and often crowded hospitals. Some communities were slow to provide their own medical facilities. To some extent, this was because they knew that they could count on the police where accidents or serious illness were concerned. The police, on the other hand, could not for humanitarian reasons turn away those in urgent need, when there was no alternative care. They tried to discourage civilians by passing an order that required them to pay 60 cents per day plus the cost of any medicine they were prescribed.[71] This did not always work however. Many civilians, in fact, ended up in the police hospitals because they were poor. There was little that Herchmer could do about the problem. It was only to be solved when more hospitals and doctors were available in the community at large.

A louder complaint of the medical officers was that their orderlies, pharmacists and hospital sergeants were required to undergo police training. In a typical case, S/Sgt. John Mercer, who worked in the Regina hospital, informed his immediate superior, Senior Surgeon Jukes, that he had been instructed to attend mounted and dismounted drill as well as lectures on police duties. Mercer, a qualified pharmacist, protested that when he had engaged in Toronto he had been told that he would only have to work in the hospital. Jukes agreed, and went to see the Commissioner. He argued that assigning the medical staff to such duties disrupted hospital routine and interfered with patient care. Herchmer would not budge. He described Jukes' request to the Deputy Minister as "preposterous". As far as he was concerned, if the medical staff was going to wear the uniform of the Force, they would have to learn how to wear it, how to deport themselves in a soldierly fashion and how to carry out regular police duties if called upon to do so in an emergency.[72]

There were more serious differences over the question of treating members of the Force who had contracted venereal diseases. In 1882, a general order was passed that authorized stoppages from the pay of men being treated for venereal disease. The deduction was to cover the cost of the treatment that was received. The attitude behind this regulation was that VD was a self-inflicted condition and therefore should not be a burden on the public purse. Those who chose to engage in what was considered immoral behaviour, it was believed, would have to pay for the consequences themselves. Some men with VD had deductions made and some did not. It was in fact difficult sometimes to determine whether the disease was self-inflicted or not. It was known that gonorrhoea and syphilis could be contracted as a result of sexual intercourse with an infected partner, but medical science was still uncertain about the other means by which the diseases could be passed on. Was it possible to become infected by touching or kissing someone, or even by a toilet seat? Many doctors were not sure of answers to these questions. In April 1886, a member of the House of Commons accused members of the NWMP of contaminating Indian women.[73] The source of his information was the Commissioner's Annual Report for 1884. In it, some of the surgeons had noted a significant increase in VD among the men. In his condemnation of the immoral activity, the member did not actually mention the police, but everyone knew to whom he obliquely referred. The administration, including Macdonald, was embarrassed. It reacted by insisting that the regulation regarding stoppages should be more thoroughly applied as a deterrent. Ottawa did, at the same time, realize that this could have a negative effect. As White said, the men must be punished for their own indiscretion, but not so severely that they will conceal their condition.[74]

Jukes and some of the other police surgeons strongly disagreed with this policy. The dispute with Ottawa became public with the publication of Jukes' annual report for 1889. The Senior Surgeon described the order authorizing stoppages as "mischievous". It increased, he wrote, rather than lessened the danger both to individuals and the community because it discouraged men who were infected from coming forward and seeking qualified medical treatment.[75] The only way to ensure that they would seek such help, he asserted, was to remove any sanction aimed at punishing those who were infected. If this was not done, they would stay hidden. Jukes did not mince his words. Unless the punitive policy ceased, he proposed to have every man in the Force examined once a month in order to prevent the spread of these diseases. Jukes was supported by Acting Assistant Surgeon Hugh Bain in Prince Albert who reported that men were concealing their condition and seeking relief from "druggists and quack" remedies.[76] The administration, however, would not be moved. Although Jukes continued to complain, the stoppages continued. The threat of monthly examinations it seems was never put into effect.

In June 1893, Jukes retired. He was 72 years of age. His health had been undermined by a severe bout of influenza he had caught during an epidemic of the disease that swept through the Territories in 1890. His condition further deteriorated when he was forced to take on extra duties for several months in 1891-92 while his assistant in Regina, Dr. Haultain, recovered from a long illness. The Commissioner also suspected with some justification that his memory was failing.[77] In the spring of 1893, Herchmer told Ottawa that Jukes was so feeble he would be unable to carry out his duties much longer. He recommended his retirement, which was agreed to, and his replacement, which was not.[78] The Commissioner suggested Dr. H. N. Bain, the acting assistant surgeon in Prince Albert, for the position. The government took no action to fill it, however, for several years. With austerity the rule in Ottawa, officials there likely saw this as a useful saving of $1,400 a year. At the same time they were probably smarting from Jukes' public criticism of their policies, and decided that for the time being it would be prudent not to have a senior medical officer.

In James B. Hendryx's story *Downey of the Mounted*, a "Stirring, Graphic Tale of the Northwest", the hero, Cpl. Cameron Downey of the NWMP, refuses the entreaties of the girl he loves to leave the Force so that they can get married. He has a long patrol ahead of him, and "I must do my duty," he tells her. She reproaches him with her reply, "You care more for your police than you do for me."[79] Nine months later when Downey returns, he finds that his beloved Margot has jilted him and married another man. In this typical portrayal of the period, the "Mountie" is shown to have a selfless devotion to the administration of justice and the maintenance of civilized order. When Downey is faced with a choice between his own emotional desires and his duty, he chooses the latter and thus forfeits his chances of future personal happiness. Such was a common literary image. The truth was something quite different. In reality, although confronted by numerous obstacles, most Mounted Policemen followed their natural inclinations and married and multiplied, in spite of their duties.

When the Force was organized in 1873 there were no regulations that prohibited the engagement of married men. It is clear that a number of original members did have wives, although the exact number is not known. After the March West, when things had settled down and posts had been established, some of these men brought their spouses and also their children out from the East to live with them. The administration encouraged this by providing half rations and quarters for the families, and paying for their transportation when their husbands were transferred to another location.

By 1877, the Force regretted this generous practice. It had found it expensive and very inconvenient. In that year, therefore, a new regulation was introduced which forbad the engagement of married men. Although once in the service a member could still marry without permission, it warned them that the wives of those that did so would not be entitled to any rations, accommodation or transportation.[80] Herein lay a source of dissatisfaction for the next several decades. In spite of the financial strain and the difficulties placed in the way of fulfilling their conjugal duties, some members continued to marry. Upon doing so, they were confronted with discouraging regulations which they attempted to circumvent in one way or another. This brought them into conflict with an administration, which would have preferred for its own reasons that everyone take an oath of chastity and lead a monastic-like existence, but upon realizing that this was impossible, grudgingly made some accommodation for the marital state. As to the proscription upon married men applying to join the ranks of the Mounted Police, with odd exceptions, it would last for almost a century.

Commissioned officers were exempt from these restrictions. Whether they entered the Force in the married state or acquired a wife later, their families would receive quarters and rations. Nevertheless, the wedded officer still could be a problem as far as the Commissioner was concerned. In December 1887, Herchmer reported to Ottawa that there were too many married Inspectors and not enough suitable accommodation to house them. He suggested that they be subject to a quota, that no more than 16 Inspectors, about 50 per cent of the total number, be allowed to be married at any one time. His superiors did not take up the recommendation.[81] Another of his complaints was that the pay of officers was too low to allow them to support their families in the manner that they should.[82] On one occasion Davin decried the unfair practice of giving privileges to the wives of officers which were not also bestowed upon the spouses of those in the ranks.[83] No serious thought was ever given, however, to rectifying this inequity.

It was not the married officers, however, that were a trial for the Commissioner, but those in the other ranks, usually NCOs. Among them were a few men who lied about their marital status when enlisting. They declared themselves to be single when in fact they had left a wife and family in the East or in Britain. Behind such circumstances there was often a tragic story of alcoholism, desertion or estrangement for one reason or another. In late nineteenth century Canada, of course, marriage was generally considered to be a life-long exclusive union for procreation and the mutual comfort of the two parties so joined together. For Roman Catholics, marriage was a sacrament which could only be annulled in very exceptional circumstances. Only Protestants were prepared to accept divorce, and then only in cases of adultery. The process of obtaining one, however, required an act of Parliament, which meant that a legal escape from an unhappy marriage was limited to the few who could afford it.

The police were not really concerned about whether a recruit lied, as long as his family did not turn up in western Canada and disrupt his ability to carry out his duties. As Comptroller White explained to D. H. MacDowell, a member of Parliament, "the rule is not to engage married men and the few that are know that their wives and families will not be recognized. I would like to see more married men in the Force," he continued, "but our experience is that they become anchored to the post at which the wife is living and discontented if a move becomes necessary."[84] Their double lives were sometimes revealed, nevertheless, under tragic circumstances. After Cst. Byron committed suicide in Calgary, it came to light that he had left behind a wife and two children.[85] Another widow with a family in England was exposed, when Cst. Scudamore drowned while bathing in the Old Man's River at Fort Macleod in 1898.[86]

By 1889, Comm. Herchmer had reached the conclusion that married NCOs had become an "intolerable nuisance in the Force". It was the sergeants that were the main problem. Staff sergeants and sergeants major were usually provided with married quarters in barracks. Sergeants had to find accommodation for their families in town, which took them away from their post at night. This, Herchmer believed, undermined discipline. In addition, it became difficult to transfer them because they invested money in their properties, acquired livestock, and became dependent upon the employment their wives obtained locally sewing, cooking or taking in laundry. The Commissioner decided to take tough measures that would discourage members from getting married. In future, he told one commanding officer, "I propose to move them around without any consideration for their families. Only one sergeant in each division will be allowed to live out of barracks at one time. They will have to take turns for the privilege of sleeping with their wives. Tell your married sergeants," he continued, "so that they can look for other employment when their time is up, if they don't like the new order of things."[87]

The *Regina Leader* had already noted the Commissioner's antipathy towards marriage in the Force in a derisive and humorous editorial. The latest exploit of Mr. Lawrence Herchmer, it reported, surpasses in brutality any of his previous achievements. The paper went on to recount the story of a young constable who had been paying attention to a young lady of the highest respectability. The pair fell in love, and decided to marry. The constable, out of courtesy, informed his superior of his intentions. The reaction of that "paternal despot" was to transfer the young man to Maple Creek. As a result, continued the *Leader*, two hearts had been broken, two lives blighted, one in Regina, and another in Maple Creek. The Commissioner had told the constable not to put a millstone around his neck. That gallant had replied that he regarded the young lady as more like a foundation stone. Although he did not look like a sentimental person, the paper wondered if the Commissioner had ever been in love. "Oysters and bears and cockroaches and cockatoos, and, to our knowledge, potato bugs feel the tender passion," it continued. "Why should not the Commissioner in his salad days have felt the exquisite glow which the girdle of Venus sent into the breast of Jupiter?"[88]

This spurious piece, of course, was written by the editor, Nicholas Flood Davin, as part of his campaign to discredit and remove Herchmer from office. In another issue, he took up the case of a sergeant who had also informed the Commissioner that he proposed to get married. Herchmer is reported to have replied that if he did he would take away his stripes. The *Leader* expressed the view that such a dictatorial threat was going against nature and promoting immorality. "God bids people marry," it stated, "but Commissioner Herchmer says: 'No; Heaven is mistaken; I know better; you must not marry; you must not increase and multiply; the decrees of Heaven must bend to my tyrannical will'."[89]

The articles in the Regina newspaper were not all rhetoric. There was a substance of truth in them. The marriage regulations could harshly affect individuals. Sgt. James Carroll had 15 years service to his credit when he came up for re-engagement in 1896. A year earlier he had married. In this case, true to his threat, the Commissioner refused to take him on again as a sergeant. Unable to keep a family on the pay of a constable, Carroll took his discharge and got a job as a street car conductor in Prince Albert.[90] Cst. James Megaffin at the Battleford post had a wife and child living in town. The infant was very ill, and Megaffin was frantically worried about it. He was unable to get a pass to spend the night with his family. It was not his turn. As a result he broke out of barracks in order to check up on the progress of the baby. His absence was discovered and the next morning he was brought before the officer commanding. His explanation cut no ice with that gentleman who summarily fined him for violating post orders.[91] In another case, the

195

Edmonton Bulletin was very critical of the Commissioner for transferring a "G" Division constable to Regina under circumstances that compelled him to leave his wife and family behind at Fort Saskatchewan.[92]

Notwithstanding Herchmer's attitude on the subject, Mounted Policemen continued to marry in increasing numbers undeterred by the obstacles confronting them. The opportunities may have been few, but they still managed to father children. In 1890, the Commissioner discovered to his consternation that all of the married men in Fort Macleod, including the constables, were receiving free issues of coal and coal oil for their families contrary to his instructions.[93] It was incidents like this that convinced him that the Force's policy on marriage should be clearly put forth in new regulations that he would be able to enforce.

In 1891, he brought his views on the matter to the attention of the Deputy Minister. White agreed with him that NCOs and constables who got married should have no right to live out of barracks, receive additional rations, or any other special considerations, except as they were considered to be in the Force's interests. Before bringing it up with the Minister, however, he asked for some statistics on the problem. These showed that there were 30 constables, 4 corporals, 6 sergeants, 14 staff sergeants and 1 sergeant major with wives, a total of 55 married men. They were distributed amongst the Divisions as follows:

"Depot"	4	"E"	5
"A"	8	"F"	10
"B"	7	"G"	7
"C"	7	"H"	3
"D"	3	"K"	1[94]

It is unlikely that any of this correspondence was ever brought to his superior's attention. A few days after White received the information, the minister in question, Sir John A. Macdonald, died. Three years would pass before the issue would be brought up again. The change in ministers no doubt had something to do with the delay. It is also very likely that the relatives and friends of married policemen used their influence in Ottawa to protect them.

In January 1894, White wrote to Herchmer to ask him once again to state his views on the marriage problem, and to provide him with the latest figures on the matter. As was often the case in such requests from the Deputy Minister, it was a signal that White believed that the time was ripe to push the issue to the fore. The numbers forwarded by the Commissioner showed an increase of 45 per cent in married men. From 55 in 1891, the total had risen in 3 years to 79, of which 69 were living out of barracks. Herchmer left no doubt that he still considered marriage to be highly detrimental to the mobility and discipline of the Force. He singled out those living out of barracks as the biggest problem. "We have no control over them after their work is done. At Calgary and Macleod all of the married NCOs and constables live in town and are really townsmen working at the barracks. At Regina," he continued, "they live close to the post and can be punished if found out of their houses at night, but you cannot enforce this elsewhere." The Commissioner referred to the fact that at Headquarters some of the married men had been given permission to build homes for their families on the police reserve close to the barracks, where he felt he could keep a closer eye on them. "Married constables cannot live on their pay," he told White. "They have to have some other form of income. Their wives take in washing and sewing but many are still hard up and in debt. It costs them at least $6.00 per month to rent a house in town, and as much again for fuel."[95]

The new regulations regarding married NCOs and constables which were approved by the Minister appeared in General Orders on 14 June 1894. The first provision merely re-affirmed the existing rule that married men need not apply. They read as follows:

1. In future, married men ineligible for engagement.
2. NCOs and men now married may purchase if they wish on 30 days notice.
3. Privilege of living out will be continued to those who are now married – provided public service does not suffer.
4. Commissioner may grant permission to marry and live out of barracks, provided service will not suffer, to a limited number of Staff Sergeants, but not to any member below that rank.
5. Commissioner may allow at his discretion the families of married Staff Sergeants to occupy quarters in barracks.[96]

A few days after the regulations were issued the Minister, William Ives, was asked about them in the Commons. His responses gave the impression that he was not too well informed as to their intent. Ives confirmed that married men would continue to be barred from enlisting, but misled the House by telling the members that those who married after joining would first have to get the permission of the Commissioner. Such was not the case. It was only staff sergeants who needed permission, if it was their intention to live out of barracks. When asked about the proportion of married men then serving, he replied that out of the total strength about eight per cent had wives. He refuted the suggestion that the government intended to place a ceiling on the percentage of men who could be married at any one time. In response to a further question about the allowances and rations provided to members, he again misinformed the House by saying that they received none.[97]

Under the regulations, the Commissioner believed that he now had the means to reverse the trend, to reduce the number of married men. Those members who wished to purchase their discharge could do so, while those who were enjoying the privilege of living out could continue to do so as long as the public service did not suffer. In future, however, this privilege would only be granted to a small number of staff sergeants. It was true that the lower ranks still did not need permission to marry, but if it was made clear to them that if they did so they would not be able to live a normal life with their spouses, they would be sufficiently deterred from doing so.

Once again it did not work. A sufficient number of men and women continued to follow their natural inclinations in spite of the difficulties, and thereby upset the plans of the administration. In keeping with the growing number of small posts in towns and villages, a new phenomenon appeared, the married detachment man. In 1898, Cst. Bill Brankley who was in charge at Okotoks wrote to his officer commanding in Calgary to ask if he might move from the hotel where a rented room served as both detachment and living quarters into a house with his wife so that they could live together. Unknown to his superiors, the young constable had recently married. He offered to pay $5 per month himself towards the rent, if the Force would agree. Insp. J. O. Wilson forwarded this unusual and surprising request to headquarters with the comment, "I don't approve of married men on detachment." To this the Commissioner replied, "I agree. How did he get there?"[98] What the verdict was on Brankley's request is unknown. He did stay with the Force, however, and raise a family. After he retired to pension in 1917, he joined the newly formed Alberta Provincial Police and eventually became its officer commanding the Calgary area.

By 1899, Herchmer was complaining once again to Ottawa about the number of NCOs marrying or about to marry and seeking permission to live out. He suggested that it was possible that they were being encouraged by the Minister, Clifford Sifton. Here was another subject upon which the Commissioner and his superiors perhaps disagreed. Herchmer called particular attention to how unsatisfactory married men were on detachment. "They neglect their patrols and duties because of the need to attend to their families," he charged, "and their wives are a perfect nuisance when allowed quarters because the other detachment men cannot get along with them."[99]

Within a few weeks of making these comments Herchmer was on his way to South Africa. Soon after his departure, he was replaced as Commissioner by Supt. Aylesworth Bowen Perry. The new commanding officer soon displayed a somewhat different attitude to the marriage issue from his predecessor. Upon hearing that Sgt. Smith, who was i/c Moose Jaw Detachment, intended to marry, Perry wrote to his superior to say that Smith was doing a good job in the area and he did not wish to transfer him. Although only staff sergeants were entitled to such privileges, "tell him", he continued, "that I am willing to grant him reasonable allowances in lieu of rations, quarters, light and fuel."[100]

In fact, within a few months of taking command, Comm. Perry had commenced plans to revise the regulations relating to married members. In doing so, he collected some interesting statistics to support his position. As expected, the total number of married NCOs and constables had continued to increase from 82 in 1896 to 102 in 1901. All those married in 1901 were serving on the prairies. At the time the figures were collected, the total strength in that area was 475. In other words, some 22 per cent of all the police serving in what would soon be the provinces of Alberta and Saskatchewan were married. What had also changed significantly was the number of them serving on detachments, only 9 in 1896 to 35 in 1901. Here was a new trend that would continue in the future.[101]

Perry used these numbers to support his recommendation that the benefits available to married men be improved, particularly as they related to the cost of moving their families and household effects when they were transferred. The regulations as revised at this time for married NCOs and constables were as follows:

1274 Married men are not eligible for engagement
1275 Any N C Officer or Constable who marries, must forthwith report the fact to the Commissioner, through his Commanding Officer.
1276 A N C Officer or Constable who is married in not entitled to any privilege on that account, but the Commissioner may, provided the public service will not suffer thereby, grant quarters in barracks, or permission to live out of barracks and draw rations separately.
1277 Any married N C Officer or Constable occupying quarters, the property of the Government, may be required to vacate them at any time, occupation is to be considered as a privilege and not a right.
1278 The following issues of fuel and light and barrack furniture are authorized for married staff-sergeants:-
(a)   One ton of coal or two cords of wood per month from November 1 to May 1, and a half ton of coal or one cord of wood per month from May 1 to November 1; coal oil, half a gallon per week when electric light is not provided.
(b)   1 axe
(c)   1 wash basin
(d)   2 bracket lamps
(e)   1 coal oil can
(f)   20 lengths of stove pipe
(g)   Use of cook stove, if one available
(h)   Use of box stove, if one available
(i)   1 wash tub
(j)   2 water barrels
(k)   1 tin boiler
(l)   2 corn brooms per year
(m)   1 galvanized iron pail
(n)   2 elbows

(o) 2 chairs

1376 Married Staff-Sergeants who are transferred from one station to another for duty, not at his own request or for cause, will be allowed travelling expenses as follows:

    (a) Transportation at public expense for wife and each child under sixteen years of age.

    (b) An allowance of $1 per diem for wife and each child above five years of age and under sixteen years, for the number of days actually travelling by train or boat, and when by trail, half rations in lieu of money allowance.

    (c) Transportation at public expense of household effects not exceeding 2,000 lbs. (907 kilos).[102]

The regulations say a good deal about the living conditions of families in the Force at the time. Few detachments at the turn of the century had a supply of electricity. Oil lamps provided the light during the long winter nights. There were no electric stoves, refrigerators or washing machines. The coal or wood burning stove was the source of heat for warmth in cold weather, for cooking and for hot water to wash clothes in the wash tub, in an age without disposable diapers. The only furniture provided to the married couple was two chairs, no marriage bed, no tables. These they had to buy or scrounge themselves. Rain collected from the roof in barrels was still an important source of water, and, of course, there was still the outside privy to sit in during all kinds of weather. Spartan as all this sounds, married members were probably better off than many of the settlers who were arriving to take up homesteads around them.

It was made quite clear in the new regulations that most of these benefits would only be granted as a privilege. No one was entitled to them. Management reserved the right to bestow or withdraw them as it thought was in the best interests of the Force. It was all very paternalistic, but nevertheless, a considerable improvement in the way married members had been treated earlier. The men still did not need permission to enter into a state of matrimony, although they were now required to report their change in status to their superiors. Perry did not strictly follow the rules as far as rank was concerned. He frequently granted the privileges to married sergeants as well. A whole new era was beginning typified by the presence of the married NCO in charge of a detachment. He must have been the envy of many. Where else at the time could a man find a job that provided him with the basics of life for himself and his family at no cost to himself, a house, heat, light, fuel, rations, and to top it off, a free pension at the end of his service. Many of those who served during this period would later remember it, however, as a time of low pay and hardship.

Why the change of attitude under Perry? Was he simply bowing to the inevitable, rather that trying to reverse the tide as Herchmer had done. At times the latter seemed to be following opposing policies.

On the one hand, he worked to improve benefits and conditions for the men. He got them pensions so that they could make a career of the Force, and then did his best to discourage them from marrying. At the turn of the century the duties of the Mounted Police were changing. They were increasingly concerned with the new settlements of white immigrants, rather than Indian reservations. Perhaps Perry had noticed that the married man was better suited to the changing conditions than the young single constables who had tended to spend their off duty hours in the brothels and bars of the frontier. The married man with his family fit in with the kind of stability and social order these new communities sought. Through his family, he became involved in a variety of local affairs, schools, church, sporting and cultural activities. Possibly Perry also observed that a detachment wife could be a valuable unpaid auxiliary, performing some of her spouse's duties while he was absent elsewhere.

Members of the North-West Mounted Police had reason to be satisfied with their chosen occupation. Pay, leave provisions and health care met at least their basic needs. Marriage regulations may not have been generous, but there was some accommodation made for senior NCOs and sufferance of wedlock among the lower ranks.

Chapter 14

Room and Board and the
Pleasures of Mounted Police Life

Life in the North-West Mounted Police no doubt was attractive to robust males. Food and lodging was spartan but met all creature needs. Diversions were available in drink and sport in the company of other men. As in the military, efforts were made to make the Force a regimental home away from home. Under Herchmer, even religious observances were facilitated by the provision of a chapel at "Depot". The formal church parade that followed, however, became another formal obligation for the men, probably not leading to an enhanced appreciation of spiritual expression.

In addition to uniform and medical care, NWMP recruiting notices also promised free rations. What they did not make clear was that the rations only consisted of basic staples like meat, potatoes, bread and tea. If members wanted pickles with the meat, ketchup on the potatoes, butter on the bread and milk in the tea, they would very likely have to pay for them themselves. The daily scale of rations per man had been revised in 1882 to consist of:

	lbs.	oz.		lbs.	oz.
Beef, Bacon or					
Pemmican	1	8	Tea		½
Flour	1	4	Coffee		½
or Bread	1	8	Sugar		3
or Biscuit	1	4	Salt		½
Potatoes	1	4	Pepper		⅟₃₆
or Beans		2			
or Dried Apples		2			
Rice		1			

In 1894, further slight changes were made to the daily issue. Pemmican was removed, the supply of buffalo meat having ceased to exist. The potatoes were reduced from one lb. four oz. to one lb. The alternatives to spuds were increased, beans from two oz. to four oz., and dried apples from two oz.

to three oz. Most mouth watering of all was the addition of a luxury item to the diet. Henceforth, every man was entitled daily to two oz. of butter to spread on his bread or melt on his potatoes.[1] The new regulations also authorized what had in fact been in practice for some time, namely the drawing of two rations by married officers and such married NCOs as approved by the minister.

The men, of course, did not line up every morning one behind the other to pick up their daily allotment of 1/36 of an ounce of pepper and other items. It was the mess cooks who drew the rations in bulk as was required to prepare meals and bake bread from the post stores. The amount was determined by multiplying the daily ration by the number of men at the post. It was widely believed, but was not necessarily true, that when the meat was being apportioned out the officers got the first choice of cuts, the NCOs the second and the men's mess the last. One of the tasks of the Orderly Officer was to oversee the weighing of all rations. At the Commissioner's discretion the daily ration could be increased. In 1888, Insp. J. O. Wilson was successful in getting an extra half ration per day for each of the men at Pincher Creek Detachment during the winter months because they were employed outside all day doing heavy work in extremely cold weather.[2]

In the House of Commons in 1888, Sir Richard Cartwright complained that prisoners in the penitentiaries were fed better than the members of the NWMP. The government, he charged, was spending $120 per head per year to feed convicts and only $90 per head on Mounted Policemen. He suggested to the Prime Minister that the amounts should be reversed. With his usual guile, in his rebuttal Macdonald deftly avoided responding to the suggestion.[3]

The scale of rations was certainly a spartan one from which the cooks were expected to provide three meals a day. Breakfast was usually served at 7:45 a.m. after morning stables, dinner, the main meal of the day, at noon, and supper at 6:00 p.m. after evening stables. These times were subject to a seasonal change of a few minutes. As one recruit wrote, the food was "plain and rough fare – in fact the plainest and roughest I think I had ever sat down to".[4] The rations certainly did not provide much room for variety. They provided a diet that was heavy on protein and starch. The main staples that filled the hungry stomachs of the young men were meat, potatoes and bread. There were no eggs, bacon or cereal for breakfast, and no fresh vegetables were provided. When bacon was available, it was eaten at the main meal. With monotonous regularity, dinner each day would consist of meat, usually beef, potatoes and rice pudding.

Cst. C. P. Dwight recalled that breakfasts at Regina routinely consisted of the leftovers from the previous day's dinner fried up into a hash which the men commonly referred to as "Mystery".[5] It was served with bread and coffee. Cst. Pennefather and his comrades did not relish the watery soup with a few beans in it that they were served for breakfast in Calgary, sometimes without bread because they had eaten it all up for supper the evening before.[6] Dinner was better, he remembered. "We got roast meat and boiled potatoes one day and boiled meat with potatoes in it the next", all washed down with good strong tea. At the sound of the bugle call for dinner, wrote Dwight, there was a rush for the mess door where everyone picked up a tin plate and stood in line to receive their portion of meat from the cook, and then sat down at the tables on which there were pots of steaming potatoes. It was probably unwise to be late for meals. The spuds would quickly disappear into hungry mouths. At some posts during hot weather, the men would move the benches and tables outside under a large tent with the sides rolled up and dine *al fresco*. Supper usually consisted of bread, cold meat and tea. The flour ration produced about one loaf of bread per man per day. At large posts like Regina and Fort Macleod, over a hundred loaves had to be baked daily by the cooks.

Generally speaking, the men were content with the nature and quantity of the rations. Cpl. John Donkin, who having served in the British Army in various parts of the world knew about such things, described them as sufficient for the voracious appetites they had.[7] Herchmer and his subordinate officers repeatedly characterized the quality of the rations in their annual reports as excellent. "Our rations are usually excellent and plentiful," wrote Herchmer in 1895.[8] One of the tasks of the orderly officer at a post was to visit the mess at meal time and enquire if there were any complaints. In 1899, the commanding officer at Lethbridge reported that the rations had been so good there had not been one single complaint all year.[9] One recruit wrote to assure his anxious parents that he was in good health. "I have gained seven pounds in three weeks," Cst. Vernon Shaver told them, "on a diet of beef, beans or potatoes, sometimes rice pudding, and all the bread I can eat."

If the men did complain about the food, it was mostly likely because of the way it had been cooked. "Cooking the rations is our great trouble, as it is extremely difficult to get competent cooks among our men," reported the Commissioner.[10] At some posts the men took turns in the kitchen. Few of them liked the job, however, and their culinary masterpieces did not always sit well in the stomachs of their comrades. Herchmer tried to overcome the difficulty by hiring experienced cooks as special constables at $25 per month with room and board. The records show, however, that they were frequently being replaced. There seem to be two reasons for this. First, the cooks did not find their employment with the police very lucrative and, second, the men did not like their cooking.

In fact, sometimes the cooks themselves were not very popular. It was the custom in Regina to assign recruits to kitchen fatigues, a duty which they detested to a man. Under the watchful eye of the cook they peeled potatoes, washed dishes, scrubbed floors and carried out any other menial task he found for them. One cook was a particularly mean and sadistic individual who seemed to enjoy making the lives of the recruits sent to him as miserable as possible. One day, two young recruits who had been the victim of his ill-temper decided that they would get even with him. The Regina kitchen at the time was described as being alive with cockroaches. On the stove was a large pot of beef stew cooking for dinner. While the cook was briefly absent, several of the black insects were added to the boiling bill of fare to improve its flavour. The intruders were not discovered until the cook began ladling out his gastronomical delight onto the plates of the hungry men awaiting their mid-day meal. The horrified shouts and curses of the diners resulted in the establishment of a Board of Inquiry to investigate the matter. The Board found that there was indeed some kind of animal in the stew. It had its suspicions, but it was unable to determine without a doubt just how they had got there. This was just as well for Csts. Christen Junget and Christopher Peters, as their careers in the Force would likely have ended there and then. As it was, they both rose to commissioned rank. Shortly after the incident the cook in question took his discharge.[11]

Sometimes the ration system did break down. In the 1880s, "B" Division used to spend the summer months at Wood Mountain. From there its members patrolled the border westward to the Cypress Hills and eastward to the Manitoba line. As soon as the cold weather approached, the division returned to Regina for the winter. Wood Mountain was an isolated spot. The quantity of food supplies required by the police could not be obtained locally. It had to be shipped in from points further north. Cpl. John Donkin recalled an occasion when the supply wagons were overdue. "After the bacon gave out," he wrote, "all we had for four days were hardtack [biscuits] and sugarless tea."[12]

It was probably because of incidents like this that in 1888 the Force decided to experiment by contracting out the food services at Wood Mountain. In the summer of that year, a Mr. Farrill agreed to purchase his own food supplies and provide all the meals for the division in return for a fixed sum of money. The exact terms of the contract are not known. The commanding officer reported that the meals were better than those prepared from the authorized ration issue. Supt. Cotton who inspected the post found that the food was abundant and of good quality. What impressed him most about the experiment, however, was that trained policemen who would otherwise have been assigned to cooking and kitchen duties were released for patrol work.[13] The contracted catering service seems to have been a success, but it was not repeated or extended to other divisions.

Of course in the 1880s and 1890s it was still possible to some extent to supplement the regulation rations by living off the land. The buffalo were gone, but other varieties of game remained abundant. Many of the men were keen fishermen and hunters. At Wood End Detachment, they found a plentiful supply of fish in the local creek, and the members on patrol brought back a deer whenever their meat rations were low or they preferred to eat venison. In season they also gorged themselves on the saskatoon berries and wild strawberries that grew in profusion around the detachment.[14] Another member on detachment in the Cypress Hills in 1886 recalled how he and his comrades dined sumptuously on pike from Elk Lake and anything they could shoot on patrol: antelope, deer, prairie chickens, ducks and geese.[15]

The police also took up gardening to add to the issue of rations. There were few divisions or posts that did not at one time or another cultivate a vegetable plot. Sometimes they were driven to it out of necessity. In 1889, the potato crop in the NWT failed. The Commissioner purchased dried vegetables as a substitute and increased the ration of beans, but the men badly missed their boiled spuds. In response, gardens were started to provide a wider variety of vegetables, especially during the winter months when they were scarce. In a typical example at Fort Macleod, Sam Steele had four acres close to the post ploughed in the fall of 1889 ready for planting the following spring. Unfortunately, the 1890 growing season turned out to be a little too dry for a bumper crop, but Steele described the vegetables they did get as "a great boon to all ranks".[16] In 1893, another dry but better year for cultivating, he reported a harvest of 4,786 lbs. of potatoes, 2,898 lbs. of turnips, 630 lbs. of beets, 360 lbs. of carrots, 63 lbs. of celery, 60 lbs. of parsnips, 58 lbs. of citron, 180 lbs. of cabbage and 214 lbs. of tomatoes.[17]

In spite of the ways and means with which the rations were supplemented, most ordinary everyday meals were monotonously the same day after day. No wonder the men looked forward to those holiday occasions like Christmas and New Year when a festive spread would replace their usual fare. Supt. Sam Steele wrote:

> Christmas was a jolly time in the west.
> Dinner was always in the evening, and this was the occasion when the NCOs and men invited their bachelor friends to accept their hospitality in return for their many kindnesses during the year at their ranches and homes. They spared no expense to make the occasion all that could be desired, and, as is customary all over the Empire, the officers, headed by the CO, visited the mess-rooms to see the decorations and wish their men a merry Christmas and a happy New Year.[18]

The additional expenses for organizing such functions were met by subscriptions from the men. In 1887, however, most of this financial burden was removed when Comm. Herchmer convinced the government to agree to an annual grant from the Fine Fund of $50 for each division to celebrate Christmas.[19] On this festive occasion, the mess room walls were decorated with flags, banners, swords, lances, carbines and green boughs. A formal menu for Christmas Dinner at "F" Division, Prince Albert, 1888 included the following traditional delicacies: Oyster Soup, Lake Trout with Red Deer Sauce, Roast Turkeys and Chickens with Bread Sauce, Boiled Ham, Plum Pudding, Mince Pies, Blanc Mange and coffee. No doubt there were also fruits and nuts of one kind or another. The Christmas season was one of the few times when suppliers would import tropical items like oranges.

Alcoholic beverages also had a part in the festivities, both as an accompaniment to the numerous formal toasts on such an occasion, and as a means of enlivening the proceedings. For Christmas the Commissioner would bend the usual rules and allow commanding officers to obtain permits to import beer. In 1891, for example, most divisions took advantage of this generous gesture and ordered 30 gallons of Carling Ale.[20] Should additional illegal supplies appear, it was usual for those in authority at these times to look the other way.

As might be expected with boisterous young men, the partying could sometimes get out of hand. It was then that wiser and more experienced heads stepped in to restore order. Cst. R. G. Matthews, a native of Dublin, Ireland, recalled two Christmas celebrations in the Force, one quite different from the other. The first took place at Fort Macleod in 1887, the headquarters of "Galloping H" Division:

> The band ushered in the day's festivities by marching through the barrack room at 6 a.m. with all instruments going full blast – it practically blew us out of bed. Stables were rather lickity-split that morning, and breakfast was just the usual mess, but when we got back to our bunks there had appeared in the corner of the room, as if by magic, a 10-gallon barrel of Montana 'Rot-gut'. Nobody seemed to know where it came from or who it came from, but there it was, and anyone who is acquainted with the old prohibition product of those far-away days doesn't have to be reminded that just the smell of it, let alone the taste, would knock almost anybody into a cocked hat.
>
> During the rest of the day a pleasant time was had by nearly all, the celebration culminating in one grand and glorious crash when one Tommy Maroney, a diminutive teamster, knocked over the red-hot Syndicate stove. While no one seemed to bother very much about this, as I supposed it may be called, unusual circumstance, it caused Sergeant-Major Bull Stewart to take a hand in the proceedings, and, it may be remarked, he was just what 'the doctor ordered' for the occasion. He made nearly every man jack of us fall in on the square and then wheeled the bunch out through the Main Gate and off up the Pincher Creek trail with a good ten inches of snow all over. Like the famous Duke of York he marched them up the hill and he marched them down again: up the trail and back again, and when he got through the cure was complete and barrack life resumed its usual routine."[21]

Two years later Matthews spent Christmas at Big Bend Detachment. He remembered it as one:

> when corned beef took the place of turkey and when our after-dinner liqueur was vinegar, and when the Cochrane Ranch cattle were dying around in the deep snow and bitter cold, and the bread froze solid in the kitchen that Christmas Eve, and had to be thawed out the next morning before we could have breakfast. It was a bad Winter that year – the Winter of '89 and '90.[22]

Among the first things issued to a recruit in Regina, and later when he was transferred to a division, were two wooden trestles, some wooden boards about six feet long, and an empty *palliasse*, or mattress. These he took to his pit, that small portion of the barrack room floor allotted to him for his personal use. There he set up the trestles a few feet apart and placed the boards on top side by side. Above these was placed the *palliasse* filled with straw from the stable. This crude piece of furniture with his blankets arranged on it in proper regimental fashion constituted his bed. Its head was placed against the wall. Above on a number of hooks and shelves hung some of his equipment and uniform along with a card on which was inscribed his name and regimental number. His personal belongings were placed in a box, suitcase or trunk under the bed. The only other furniture in the room apart from the stove and wash stand would be a table, also constructed of trestles and boards, and one or two benches. These items were constructed by the division carpenter. At one end of the room the corporal in charge enjoyed a degree of privacy with his bed behind a screen. By contrast, the senior NCO's quarters usually contained factory-made furniture, chairs, tables with legs, dressing tables and beds with springs.

The trestle beds were a source of many practical jokes. It was common to rearrange the position of the trestles and the boards so that if the slightest weight was put on them they would collapse. Many a constable returning from a late night pass or coming off a stint as night guard had wearily plopped on to his bed only to end up on the floor entangled in his bedding and boards. A "blue flame of profanity" usually erupted from those on the receiving end of such tricks, recalled Cst. Percival Pennefather.[23]

Apart from these amusements the trestle beds pleased no one. The men found them uncomfortable. The straw would not stay in one place. The sharp stems stuck into them and they attracted vermin. Herchmer and his sergeants major did not like them because it was impossible for the men to make the lumpy beds up in a uniform and smart military fashion. Year after year the Commissioner pleaded for iron bedsteads like those in use in the Imperial Army to replace them. "Even the convicts in the prisons have iron cots," he told the Minister, "as do the Indian children in the industrial schools and the U.S. troops south of the border." He wrote on one occasion, "I am ashamed to show strangers, particularly military men, over them, on account of the very disparaging remarks they invariably make on our sleeping accommodation."[24] It was not until 1893 that Ottawa agreed to the purchase of iron bedsteads, and then only for the divisions at Regina, Calgary and Lethbridge. These were bought the following year from Geo. Gale & Sons of Waterville, Quebec at a cost of $5.10 each.[25] In 1894, the government also consented to the Fine Fund being used to buy tables and chairs for the barrack rooms. As the century came to a close, however, Herchmer was still asking for another 500 cots to complete the distribution to all divisions.[26]

Constables often found their accommodations improved when they boarded out on detached duty. Many detachments were located in courthouses, hotels, boarding houses, even the homes of settlers. The general rate paid by the Force for room and board for a member was 50 to 75 cents per day per man, $1 if stabling and hay were provided for his horse. The detachment at Moosomin was located in the courthouse. The sheriff allowed the men there to use the iron cots from the attached jail, provided they were not needed for prisoners.[27]

The Swift Current Detachment in 1887 was situated in Mrs. Paskett's Boarding House. The arrangements there were typical of the time. The corporal in charge had a room to himself. The two constables shared one, but had separate beds. For this they were each charged $5.50 per week. Mrs. Paskett evidently felt that they were living high off the hog. She wrote to the Commissioner to explain that the two constables could share one bed, like the railways workers she also boarded, for considerably less. This she seemed to feel would not only be a saving for the NWMP, but would also provide her with another bed that she could rent. Herchmer was always anxious to reduce expenses, but not where the well-being of his men was concerned. He explained in reply that the corporal must have a room to himself because the room also constituted the detachment office, and he must have privacy to conduct his police duties. As to the constables, he informed her that they must continue to occupy separate beds as that was a comfort they were entitled to in barracks.[28]

Sometimes, of course, the living conditions on detachments, or outposts as they might be more accurately called, could in fact be worse than living in barracks. In May 1887, Cpl. John Donkin was detailed to establish a post with two constables at the Souris River where it crossed the international boundary into North Dakota just west of the Manitoba line. This was the most easterly of the chain of detachments that maintained a system of patrols along the border with the United States from Manitoba to the Rocky Mountains. The party travelled by train with their horses and supply wagon from Regina to Moosomin. From there they had a 90 mile ride to their destination via Carlyle and Almeda. A merchant in Carlyle was to deliver their rations once a month. While in the settlement they arranged to substitute some items on the official list for eggs at ten cents a dozen. The storekeeper was paid a flat rate by Regina. It made no difference to him in what form they took their rations as long as they did not exceed the amount he received. Following their arrival at the detachment site, Donkin found a beautiful location close to the river on which to pitch the tents that would be their home for the next several months. Not far away they encountered a Scottish settler and his family. His two Highland daughters agreed to take their flour supply and bake fresh bread for the men every morning.[29]

Apart from the oppressive heat everything looked rosy. They would spend a relaxed summer far from the regimental ways of Regina, riding the old Boundary Commission trail westward to meet the patrols from Wood End Detachment.

Somehow, someone had even managed to bring along a keg of cider. They soon discovered, however, that it was not going to be as comfortable as they had expected. As the sun went down they were attacked by "noisy swarms" of mosquitoes who settled on their and hands and necks until "their bloated bodies gleamed crimson with blood". Their painful and irritating stings became a nightly torment. With the arrival of wet weather, the "swarms" turned into "clouds" of mosquitoes. The only way to get any sleep was to place burning oil smudge pots in the tents until all of the mosquitoes had been killed, remove the pots and dive into the tents being sure to leave not the slightest crack open through which more of the critters could enter. Later on, the mosquitoes were joined by blood-hungry black flies who bit both men and horses. The latter had no respite from the pests as they were tethered in the open. The weather stayed wet so the insects continued to multiply all summer. There were frequent thunderstorms. More than once their tents were flooded and bedding, food and clothing soaked. On top of it all, the water from the river, their only supply, upset their stomachs. In spite of these kinds of discomfort, however, many men still preferred life on a detachment to the parades, drills and routine of their division headquarters.

The lives of Mounted Policemen were plagued from time to time by two other common pests of the period. The first of these they encountered on the March West. "At Sweet Grass Hills by bad luck we camped for a couple of days on an Old Indian Camping Ground. Here the men became infested with vermin [lice], the officers being no exception," wrote Surgeon Kittson.[30] There were two principle types of lice that lived off humans. One preferred the head, the other the body. They could be passed from one person to another by contact. They could also rest in an inactive state for long periods until aroused by the presence of a human body. A common source for them was the sites used by patrols for camping. They are "a great nuisance to the Prairie wanderer," continued Kittson, "and against catching them it is useless to guard one's self. They lie dormant on Camp grounds, long deserted, and brought to lively and tormenting activity by coming in contact with a warm body."

Body lice infested the clothes and bedding of the carrier. They caused severe and persistent itching. Scratching brought some relief, but it also assisted in the spread of the vermin. Lice could also be the source of other diseases, typhus in particular. Washing clothing or blankets had no effect upon them whatsoever. The surgeons found that the only successful way of completely eradicating them was the liberal use of either Mercury Ointment or Oil of Juniper. The Sweet Grass Hills witnessed a very unusual scene, one that was never to be repeated.

Surgeon Kittson had almost the entire Force paraded in the open air, one division was on its way to Edmonton and a few men had been left in Manitoba. The men were then ordered to take off all their clothes, and rub their bodies from head to toe with Oil of Juniper. The oil was also sprinkled on their clothing and their blankets. What any passing Indian may have thought had he beheld this spectacle of white behaviour is hard to imagine. By this means, however, the NWMP was able to defeat the first enemy to attack it in western Canada. Although the numbers would be considerably smaller, the line-up to get oil or ointment from the doctor to get rid of lice would be a frequent occurrence in the years ahead.

The other equally distasteful insect that was host to man was the bed bug. One young recruit from Ontario recalled that upon his first acquaintance with the "Northwest Bed Bug"; it literally chased him out of bed and he spent the night on the floor.[31] This tiny member of the Cimicidae family lived by sucking the blood of humans. During the day it hid itself from the daylight, usually in the walls of the bedroom. At night it came out in search of a victim. Although its bite could be quite painful, rousing the sleeper suddenly from his dreams, sometimes it was not felt at all. Once it had blown itself up to several times its size with blood, it retreated to its hideout to digest it. It could, if necessary, go for long periods without food. Apart from its bite, its presence could also be detected by the droppings it left on the bedclothes and the floor, as well as the sickly sweet smell it emitted.

Infestations of bed bugs in NWMP barracks and detachments were quite common, especially in hot, summer weather. The insect found holes in the trestles and boards that made a handy refuge during the daytime. Not for the first time, Herchmer complained to Ottawa in 1892 that some of the barrack rooms in Regina were overrun with bed bugs. He moved the men out into tents temporarily, and he asked for permission to burn some of the trestle beds and the wainscotting in some of the rooms. A favourite hiding place for the insects, the wainscotting was the wooden panel or board that covered the wall for several inches from the floor.[32] In August 1893, it was the turn of Milk River Detachment members to be driven from their quarters. They too set themselves up in tents while oil of cedar was brought from Fort Macleod in an attempt to expel the insects from their building.[33] Bed bugs would continue to plague the police until iron beds replaced the trestle ones and more effective insecticides were produced.

Another development for which Herchmer must take most of the credit was the introduction of division canteens. Although their establishment brought him a great deal of criticism and personal abuse, they contributed to the welfare and benefit of the men in many, many ways. The idea of operating a non-profit general store at a military post to provide the men with a variety of goods that they needed at reasonable prices was not new. As Macdonald explained in the Commons in defending them, the canteen had long been a successful feature of the British military system.[34] In the canteen one could buy boot polish, brushes, soap, tobacco, razors, matches, envelopes, postage stamps and other daily necessities at a little over wholesale price. Its operation was regulated by a committee headed by an officer, which also appointed a manager and used the small profits as a means of improving recreational facilities for the men.

Herchmer also knew that canteens had been organized and promoted by the military authorities as a temperance measure. The only place on a Mounted Police post where alcoholic drinks could be served was in the officers' mess. This privilege was not extended to the sergeants' or division messes. If the NCOs and constables wished to buy a drink, they had to go to a saloon. It was customary in a military canteen, on the other hand, to sell beer to the men, but not wines or spirits. It was argued that if beer was made available on police posts this way, at a reduced price, it would induce the men to spend their drinking time in barracks. There would be less carousing in local saloons, where they were liable to spend their money on expensive hard liquor, get drunk and make spectacles of themselves in public. It was in the hopes of attracting such trade that an entrepreneur from "down East" opened a saloon near the Regina barracks in 1884. It was described as having all "sorts of canned goods, such as lobster, sardines, and salmon" at very high prices, as well as "a flash bar, gorgeous with mirrors, and photographs of American danseuses".[35] In a properly regulated canteen an NCO would always be on duty to see that no one drank too much. However, the canteen system was open to abuse. It does seem to have reduced drunkenness, but it did not eliminate it. When it did still occur, however, it did so on home turf.

The first NWMP canteen opened at Headquarters in Regina in May 1888 under the management of Sgt. T. H. Dunne, a former hotel-keeper. Its organization set the pattern for the establishment of canteens at other large posts. Dunne was responsible to a committee of members who drew up the rules for its operation, set the prices on the articles to be sold, and decided to what use the profits would be put.[36] Goods were sold a little above their cost price in order to provide a small profit to be used for the benefit of the men. It started with a modest selection of merchandise: cigars, cigarettes, soap, polish, razors, toothpaste, clay pipes, to mention a few, and of course beer. In the canteen a thirsty constable could get a glass of Carlings Winnipeg Ale for five cents, a considerable saving. A similar size glass in one of Regina's saloons would have cost him 12½ cents.[37] The beer of course was sold in accordance with the territorial regulations. It had to be obtained with a permit issued by the Lieutenant-Governor, and its alcoholic content could not exceed 4% by volume. Later, the selection of articles for sale expanded. A list of these that has survived tells something of the diet and habits of mounted policemen a century ago.

In 1895 Comm. Herchmer approved a set of regulations for the operation of all NWMP canteens. The managing committee was to comprise one officer, who was president, the sergeant major of the division, and three others elected by a general meeting of the division mess. The canteen manager was appointed by the officer commanding the division, and placed under the control of the committee. The latter was required to meet once a month to keep track of the stock and audit the accounts. All sales were to be paid for in cash, except for officers, NCOs and married constables who were permitted to run a monthly account. Only members of the Force and their families were permitted to make purchases. The canteens were open from 8:30 a.m. until 9:15 p.m. Monday to Saturday. Beer was only sold, however, from noon to 1:30 p.m. and from the end of evening stables to 9:15 p.m. Whenever beer was being sold, a duty NCO had to be present to see that there was no intoxication. The canteens were closed on Sundays in keeping with the observance of the Sabbath Day.[38]

By 1890 canteens were operating at Regina, Calgary, Fort Macleod and Lethbridge. They did attract some criticism from the churches. They caught the attention of the Presbyterian Synod of Canada which, at its annual meeting, passed a resolution calling for an end to the serving of liquor in NWMP canteens. The church fathers seemed satisfied when it was pointed out to them that liquor in fact was not served, only beer, and that the canteens existed in order to deter men from going into town and getting stronger drink.[39] In fact the officers commanding at these posts reported favourably on them as producing more temperate drinking habits among the men.[40] In 1891 Herchmer noted a reduction also in disciplinary offences at those points with canteens as opposed to those without them.[41] Eventually a canteen was established at every divisional headquarters.

The men were soon experiencing some of the benefits of the canteen profits. Between March 1891 and September 1892, the canteen committee at Fort Macleod expended over $1,000 on improving the recreational facilities there, including the erection of an 87 foot bowling alley.[42] Regina of course had the largest complement of men. In 1890 alone, the canteen there produced $180 a month for luxuries for the messes, and provided $200 for the purchase of sports equipment, $400 for a gymnasium and $250 towards the expense of sending the football team and band to play in Winnipeg.[43]

The canteen was a welcome addition to barrack life. It gave the men a place where they could relax in their off-duty hours with a glass of beer. One member perceptively described it as "a harmless safety valve each night for the pent-up grievances and complaints accumulated during the course of the day".[44] It was a place for comrades to gather, shake dice for schooners of 4% beer, puff on their clay pipes around the pot-bellied stove and exchange gossip and stories to unburden themselves. At Regina, it was also the site for the initiation of recruits. After being plied with a few drinks, the unseasoned newcomers were hoisted up on to a table and required to sing for the entertainment of their seniors.

Recreation rooms were another improvement that became a permanent feature of barrack life under Herchmer. They had existed before from time to time whenever room and money was available. The post-rebellion building program provided an opportunity, however, for seeing that space was specifically allocated for them, or that older buildings might by renovated for the purpose. Recreation rooms were included in the new barracks under construction at Regina, Lethbridge and Battleford in 1886. At Prince Albert and Calgary, meanwhile, the men built them themselves in their spare time using discarded materials.[45]

The profits from the canteens and grants from the Fine Fund provided the financial resources to maintain them. Just as with the canteens, the Commissioner realized that there would be less chance of men getting into trouble if their spare time was spent amusing themselves rather than in idleness. In 1886 he received requests from several divisions for sports equipment, checkers, chess, playing cards, dominoes, dumbbells, foils and boxing gloves for their recreation rooms.[46] Two years later Maple Creek purchased a billiard table from its canteen profits. One member left an affectionate description of the recreation room in Regina at this time:

> We had a recreation-room, which was very cosy and well looked after, and attached to this was a lending library. One of the buglers had his quarters here, and kept the place in order. There was a bagatelle table in the room, and also draught-boards and cards. A large stove gave out ample heat.[47]

Many of the recreation rooms also included a library, or had a library attached to them in a separate room where it was less noisy. In the days before radio and television, newspapers were the principal means of keeping abreast of world events and the sporting results. Novels and magazines with their articles and serials were widely read as a pastime. Supt. P. R. Neale saw libraries as a necessity to relieve the "terrible monotony of the life, especially during winter", and "to keep many of the men out of trouble".[48] There was too the wide-spread belief of the time that reading was a form of self-improvement, that it was the duty of the educated classes to make books available for those less fortunate. As Comm. Irvine said in support of establishing libraries, they "encouraged men to employ their leisure hours in a manner that combined amusement with useful knowledge and taught them the value of sober, regular and moral habits".

There had been libraries in the Force almost from its beginning. In 1875, the officers had donated $100 to purchase books for the men. A year later a well-wisher had arranged for an appeal to appear in eastern newspapers for books and magazines for members of the NWMP. These efforts were welcomed, but reading material that was passed from post to post soon fell apart. As with the recreation rooms, it was not until the Fine Fund and the canteen profits provided a constant flow of funds, and subscriptions were obtained from the men that libraries became permanent fixtures.

One of the finest and best organized of the period was the division Library in Battleford. It set the example for other posts. By 1893 it had acquired a collection of 300 books of the "leading authors". Each member of the division subscribed 25 cents a month to the library fund. The books were circulated to those on detachment. Members were allowed to borrow one book at a time for one week. To maintain marital harmony, however, married men could take out two. The penalty for those who did not return their book on time was five cents a day. This was deducted from their pay. New books and magazines were purchased with the money provided by the monthly subscriptions and fines. The Rose Publishing Company of Toronto gave the library a 40 per cent discount. The Division Librarian was Cst. George Alleger.[49] By 1898, the collection had increased to almost 1,000 books, and the officer commanding reported that the men were very "proud" of their library.[50]

In 1895, the officer commanding in Calgary received $100 from the Fine Fund to renovate an old barrack room into a reading room. It was furnished with linoleum, tables, chairs and curtains. Four years later he reported that it was a credit to the division, and only leather bound books were purchased.[51] At Lethbridge the canteen profits were used to buy a new edition of the Encyclopedia Britannica for the division library. The "A" Division Library in Maple Creek included books by Conan Doyle, Scott, Dickens, Dumas, Melville,

Kipling, Byron, Milton and Tennyson, as well as works on European and British History.[52] In Prince Albert the following magazines were subscribed to: *The Sketch, Black and White, Harper's Weekly, Puck, Judge, The Strand Magazine, The Illustrated London News, Life, The New York Sunday Herald* and *Lloyd's Weekly.*

In 1893, Comm. Herchmer got the Minister's approval to spend $2,000 from the Fine Fund on the establishment of a central circulating library in Regina. It was designed to supplement those in the divisions by exchanging books with them. The help of the Parliamentary Librarian in Ottawa, Mr. Griffith, was sought in selecting and purchasing books.[53] Ottawa also agreed to use the Fine Fund to buy newspapers and magazines; $100 a year was allocated to each division for this purpose. Regina and Macleod received $125 because of the larger complement of men at those posts. By the turn of the century there would appear to have been ample reading material available for all who were inclined to use it.

The NWMP had an influential role in the development of sporting life and organized sport on the prairies. As was to be expected, groups of young men living together in barracks soon found the means to enliven their routine existence by playing the games they were familiar with at home. It was such groups that often provided the catalyst in many western communities for the start of team sports. At first, the police competed amongst themselves, perhaps one troop against another, or the constables versus the NCOs, the losers buying the drinks. As the settlements grew, teams of local citizens began to appear to challenge the police at their favourite game. The big sporting holidays of the year were the Queen's Birthday in May and Dominion Day in July. To highlight these occasions, football, cricket or baseball matches would be accompanied by community picnics, band concerts, athletic meets, including races for the children, and other events. Finally, with the spread of railways after the rebellion, inter-settlement competition became a possibility, which added to the growing sense of a western identity.

While patterns were by no means rigid, the choice of sport tended to reflect the social, educational and cultural background of the players. As in other matters, the commissioned officers often took the lead in organizing sports. Supt. A. B. Perry and Insp. A. C. Macdonell are two good examples. Both were graduates of the Royal Military College, Kingston who brought their college recreational preferences west with them. Perry was an enthusiastic curler and cricketer. He was directly involved in promoting both games, and continued to play them long after he became Commissioner. A leg injury kept Perry from playing football, but this was Macdonell's forte. He was the leading light in organizing several police football teams, including the one which under his captaincy won the championship of the NWT and Manitoba in 1894. Most Mounted Police divisions had a football team at one time or another. Football, as it was widely called then, was actually British rugby. This game, of course, as well as cricket, would have been quite familiar to those members who came from the British Isles and had attended public schools.

Another active sportsman whose preferences probably derived from his formative years was Surgeon R. B. Nevitt. He was somewhat unusual in that he had a passion for both baseball and cricket. His love of the former no doubt stemmed from his childhood in Savannah, Georgia. As to the latter, after his family fled to Canada at the end of the American Civil War, he was a scholar at Bishop's College School and later Trinity College, Toronto. Baseball seems to have been the choice of the farmers' sons, or working class lads, of Ontario, supported by the few Americans in the Force like Nevitt. Cst. J. D. Nicholson from Massachusetts, for example, was the principal spirit behind the formation of a baseball team at Battleford in 1888. Soccer, or association football, as it was often called at the time, appears to have been the preference of the members of British working class origin.

Sport was one of the few things that penetrated the class structure that kept commissioned officers from contact with the other ranks on a social level. On the playing field, ability was the great equalizer. Most police teams of the period were mixed, consisting of both officers and men. The one exception was polo. It had been brought to Europe in the nineteenth century by British army officers who had learned the game while serving in northern India. It was first played in Canada in 1878 by British officers of the Halifax garrison.[54] During the 1880s and 1890s, it became very popular with the large ranchers of the Alberta foothills, who had British upper class connections. The first civilian team was organized at Pincher Creek in 1889. The rank and file of the police had neither the money for polo ponies, nor the social standing to mix in these circles. The officers, on the other hand, provided the initiative for the formation of the Fort Macleod Polo Club in 1891.[55] At least three of them played on the team – Insps. Baker, White-Fraser and Davidson. All of these were of respectable British origin. In fact, Davidson, the son of a British Army general, was born in India.

By the early 1880s, cricket, baseball and football (rugby), were being played frequently at the larger Mounted Police posts. Surgeon Nevitt, who was the medical officer at Fort Macleod, described in a series of letters in the spring of 1875 what were probably the first baseball and cricket games played in what would later be the Province of Alberta. In the afternoon of March 3rd, he wrote, "We had a fine game of baseball, the ball being made by a member of the force, and the bats pieces of green wood. We enjoyed ourselves very much."[56] In the weeks that followed Nevitt took a leading role in several games of both baseball and cricket in Canada's colonial outpost in the foothills. The season culminated on May 24th, the Queen's Birthday, with what was likely a double first, the first intertroop, or division, sporting fixture, and the first game between members of the NWMP and a team of civilians. Nevitt recorded it as a clear and sunny day. The first event was a cricket match that pitted "C" Troop, captained by its commanding officer, Supt. W. Winder, against "F" Troop led by Nevitt. The game commenced at ten in the morning, paused for the mid-day meal, and continued in the afternoon with "F" emerging as the winners. The holiday sports program was capped off with the baseball battle in which nine stalwarts of Fort Macleod were badly beaten by the police team.[57]

What was happening at Fort Macleod was also likely taking place at some of the other bigger posts in the same period. Some cricket equipment and at least two footballs had been brought west by the second contingent of recruits in June 1874. Sub-Cst. William Parker, the son of an English clergyman, recorded that this equipment had been used by the recruits at the New Fort in Toronto whilst they awaited their departure, most likely the first such games ever played by members of the NWMP.[58] Parker later noted that while at the Force's headquarters at Swan River in 1876 an athletic sports day was held on the Queen's Birthday and cricket was the chief diversion of the men during the summer evenings of that year. It was at a similar athletic contest at Fort Walsh a year or two later that Cst. Jack Simons was said to have broken the world record for throwing the cricket ball with a toss of 170 yards, 2 feet.[59]

The police participated in the first game of baseball played at Fort Battleford in 1879. In the same year cricket was introduced at "G" Division, Fort Saskatchewan by Sgt. Maj. Bobbie Belcher, a former English public school boy.[60] In the summer of 1883 the *Regina Leader* reported that the police at the headquarters there were regularly practising cricket and baseball. In October of that year it also carried a brief account of a football (rugby) match between a Mounted Police team and one from the town, which the latter won two tries to one.[61]

Organized sport took a big step forward in the years following the rebellion, not only in the Mounted Police but also in the community at large. The increase in population and the improvements in communications had a lot to do with this. For the police, however, another important factor was the establishment of canteens at the main posts. One of the arguments that Herchmer had put forward in favour of their operation was that some of the profits could be used for recreational purposes. As a result of their success, money became available for the purchase of regular supplies of sporting equipment, the maintenance of rinks, pitches or fields, and for travelling expenses. In 1887, for example, the Commissioner ordered complete sets of equipment for tennis, quoits, football, cricket and baseball for "H" Division.[62] An example of the changing circumstances was the baseball team at headquarters in Regina. It was reorganized as a "Club" with Mrs. Herchmer as its "President" in 1887. Both the Commissioner and his wife encouraged sporting activities among the men. In the fall of that year it toured the annual fairs and exhibitions in the area playing against local teams. The team members missed so many parades and other duties in the process that they became known to their envious comrades as "Mrs. Herchmer's Pets".[63]

With a population of over 3,000 in 1891, making it by far the largest urban centre in the Territories, a variety of sports developed in Calgary with the help of the Mounted Police. Soccer and football (rugby) were being played at the barracks there as early as 1884, sometimes with the townsmen joining in.[64] In 1890, a town cricket team competed against the police.[65] Later that year one local newspaper called for the formation of a town football (rugby) squad to play against the police. The latter won the contest that resulted.[66] In 1896, the city team and the NWMP team amalgamated to form the Calgary Rugby Football Club.[67] By this date the police had organized football (rugby) squads in Regina, Calgary, Edmonton, Fort Saskatchewan, Battleford and Lethbridge.

The police were also instrumental in bringing lacrosse to Calgary. Many Canadians of the time considered it their national sport. The leading figure behind the formation of the Calgary Lacrosse Club in 1891 was Sgt. Steve Garnham, who had made a name for himself as a master of the game in his home town of Toronto before enlisting.[68] By the winter of 1890, curling was also being regularly followed in the town. One of its most enthusiastic supporters was the commanding officer Supt. J. H. McIllree. This same gentleman had a passion for hunting game birds and was a co-founder of the Calgary Rod and Gun Club.[69] During the early 1890s, the Mounted Police helped the Calgary Turf Club run its periodic race meetings. In the winter of 1889-90, a skating club was started at the police post with Insp. Sanders, another RMC graduate, as its secretary. A slough close to the barracks was used as a rink.[70] Long distance running was another popular spectator sport of the time. Many towns had their own champions. There was considerable rivalry and

challenges were made which included large monetary prizes for the winners and heavy betting by their supporters. The Indians excelled at the sport, and runners like Deerfoot and Bad Dried Meat established reputations that went far beyond the borders of the Territories. The Mounted Police hero in Calgary was Cst. Alfred Green, a native of England who had grown up in Montreal. At 5 feet 6 inches and 138 lbs., "Green the Runner" was ideally built for long distance running.

In June 1886, Claxton's Arena in Calgary was crowded for three days to watch a challenge between Bad Dried Meat, Green and another Indian called Little Plume. Long distance races were not always run from point to point, but often around a track before a paid audience. This contest was to see who could run the farthest around the arena in three days. The contestants were allowed to stop to rest, sleep or eat as they felt necessary. At night the spectators were entertained by the Mounted Police band. The crowds grew larger as the race advanced. After two days Bad Dried Meat had completed over 84 miles, Green 83 and Little Plume 76. At the end of the third day, Bad Dried Meat hung on to his lead to win, with Green finishing second.[71] During the winter when Claxton's Arena became Claxton's Skating Rink, Green the long distance runner became Green the speed skater. In 1886-87, he engaged in several hotly contested one-mile races before large crowds.[72]

Calgary was also the centre of hockey activity. As early as 1893 there was a contest between the police and a city team, which the mounted men won 4-0. Thereafter, the police and the locals competed regularly. In 1896, the city beat the police 9-1. Later that year the NWMP side also played a local team known as the "Typeslingers".[73] In Edmonton, meanwhile, the "G" Division squad lost to the Edmonton "Thistles" Hockey Club in a game played on the Saskatchewan River before 150 fans in 1895.[74] With the largest complement of men at Headquarters, Regina also saw a lot of participation by the police in sporting events. Comm. Herchmer took a lead in promoting inter-town football (rugby) tournaments. In 1890, the Regina Mounted Police team, known locally as the "Rough Riders", sent out a challenge to the Winnipeg Football Club. The gauntlet was picked up not only by the latter, but also by the Royal School of Mounted Infantry. The three sides agreed to play each other at both football and cricket. As a result, in September of that year, a party of 40 Mounted Police, including the band, the Commissioner and several officers, descended on the "Queen City of the Prairies" for six days of sports, parades, partying and amateur theatricals as guests of the host teams.[75]

Judging from the press accounts the visit made quite an impact on the social life of Winnipeg. The

Lieutenant-Governor of Manitoba, the city fathers and other local dignitaries attended many of the events. At cricket the police defeated the Mounted Infantry, but lost to the Winnipeg Cricket Club. Supt. A. B. Perry, the future Commissioner, was bowled out before he could put a run on the scoreboard, out for a duck. The football matches attracted the largest crowds for what one Winnipeg newspaper described as the "supremacy of the Northwest".[76] The first to claim that honour was the Winnipeg Football Club which defeated both the Mounted Police and the Mounted Infantry.

In an effort to turn the football (rugby) tournament into an annual affair, Herchmer decided that the police would host it in Regina in 1891. Responsibility for organizing the games and the entertainment that accompanied them rested largely upon the shoulders of the RMC graduate, Insp. A. C. Macdonell, who was also captain of the police team. Macdonell tried to expand the contest by sending out invitations to several prairie towns. A number of them expressed interest in participating, but in the end only three turned out: Winnipeg, Moosomin and the Mounted Police. As a symbol of the championship of the NWT and Manitoba, the president of the Winnipeg Club, Mr. C. L. Hamilton, presented a cup, henceforth known as the Hamilton Cup, to be awarded to the winner. Once again the men from Winnipeg proved too strong for the opposition and emerged as the first holders of the Hamilton Cup.[77]

In the years that followed, the tournament continued intermittently. Moosomin won the cup in 1892. There was no contest the following year. In 1894, the police triumphed, beating Moosomin two tries to nil at the Barracks in Regina. Once again, there was no contest in 1895. Some of the teams likely had difficulty in raising enough money for travelling expenses. The Regina police team, however, found other outlets for its energy. In April 1895, it journeyed to Calgary to play three matches against the "E" Division squad. The local police band entertained, and the sports spectacle was rounded off with a banquet. In 1897, Herchmer organized a Jubilee Cup Tournament in Regina in honour of the Queen's Diamond Jubilee.[78] In the years that followed, the Mounted Police continued to play and promote the game of football in many communities.

As in the case of band concerts and other entertainment at the barracks in Regina, the police were always happy to invite the local citizens to participate. In 1889, an outdoor rink was constructed for skating, hockey and curling. The *Regina Leader* announced that it would be open to the public for skating on Monday and Friday nights. A tent was erected nearby, it continued, in which coffee and refreshments were provided for the skaters.[79] The rink was also the scene of numerous curling matches involving the police and civilians. In 1895, the annual curling competition was won by a police team comprised of Asst. Comm. McIllree, Supt. Perry, Insp. Gilpin-Brown and Cpl. "Biff" Heffernan.[80]

During the 1890s, the Annual Athletic and Military Sports Day at the Barracks became a regular feature of Regina life. The 1898 event was similar to many of the period. It was treated as a festive occasion. A large crowd of citizens came out from the town both to watch and participate in the proceedings. Many brought their picnic baskets with them. Refreshments were available. The Mounted Police Band under S/Sgt. Harry Walker entertained, and the presence of the Lieutenant-Governor and his retinue added a stately touch to the company.

The program comprised events for both police and civilians, including races for the ladies and the children. Among the results, "Biff" Heffernan, the son of Admiral Sir John Heffernan, R.N., and recently promoted to sergeant, kicked the football 75 yards to win that event. Cpl. Purves won the quarter mile race in 58 seconds, and the high jump with a leap of five feet, three inches. The fastest man of the day was Cpl. Browning. He covered the 100 yards in 11 seconds. Two events which are now a little obscure were the Umbrella and Cigar Race and the Ladies Boot Race. The crowd was thrilled by the mounted contests, especially the Balaclava Melée and the Horseback Wrestling. These two events were won by teams led by Sgt. Frank Church, the Riding Instructor. As on other occasions, the day ended with the presentation of prizes to the winners by Mrs. Herchmer.[81]

The NWMP followed the military practice of making it obligatory for all members to attend church services on Sunday. It was assumed, of course, that everyone subscribed to the Christian faith, either as Church of England, Roman Catholic or Dissenter. The officers often took an active role in the organization of their respective churches. In earlier days, when there were few clergy in the Territories, the officers themselves led the men in worship. They placed emphasis on the moral benefits of religious instruction, rather then the spiritual ones. In encouraging Christian worship, the Commissioner was supported by Ottawa, which seemed to feel that it had some duty to fulfil in this regard on behalf of the government, although it was hesitant about advancing funds for the purpose in case it should violate the principles of the separation of church and state.

The growth of post-rebellion settlement around the larger police centres was accompanied by the appearance of clergy and places of worship. Most Mounted Policemen were now able to attend regularly the church of their choice. On Sunday mornings, the men were paraded in uniform, inspected, and then marched off to their different houses of prayer. "A large number of Mounted Police attended the Presbyterian Church in Regina last Sunday," reported the *Regina Leader* in May 1887. Rev. Urquhart used the opportunity to preach a sermon on the "Soldiers of Christ".[82]

Religious freedom was recognized for mainstream Christian denominations, Roman Catholics, Anglicans, Presbyterians, Methodists and Baptists. Those whose spiritual affiliations were less common, usually joined the Church of England detail, whether they liked it or not. One young Dane recalled his sudden conversion. On his first Sunday morning in the Force, he was lined up with the other new recruits. The sergeant major proceeded to question each one as to his religious persuasion. When his turn came, he replied "Lutheran, Sir." To this response, the sergeant major bellowed "Lutheran, 'aint no such damned religion'," and he was ordered to fall in with the Church of England party.[83] Certainly no one was allowed to remain in bed on a Sunday morning on the pretext that he was a follower of Swedenborg or Mary Baker Eddy, and as there was no one else in the district who shared his beliefs he had no church to attend.

Comm. Herchmer started holding regular Sunday services at the barracks in Regina shortly after his appointment. His example was followed by others. In 1886, Supt. Perry reported that Divine Service had been observed at his headquarters in Prince Albert twice a month during the winter. In 1888, a general order was promulgated that made religious worship mandatory for everyone. This was incorporated into the "Regulations and Orders" of the NWMP the following year. It stipulated that a full dress church parade would be held every Sunday at the headquarters of each Division. Commanding officers were authorized to provide transportation to the places of worship of each denomination, where necessary.[84] It is evident that the divisions were not always as well equipped as they might have been to carry out these responsibilities. The CO at Fort Macleod complained that his men could not fully participate in the Church of England services held by the Rev. Canon Newton as they only had two prayer books between them. His counterpart at Fort Saskatchewan was even worse off. His men had no prayer books at all. As a result, efforts were made to secure a supply of the necessary items from the Society for the Promotion of Christian Knowledge.[85]

The divisions used whatever suitable space they could find for religious services. It was only at headquarters in Regina that a permanent structure was established. This was partly because of the large number of men there and the distance between the barracks and the churches in town. On Sunday mornings, the small groups of Roman Catholics and Protestants were provided with wagons to take them to Regina, but it was impossible to find transport for the members of the Church of England because there were too many of them. It was necessary, therefore, to induce a clergyman to come out from town and officiate.

By 1887, the Rev. H. H. Smith was acting as chaplain, conducting services at the barracks every Sunday and presiding over weddings and burials.[86] The following year some members of the band formed the nucleus of the first choir. The Bishop of Qu'Appelle suggested that the chaplain's position be made an official appointment, presumably with the object of obtaining some financial benefit for the incumbent and thus making the situation more permanent.[87] Herchmer tried to secure funds from the government, but Ottawa was unwilling to place a chaplain on the payroll. He next attempted to give him $2 each Sunday from the money taken up in the collection. Unfortunately, Mounted Policemen were not easily parted from their hard-earned pay. On many a Sunday not enough was found in the collection plate to meet this modest objective, let alone purchase books and other necessities for the services.[88] As a consequence, throughout this period, the police often had to depend upon the goodwill and dedication of the clergy in Regina for their religious worship.

Until 1895, the Church of England devotions were held in one building or another. In March of that year, the wooden frame structure on the southwest corner of the barrack square which served as a canteen and recreation room was badly damaged by fire.[89] It had been originally built in 1883, and was used as a mess hall until the new barrack buildings were completed in 1887. Upon Mrs. Herchmer's suggestion, the Commissioner received permission to renovate the remains and convert it into a chapel, something he had wanted for some time.

The task of remodelling fell to S/Sgt. George Service, the Head Carpenter, and Cst. (later Insp.) Bill Cunning. Together they rebuilt the charred portion of the walls and roof, added a small addition at the rear for a chancel, and constructed pews and a pulpit.[90] The result was a small chapel capable of seating about 120 persons comfortably. Later, stained glass windows were provided from out of the Church Fund, which obtained its assets from such money raising projects as the plays put on by the NWMP Dramatic Club. An organ was obtained with a grant from the Fine Fund.[91] The NWMP Chapel was officially dedicated and opened by the Bishop of Qu'Appelle, the Right Rev. William J. Burns, on the second Sunday of Advent, 8 December 1895.[92]

The Chapel would eventually become a cherished Mounted Police institution, but not everyone welcomed the new place of worship at first. Asst. Comm. McIllree believed that it would have been more beneficial had the building been converted into a bath house, something he felt the men needed badly.[93] As for those in barracks who were Church of England, many would rather have stayed in bed on Sunday morning, recovering from the revelries of the previous night. As it was, the opening of the Chapel enabled the Commissioner to hold a more formal and ceremonial church parade. "Everyone hated church parade," wrote one recruit, "because you had to gild the lily for that."[94] The men formed up in front of the barracks in their full dress uniform, where they were inspected by Herchmer himself. Heaven help anyone who was not spotless and caught his attention. The band then led the parade once around the square and into the church. Another recruit of the period recalled that the voice of the wife of the Assistant Commissioner drowned out all others in the choir, making the service an unpleasant experience for the congregation.[95] Her husband, meanwhile, noted that on one occasion when the attendance was made voluntary, "very few" of the men attended.[96]

Comm. Lawrence Herchmer was probably not a popular leader of men. He had no natural charisma, nor did he strive to attract the loyalty of the other ranks. But he did try to ameliorate the lot of his men through improved conditions of service and he achieved this objective.

Chapter 15

Without "Fuss or Feathers": Kit and Clothing

The original NWMP uniform was designed to be practical and without any "fuss or feathers", as Sir John A. Macdonald was reputed to have said. After all, the Force was only intended to be temporary so there was no point in spending more money than was absolutely necessary. Once order had been established in the Territories, it would be disbanded. The loose fitting scarlet Norfolk jacket, tan breeches and brown boots with little in the way of braid or brass adornments was a rather plain outfit compared to the Canadian Militia uniforms of the day, which aped those of the British Army. As soon as it became clear, however, that the NWMP was going to be around a great deal longer than its founder had ever thought possible, this circumstance changed.

Considerable significance was attached to the wearing of uniforms in the nineteenth century. Among other things they could be the outward and visible sign of a certain desirable social status. Most of the officers and NCOs of the NWMP had previously served in the Militia. Like their former military comrades they sought to be associated with the traditions and prestige of the Imperial Army. They were intent upon imitating the appearance, manners and style of the famous regiments that had built the Empire. The British soldier was their role model. One of their first acts was to ignore the police rank structure laid down in the Force's original organization in favour of the more pretentious military one with which they were familiar. Constables became sergeants, and Inspectors and Superintendents captains or majors. Not long after, there was pressure from officers and men to abandon Macdonald's lack-lustre uniform in favour of a more elaborate military style of dress. Changes followed, but the "red coat", which early observers had recommended because of its association by the

Native people with the British Crown, was retained.

One of the loudest complaints about the first uniform was that there was little difference between the officers and the men. This was rectified in 1876 when the officers opted for an ornate uniform patterned after that of a British regiment, the 13th Hussars, which set them apart in unmistakable splendour from their humble subordinates. Later this was replaced by a dragoon-style order of dress. The constables and NCOs, meanwhile, were also provided with a new and more military mode of uniform in 1876. Like that of the officers, it too imitated current British military styles and, with slight modifications, would remain their official uniform until almost the end of the century. The only thing that was distinctly identifiable as Canadian about this uniform was the buffalo coat.

The official uniform was a spectacular sight on the parade square or at a state function, but most of it was useless and impractical as attire for the everyday duties of the Mounted Policeman. On patrol he encountered heat, dust, rain and, in winter, bitterly cold temperatures. To combat the environment and carry out their duties more comfortably, the men purchased additional items of clothing out of their pockets. Gradually, an unofficial uniform evolved from their experience, which was seen as being characteristically Canadian. By the time of the Boer War, the "prairie dress", as it was commonly called, had replaced the British military style in the minds of Canadians and others as the distinctive uniform of the NWMP.

In its day the cut and colour of the British-style uniform was much admired by contemporaries. One experienced observer, J. G. Donkin, who had served with the British Army in several parts of the world, remembered his first sight of a mounted policeman in 1884:

> His buttons, spurs, helmet spike, and chain glittered in the sun, his brass cartridges, peeping in even rows from his belt, gleamed with a brilliant lustre; his white helmet was pipeclayed without a speck; while his scarlet tunic and long boots were perfect in fit.[1]

The *Regina Leader* commented on the splendid effect the colour of the uniform had on its surroundings when an honour guard of over 200 Mounted Policemen assembled in Regina to welcome the Governor General in 1889: "the bright red of the coats and dazzling white of their helmets and gauntlets making a brilliant contrast."[2] Describing the uniform in an American magazine of the period, one author wrote of its wearer:

> As he swaggers down the street of some little Northwest town, there is not a crack regiment in Her Majesty's service that can show a smarter trooper.[3]

The man who more than anyone else at the time brought the appearance of the NWMP to the attention of the public was the American frontier artist Frederic Remington. He produced a number of sketches from life which were printed in newspapers and magazines in Canada and the United States.[4] His mounted policemen were a bit dashing, but otherwise realistic and their uniforms accurately detailed, unlike the romantic image of the "Mountie" that would become stereotypical of the work of later artists.

As a symbol of authority the red tunic could command considerable respect. Edward Braithwaite was a former medical student from Britain who came to Canada to join the Mounted Police. After completing recruit training, he was promoted to hospital sergeant, a common fate for anyone in the police with medical experience. One day whilst travelling on the train from Regina to Winnipeg, an excited railway official asked his assistance to stop several men from fighting in another car. Braithwaite had never done any actual police work and was very unsure of what to do, but agreed to accompany the train man to the scene of the brawling. Upon opening the door of the car and without even uttering a word, to his complete amazement, the men "went back to their seats like a flock of children",[5] upon seeing his red tunic.

The men themselves were very proud of their uniform and often spent their own money on additional articles and extra tailoring for a better fit. "We were very 'fussy' about our dress," wrote one of them, "everybody wanted to look as 'slick' as possible. We were allowed to wear long pants with boots and spurs. These you had to supply yourself out of 15 bucks. Most of the men had them. Your riding breeches for dude wear were skin tight. The ones you rode were not so tight."[6] They saw the red tunic in particular as a unique symbol of their elite status and, as a result, resented its unauthorized use by anyone, be he Indian or white. Supt. Sam Steele protested vigorously to the Commissioner after the Department of Indian Affairs handed out discarded tunics and helmets to the Indians saying that it would lower morale and bring ridicule upon the Force.[7] Even special constables were not considered worthy enough to wear the scarlet dress. When Asst. Comm. J. H. McIllree discovered that red serges had been issued to Indian scouts in "E" Division, he ordered the practice stopped at once.[8] There was also opposition to the wearing of old tunics by the Regina Boys' Brigade, even though they had been altered.

Following his enlistment in Regina, the recruit was issued with a variety of articles to equip him for his new vocation. Collectively, they were commonly referred to as his "Kit and Clothing". As well as uniform, there were blankets, bedding, eating and cleaning utensils, saddlery, firearms and other necessary accoutrements. He could not sell or exchange any of these items, most of which had to be marked with his regimental number. In July 1886, the Quarter Master Stores of each Division were supplied with a set of indian rubber dies and ink for this purpose.[9] On inspection day, all of his uniform, apart from what he was wearing, and other items were required to be laid out on his bed in spotless condition, polished where necessary, for the sharp eye of the inspecting officer. In the interests of uniformity, Herchmer had a diagram drawn up in 1893 illustrating the order in which the articles should be displayed. Copies were made available to every member. Anyone who failed to lay things out in the prescribed order, or did not have them in an immaculate state, was likely to find himself the recipient of a small fine.

The order of dress for constables when Herchmer became Commissioner in 1886 laid down a basic schedule for issue of kit, uniform and equipment.[10] Basically, most articles ranging from spurs to buffalo coats were issued upon engagement and were expected to last for a five-year term of service. Other items such as boots and the red tunic were scheduled for replacement periodically.[11]

Herchmer sought to achieve complete uniformity in matters of dress throughout the Force for both officers and men. Like his predecessors, however, it was an objective he was never entirely able to meet. The uncertainty of supplies often resulted in some men still wearing the "old" style cap, tunic, belt or whatever, while others had been issued with the "new" style. There was also the problem of quality control. Under the government's system of patronage, contracts for supplies of articles of uniform went to numerous manufacturers. Over a short period of time the tunics, boots, breeches and other items obtained by the Force could come from several sources. One manufacturer might, for example, produce a tunic of slightly different cut, colour and texture from the next. It is for this reason that photographic evidence of NWMP uniforms must be evaluated with extreme care. What appears in a photograph may not conform to the official regulations on the day it was taken.

Acknowledging the possibility of slight variation, the constables' full dress uniform in 1886 consisted of a close-fitting scarlet tunic edged with yellow cord braid, seven brass buttons in front and a single yellow braid Austrian knot on each sleeve, brown leather cartridge belt with steel buckle and holster, white canvas haversack, white buckskin gauntlets, blue breeches with yellow braid stripe, long black laceless riding boots with steel spurs and white helmet with brass spike and chain. In 1889, this outfit alone cost $35 to $40 for each man.[12] In the undress or service order of uniform, the cloth tunic was replaced by a plainer and heavier one of scarlet serge with five brass buttons in front, but no braid around the edge or on the sleeve. Instead of the white helmet, a round pillbox cap with a yellow band was worn on the right side of the head two-fingers breadth above the right eye. Its strap, like the chain of the helmet, was to be worn around the point of the chin.

In winter, a fur cap of sealskin with a yellow bag on the right side and ear flaps inside that could be drawn down over the ears in very cold weather, or a red woolen tuque took the place of the helmet or pillbox. Moccasins with woolen stockings replaced the riding boots. A grey overcoat or buffalo fur coat was also worn during the winter. The latter were very popular with the men because they were capable of keeping the body warm in the coldest of prairie temperatures, an essential garment when one had to visit an unheated outhouse or latrine on a winter's night. With the rapid decline of the buffalo herds, however, they were becoming difficult to obtain. Strange to say that apart from the ankle boots there was nothing on the schedule of kit and clothing that was suitable for wear when the men were engaged in carrying out the numerous "dirty jobs" that often made up their daily routine. It was assumed that they would wear the service order of dress when cutting firewood, hauling ice, washing their clothes, cooking, cleaning stables or chinking the sides of the detachment with mud.

In 1889, it was calculated that the entire expense of outfitting a recruit with kit and clothing for his five-year period of service came to a total of $268.51.[13] During the years 1886 to 1900, the annual cost of issuing uniform and related articles to the NCOs and men (officers paid for their own) averaged eight per cent of the yearly police expenditure.[14] Except when he was in bed or in the bathtub, if he was lucky enough to have one, a constable was never out of some kind of uniform. Regulations forbade the wearing of mufti (civilian clothes), even when courting his best girlfriend on a Sunday afternoon.[15] Only officers were permitted to wear plain-clothes when off duty. All members were also forbidden to display any party emblems on their uniforms that indicated their religious, political or fraternal affiliations. This was in keeping with their Oath of Office to "faithfully, diligently and impartially execute and perform the duties required . . . without fear, favour or affection of or towards any person or party whomsoever."[16] The only exception to this was the wearing of the floral emblem of the patron saints of England, Ireland, Scotland, Wales and Quebec on their feast days.

The uniforms of the NCOs were almost identical to those of the constables. There was really no difference as far as footwear, headgear and breeches were concerned. What set them apart was a generous application of resplendent Russia gold braid to their tunics. It was used on the collars, around the edge of the garment and for Austrian knots and badges of rank, instead of the yellow of the constables. The pillboxes of the NCOs were also adorned with the gold rather than the yellow. There was one small difference between junior NCOs (corporals) and senior NCOs (sergeants and staff sergeants). The former had shoulder straps on their tunics like the constables, although edged with gold braid. The latter had shoulder cords made by twisting the gold braid into a knot. The effect was to make the sergeants and staff sergeants the most resplendent of the NCOs.

Senior NCOs had other accoutrements which also set them apart from the constables and corporals. When in full dress they carried swords, usually the British Light Cavalry pattern of 1822 in a black leather scabbard. In addition, in both full and service order they wore a brown leather pouch belt across their chests to which were attached in the middle of their backs, the most awkward place possible, a leather pouch or binocular case. Finally, they also had a dark blue cloth patrol jacket edged with black mohair. These were officially approved for issue at public expense in 1895, but from photographic evidence it is clear that they had been worn for several years before this, probably at the wearer's own cost.[17]

In the early 1880s, a new brass button that was identifiably NWMP was issued to the constables and NCOs. The buttons worn earlier had either been militia issue or had a crown in the centre with the letters "NWMP" above and the word "Canada" below. The new ones had a buffalo head in the centre. Below it were the letters "NWMP", and above it, the word "Canada" surmounted by a crown. The pouches or binocular cases of the senior NCOs were adorned with either a monogrammed badge of the letters "NWMP" in brass surmounted by a crown, or a pouch badge similar to that of the officers. Like the other officers' badges, the central motif of this was the head of a buffalo, or American bison as it was sometimes referred to, surrounded by a buckled garter inscribed with the motto *Maintien le Droit* enclosed in a wreath of maple leaves. Above this device was the name "Canada" surmounted by a crown and below it on a scroll the words "North-West Mounted Police". The origin of this badge, its composition and the choice of the elements remain obscure. The number of maple leaves seem to have no significance in this early period of the Force's history. The very apt motto is a traditional one from fourteenth century England of French derivation with an archaic spelling of the verb *maintenir*.[18] These badges, the "NWMP" monogram and the buttons were the only NWMP insignia worn by members, with the exception of officers and bandsmen, until the helmet plate came into general issue in the late 1890s.

By 1886, badges of appointment had been in use for sometime. They were identical to those worn by the militia cavalry. The earliest of these issued to members were Bugler, Saddler, Roughrider, Armourer and Farrier. Bandsmen's badges were approved in 1887. In 1898, the Commissioner agreed to a request from Sgt. Nichols, the foot drill instructor at "Depot", to wear the familiar crossed swords badge of his appointment, provided he paid for them himself.[19] A decade earlier, Asst. Comm. McIllree had suggested that detectives be issued with a metal badge with which to identify themselves when working in plainclothes. Herchmer did not agree, probably because of the cost. Commanding Officers were instructed to give them a signed note certifying who they were instead.

The badges of rank of NCOs had at one time been worn on both arms, but by Herchmer's time, like the badges of appointment, they were restricted to the right arm only, and once again were similar to those worn by the military. In the case of corporals, the badge consisted of two chevrons with their points down worn above the elbow. Sergeants sported three chevrons, points down, surmounted by a crown, also above the elbow. Staff sergeants had four chevrons points up sewn on the lower part of the sleeve. Sergeants major also wore their badge below the elbow, four chevrons points down surmounted by a crown. The regimental sergeant major had no distinctive emblem during the Herchmer years. He continued to wear the insignia of a sergeant major.

In 1894, the Commissioner obtained approval for some additional badges. These were worn on the left arm. The first was the Good Conduct Badge, a yellow five-pointed star, one of which was awarded every five years that a member served without being convicted of a serious disciplinary offence. The oth-

ers were the marksman's badges, crossed rifles and crossed revolvers for those who attained the required score with each weapon at their annual shoot.[20] The best shot in the Force each year with either rifle or revolver wore a crown above the respective marksman's badge.

To encourage the men to look after their kit and clothing, Herchmer got approval for a system of compensation shortly after he became Commissioner in 1886. For each article that was still in good usable condition and did not have to be replaced at the end of its authorized term of service, the owner was paid two-thirds of its replacement value in cash. This was a saving for the government of one-third of the cost of issuing a new article to the member.[21] For example, suppose that forage caps cost $9 each. According to the schedule, a constable was entitled to receive a new one every year. If he looked after his forage cap and at the end of the year it was still serviceable and did not have to be replaced, he would be paid $6 and the government would save $3. As the Commissioner said, the system gave prudent and careful men a chance to make a little money.[22] They found ways to extend the life of articles. A common practice, for example, was to hammer metal studs into the bottoms of their boots to protect the leather soles. In fiscal year 1889-90, almost $2,300 was paid out to constables and NCOs for items of uniform that did not have to be replaced, a saving of over $1,100 on the public purse.[23] This no doubt gave the parsimonious Macdonald much satisfaction.

Recruits were reminded of the manners which were commonly observed by the military of the period as to the wearing of uniforms. There was to be no foppery or exaggeration in their attire. Their dress and appearance should at all times be such that it created respect for the Force. Neatness and smartness promoted respect. An untidy and slovenly looking constable, on the other hand, brought contempt upon the organization. A uniform was to be worn in a manner which indicated to all that the wearer was proud of it. When out in public they were to hold their heads erect. As noted many members purchased overalls, tight-fitting blue trousers with a yellow stripe, and black ankle boots with box spurs at their own expense to wear when off duty and out on the town. These items of unofficial issue were worn with the pillbox cap and the scarlet serge tunic. The whole outfit constituted what was known as "walking out" order of dress. This was topped off by the purchase of a bone or silver handled riding crop to be carried on such occasions. The result was a dashing-looking constable with a swagger in his step, an appearance much admired by young ladies of the time. Smoking habits of the period were largely confined to pipes. The division canteens sold a great many clay ones to the men. Smoking, however, was strictly forbidden when in public in uniform.

The original members of the NWMP had been a hairier lot than those who followed them a decade or so after. In the later years of the Victorian era there was decline in the popularity of beards, goatees and mutton chops, especially among younger men, but a bushy growth on the upper lip was still much admired as a sign of masculine maturity. The 1889 regulations placed no prohibitions on the length of hair. It is clear, however, from photographic evidence that certain standards were imposed under the watchful eye of the division sergeants major. Contemporary military opinion favoured short, neatly cut hair as promoting comfort and coolness. Moustaches and sideburns of moderate length were acceptable, but the chin and under the lip had to be shaved.[24] As noted, a shaving kit was part of the scheduled issue of equipment.

By Herchmer's time, short hair and a clean shaven face, with the option of a moustache, had become the norm for young constables. The luxuriant beards once cultivated by senior NCOs were passé. Their hair, too, was now cut short, and the beards replaced by large moustaches, sometimes waxed. The beards that remained were now well trimmed and restricted to older officers as a symbol of their authority and dignity. Comm. Herchmer wore a beard throughout his service. When RSM "Bobbie" Belcher was appointed an Inspector in 1893, he immediately grew one as testimony to his new status. Asst. Comm. McIllree allowed his beard to grow during the winter months and shaved it off in the spring.

Herchmer was always looking for ways to economize on the cost of uniform and equipment, but not at the expense of quality. Each shipment of items that was received at Regina was examined by a board of officers, usually headed by the Supply Officer, to determine whether it was of the desired standard, or defective in any way. It was not unusual for the board to reject articles. In 1887, for example, a large shipment of boots from J. C. MacLaren of Montreal was returned because some of them came apart after only being worn for a few days.[25] Samples of clothing supplied by manufacturers seeking contracts were worn for several weeks by an NCO. The board then examined them to see how they had stood up to the wear and tear. To save money, many of the leather accoutrements required by the Force, belts, bandoliers, holsters and the like, were made by the saddlers at headquarters.[26]

Almost all articles of clothing were purchased in Canada. Although the choice of provisioner was subject to government patronage, the same suppliers were frequently used. Some of the commonest names of the period appeared in the auditor general's report for 1891-92:

T. A. Code (Perth, Ont)	5,354 socks @ 15 cents per pair
R. J. Devlin (Ottawa, Ont)	500 helmets $598.19
J. M. Garland (Ottawa, Ont)	2,000 stable jackets @ $1.09 each
Jas. Hall (Brockville, Ont)	1,000 mitts at $1.25 each
James O'Brien (Montreal, Que)	2,617 breeches @ $5.56 each
Gillespie, Ansley & Dixon (Toronto, Ont)	1,200 forage caps @ 59 cents each[27]

Until Henry Birks & Son of Montreal began producing brass badges for the Mounted Police in 1901, these as well as buttons, chevrons, service stars and badges of appointment and rank had usually been obtained from England. Some of the principal suppliers during the Herchmer years were: Hobson & Son, London; James Inch & Co., London; and Baxter & Hicks, London.

The system of supply sometimes broke down, leaving men without a complete issue of kit. The commanding officer at Battleford in 1896 complained that 27 of his men had been without red serges for over ten months.[28] His counterpart at Fort Saskatchewan advised Regina that his supply of fur coats and caps was unfit to be worn, but were issued anyway as there were no replacements. In April of the same year, Herchmer told White that only ten per cent of a recent shipment of boots from Hamilton were fit for use, that it was a waste of money and would be embarrassing if the newspapers found out. A shortage of boots in 1898 prevented a number of men in several divisions for a time from going on duty.[29] One division, meanwhile, ran out of blankets and had to give out horse blankets to the men for bedding instead.[30] These were exceptions however. The comments of the commanding officers in their annual reports show that the quality and supply of uniforms and equipment was, on the whole, satisfactory.

Herchmer frequently experimented with new items of uniform in an effort to improve the existing one and make it more serviceable. Change was also necessary when some articles became difficult to obtain. In the process, a distinct working order or dress gradually evolved. One of the Commissioner's first innovations was the lanyard. It resulted from a few instances of carelessness that greatly angered him. Some members, while out on patrol, lost their revolvers because their holsters were broken or not properly secured. The cost of the firearm was deducted from their pay, but Herchmer was still determined to put a stop to their negligence. If they were going to act like children, he would treat them like children. Their revolvers would be fastened to a piece of string and tied around their necks. In June 1886, an order was sent to every commanding officer to purchase a supply of cod fishing line, stain it with coffee, and make a lanyard for each man under him. These were to be fastened to the ring on the butts of their Enfield revolvers and looped over their heads whenever the weapon was carried.[31] Lanyards had, of course, been used by the military long before this to prevent the loss of the revolver during battle, but this was the way the lanyard came to the NWMP. What is also interesting is that so much cod line was evidently obtained hundreds of miles from the nearest cod fish.

One of the biggest difficulties Herchmer faced with respect to the uniform was to find a suitable replacement for the buffalo coat. With the growth of settlement and the spread of rail lines and fences, the vast herds that had been a ready source for this garment had been reduced to a few scattered survivors. According to the 1882 schedule of free kit issue, every recruit was entitled to a buffalo coat. Although heavy, they were warmer than the greatcoats, and very popular as a result. In 1886, White was able to purchase 50 from a supplier in Chicago. He warned Herchmer that it would no longer be possible to provide one to each recruit.[32] The following year they were removed from the list of free kit. Henceforth, all new supplies of buffalo coats were to be retained in division stores and only loaned to the men when their duties necessitated them, on sentry duty or patrol in winter, for example.

In 1887, a board of officers examined samples of kangaroo, sheepskin and calfskin coats as possible substitutes. Its report was not favourable.[33] The black dye used on the sheepskin and calfskin coats came out on the hands, faces and tunics of the men in wet weather.[34] For a time, kangaroo coats were considered as a replacement, but the idea was eventually rejected because they were too expensive.[35] Although it continued to be criticized for a number of reasons, sheepskin, because of availability and low cost, became for a time the principal official successor to the buffalo coat. In 1890, the Force's total stock of fur coats amounted to 298 sheepskin, 30 buffalo, 6 Austrian bear, 1 calfskin and 1 of Russian dog.[36] In an effort to extend the life of the fur coats, it was ordered in 1891 that they should all be turned in to division stores at the end of the winter and kept in moth balls until they were needed again.[37] A few buffalo coats were obtained from time to time, but they never became general issue again. In 1898, it was reported that some of the last of them that were still in usable condition were supplied to the men transferred to the Yukon that year.[38]

Actually, the disappearance of the buffalo coats was not all that serious because it was being overtaken in popularity by an unofficial article of uniform. As early as 1887, Supt. Sam Steele had suggested that the buffalo coat be replaced by a pea jacket, a short dark blue double-breasted overcoat of coarse, woolen cloth, sometimes referred to as pilot-cloth because of its association with sailors and shipping pilots.[39] They were already being worn by a few sergeants at their own expense. A year later, Steele asked for permission for all men in his division to wear them, saying that they were prepared to buy them with their own money.[40] The Commissioner replied that they were for NCOs only.

In spite of the refusal, the use of the pea jacket began to spread throughout the Force. The men found that if well-lined they could be very warm in cold weather, and they looked particularly smart worn over the serge tunic when "walking out" on social occasions. Once again, because of their experiences and preferences, the men were asserting their influence over the future of the uniform. In May 1889, White sent a sample pea jacket to Regina. The examining board was favourably impressed and recommended their official adoption, commenting that they were already worn throughout the Force at the expense of the members.[41] Ottawa, however, did not rush to buy any. At $10 to $12 apiece, the official endorsement of pea jackets would have added about $10,000 to the cost of maintaining the Force. The willingness of the men to spend their own money probably encouraged this kind of bureaucratic penny-pinching. Finally, in 1893, the department purchased 100 of the jackets from James O'Brien & Company of Montreal at $10.50 each and distributed them to "B", "E", "A" and "K" divisions.[42] Further issues followed, and by 1900, the pea jacket had replaced both the sheepskin and the buffalo coat as the common winter outer garment.

Another innovation during Herchmer's time was the issue to the ranks of a khaki duck suit consisting of a jacket and trousers made from strong, hard-wearing, untwilled cotton. A similar suit was also adopted by the officers. When worn they were commonly referred to as fatigue or stable dress and, although not very flattering in appearance, became standard wear for all kinds of manual work. They were also worn on patrol by many of the men in place of the red serge tunic and the breeches. A distinct advantage of the cotton items over the woolen ones was that they could more easily be washed and dried.

The first duck suits were ordered in 1886.[43] The following year the Commissioner reported that their introduction had been a resounding success. By 1890, he was able to tell Ottawa that the red serges were no longer being used for prairie work as the duck jackets were warmer and more serviceable.[44] Earlier, many of the men had to have their serges lined at their own expense to keep out the cold when on patrol in winter.

The duck suits were supposed to be worn with a soft khaki cap of similar material. To Irvine must go the credit for its introduction. The pillbox and the helmet gave little protection from the hot sun or rain when riding across the prairie. In 1884, Irvine recommended the adoption of a new cap which he believed would protect the eyes and the back of the head and neck when on patrol.[45] It was familiarly called the "fore and aft" or "deerstalker" cap in that it had a peak at both front and rear resembling the traditional style of headgear associated with deer hunting in the British Isles.

Herchmer and some of his officers did not, however, share Irvine's enthusiasm for them. They found that the caps were quite suitable for fatigues, but were just as useless as the pillbox and the helmet in sun or rain.[46] Most of their subordinates seem to have agreed with them. Photographic evidence suggests that they continued to prefer the broad-brimmed felt hats that they bought themselves. By 1894, the use of the helmet had decreased to the point that Herchmer felt an issue of one every five years instead of one every two years would be quite sufficient because it was "seldom required."[47]

The members were generally dissatisfied with the issue of grey greatcoats that replaced the blue ones in 1888. Like the old ones they came with a cape that could be attached or detached as the needs required. The grey cloth was lighter than the blue and, as a result, there were complaints that they were not as waterproof.[48] A slicker, a long, loose-fitting oilskin raincoat, was suggested as the remedy for wet weather. Ottawa sympathized, but the cost kept it from being added to the free issue schedule until after the turn of the century. In the meantime of course, the men could always buy them out of their pay, if they wished to stay dry.

Comm. Herchmer did not like the moccasins which the men wore in winter with breeches and woolen stockings in place of boots. He felt that they looked untidy and were associated with the cruder, less cultivated days of the frontier. "The Territories have changed," he told White. Moccasins were all right on patrol, but they looked unsightly in public places. He wanted them replaced by long felt boots, but he knew that Ottawa would not pay for them nor issue them free. He suggested to White, therefore, that he obtain a supply of them and make them available for sale to the men in the division canteens at their own expense.[49] As a result, an order was placed with the Dolge Felt Boot Co. and yet another "semi-official" or "unofficial" item found its way into the uniform of the NWMP at no cost to the government.

Two other items that were experimented with were khaki breeches and leather tunics. It was a frequent complaint that blue breeches very easily became discoloured. Cpl. Donkin described them as becoming filthy in a few minutes around a camp fire. He suggested that they be replaced by brown ones similar to those worn by the Cape Mounted Rifles.[50] His views were echoed by Supt. John Cotton who recommended cord breeches of a "neutral" colour.[51] It was not until 1899, however, that some sample khaki breeches were obtained.[52] In the search for the ideal patrol jacket or tunic, some leather ones were tried in 1890, but they were not found to be suitable.[53]

An essential figure in the matter of appearance was the division tailor. Each division was supposed to have one, but a qualified tailor was often difficult to engage. What was even harder to find on the prairies was a "regimental" tailor, one who knew the intricacies of military styles and customs. A constable employed as a tailor would receive 15 cents per diem extra pay. If he were engaged as a special constable, he could expect $25 per month with rations. He was usually a senior NCO or special constable with comparable pay.

Tailors could make additional money doing alterations on the clothing that the men bought themselves, or fitting officers' uniforms. Operating their own business, however, could often be more lucrative than working for the police. As a result, divisions frequently found themselves without the services of a tailor. In 1889, the commanding officer at Prince Albert had to send his men to a private tailor in town to have their uniforms fitted at a cost of 75 cents each.[54] His counterpart in Battleford, meanwhile, complained that Cst. William Parks had such a peculiar shape that he would not let him out in public until his uniform had been properly fitted by a tailor. To assist White in ordering supplies of clothing, a size roll was compiled in 1886 of the height and chest measurements of all the men.[55]

Throughout most of Herchmer's term the position of Master Tailor was held by one of the original members, S/Sgt. John A. Martin, a native of Prince Edward Island.[56] Before joining the Force in 1873, he had served as a tailor with "A" Battery of the Canadian militia at Kingston. It was Martin who made clothes out of buffalo robes at Fort Macleod in 1874 to replace the "rags" the men were in after the March West. Martin retired in 1898. He was briefly succeeded as Master Tailor by Special Cst. John Armstrong who, in turn, was replaced by Special Cst. James Chatwin in 1901.

The debate over tradition versus practicality with respect to military uniforms was by no means limited to the NWMP. There was considerable discussion on this subject at the time throughout the Empire. As early as the 1840s, some British troops in India had started to wear uniforms made from hard-wearing cotton that was dyed a khaki colour by the use of substances like coffee or curry powder. The word "khaki" came from Persian and Urdu, meaning a dusky brown colour. The khaki uniforms were practical, easily washed, cheaper, did not discolour and blended with the landscape. They were not always popular with the troops or the top brass, however, because they felt that they looked scruffy compared to traditional regimental dress. A khaki tunic did not have the same effect on the ladies as a blue or red one. There was a resistance to the change and the transformation to khaki was a slow one. The Khartoum expedition of 1884, which unsuccessfully sought to relieve General Gordon, was one of the last occasions on which red tunics were worn on active service by the British Army. When Khartoum was finally taken 14 years later following the Battle of Omdurman, all the British troops were dressed in khaki.

Year after year the commanding officers complained in their annual reports of the inadequacies of the official uniform for patrol work and recommended the adoption of a new order of dress. However, the changes that came were piecemeal. The biggest obstacle to a more workaday outfit was that every item added to the official issue list would mean an increase in public expenditure, and Macdonald and his successors were committed to a policy of holding the line or even retrenchment in this regard. The adoption of the duck suit was an attempt to introduce some practicality into the dress of the men, but it did not go far enough. As a result, the men were forced to take matters into their own hands by supplying themselves with a variety of articles which came to constitute what was commonly referred to as "prairie dress" or "prairie service order".

There were individual variations, but this unofficial patrol outfit usually consisted of some or all of the following items: buckskin jackets with fringes; leather chaps or chaparejos, as the Mexicans called them; colourful bandannas; oilskin slickers; western gunbelts and holsters and wide-brimmed felt hats, variously described at the time as "prairie hats", "cowboy hats", or "slouch hats". In fact, were it not for the blue breeches that some continued to wear, the Mounted Policeman of the era on patrol seated in his western-style saddle could easily have been mistaken for a cowboy of the American West. A British journalist in 1889 described them thus:

> I saw four of them ride out from the police station on some important duty. They did not wear the smart red jacket and white helmet, but were dressed somewhat like Garibaldi's men, in loose shirt and slouched hat, knicker bockers and leather leggings, blanket, canteen, rifle & carbine were fixed fore and aft on the Mexican saddles. The horses were dark bays, full of power and action. Round the men's waists were stout leather belts, from which I noticed various ominous-looking weapons project.[57]

The most significant item of the prairie dress as far as the future development of the Force's uniform was concerned was the wide-brimmed felt hat. From the highest to the lowest, the members had complained about the helmet's inadequacy. One went as far as to charge that continuous use of it in sunlight could injure the eyesight.[58] Another pointed out that U.S. troops across the border had already wisely discarded helmets and kepis in favour of felt hats. As the government would not provide them the men were forced to purchase their own. They were usually sold in the division canteen at a cost of from $4 to $6. There was no uniformity in style. As they were unregulated, the men pleated them or knocked them into any shape that they wished. In fact, finding a felt hat that would keep its shape turned out to be a problem for a while. In 1891, the Commissioner reported that felt hats were in general use throughout the Force, but it was hard to find one that would retain its shape at a reasonable price.[59] Several types and makes were experimented with over the years. In 1888, a supply of white ones was tried.[60] Three years later samples that were obtained from a company in New York City proved unsatisfactory.[61] In 1893, an order was placed with W. D. Dineen of Toronto for a quantity of khaki prairie hats described as the "Belinda" model at a cost of $4 each.[62] A year later, Supt. Sam Steele purchased a supply of "cowboy hats" for his own division while in Helena, Montana, at $66 a dozen. He reported that they were made by I. B. Stetson of Philadelphia and were "far superior" to anything made in Canada.[63] By the late 1890s, the "Stetson" seems to have been the most commonly used hat, although the blocking or pleating still remained a very individual affair.

The most influential event of the period in determining the future development of the uniform was Queen Victoria's Diamond Jubilee in 1897. Herchmer was anxious that the NWMP contingent which would travel to London to participate in the festivities would be able to hold its own in appearance with the best of the military regiments that would come from all over the world to rejoice in the power and glory of the British Empire that was associated with Her Majesty's long reign. He received the support of Laurier for the men to wear both full dress and "Prairie costume".[64] His appeals for money to buy new equipment and uniforms for the contingent were also approved. Some of the items he had wanted the government to add to the official issue for years would be so for the first time. The Commissioner was determined that the men would look their finest in whatever they wore. He wanted to show them off to the world.

What the Jubilee did was to force the police to formalize the prairie dress. Individual choice was replaced by uniformity of attire. What emerged as a result was a mode of dress that was recognizable both at home and abroad as distinctly Canadian. The *Edmonton Bulletin* understood this in its own parochial way. It saw the contingent as a true representative of the Canadian prairies and applauded with pride the decision to allow the men to wear the "Stetson" hat while in England. This item, it continued, is the typical head gear of the "great West" from which the police come.[65] The style of hat was indeed being worn by many civilians on the prairies, and the name of one manufacturer, Stetson, was most often used to describe it.

The new official prairie dress consisted of the now familiar brown broad-brimmed felt hat with a brown leather hat band buckled on the left side with end to the rear. From photographic evidence, it appears that the Jubilee brought uniformity to its blocking. The predominate arrangement is four indentations or pleats running down from a point in the top centre of the hat. A somewhat similar style was also coming into use about this time in the United States Marine Corps and with troops in Australia and New Zealand, although in the latter cases, one side of the brim was often fastened upwards. As to the NWMP, Herchmer and his officers no doubt had some part in determining the choice of style, but no written record has survived to explain why or by whom the decision was made. Tradition would later say that the hat was pinched or pleated in four places to signify the four initials of the Force. Herchmer purchased the "prairie hats" for the contingent in the Regina Canteen for $4 each. The source of this particular supply is uncertain.[66]

The new order of dress also included a brown duck stable jacket to which a patch pocket had been sewn on each breast by the tailor in Regina. The rest of the uniform consisted of white lanyard instead of brown, brown leather bandolier, brown leather ammunition belt, white buckskin gauntlets, blue breeches with yellow stripe and long black boots with steel spurs. The contingent was also supplied for the first time at public expense with blue overalls and congress boots with box spurs for "walking out" while in London. These boots were obtained from G. Breese and Company of Quebec at $2.85 a pair. When dressed in prairie service order, the men attached their Winchester carbines to the sling on the front of their saddles. In full dress, however, they were carried in carbine buckets. There were no innovations in the dress of the two officers who accompanied the party, except for Supt. A. B. Perry who can be seen wearing a "Stetson", very likely the

first officer to do so officially, when the other ranks were in prairie dress.

Photographs show that the full dress worn by the contingent consisted of the usual authorized items: long black boots, steel spurs, blue breeches, red tunic, white buckskin gauntlets, brown ammunition waist belt, white helmet with gold chain and spike, carbine and revolver. The white haversacks usually required with full dress were not taken. White lanyards were worn instead. There were also two new features. Herchmer obtained pouch badges and blue overcoats with cloaks for the group from England. The overcoats were the older heavier type that had earlier been replaced by the unsatisfactory grey ones. The NWMP pouch badges were attached to the front of the helmets of the contingent. Previously, these had only been worn by officers and bandsmen. After the Jubilee they came into general use.

Just prior to departure from Quebec City in June 1897, the contingent was paraded in full dress before the Governor General, Lord Aberdeen, and Major General W. J. Gascoigne, the British officer who commanded the Canadian militia. They both expressed their satisfaction with its appearance, and asked out of curiosity for one of the men to be paraded in prairie dress. Perry ordered S/Sgt. Fred Bagley to change his clothes quickly. The two dignitaries were impressed by what they saw when the NCO, who had started as a boy bugler on the March West, returned. Gascoigne described the outfit as "most workmanlike".[67] In Bagley, the general saw a fine example of the experienced frontiersman, the irregular soldier or scout, whose qualities would be much admired and much in demand as the war clouds gathered over southern Africa. As far as the uniform was concerned, the NWMP found itself among the trend-setters of the day.

The success of the prairie dress before a world audience in London in 1897 accelerated change in the uniform of the Force. The formalized version of the "cowboy suit" was soon in widespread use. By 1899, breast pockets with flaps had been added to the stable jackets of most of the men by the division tailors at a cost of 20 cents each.[68] In the same year a new cavalry pattern khaki patrol jacket was proposed for the officers to replace the red one. The Stetson hat gradually became general issue, and the shape uniform. Its new status was recognized by its increasing use on formal occasions. During the Governor General's tour of the Territories in 1899 he was provided with a 16-man escort wearing Stetsons with the red serge tunic. It was this attire that was becoming more and more identified as the uniform of the NWMP.[69]

Yet another influence was also having an impact on the future dress of the Force. The men transferred to the Yukon found that several items not on the free issue were absolutely necessary because of the sub-Arctic environment. As on the prairies, they purchased some of these at first out of their own pocket. By 1897-98, however, they were being supplied with deer skin parkas, fur mitts, pea jackets, lined stable pants, sweaters, Mackinaw coats, Yukon-style fur hats and brown "Klondyke laced boots".[70] The first supply of riding boots with a laced instep arrived at headquarters in Regina in 1894.[71] They were probably purchased from Dolan & Company of England. Whether they went to the Yukon or not is not known.

Some of these changes in the dress of the NWMP influenced the choice of clothing made by the two regiments it spawned for service in South Africa. Both the Lord Strathcona's Horse and the Canadian Mounted Rifles adopted Stetson hats, khaki jackets and brown-laced riding boots. In fact, what had earlier been referred to as "Klondyke laced boots" would become better known as "Strathcona Boots". These Canadians made their mark in South Africa looking like Canadian soldiers not British ones, and their experiences confirmed the utility of their uniforms.

By 1900, official recognition of the modifications in the dress of the police was long overdue. During the spring of that year, White and McIllree, in the Commissioner's absence in South Africa, and later Perry considered the required alterations. On 25 August 1900, a few short weeks after Herchmer's enforced retirement, an order-in-council approved a new schedule of kit and clothing. These changes were published a few months later in the NWMP Annual Report for 1900.[72] They reflected in some degree or another not only the victory of common sense over tradition, and a new sense of identity among Canadians, particularly westerners, but also in a Turnerian manner the influence of the frontier over more conventional styles.

As Perry wrote in the Annual Report, "The object is to make the uniform more serviceable, suitable for the work we have to do . . . Pipeclay and blacking are discarded. Gloves and boots are of brown leather and can be readily cleaned."[73] These changes only applied to the rank and file. In his report Perry announced that new regulations for the uniforms of the officers would be presented later. In fact, although the officers did adopt a practical patrol or service dress, they did not break so sharply with the past as the men did. They continued with the ornate dragoon-style full dress for some time. Officers were slower to agree to changes in their uniform, because every such change had to be paid for out of their own pockets.

Actually 1900 was only the beginning of a short period of considerable experimentation and further change in the uniforms of the NWMP. These changes were influenced by the continuing experience of the troops in South Africa, modifications in Canadian Militia regulations, the coronation of King Edward VII and the grant of the title "Royal" to the Force in 1904. Throughout all of this, however, the image of the "Mountie" that had been established nationally and internationally as a man wearing a Stetson hat and a red tunic would survive.

A military uniform attracted more attention if its owner was entitled to adorn it with medals and decorations. The former were usually awarded for participation in particular battles or campaigns, the latter for individual acts of heroism. The medal wearer stood out a little bit more than his comrades on parade. In the early years of the Force, Sgt. Maj. Joe Francis had been singled out because he wore the Crimean War Medal. Every school boy in Britain and every English-speaking one in Canada knew about the Charge of the Light Brigade. Most of them had been forced to learn Tennyson's immortal lines:

> All in the valley of death
> Rode the six hundred.
> Some one had blundered:
> Theirs not to make reply,
> Theirs not to reason why,
> Theirs but to do and die.

It was perhaps the most famous military engagement of the century. Francis was the focus of attention for young recruits who listened in awe to his first hand account of the attack upon the Russian guns at Balaclava by the 13th Light Dragoons in which he served. Since a number of ex-British soldiers served in the ranks, there were always a few shiny medals to be seen on a full dress parade, awards for Imperial campaigns in India, Afghanistan, Egypt and other parts of Africa.

Shortly after the 1885 Rebellion, the government decided to award a medal to those who had taken part in its suppression. In addition to the medal, the participants were to receive a land grant or scrip to the value of $80 with which to purchase land. When the terms of the award were made public, however, a controversy arose because the members of the NWMP were ruled ineligible for the medal and the other benefits. The move to exclude the Mounted Police from recognition for its part in the rebellion was seen as another slap in the face by Gen. Middleton, who was popularly believed in the West to be the villain behind the ruling. Many were angered by the decision. After all, their supporters argued, eight Mounted Policemen had been killed and eleven wounded in the fighting.

Agitation started almost immediately to have the qualifications for the medal changed. Nicholas Flood Davin, in his influential newspaper, called upon the government to remove the injustice and treat the police in exactly the same manner as the militia.[74] As a result of this and other protests, Ottawa gave the matter second thought. In July

1886, an Order-in-Council was approved which extended the award to the NWMP, but only to those members who were actually under fire.[75] About 187 medals were eventually presented under these terms, leaving several hundred who had served during the rebellion without seeing action with no recognition whatsoever.

The members of the Force and those who championed their cause still strongly believed that this change of heart did not go far enough. They continued to argue that all the police should receive medals, land grants and scrip. As far as the militia was concerned every soldier was treated alike. It did not matter whether one private spent the entire campaign peeling potatoes in the cookhouse, whilst another took part in the charge at Batoche. They both received the medal and other benefits as long as they were at a point west of Port Arthur when hostilities officially ceased on 3 July 1885. In refusing to treat the Mounted Police on an equal footing, successive governments argued that in leaving their homes, employment and families in the East the volunteer militiaman had sacrificed more than the police who were on the spot simply doing the job they were paid to do.

Many westerners, however, continued to see the issue as another injustice imposed upon them by an insensitive federal government and periodically kept up the agitation for a change in policy. During November 1886, the Council of the NWT passed a resolution in favour of medals and scrip for all members of the NWMP.[76] In 1894, Davin, now the sitting member for Assiniboia West, brought the subject up in the House of Commons. His demand for equal treatment was turned down.[77] After the Liberals came to power, Frank Oliver, another western member, raised the issue again in the Commons. Replying for the government, the Minister of the Interior indicated that his party would stick by the decision made earlier by the Conservatives.[78]

Unforeseen events, however, were about to occur that would lead to a modification of the government's position. Following the Diamond Jubilee in 1897 there was an upsurge in imperial sentiment in Canada. When war broke out in South Africa in 1899, public pressure forced a reluctant Laurier to agree to send Canadian troops. The NWMP played an important role in recruiting for the Canadian contingents, and over 200 of its members were given leave of absence to serve in the Canadian Mounted Rifles and the Lord Strathcona's Horse, two mounted regiments. Many of them served with distinction, most notably Sgt. A. H. L. Richardson who, in 1900, was awarded the Victoria Cross for valour. At home, the contribution of the Mounted Police to the war was applauded with pride. It was probably no coincidence that only a few days after

Richardson's heroic action was made public, that the government passed an order-in-council granting the 1885 medal to all members of the NWMP who were serving during the rebellion regardless of their duties.[79] The *Edmonton Bulletin* linked the change of heart to the record of the members in South Africa and congratulated Ottawa on removing an injustice.[80]

The decision was welcomed but it still did not end the controversy. Although all the police were now entitled to the medal regardless of whether they saw action or not, they were still denied the land grant or the financial remuneration that had been offered to the militia. They, their families, friends and later their veterans' association continued to lobby for what they insisted was injustice. The dispute would be raised again and again, both in and out of Parliament for another 30 years until it was finally resolved. In July 1931, Prime Minister R. B. Bennett, a long time resident of Calgary and its member in the House of Commons, announced that the government would make a grant of $300 to every surviving ex-member of the NWMP, or his heirs, who had served during the rebellion.[81] As land grants by this time were out of the question, this amount was agreed upon as fair and just compensation for what had been originally available to the militia. To many a needy police pensioner or his descendants in the middle of the Great Depression, the sum represented a small fortune. The deadline for grant applications was 1 December 1934, and by that time, 194 claimants had come forward and accepted the settlement.

Incredible as it may seem, this was not the end of the medal story. When the government in 1900 extended the award to all members who had served during the rebellion, several hundred men became eligible. Fifteen years had passed, however, since Louis Riel and his followers had taken up arms against the state. Some of the men were still serving in the police, but others had died or taken their discharge and disappeared. A few had deserted, and others had been dismissed. The latter two categories were ruled ineligible to receive the award. Although it was widely publicized in the newspapers at the time, many former members did not claim their medal. The task of tracing them or their next of kin was to take many years. From time to time a veteran or his descendent did come forward. As late as 1935, the *RCMP Quarterly* published a list of ten names of former members whose medals were still unclaimed.[82] The last presentation to an ex-member of the NWMP was made in October 1945, more than 60 years after the last shot in the rebellion had been fired.[83]

Chapter 16

Mounted Men at Arms

> I don't know the actual musketry standard required from the N.W.M.Police, but I should think it is very low . . . I was amused to see the English newspapers talking of our first Contingent as 'Canadian marksmen'. I suppose the popular idea is that Canada is a wild country full of good shots – the fact is that musketry is at the very lowest ebb here.
>
> Lord Minto 17 December 1899[1]

The Governor General, Lord Minto, did not have a very high opinion of the shooting abilities of the Canadian Forces, including the Mounted Police, who at the turn of the century were being sent to South Africa to fight the Boers. He knew that many Britons regarded Canada as a forest wilderness inhabited by savage Indians and wild beasts. When they conjured up an image of a Canadian settler or a Mountie with a gun in his hand, they likely thought of the novels of James Fenimore Cooper and his woodsman hero Hawkeye who could hit a fly at a hundred paces with his trusty musket. The Americans, on the other hand, came to see the Mountie's prowess with a gun in the image of their own western epics. Sgt. Preston and Sgt. King, the comic book heroes, were quick on the draw with their pistols. They could shoot a gun out of the hand of an outlaw faster than one could blink an eye. The truth, of course, was somewhere else. In fact, during the Herchmer years the police rarely resorted to the use of guns in carrying out their duties. The primary reason that the NWMP carried firearms was not to assist in capturing criminals, but rather because of the possibility that they might be attacked by Indians. In their relations with Native people, however, the police took pride in their being able to defuse potentially violent confrontations without the use of weapons. The down side of this was that their reluctance to resort to that kind of force may well have cost Sgts. C. C. Colebrook and W. B. Wilde their lives. As to their expertise with firearms, for the most part they did not have

enough opportunity to practise to develop into a body of exceptional marksmen.

The first shoulder arms[2] issued to the NWMP in 1873 were the British-made Snider-Enfield Carbine Mark III and the Snider-Enfield Short Rifle. A year later a handful of Martini Henry Rifles were acquired. Apart from a few weapons privately owned by some of the officers, these weapons were all .577 calibre single shot breech loaders, far inferior in firepower to the Spencer, and Winchester repeating rifles which the Plains Indians were beginning to acquire at the time. Just how far they were out-gunned was brought home to the Force in dramatic fashion in 1876 when the Sioux destroyed five companies of the U.S. Seventh Cavalry under Custer at the Battle of the Little Bighorn.

The danger of violence erupting on the prairies became acute after the Sioux crossed the border to seek refuge in Canada. The police decided that it was time to improve their firepower. The make of weapon they chose was later to have an adventurous and romantic association with the frontier days of the American West. In 1878, the first shipment of .45-75 calibre Model 1876 Winchester Military Carbines was received. Made by the Winchester Repeating Arms Company of New Haven, Connecticut, these repeating rifles had a magazine capacity of eight rounds. In 1882 the company modified the model expressly to meet the needs and suggestions of the Force.[3] Comm. Irvine described the "new pattern" as a "most excellent arm . . . well adapted to our use".[4]

Unlike the Sniders which were carried in a leather scabbard or bucket strapped to the right side of the saddle, the Winchesters were attached to the horn of the western-style saddles then in use by a sling. By 1885, the Winchesters had replaced the Sniders as general issue throughout the Force. Those of the latter that remained were placed in storage, loaned out to rifle clubs, and gradually sold or otherwise disposed of.[5] Comm. Herchmer reported in 1895 that 45 Sniders were being used by local rifle associations. He also recorded 20 Martini Henrys still held by the Force, 10 at Prince Albert and 10 at Fort Saskatchewan.[6] Two years later the Force still had a few Sniders in its inventory.[7]

The durability of the Winchesters was not really tested until the 1885 Rebellion, when they do not appear to have fared very well. Supt. W. M. Herchmer who was with the police at the engagement with the Indians at Cut Knife Hill reported that the Winchesters did not stand up to hard work, the extractors sometimes breaking after a few rounds and rendering the weapon useless. He recommended their replacement with a more serviceable arm.[8] Other faults were noted as they aged. Cpl. Donkin found that the sighting on them was inaccurate, especially at ranges over 500 yards.[9] In 1887, Comm. Herchmer stated that:

> The favourite arm with the western prairie men is not giving good satisfaction in the Force, the ease with which it gets out of order and its liability to break off at the stock, are serious drawbacks to its efficiency.[10]

The older issues were gradually wearing out, he continued, and it was time to look for a better weapon.

It was a recommendation he was to repeat for several years. The big problem with replacing the Winchesters was of course the cost. While Ottawa delayed a decision in the matter, the armourer at Headquarters was kept busy fitting new barrels and other parts to the carbines to keep them serviceable.[11]

The NWMP had a difficult time finding and retaining an armourer, a qualified firearms expert. The position was a vital one if the weaponry of the Force was to be kept in working order. Under the supervision of the supply officer, the armourer sergeant or staff sergeant was responsible for the repair and maintenance of all firearms. In 1883, the Force was fortunate to engage a former Winchester employee named John McNamara to fill the position. Earlier that year Deputy Minister White had sent a notice to the American company advertising the vacancy. It set out the pay at $1 per day, that of a staff sergeant, and promised free passage to Regina. As further inducement, it informed those interested that a married man would be acceptable, although the Force would not be responsible for the wife's transportation. The duties were described as the repair and refitting of the arms of the Force. It was further stipulated that the successful applicant would not have to do any "military duties" except in an emergency, and that he would be able to earn extra money by taking on private work.[12]

The Winchester Company recommended John McNamara and he was duly sworn in at Ottawa on 27 June 1883. McNamara turned out to be just the expert the Force was looking for, but he eventually became disaffected by Herchmer's dictum that anyone who wore the uniform and looked like a member of the Force should also be able to act like one. Just like the other specialists, the veterinarians and hospital stewards and pharmacologists, he resented having to do drill and attend parades. In 1888, when his time expired, he refused to re-engage unless he was excused from them. He claimed quite rightly that he had been promised this in 1883. The Commissioner refused to make an exception, however, and McNamara was sent on his way.

Ottawa was eventually forced to replace some of the Winchesters. The company was no longer making the Model 1876; it had been superseded by others and was becoming obsolete. In 1891 A. W. Hooper, the President of Winchester, wrote to Fred White to warn him that the stock of spare parts for the police model was getting low, and the company did not intend to manufacture any more once they were sold.[13] Their replacement it was decided would be the Lee-Metford Magazine Carbine, a .303 calibre bolt action weapon with a magazine capacity of six rounds. This British-made firearm had already been adopted by the British Army and the Canadian Militia. With the Winchester the police had been dependent upon an American manufacturer, and out of step with the arms used by their own militia and the British Forces. The change to the Lee-Metford was encouraged by contemporary calls for closer imperial unity in military and other matters.

The Lee-Metford was first recommended by Supt. A. B. Perry in 1888. He expressed the view that it was a most superior arm that would fill the Force's need for a magazine rifle of exactness, precision and strength. In 1894, authority was obtained to buy three of the weapons as samples.[14] These evidently satisfied the board of officers that oversaw their testing, as the following year 200 of the Lee-Metfords were purchased from the imperial authorities at a cost of $18.47 each.[15] In his annual report for 1895 the Commissioner noted that the receipt of the new carbines enabled him to retire a large number of the worst Winchesters. Of the 200 Lee-Metfords, 150 were issued to "D" Division at Macleod, still considered the most likely area of confrontation with Native people, 20 went to the Yukon with Supt. Charles Constantine's detachment, and the rest were retained at Headquarters in the hands of "crack shots".[16]

The annual shoot at Regina that year between the best shots in each division gave Herchmer an opportunity to put the new weapons to the test. He divided the marksmen into two teams, one armed with Winchesters and the other with Lee-Metfords, and arranged a match between them at distances up to 700 yards. The demonstration showed that the Winchester was more accurate than the British firearm at ranges up to 500 yards, while the Lee-Metford was superior at distances beyond that.

Faced with these results, the Commissioner suggested that the Lee-Metford should be more thoroughly tested before any more of them were purchased.[17] They also turned out to be something of a problem when carried on mounted patrols. The police soon found from experience that if carried all day in a scabbard, the Lee-Metford would rub against the back of the horse and produce sores. When attached to the horn of the saddle like a Winchester, its mechanism was liable to be damaged. The cumbersome answer they came up with was to place the muzzle in a short seven inch leather bucket attached to the front of the saddle, the butt being supported by a strap that went around the elbow of the rider.[18]

As it turned out, with the period of fiscal restraint that followed and the reduction in strength, no more Lee-Metfords were purchased. The police had to make do with the increasingly obsolete Winchesters that remained, refitting and repairing them with such parts as the company still had. It was the Winchester that were taken to London by the Diamond Jubilee Contingent in 1897. In fact some of them were still in service when the First World War broke out in 1914. In 1901, after the disruption of the war in South Africa, Comm. Perry proposed buying more Lee-Metfords, but by then they had been superseded by the Lee-Enfield Magazine Rifle Mark I.[19] The police acquired a quantity of these in 1902 as well as some samples of the controversial Canadian-made Ross Carbine Mark I.[20] Their arrival opened up a new chapter in the history of shoulder arms in the Force.

In 1882, the authorized strength of the NWMP was increased from 300 to 500 men. Additional uniforms, weapons and other items of equipment were needed to outfit the new recruits. To meet their needs for a side arm, Comm. Irvine requested a further supply of 200 Adams revolvers, the British-made weapon that had been in general issue throughout the Force since its inception in 1873. He discovered, however, that the Adams had already been discarded by the imperial military authorities in favour of a new pattern Enfield, and it was 200 of these that arrived from England later that year. Irvine was entirely satisfied with their performance. The Enfield Mark II was a double or single action .476 calibre revolver with a cylinder capacity of six rounds. Like its predecessor the Adams, it was on the heavy side, weighing 36 oz. Gradually the Enfield replaced the Adams. Another 600 of them were purchased in 1885 at a cost of $9,453.49, and a further 300 in 1886 at $19.95 each, all through the War Office in England.[21] At the end of his first year in office Herchmer was able to report that the entire Force had been supplied with Enfield revolvers which were "eminently adapted for our use."[22]

Satisfaction with the Enfield seems to have slowly eroded away. By 1896, it was receiving more and more criticism. Many of the complaints concerned its weight. The commanding officer at Battleford described the Enfield as a "heavy" and "clumsy make" compared with other revolvers that were available. He reported that although they were kept cleaned and oiled, they were constantly out of order.[23] The Commissioner agreed that they were "much too heavy" and a year later recommended their replacement with a "lighter and more modern weapon".[24] Firearms manufacturers of the day were frequently bringing out new and improved models. It seems that the Enfield had in so short a time become obsolete. There were new and better weapons on the market. If the police stayed with the Enfield, they would encounter the same problem they were having with the Winchester rifles, that of a dwindling supply of spare parts. The British forces had already abandoned the Enfield in favour of the Webley and this, as one authority has explained, no doubt had something to do with the call for a new side arm.[25] As with the rifles, however, uncertainty over the Force's future delayed any decision in the matter, and there were several years of experimentation with various types of weapons including Colts and Lugers and automatic pistols before the Colt New Service Revolver began to replace the Enfield as the general issue side arm in 1904.[26]

In addition to the Enfields, the NWMP also acquired in the 1880s and 1890s a number of pocket revolvers. Their purchase was another sign of the changing role of the police. Until this time the choice of weapons had largely been determined by their suitability for military action. The pocket revolvers were designed to assist them in carrying out their increasingly civil role as peace officers. In 1887, Comm. Herchmer remarked that he proposed to arm the men who searched trains for illegally imported supplies of alcohol with a smaller weapon than the Enfield which could be carried in a less conspicuous manner. Working in plain clothes they would thus draw less attention to themselves.[27] Three years later he asked for a supply of small pocket revolvers to be issued to detectives and others working in towns in plain clothes.[28]

In 1886, two sample guns of unknown origin were purchased at a cost of $12 each.[29] The following year $5.50 was spent on a Winchester pistol.[30] The police seem to have found what they were looking for in 1888 when they acquired 24 Smith & Wesson .38 calibre pocket revolvers.[31] These weapons became very popular with members of the Force since they were considerably lighter and smaller than the Enfields. Whereas the latter weighed 36 oz. and had a barrel length of 5¾ inches, the Smith & Wesson weighed only 20 oz. and had a barrel 3¼ inches long. An additional 25 of these revolvers were purchased in 1890,[32] and a further 25 in 1900.[33]

"When 'arf of your bullets fly wide in the ditch, Don't call your Martini a cross-eyed old bitch."[34] The finest firearms in the world are of little use unless accompanied by an adequate supply of reliable ammunition. During the last two decades of the nineteenth century the ammunition provided to the NWMP was at times of such poor quality and in such short supply that not only were the men unable to practise sufficiently enough to become good marksmen, but commanding officers feared that if there was an Indian uprising, the Force would be at an embarrassing disadvantage.

Lack of ammunition seems to have been an early problem of the Force. In 1878, Comm. Macleod reported how much he liked the new Winchesters which had arrived, and then went on to state that he had not been able to allow the men to practise with them as he did not feel that he could spare the ammunition.[35] Two years later Supt. Winder in command at Fort Walsh recorded that although his men had practised with their rifles they had not been allowed sufficient bullets to make them into proficient marksmen.[36] Out of necessity, empty Winchester cartridges were sent to Headquarters for reloading by the armourer. In 1881, Comm. Irvine set the allowance for rifle practice at 120 rounds per man annually, which was more than that provided for under Queen's Regulations for the British Army.[37] The threat of rebellion seems to have loosened the government's purse strings and the Force received large and adequate supplies of ammunition just before its outbreak in the spring of 1885.[38]

Ammunition for the Snider Enfield Carbines and the Adams Revolvers had come from Britain via the Canadian militia stores in Ottawa. The Winchester ammunition was purchased from the company or its agents in the United States. There had occasionally been minor problems and complaints about these supplies, but nothing like the criticism that would arise after the government decided that, in an effort to promote Canadian manufacturing, the police should obtain at least some of their ammunition from a domestic source.

In February 1888, Fred White sent 1,000 rounds of Winchester ammunition made by the Dominion Cartridge Company of Montreal to Regina for testing. "This is the first of its kind made in Canada," he told the Commissioner, "and we want to 'encourage our manufacturers'."[39] The report by the examining board was not favourable. Its principal criticism was that cartridges did not contain enough powder, only 69-70 grains, instead of 75, which made accurate shooting difficult. It further noted that the powder was dirty and the rounds not waterproof.

Use of the ammunition in the divisions simply confirmed the findings of the board. At Maple Creek in 1889 the cartridges were so bad that even the best shots made "wretched scores" at the annual rifle shoot, reported the commanding officer. It was so discouraging for the men, he stopped the practice until better ammunition could be obtained from Regina.[40] Supt. E. W. Jarvis, another division commander, agreed. "It was impossible," he recorded, "to shoot well with bullets supplied by the Dominion Cartridge Company."[41] When Supt. A. B. Perry, the future Commissioner, examined a shipment of Winchester ammo from Montreal in 1891, he found that some of the cartridges were so large they could only be used by forcing them into the breech of the firearm. The company sent an expert out to inspect the supply. He found that 18,200 of the cartridges were defective.[42] In fact, some of them were so flawed that at the annual shoot at Fort Saskatchewan a number of bullets failed to reach the targets.[43]

In 1892, a bullet exploded in a carbine being used by Sgt. Bill Bruce, the Riding Instructor in Regina. Fortunately he was not seriously hurt. The board that investigated the accident found that ammunition manufactured by the Dominion Cartridge Company was unreliable and dangerous to use. In forwarding the findings to Ottawa the Commissioner told his superiors that the quality of the domestic cartridges was producing poor marksmen, and he warned that if trouble arose with the Indians, they could find themselves in an embarrassing position as a result.[44] In spite of the complaints about the Canadian-made Winchester ammunition, Ottawa continued to insist that the police use it in addition to the supplies it purchased from the United States. On the other hand, the ammo obtained from the militia for the Lee-Metford Carbines after their introduction in 1895 proved entirely satisfactory.

The Force experienced similar problems with the Enfield revolver cartridges made by the Dominion Cartridge Company. The first shipment of this ammunition arrived in Regina in 1891. Prior to this the bullets for this handgun had all originated in England. They had been found reliable, although they had been criticized from time to time for having too much powder, which caused a greater recoil and resulted in the arm being thrown high when fired.[45] The police did not find, however, that the domestic replacement was an improvement. For the rest of the 1890s they repeatedly expressed their dissatisfaction with the quality of the ammunition produced by the Dominion Cartridge Company, but it did little good. In 1901 Perry, now

Commissioner, prepared a litany of complaints that went back to 1896, but by then the history of firearms and ammunition was entering a new phase.[46]

To maintain proficiency in marksmanship the police followed the military practice of having an annual target shoot. Each year during the summer months the men were called in to their division headquarters for several days to compete amongst themselves at shooting with rifles and revolvers. For the rifle competition they were issued 90 rounds of ammunition to fire at targets ranging from a distance of 100 to 500 yards. The highest possible score in the rifle contest was 360 points. They were issued 54 rounds for the revolver competition to fire at a much closer range of targets with a total possible score of 216 points. In 1886, there were no prizes for the winners and no inter-divisional contests.

Some officers like Supt. Sam Steele argued, with justification, that bringing the men together once a year to practise in this way was not likely on its own to produce good marksmen.[47] Any other ammo issued to the men was to be used in carrying out their duties. It was carefully accounted for, in fact, many of them would complete their service in the Force without drawing their weapons to enforce the law. If they wished to practise independently or hunt, they had to buy their own ammunition. Steele was right in claiming that for many men the only time they fired a weapon was once a year at the annual shoot.

As the years went by, however, there was more and more danger that they could no longer even be assured of this amount of practice. In 1886, every division managed to hold an annual shoot. By 1888, it was discontinued in Calgary and two years later in Lethbridge too because both divisions were unable to use their ranges. Originally built on the edge or just outside these towns, these posts and their ranges were slowly being surrounded by urban development.[48] Eventually they would find alternate sites to practise shooting, but in the meantime it was suspended. The increase in patrol work and the number of detachments also had a detrimental effect. "Too many men out on patrol this summer," reported Steele in Fort Macleod in 1887, "for the musketry course to be held."[49] "Not much target practice," recorded Deane from Lethbridge a year later, "because the men are on outpost duty." Maple Creek had the same problem in 1891. The annual shoot was not held as most of the men were at detachments and it would have been too costly and disruptive of their duties to bring them in to division headquarters.[50] Comm. Herchmer summed up the situation for Ottawa in 1893:

> It is very hard now, to get all the men through the annual target practice because of the reduction in numbers, the increase in duties and the fact that sever-al posts no longer have ranges. As a result, the Force does not shoot as well as it should.[51]

There were individual exceptions of course, men who were keen on hunting or target shooting purchased their own ammunition and became crack shots. Supt. R. B. Deane left an appreciative account of the exploits of one of these. Cpl. Tom Dickson was one of four brothers from Keene, near Peterborough, Ontario, who served in the Force at this time. Deane described him as *facile princeps* with both revolver and carbine, and an "extraordinary quick and sure shot at deer and antelope". The Superintendent went on to recall an occasion when Dickson was out with a shooting party near Lethbridge. An antelope was disturbed by the hunters and it took off across the prairie bounding and weaving as fast as it could. Dickson had earlier broken the trigger on his carbine. Two or three of the men took a shot at the animal, but missed. At this point Dickson raised his seemingly useless weapon drew back the hammer with his finger far enough so that it did not cock and then released it. The carbine fired bringing down the antelope which was by then no doubt swiftly receding into the distance.[52]

There were various suggestions on how to stop the decline in marksmanship and stimulate more interest among the men in target practice. One of the most frequent put forward was that there should be more competitive shooting with prizes and badges or extra pay awarded to the winners as was the custom in the militia.[53] Herchmer pushed the idea year after year and finally in 1894 the Minister agreed to an annual competition in which all members would be eligible to qualify for medals and badges, but not extra pay.[54] Under the scheme a shoot-off would be held in each division once a year to determine the best shots with carbine and revolver. The winners or winner, sometimes one individual won both categories, would be awarded gold marksman's badges of crossed carbines or revolvers to be worn on the left sleeve of their tunic as a mark of their distinction. In addition, the top ten per cent in both classes would be entitled to wear similar badges made of worsted. As a further incentive, the winners from each division were to meet in Regina to decide who was the best revolver and carbine shot in the Force. To the victors went a gold medal in the carbine category, a silver medal in the revolver, to be worn on their uniforms, and gold crown badges to be placed above their marksman's badges.

The first competitions were held in the summer of 1894. The best man with a carbine turned out to be Cst. Ken Sinclair of "A" Division, a former Seaforth Highlander from Rosshire in Scotland. The champion with the revolver was Sgt. Maj.

James Flintoff of "G" Division, Fort Saskatchewan, a native of Newmarket, Ontario.

Such was the interest in the outcome of the championships, that Sinclair's comrades at Maple Creek had bought him 2,000 rounds with which to practise. The carbine competition was shot with Winchesters using the reliable American ammunition.[55] Sinclair and Flintoff also won the same categories in 1895 and 1896, but failed to receive any medals. For some unknown reason Ottawa had not procured them. Just prior to the 1896 competition, when Lee-Metfords were used for the first time, the Commissioner complained to the Deputy Minister that it was very discouraging for the men to be promised them and not get them.[56] Nevertheless, it was another two years before they finally received the medals.[57]

As the years went by various other shooting events were added to the annual individual competition at Headquarters in Regina. These included mounted as well as team contests. Monetary prizes, usually $20 for first place, $10 for second and $5 for third, were provided from the Fine Fund or put up by private citizens. A silver challenge cup was presented for rifle competition at distances of 200, 400 and 500 yards by Mr. E. L. Drewry, President of Redwood Factories in Winnipeg, the makers of Redwood Ale and other beers.[58] Another medium used to promote marksmanship was the formation of rifle clubs. Most divisions had one by the end of the century. The clubs led to more inter-division competition and contests between the police, the military and civilian teams. In the post-frontier period most people were familiar with the use of firearms, and hunting was still an important source of food for many families. There were clubs at "F" Division, Prince Albert, where the officer commanding, Supt. A. B. Perry, was himself a shooting enthusiast, and at "G" Division in Fort Saskatchewan by 1890. At the latter place, the club's annual meeting that year was opened by the wife of the officer commanding, Mrs. Griesbach, who fired the first shot and astonished everyone, according to the newspaper, by hitting the bull's eye with it.[59] A rifle club at "Depot" Division in Regina was also active by 1891.

One of the things that discouraged shooting practice was the high cost of ammunition. In 1891, Herchmer wrote to Ottawa to say that a number of other divisions were considering the formation of clubs but felt the members would not get much practice because of the price of ammunition. He asked the Deputy Minister for an annual allowance of 50 free rounds for each club member. To this White agreed and later ammunition was also made available to the clubs at a reduced cost. These changes seem to have spurred the organization of other groups. One of the most active of these was the "E" Division Rifle Club in Calgary. It frequently competed against the local town marksmen, and in 1896, beat a team representing the Alberta Rifle Association.[60]

The most successful of these early police shooting fraternities was located at "F" Division in Prince Albert. On more than one occasion it defeated the "Depot" club. The fact that it had one of the best ranges in the Territories may have had something to do with this. In 1890, it entered a team in the Canadian Military Rifle League for the first time, but only finished 19th out of the 42 contestants in its category.[61] During the next few years its members improved considerably. In 1897, it won first place in its category in the country-wide contest. Cst. Odilon St. Denis, a former butcher from Montreal, posted the highest individual score in the entire league. Two years later the team repeated the feat, adding another silver cup to its growing collection of awards.[62]

There is no doubt that the introduction of competitions, prizes and clubs aided in producing some first-class marksmen in the Force. In general, however, the standard of musketry of most of the men justified Minto's assessment. The quality of the ammunition continued to be discouraging[63] and the increase in detachment and other police duties prevented many men from attending shooting practice year after year.[64] Those of them who went off to fight in South Africa in 1900 had many fine qualities, but they were not the crack shots that their admirers around the world believed them to be.

During the latter part of the nineteenth century controversy raged in military circles as to the effectiveness of swords as weapons and whether or not they should continue to be carried by mounted troops. Both sides in the discussion frequently referred to the fate of the Seventh U.S. Cavalry under Custer at the Little Bighorn in 1876 to support their argument. Their proponents argued that swords never jammed or misfired as many of the Springfield carbines carried by Custer's men had. They agreed with Major General Selby Smyth of the Canadian Militia when, in 1875, he recommended that the officers of the NWMP be armed with swords because they have a "great effect on the Indian mind".[65] The sight of cold steel, it was believed, would demoralize the Indians, be it sword or lance. Custer, they opined, would have survived had his troops been equipped with swords.

Their detractors claimed that swords were cumbersome, heavy and noisy to carry. It was further said that because of the hit and run manner of Indian warfare, a soldier seldom got close enough to the enemy to use such a weapon. Custer, they agreed, was right in not issuing swords to his men because the rattling of the steel scabbards would have given his position away.[66]

In 1880, after weighing the pros and cons of these arguments, Comm. Irvine decided in favour of swords. He wanted the police armed with them because, in spite of all the drawbacks, he still believed that in any confrontation with the Indians the men could find themselves in "tight places", where a sword in addition to his carbine and revolver might be "invaluable" to him.[67] The problem of noise, he suggested, might be overcome by using wooden scabbards.

Both swords and lances had been taken on the March West in 1874.[68] Commissioned officers purchased their own as evidence of their gentlemanly status, their right to bear arms and their call to serve the Crown. The first pattern approved for officers was the 1822 British Light Cavalry model, which was encased in a steel scabbard. These were purchased by most but not all officers, while some continued to carry the sword that they had used as military officers. The NCOs were issued with the British 1853 pattern. It was also carried in a steel scabbard. Twenty-five British Army 1868 pattern lances were purchased. These had bamboo shafts and traditional red and white pennons. They were used to outfit a troop of lancers, whose appearance it was believed would have a salutary effect on the Native peoples. After the March they were used again from time to time by parties of men to again make an impression on the Indians.

Although numerous posed photographs have survived of constables holding a sword, neither that nor the lance ever became general issue throughout the Force. Comm. French was opposed to such policy, although he thought it was a good idea to keep a few in reserve. Comm. Irvine did not agree with him and, in 1880, he recommended that all members be issued with swords.

Ottawa did not fully support his plan, but during the 1880s it did purchase supplies of the 1822 pattern in wooden scabbards bound with leather both to issue to NCOs and to retain in stores. The only other significant change in these weapons occurred in 1896 when British cavalry officers adopted the 1896 pattern. Newly appointed officers of the NWMP and the Canadian Militia immediately followed suit.

Both weapons came to be used primarily as ornaments for inspections, parades and ceremonials and it was here that they were to find, especially the lances, a permanent place in the traditions of the Force. Swords and lances were frequently used in displays of mounted sports put on by the police at the annual exhibitions and fairs. The riders demonstrated their skill with them in such events as tent pegging, tilting the ring and splicing the Turk's head. More significant, however, both were used in

the first performances of the NWMP Musical Ride in 1887.[69] Frederic Remington's contemporary engraving captured all the power and excitement of the final scene as the riders advance with their lances at the charge. It was a scene that was to thrill audiences in the decades to come.

The initial objective of the NWMP as it proceeded westward on its famous march in 1874 was to capture Fort Whoop-Up and the other "whisky forts" from which American based traders plied the Native people with cheap alcohol. It was in anticipation of having to dislodge the desperadoes from these fortified positions that the Force took with it two 9 pounder Mark I muzzle loading field guns which the government had purchased from the imperial military authorities for the task. With them also went two 5.63 calibre brass mortars that had been obtained from the same source. It turned out to be quite a struggle getting the guns from Manitoba to the foothills of the Rockies. They each weighed almost 1,000 lbs. and it took four horses to pull each one of them.

They were never used against the desperadoes of course. The police arrived to find Fort Whoop-Up undefended, the existence of other forts greatly exaggerated, and the whisky traders either back across the border, or transformed into respectable businessmen overnight. The guns and mortars were retained, however, at Fort Macleod, the post that was subsequently built on the banks of the Old Man River. The site was in the midst of Blackfoot country. It was the Blackfoot tribes that the police saw as the most formidable in terms of possible confrontation. The guns were kept at Fort Macleod as a deterrent. In 1877, they had a ceremonial role in the signing of Treaty No. 7 at Blackfoot Crossing. One of them saw action in the 1885 Rebellion as a part of the Alberta Field Force. Other than that, they and the mortars remained at Fort Macleod being used for drill and firing salutes on holidays until well after the turn of the century.

The next acquisition by the Force as far as artillery was concerned was four 7 pounder bronze Mark II field guns, sometimes referred to as "mountain guns", in 1876.[70] These were obtained from Militia Stores in Winnipeg. They had been purchased by the government in 1870 from the War Office in London to accompany the Red River Expedition under Col. G. J. Wolseley. It seems fairly certain that prior to their arrival in Canada they had served with the British Army in India and had been a part of Lt. General Sir Robert Napier's force in the Abyssinian campaign of 1867-68.[71]

The four guns were taken from Winnipeg to Fort Walsh by ox cart in September 1876. An urgent need had arisen to strengthen the Force at that point. Three months earlier the Sioux had defeated Custer at the Battle of the Little Bighorn. The defeat of the American troops had created great excitement among the Canadian Indians, and it was feared that the Sioux might cross the border into Canada. Following the return of the Sioux to the United States in 1881 and the abandonment of Fort Walsh as the headquarters the year after, the 7 pounders were moved. Two went to the new headquarters in Regina and two to Calgary. Three of these guns subsequently saw action in the 1885 Rebellion. Two of them were used by "B" Battery of the Canadian Militia at the Battle of Cut Knife Hill, but lost their usefulness when their carriages broke under the heavy pounding.[72] The other was with Supt. Crozier and his command on the road to Duck Lake on that fateful day in March when they encountered a force of Métis and the first shots were fired in the insurrection.

It has been stated that on this occasion the 7 pounder, after firing a few shots, had a shell mistakenly rammed down its barrel before the powder charge was inserted which rendered it "useless for the remainder of the engagement".[73] The truth was revealed some years later by Supt. Joe Howe, who at Duck Lake was the officer in charge of the gun squad:

> The facts of the case are as follows. I brought up the 7 pounder Gun by order of Supt. Crozier and brought it into "Action Front". Nearly the whole fire of the enemy was directed at the Gun as we came up. I fired two rounds of Shrapnel and two rounds of Case when No 3 of the Gun Squad Const. Garrett was shot through the lungs and had to fall out. I called upon Const. Fontin who was one of the spare men to take Garrett's place. Then I gave the command to load with Case shot and in the excitement Const Fontin put Case shot in the barrel before the Cartridge. He turned to me and told me what he had done. I simply ordered Sergt. Smart who was in charge of the Gun to raise the trail and allow the Cartridge and shot to fall out, which they did. As the fire was very hot and we were at too short a range to be of any use with the Gun and were fast becoming surrounded by the enemy Supt. Crozier ordered me to retire with the Gun which I did, telling Sergt Smart to take the gun to the rear.[74]

In the aftermath of the rebellion the government decided to once again strengthen the armaments of the police in the event of further outbreaks of violence. Comm. Herchmer believed that the most suitable weapon for this purpose would be the recently developed Nordenfeldt machine gun, but Ottawa decided to stay with the traditional artillery pieces.[75] Through the offices of Charles Tupper, the High Commissioner for Canada in London, White ordered two 7 pounder steel Mark II field guns from imperial stores in April 1886.[76] These arrived in Regina in October of the same year and were subsequently transferred to Calgary. In March of 1886, White also arranged for two 9 pounder Mark II guns which had been used in the rebellion to be taken over from the Canadian Militia.[77] These were retained at Battleford. The addition of these

weapons did not, in fact, substantially improve the fighting capabilities of the police. The truth was that the carriages of the bronze 7 pounders, although patched up and repaired after the rebellion, were in such a condition as to render them militarily unserviceable. As White said, it would be embarrassing to go into action with them. It was estimated that it would cost $2,000 for new carriages. In November 1888, White and Herchmer pondered whether it might not be more economical to replace them with two more steel 7 pounders or with machine guns.[78] Eventually it was decided that both new carriages or new weapons were too expensive and the Force would just have to make do. The four bronze guns were declared "non-effective" and orders were given that they were only to be used for drill and salutes.[79] Ottawa was anxious, however, that the Indians should not become aware of their true condition. It would be better for security reasons that they still believed them to be a threat.

One of the 9 pounders and the 7 pounder bronze which had been used at Duck Lake during the rebellion were the last Mounted Police artillery pieces to be used on active service. In May 1897, the Cree Indian, Almighty Voice, who was wanted for the murder of Sgt. C. C. Colebrook, was run to earth and surrounded with two of his companions in a poplar bluff 17 miles from Duck Lake. After a bloody battle that left one civilian and two policemen dead, a bombardment of the Indian position by these two guns brought their heroic stand to a tragic end.

It has been stated that from time to time during this period the NWMP was in possession of a Gatling Gun, one of the forerunners of the machine gun. This in not true, although one was employed by the Canadian Militia during the rebellion. In 1884, Supt. L. N. F. Crozier had recommended the purchase of one of these weapons. Comm. Irvine, however, opposed the suggestion. For reasons not given he considered them to be unsuitable.[80] Three years later the Gatling Gun Company did send the Force information on its latest model in hopes, no doubt, of making a sale. Herchmer showed no interest in acquiring one, perhaps because the weapon had not lived up to its earlier reputation.

However, he did see machine guns as a replacement for artillery. One of the reasons for this was that a gun squad consisted of eight men. At Fort Macleod, for example, where there were two 9 pounders, 16 men would have to be kept on the post and trained and drilled in the use of the guns, quite apart from the horses that would be needed to draw them. What with the reduction in strength and the need for more and more men on patrol or detachment, this became a drain on manpower that the Commissioner could ill-afford. Machine guns, as well as being an advance in firepower, also required fewer men to handle them. Herchmer wanted every division to be provided with one.

After repeatedly recommending them, the purchase of two Maxim automatic machine guns was approved in November 1894. These weapons arrived in Regina from imperial stores in 1895. The Maxims had already been tested and adopted by the British Army. They were water cooled .303 calibre guns that could fire up to 500 rounds per minute. For Herchmer and his officers they had the advantage of mobility, and their accurate and sustained fire power suggested that they would be more effective against mounted warriors than field artillery.

Although purchased with the Indian problem in mind these guns did not remain long on the prairies. In August 1896, large quantities of gold were discovered on a tributary of the Klondike River. By 1897, the Yukon Gold Rush was under way, and the Mounted Police who were already on the spot found themselves with another frontier to tame. Almost over night the threat of prairie Indians receded as the police were confronted with the possibility of annexation of the Yukon by American miners and the undermining of law and order there by violent elements such as the notorious Soapy Smith and his gang. In 1897, the two guns were shipped north from Victoria by the Canadian Pacific Navigation Company.[81] One ended up in Tagish, the other in Dawson City. Two more of these Maxims, the air-cooled variety, were obtained in 1897-98. One of these was also sent to the Yukon where it was positioned on the border at the summit of the White Pass to protect Canadian sovereignty.[82] In 1900, the disposition of the artillery and machine guns was as follows:[83]

9	Pounders	1	Regina
		1	Battleford
		2	Macleod
7	Pounders	1	Regina
		1	Prince Albert
		2	Battleford
		2	Calgary
		2	Dawson*
	Mortars	2	Macleod
	Machine Guns	3	Yukon
		1	Unknown

* Two bronze 7 pounders were handed over to the NWMP by the Yukon Field Force when it left the Yukon.

To fulfil its role as a frontier police force, the NWMP in the Herchmer era was reasonably well armed. After some experimentation, efficient shoulder and side arms were acquired for its members. For emergency purposes, artillery pieces and machine guns were available. Lances and swords, originally considered to be useful ancillary weapons, were relegated to ceremonial roles. However, infrequent occasions to practise and shortages of good ammunition limited the marks-manship of most Mounted Policemen. This was not a grievous shortcoming, as the NWMP methods of law enforcement called for use of arms only as a last resort.

Chapter 17

Desertion

One of the chronic management problems that Herchmer inherited in 1886 was that of desertion. Every recruit who engaged in the Force agreed to serve for a stated period of time, usually five years. Once he was engaged he was legally bound to complete the term for which he had contracted. The only way he could obtain his discharge before his five years were up, apart from either dying, being medically unfit or dismissed for bad behaviour, was to purchase it. Purchasing one's discharge was a practice, like so many others, that the Mounted Police adopted from the military. By agreeing to pay a set amount for each month of his period of service that remained, a member could buy his way out of the Force. The trouble with this practice as far as the administration was concerned was that there were always too many men wanting to purchase their discharges. It was impossible to comply with all the applications without reducing the strength of the Force to the point where its efficiency would be diminished. As a result, a rule was applied that limited the number of purchases that would be approved each month. For those unable or unwilling for a variety of reasons to wait for their turn, and it could take several months, the only alternative was to desert, go AWOL, absent without leave, or take "French Leave", as it was often called. Desertion was a problem almost as old as the Force itself. Comm. George French wisely recruited more men than he was authorized to do in 1874 because he anticipated that some of them would lose their eagerness for adventure and hardship as the day for setting out on the great westward trek approached. As it turned out, he was quite correct. Just prior to leaving Fort Dufferin on the March West, 31 men deserted after hearing reports that the Sioux had attacked and killed white settlers on the American side of the border.[1] Even though he had brought spare men to take the place of those who were faint-hearted, French knew that he had to take action to punish those who had broken the terms of their engagement. He had to deter others. Once out on

the western plains it would be impossible to replace anyone who followed in their footsteps.

Before his departure the Commissioner gave orders to Insp. E. D. Clark, the officer in charge of the small detachment left at Fort Dufferin, to make an example of any of the deserters he could apprehend. Clark found an obvious target in Sub-Cst. J. G. Stone, who had not even bothered to flee across the line into the United States, but had thumbed his nose at the Mounted Police and returned openly to Fort Garry (Winnipeg) to live with his wife and children. The officer had him arrested by the local authorities and lodged in jail. Stone, however, was a former soldier and a bit of a barrack room lawyer. He hired a lawyer who soon had him released on the grounds that there was no warrant for his arrest. With respect to discipline, he had rightly calculated what others were coming to realize: that the disciplinary regulations in the *Mounted Police Act* were ill-defined or unenforceable.

Stone escaped punishment, but the failure to bring him to account started a process of clarifying the procedures to be taken with regard to deserters and increasing the penalty so that those who emulated him in the future would not so easily escape the consequences of their actions. The 1874 regulations had only provided for a fine of up to 30 days' pay or suspension from duty as a punishment for being absent without leave. When the disciplinary code was thoroughly revised in 1875, desertion was specifically listed as an offence and the penalty was increased to up to one month pay and/or up to six months imprisonment with hard labour. Furthermore, should the deserter be apprehended outside the NWT he faced an even stiffer sentence of up to $100 in fines or one year in jail, or both.

It had not been clear in the earlier legislation whether deserters could be arrested and proceeded against outside the Territories. As a result, men who were able to return home to the eastern provinces had been safe from prosecution. The 1875 amendment closed this loophole. Upon receipt of evidence of desertion from the Commissioner, a deserter could be arrested anywhere in Canada and brought before any justice of the peace.[2] The evidence took the form of a declaration signed by an officer who attested that an individual had engaged in the Force on a certain date and had absconded before his term of service was complete. His name would then be added to the list of deserters kept in a ledger at Headquarters and known as the "Deserters' Roll". As a further deterrent in 1882, the possible prison sentence was also increased to one year with hard labour for deserters apprehended in the NWT.[3]

In spite of the penalties desertion continued to attract numbers of men who were anxious or desperate to sever their connection with the Force. Between 1881 and 1885, it averaged five per cent of the total strength annually. In 1886, the year that Herchmer took command, it reached a high of eight per cent. Out of the total establishment of 1,005, 84 men deserted that year.[4] Although the railway had opened up the country and established reliable communications with the East, it was still difficult for the police to replace deserters quickly. In addition, their truancy represented a material loss in terms of the time and money spent training and equipping them.

Comm. Herchmer blamed the rise in desertion in 1886 on the hurried increase in the strength of the Force the previous year caused by the rebellion, "when many men of a class were engaged who, otherwise, would not have been accepted".[5] He went on to describe the deserters as having only a few months service and being men of a "wandering disposition, who would not be contented in any sphere of life". The officer commanding at Fort Macleod attributed the ten desertions in his division to reports that $4 to $6 a day could be earned in the mines in Montana.[6]

The number of deserters in 1887 dropped to 66 or 6 per cent of the total strength. In his annual report that year Herchmer described most of them has having very little service and being "town-bred" and therefore not fitted to the lonely life of a Mounted Policeman. Unsuitable recruits were at the root of the problem. He recommended greater care in selecting men, and in particular, a closer scrutiny of the glowing character references they presented. However, the recruiting system was riddled with political patronage and certificates of character were often not worth the paper they were written on, but the Commissioner was obliged to accept them.

Another major cause for desertion he found was the difficulty men had in purchasing their discharge. Men were constantly seeking to leave the Force because of more lucrative offers of employment, the illness or death of parents, inheriting property and the like. However, as only three per month under the regulations were permitted to purchase and they needed a speedy release, they deserted. Herchmer suggested that all men be allowed to purchase upon giving 30 days' notice, but recognized that such a course of action could not be allowed as it would reduce the strength of the Force to the point where it would no longer be able to maintain order.[7]

The haven sought by most deserters was the United States of America. Once across the line they were safe from prosecution and extradition, unless they wished to return home. They were in a situation rather like the U.S. draft dodgers who came to Canada a century later. Fewer men tried to escape westward into B.C. or eastward to Manitoba as they knew the long arm of the Mounted Police could follow them there. As a result the overwhelming majority of desertions occurred from the four divisions that bordered on the boundary: Regina, Maple Creek, Lethbridge and Fort Macleod. Very few tried to escape from the northern divisions. They were too far from the line. The telegraph would carry news of their desertion and patrols from the southern divisions would be out scouring the country for them long before they could reach the sanctuary of the "Stars and Stripes".

The men who had the best opportunities to desert were those employed on patrols close to the border, or posted to detachments a short distance from the line, like St. Mary's, Writing-On-Stone, Wood End and Milk River. Commanding officers chose the men for these outposts with care, taking into account any rumours or gossip the sergeant major may have heard around the barracks. It was not unknown, however, for the entire complement of such a detachment, perhaps three or four bored and disheartened men, to desert together.

It was harder for those at division headquarters. They often had to slip away at night leaving a carefully prepared bundle under their blankets, which they hoped would fool the night guard long enough to give them a head start on their way to the boundary on the horse they had quietly taken from the stables. Once their absence was discovered, a mounted patrol would be hard on their trail. The horse and the saddlery they took were a necessary part of the escape plan, but they were also a liability. If caught with them before they reached the line, or if they later returned to Canada, they could be charged in criminal court with theft of government property in addition to any punishment they received for deserting. It was the practice, therefore, for deserters to leave the animal and the equipment in the care of a rancher or settler close to the boundary, who would turn them over to those in pursuit. In 1887, Cpl. O'Brien from Lethbridge just failed to catch three deserters before they reached the border, but he did recover their horses, saddles and weapons from the hotel keeper at Marias River, Montana.[8]

Common stopping places for deserters from the Mounted Police were the U.S. Army posts at Fort Assiniboine and Fort Belknap to the south of the Cypress Hills. There they could not only leave their mounts and other gear, but count on a meal and some temporary shelter after their sometimes exhausting ordeal. The American commander would telegraph Regina of their arrival and someone would be detailed to pick up the horses and equipment. When U.S. Army deserters turned up in Canada, as five did at Maple Creek in 1888, the NWMP reciprocated by notifying the authorities at Fort Assiniboine and arranging for their animals and other things to be returned.[9]

As well as having a variety of reasons, men found a variety of means to desert. Some later regretted their action. Others went on to fame and fortune. Cst. John Clarence Geldert, a native of Saint John, N.B., took French Leave from Calgary in July 1886. He headed for California where he eventually became a Hollywood actor. Geldert appeared in many early western movies, often as the father of Mary Pickford, and continued to act until his death in 1935.[10]

Five other men who deserted from Regina in 1886 caused quite a sensation when the press reported that they took $2,000 of the Force's pay roll with them.[11] In spite of strenuous efforts to repair the damage done to the Force's reputation, they managed to get across the line. Actually the missing sum only amounted to $487.50, and only one man was implicated in its theft. He eventually surrendered and was charged with theft, but acquitted. The money was never recovered.

Four young members foolishly tried to desert from Prince Albert, which was almost 300 miles from the U.S. border. They were captured three days later not far from where they had started. Their officer commanding, Supt. A. B. Perry, sentenced each one to a year in prison with hard labour. In view of their short service, however, he recommended that their sentences be reduced, if they behaved themselves. At their disciplinary hearing each one gave a short explanation of the reasons for his action. Their story is one of unfulfilled expectations and disenchantment, which suggests that the recruiting system may have been at fault. All four claimed that life in the Force was not what they had expected when they enlisted in eastern Canada. One stated that he was actually deceived when he joined: "I thought it was a Civil Force to fill the duty of Policemen. I found it more like soldiering. I am not cut out to be a soldier." All asserted that they had tried to make a go of it, but that it did not work. They had considered trying to purchase their discharges but had neither the money nor necessary

political influence that they assumed was required to succeed. Applications for discharge by purchase did have to be approved by the Minister. As a result they decided to desert out of desperation. One of them actually tried again and succeeded a few weeks later by cutting his way through the ceiling of the Regina guardroom.[12]

Some men went AWOL to escape impending punishment for falling afoul of the regulations. Cst. George Keator deserted from Fort Macleod in January 1889 because he knew he was about to be charged with theft. He joined the U.S. Army and committed suicide a few months later.[13] The sergeant major at Fort Macleod in 1889 got into a "bar room fight" in the Wentworth Saloon which was watched with great excitement by a large crowd. He deserted after being charged with drunkenness and disorderly behaviour. Two constables who took French leave from Lethbridge in 1892 were described as "incorrigible drunkards" who were about to be dismissed.[14] If it was felt that a man had only absented himself from his duties and might return, the Force followed the military custom of giving him seven days to do so before declaring him a deserter.

It was not unusual for men to be induced to leave by others. A constable at Calgary in 1890 was reported to have encouraged another to desert in order that he could get the latter's job as division blacksmith.[15] Letters giving glowing accounts of the high wages to be found in Montana from members who were already across the border were a temptation to others. One man at Writing-on-Stone in 1892 decided to join his comrades in deserting after they humiliated him by accusing him of not having enough "sand".[16] Yet another constable, who was a capable musician, deserted to join a minstrel show in Washington State, which was being managed by another deserter who promised him financial advancement.[17] Cst. Lackie, meanwhile, was lured away by the excitement of the 1893 World's Fair in Chicago, taking all his savings with him.[18]

Officers were often glad to see some men go. Supt. Sam Steele was happy to see the last of two constables he described as "slovenly and useless".[19] The officer in command at Maple Creek in 1889 said "good riddance" to another one who was more trouble than he was worth.[20] A young recruit deserted from Regina whilst undergoing training because, as he later wrote, Sergeant W. B. Wilde kept picking on him and made his life miserable.[21] As might be expected, romantic entanglements were frequently the cause. Cst. George Wilson deserted from Stand Off in 1887 with a woman from the Blood tribe.[22] Cst. John Albert from Billings Bridge, Ontario, meanwhile, deserted from the Force twice. His departure on the second occasion was attributed to his involvement with a young lady.[23] In another case, a man from Regina was said to have left on account of "trouble with a woman".[24] In 1896, the *Calgary Herald* reported that a constable eloped from Lethbridge accompanied in his flight by a "married woman".[25]

Desertion also had its dangers. Cst. T. Frayer went AWOL from the outpost at Battle Creek, which was quite close the border, in February 1890. Shortly after his departure the weather turned very cold. By the time he reached Fort Assiniboine he was badly frostbitten. The American troops took him in and placed him in their hospital. It was several weeks before he recovered. Upon doing so he re-crossed the boundary and gave himself up. After a term of imprisonment, he was returned to duty.[26] Cst. Fisher faced a danger of a different kind. He was serving 12 months with hard labour in Calgary for deserting. One day while out of the guardroom on a work detail he decided to make a run for it again. The guard called upon him to halt, but he paid no heed to his threat that he would shoot. Just as he was about to dive into the Bow River he was hit in the back by a bullet. The wound was serious, but he eventually recovered and completed his prison term.[27]

The consequences of desertion were tragic for more than one young man. Cst. Vickers was tempted by the stories of high wages to be had on railway construction in Montana. He deserted from Fort Macleod on 6 June 1888. Unfortunately, he never reached his Eldorado. He drowned while attempting to ford the Kootenay River during high water.[28] In another instance, the results were permanently disabling. In March 1887, three constables deserted from Lethbridge. They were recent recruits from the East who were still "greenhorns" to the ways of the prairies. Not being familiar with the landmarks, they took the wrong trail. Their horses then managed to get away from them and they were soon lost. The patrol sent in pursuit picked up their mounts, but was unable to locate the deserters. News was later received in Lethbridge that they had managed to cross the border and reach Fort Assiniboine in a "fearful plight". It was said that one would die, one lose his feet and eyesight and the third his feet and hands from frostbite.[29]

Fortunately things did not turn out as badly as first reported, but Cst. Stephen Owens did have to have both of his feet amputated at the ankles by the U.S. Army surgeon. Friends and relatives at his home in Wellington, Ontario, started up a petition calling upon the government to allow him to return to Canada without prosecution. Owens himself wrote to Comm. Herchmer pleading for a free discharge, stating that unless he got back to his family he would starve. Even Herchmer's heart was softened by his predicament, and he forwarded the letter to Ottawa recommending his discharge.

Mercifully, Sir John A. Macdonald approved it. Owens was the only exception that was made to the rule to prosecute all deserters who were apprehended.[30]

Another deserter fell in with bad company and it almost cost him his life. Cst. Robert Maxwell from Pembroke, Ontario absconded while on duty near Banff in June 1886. Shortly after, he joined up with two tramps who were heading for the west coast. The three made their way by stealing rides on trains. At Lytton, B.C. they robbed and beat to death a rancher. A few days later they were arrested and charged with murder. At their trial before the Lytton Assizes in October they were found guilty and sentenced to be hanged.[31] At the eleventh hour Maxwell's punishment was commuted to life imprisonment. It was adjudged that he had been less responsible for the killing than the other two.[32]

Herchmer recognized that the principal cure for desertion was greater care in the selection of recruits, but he also saw, as with other disciplinary problems, that it could be reduced if the conditions of service could be improved. Duties were often monotonous, and when not working there were few diversions for the men. The establishment of canteens and recreation rooms, he wrote, would certainly stop a great deal of desertion.[33] Supt. Sam Steele agreed with him, "If recreation-room accommodation were increased, gymnasium and libraries established, canteens carried on as in the army, there would be very few desertions."[34]

Until such improvements occurred, however, the Force still had to deal with the problem of men who persisted in trying to sever their connection with it by deserting. One response to the situation was to maintain an effective deterrent. Both Comm. Herchmer and Comptroller White were determined to continue the practice of prosecuting and severely punishing all deserters who were caught, without exception. It was essential in this respect that it be clearly understood that no one, regardless of his political influence, could escape the long arm of the law. In this course of action they needed and got the support of the Minister, Sir John A. Macdonald.

From time to time politicians tried to use their position to obtain some kind of dispensation or clemency for Mounted Police deserters. Cst. Samuel Sutton took French Leave in 1886. Within a few months Sir John Carling, the Minister of Agriculture, approached White on behalf of Sutton's family, who were "good friends of the government", and asked that the "foolish fickle minded fellow" be allowed to return to his home in Ontario. The plea was made on the grounds of "humanity". His mother was described as being on her death bed, his father aged and infirm.[35] White told the Minister that since the beginning of the Force every deserter captured in eastern Canada had been prosecuted, and all those in the United States who had tried to get permission to return had been refused.

A few months later it was the turn of Mackenzie Bowell, the Minister of Customs. He wanted to arrange for the repatriation of a deserter upon payment of a $150 fine. White replied, as he did to others, that there was no exception to the rule. If the young man surrendered himself in Regina, he would be treated leniently with a six-month sentence. If caught in the East, he was liable to receive 12 months with hard labour.[36] In 1911, Philip Short, who had deserted 25 years earlier in 1886, sought a pardon from the Department of Justice. Short had become a successful and wealthy Montana rancher who wished to visit his native Montreal. White, still Deputy Minister of the police, resolutely refused to agree to such action, telling the Minister of Justice that the only deserter ever absolved of the offence was one who had to have his feet amputated because of frostbite. White did promise, however, that if Short stayed in eastern Canada and did not attract attention to himself, the police would not go looking for him.[37]

Not even a cousin of the Queen's representative could pull strings. In 1898, Cst. Robert Baillie got into a nasty entanglement with the fiancée of a saloon-keeper in Gleichen. He decided to extricate himself from his difficulties by deserting across the line. The 20-year-old Baillie was a cousin of the Governor General then in office, the Earl of Aberdeen. Herchmer had been asked to keep a fatherly eye on the young man, but nothing came from Ottawa seeking any favours for the deserter. Eventually Baillie surrendered and served out the mandatory prison sentence. Ex-Constable Robert Baillie was killed in action in 1915 whilst serving with the Australian Forces in Europe.[38]

To reinforce his position White would often recount the details of the Macpherson case to petitioners. Cst. David Macpherson was the ne'er-do-well son of Senator Sir David Macpherson, wealthy railway promoter, businessman, friend of Macdonald and Minister of the Interior from 1883 to 1885. His mother was a member of the Molson family.[39] The young Macpherson deserted from the police in October 1880, just four months after he joined. For a time he remained safely in the United States. Eventually, however, he tired of his sanctuary in Buffalo, N.Y. and wanted to come home. Pleas made on his behalf to the Department for immunity from prosecution had no effect. Those pushing his case were simply informed that his only recourse was to surrender and take his medicine. At one point he tried to sneak back into Canada across the international bridge at Niagara Falls, but was recognized, or thought he was, and ran back to the American side. Finally, when it was clear that polit-ical influence would not succeed, he returned to Regina and gave himself up. He took his punishment and then returned to duty. The point of the story as far as White was concerned was that if Macpherson with all his connections could not escape prosecution, no one could. By contrast, his father's influence with Macdonald did later succeed in getting him a commission in the Force. Evidently the Prime Minister drew the line at using the spoils of political power to exculpate NWMP deserters. Macpherson, incidentally, was not the only commissioned officer to have been at one time a deserter from the ranks.

It became the standard practice to punish those deserters who turned themselves in to six months imprisonment with hard labour and those who were caught to twelve months. This standard was rigorously applied by the Commissioner, but justice could be tempered with mercy. Men who had a good record previously and who behaved themselves during their incarceration in the guardroom could have as much as four months of their sentence remitted.[40] Sentences were also sometimes reduced in honour of a special occasion, like the Governor General's visit to the West in 1894. On the other hand, any member who assisted another to take French Leave could expect no mercy. Cst. Seymour who helped his friend Cst. Goodwin make good his escape from Calgary in 1890 received six months with hard labour for his efforts.[41]

Where hard cases or repeat offenders were concerned Herchmer was likely to take draconian measures. One incorrigible who was recaptured in Calgary and given 12 months was sent to the guardroom in Regina in leg irons. Another who deserted twice was given nine months upon surrendering for the second time. The case that attracted a lot of public attention because of it harshness, however, was that of Cst. Emille Dubois from Ste. Adele, Quebec. Dubois was a disciplinary problem with numerous defaults to his credit and was clearly not suited to the military life. On 14 July 1886, he deserted from Battleford, but his freedom only lasted two weeks. An angry Commissioner decided to make an example of him for reasons that are not fully explained. Perhaps it was his obvious contempt for authority. Herchmer sentenced him to 12 months hard labour in the Regina guardroom with "ball and chain".[42] The punishment may have deterred others, but it did not dampen Dubois' resolve to terminate his connection with the NWMP at the first opportunity. On 9 October 1886, in spite of the manacles, while still serving his sentence, he managed somehow to give his escort the slip and take flight again. Once again his liberty was short-lived. For this escapade the Commissioner gave him two months additional imprisonment and put him on a diet of "bread and water" for a week. The provost guards managed to keep him in the guardroom this time until he completed his sentence, but Dubois had the last laugh. On 29 August 1887, he deserted from Langenburg Detachment and was never heard of again.

The treatment of Dubois provided Nicholas Flood Davin, the Member of Parliament for Assiniboia West and the editor of the *Regina Leader*, with more ammunition to use in his quest for an official enquiry into Herchmer's management of the Force. The public was aware of the punishment handed out to Dubois and sympathized with him. As even the Commissioner admitted, "All civilians consider that our sentences for desertion are excessive."[43] Davin made the most of the Dubois case in his campaign against Herchmer, as yet another example of his tyrannical and unlawful conduct. It was brought before Judge Wetmore in his investigation of allegations against the Commissioner as charge 78, "Irregularity" in sentencing Cst. Dubois to "ball and chain" in addition to 12 months imprisonment for deserting. Herchmer defended himself against the severity of the penalty by claiming that it was only intended that the ball and chain should be worn by Dubois when he was out of the guardroom on a work party and liable to make a desperate run for it. In his findings the judge agreed that the Commissioner had acted irregularly. There was no provision, in his opinion, under the *NWMP Act* by which members could be sentenced to wear a ball and chain for infractions of the disciplinary code. If the Commissioner wished to award such punishment, he should have done so under the regulations provided for the operation of a territorial jail, of which the Regina guardroom was one. In other words, the Commissioner could subject members to such penalties provided he did so under the appropriate legislation.[44]

The sanctions against desertion could not be undermined by political influence and the punishment for those caught in the Territories was usually severe. Desertion, nevertheless, continued to be a headache for the Commissioner. The problem was that there were loopholes in the law. To start with, no action could be taken against those who were granted leave to return to their homes in the British Isles and did not come back. These were not too much concern to him however. They were out of sight and out of mind and, in any case, the costs of bringing them back to face the music would have been prohibitive. It was the deserters who managed to get as far as Manitoba or Eastern Canada, circumvent statutory authority in some way or other, or obtain a light sentence and thumb their nose at him, that stuck in his throat. Apart from being personally insulted, he knew that their success only encouraged others to follow them. Something,

therefore, had to be done about the state of the legislation.

The *NWMP Act* as it was revised in 1886 had two sections which provided for the prosecution of deserters.[45] These divided them into two groups as far as procedures and penalties were concerned: section 18 related to those who were captured or surrendered in the NWT, and section 24 to those taken into custody elsewhere. Under section 18, desertion was treated as a matter of internal discipline. It provided that in the NWT only the Commissioner, or a commissioned officer empowered by him, had the jurisdiction to try a deserter. Such officer could proceed to investigate the charge in a "summary way", under oath or not, as he felt fit, and upon conviction could sentence the offender to a penalty "not exceeding one month's pay, or to imprisonment with hard labour, for a term not exceeding one year, or to both".

In addition, offenders forfeited their pay whilst in prison. There was no provision for appeal over the Commissioner's head. With such control Herchmer was able to ensure that severe penalties were handed down as a deterrent to desertion.

Under section 24, the procedures were significantly different. A deserter who was arrested outside the NWT could be brought before a "stipendiary magistrate, or any justice of the peace in any part of Canada", or could surrender himself to such an official. If he was taken into custody, a written statement from the Commissioner or other commissioned officer certifying the date and term of his engagement was acceptable as *prima facie* evidence of his engagement and he would be held for trial. If he surrendered and was prepared to plead guilty, his trial could also proceed. In neither case was it necessary to return the accused to Regina. The local magistrate or J.P. had jurisdiction to hear the case and could proceed under the "Act respecting summary proceedings before Justices of the Peace".

Upon conviction the maximum penalty was also different from that provided in section 18. Instead of a fine of one month's pay, the offender was liable to be fined up to $100 in addition to 12 months hard labour, or both. A month's pay ranged from $15 to $45 depending on the rank. The higher fine for being convicted outside the Territories seems to have been put in the Act in order to encourage deserters to return to Regina and give themselves up. If that was the reason, it did not work very often.

The public tended to consider the punishment handed out by Herchmer to deserters as cruel and unjust. It seems clear that many deserters surrendered to officials outside the Territories because they anticipated more lenient penalties, or even getting off scot-free. There is no documentary evidence, but it is reasonable to assume that in some cases deals were struck between sympathetic local justices and friends or relatives of the deserter before he turned himself in. In respect to the punishment provided under section 24 it is important to note that no minimum was set on the fine or period of imprisonment that could be imposed.

In April 1887, Cst. George McCurdy, formerly a carpenter from London, Ontario, who had just completed a prison sentence for being absent without leave, deserted from Regina. He managed to elude the patrols hunting for him and reach Winnipeg. There, he gave himself up to the local police as a deserter from the NWMP. He was brought before a magistrate in the Manitoba capital, pleaded guilty, and was sentenced to five months imprisonment without a fine. When the news reached Herchmer, he was beside himself with anger. Had the Mounted Police patrols captured McCurdy, he would have received 12 months without a doubt. A few months later it was the turn of Cst. Newton. He decided to take his chances before a justice of the peace just across the border in Virden, Manitoba. It was his lucky day. The worthy gentleman on the Bench sentenced him to one month in the local jail and a fine of $25. The press reported Newton as saying that he was very happy to be out of the NWMP at that price.[46] Comm. Herchmer responded by asking the Deputy Minister to have the legislation amended so that all deserters had to be brought back to the Territories and there was no option of a trial elsewhere.[47]

In 1888, further difficulties surfaced during the prosecution of two deserters in Halifax. In June of that year Cst. William Walke was given a month's leave to visit his sick mother in Nova Scotia. While on leave he wrote a letter directly to the Deputy Minister in Ottawa seeking permission to purchase his discharge on account of his parent's illness. White agreed to the request and replied that he could have his discharge upon payment of $66. It cost $3 a month to purchase for every month that remained to be served by the member. Walke still had 22 months to go before he would complete his five-year term, hence the $66. Unfortunately, he had trouble raising the cash and his leave expired in July before he had done so. Instead of returning to Regina as he should have, he decided to take French Leave and stay in Halifax.

In October 1888, S/Sgt. Bill Bremner, the Commissioner's clerk, arrived in Halifax to visit his relatives. In addition to a well-earned holiday, there were two other reasons for Bremner's presence in the Nova Scotia capital. First, he was to keep his eyes open for any suitable recruits. Second, he was to endeavour to locate Walke and another deserter named Crockett, who was also believed to be in the city, and take steps to have them prosecuted. In doing so the Commissioner hoped to make an example of two shameless and embarrassing offenders.

Bremner had no trouble finding Walke and upon doing so telegraphed Regina for instructions. The prompt reply ordered him to arrest the deserter and charge him before a local magistrate. Haligonians were about to witness an unusual sight as probably for the first time a member of the NWMP was going to exercise his authority within the precincts of their metropolis. In fact, it is unlikely that such an act had ever taken place before in the Maritime provinces. Bremner, of course, did have the power to make the arrest. Under section 9 of the *NWMP Act* every constable of the Force was a constable in every province for the purposes of enforcing the criminal and other laws of Canada. The *NWMP Act* was a federal statute.

On 6 October 1888, the staff sergeant placed Walke under arrest and took him to the city police court where he charged him before Stipendiary Magistrate Mottow with being a deserter from the NWMP under section 24 of the statute. According to one local newspaper Bremner executed his duty in "full regimentals".[48] As *prima facie* evidence of Walke's guilt, he placed before the magistrate the sworn declaration signed by Supt. S. Gagnon, the CO of "Depot" Division, which Bremner had brought with him, that upon the expiration of the prisoner's leave on July 7th, Walke had deserted from the NWMP.

Bremner was able to identify the accused as Walke. It looked as if there could be no doubt about the outcome. The conviction would be a warning to others contemplating desertion. Unfortunately, there was a big hitch in the Crown's case. Walke must have chuckled to himself when he found out about the evidence against him. Upon being asked if he had anything to say in his defence, he placed before the magistrate his duly authorized leave pass. It granted leave from June 7 to July 9. The Crown was contending that he deserted on July 7, while his pass certified that he was still on leave on that date. Bremner rightly concluded that the date on the pass was a clerical error, and protested on those grounds to the Bench. The magistrate, however, would have none of it. He very properly adjudged that the evidence was conflicting and that the accused should have the benefit of the doubt. Walke was acquitted. No doubt delighted at having wriggled of the hook as it were, he quickly assembled the necessary $66 and purchased his discharge. Walke had the last laugh in more ways than one. Twelve years later in 1900, with the help of several politicians, including Clifford Sifton, he obtained a commission in the Force as an Inspector, and served until ill-health forced his retirement in 1911.[49]

If the Walke case was discouraging, the Crockett case was a disaster for the future prosecution of deserters. Cst. W. P. Crockett came from Moncton, N.B. He deserted from Fort Macleod on Christmas Eve 1886. By the time that Bremner ran him to earth in Halifax, he had been absent for almost two years. Whether Crockett knew that the NCO was looking for him is unknown. In this case Bremner had not brought the necessary sworn statement attesting to the desertion with him. This took several days to come from Regina by post. Upon its receipt the staff sergeant laid information before a justice of the peace accusing Crockett of being a deserter from the NWMP. The accused was then arrested by members of the local police.

The case against Crockett came up in the Halifax County Court before County Magistrate Griffin on 24 October 1888. From the events that followed it would seem very likely that this learned member of the bench had never had an alleged deserter of the famous Mounted Police appear in his courtroom before. S/Sgt. Bremner was the sole representative for the Crown. Crockett had retained a lawyer to defend him.

The information charged the accused with having deserted under section 18 of the *NWMP Act*. Bremner presented the certified declaration to the court in support of the accusation. Once again he must have felt that it was a cut and dried case. Crockett, however, had found himself a keen-eyed representative of the legal profession. Defence counsel argued quite rightly that under section 18 of the *NWMP Act* anyone accused of deserting from the police in the NWT could only be tried by the Commissioner of the Force, or other officers appointed by him, and the magistrate, as a result, had no authority to hear the case. His second contention was even more damaging. According to section 11 of the *Summary Convictions Act*, he asserted that the charge was subject to a statutory limitation of three months. In other words the accused had to be brought to trial within three months of his having deserted. In Crockett's case nearly two years had passed. The magistrate accepted both arguments and the charge was dismissed.

Bremner knew enough law to know that something was badly wrong with the decision. Not feeling capable of sorting out the legal tangle himself, he astutely and on his own initiative immediately hired a lawyer who happened to be sitting in the courtroom to represent the Crown. This gentleman advised laying a new charge under section 24 of *NWMP Act*, which Bremner did forthwith.

Crockett appeared in the same courtroom before the same magistrate three days later on 27 October 1888. Crown counsel argued that the charge under section 24 was a new one and should not in any way be confused with the earlier one under section 18, that having been found in the city of Halifax the accused could be brought before any magistrate or justice of the peace. Magistrate Griffin disagreed. He ruled that the charge was not a new one, that Crockett could not as a result be charged with the same offence twice and that, in any event, the statute of limitations still applied. In an explanatory letter to the Commissioner, the Crown counsel informed him that although he believed Griffin to be clearly in error the only way to rectify the matter would be to appeal the case to a higher court, which would take several months. No appeal was made.[50] Crockett had got away with deserting from the NWMP, a fact that would not have gone unnoticed by other deserters still in hiding, or those members contemplating following in their footsteps.

The Crockett case left the Force's policy on prosecuting deserters in disarray. As a result it compelled the administration to do something quickly about the defects and ambiguities of the legislation. "It is of course a waste of time and money to attempt to prosecute deserters until we can get an amendment to the Act," wrote the Deputy Minister to the Commissioner on 29 November 1888.[51] All a deserter had to do was hide for three months, and he could get off scot-free. White asked for a full report on the Crockett trial and a list of any other cases which would illustrate the difficulties met under the existing statutes. Earlier Herchmer had asked for a ruling from the Department of Justice on another uncertain point, namely whether a deserter could still be proceeded against even though his term of engagement had expired.[52]

The remedial legislation was not long in coming. Amendments to the Act were introduced in the Senate in April 1889, by John J. C. Abbott (later Prime Minister Sir John J. C. Abbott), who was the Government House Leader in the upper chamber. Why Abbott and not Macdonald, the Minister responsible, initiated the measure is unclear, but it likely had something to do with the fact that the 74-year-old Prime Minister was embroiled in the passionate and turbulent uproar involving race and religion over the *Jesuits' Estates Act*.

Whoever was directly responsible for the amendments to the *NWMP Act* in 1889 was clearly determined to use the law as far as it was possible to see that deserters would no longer escape prosecution and that, upon conviction, they would be severely punished no matter where they were in Canada. White and Macdonald appear to have supported this punitive position, while Abbott took a more humane approach. The new legislation did not change section 18 which applied to deserters apprehended in the Territories. The Commissioner and his staff retained sole jurisdiction there and thus could continue to impose harsh penalties.

It was section 24 that was the problem and it was that provision that was significantly altered.[53]

239

To start with, both a minimum fine and a minimum prison sentence were introduced. Under the earlier legislation there had been no minimum in either case. This had resulted in men convicted outside the Territories being fined as little as $25, or sentenced to only one month in prison. Under the new measure, magistrates and justices of the peace would be required to give them a minimum fine of $100 and a minimum of six months hard labour. If local authorities were unwilling to prosecute NWMP deserters, another amendment provided that they could be handed over into the custody of another member of the Force and returned to Regina to be dealt with by the Commissioner under section 18. To put a stop to relatives and friends hiding or helping deserters in any way a totally fresh provision was introduced. It provided for up to six months imprisonment for any person enticing or aiding a member to desert, or concealing or assisting a deserter.

Finally, there was the crucial question of limiting the time during which deserters could be prosecuted. Comptroller White was in favour of no time constraints. He evidently drafted the amendment so that a deserter would be permanently liable for indictment regardless of how many years passed. White believed that they should either surrender and take their punishment, or stay in the United States. Abbott, however, was strongly opposed to what amounted to permanent exile, and rewrote the clause before presenting it in the Senate.[54] Under the new clause, a deserter who remained in Canada was liable to arrest during the period for which he originally engaged and up to 12 months thereafter. In the case of those who took refuge in the U.S., they remained liable during their term of engagement if they returned home. If they went back after it expired, they were still liable for up to 12 months from the date they entered Canada.

As an example, a member who enlisted for five years, deserted from Fort Macleod after one year and hid out in Vancouver would be liable for prosecution for the remaining four years of his engagement and for one additional year immediately thereafter. Had he crossed the line into Montana, he remained liable for the four remaining years and for one more year from the date he re-entered Canada. In theory at least, if he did not return to the Dominion for another 25 years, he was still open to prosecution as a NWMP deserter. In practice no one was ever charged under such circumstances. The Mounted Police simply did not hunt down old deserters, providing they did not draw attention to themselves. The risk of public criticism, for one thing, would have been too great to hound men to the grave. Rather it became a matter of forgive and forget as the years passed. Decades later the obituary columns of the *RCMP Quarterly* would record

the service of men from this era as though they had been honourably discharged when in reality they had deserted. The new legislation, in fact, still left enough of a loophole that any deserter who kept his head down and avoided detection could still get away with the offence. The difference was that fewer were able to do so or tried to do so than had been the case before.

Macdonald was questioned on the new clauses on desertion when the legislation reached the House of Commons by Sir Richard Cartwright for the Opposition. The Prime Minister explained that it was hoped that the changes should remove any doubt as to whether a deserter could be arrested after the expiration of the term for which he engaged. When Cartwright asked him if it was intended to keep the charge hanging over a man's head forever, Macdonald replied in the affirmative. Clearly, Cartwright had not read the legislation thoroughly, and the Prime Minister was not about to enlighten him as to the details. He went on to explain that justices of the peace in eastern Canada had been letting men off with as little as a $5 fine. With these provisions, he further observed, he was merely trying to improve discipline.[55] The amendments were then passed without further comment.

As it turned out, Cartwright was not the only one who did not look closely at, or fully understand, the intent of the new section in the Act placing a time limit on prosecutions. As the years went by White received numerous letters from the friends of deserters, or from deserters themselves in the U.S., seeking an explanation of the penalty clauses. He found that it was evident from this correspondence that very few people reading the Act "catch on" to the fact that the possibility of prosecution did not permanently hang over their heads. As he did not agree with Abbott's amendment, he did not feel, in responding, that he was obliged to offer a fuller exposition on the matter. Instead, he answered such enquiries on what he called the "scarecrow" principle, keeping his explanation as lean as possible.[56] As far as White was concerned, if deserters continued to believe that they were permanently liable to arrest, so much the better for the discipline and the administration of the Force. Just how many men as a result continued to hide or remain in the United States long after it was necessary is not known.

There was only one other major change in the *NWMP Act* before the turn of the century relating to desertion. When the legislation was again amended in 1894, the prohibition punishable with up to six months in prison for anyone enticing a member to desert or aiding a deserter which had only been introduced in 1889 was entirely omitted.[57] No documentary evidence has been found to explain this.

The exact same provisions were included, however, in the new *Criminal Code of Canada* which came into use in 1892.[58] Why the switch from one piece of legislation to another? It certainly would not have been a popular law in the NWT, or anywhere else in Canada. One cannot imagine local police forces in Ontario or the Maritimes charging the father or brother of a deserter with providing him with food and shelter. On the other hand one can see an angry Herchmer doing it, and bringing a great deal of criticism on himself as a result. Putting it in the Code did give it more weight and prominence than just being a regulation under the police statute. Even so, there is no known record of a civilian ever being charged or convicted of an offence under the provisions in almost a century since it was promulgated. Perhaps it was simply that because it did relate to civilians that those responsible felt that its proper place was the *Criminal Code of Canada*.

White believed that the 1889 amendments had tied up all of the legal loose ends as far as desertion was concerned, but this was not the case. In 1898, a Department of Justice ruling put another scare into him that led to yet a further legislative amendment. During September of the latter year, Cst. H. A. Hetherington of Innisfail Detachment recognized one of his former troop mates living in the district. He immediately notified his superiors and asked for direction. The person in question was Clarence Fisher, who had engaged in Sherbrooke, Quebec, in April 1885. He deserted the following year, was captured, did his time in the guardroom, returned to duty and then deserted for the second time in 1888. As far as the police were concerned, nothing more was known of him until he was spotted in Innisfail a decade later.

Hetherington was able to determine that he had been living in the area for over 12 months. Could he still be prosecuted? The limit on time had only been attached to section 24 of the Act, to those who resided outside of the NWT. Did it also apply to section 18 under which the Commissioner or other officers could proceed against deserters found in the Territories?

Herchmer and White both wished to arrest him and punish him. Fisher it appears was not alone. Several other deserters had also been detected on the prairies. Before doing anything White prudently decided to ask the Department of Justice for an interpretation of the law.

As White later wrote, "I asked for advice and got more than I wanted."[59] In his reply E. J. Newcombe, the long-time Deputy Minister of Justice, advised the Comptroller that the time limitation in section 24 on prosecutions in other parts of the Dominion did not protect deserters found in the NWT. This was just what White wanted to hear, but unfortunately that was not the only thing Newcombe had to say. He went on to opine that section 18 had, in his view, a limitation of another kind arising from its language. Under that provision, he ruled, proceedings could only be taken by the Commissioner and his officers against a "member of the Force". A deserter who remains absent after his period of engagement expires, he continued, is no longer a member and therefore not liable to prosecution.[60]

This was bad news for White, who advised Headquarters in Regina that the Act would have to be amended to close up yet another loophole. Neither Fisher not any of the other deserters identified as living in the Territories at this time were brought to trial. The act to amend section 18 was passed in 1902.[61] Under it, deserters found in the Territories could be prosecuted under the same circumstances that applied to those caught in other parts of Canada. That is they would be liable for up to 12 months after their period of engagement expired, and if they deserted to the U.S. and later returned to the Territories, they would remain liable for up to 12 months from the date of their return. These provisions were later extended to the Yukon Territory as well. The only differences that remained between deserters arrested in the Territories and those elsewhere were the trial procedures and the possible penalties. In the Territories desertion remained a disciplinary matter to be dealt with by the Commissioner and his officers. In the rest of Canada the accused could be brought before any justice of the peace or magistrate. In the Territories the guilty party could be fined up to one month's pay, and/or be imprisoned with hard labour for up to twelve months. Elsewhere, he was subject to a fine of between $100 and $200, and/or imprisonment with hard labour for up to 12 months.

During the Herchmer years desertion gradually declined from a high of eight per cent in 1886 to an almost insignificant one per cent in 1900. To what can this reduction be attributed? There was without question a number of factors that offer a partial explanation. The determination of management to apprehend deserters, and punish them severely was no doubt a forceful deterrent. But just as important were the improvements in living conditions brought about to a large extent by the Commissioner. The addition of canteens, recreation rooms, libraries, sporting and other entertainment activities considerably bettered the quality of life of the ordinary Mounted Policeman. Like the increase in settlement and urban growth, these changes helped remove some of the boredom and loneliness that was often the immediate cause of desertion. Better recruiting had an impact, as did the introduction of a probationary period of engagement. Starting in 1898, all recruits spent the first two months of their service on probation. During that time they could obtain their discharge freely. No longer should young men who signed up one day for five years' service, awake the next to find that they were not cut out for life in the Mounted Police, and later desert. These things, however, by no means offer a complete explanation. In spite of the changes, desertion strangely enough started to increase again after 1900, reaching as high as six per cent by 1907. Through these years desertion was also a chronic problem in the Canadian Militia. There it was usually over ten per cent annually, and in 1904 amounted to 20 per cent. Poor pay has been adjudged as the main reason for this circumstance.[62] No doubt the police were also effected by the prospect of higher wages in civilian life. Even so, there would always remain that unpredictable side of human nature which would always cause some men some time to cut and run.

Chapter 18

Discipline

We cannot have a body of 300 soldiers all saints.
Sir John A. Macdonald
House of Commons, 1882

As the Minister responsible for the North-West Mounted Police for many years, Sir John A. Macdonald frequently had to face criticism from the opposition benches in the House of Commons about the conduct of its members. The two commonest accusations of the time were that of drunkenness and immoral relations with Native women. In 1880, the Prime Minister was asked to verify reports that the police themselves were a source of alcohol for the Indians, and that a constable and an officer had come to blows over a Native woman. If true, stated the questioner, the Force was clearly in need of stricter discipline. Although he stressed that they were greatly exaggerated, Macdonald was forced to admit that there was some truth in the assertions.[1] A year later, Edward Blake, the Leader of the Opposition, again raised the issue of insobriety among members of the NWMP. Once again the Prime Minister had to acknowledge the fact. There "is still a good deal of drinking at some of the posts", he replied. He went on to blame the situation on the "too kindly" disposition of the former Commissioner of the Force, James F. Macleod. His successor, A. G. Irvine, he assured the House, was in the process of restoring discipline.[2]

During the nineteenth century public disclosure and debate on the disciplinary problems of the Mounted Police was commonplace. In the small prairie communities it was very difficult for anyone to keep anything secret. No doubt the Commissioner and his officers would have preferred that what went on when men were brought before them in Orderly Room for breaching the regulations would remain confidential. Such was not the case, however. The miscreant's transgressions and his penalty would soon be gossiped all over town and, if the editor of the local newspaper found it newsworthy, it would be reported and commented upon in its columns the next day. Oddly enough, this washing of its dirty linen in public does not seem to have effected its overall reputation. Opposition critics might cause momentary embarrassment by revealing the misdeeds of individuals, but they would later join with the Government in praising the country's famous Force. Even when it was being hailed abroad for its accomplishments, its entrails were still open to public scrutiny. It seems that there was an acceptance that no one was perfect, not even members of the NWMP. A few rotten apples could be found in every barrel, or as Macdonald said, "We cannot have a body of 300 soldiers all saints." It was expected, however, that the sinners, the worst of them at least, would be weeded out and punished.

To later generations this realistic appreciation of the North-West Mounted Policeman became obscured by the development of the image of the heroic Mountie. Both in the nascent silent film industry and in popular literature of the same period the Mounted Policeman appeared as a stereotypical, one-dimensional flawless character who could do no wrong. Of the hundreds of films and adventure stories that were produced, few featured a bad Mountie. If they did, it would turn out that he had been framed or tricked in some way and his moral superiority would win out in the end. Of course, much of this was due to the Americanization of the image by the Hollywood movie industry. As one authority on the subject has written, "The movie Mountie was almost invariably brave, noble, honourable, courteous, kind, and trustworthy - all the standard Boy Scout qualities, to go with the hat."[3]

Americans were not entirely to blame, however. Canadian writers too had a role in the first decades of the twentieth century in promoting a romantic and heroic view of the NWMP which consciously and carefully omitted references to behaviour that they had become ashamed to admit. One will look in vain in the first popular histories of the Force, in books like Chambers' *The Royal North-West*

Mounted Police (1906), Haydon's *The Riders of the Plains* (1910) and MacBeth's *Policing the Plains* (1931), for a description of a Mounted Policeman, "warts and all". Reference has already been made to the quarrel between Sam Steele's son and T. Morris Longstreth over the latter's comments on the drinking habits of the famous Superintendent in his book *The Silent Force* (1927). Apart from those comments, however, Longstreth's work was simply another typical heroic account of the history of the NWMP. As for the son, Harwood Steele, he produced a hagiographical history of the Force's exploits in the North entitled *Policing the Arctic* (1936), in which the characters of the men are blessed throughout with divine purity. Writing of the members who manned the posts at the top of the Chilcoot and White Passes in 1898, he compared them to "angels" guarding the "gates of Paradise".[4]

Perhaps because of their sense of loyalty to the "Old Force", autobiographies by ex-members were even more reticent to reveal matters that would not only tarnish their own reputation but the image of the police that was, by then, widely accepted. Sam Steele's autobiography, *Forty Years in Canada*, appeared in 1915. It was followed a year later by Supt. R. B. Deane's *Mounted Police Life: A Record of Thirty-One Year's Service, 1883-1914*. Both were proud and conceited men who had no difficulty casting their careers in the Force in the courageous mould that the world by then expected, without revealing their own shortcomings. A better case in point, however, was ex-Insp. Cecil Denny. In 1905, he produced a partly autobiographical account of the early years of the Force entitled *The Riders of the Plains*. He later expanded this work and it was re-published in 1939, several years after his death, under the title *The Law Marches West*. Denny served as an officer in the NWMP from 1874 to 1881. He took part in the March West, and his account of this and the other stirring events in the early history of the Force in which he personally participated is a valuable one. Like many others, however, it carefully avoids certain subjects.

At the time of his death in 1928, he was an honoured and respected pioneer who was recognized as having played an important role in the development of the prairies, which indeed he truly had. Upon his tombstone in Union Cemetery, Calgary are the words:

> Captain Sir Cecil Edward Denny Bt.
> Crossed the plains in 1874 as Inspector in the original North West Mounted Police Co. founder of Forts Macleod and Calgary
> Honorary Chieftain in Blackfoot Nation
> Indian Agent, Government Archivist, Explorer, Pioneer, Adventurer & Author

Denny had succeeded to a baronetcy in 1922 when a half brother had died without issue. All that the epitaph says is deservedly true. It is what it does not say that is illustrative of how times had changed.

Denny's service as a commissioned officer in the NWMP did not end nobly. In 1881, he was forced to resign his Inspectorship for what his immediate superior described as "disgraceful" behaviour "unbecoming an officer and a gentleman". Although he had done some exceptionally good service, he continued, the sooner "he is out of the Force the better". The conduct in question involved his having "criminal connection" with a married woman, and breaking into her husband's house in an attempt to assault him. He was convicted of the latter offence before his former commanding officer, Colonel Macleod, in his capacity as a magistrate, and fined $50.[5] Denny later became the Indian Agent for the Blackfoot Reserve. In 1886, the Oblate missionary Father Lacombe, who knew him well, informed officials of the Department of Indian Affairs in Ottawa that Denny was a "notoriously dissolute character, a libertine and addicted to excessive use of alcohol". The priest's views agreed with similar reports the Department had had from other sources, which was one reason why Denny lost his job on the Blackfoot Reserve not long after.[6] In the years that followed, Denny had several brushes with the law. In 1888, he was convicted of illegally possessing alcohol.[7] Four years later, he was charged with shooting with intent to cause bodily harm, but acquitted.[8] In 1893, he was so badly beaten up in a bar room fight in the Macleod Hotel in Macleod that he spent several days in the local police hospital recovering.[9] A few months later he was accused of selling liquor to Indians, but once again the case was dismissed. For much of the remainder of his life he lived on the edge of poverty, begging odd jobs from time to time from the police or the Department of Indian Affairs.

Denny's case was not unique in the Mounted Police and other police forces, but by the end of the First World War there were strong social sanctions against exposing the disreputable side of their past. In 1919, Lasky Films produced a movie entitled *Tyrant Fear*. This was the same studio that had made *The Squaw Man* in 1913, a big hit and generally considered an historic milestone in the Hollywood film industry. *Tyrant Fear* had a scene in it which showed a member of the NWMP drinking in a brothel. Such an event had actually happened many times in the past, but there was such a public outcry over the portrayal that the distributors, Famous Players, withdrew it from circulation in Canada, and in Britain it was edited to remove all reference to the Force.[10] The reputation of the Mounted Police had become a sacred cow, and attempts to sully it would no longer be tolerated.

In the nineteenth century the London Metropolitan Police and the Royal Irish

Constabulary were used as models for organizing police forces throughout the British Empire. Sir Robert Peel's role in founding the famous London force based upon his idea of the "new police" is well known. What has not received as much publicity is that, as Under Secretary for Ireland in 1814, it was he who was responsible for the passage of the *Peace Preservation Act*, a bill that provided for fundamental reorganization of the police in Ireland and led eventually to the creation of the Irish Constabulary in 1836. The Force was granted the prefix "Royal" in 1867.

These two bodies were in many ways quite different. The London Force unarmed and civilian in organization contrasted with the para-military structure and weaponry of the Irish Constabulary. In part this was due to the fact that they had been founded to police very different communities. They did have one thing in common, however, a rigid disciplinary code. One of the things that had discredited the early forms of policing in Britain was that the watchmen, the magistrates' constables and the Bow Street Runners were often considered little better than the criminals themselves. As Peel saw it in his nine principles of policing, if any reform of the police was to gain public acceptance and be successful, the policemen would have to observe standards of behaviour that the people they served would respect.[11] Both the RIC and the Metropolitan Police developed authoritarian systems of discipline which stressed rigid adherence to rules and unquestionable obedience towards superiors. These practices set the standard for other police forces for decades to come. More than a century would pass before progressively minded lecturers in police management courses would disparage this "ours is not to reason why" military type of discipline as negative and punitive, promoting in its place a persuasive management style that used indirect techniques of control and positive incentives.[12]

It is quite clear from the private papers of Sir John A. Macdonald that he used the Royal Irish Constabulary as a model in planning the Force that he hoped would bring about the peaceful admission of the western prairies into the Dominion of Canada. As early as 1869, he wrote to a friend saying, "It seems to me that the best Force would be, Mounted Riflemen, trained to act as cavalry . . . this body should not be expressly Military but should be styled Police, and have the military bearing of the Irish Constabulary."[13] He later obtained material on the organization of the Irish Force from an old cabinet colleague living in England.[14] The Prime Minister was likely aware that in 1858, British Columbia had obtained an ex-member of the RIC to organize its colonial police force and that

Newfoundland in 1870 was in the process of doing the same thing.

The influence of the RIC can be seen in the disciplinary procedures found in the act providing for the establishment of the NWMP in 1873.[15] Under section 20 of the legislation the Governor in Council was given authority to make "rules and regulations for . . . the good government, discipline and guidance of the Force". It also provided for fines of up to 30 days' pay for those guilty of contravening such regulations. Section 22 gave the Commissioner, or any officer delegated by him, authority to suspend from duty or dismiss any member. Under section 24 the Commissioner, or an officer delegated by him, could, at his discretion, hold a special enquiry, in which all evidence would be taken under oath, into any complaint against a member or into the conduct of any member dismissed or under suspension.

These provisions were by no means clear and comprehensive, no procedure was set out for trying offenders, for example, but they did follow the civil principles set out in the rules and regulations of the RIC. Those accused of serious breaches of discipline would be tried by courts of enquiry. Punishment was limited to dismissal, suspension, demotion or fine. There were no provisions, as under military law, for imprisonment, solitary confinement, punishment drills, flogging and even execution in time of war. Two things should be noted about the original disciplinary system as they would become controversial later during Herchmer's command. Firstly, the Commissioner could delegate his authority to administer discipline to other commissioned officers. Next, when enquiries were held to look into charges and complaints, all the evidence brought before them was to be given under oath.

In the haste to organize the Force in the fall of 1873, nothing further was done about establishing a disciplinary system. In November Comm. French complained to Ottawa from Lower Fort Garry where he was with the first contingent of recruits that he was unsure as to whether he could impose the penalties set out in the Act as there were still no regulations setting out the offences and no trial procedure had been formulated. Obviously he was having difficulty with a few troublemakers. The government responded by amending section 22 of the legislation in the spring of 1874 so as to include some 50 offences such as disobeying an order, being intoxicated, making false statements, grossly immoral conduct, striking a superior, gambling and communicating with the press.[16] This list of offences was adopted almost word for word from the "Rules and Regulations" of the Royal Irish Constabulary.[17] The punishment, too, for those found guilty of transgressing these regulations remained the same as in the Irish Force, either dismissal, suspension, demotion or fine.

A year later, however, the disciplinary system that was evolving in the police took a turn in a different direction. In 1875, section 22 was amended yet again and the civilian style of discipline abandoned in favour of one closer to that of the military. The number of offences was reduced and a procedure for trying offenders introduced. Under the latter provision, all charges against members, except officers, were to be put in writing. The Commissioner, Assistant Commissioner, or the officer commanding any post was then empowered to hear the charge in a "summary way", under oath. The most important change related to punishment. If the adjudicating officer convicted the offender, he now had the option of sentencing him for up to six months imprisonment with hard labour, in addition to any fine of up to one month's pay. A prison term of up to one year was also introduced for desertion. In an amendment to section 25 members, other than commissioned officers, also became subject to arrest in certain circumstances.[18]

Under the new provisions the procedures for dealing with offending commissioned officers were to be different from those for the other ranks. Officers would remain subject to suspension from duty and an investigation into their conduct by way of enquiry. The legislation did not make them liable to fine or imprisonment. The other ranks, meanwhile, could now be arrested, charged with an offence and investigated "then and there" in a "summary way" free of too many formalities and fined and/or imprisoned if convicted. No provision was made for appealing the results of the summary trial or the penalty.

Clearly the civilian style of discipline had in the eyes of those in authority not worked. The truth was the March West and the other events of 1874 had been a great learning experience for all concerned. The NWMP had, in the process, lost its innocence. The problem of punishing deserters under the existing legislation has already been noted. In addition, there were several incidents that year of men refusing to obey the orders of their superiors. In two cases the disobedience was organized and collective, amounting in the opinion of Comm. French almost to mutiny. To describe such events the Mounted Police usually used the word "Buck" rather than "Mutiny", from the phrase "bucking," i.e., resisting the system.

In December 1874, all of the sub-constables and one NCO at Fort Macleod had refused to turn out on parade. The NCO, who was the ringleader, drew up a list of grievances which complained of the poor working conditions and the fact that the men had not been paid since they had left Manitoba several months before. The commanding officer, Asst.

Comm. J. F. Macleod, met with the malcontents and persuaded them to return to duty. The NCO he later demoted. In reporting the matter to Ottawa, Comm. French expressed regret that he did not have more power to punish the offenders.[19] A few weeks later, in February 1875, 13 sub-constables of the detachment under Insp. Carvell at Swan River also refused to obey orders, and put their demands in a written petition. Once again the protest was smoothed over, but in his report Carvell admitted that he had been uncertain as to how to act because the Commissioner had not delegated to him any disciplinary authority. These, and other incidents, appear to have convinced Comm. French that the existing penalties were insufficient to maintain order. In March 1875, he wrote to the Minister in Ottawa recommending that he be given power to imprison members for gross breaches of discipline.[20]

The problems of discipline in the NWMP had, in fact, already been aired both in the newspapers and in Parliament. In the House of Commons on 25 February 1875, Conservative MP, Charles Tupper questioned Télésphore Fournier, the Minister of Justice, on the state of affairs in the Force. Having heard that the present legislation did not give officers enough power to preserve subordination and prevent desertion, he asked if the Government intended to change its constitution. He went on to suggest that the difficulties over discipline might better be resolved if the Force was incorporated with the militia. Replying on behalf of the Government, Fournier denied any suggestion that the Mounted Police had not been a success. He admitted that there had been some disciplinary problems. However, he put these down to the "novelty" of the organization, and made it quite clear that there was no intention of transforming the Force into a regular military unit. Another member agreed that it had been a success, but suggested that the government should give more power to officers to punish men for deserting and refusing to obey orders. The Minister responded by revealing that it was, in fact, the government's intention to bring in a bill to do just that.[21] A few days later Fournier introduced the amendments that resulted in the changes outlined above. On 8 March 1875, they passed second and third reading in the House without any debate.[22] Everyone, it appears, agreed that discipline in the NWMP needed stiffening up.

It would be later argued that the evolution of a more military style of discipline was due to the fact that so many of the officers and senior NCOs were ex-soldiers, who knew and preferred military ways. This was true and their presence undoubtedly served to strengthen and confirm the military style once it was introduced. They were the same men, after all, who quickly replaced their police ranks of constable and Inspector with sergeant and captain.

Far more important in bringing about the changes, however, were the frontier conditions the police found themselves in. The disciplinary practices of the Metropolitan Police and the RIC were simply not suitable to the role it had to play. The NWMP was not policing the streets of London, the counties of Ireland or the farmlands of Ontario. It had taken up position in a remote and sparsely populated territory to keep the peace among reputably hostile Indian bands whose warriors were better armed and vastly superior in number. There were no lines of unemployed men in the foothills of the Rocky Mountains from which replacements could be found for deserters and troublemakers. A violent confrontation was always considered a possibility. Mutinous behaviour and desertion could not be allowed to threaten the Force's survival. The answer was to give the Commissioner greater power to deal with misconduct quickly and in a manner that would deter others.

There were several other changes to the disciplinary procedures before Herchmer took command in 1886, some of them later controversial. In 1879, the "if he thinks fit" clause was added to the Act. The earlier changes in the legislation had provided that the officer investigating the charge against a man would hear all of the evidence under oath. With this amendment he could now use his discretion in deciding whether it would be given under oath or not.[23] The government gave no reason for this adjustment. The subject was not raised in Parliament.

In 1882, Macdonald introduced further amendments which appear to have been aimed at increasing the deterrent effect of the penalties by making them more severe. They no doubt were related to the criticism in the House of Commons in 1880 and 1881, which has already been noted at the beginning of this section, on the drunkenness among the police and their relationships with Native women. The first amendment raised the maximum prison sentence with hard labour for breaching the regulations to the same as that for desertion, one year. Secondly, those undergoing prison sentences would in future not be paid during their period of incarceration. Lastly, the Commissioner was given the power to reduce or increase at his discretion any prison sentence of more than one month imposed upon an offender by officers of the Force.[24]

Here is a summary of the disciplinary system as described in the *NWMP Act* in 1886 when Herchmer was appointed Commissioner. The Governor in Council was given the authority to make rules and regulations for the discipline of the Force. The legislation identified 22 offences as constituting breaches of discipline. These were adopted from the rules and regulations of the Royal Irish Constabulary. Some of them like "scandalous behaviour" were so vague as to cover any form of conduct that the administration wished to discourage.

Under the trial procedure, a member of the Force had to be charged in writing with having committed one or more of the offences. He could then be brought before the Commissioner, Assistant Commissioner, Superintendent commanding a post or other officer empowered by the Commissioner to investigate the charge. Such officer could then proceed in a summary way to hear the evidence, under oath only if he felt it was necessary, and decide upon the guilt or innocence in the case. If he found the accused guilty, he could sentence him to up to one year in prison with hard labour, or a fine of up to one month's pay, or both. The legislation did not provide for any means of appealing the decision, although in 1885, Irvine asserted that an offender could appeal his sentence to him, and through him to the Minister. The latter also held that an accused did not have right to counsel, nor was the Act subject to any writ of *habeas corpus*. While in prison the offender forfeited his pay.

As to commissioned officers, their misconduct was to be investigated by way of a special enquiry. No procedures were prescribed for this in the legislation, nor any punishment for those found guilty. In practice the Commissioner usually gave such tasks to the Assistant Commissioner, who acted as a one man board of enquiry. He took evidence, under oath if he felt it was necessary, and forwarded his findings to the Commissioner. He in turn sent them on to Ottawa with his recommendations. The Minister decided on the penalty. At the worst it would be demotion to a lower rank, reduction in seniority, which could effect promotion, or dismissal. Of course, officers who were accused of immoral conduct could be pressured into resigning their commission which would remove the need for an enquiry that both sides, for their own reasons, would prefer to do without.

The reason that the adjudicating officer was given discretion as to whether or not he would hear the evidence against offenders under oath or not was to enable minor offences to be dealt with expeditiously in a military fashion. The responsibility for ensuring that all regulations and orders were obeyed fell upon the shoulders of the division sergeant major, with the help of the other NCOs. Should it be discovered that a constable appeared on parade with a dirty rifle barrel or improperly dressed, his name would be taken, he would be placed under open arrest, which meant that he was confined to barracks, but not excused duties, and ordered to appear with other defaulters like himself before the orderly officer the next day. Parades for defaulters were normally held at large posts every day from Monday to Saturday at 10 a.m. At the appointed time he would be marched into the Orderly Room in soldierly fashion by the sergeant major without sidearms or headdress. There he would be brought abruptly to attention before the officer on duty. The sergeant major would inform the latter in a loud staccato voice what a horrible little man the offender was for daring to appear on parade in such a condition. The constable would then be asked if he had anything to say in his defence. If he was wise, and most were, he would reply, "No Sir", receive his punishment and be marched away. If he were foolish, he would try to offer an explanation. This would likely result in an increased penalty. It was an arbitrary process which did not accept excuses. If a mistake had been made, one should accept it, and put it down to experience.

It was only for more serious offences like drunkenness, breaking barracks, disobeying orders or striking a superior that more formal procedures were held. The accused in these cases had usually been put under close arrest which means he had been placed under lock and key in the guardroom until his trial came up. On such occasions, a charge would be laid in writing, and a written record kept of the proceedings. The evidence would be given under oath and the accused would have an opportunity to cross-examine the witnesses as well as make a statement himself. He could not obtain a lawyer or anyone else to act as his defence counsel. As to the question of placing men under arrest it was probably illegal, although like everything else in the disciplinary system to this time it had not been challenged in the courts. The Act only provided for arresting men when they refused to obey the lawful order of a superior. In practice, however, they were placed under arrest for all kinds of offences under the legislation.

By 1886, a disciplinary system had evolved in the NWMP that was largely military in character. It dispensed justice in an authoritarian way from the top down. It was strongly believed by those in command and supported by their masters in Ottawa that the ability of the police to carry out its duties was closely related to the maintenance of strict discipline. As the first published *Regulations and Orders of the Mounted Police* said in 1889 in its general instructions,

> Towards the attainment of complete police efficiency, it is essential that members of the Force should cultivate and maintain the good opinion of the country at large, by . . . prompt obedience to all lawful commands, by pursuing a steady and impartial line of conduct in the discharge of their duties, by their cleanly, sober and orderly habits, and by a civil and respectful bearing to all classes.[25]

The police administration would also have agreed whole-heartedly with the meaning and need for discipline expressed in *The Guide: A Manual for*

the Canadian Militia which was compiled by Lt. Col. W. D. Otter, the commanding officer of the Queen's Own Rifles, and published in 1880. Where the word "soldiers" appears, simply read "police":

> Discipline means obedience to orders, which is the first principle and duty of all soldiers. The best disciplined soldier is he who most implicitly obeys, not only in the letter, but in the spirit, all orders which he may receive. Without discipline there can be no real bond of confidence between Officers and men, or even between men themselves, and without it no great results can ever be attained. Life in a highly disciplined corps is always more pleasant than in one where order and regularity are not strictly maintained.
>
> Respectful obedience is the only true basis upon which sound discipline can rest. It must not have its origin in fear or dread of punishment, but should be rendered from the conviction that the orders emanate from a superior not only in rank but in knowledge.[26]

This kind of relationship that proper discipline could foster between officers and men was echoed in the memoirs of a constable who served under Supt. Sam Steele in the 1880s. Writing with admiration for his commanding officer, he described him as a "strict disciplinarian" but one who was very human and understood his men well. He knew when to look the other way, or take a lenient view of their off duty diversions.

> But oh ye Gods. When it came to a man failing in his duty, look out. You could be sure of one thing and that was cooling your heels in the Guard Room and plenty of time to think about your folly. He would hand you six months without batting an eye.

What is more, he continued, Steele would accept no criticism of his men from outside. He would stand up for them and make it clear that he considered them the best in the Force. As a result "his men would follow him to hell if need be".

"It is really wonderful," he recalled, "what men will do for an officer who is beloved by his men and it is also true what devils they can be when the officer is a sneak and hated."[27]

Of course not everyone subscribed to this philosophy of discipline. One of the few to kick against it was Cst. Charles Dwight who engaged in April 1891 at the age of 19. His father expressed the hope that life in the Force would "make a man of him." Dwight, however, was "disgusted" by the unjust and arbitrary system of discipline he encountered as a recruit in Regina. He soon ran afoul of Regimental Sergeant Major Belcher, who he described later as a "repugnant personage", and ended up in the Orderly Room on a charge. There he found that punishment was often meted out according to the whim or "humour" of those in authority without considering "any explanation which might be offered on the defence". Within a few weeks Dwight was very anxious to leave the NWMP. Through the influence of his father, a Toronto business man, he managed to purchase his discharge in October 1891. A year later he recorded his experiences and vented his spleen on the Force in a book entitled *Life in the North-West Mounted Police and Other Sketches*.[28]

Herchmer set out to tackle the problem of discipline with the same energy and optimism he put into other matters. The incidence of misconduct he found on taking command was put down to the influx of unsuitable men as a result of hasty recruiting in 1885. The principle cause of their misbehaviour, he soon found, was the same as that that infected the RIC, Scotland Yard and other police forces of the time, drunkenness. Nearly every instance of bad conduct, he wrote in 1887, was "attributable to whisky", and he found it necessary "to summarily dismiss several men".[29] The long term solution to this situation he believed was the introduction of libraries, recreation rooms and bands that would keep the men on their posts in the evenings and away from the temptations of the billiard saloons in the nearby towns.[30] He also hoped that the eventual passage of a "Pension Bill" would attract better men seeking a career and end the necessity of sending men to prison altogether.[31] In the meantime, he proposed to enforce discipline strictly and see that the men were regularly drilled.

It was strongly believed by military leaders of the day that foot or mounted drill fostered obedience in the soldier and hence improved discipline. As a result, recalcitrant individuals or squads of men were commonly punished by being given extra drills as a corrective for their misbehaviour. The constant response to words of command, it was thought, reduced the drill movements to the subconscious and instilled instinctive obedience in those on parade. As Otter expressed it in his manual for the militia:

> Drill is the discipline of the body, but tends also materially to discipline the mind, and, as the discipline of the mind is a hundred-fold more important to the efficiency of the soldier, the constant practice of drill, in which all ranks have to render spontaneous and silent obedience to the commands of their superiors, is absolutely necessary.[32]

Once again the police adopted military procedures with which many as ex-soldiers were familiar. Drill, drill and more drill was one of Herchmer's maxims as a cure for poor discipline. The police regulations specifically noted that it was the duty of the officer commanding every division to see that his men were thoroughly drilled. In his annual report for 1886, Supt. Sam Steele recorded that he had had a number of cases of insubordination among his men during the winter months. Once the weather improved, however, and he was able to commence spring drills, he found that the discipline got better.[33]

Comm. Herchmer soon left no doubt that, unlike his two most recent predecessors, he intended to handle disciplinary matters with a very firm hand, some would later say an iron fist. Only two weeks after taking over from Irvine he sent a circular memorandum to all of his division commanders informing them that the sentences they were handing down were too lenient. He reminded them that only he had the power to alter punishment. If it was to be effective, he explained, discipline must be severely administered. In future, he ordered, they were to award the maximum sentence in all serious offences.[34]

Herchmer's action exposed two differing views on the power of the Commissioner's office. As has been noted, no reason was made public for amending the legislation to give the Commissioner authority to increase or decrease sentences. Some believed the primary responsibility for sentencing an offender lay with the officers in the divisions who actually heard the charges. It was their task to judge each case on its own merits and punish accordingly. Those who took this view claimed that it was only intended that the Commissioner should later change the sentence in exceptional circumstances, where perhaps it later developed that a miscarriage of justice had occurred, or there appeared a need for mercy and compassion. Herchmer, on the other hand, wished to use this authority to establish centralized standards of discipline. In the process he was reducing the power of his officers to adjudicate serious offences and turning them instead into administrators of headquarters' disciplinary policy. This development, of course, did not go down well with some members of the public who saw too much power going into the hands of one man. This tug-of-war between the divisions and Regina over authority was a familiar theme of the Herchmer years.

Another criticism was the increasing use or misuse, according to one's viewpoint, of the disciplinary code under Herchmer to punish men for actions which were really criminal in nature. The regulations of the Royal Irish Constabulary were quite explicit with regard to such matters. A member of the Force who was suspected of having committed a theft, for example, was to be charged with theft in a civil court just like any other citizen.[35] While his case was before such courts he was suspended from duty. In the RIC only actual breaches of its internal regulations were tried before its own courts of inquiry.

Herchmer recognized the public discontent on the subject. He disclosed his forthright views on the issue in a letter to the Deputy Minister in 1887:

> There is a feeling among certain people that the officers are exceeding their powers when trying some members under the *NWMP Act*. They believe that members guilty of criminal acts should appear in civil courts. In the past men caught stealing, for example, have been charged with "disgraceful conduct" under the police regulations, which is what theft is considered to be. If we cannot continue to do this, it will be impossible to maintain discipline. In the civil courts

they will be treated like civilians and punished like civilians with lenient sentences compared to those under the police regulations. What is more, there could be a delay of up to two months before their case would be heard. It is essential, he concluded, that punishment is prompt, if discipline is to succeed.[36]

The Commissioner might also have added that it was probably better for the Force's reputation, if its rotten apples were not disposed of too publicly.

Herchmer need not have worried. Whether White responded to the concern raised in his letter is not known. Past procedures continued, and there is every reason to assume that Ottawa agreed with them. Only a few weeks earlier the Deputy Minister in a note to a leading Conservative politician in Ontario expressed himself in favour with the severity of the punishments that could be handed out under the police regulations. He referred specifically to a case in which a constable had been caught stealing from the men in the same barrack room in which he was quartered. Both in the military and in the Mounted Police this was considered a very serious offence because until the petty thief was apprehended a cloud of suspicion would hang over everyone's head that could undermine morale.[37]

Having singled out the curse of drunkenness as the principle cause of disobedience, the Commissioner paid special attention to the punishment of those who over-indulged. Under the regulations the offence was officially designated "Intoxication, however slight." In June 1887, he instructed his officers to stop issuing warnings or reprimands in such cases. In future he wanted all those found guilty of drunkenness to be fined.[38] A year later as a further deterrent he set the fine for first offenders at $10, about half of a month's pay for a constable.[39] As in other matters he closely monitored the reports from his officers regarding their action in disciplinary cases. In 1887, he noticed that Supt. A. R. Macdonell, who was in charge at Lethbridge, had only awarded two months with hard labour for intoxication to a constable who had been convicted of the offence several times before. Herchmer did not think that this was sufficient. He told Macdonell that the sentence was a "gross miscarriage of justice" because it was not severe enough, and ordered him to change it to six months followed by dismissal. He warned him that, if he continued to be so lenient, he would take away his power to try his own men.[40] It was not unknown for the Commissioner, upon hearing of a serious case, to order the prisoner brought to Regina under escort so that he could personally investigate it and see that a suitable sentence was handed out.

It was Herchmer's hope that he would be able "to dismiss all men with dissolute habits as they are only an encumbrance to the Force".[41] Given the social customs of the time, this was to be a harder task than he may have anticipated at the outset of his command. In 1889, a constable at Maple Creek who paraded for mounted drill after lunch was arrested and taken to the guardroom when it was found that he was too drunk to mount his horse and was unable to speak coherently.[42] There are many such examples of the use of alcohol, which were widely practised and tolerated at the time. On one occasion, when the less than abstemious habits of the NWMP were being discussed in the House of Commons, a member rose to defend their right to "a glass of grog". In fact he went further and suggested that they should receive a ration of rum twice a day just like the Navy.[43] Sam Steele claimed that over half of the men in his division were total abstainers, and identified the few drinkers as the main troublemakers.[44] Other commanding officers made similar claims. On the other hand, when the Sons of Temperance attempted to establish a branch of their organization at Headquarters in Regina, the largest post in the Force, they were unable to sign up one single member.[45]

If the same commanding officers are to be believed, the drinking problem in fact grew worse when prohibition ended in the Territories in 1892. Prior to this the men often had to take the risk of getting their whisky from smugglers who charged high prices. Under the new licence laws bars were permitted to open and sell cheaper liquor legally. The easier access, according to Steele and his brother officers, resulted in more drunkenness and more dismissals.[46] In any event, it is unlikely that the Commissioner could have ever eliminated drunkenness. It was an endemic social problem which even the temperance movement was still far from eradicating. As one of his NCOs later wrote, drink was the most important disciplinary problem in the Force, but in trying to put a stop to it Herchmer was expecting too much in a society where it was used so generously, both socially and medicinally.[47]

Another maxim of military discipline that was adopted by the NWMP was that a commanding officer was ultimately responsible for the conduct of the men in his charge. In referring to the duties of Superintendents in command of divisions the police regulations made it quite clear that "laxity in command will betray itself in the demeanour of the men".[48] From the flow of reports now coming into his office, the Commissioner was able to maintain a vigilant watch upon his commanding officers in this respect. If he detected any "laxity", he was quick to browbeat them and correct them as he did in other matters.

A typical such case occurred at "A" Division, Maple Creek, in November 1888. Cst. Edwin Blackmore was a trouble-maker with a long list of defaults to his credit. His commanding officer, Supt. W. D. Antrobus, described him as the worst man he had ever had under his command. It appears that

Blackmore had become increasingly insolent in his manner towards the NCOs at the post, thereby undermining their authority. For a while he got away with it. One day, however, upon refusing to obey the orders of Sgt. F. W. Spicer and Sgt. Major H. Des Barres, there was an angry exchange of words and Blackmore was placed under arrest. He was subsequently charged with uttering insolent language towards the two NCOs, disobeying an order and calling Sgt. Spicer "a son of a Bitch and a Bastard". He was summarily tried by Antrobus, and found guilty. His original sentence is unknown as it was later changed. When copies of the proceedings reached the Commissioner's office a couple of days later, Herchmer became enraged. From the evidence given at the trial, Herchmer concluded that discipline in the division had in fact become very lax because the NCOs were not doing their job. He immediately wrote angrily to Antrobus to tell him that the case showed a gross want of discipline in his division, and that Blackmore should have been dealt with more severely. He further ordered him to do three things:

1. Charge Sgt. Major Des Barres with neglect of duty and "If found guilty as I am sure he will be, you will fine him $30";
2. Charge Sgt. Spicer with neglect of duty, fine him $20 and transfer him to Regina;
3. Increase the penalty for Cst. Blackmore to a fine of $10 and three months imprisonment with hard labour.

Finally, he made it clear to Antrobus that he held him responsible for a situation that resulted from his own lack of tact, discipline and judgement.[49]

Although his reputation both in and out of the Force was growing as a pitiless disciplinarian, Herchmer would occasionally surprise everyone by taking the side of a constable against an officer, when he believed an injustice had taken place. In 1887, he intervened in the case of Cst. J. R. Warren of "K" Division, who had been imprisoned for refusing to clean Insp. Henry Likely's boots. Officers were allowed to employ a constable as a servant, called batman in the military, to clean and keep their uniforms and other kit in good order. For these services the officers usually paid their servants $5 a month. The regulations made it clear, however, that officers' servants had to be volunteers. Warren, it transpired, had not chosen to be the Inspector's servant. Likely had exceeded his authority. Therefore, when the Commissioner discovered what had happened, he ordered Warren released and punished Likely by transferring him to another division.[50] Cst. Warren, incidentally, was the son of Sir Charles Warren who was, at the time, Commissioner of the Metropolitan Police in London.

Reference has already been made to incidents of collective disobedience, known as "Bucks", following the March West. In February 1886, another "Buck" occurred at the headquarters of "G" Division in Edmonton, which was probably the most serious example of organized resistance to authority in the history of the Force. At the time it stood out as a glaring example of the discontent and poor morale that had infected the police in the months following the rebellion. As such, it likely hastened the desire in Ottawa to find a replacement for Comm. Irvine. Although the event took place some seven weeks before Herchmer took over command, it undoubtedly had some influence on his determination to take a very tough line as far as discipline was concerned.

The trouble started on the evening of Thursday, February 4th when three constables who had been detailed for night guard refused to obey the orders of the acting corporal in charge, W. F. Carstairs. During the night the rebellion fever spread. By morning the mutineers were too numerous for the NCOs to regain control. The men continued to do their duties, but ignored their superiors and showed the truculent mood they were in by wearing their sidearms. Somehow they managed to get a message to the 15 constables who were at the Fort Saskatchewan Detachment, 30 km away, inviting them to join in. In the meantime the commanding officer, Supt. A. H. Griesbach, agreed to receive a deputation of the malcontents and hear their complaints.

Complete and accurate information about what happened over the next two or three days is difficult to find. The immediate cause of the mutiny appears to have been the promotion of six constables who were unpopular with the men to the rank of acting corporal. Carstairs was one of these. In addition, it was claimed that in selecting the promotees Supt. Griesbach had passed over men with longer service and more experience. Conditions in the barrack rooms were also said to have contributed to the growing feeling of dissatisfaction at the post. The quarters were overcrowded and infested with bed bugs and fleas. They were so badly constructed that those sleeping nearest to the stoves suffocated whilst those by the doors were frozen. This, combined with the fact that Edmonton was going through a very cold spell of weather with temperatures in the -30°F range, had got some of the men into an extremely fractious mood.

At the meeting with Griesbach the six new acting corporals offered to give up their promotions. This appeared to satisfy the complainants who then agreed to resume normal duties. Before this could be accomplished, however, nine men turned up from Fort Saskatchewan with their own list of grievances. Principle among these was their desire to have the conduct of a corporal at the detachment investigated. Until this was done they refused to return to duty. As a result, the Edmonton rebels, believing no doubt that there is strength in numbers, decided to join them. By now it was Friday evening. Griesbach evidently consented to the wish for an inquiry into the complaint about the corporal, but put off taking any action until Monday morning. Over the weekend the mutineers continued to thumb their noses at authority. They fed and watered the horses, but otherwise ignored the post routine and the entreaties of those with wiser heads to bring the lark to an end. Their spirits were enlivened and their determination to buck the system kept up by a liberal supply of whisky obtained from the town. At some point they removed the Union Jack from the flag pole and replaced it by "a flag showing disregard for authority". Some reports say that this was a skull and cross bones painted upon a piece of canvas.

Griesbach faced a serious challenge to his reputation as well as his authority. As commanding officer he would be held responsible for the state of affairs. His culpability would be considerably reduced, however, if he could restore order himself, without the need for outside help. So far he had not tried to have any of the mutineers arrested. He evidently did not wish to provoke a confrontation that could lead to bloodshed. He was content to bide his time, waiting for an opportunity to resume control peacefully. He probably hoped that during the weekend as the supply of alcohol dried up the mutineers would sober up and quietly return to their duties. Regina had been notified by telegraph of what had happened, and he knew that Supt. W. M. Herchmer was on his way with 25 reinforcements, if he should fail.

On Monday, Griesbach looked into the charges made by the Fort Saskatchewan men against their NCO. He found that they were frivolous, however, and refused to take any action to remove him. The decision put the mutineers on the spot. Would they back down or force the issue further. Perhaps Griesbach detected that they were losing their resolve, that the unity among them was disintegrating. At any rate on Tuesday morning he was able to persuade them to take their horses out on an exercise ride without their sidearms. It was a carefully prepared trap. While they were away he organized the loyal men who remained behind. The barrack rooms were searched and all firearms found there collected and locked away. When the mutineers returned they were surrounded by armed loyalists. The ringleaders were arrested and placed in the guardroom, the rest confined to their barracks. The Edmonton Buck was over. Griesbach had managed

to reassert his authority without assistance, and the subsequent enquiry exonerated him of any serious fault. Eighteen constables were eventually convicted of participating in the affair and sentenced to long terms of imprisonment.[51] In his published annual report for 1886 the seriousness of the affair was carefully down played and accounted for in one sentence: "During the early part of the year there were several cases of insubordination which were promptly suppressed, and those implicated sentenced to severe punishment."[52] Researchers beware! In their published reports mounted police officers could, at times, write no more and no less than it was in their interests to do.

One of the ringleaders of the mutiny in Edmonton was Cst. John Henry Beggs. It has been claimed that the disciplinary problems of the post-rebellion years were in part due to the hasty recruitment of unsuitable men in 1885. Beggs seems to have been a case in point. He engaged on the 4th of February of that year. Prior to joining he had worked as a farmhand near Pembina, which was just south of the Manitoba border in North Dakota. In spite of his previous address, his religious affiliation, which he gave as Church of England, would suggest that he was a Canadian. Beggs was disciplined several times in 1885 for minor infractions of the regulations. On one occasion at Prince Albert, however, he was found guilty of refusing to obey an order. For this he was only fined five days' pay. One authority feels that it was light sentences like this under Irvine for such serious offences that encouraged Beggs and others in their insubordination in Edmonton.[53]

For his part in the mutiny Beggs was charged with the following offences:

> Refusing to obey orders.
> Mutinous conduct by inciting men by words and deeds to set at defiance their CO and disobey orders, also present at the hoisting of a flag showing disregard for authority and showing by this emblem that Judge Lynch was in command of the post at Edmonton.
> Giving a letter to a civilian to take to Fort Sask. to incite the men there to mutiny.[54]

He received from Irvine the maximum sentence allowable under the *NWMP Act*, a fine of one month's pay and twelve months imprisonment with hard labour. Like several of the other mutineers he was transferred to Regina to serve his time in the guardroom there. On March 16th he was given an additional month with hard labour after he stole a pipe from the canteen whilst employed to clean it.

Beggs still had several months of his sentence to serve when Herchmer arrived to take command in April. What transpired over the next several months was perhaps the most extreme example of how severe the military style of discipline could be administered under the new Commissioner. Herchmer was merciless in his treatment of Beggs.

He evidently wished to send a message to anyone who had any thoughts of bucking the system or participating in a mutiny in the future. On 7 May 1886, Herchmer put him on a diet of bread and water for four days, forced him to wear leg irons for fourteen days and ball and chain for two months for creating a disturbance in his cell. On July 15th, for using threatening language towards one of the provost guards, he got five days on bread and water and an additional two months wearing a ball and chain, presumably when out on work parties. On the 21st of July, he refused to obey an order and received two more months in leg irons and bread and water three times a week; in September yet another month in irons for refusing to obey orders; and in October two additional months hard labour and one week on bread and water for the same offence. The 23-year-old Beggs, however, still seemed to be driven by a defiant hatred of authority. His next offence was to bite one of the provost guards while handcuffed. For this Herchmer sentenced him to be put in "Irons until he behaves". In November he ordered him to be kept in irons until the term of his imprisonment expired after a knife was found concealed in his cell. Not long after this, in a letter to the Commissioner, the Deputy Minister opined that it was a pity that the *Police Act* did not provide the power to inflict greater punishment on characters like Beggs. His final act of defiance was to create a disturbance in his cell again in February 1887. For this yet another month with hard labour was tacked on to his sentence.[55]

Beggs was finally released from the guardroom in Regina and dismissed from the Force on 3 June 1887, after serving a total of 16 months in prison. During this time he was not entitled to any pay. The only money due to him was $1.50. It represented his pay of 50 cents per day for the first three days of February 1886 as his sentence had commenced on the fourth of that month. Beggs did not get the $1.50, however. It went towards the fine of one month's pay. What happened to Beggs after his release the records do not say.

Beggs appears to have been an incorrigible mischief-maker. He clearly was not suited to service in the NWMP. Herchmer described him as a representative of the criminal class. Be that as it may, his case was an example of the way the disciplinary system was developing under the new Commissioner. Could Herchmer have kept him in prison indefinitely? Were the punishments he handed out legal under the police regulations? Beggs had no means by which he could appeal against the actions of an arbitrary superior who was at one and the same time his accuser, judge and jailer. The regulations provided that any member who had a complaint or grievance could put it in writing and forward it to the Commissioner. This simply made Herchmer the

appeal court in addition to all the other positions noted above. Beggs did write a letter offering to behave if the Commissioner would mitigate his sentence. Herchmer ignored it. Beggs seems to have got no sympathy from any quarter, not even the press which often took up the cause of members it felt had been unjustly treated. He also had no friends in high places or influence in Ottawa to defend him. It looked as if everyone agreed that he only got what he deserved. Herchmer received no criticism over his treatment of Beggs, but it would not be long before his disciplinary action in other cases would be challenged.

Disciplinary offences reveal a good deal about the conditions of service and life in the Mounted Police during Herchmer's time. Supt. Percival Pennefather recalled how strict discipline was at Regina when he served there as a constable:

> A man was placed under arrest for the least inattention to duty. A sentence of one month or two months and even six months was a common thing to be handed out by Larry [Herchmer] and the Fine Fund was contributed to daily by anywhere from a day's pay to a month's.[56]

Punishments for minor offences ranged from a 50 cent fine for having an untidy bed to seven days hard labour for bearing a dirty carbine.

The police were particularly sensitive about prisoners escaping as a result of members neglecting their duty. The hunt for escapees was often embarrassing and brought public criticism on the Force. A case in point is the 1886 escape of Cst. Anthony Gallagher, who was serving six months for his role in the recent mutiny, and a vagrant with the colourful sobriquet of Crackerbox Johnson.[57] Two NWMP members, Sgt. Gordon and Cst. Baker, were convicted of neglecting their duty and allowing their prisoners to escape. Sgt. Gordon was reduced to the rank of constable and Cst. Baker was sentenced to four months in prison with hard labour.[58]

The administration was also anxious that men did not discuss police matters with the press or the public without permission. Cst. Hea received seven days hard labour after he made statements at a public meeting which brought the Force into disrepute.[59] Improper treatment of prisoners was another disciplinary matter. Sgt. Green was reduced five places in the order of seniority and relieved of his duties as provost sergeant after he struck a civilian prisoner.[60]

As might be expected, fighting was a frequent occurrence between men living in barracks. In the cramped and uncomfortable quarters they became irritable and tempers could easily flair up. Sgt. Doyle was reduced to the rank of corporal for striking a constable, as was Sgt. Dunne. When the ranks were reversed, the penalty was harsher. Striking a superior was considered more serious than striking an inferior. Cst. Power was fined one month's pay and sentenced to six months hard labour for punching Sgt. Cameron in the mouth.[61]

Fights were sometimes settled in the hay corral, and the officers looked the other way providing the Queensberry Rules were observed. The record of such a fight at Lethbridge in 1897 reveals something of the sense of fair play that was expected. Whilst eating their dinner in the mess Cst. Peirce and Cst. McCulla got into a quarrel over a letter. The contents are unknown. Angry words were exchanged. Tables were pushed aside and chairs knocked over as they tried to exchange punches. They were restrained by others in the mess. Peirce then invited McCulla to meet him in the hay corral after the meal. What followed was reminiscent of Tom Brown's School Days. In the corral the two men squared-off against each other surrounded by some of their comrades. After a few punches had been thrown, McCulla knocked Peirce down. He then jumped on to him pinning his arms to the ground with his knees and proceeded to pummel his face and head viciously until some of the spectators pulled him off. One constable called McCulla "a dirty low coward" for fighting the way he did. Peirce was so badly cut he had to go to the hospital to be patched up. News of the fight was soon all over the post and the commanding officer, Supt. R. B. Deane, had no choice but to intervene. He clearly would not have done so had it been a "fair" contest. McCulla was the villain of the piece, but Peirce would have to be disciplined too. Deane charged McCulla with assaulting Peirce and fined him $10, and Peirce with creating a disturbance in the mess and fined him $5. Everyone seemed to feel that justice had been done. In reporting the matter Deane described McCulla's behaviour in not obeying the rules of the prize ring as "revolting".[62]

Swearing at NCOs, or indeed anyone else, was a punishable offence. The two commonest epithets used were "bastard" and "son of a bitch". Cruder language was used from time to time. Cst. Edward Jones posed a particular problem with respect to swearing. He was described by his CO as "a very low stamp of a man, and totally unfit for the Force". In April 1898, Jones was admitted to the Calgary General Hospital for treatment. While there, he loudly shouted obscenities, knowing full well that the nurses could hear him. They complained to the matron about him. She complained to the doctor, who told Jones to stop his "unseemly behaviour". When the news of his conduct reached Regina, the Commissioner angrily asked the commanding officer in Calgary why Jones had not been charged. In reply, that officer explained that Jones would call the nurses as witnesses at his trial, and ask them to repeat what he had said. This, they would be too embarrassed to do and hence the case could not be proved against him. Shortly after, Headquarters agreed to Jones' discharge as unsuitable.[63]

Theft in barracks was also considered a very serious matter. A sentence of six months with hard labour was common for stealing an article of little monetary value from a roommate.[64] When Cst. Jim McAuley stole $35 from the trunk of a corporal in Prince Albert, however, his superior decided a much stiffer sentence was needed. Here was an example of the double jeopardy faced by members under the disciplinary system. McAuley was originally tried under the police regulations with disgraceful conduct in that he stole the $35. Upon hearing the evidence, Supt. A. B. Perry adjourned the internal investigation and had McAuley indicted for larceny in the civil court. The maximum sentence for larceny was seven years. McAuley was eventually found guilty by Mr. Justice Maguire in Prince Albert and sent to Stony Mountain Penitentiary for two years. It was only after the conviction that the police dismissed him from the service. If the civil court had failed to convict him, the disciplinary proceedings could have been resumed, and he would still have been liable for up to one month's pay and one year in the guardroom.[65] In another case, for reasons that are not clear, the thief got off comparatively lightly, although the value of the goods stolen was approximately the same as that taken by McAuley. The winter of 1886-87 was a particularly cold one. Perhaps that partly explains why Cst. Bill Shaw tippled away from time to time at the hospital's medicinal liquor supply in Supt. Sam Steele's quarters in Lethbridge. The irony of it was that Steele had deliberately locked the hospital comforts in his room for safekeeping. As Steele's servant, Shaw had a key to the place in order to carry out his duties. It was several weeks before his secret drinking was discovered. Shaw avoided detection by removing the liquor and then refilling the containers with water. By the time the discrepancy was noticed, he had filched one gallon of alcohol, one gallon of wine, six and half pints of whisky, one gallon of methylated spirit and three and three-quarter pints of brandy. For his transgression Shaw had to pay for the cost of replacing the liquor and spend only one month in prison with hard labour.[66]

Insubordination and mutinous conduct still continued to be treated severely. Cst. Pat Power refused to obey the order of Cpl. Pollock to get on with his work. When brought before his commanding officer and sentenced to seven days in prison, Power lost his temper and said, "Send me for the rest of my life. I won't do another stroke of work." Supt. Antrobus immediately added another year to his penalty for mutinous language.[67] Cst. Ronan got one month with ball and chain simply for refusing to answer his name.[68] Cst. Harry Stephens also had a problem controlling his temper. In 1887, he threw a plate of meat into the face of Cpl. Mcleod. For this he was fined $2.50 and confined to barracks for 14 days, but he could not keep his mouth shut. When asked by his commanding officer if he had anything to say, he told him that he hoped that the blankety blank barracks would burn down. He, too, received a year in prison for his careless remarks.[69] Cst. John Potter from Birkenhead in England broke out of barracks in Lethbridge one night in January 1889 to paint the town red. Up before Supt. Deane the next day he was sentenced to three months. Potter responded by calling Deane a "damned son of a bitch" and took a swing at him. Deane described this as the most serious offence a man can commit. He charged Potter with striking his commanding officer and gave him another 12 months. Actually Deane over-dramatized the incident a little. Potter's fist never struck him. An NCO who was present grabbed his arm before the punch landed.[70]

There were isolated incidents in which members of the NWMP were involved in homosexual activity. Before the appearance of the *Criminal Code* in 1892, such acts were punishable as either "sodomy" or "unnatural offenses" under the criminal law. In the new code these offences reappeared as "buggery", section 174, which carried a maximum sentence of life imprisonment, and "acts of gross indecency", section 178, which had a maximum sentence of five years and the option of whipping.[71] Under the police regulations men who were believed to have committed homosexual acts were charged with "grossly immoral conduct".

As was not unusual in the nineteenth century, when clergymen, soldiers and other members of established institutions were caught engaging in homosexual behaviour, efforts were made to try and "hush up" the matter. The offender was quietly discharged or otherwise removed unobtrusively from the scene to protect the reputation of the church or the regiment, and because of the fear that his unnatural desires might be contagious. There was also concern for the family of the offender. It was the one repulsive crime that the police, among others, were anxious should not be made public. In the process, therefore, criminal prosecution was sometimes deliberately avoided. Such action would have been widely approved of by the public of the time.

The NWMP disciplinary system with its summary in camera investigative procedures from which there was no appeal was particularly suited to ridding the Force of an undesirable quickly and effectively. In 1882, Comm. Irvine had so discreetly charged and convicted a sergeant of "grossly immoral conduct" that not even the senior officers who made up the Discharge Board that processed the offender's dismissal from the Force were aware of the reason for his departure. In another case in

1887 the Force was not able to act quite so secretively.

In April 1887, a corporal on duty in Regina discovered a constable performing oral sex upon a local saloon keeper in an hotel room in the town. The constable was immediately arrested and tried the same day before Supt. W. M. Herchmer with "disgraceful conduct in having committed an unnatural offence". From the evidence given by the corporal it was clear that several citizens in Regina were aware of the constable's activity. The whole affair was public knowledge and there was no possibility of covering it up. Whether this fact influenced Herchmer in deciding upon the punishment is not recorded, but it is reasonable to assume that it did. The constable was sentenced "to be dismissed the Force with ignominy - case to be dealt with in civil court". In his defence the accused had pleaded that he was too drunk to remember what had happened.

There was no provision either in the *NWMP Act* or the rules and regulations of the Force for discharging a member with ignominy. This was simply another military practice which the police adopted. On 12 April 1887, a General Parade was ordered at four p.m. on the square at the barracks in Regina so that all ranks could witness the dishonourable discharge of the constable. Following military procedures his crime and sentence were read aloud to all those assembled. His uniform was then stripped of buttons, badges, medals and any other distinctive markings, and he was marched down the ranks and off the square, where he was then charged with committing an "unnatural offence" and placed in the cells. The charge was later dropped, however, when the crown prosecutor advised the magistrate who was to hear the case that the act for which he had been arrested was not an offence under the existing criminal statutes. Although Fred White then took up the "beastly" matter with the Deputy Minister of Justice to see what else could be done to prosecute him, no further charges were laid.[72]

Each division usually had one or two "barrack room lawyers" who were cunning and crafty enough, or had such a glib tongue, that they somehow just managed to escape punishment by one means or another. They were usually unpopular with the other men. Supt. Deane described such a slippery customer to the Commissioner in 1895:

I strongly recommend that we get rid of Cst. Crafter. He "is a barrack room lawyer, rather more ignorant than most of them and a most disagreeable man". I had to remove him from Little Bow Detachment because he was so offensive to his comrades. He was charged with being absent from stables. He pleaded that he had neuralgia. I gave him the benefit of the doubt. He was then brought before me for neglecting his sentry duty. This time he claimed that he had an ulcerated tooth. He is testing me to see how far he can go. I decided that I had had enough. I fined

255

him $15.00 and arranged for him to receive a comprehensive education in sentry duty for the next few days. For his next offence Crafter was imprisoned for one month and then dismissed.[73]

A constable who was sent to prison for a disciplinary offence could find himself sharing the same cell as a thief or burglar he had earlier arrested. There was no separate prison accommodation for policemen. They served their time in the guardroom which was also the territorial jail for all criminals who received a sentence of less that two years. Those with longer terms were sent to Stony Mountain Penitentiary in Manitoba. The policemen serving time in the guardroom did not have to don prison uniform like the convicts did. They wore their cotton fatigue dress, but in every other respect they were treated like common criminals. They ate the same food, were subject to the same routine, and worked side by side with them at cutting wood, repairing roads, or whatever else was found for them to do as hard labour.

One former sergeant who had been reduced to the rank of constable and given four months with hard labour for neglecting his duty decided to protest against these conditions. He wrote a letter to the Commissioner objecting to being kept in a common jail with felons, vagrants and lunatics. The prisons, it should be noted, were usually overcrowded during this period. The *NWMP Act* provided for the imprisonment of policemen for breaches of the regulations. The legislation stipulated that and no more. It said nothing as to whether they were to be incarcerated with those convicted of criminal offences, or whether they were subject to prison discipline. Herchmer forwarded the complaint to Ottawa, noting that unless new facilities were to be built at every post he had no choice but to confine police prisoners in the guardroom with the criminals. As there was little chance of the government agreeing to provide separate accommodation, the Deputy Minister proposed a compromise. Provide the complainant with a cell to himself, he replied, and allow him to eat his meals with the guards. "This is the best we can do," he told Herchmer.[74] The treatment of members of the Mounted Police while undergoing imprisonment caught the public eye in the spring of 1896 when an ex-constable brought a charge against his former commanding officer. This incident revolved around Cst. Robert Casmir Dickson being charged for negligence in allowing his prisoner Almighty Voice to escape from detention.[75]

Dickson was tried under the police regulations for allowing the prisoner to escape by his commanding officer, Supt. Moffatt, and sentenced to two months hard labour followed by dismissal from the Force. Several of the newspaper accounts also stated that as part of his sentence he had been forced to dig the grave for Colebrook in the cemetery in

Prince Albert where he was buried.[76] Comm. Herchmer was at pains to correct this misunderstanding. He wrote letters to the newspapers concerned rightly pointing out that the grave digging had not been included in his sentence. He had only helped to dig the grave, he explained, along with other prisoners as part of their requirement to perform hard labour.[77] Be that as it may, he had been forced to dig the grave, and the public continued to believe, not that it necessarily disapproved, that this was additional punishment vindictively imposed upon him by the police. Dickson probably had good reason to feel that he had been victimized, and it so happened that prior to joining the NWMP he had worked for several years in a law office.

Not long after his release from the Prince Albert guardroom and his dismissal from the Force, Dickson laid a charge against Moffatt under the *Post Office Act* for illegally opening his mail while he was a prisoner.[78] The magistrate who heard the information committed Moffatt for trial at the next sitting of the territorial Supreme Court in April 1896, and then released him on his own recognizance for a sum of $600. The decision sent a shock wave through the Force, especially after Comm. Herchmer learned from a confidential source that the presiding judge on the court, Mr. Justice McGuire, who had a reputation as an enemy of the police, had privately let it be known that he intended to convict Moffatt.

What was at stake was the right of the police as jailers to intercept the mail of prisoners, both civilian and police. Although no regulation had been laid down, commanding officers had been routinely reading the letters of those committed to the guardrooms under their control for at least 20 years. Should a prisoner object to the practice, his mail was held unopened until his sentence expired, and then handed to him. Comm. Herchmer considered that the authority to continue this practice was absolutely necessary in order to prevent prisoners from conspiring with outsiders to escape. In fact, shortly after assuming command he had drawn the attention of his commanding officers to the necessity of continuing to intercept the mail for this very reason. Pending the outcome of the trial he issued a general order instructing them to hold all correspondence, unless the prisoner in question agreed in writing to his letters being opened. In the meantime he waited anxiously for the Department of Justice, which had been telegraphed for its advice, to sort the matter out.[79]

The *Post Office Act* made it an offence for anyone to unlawfully open, wilfully keep, secrete, delay or detain a letter. The question was whether Moffatt did or did not have the legal authority to do these things. After reviewing the case, justice officials decided that he had indeed acted quite lawfully.

Much to White's relief, the Deputy Minister of Justice notified him on April 11th, just five days before the case was to be heard, that the crown prosecutor in Prince Albert had been instructed to enter a *nolli prosequi*, a stay of proceedings. The department's rationale for this was that under the *North-West Territories Act* NWMP guardrooms were constituted "territorial gaols". It further followed from this that the officer in charge of the guard room also held the status of "warden" or "gaoler". Under the *Penitentiaries Act*, meanwhile, the Inspector of Penitentiaries was empowered to make rules and regulations for the operation of jails and prisons. It so happened that one such rule permitted the wardens or jailers of such institutions to open the mail of prisoners. The police, therefore, according to the Department of Justice had been acting quite legitimately.[80]

Dickson remained unconvinced. He wrote a letter to the Prime Minister, Sir Mackenzie Bowell, who was also the minister responsible for the Mounted Police, protesting against the decision not to proceed with the case. He argued that the authorities cited by Justice did not abrogate the provisions of the *Post Office Act*. That question, however, would have to wait to be answered another day. Dickson also charged that he had not received a "fair trial" and that Herchmer tended towards "Russian methods" in disciplinary hearings.[81] His complaint was ignored. The implications of all this for the disciplinary system was that police prisoners were indeed subject to the same prison regulations as criminals - mail opening, low diet, manacles, ball and chain and the like.

A much more serious legal challenge against the military system of discipline that had developed in the Force was launched in 1898-99 by Cst. Basil Nettleship, the son of a Church of England clergyman. Once again, as in the Craig case, the issue that was raised was whether the civil courts had any jurisdiction over the internal tribunals of the police. Nettleship's period of engagement was due to end on 29 November 1898. He had recently come into an inheritance, and intended to use the money to set himself up in business in British Columbia. As a result he was anxious to leave the Force as soon as possible. With the blessing of his commanding officer at Fort Macleod, Supt. R. B. Deane, he arranged to take the last few days of his service as leave. Deane also agreed to his request to go through his discharge proceedings prior to going on leave so that he would not have to return on the 29th. There was nothing unusual about this request. It had been frequently granted before to men whose term of service was about to expire. Nettleship would be free of the Force a few days early and on his way to a new life.

His last day was to be the 23rd of November. Although in recent months Nettleship had had no disciplinary problems, he had in the past received several convictions for drunkenness. On the morning of his departure he stopped in at the division canteen for a farewell drink. It appears that he had a few too many and became intoxicated. His next stop was to appear before the Discharge Board headed by Insp. Cuthbert. It verified his service and processed the necessary papers for his discharge. Nettleship would later claim that at this point Cuthbert told him that he was a "free man". Cuthbert later denied making any such statement. In any event his discharge papers were quite properly post-dated by the Board for 29 November 1898.

Nettleship's last stop was the pay office where he was to pick up any money that was owed to him. This would only take a few moments and then he would be off through the gates of the post and nothing more would likely have been heard of him. Unfortunately for Nettleship, as it would turn out later, by the time he reached the pay office the drink had got the better of him and he had become quite truculent. When the paymaster seemed to take a little longer than he thought was necessary to process his account, he shouted in a loud and rude manner, "Hurry up! Hurry up, Sergeant! I cannot wait here all day!"[82]

By coincidence, Deane, who was working in an adjacent office, happened to overhear this unseemly outburst. Upon investigating its cause, he placed Nettleship under arrest for intoxication, informed him that his leave was cancelled and ordered him to return to duty. The latter returned to his barrack room. Had he remained there he likely would have received a fine for his transgression and have been discharged at the end his term on the 29th. Instead, he decided to proceed upon his way as planned. Within a short time of skipping from the post he became ill with diphtheria. The local doctor who attended him put him in quarantine in the home of the settler he had been hiding with. The police, however, soon discovered his whereabouts. After he refused to place himself in the care of the police surgeon, Deane followed routine procedures and had him declared a deserter. As soon as the quarantine was lifted, the police would arrest him. Instead of just having six more days to serve, he now faced up to a year in prison.

Rather than return and face this possible punishment, Nettleship retained a Fort Macleod lawyer, Charles Harris, as his counsel. His recent inheritance no doubt influenced this decision. It is possible that, as he later attested, he really believed that he had been discharged and that Deane was unjust-

257

ly pursuing him. On 9 January 1899, Harris persuaded Mr. Justice Rouleau of the Territorial Supreme Court in Fort Macleod to issue a "Rule Nisi" which temporarily protected Nettleship from arrest by Deane or any other police officer. Having secured a brief immunity from the disciplinary system, he left the sanctuary of his quarantine and proceeded on his way to British Columbia, leaving his lawyer to secure his permanent freedom through the courts.

Nettleship's action touched off a protracted legal battle. As far as Herchmer was concerned there was a great deal at stake. Was the military system of discipline which he had advanced and considered so essential to the efficiency of the Force to be subject to the jurisdiction of the civil courts. "If the judges are to interfere in police discipline," he wrote, "it will be an end of it, as every man will get a lawyer, and interview the judge."[83]

It was the most serious such challenge to the Force since Mr. Justice Macleod, the former Commissioner, had issued a writ of *habeas corpus* for the release of Cst. Craig from the Fort Macleod guardroom in 1887.

The next round in the legal confrontation took place in Calgary on 30 January 1899. In his temporary restraining order Mr. Justice Rouleau had called upon Deane or any other officer of the Force to appear before him on that date, if they wished to show cause why he should not issue a "Writ of Prohibition" that would permanently prevent them from arresting or punishing Nettleship. In his deposition to the court Deane rightly argued that neither he nor the Discharge Board had authority to release Nettleship before his term of service expired, that his discharge papers had been properly post-dated 29 November 1898, that as a favour he had permitted him to take his last few days as leave, and that during that period he was still a member of the NWMP subject to its rules and regulations. Nettleship for his part claimed that he had been discharged on November 23rd, and that the subsequent charge of desertion resulted from Deane's personal prejudice towards him and was therefore illegal. In his decision Rouleau rejected the police representation and accepted Nettleship's argument, granting him a "Writ of Prohibition" on 27 February 1899.[84]

To say that Herchmer and the officials in Ottawa were perturbed by Rouleau's verdict would be to put it mildly. The assistance of the Department of Justice would have to be sought to appeal this challenge to their power to a higher court. In the meantime Deane had a charge of perjury laid against Nettleship. It was the contention of the police that in his affidavit to Rouleau the latter had lied when he swore that at the Discharge Board Cuthbert had told him that he was no longer a member of the Force. Cuthbert of course denied this. The judge and jury that heard the case, however, accepted Nettleship's claim that the words in his sworn statement were only intended to convey his understanding of the consequences of his appearance before the Discharge Board. He was acquitted. The police had lost the second round.

The final battle would now take place at Regina in July 1899 when the Justice Department lawyers would appear before a full sitting of the Supreme Court of the NWT to argue that Rouleau's "Writ of Prohibition" should be set aside. The basis of the Crown's case rested upon a lengthy brief prepared by Supt. R. B. Deane. According to his own account of the affair, all of the setbacks for the Force up to this point were due either to the bias of the judiciary, or the incompetence of the Crown prosecutors involved. Deane, who had a highly exalted opinion of himself with respect to almost any subject one could think of, relished the opportunity to show them that he could do better. If they could not bring Nettleship to heel, he certainly would.

Although he had no formal legal training, the Superintendent was well qualified for the task. While an officer in the Royal Marines he had served as adjutant of its Chatham Division. After being appointed an officer in the NWMP, he was for a time its adjutant in Regina. It was while there that he had compiled the first *Regulations and Orders of the Force* which was published in 1889. Deane had picked up a good grounding in the administration of military law. With the help of the legal library of his friend C. F. P. Conybeare, the Crown prosecutor in Lethbridge, he put together a formidable argument for overturning Rouleau's judgement that was based upon precedents in British law going back several centuries.

The essence of Deane's reasoning was that ordinary courts of law had no jurisdiction over the internal disciplinary and regulatory affairs of a military organization. He wrote in the conclusion to his brief:

> I submit that the N.W.M. Police, if not a military body, are as nearly military as it is possible for an armed body of Constabulary to be; that the Statute by virtue of which they exist enjoins and provides for the maintenance of discipline, and that their discipline is essentially of a military character.

If, as he claimed, the Force was a military body just like the British Army then it followed that the issues involving Nettleship's leave and discharge were "purely matters affecting the interior economy and discipline of the N.W.M.Police". Being thus a question "purely of a Police character", he concluded, it is "cognisable only by a Police tribunal, and not by a Court of Law".[85]

The appeal before the Supreme Court in Regina was successful. Their lordships ruled that Nettleship had not been discharged on the 23rd of

November, and as a result he was still subject to police discipline when he left the barracks without permission and failed to return. The "Writ of Prohibition" was set aside. Nettleship could now be arrested and charged with deserting the NWMP. Deane claimed a great and complete victory for the arguments he had set forth. This however was not really the case. The judges overruled Rouleau's order because they found that he had granted it "incautiously". They did not say that he had exceeded his jurisdiction. The question, therefore, of whether the disciplinary system of the NWMP was subject to the authority of the civil courts still remained unanswered.

Finally, the police decided after all not to drag Nettleship back from British Columbia to face the music. His legal fees which were reported at between $1,200 to $1,300 were believed to have eaten up most of his inheritance. Deane seemed to feel that this was punishment enough, and that to have pursued him further would only have looked like malicious "persecution".[86] Whether that was the official reason for not treating him as a deserter is not clear. Perhaps, too, the police felt that it would be prudent and in their best interests to allow the whole affair to be quietly forgotten. They would have had no desire to revive or encourage further such legal challenges. As for Nettleship, his alcoholism brought him to a tragic end. On 20 November 1902, he died from the effects of drinking methyl alcohol while working for a coal company in Michel, B.C.

With respect to the campaign in the late 1880s to have Herchmer removed from office, much of the criticism aimed at him concerned the misuse of his authority in disciplinary matters. Nicholas Davin, editor of the *Regina Leader* and local member of Parliament in particular felt that the *NWMP Act* put too much power in his hands, and agitated to have the legislation changed. Macdonald, however, defended the Commissioner and even went so far as to say that discipline in the Mounted Police needed to be more severe than in the military. The Wetmore Inquiry showed that the Commissioner's temperament had at times led him to overstep his authority, but no substantive changes were made either to the legislation or the regulations and orders that related to discipline. In 1894, with Macdonald gone from the political scene there was one small reversal in the general trend towards a more and more authoritarian code.

Several amendments to the *NWMP Act* were introduced into the House of Commons that year by the government. None of the changes effected the provisions relating to discipline, but during the debate some members chose to focus attention upon these. In particular they objected to the "if he thinks fit" clause. This was put in the legislation in 1879 without any explanation or discussion. Under it, the officer hearing a disciplinary charge could decide on his own discretion whether or not the evidence presented to him would be given under oath or not. It was no doubt intended to give him the power to dispense with the oath when trying men for minor offences that he had witnessed himself. The legislation did not, however, make this clear.

The attack on the clause was led off by Louis Davies, a Liberal member from P.E.I., the former Premier of that province and later Chief Justice of the Supreme Court of Canada. He told the House that in his opinion it was unfair to fine or imprison a man without hearing the evidence against him under oath.[87] W. B. Ives, the minister responsible for the police, objected. He pointed out that the clause was not a new one, and that it would be very inconvenient to have formal proceedings in every trivial case. He cited the example of the Orderly Officer who might find an untidy bed or a dirty rifle barrel during his inspection. Davies persisted, however, with the view that, as the legislation stood, a man could be charged with a very serious offence and given severe punishment without one word of evidence being given under oath. Other members, including Nicholas Davin, agreed with him. It was suggested to the government that if the clause was to be retained, the disciplinary offences in the Act should be classified as major or minor ones. Davin had argued for such a system of classification during the debate on Herchmer's conduct in 1889. In this way it would be made clear that sworn testimony would be mandatory where all major offences were concerned. To have consented to these demands would have required the government to withdraw the legislation and extensively revise it. Rather than do this Ives agreed to strike out the offending clause, "if he thinks fit".[88] Henceforth, the evidence in every charge against a member of the NWMP under the disciplinary code would have to be heard under oath.

One of the few years for which statistics on discipline are not only complete but easily obtained is that from December 1894 to December 1895. During that year there were 326 convictions for breaches of the regulations. These offences were committed by 217 men. Several men were guilty of more than one offence; one man was convicted seven times. With a total strength among the rank and file in November 1895 of 675, the 217 offenders represented about 32 per cent of the Force. Of those 217, 30 were fined and/or imprisoned followed by dismissal. The charges against those so dismissed were as follows:

Drunkenness	21
Absent without leave	2
Refused to assume duties of cook	1
Disobeying orders	1
Asleep on sentry duty	1
Neglect of duty	1
Obtaining a pass by fraud	1
Stealing from the mess fund	1
Immoral conduct by associating with a woman of ill-fame	1
Total	30

The 30 men who were dismissed represented approximately five per cent of the Force. As might be expected, the commonest offence among those who were not dismissed was "being intoxicated however slightly", 96 convictions. During the year a total amount of $1,644 was levied in fines.[89] This of course went into the Fine Fund. In 1893, a year for which the figures are available, the Fine Fund stood at almost $5,000.[90] The above, of course, are just the statistics for one isolated year. Whether it was typical of others is not known.

As an incentive to better discipline, good service pay had been introduced into the Force in 1881. For every year that a member served without committing a serious breach of discipline, the Commissioner could at his discretion award him five cents per day good service pay to a maximum of twenty-five cents. From his basic pay of 50 cents per day, a well-behaved constable could move up to 55 cents per day at the end of his first year, 60 cents per day at the end of the second year, and so on until he reached 75 cents per day at the end of the fifth year. In the latter case, the good service pay represented a 50 per cent increase over the base pay that an habitual troublemaker would continue to receive. It paid to follow the rules. An extra 25 cents a day gave a constable a lot of extra buying power. Of course, the regulations gave the Commissioner complete authority to suspend or cancel the good service pay when misconduct occurred.

Not long after taking office Herchmer recommended that Good Conduct Badges be awarded to the men as a more visible sign of their good behaviour.[91] Good Conduct Badges or Stripes had been introduced into the British Army as early as 1836. It was hoped that the recipients would take more pride in themselves; that they would stand out as a role model for others; that the badges would thereby promote better discipline and morale. The Commissioner's suggestion was not approved by Ottawa until 1894. It must not be forgotten that badges cost money.

Under the new regulations every NCO and constable would be entitled to wear one Good Conduct Badge on his left arm above the elbow for every five years that he served without being convicted of a major disciplinary offence.[92] The badge itself consisted of a five-pointed gold star. In the beginning no limit was put on the number of stars for which a member might qualify. As with good service pay, the Commissioner could deprive a member of the badge for misconduct. The first rules in this respect were issued in 1895. To qualify for the badge the member had to have served for five years without receiving a prison sentence for a breach of the regulations, and without a conviction for drunkenness for the last four of those five years.[93] In August 1895, the first award of the badge was made to 116 men.[94] Given this and the statistics above on offences for the year 1894-95, it would appear that the Commissioner was right when he frequently commented that the disciplinary offences were committed by a minority of the members. The vast majority it seems went soberly through their years of service without being convicted of a serious breach of the regulations.

During the Herchmer years, in spite of public criticism in the press and in parliament, and the revelations of the Wetmore Inquiry, the strict military style of discipline which evolved under his predecessors was consolidated and expanded. For many, both in and out of the Force, this must have appeared as a perfectly natural development. By 1900, the NWMP had long lost any semblance of the civilian body its founder had originally intended it to be. It had become recognized around the world as an outstanding military corps. It was considered a self-evident truth at the time that a regiment's efficiency rested upon its discipline. In his last few annual reports Herchmer noted that with the exception of drunkenness the conduct of the men was on the whole excellent. In that of 1898 he wrote, "As a rule the men take a pride in the Force, and even those inclined to be dissipated, hesitate before jeopardizing the good reputation in which we are held at home and abroad."[95] It appears that morale was high as the Force was about to be called upon to serve in a military capacity in South Africa.

Chapter 19

The Officer Cadre, 1893-1900

With the Wetmore Inquiry behind him, Comm. Herchmer was able to make something of a fresh start in his relations with his officers. He had been cleared of any serious wrong doing, and those who felt they had been unjustly treated had had their day in court. The *Regina Leader* claimed that the public airing of their accusations had achieved nothing, that the old antagonisms persisted, but it was merely expressing Nicholas Davin's continued vindictiveness toward him.[1] The truth was, there appeared a general willingness on both sides to bury the hatchet and get on with the job. Supt. R. B. Deane probably echoed the thoughts of others when he wrote that he now had more respect for his superior, although he still did not personally like him.[2] Herchmer would still have disciplinary and other problems with some of his officers, but their differences would never develop to quite the same intensity of feeling or degree of public exposure as in the earlier period of his command.

As the nineteenth century drew to a close, commissioned officers of the NWMP continued to have a prestigious and influential role in the nascent prairie society. They also remained a strong force in the development of its social and cultural activities. Their material benefits improved slightly, particularly as far as pension provisions were concerned, and, in spite of the calls for disbandment, the opening up of the Yukon suggested that the Force might still be around for some time to come. The only really black cloud on their horizon was the possibility that the Liberals might defeat the faltering Tories in the 1896 federal election. If this happened, they worried, what would become of their futures? Would there be a purge of Conservative appointees? Would the police become a job market for the friends and supporters of the Liberals, as it had been for the Tories? What would be their chances for advancement under the new government? And what of Comm. Herchmer who had been so closely associated with the Grit's arch enemy, Sir John A. Macdonald? If Laurier did not remove him, which

seemed very probable, how much would political influence once again override his authority.

From 1893 until Herchmer's superannuation in August 1900, there were 19 appointments to commissioned rank. Six of these were surgeons. The first seven vacancies were filled in 1893-94 by the Conservatives while still in office. Three of these went to experienced NCOs recommended by the Commissioner. They were Regimental Sergeant Major Robert Belcher, Sergeant Major A. M. Jarvis and Staff Sergeant W. H. Irwin.

Although born in England and a former ranker in the British Army, Belcher had been in the police since its formation in 1873. He was a veteran of the March West and other historic moments in its early days. More recently as RSM at "Depot", his tall, authoritarian figure had become an unforgettable sight for many a recruit. The *Regina Leader*, which applauded his elevation as "A Well Merited Promotion", remarked that although a "glance from the R.S.M's eye was usually sufficient to quell the slightest tendency to unsteadiness in the ranks", he nevertheless "carries a warm heart" under his severe military manner.[3] Jarvis was another of the several scions of the prominent Toronto family of that name who served in the police at one time or another. Irwin was the son of a former head of Kingston Grammar School. He and Herchmer had attended the school together when they were boys. Although these promotions came from the ranks, their advancement was in each case, as in the past, supported by one or more Conservative members in Ottawa.

The other four vacancies filled by the Tories before they left office were all from outside the Force. The first appointee was A. E. Wills, M.D., C.M., a graduate of the University of Toronto, who obtained a position on the medical staff made possible by the death of Surgeon Dodd in 1893. A general practitioner in Belleville, Ontario, Wills had some powerful friends with influence in Conservative circles. In addition, his father was a Tory member of the Ontario Legislature. Nevertheless, the *Regina Leader* complained that the appointment should have gone to one of the three qualified applicants in the Territories, each of whom had the support of their local Conservative member.[4]

Whilst a growing number of westerners protested about easterners getting preferment over local boys for local jobs, the latter, particularly Ontarians, objected to the British, especially Englishmen, using their connections to treat Canada as a colonial employment preserve. It was not surprising, therefore, that there was a spirited outburst of complaint from that quarter over the appointment of Captain E. G. Brown, a former officer of the Gordon Highlanders and an Englishman, as an Inspector in February 1894. Representing opinion in the Militia, *The Canadian Military Gazette* grumbled about the advancement of a "rank outsider" over a graduate of RMC, or a home-grown militia officer.[5] The *Toronto Telegram*, meanwhile, thought that there were many in the ranks of the police with abilities equal to this political favourite.[6] Neither journal used the word "Englishman", but they left no doubt that it was Brown's origins they were dissatisfied with. The tone of their objection echoed the feeling that as far as the NWMP was concerned, only Canadians need apply.

In the House of Commons, the appointment was questioned by a Liberal member from Ontario. He forced the minister responsible for the NWMP to admit that Brown was indeed an Englishman. The government defended its action, however, by stressing his suitability based upon his military experience. There was no question that these were first class. Brown had been an officer in the Gordon Highlanders from 1874 to 1884. He had served with distinction in the Afgan War of 1878-1880, and had also seen action in the Boer War of 1881 and the Egyptian campaign of 1882. Not having the financial resources to maintain the lifestyle expected of an officer of a famous Scottish regiment, he had resigned his commission in 1884 and moved to Canada. A year after his arrival he commanded a troop of the Rocky Mountain Rangers during the North-West Rebellion.[7] What was not publicly admitted at the time, was that Brown had support from the highest levels of the Tory party and the upper crust of Toronto society. Among his backers for the job were T. C. Patteson, Senator George Allan, representatives of the Gooderham and Denison clans, the Conservative members for the Toronto area, and, to cap it off, he had just married into the Boulton family.[8] With such impeccable connections, one could not help but get ahead.

The Conservatives made two more appointments before going out of office. The first was Insp. Walter Martin de Ray Williams, a militia officer from western Ontario who had commanded the 7th Fusiliers from London in the rebellion. He was supported by Sir John Carling and several London area Tory members. The other was Surgeon G. P. Bell, an M.D. of the University of Aberdeen, who arrived on the prairies in 1886 and set up practice in Fort Qu'Appelle. His claims were put forward by Senator George Perley and the two Conservative members for Assiniboia. In this instance the westerners got their share of the spoils. It is interesting to note that at the time of his appointment Bell was also president of the Assiniboia Liberal Conservative Association. Actually he turned out to be a very capable and conscientious disciple of Hippocrates, who was much praised by the Commissioner of the day when he retired 20 years later.[9]

Following the success of the Liberals in 1896, their leader, Wilfrid Laurier, returned to Macdonald's practice of retaining control of the Mounted Police in the hands of the Prime Minister, on this occasion as part of his responsibility as President of the Privy Council. Laurier privately believed that the police should be free from political influence as far as appointments to the Force were concerned. He was even prepared to consider disenfranchising its members to achieve this objective.[10] As head of the government, however, he had to put his private views aside in the face of the determination by his cabinet colleagues and supporters to have their share of the booty following their election victory.

The new government was soon put on the spot on this very point. In 1897, N. F. Davin mischievously proposed in the House of Commons that the *Police Act* be amended so that only men in its ranks and graduates of RMC would be eligible for appointment as commissioned officers.[11] The Conservative member for Regina shrewdly reminded Laurier that his party had frequently suggested such restrictions on appointments when in opposition. Such a legislated limitation, he pointed out, would have its advantages. It would tie the Prime Minister's hands, and he would be able to turn away many office seekers without losing face.

Laurier responded by defending the status quo, that is the practices of his Conservative predecessors. In other words, when in office he did not do as he said he would do when in opposition. He agreed that politics should be eliminated, but saw no reason to limit the selection of candidates as Davin proposed. In the past men had been chosen from the ranks, RMC, and the Active Militia, with an occasional "special appointment". He produced statistics on the 42 officers then in service, excluding surgeons, to show that there had been no abuse of appointments based upon this selection criteria. Seventeen (40 per cent) had been promoted from the ranks, six (15 per cent) commissioned from RMC and thirteen (30 per cent) from the Active Militia. The remaining six (15 per cent) appear to have been the special cases to which he referred. They consisted of one from the Indian Department (Herchmer), one original officer (Gagnon), two former British Army officers and two farmers from the Territories.[12]

In fact, the Liberals had already given a clear signal that they were going to be just as rapacious in handing out NWMP commissions as the Tories. On 15 February 1897, the Laurier government appointed its first Inspector. He was Francis Lennox Cartwright, a militia officer. The choice followed past practices, although he did have rather poor eyesight. There was more to Cartwright than that, however. He was the son of Sir Richard Cartwright, Minister of Trade and Commerce, the senior English-speaking member of the cabinet, acting Prime Minister and one of the wealthiest men in the country, who had often criticized the Conservatives in the past for choosing such candidates.[13]

The next two Liberal appointments also had strong political overtones. Behind both was a new force to be reckoned with in Mounted Police affairs. This was the energetic and strong-willed Minister of the Interior, Clifford Sifton. In June 1897, an order-in-council placed the control and management of the police in Sifton's hands during the Prime Minister's absence.[14] In reality, however, Sifton managed to manipulate the administration and organization of the police whenever it suited his purposes, much to the consternation of the Deputy Minister, Fred White, who seemed quite unable to stand up to the Minister or bring the situation to Laurier's attention. Part of the problem was that, although the Prime Minister was genuinely interested in police affairs, he simply did not always have the time to devote to them that was necessary. Laurier later denied Sifton's interference, but the assessment of the Governor General, Lord Minto, that the Prime Minister allowed the police "to drift under his [Sifton's] influence" seems closer to the truth.[15]

The Liberals rise to power coincided with the discovery of gold in the Yukon. By the spring of 1897, the stampede to the Klondike was well underway. The situation called for additional police to reinforce those already there under Supt. Charles Constantine, who had surveyed the district with an NCO in 1894 and returned with a party of 20 men in 1895.

As Minister of the Interior, Yukon affairs were Sifton's responsibility. In August 1897, he secured a vacancy as a surgeon among the reinforcements for Dr. Hector Bonnar, the defeated Liberal candidate in the Ontario riding of Bruce North in the federal election.[16] A few days later his influence also resulted in the re-appointment of James Walsh as a Superintendent in the police. Walsh was one of the first officers named to the NWMP in 1873. He had been forced to resign in 1883 by Macdonald because he believed that the officer was deliberately undermining the government's policy to induce the refugee Sioux under Sitting Bull to return to the United States. After he left the police, Walsh became a successful coal merchant in Winnipeg, where he established a friendship with Sifton. The former officer had no love for the Conservatives. In fact he became a critic of their management of the police, privately urging the Liberals to reduce it because it was inefficient.[17]

Walsh's appointment had important consequences for the organization of the police. Through it, Sifton secured control of the Force in the Yukon for himself. The Order-in-Council of 26 August 1897, first of all named Walsh Administrator of the Yukon District, the government's chief executive officer responsible to Sifton. Secondly, it re-appointed him a Superintendent, without salary, in the NWMP with precedence in rank in the Yukon. Thus making him senior to Supt. Charles Constantine who was in command there. Thirdly, it relieved Herchmer of his authority over the police in the district.[18]

With about a third of the Force's strength transferred to the Yukon by 1898, Sifton's action had divided the NWMP into two separate commands, which were united in name only. Unhappy with losing control of the men in the gold rush country, Herchmer wrote to White for clarification of his position. The Deputy Minister's reply made it clear that yes indeed Walsh was in charge of all police matters in the Yukon.[19] Even after Walsh's resignation in 1899, Sifton continued to control most of the police activity in the new territory until he left office in 1905.

In the remaining years of Herchmer's somewhat truncated command the Liberals filled nine more vacancies for commissioned rank. Three of these were surgeons. In every case the candidates had friends and supporters of the party behind their appointment. Of the six field commissions, only one came directly from the ranks. He was Sergeant Major A. E. C. McDonell, who had been the senior NCO with the Diamond Jubilee Contingent. A native of Quebec with French-Canadian ancestry, he was one of the small number of members who was fluent in both English and French. Herchmer, who recommended him, considered him an outstanding candidate for promotion. In later years he became the first commanding officer of the Alberta Provincial Police.

Two of the other new Inspectors were former NCOs who had been discharged a few months before their appointment. Ex-S/Sgt. C. H. West was another son of a British major general. He was also a former medical student of Guy's Hospital in London, England. The other was ex-Sgt. Sam Crosthwait, a native of Ireland. Both men had served for many years in the ranks. It was not unusual for NCOs to take their discharge in order seek a commission with the help of their friends. It was a gamble, but they hoped in this manner to overcome the objection that they did not have enough seniority as NCOs.

All of the three men commissioned from outside the police had served as officers in the Militia. One of them, Insp. F. J. A. Demers, was a French-Canadian from Quebec. Laurier was anxious to increase the number of Francophones among the officers and was always on the look out for suitable candidates, with the right connections, of course. Another appointee, F. J. Horrigan, was a dry goods merchant from Picton, Ontario. His friends claimed that his nomination would go down well in the Irish Roman Catholic community from which he came, and bring in a few more votes for the local Liberal candidate at the next election.[20]

From 1885 to 1900, a total of 68 men were commissioned as officers in the NWMP, 17 of these were veterinary or medical surgeons. As a group they by no means constituted a social caste. As long as political influence was a prerequisite for advancement, the successful candidates would come from the diverse regional, racial, social and religious groups that were reflected in the political system itself. Canadian democracy had a significant levelling effect upon Canadian society. At one end of the spectrum of those appointed were the RMC graduates with their Loyalist ancestry, their education, their correct manners and standards of behaviour. At the other end, as we have seen, anyone with enough "pull", the son of a self-made man, a pay clerk, an insurance salesman or a dry goods storekeeper, with little more than elementary schooling and a rudimentary knowledge of military procedures obtained at annual militia camps, could obtain a commission in the NWMP.

As long as the Force was considered primarily as a military garrison maintaining order in Canada's uncivilized colonial territory, the need for its officers to have experience as policemen was hardly ever thought about. Not all of them were even gentlemen, as that term was then understood. More than one had to be removed from office for incompetence, immoral behaviour or alcoholism. As to aristocratic lineage, there was more of that among the ranks than the officers. What they did have in common, apart from military experience and political influence, was a strong conviction that the British political and legal system that Canadians had inherited was far superior to that adopted south of the border. They believed that they had an almost divine mission to prevent any American "ways"

from sullying the purity of Canadian institutions. Gun toting, lynching, vigilantes, gun fights or the taking of the law into the unauthorized hands of anyone were anathema to them. It was their duty to see that western society would mirror that of central Canada from whence most of them had come.

The following tables provide a statistical look at some factors in the background of the 68 appointments to commissioned rank in the years 1885 to 1900. Military service seems to have been a prerequisite. All of those selected had some kind of army experience. The largest group (45 per cent) had had an active role in the North-West Rebellion. Their elevation was, no doubt, a reward for answering the call to arms. It is also interesting that the next largest section (35 per cent) were men promoted from the ranks. Rigid social barriers to advancement were breaking down. Almost any intelligent, hard-working young constable could aspire to be an officer. In 1894, for example, Herchmer recommended S/Sgt. William Parker for a commission, although his wife was a Métis.[21] Herchmer was perhaps more egalitarian than others of his day. Parker's mother, as a matter of interest, strongly opposed her son's match. Nevertheless, Parker was eventually commissioned. It would be many years, however, before anyone else would be considered who was married to a Native or a non-white.

The birthplace of officers is also a matter of interest. It was often claimed at the time that there were too many former British soldiers in positions of authority in the Force blocking the advancement of home-grown lads. Later Mounted Police literature and films would sometimes portray the officer of this period as a sort of stereotypical British "Colonel Blimp". In fact, there were more RMC grads (ten per cent) than ex-members of British regiments (nine per cent). In total, (65 per cent) of the men appointed to officer rank were Canadian by birth, the largest group of (38 per cent) coming from Ontario. The NWMP, it seems, was more Canadian than was generally perceived at the time.

Appointments to Commissioned Rank
1885 - 1900

Table 1	Place of Birth	No.	Per Cent
	PEI	-	-
	Nova Scotia	3	5
	New Brunswick	1	-
	Quebec	15	22
	Ontario	26	38
	NWT	-	-
	Manitoba	-	-
	British Columbia	-	-
	Ireland	2	3
	England	11	16
	Scotland	2	3
	United States	2	3
	India	3	5
	Unknown	3	5
		68	100

Table 2	Previous Military Service	No.	Per Cent
	British Army	6	9
	Royal Military College	7	10
	Canadian Militia	20	30
	Ranks - NWMP	24	35
	North-West Rebellion	30	45
	No Previous Service	-	-

* Note that some individuals are found in more than one category, i.e., Insp. E. G. Brown served in the British Army, the Canadian Militia and the North-West Rebellion.

Table 3	Religion	No.	Per Cent
	Church of England	27	40
	Roman Catholic	14	21
	Presbyterian	4	5
	Methodist	1	1
	Unknown	22	33
		68	100

Table 4	Mother Tongue	No.	Per Cent
	English	60	88
	French	8	12
		68	100

The material benefits of serving in the commissioned ranks, with one exception, changed very little during the last years of the century. The rates of pay, for example, remained the same as they had been since the formation of the Force in 1873. They were not increased for officers until 1905. There were no increases for length of service, experience or merit. Unless promoted to a higher rank, an officer could serve 10, 20, or even more years, without a pay raise. These circumstances, of course, were also true for most permanent employees of the federal government. There was one notable exception, however, to this state of affairs. There was a significant improvement in the conditions under which the officers and their families were provided with a pension.

As previously noted, from 1880 the commissioned ranks were covered by the provisions of the *Civil Service Superannuation Act*. By paying two per cent of their annual salary into a fund, they became eligible for an annual pension after a minimum of ten years service. This pension amounted to one-fiftieth of their annual rate of pay for each year of pensionable service. The first officer to retire under this scheme was Surgeon Augustus Jukes who went to pension in 1893 after serving for 11 years. His annual pay was $1,400. One-fiftieth of this amounted to $28. By multiplying this by 11, he received an annual pension of $308.[22]

As basic as such a system of social security might seem later, it was an exceptional and progressive measure for the late nineteenth century. The overwhelming majority of Canadians of the time had no pension of any kind to look forward to as they grew older. Unless they provided for themselves for the time they would no longer be able to work, they would have to depend on their families and friends, or fall back upon the goodwill of various charitable organizations.

When the pension plan for the constables was debated in the House of Commons, there were those who asserted that the government had no business getting involved in such schemes. There were others though, like Nicholas Flood Davin, who believed that these measures did not go far enough. As far as the plan available to officers was concerned, there were two criticisms that were frequently heard. First, when an officer who was retired on pension died, his pension died with him. The widow, if there was one, got nothing, and could be left without any support whatsoever. The second concern was related to the first; the widow of an officer who died while he was still serving, after having paid into the pension fund for 25 years, for example, also did not receive a pension. All that a deceased serving officer's family would get in such a case was a lump sum payment or gratuity amounting to one month's pay for each year he had served.

In 1892, Asst. Comm. W. M. Herchmer died suddenly of heart disease in Calgary while still serving. He was 47 years old. Although he had paid into the pension fund for nearly 12 years, his widow only received a gratuity payment of one month's pay for each year he had served upon which to provide for herself and her two daughters. In such circumstances, there were strong pressures at the time for women to remarry out of economic necessity.

A more poignant case was that of 41-year-old Insp. Tommy Wattam. He was forced to retire in 1891 with less than ten years service as an officer because of an incurable debilitating illness. His gratuity amounted to $437.49.[23] As he had to remain in an institution and was unable to work, this sum was soon eaten up by the mere necessities of life. He soon became destitute, relying upon charity for his medical treatment. As he was a widower, his two young daughters were taken in by his brother-in-law. Wattam finally died in 1895. It says something about the sense of responsibility that existed at the time to help unfortunate neighbours or ex-comrades in arms that a voluntary subscription was started to pay for his funeral, purchase a headstone and provide something towards the support of his children. Charity played a major role in the well-being of many Canadians. Asst. Comm. McIllree who organized the fund raising set a target of $200. Actually over $300 was finally collected, or more than a year's pay for a constable.[24]

The inadequacy of the government pension scheme was brought before the public during this period by the unexpected death in 1894 of the Hon. Justice James F. Macleod of the Supreme Court of the NWT. A leader on the March West, former

Commissioner of the Mounted Police, and the one white man who had done more than any other to secure peaceful relations with the Blackfoot Confederacy, Macleod, by the time of his demise, had become one of the most respected men in the Territories, a revered and legendary figure of the frontier days. A huge crowd attended his funeral at Fort Macleod, which was of course named after him, including scores of serving and ex-members of the police. Shortly after his death the NWMP Veterans' Association in Calgary started a fund to raise a monument to his memory.[25]

As Commissioner of the Force, his financial mismanagement had led to his removal from office by Macdonald. Well-known for his hospitality, it appears that he was no better at running his private affairs. Although as a justice of the Territorial Supreme Court he received a salary of $4,000 a year, making him one of the highest paid officials in the public service, he left his family, according to a close friend, "without a dollar".[26]

As his widow was not entitled to a pension, a public petition was started in Calgary to ask the government to grant her one in view of the exceptional nature of his services to the country. Fred White warned Comm. Herchmer not to let police members sign the suit as they would likely do more harm than good.[27] Among those who did add their signatures were two former governors general, Lorne and Dufferin, who were acquainted with Macleod's contribution to the Territories, but Ottawa still refused to budge on the issue. The government knew that if it granted a pension to Mrs. Macleod, it would soon be besieged by similar demands from many others. The plight of the former Commissioner's family did, however, focus public attention on the deficiencies of the existing pension provisions.

One significant difficulty of having the officers in the Civil Service plan was that the NCOs who were commissioned were unable to count their service in the ranks in calculating their pensions. In 1897, Insp. Robert Belcher sought the help of Frank Oliver, the member for the District of Alberta, in getting an amendment to the legislation.[28] Belcher had good reason to complain. He had joined the ranks in 1873. When promoted to Inspector in 1893, he already had 20 years of service. If he had turned down the commission, he would have been eligible for a free pension in five years as a sergeant major under the 1889 legislation governing the superannuation of NCOs and constables. In accepting the promotion those 20 years were simply wiped out as far as pension credits were concerned. Under the plan for officers he simply started afresh with no pensionable service to his account at all.

Comm. Herchmer was aware of the inequities of this system. Not only was it unfair to officers like Belcher, it also discouraged some good NCOs from seeking further advancement. In 1897, he recommended that the regulations be changed so that those commissioned from the ranks could count their time from the date they were promoted to sergeant.[29] The response of the Deputy Minister was not encouraging. There was a larger issue at stake. It was not only service in the ranks of the Mounted Police that was not covered under the *Civil Service Superannuation Act*, but also employment in many positions in other federal government departments. When Insp. White-Fraser decided to retire for health reasons in 1897, he urged White to recommend to the Minister that he be allowed to count his employment in another department before he was commissioned. The Deputy Minister replied that it would do no good. The government, he told him, had in the past been under extreme pressure to allow individuals to count such time for pension purposes but had refused in every case.[30]

Officers' pensions was another issue that Davin, one of the members for Regina, took up in Parliament on behalf of his many police constituents. If anyone of the time deserved to have a monument erected in his honour for his efforts to better the conditions of the NWMP, it was Davin. In April 1897, he brought a resolution before the House of Commons that would allow officers to compute their time for pension purposes from the date they engaged in the ranks. The government might have been sympathetic to the change, but there was a second part to Davin's motion which it would not support. It called upon all commissions in the Mounted Police in the future to go to men in the ranks, or graduates of the Royal Military College.[31]

The member for Regina refused to separate these two issues. He introduced a similar resolution in 1898 and again in 1900.[32] On each occasion the administration declined to proceed with them. Laurier argued that restricting commissions to men from the ranks or RMC would deprive the Force of the opportunity of obtaining the service of experienced militia officers. Davin countered that eastern militia officers were little better than civilians, and knew nothing about conditions in the West.

Pension reform, however, was on the way. With talk of Canada contributing to imperial defence and with the country's credible performance in the South African War, the permanent active militia was slowly being improved and expanded. The Minister of Militia, F. W. Borden, sought to attract better men to the service by improving conditions and benefits. One of his initiatives was the introduction of a pension plan for militia officers in 1901. The terms of the measure paved the way for reform of the police plan.

In 1902, Laurier brought forward a bill entitled the *Mounted Police Officers Pension Act*.[33] With the passage of this measure in May all serving officers had the option of continuing under the Civil Service Superannuation scheme or becoming subject to the provisions of the new legislation for their future pensions. Everyone chose to come under the new plan. Those commissioned after its terms came into effect on 1 July 1902, had no such choice. One long-term consequence of the measure was that it perpetuated the circumstance whereby the officers' pensions were provided for under separate legislation from that of the others ranks. The two plans tended to develop differently in some respects and one result for the future was that they were not always as compatible as they might have been.

In some respects the terms of the new measure were not as generous as the old one. The minimum period of service required to qualify for a pension was raised from 10 to 20 years, and a limit of 35 years was set on the maximum that could be counted for pension purposes. An officer could serve more than 35 years if he so desired, as there was still no compulsory retirement age. Theoretically an officer could hold his position as long as he was physically and mentally able to carry out his duties.

The basic calculation for determining the amount of the pension remained the same, one-fiftieth of the annual salary at the time of retirement for each year of pensionable service. Where the new scheme was a vast improvement over the former one was that it enabled officers not only to count any time they had served in the ranks, but also their employment in other areas of the federal civil service. Furthermore, it provided for pensions for widows, as long as their husbands were on pension when they died, or were entitled to a pension, if still serving at the time of their death. These additional benefits were not without their cost. Under the Civil Service plan two per cent of their annual salary had been deducted for pension purposes. The new rate of contributions was set at five per cent.

At the time the *Mounted Police Officers Pension Act* was considered a progressive reform. Some of its provisions, however, would be considered by future generations as highly unjust and discriminatory. Under the legislation an officer was "entitled" to a pension upon fulfilling the necessary conditions. Once he received it, he could not be deprived of it for any reason whatsoever. In the case of the widows, it was a different story altogether. The Act only provided that they "may" receive a pension. They had no right to one, and would not be granted one if they were already wealthy, or were deemed "unworthy" to receive one. The latter condition referred to their state of respectability. In addition, once having been granted a pension, it could be discontinued if the widow came into a fortune, followed a "scandalous" way of life, or remarried. Except for the last reason, there is no record of a woman losing her superannuation under these provisions. Only seven officers of the NWMP were retired to pension under the terms of the *Civil Service Superannuation Act*.

With governments seeking to reduce the police in the 1890s, promotions within the commissioned ranks were few and far between. In 1892, Supt. J. H. McIllree had succeeded to the one Assistant Commissioner's position made vacant by the death of the Commissioner's brother, W. M. Herchmer. In 1893, two Inspectors were promoted to Superintendent following the death of one Superintendent and the demotion of another. With the exception of those in the Yukon, there was only one other promotion to commissioned rank during the remaining seven years of Herchmer's command. One of the reasons that some officers were anxious to go to the Yukon was that the expansion of the Force there opened up the possibilities for advancement. The Commissioner would have liked to have created more opportunities in the Territories by retiring some officers that he believed were no longer fit enough to carry out their duties, but Ottawa seemed reluctant to take action in such cases.

In 1898, he complained of two Superintendents. "One," he told Ottawa, "is too fat to ride and has been sick for months and has done no work whatsoever during this time." The other had also been incapacitated for a long period due to recurring fits, which the medical experts of the day at first diagnosed as nervous exhaustion, but were later found to be epileptic. The Commissioner suggested that in the interests of efficiency they should be superannuated. Both men, however, had Liberal party connections and nothing was done.[34] In the meantime, the command of their divisions was taken over by subordinate Inspectors, who had all the extra work and responsibility without receiving one cent of additional pay.

A year later the Commissioner brought the condition of one of the officers to the attention of his superiors once again. "Because of his 'extreme corpulence'," he reported, "he has not been on a horse in years, is going paralytic and the surgeon says his case is hopeless." He recommended six months' sick leave followed by retirement. Before Ottawa had time to reply, the Superintendent died. The *Regina Leader* pointedly noted that after a long illness his death had finally resulted from "locomotor ataxia".[35]

His expected demise had already sparked off a vulture-like competition among some of his fellow officers for the only promotional opportunity in the officer ranks to come along in years. Laurier was under considerable pressure from western Liberals to give the step up to an Inspector who was said to be one of their supporters.[36] The Commissioner, meanwhile, recommended Insp. Gilbert Sanders, an RMC graduate, who, later in life, following his retirement from the police became a respected magistrate in Calgary. Seniority usually played an important role in promotions. Sanders was not the most senior Inspector but, in Herchmer's opinion, he was the most deserving candidate.[37] Sanders, as it so happened, was also the choice of the local Liberals. On this occasion, therefore, the Commissioner's desire to advance the most efficient officer coincided with Ottawa's political needs and Sanders got the promotion.

> I propose to bring your conduct to the notice of the Rt. Hon. the Minister, in order that he may decide whether officers serving in this Force are not bound to obey the ordinary rules of gentlemen, and whether the two titles shall not go hand in hand "Officer and Gentleman".[38]

Although they were written by his successor, Comm. Lawrence Herchmer would have endorsed the sentiments behind these words with a loud "Amen". With the passing years he continued in his cause to impose a code of gentlemanly conduct upon his officers that would conform to the commonly acceptable behavioural standards of middle class, late-Victorian society. He had run into two obstacles in furthering this objective. To begin with he did not entirely control the selection of officers. Many of those chosen by the government for commissioned rank were gentlemen, but some were not. Secondly, while political influence continued to have a powerful role in determining police affairs, he never had complete authority over the disciplining of his subordinates. Of course, after the revelations of the Wetmore Inquiry, his enemies would argue that such power should never be put into the hands of someone with such a vengeful and ill-tempered nature.

When the Liberals came into office, however, he had reason to hope that he might get more support in his efforts to get his officers to set a better example of behaviour. He desired this not only for the effect it would have on the other ranks, but also because he believed they had a role as leaders in the community at large. One of the consequences of Judge Wetmore's report was that when the *NWMP Act* was amended in 1894, White's position was given statutory authority so that there would be no doubt publicly or legally that the Commissioner was subordinate to him. It did not change what had already existed in practice, but it did remove any misunderstanding on the subject. It was also useful politically in that it gave the impression that the government had punished him for his overbearing conduct by demoting him. The new legislation provided for the appointment of a "Comptroller" who "shall have the rank and salary of a deputy head of a department, and shall, under the Minister have control and management of the Force".[39]

The Comptroller and his staff occupied offices in the West Block of the Parliament Buildings. In 1897, the personnel apart from White consisted of six civil servants, three staff sergeants, one sergeant, one constable and two packers. White's immediate subordinate was Laurence Fortescue, the Chief Clerk. Fortescue had joined the Mounted Police as a sub-constable in 1873. At Fort Dufferin the following year he came down with typhoid a few days before the historic March began. Eventually he was shipped back east to convalesce. Upon recovering, he reported to the Comptroller in Ottawa for further orders. While he was awaiting instructions from the West, he was given some clerical duties to keep him busy.

As it turned out, he did them so well that he stayed in the Ottawa office for the next 42 years, eventually succeeding White as Comptroller.

The staff in the Comptroller's Office had two primary functions. The first was financial management, keeping account of all pay and expenditures and carrying out an audit. The second was the purchase of uniforms and other supplies, which were then forwarded to Regina, hence the two packers. For this purpose a storage building was also maintained in Ottawa. In 1897, there was a serious fire in the West Block of the Parliament Buildings. The Comptroller's offices were badly damaged. Although the staff threw ledgers, files and other records out of the windows, they were not able to save everything. Among the things that went up in smoke were two or three drawers of memoranda regarding the origin and development of the NWMP that White had been saving for many years because of their historical significance.[40]

White's apparent elevation in fact augured well for Herchmer's hopes of establishing an enforceable code of conduct for his officers. The Comptroller, as it happened, strongly supported his belief that the disciplinary process should be free from political manipulation. With the coming to power of the Liberals, White had good reason to believe that they might indeed achieve their objective. Upon discussing the problem of political influence in the police with his new mMinister, Laurier, he received an assurance that a determined effort would be made to discourage it. This pledge was good news, and he was quite buoyant when he reported the Minister's commitment to Herchmer:

> I feel that we have in Mr. Laurier a Minister who is disposed to back us up on disciplinary points and to stamp out politics in the Force.[41]

As it so happened, the Liberal Leader also believed that Mounted Police officers should act like gentlemen. If anything, the French-Canadian, Roman Catholic Prime Minister was more puritanical in his attitude toward matters involving misconduct by officers, especially where sexual indiscretion occurred, than the Protestant Macdonald had been. Laurier, however, was unable to ignore the well-entrenched practices of the Canadian political system overnight. The Liberals had waited a long time for their chance to pull the strings. Many of them on the prairies wanted to see a little blood-letting now that they were in power. On top of that there was Sifton's ruthless manipulation of police affairs. Laurier seems to have exerted a restraining influence on all of this, but all in all the Liberals were just as bad, perhaps marginally worse than the Conservatives in their political interference into the management of the NWMP.

From almost the beginning of the Force, Mounted Police regulations had included a list of disciplinary offences with which constables and NCOs could be charged and tried summarily by their commanding officer. If found guilty, they could be punished. Such was not the case with commissioned officers. There were no specified disciplinary rules in the regulations to which they were subject. The Commissioner could not charge them with having committed a transgression and fine or imprison them as he did the other ranks. He had long considered that this was an unsatisfactory state of affairs and, in 1894, his wishes in this regard were partially fulfilled. When the *Mounted Police Act* was amended that year section 21 was changed so that commissioned officers were subject to the same offences as their subordinates.[42]

The change removed some of the doubt about what an officer could or could not do, but it still did not give the Commissioner authority to charge them with an offence and try them as he could with other ranks. As in the past, all he could do was to place the accused under open arrest, he was not confined to his quarters or placed in custody, and appoint a senior officer to hold an enquiry into the charges. While this took place the defendant was suspended from all duties and ceased to draw pay. There was no regulatory authority for the latter course of action and Herchmer thought that there should be in case someone challenged it.[43]

Another problem with the process was that an officer could be under suspension for several weeks until the charges against him were settled. In the meantime his post was left shorthanded. First of all the senior officer had to complete his enquiry and forward his report to the Commissioner. He in turn added his recommendations and then sent the findings on to Ottawa for the Minister's decision. It was at this point that political influence came into play. Herchmer grew accustomed to waiting when a minister was absent from the capital, too busy with

other matters or just simply procrastinated for a variety of reasons before informing him of his verdict.

Occasionally men obtained commissions who were totally unsuited for the role. In these exceptional cases no amount of political pull was likely to protect them. One such young man secured an Inspectorship with the help of several members of Parliament and his father who was a senator. He eventually proved to be so "useless and unreliable" that even the redoubtable Sam Steele, his commanding officer, could do nothing with him. "He associates with the worst class of people, plays billiards with a well-known criminal and visits brothels when the men are there," reported Steele.[44] Later he was suspended after he left his post as duty officer at Fort Macleod to attend a race meeting. His departure from the Force occurred not long after, when in 1895, it was decided to reduce the number of Inspectors in an effort to promote economy.

Excessive use of alcohol continued to be at the root of most of the officers' disciplinary problems. What made the Commissioner very angry was that they tended to make a public spectacle of themselves when in their cups. One Inspector came out of a Regina Club one night so drunk he caused a serious disturbance in the streets. The Chief of the Town Police found it necessary to complain of his conduct to Herchmer.[45] When the opportunity presented itself, the officers of one division looked forward to meeting with the officers of other divisions. It gave them an opportunity to meet old friends they may not have seen for several months with whom they could exchange news and gossip. Inevitably some form of libation would appear to warm their spirits, and they would commiserate with each other over their low pay, hard work and poor quarters, or complain about the latest orders emanating from Headquarters in Regina.

Herchmer was well aware of the danger of such gatherings, and he often took steps to prevent them from occurring, unless he knew that a steady senior officer was also in attendance. It was with reluctance, therefore, that he agreed to allow a number of officers from various posts to travel to Calgary in November 1894 to participate in the funeral of Supt. E. W. Jarvis; his worst fears were realized. Several young Inspectors made a public exhibition of themselves by drinking too much. The most outrageous example was reported to him as being stoned out of his mind in uniform in the crowded dining room of the hotel where he was staying at nine o'clock in the morning.[46] This rakish young officer soon joined the billiard player and race horse fan from Fort Macleod in helping to promote the Force's economy.

Some officers, however, had too much political influence to be removed, no matter how much they drank. One such alcoholic was reported off duty for several days with delirium tremens. The Commissioner exacted a promise from him that he would abstain from further drinking, but he doubted that he would keep his pledge. If he did not, there was little he could do about it. The brother-in-law of the officer in question was a "great friend" of the Minister of the Interior, Clifford Sifton.[47]

From time to time attempts were made to rehabilitate both officers and men whose addiction to alcohol was out of control. The most common course of treatment of the period was known as the Gold Cure. Herchmer reported that it had been successful with most members who had tried it.[48] Each individual had to volunteer to take the treatment, pay the cost out of his own pocket, and apply for the necessary leave, usually about a month. Ottawa seems to have given its approval willingly to all who applied.

The so-called Gold Cure or Keeley Cure was allegedly discovered by Dr. Leslie Keeley. Born in Ireland, Keeley was brought to the United States as a child by his parents. He obtained a medical degree and served with distinction as a surgeon in the Union Army during the Civil War. Following the conflict between the States, he claimed to have found a remedy for alcoholism and opened a treatment centre, the Keeley Institute, in Dwight, Illinois. His opponents called him a quack, but by the 1890s similar institutes had sprung up all over the United States and Canada. Many were established by other doctors who either copied Keeley or dispensed their own version of the formula. Thousands of individuals flocked to these centres in the hope of being cured of the worst social ill of the time.

The cure itself consisted of a mixture of gold salts, vegetable compounds and other drugs which were injected intravenously into the patient. Its proponents argued that properly scheduled doses over a period of treatment could break the addiction. Extravagant claims were made about the success rate of the cure and for a time it was the most popular form of treatment for alcoholism. In the long run, however, the cure did not live up to its reputation. The benefits for many were found to be only temporary. The medical establishment continued to denounce it and eventually it fell into disrepute.[49]

Nonetheless, in 1894 with the Gold Cure at the height of its popularity, Herchmer worked out an arrangement with a Dr. Hunt of Indian Head for both officers and men to pay for a course of treatment by instalments. According to the Commissioner he had a number of members who were anxious to undergo the medication but were unable to pay the full fee of $75 up front. Hunt agreed to take them for the month-long remedy upon down payment of $35 with the remainder to be paid later in instalments. While undergoing the cure the patients boarded at a hotel in Indian Head.[50]

Comm. Herchmer also introduced a temperance measure of his own to discourage excessive drinking following the disgraceful incident in Calgary. He issued an order stopping the serving of spirits in all officers' messes. "Liquor was no longer to be kept in the mess," he told Insp. Starnes, the Mess Secretary in Regina. "If the mess steward violates this rule he will be dismissed. Henceforth only beer and wines will be served to officers with their meals and at mess functions."[51]

The officers' mess was an important institution through which the Commissioner could inculcate standards of conduct. By 1894, the largest of these the one at Headquarters in Regina had drawn up with Herchmer's approval a formal set of rules. These became standard for officers' messes at other posts. All officers upon appointment were required to join the mess at their location.

The entrance fee was set at $10. The rules also provided for monthly subscriptions, the election of a managing committee, monthly meetings of the members and the hours of meals. All single officers, of course, lived in the mess. The regulations were very strict about bills and other financial matters. Officers who did not pay their bills on time received a stern warning from the Commissioner, and their credit was stopped at the bar until their debts were paid. Discipline and good order in the mess was the responsibility of the senior officer present on any given occasion. As in so many other things, mess rules were largely adopted from military customs.

One thing that the regulations made clear was "strictly forbidden" was the "practice of officers treating each other". Treating was a special target of temperance organizations at the time. It was the habit whereby a man joining a group of friends for a drink felt obligated to treat all of those in the party. His friends were equally expected to reciprocate. Thus instead of perhaps just having one or two drinks, he became involved in several "rounds" to the detriment of his purse and his sobriety.

By tradition military messes also had unwritten rules. The Mounted Police was no exception. One of the most time honoured of these was the proscription against the discussion of certain subjects which might provoke discord and endanger the fraternal bond that united all officers in the service of the regiment. The most obvious of these were indiscreet remarks as to politics, religion or the reputation of respectable women. Equally frowned upon was irresponsible gossip or innuendo regarding the character of a fellow officer. The *Regulations and Orders* of the NWMP instructed that "Officers are to cultivate that spirit of unanimity and good fellowship among themselves for which every force should be distinguished".[52]

In 1894, rumours began circulating in Regina about the character of an officer. They caused the Commissioner to enquire into a case that he believed could have ruined the Force's reputation. He perhaps exaggerated, but it was a serious incidence of misplaced confidence, vindictive story-telling and false sense of honour that turned a dispute over cards into the impugnment of an officer's honesty.

One day in November the commanding officer of "Depot" Division reported to Herchmer that he had heard that a story was going around that one of the Inspectors had stolen money from the Division Orderly Office.[53] The Commissioner's instinctive reaction was to hold an enquiry under oath, not only to clear the officer's character but also to determine if a criminal offence had been committed. Unfortunately, he immediately ran into an obstacle to such a proceeding which made him very angry. The commanding officer refused to name the source of his information on the grounds that he had received the story in confidence and was honour bound not to reveal the informant. Herchmer responded by giving him until 9:30 the next morning to change his mind. When the deadline arrived and he still refused to identify the source, the Commissioner suspended him, warning him that his false idea of honour could ruin a fellow officer's reputation.

This impasse and the suspension came to an end when the Commissioner learned the source of the tale from another party. He immediately called for an enquiry under section 22 of the *NWMP Act* to investigate the whole affair. It eventually revealed that two officers had got into a dispute over a card game in the mess. Out of pique, one of them subsequently gave out an account of the quarrel which led others to believe that the other officer had stolen some money. The rumour was helped on its way around the barracks by the injudicious gossip of the commanding officer's wife. The enquiry made it clear that no theft of any kind had occurred. As a result of its findings one officer received a reprimand for telling "stories", a Superintendent was sternly told to see that his wife guarded her tongue in the future and the Minister agreed to Herchmer's recommendation that card playing should henceforth be forbidden in officers' messes.[54]

During these years the officers' mess in Regina began to have an important social role for the police. The Lieutenant-Governor, the Justices of the Territorial Supreme Court and other dignitaries were admitted as honourary members. The officers entertained these and other bigwigs who visited Regina to lunch or dinner, or perhaps a "Smoker" in the evening. There were as yet, however, no formal regimental dinners or levees. On New Year's Day the Commissioner and the other officers attended the levee at Government House. In keeping with its growing sense of decorum, no one was allowed to bring dogs into the mess. All drinking, except when eating, was confined to the billiard room, and meal hours were to be strictly observed - breakfast 8 a.m. to 10 a.m., luncheon at 1 p.m., dinner at 6 p.m.

An early concern of the Mounted Police was officers engaging in business activities that conflicted with their duties. Following the March West some officers had started cattle ranching. In effect this put them in charge of protecting their own property. It left them open to the accusation that the men under their command were more concerned about the safety of their herds than they were about those of their neighbours. Eventually the regulations were changed and one of the few proscriptions that applied directly to officers was that they were not to operate ranches or deal in livestock. In 1893, a report that an officer had started a sheep ranch brought him a strongly worded memo reminding him that such conduct was forbidden.[55]

As an exception Mounted Police surgeons were allowed to run a private medical practice in addition to their official police duties. There were two reasons for this. First, as doctors were sometimes few and far between, it would have been inhumane to deny the public the benefit of their services. Second, it was hard to keep a good doctor in the police service on the salary he received. They were permitted, therefore, to make extra money on the side. They needed watching, however, to ensure that their private interests did not grow to the detriment of their police responsibilities. As well as operating a livery stable, one surgeon opened up his own drug store. On one side of the counter he was the druggist selling drugs. On the other side he became the police doctor buying them. The Commissioner felt that this went too far, that there was a conflict of interest. With Laurier's approval he was told to cease his business ventures or hand in his resignation.[56]

The question of officers becoming involved in more complex entrepreneurial schemes arose in 1896 when the Commissioner saw a report in the *Calgary Herald* that announced that the Ibex Mining and Development Company had just been organized in Kaslo, B.C. to take over the famous Brennard group of mining claims. It went on to state that Supt. Sam Steele was the president of the new company and Insp. A. M. Jarvis was on the board of directors.[57] The Kootenay area had experienced a short boom in silver mining a few years earlier. In 1895, a sudden rise in the world price of the metal awakened interest in re-working the old claims.

The Commissioner wrote to Steele to inform him that he did not believe that officers should

271

occupy official positions in business ventures, and to ask for an explanation for the Minister.[58] Steele's reply revealed that a number of the men of his division had also purchased shares in the company, and that S/Sgt. Hilliard was also on the board of directors. Fred White raised the possibility of the enterprise going "bust" and the disappointed shareholders claiming that they were induced into speculating in them by their commanding officer. Laurier's ruling on this matter came quickly and firmly. Officers, he decided, may invest their money in businesses, but they should not become involved in their management.[59] Steele and Jarvis had to resign from the board. On the other hand, Hilliard, who was only an NCO, was allowed to retain his position.

Mounted policemen of all ranks were always on the look out for ways to make money. Some of them tended to be attracted to get rich quick schemes like bees to honey. Very few of them did in fact become wealthy as a result, but they never seemed to lose their optimism. Comm. Herchmer was no exception. Having cleared up the matter of investments, he decided to put some money into the mining undertaking himself. He was discrete about it, however, purchasing 800 of the 25 cent shares in the name of his wife and his daughter.[60] It was all to no avail as the Ibex Mining and Development Company did not, as it turned out, make a fortune for anyone.

There was one source of wealth from which a few mounted policemen did benefit and that was the Klondike. The lucky ones were those who were among the party of 20 which accompanied Supt. Charles Constantine on his return to the Yukon in 1895. They were on the spot the following year when George Carmacks registered his fabulous claim that started off the last great gold rush. When some of them came out of the Yukon in 1897, the newspapers carried stories about sacks of gold, and of five of them having $200,000 between them.[61]

Naturally, the other officers and men wanted their share of the pot of gold. Later reinforcements of police to the Yukon were forbidden to stake claims, but there were other ways to get in on the action. Although far from the diggings, Comm. Herchmer quite legitimately tried to benefit from the discovery. He and Supt. Constantine agreed to stake a former NCO to try his luck on the Klondike. In return for paying his passage to Dawson City and providing him with $200 for supplies, they were to get one-half of all the gold he found. The ex-member in question was a tall Australian named Charlie Ross, a rough, tough, colourful character who was probably a bit of a rascal. Ross later distinguished himself in the South African War, leading a force of Canadian Scouts and rising to the rank of colonel. Judging from the Commissioner's later complaints about his financial state, the Yukon enterprise like the mining shares did not make him a rich man.

The Commissioner's disciplinary action with regard to his officers was often reported in the press as it had been in the early years of his command with accusations of unjust treatment. This criticism reached a peak in the winter of 1896-97 as a result of a spectacular crime in Calgary. On the night of the 12th of November that year the safe in the Orderly Office at "E" Division Headquarters was robbed of $629.16 in cash and cheques to the value of $306.40. To say that the police were embarrassed is to put it mildly. One of the most serious robberies of the period had taken place right under their noses. What was worse, the circumstances surrounding the theft suggested that it had been an "inside job".

The money had been locked in the safe at 3 p.m. by the Superintendent in command, Joseph Howe. Its loss was not discovered until he opened it again at 10 a.m. the next morning. The lock had not been tampered with. Whoever had committed the crime must have known the combination.[62] The investigation that followed revealed flagrant breaches of the regulations and inexcusable carelessness on the part of the officer commanding. In punishing those responsible Herchmer was once more accused of tyrannical conduct, political bias, and the press, especially the Liberal organs, revived the clamour for his removal from office.

As soon as he received the startling news, the Commissioner despatched Supt. A. B. Perry from Regina to lead the investigation into the theft. The first suspect was a corporal who had previously been a bank clerk in Toronto, but contact with the police authorities there revealed nothing incriminating. Inquiries were also begun into the background of several other members at the post. Meanwhile, Perry discovered that, on the night of the misdeed, the duty NCO had failed to make the required rounds through the barrack rooms to see who was in bed and who was not. He had also omitted to see that the sentries were properly relieved, and had not kept track of the time that the men who were out on pass returned. As a result Perry could not determine just who was where at the time the offence was most likely committed. In short, the thief could have been anyone of the about 40 men serving in Calgary.

The actions of the officer commanding only compounded the problem of catching the culprit. Although he had been ordered by the Commissioner not to leave large sums in the safe overnight, he had neglected to transfer the money to the bank in town for safekeeping. It was likely that several members were aware of this. Worst of all, however, was the way he carelessly left a slip of paper on which the safe's combination was written in an easily accessible place in his office. The combination was supposed to be known only by the Superintendent and the two Inspectors at the post. Perry's investigation showed that it could have been discovered by anyone who had access to the office. Among these was a civilian prisoner from the guardroom who cleaned it regularly every morning without an escort. In fact, the Superintendent's negligence in securing the identity of the combination was so well known that the two other officers preferred to keep large sums that they were responsible for on their persons until they had an opportunity to go to the bank, rather than put them in the safe.

In the end Perry's detective work was unable to identify the thief and no charges were ever laid. Not for the first time, the Mounted Police had failed "To Get Their Man". Comm. Herchmer, however, had no doubt where the blame lay for allowing the conditions to exist that enabled the crime to go unpunished. In a stern note to the officer commanding, he reprimanded him for the slackness at the post and his disobedience in not securing the money. He threatened that unless the cash was recovered he would recommend to the Minister that he repay every cent himself.[63] The cash amount was made up of $358 from the men's canteen fund, $159.66 pay for the men on detachment and $111.50 which was security on a contract. The total of $629.16 was almost half of a year's pay for a Superintendent. As to the other ranks who had been guilty of breaches of post orders, they were quickly and summarily dealt with through fines, demotions and transfers. The most serious offender, the duty NCO, was reduced from sergeant to constable and sentenced to four months imprisonment with hard labour.[64]

After reading Perry's report the Prime Minister agreed with Herchmer that the officer commanding should be punished for his carelessness by having to make good the cash that was taken.[65] Later, however, he began to have second thoughts about this decision. First of all the officer responded to the verdict by protesting that he had been found guilty without an opportunity to defend himself. Herchmer had not formally charged him with a breach of the regulations as provided for in the 1894 changes to the *Police Act*.

Another thing that caused Laurier to waver was the public outcry against what was felt was the Commissioner's harsh treatment of the other members. The *Calgary Herald* described his action as "Tyranny at the Barracks".[66] The paper claimed that since the thief had not been caught Herchmer was making everyone suffer, treating all the men like abject slaves and disciplining others without cause. It called for a public enquiry into the robbery and the Commissioner's subsequent action. The *Edmonton Bulletin* under its owner, Frank Oliver, the new Liberal member for Alberta, went even further. It not only lashed out at the unjustifiably severe punishments for "minor breaches" of discipline and the transfer of men without consideration for their wives, but claimed as well that those being punished were being so because they had voted Liberal in the recent federal election.[67] "It is time that Comm. Herchmer went to pension," it concluded. Privately, Oliver advised the Prime Minister that Herchmer and White were not telling him the truth about the events connected to the theft. "The officer commanding," he charged, "was being singled out for supporting the Liberals."[68]

Upon hearing that Laurier was relenting on the question of the officer's punishment, the Commissioner penned a bitter complaint to Ottawa about the injustice of such action. He could hardly be expected to maintain discipline, he protested, when an NCO gets four months with hard labour for disobeying orders and his superior who had committed the same offence gets off scot-free.[69] In the end Laurier reached a compromise. The officer had to repay in instalments the $271.16 that was considered "public money". This was made up of the $159.66 destined as pay and the $111.50 security on a contract. The $358 in cash from the men's canteen fund was written off, a further punishment on them all. It was not everything that the Commissioner had recommended, but it was enough to give him good reason to believe that the new Prime Minister would back him up where glaring infractions of the disciplinary code by officers were concerned.

There was still little that any Commissioner could do about the few officers who had so much influence they could thumb their nose at his authority, unless they became involved in a scandalous affair with a woman, committed a criminal act, or were guilty of a serious breach of regulations like that in Calgary. In 1895, for very good reasons, Herchmer refused an application for leave from Insp. Macpherson. The young man responded by asking his father, Sir David Macpherson, to go and see the Minister. Shortly after, the Commissioner received an order from Ottawa to grant the requested leave. The following year the same selfish officer decided that Banff was a desirable location to which he would like to be transferred. It was indeed a plumb of a posting. The officer in charge of the detachment there could avail himself of the very fine facilities at the Banff Springs Hotel, as well as participate in the varied social events put on for the guests. Using his influence behind the Commissioner's back, he arranged to have the incumbent at the mountain resort removed and himself sent in as his replacement. Herchmer was furious when he found out, but all he could do was fume and threaten.[70] These were the realities of the political system that he reluctantly had to accept.

Fortunately, the overwhelming majority of his officers were hard-working, dedicated and honest men. As he wrote in 1895, "All ranks have done their duty with cheerfulness and alacrity, and I have received the strongest support from Asst. Comm. McIllree and all the officers and non-commissioned officers in the Force."[71]

Chapter 20

Horses and Music: The Force's Evolution from Function to Ceremony

The majority of saddle horses now used by the Force are bronchos or natives; they having been found very much superior to the eastern horses.[1]

In the 15 years before 1900 the use of the horse by the Mounted Police reached its zenith. The horse was as important to the police then in carrying out their duties as the automobile would be later. Comm. A. G. Irvine put the matter very succinctly, "The usefulness of this force depends upon its mobility, and mobility depends upon the quality and sufficiency of horses."[2]
The dependence increased as the number of communities and settlers grew and the patrol system expanded to serve them. Upon another level, it was the period in which the first Musical Rides were produced, and the Mounted Police acquired an international reputation after its members participated on horseback with the military elite of the British Empire in the pomp and pageantry of state occasions like Queen Victoria's Diamond Jubilee. It was also a time when the "Mountie" became an established literary figure. The scarlet rider and his trusty steed became inseparable in the public mind. The stereotypical image that ensued would continue long after the horse had ceased to have any practical use in the performance of his police duties. During this time also, several divisional headquarters organized bands which became popular musical attractions within the Force and to the public.

Between 1886 and 1900, 10 to 15 per cent of the annual expenditure of the NWMP went to the purchase and maintenance of horses. In most of these years more was spent on feeding horses than on food for about the same number of men.

The establishment for horses was set at 90 per division, or 900 in total. The actual strength during the period, however, averaged a little over 800.

About 100 new horses, termed remounts, had to be purchased each year to replace those that had died or become unsuitable for further service. Horses were so vital to the effectiveness of the police that as much effort was put into selecting remounts as was in finding recruits, and they certainly received care equal to that of their riders. To protect this capital investment by keeping it in good health, the NWMP developed a first-class veterinary service.

Concern for the welfare of the horses is attested to by the lengthy instructions relating to them to be found in the 1889 *Regulations and Orders*.[3] Upon purchase, a description of the animal was entered in the Register of Horses at Headquarters. Recorded was the age, height, previous owner, cost, identification marks and final disposition, when either sold or destroyed. Once entered in the Register it would be given a "register number" which would identify it throughout its service. In the early years, horses had been registered and numbered by division and, upon leaving the service, their numbers had been allocated to their replacements. As with the early regimental numbers of the men, this led to confusion when it came to identifying individual horses. As a result, in 1883, all of the horses were re-numbered consecutively throughout the Force, and upon being cast, that is discharged from service by being sold or destroyed, their numbers were not assigned again. It became a case of one horse, one number. Horse No. 1 under the new system was Comm. Irvine's mount "Jack", who died in 1890, aged 17, having travelled many thousands of miles.[4] Mules and ponies were given their own register numbers preceded by the letter "M" or "P" as the case may be.

From time to time, horses like "Jack" who had given long and faithful service were not sold or destroyed when no longer able to carry out their duties. Instead, they were turned out to pasture to be kept as pets. Another of these was "Crowfoot" (regimental number 70), an "old favourite", who at age 20 being no longer fit for work, was handed over to the NCOs and men of "Depot" to be cared for until he died.[5] The most venerable of them, however, was "Old Buck" (regimental number 199), described as the "patriarch of the police force". "Old Buck" had been ridden on the March West in 1874 by Trumpeter (later S/Sgt.) Fred Bagley. Twenty-five years later he was still working. Finally, in 1899, at the age of 32 the Commissioner sanctioned his being destroyed at Lethbridge because of his infirmities. Insp. Morris lamented that, "Horse flesh in the police force has deteriorated to a marked degree since 'Buck's' advent."[6]

Once registered, a remount was branded with the fused "MP" brand of the NWMP on the near shoulder, and its register number marked on the near fore hoof. The brand had officially been allotted to the police in 1887 under territorial regulations.[7]

Photographic evidence shows, however, that it had been used for many years before this by the Mounted Police, not only on horses but accoutrements as well. Actually, some horses did not have the brand applied as they already had one or more brands from previous owners. It was used, though, on the few cattle the police acquired or bred from time to time.[8] The horses of the scouts employed by the Force were branded with the letter "S" on the near shoulder.

The naming of horses was left to the divisions where they would serve. It was common practice there to allow the name to be chosen by the first member to whom it was assigned. It had become customary by 1886, however, that whatever name was chosen it would commence with the same letter as that of the division. Hence all the horses in "G" Division had names beginning with "G".[9] The name of each animal was printed on a card above its stall.

The regulations were very specific about many other things. Stables were to be kept thoroughly clean and well ventilated at all times. Horses were to be fed and watered three times a day, morning, midday and evening. "Full time is to be given the horses while drinking, and care must be taken that the men do not hurry them."[10] Each horse received about 900 lbs. of hay a month. Not all of this was eaten; a small portion was used as bedding. The daily ration of oats for a saddle horse not on patrol was two to four kilograms, and up to six kilograms when on patrol. Team horses were fed up to seven kilograms when working.[11] The veterinarians in each division were required to inspect every horse in their care once a day. They also supervised feeding, shoeing and the treatment to be given sick animals.

By 1885, the Mounted Police had come to rely almost entirely on outside sources for their supply of remounts. Any serious attempt to breed their own was abandoned in 1882 when the breeding station at Pincher Creek was leased to the Stewart Ranching Company. The breeding farm had taken too many men to operate. A stallion was kept for a while and a few mares bred to it from time to time. "Clandeboye", the stallion, was sold in 1887, however, for $125 to a settler at Whitewood.[12] Thereafter, mares were occasionally bred to the stallions of local ranchers and a fee of $15-20 paid.

The increase in men from 500 to 1,000 in 1885 resulted in an urgent need for horses on which to mount them. Over 400 remounts were hastily purchased that year. The majority of them were of poor quality. One of Herchmer's priorities was to weed out the unsuitable ones and find good replacements. He explained that the Force needed saddle and team horses capable of travelling 50 miles a day and more for several days at a time even in the extreme cold of winter.[13] Unfortunately, he was unable to find all the new stock he needed in the Territories. He had to import 125 team horses from Ontario. Like his predecessors, he found that these eastern animals took about a year to acclimatize. The first winter was especially hard on them, and they often reacted adversely to the change in feed and the alkaline content of prairie drinking water. He was more fortunate where saddle horses were concerned. Over 200 were purchased from ranchers in the Territories, British Columbia and Oregon. They gave every satisfaction, were cheaper than Ontario horses, and were less liable to illness or death from bad water and extreme temperatures.

The horses the Commissioner was so pleased with were western bronchos, the offspring of thoroughbred stallions and the Indian-bred descendants of Arabian stock brought to the New World three centuries earlier by the Spaniards. The word "bronco" or "broncho" derived from Spanish signifying something wild, rough or half-tamed. They averaged 15 hands, had good heads, short backs and weighed around 1,000 lbs. In addition, they could drink water that would make eastern horses ill, and survive on herd during the winters by digging through the snow for forage with their feet. The western broncho would be the equine mainstay of the police for several years to come.

The Commissioner purchased many of the horses himself. He travelled around the horse ranching country two or three times a year, usually accompanied by the senior veterinary officer. The local press followed his activities closely as the sale of horses to the police was an important source of income to the ranchers.

"The Comm. of the NWMP will purchase a few good saddle horses at the Barracks on Wednesday," announced one paper.[14] "They must be sound, well-broken, four to seven years old, 14.3-15.2 hands and of good colour," it continued. Another report stated that he had been buying horses in Fort Macleod and High River. Thirty-four had been purchased at prices from $80 to $140 each, most from the Davis, Patrick and Cross ranches. Herchmer was quoted as describing them as the best he had ever bought for the police.[15] On another occasion it was noted that he had rejected most of the horses offered to him because they were too weak-backed and too young.[16] He preferred remounts four to five years old.

As the supply of suitable horses increased in the West, the need to import animals from Ontario declined. In 1887, Veterinary Surgeon Burnett reported that most of the saddle horses purchased were bronchos, superior to those from the East, cheaper to buy and ate less food. The best, he believed, came from British Columbia and Oregon because breeders there had been using thoroughbred stallions with native mares longer. He noted though that breeding in the Territories was rapidly improving.[17] The following year, almost all of the 125 remounts obtained came from the NWT. The average price was $125 for saddle horses, $150 for team.[18] In 1889, for the first time, all of the horses purchased were bred on the Canadian prairies. The best of them came from some of the well-known ranches of the time, Frank Strong's at Fort Macleod, the North-West Cattle Company at High River, the Quorn Ranch near Calgary and the Oxarat Ranch south of Maple Creek.[19] These were among the principal suppliers of remounts to the Mounted Police of the period.

The horse ranchers were very happy with the published statements of the police about the virtues of bronchos. They and their backers hoped to promote western Canada as a major producer of horses for the military. One of their fondest hopes was to turn the prairies into a remount station for the cavalry regiments of the British Army. The *Calgary Herald* went so far as to urge the government to send a detachment of police and their mounts to perform at the annual Military Tournament in Islington, London as part of an advertising campaign.[20] Ottawa did not take up the suggestion. When the police and their horses did go to London in 1897 they were much admired, but the British did not rush to buy bronchos from western ranches. The truth was the cavalry had almost become obsolete as a fighting arm.

In 1892 came the first warning that suitable horses were no longer available as plentifully as they had been earlier. "First class troopers are now hard to get," reported the Commissioner.[21] In the years that followed, finding remounts became more and more difficult. The problem of supply went far beyond the Canadian prairies. The fact was the age of the horse as a principal means of transportation was rapidly coming to an end. The immediate cause of the difficulty was the replacement of horse-drawn buses in North American cities with electric street cars. There was a glut of common horses in eastern Canada. As a result, prices dropped sharply and cheap Ontario animals were readily available in the Territories. Local ranchers there found it more and more profitable to breed cattle rather than horses.

By 1894, the demand for saddle horses had declined to the point where the police had trouble selling all the horses they cast. In earlier years the proceeds from the sale of cast animals usually accounted for about half of the cost of their replacements. As a result, Herchmer approved the destruction of those unsaleable, who would otherwise "eat their heads off".[22] Those destroyed were used as meat for the dogs around the barracks.

As a solution, Herchmer suggested that the department award cash prizes annually for the best three horses for police purposes presented at the Territorial Fair in Regina.[23] Following Ottawa's approval, the first competition was held in 1895. There were 14 entries. The first prize of $50 went to a five-year-old bay gelding bred by the Quorn Ranch. A four-year-old bay gelding sired by "Nuremburg" and presented by a Mr. Thomas of Cut Arm Creek, Regina won second prize of $25.[24] The Commissioner purchased both horses for $125 each, as well as several other of the entrants. He commented favourably upon the horses presented, but although the competition continued, it did little to reverse the general decline in breeding suitable remounts for the police.

The situation improved briefly in 1896. Ninety-one "re-mounts, all young, and sound, generally by thorough-bred stallions" were obtained at an average price of $60. Most of them came from the Quorn Ranch, offspring of the stallions "Eagles Plume" and "Scottish Chief".[25] In subsequent years, however, Herchmer complained again and again of the difficulty of finding suitable animals and the deterioration of breeding on western ranches. Eventually his successor would have to go outside the Territories to find remounts.

The training of the horses and the recruits to ride them was the responsibility of the riding staff at "Depot" Division in Regina. The staff usually consisted of one experienced senior NCO who was appointed "Riding Instructor", and as a result wore the traditional "Roughrider" badge, a spur, on the right arm. Between 1885 and 1887, this position was held by George Kempster, who had had many years of experience in British mounted regiments. In 1886, the office of "Riding Master", the senior position in a riding school, was revived with the appointment of Insp. W. G. Matthews to that post. When the latter was transferred to Lethbridge in 1889, the position fell vacant and remained so for several years.

Kempster's successor as Riding Instructor was S/Sgt. W. D. Bruce who, as a native of Guelph, Ontario, was an exception to the British cavalry types who usually filled the position. Bruce was admired by his contemporaries for his ability to break difficult horses.[26] When he took his discharge in 1897, he was replaced by Frank Church, a former corporal major in the Royal Horse Guards. Church learned of the need for a riding instructor in the NWMP while talking to members of the Mounted Police Jubilee Contingent in London. Quickly obtaining his discharge from his own regiment, he high-tailed it to Regina at his own expense and was successful in obtaining the position. He was a fortunate acquisition. Sgt. Major Church (later Inspector) would maintain the best standards of horsemanship, and eventually revive the Musical Ride.

The majority of remounts purchased by the police were completely untamed. Since birth they had grazed on the prairie with the ranch herds without any close contact with a human being. They had never felt bits in their mouths, or saddles on their backs. There were those who argued, like Veterinary Surgeon Burnett, that all remounts should be sent to Regina for a period of training by experienced riders who would gently obtain the horse's confidence and hence its trust and obedience.[27] Unfortunately, there was such an urgent need for them that there was no time for a process of schooling. Most horses were "broken" rather than "trained". Their cooperation and obedience was obtained through force instead of trust. A few did not even get to Regina. They were broken in the divisions by members who had experience as a "broncobuster", or by local cowboys engaged briefly as special constables for the task at $35 per month.

One recruit who witnessed a number of remounts being broken at Regina in 1891 has left a detailed account of what he described as an exhibition of rough riding and bucking that exceeded anything he had ever seen in the Wild West Shows that came to his native Toronto. The broncobuster on this occasion was Special Constable Louis Cobell, probably the finest horse breaker ever to serve in the police. The remounts were first driven into a small corral. One by one a rope was thrown around their necks. Holding on to the end of it, Cobell endeavoured to reach the animal's head, while it retreated quivering with fear at the sight of the approaching two-legged monster. After a struggle, he managed to attain his objective. A few moments were spent trying to gain its confidence then a blanket was thrown over its eyes, and one leg pulled up under it to restrict its movements. Deprived of sight and hobbled, a saddle was placed upon its back and a bridle forced upon the head of the terrified creature. Cobell then sprang into the saddle and readied himself. The blanket was removed and the leg released:

The first movement on the part of the broncho after finding himself thus encumbered, was to shake himself – after the fashion of a dog coming out of the water – expecting in this manner to rid himself of the burden upon his back. Finding himself unsuccessful in this, however, he would attempt to roll, but a vigorous touch from well-appointed spurs would bring him sharply to attention. He would then remain passive for a few seconds, and then wildly toss and twist his head in a vain effort to shake off the bridle. With his head hanging between his fore legs he would then remaining standing motionless in that position for about half a minute, as though in deep and anxious thought, his eyes shining the while like fire, and his whole frame quivering with nervous excitement. Then, as a sleepy dog is often seen to stretch himself, placing his fore legs in front and bending its back like a bow, so did the horse, but it was a preparation on his part for a wild leap in the air, which would immediately follow, accompanied by a loud, indescribable snort or scream of rage. The suddenness and velocity of these leaps was sufficient to unseat any but a born horseman. He [Cobell] was immovable. The animal after these leaps in the air would land upon the ground with his four feet so bunched that a square foot would have contained them all, but no sooner would he touch the ground than in a twinkling the operation was repeated with equal vigor and energy. He [Cobell] remained upon his back during this frenzy of bucking, as though part of the animal, and seemed to experience not the slightest discomfort or anxiety through it all. The broncho would continue his "bucking" without the slightest intermission for a space of about ten minutes, and then with a mad kick and snort, and his head hanging between legs, would rush off in a wild chase over the prairies, stopping occasionally only to indulge himself in a spell of vigorous and earnest kicking, after which, with a few wild buck leaps in the air, he would rush off again as though driven by a hundred demons. These antics he would continue with perfect equanimity of purpose without the slightest intermission for nearly two hours when, cut and bleeding at the mouth and sides, and in some cases absolutely blind for a time with his own rage and madness, he was about ready to abandon the fight. The saddle and bridle were then removed, and the horse turned loose again in the corral.[28]

The same procedure was then gone through with the next horse. No wonder that following the arrival of a bunch of remounts the *Regina Leader* reported a "lively time" at the barracks breaking them in.[29]

The initial riding instruction given to recruits was similar to that administered in the schools of the cavalry regiments from which the instructors had come. On the one hand, it stressed the practical techniques of the art of horsemanship based upon the control of the animal by the proper use of the legs, hands and position of the seat. At the same time, it observed the traditional school of hard knocks belief that the ability to learn to ride was somehow related to the number of times the recruit had fallen off a horse. As one authority has written, the cavalry riding school of the day was a place of terror for many young men. The aim of the instructors being to cause as many falls as possible.[30]

Shortly after being appointed Riding Master in 1886, Insp. Matthews secured the Commissioner's permission to change the equipment used by recruits during riding instruction.[31] They had been riding with California saddles and Whitman bits. Matthews believed that it was dangerous for inexperienced riders to use these bits as too much pressure could easily cause the horse to rear. What he objected to most of all, however, was the use of western- or California-style saddles by recruits. Learning to control a horse by means of pressure applied by the rider's legs was an essential feature of traditional cavalry training. The Riding Master complained that the skirts or flaps of the western saddle were so thick that the legs could not make sufficient contact with ribs of the mount. As a result, the western tack was replaced during training by universal-style cavalry saddles and bits, and the recruits were taught the movements and formations of regular cavalry drill. Once through training they would switch to the more innovative mounted infantry drill that Herchmer had decided the Force should adopt.

The recruits' first acquaintance with the horses began with the thrice-daily parade to the stables to water, feed and groom them under the critical eye of the riding staff. Efforts were made to keep a group of well-trained, steady mounts at "Depot" for the trainees.[32] Instruction began in the riding school twice a day, morning and afternoon rides. No saddles were used until the recruits had acquired a sense of balance and were able to stay mounted at least some of the time by gripping their horses with their knees. Even after they graduated to the comfort of a saddle it would be several weeks before they were allowed stirrups, and later still, spurs.

The instructor took his position in the centre of the riding school. As the recruits circled around on their horses, his eyes searched for the slightest error. Failing to follow his instruction exactly was considered disobedience. Censure and ridicule were sternly administered to those unfortunate enough to catch his attention for some wrong movement. Punishment was meted out to the repeat offender. No excuses were accepted. One recruit recalled, that while proceeding at a walking pace during the first few days, he felt "tolerably secure". There

came one morning, however, when for the first time the instructor in a "stentorian" voice gave the order to "trot".[33] At the sound of his command the horses broke into a brisk trot. Any that lagged behind would hear the crack of his whip at their heels. In a few moments recruits were coming off their steeds in all directions. Upon picking themselves up, they were confronted by the angry autocrat of the riding school who demanded to know who had given them permission to dismount. Those who tried to retain their seat by wrapping their legs around their horses only succeeded in making them trot all the faster, and soon joined their companions on the ground.

Cst. C. P. Dwight found, however, that after a few weeks of riding without stirrups he and his fellow recruits had begun to acquire something of a "seat". There were many falls, a lot of sore limbs, but no serious injuries. A few recruits tried going on sick parade to avoid the terrors of the riding school, but the surgeon warned them that they would be reported for malingering. Dwight himself found that the constant friction between the tender skin of his posterior and the leather saddle resulted in the latter being dyed with his own blood. Upon complaining of this he was informed that his condition was "trifling", and that it was the only way to learn to ride.[34]

After a few weeks the recruits were switched to California saddles and Whitman bits, and were taken outside to ride on the prairie. They were now permitted to wear spurs, but they were warned of the danger of applying them too forcefully on bronchos. Dwight recalled that one of his fellow recruits accidentally spurred his mount. The broncho bucked three times and then took off at full gallop with its rider hanging on for dear life, finally disappearing over the horizon. Several hours passed before recruit and horse returned wearily to the stables.[35] Misapplication of spurs was a cause of serious accidents.

Bronchos could also be stubborn and balky. Two greenhorn young constables were once in charge of a horse and sleigh. They tried everything they knew but they could not get the animal to budge. The sergeant major, upon seeing their difficulty, proceeded to give them a lesson in the care and management of horses that would not be found in any manual of instruction. Marching into the post kitchen, he returned with a hot potato from the stove. He raised the horse's tail and slipped the spud under it. Off went the poor beast like a "flash of lightning". The tighter the animal pressed its tail down, the more the hot steam came out of the squashed potato.[36]

During the winter months, groups of men were sometimes brought into Regina for a period of remedial riding instruction. The experienced older hands resented the efforts of the regimentally minded staff to cure them of their "bad habits". After being on detachment for a while, they rode in the relaxed manner of the cowboy, their arms going up and down from the shoulder like a bird flapping its wings. One remembered that on his first morning in the riding school the disgusted instructor shouted, "Orderly! Open the windows and let them fly."[37] Another complained that the "genius of the manège", the Roughrider, "had not left the barrack square since he landed", and did not understand that it was impossible to sit on a horse in a stiff regimental manner when out on patrol all day, day after day, in all kinds of weather.[38]

Although they were generally well cared for, Mounted Police horses were expected to work hard and suffer hardship from time to time. In 1887, Herchmer issued an order that except for unusual circumstances a horse was not to travel more than 40 miles a day.[39] Records indicated, however, that this figure was frequently exceeded. From May 1888, divisions were required to keep a daily record of the mileage of each horse.[40] Considering each animal spent some time on herd and did not work every day, some remarkable mileages were tallied. Four horses driven by Cst. Aylesworth at Lethbridge hauled their heavy wagon just over 5,000 miles for the year 1888. Four-horse teams were routinely used in the Lethbridge area because of the steep grades on many roads and trails. In 1895, the only year for which a record of every horse could be located, the total mileage for the whole Force was 1,719,630 miles. Supt. Perry reported that three saddle horses in his division that year patrolled over 6,000 miles each, and nine others over 5,000 miles.[41] At Lethbridge, meanwhile, Supt. Deane praised horse Reg. No. 1873 which "has never been sick or sorry", and was ridden 4,898 miles in the year by Sgt. Higinbotham whilst employed taking the census, rounding up seized American cattle and hunting for stolen horses.[42]

Bronchos were tough but so too was the prairie environment. The winter of 1886-87 was an extremely severe one on the Canadian plains. Comm. Herchmer noted that although they had received excellent care several horses had died as a result of exposure, or the effects of extended patrols in badly watered country.[43] Cpl. Donkin described a forced march of about 120 miles from Wood Mountain to Regina by "B" Division during that winter. There was little snow on the ground but many of the springs had either dried up or were frozen hard. On the first day the party reached Willow Bunch, a distance of 45 miles. Here they were lucky to find some drinkable water. After noon on the second day, however, the water they found in the ice-covered ponds along the route had so much alkali in them that it was fit for neither man nor beast. It was not until they reached the Moose Jaw Creek on the night of the third day that they found suitable water. The horses had not had a drink for 36 hours. On the fourth day, with 32 miles to go to reach Regina, it began to snow and the temperature dropped to -40°F. The men had to dismount and walk beside the animals in order to keep their legs and feet from freezing. The poor horses, meanwhile, suffering miserably from the cold, plodded on with icicles hanging from their nostrils.[44] On such occasions it was not unknown for men to cover their mounts with their own blankets.

Summer could bring its own particular problems. The report of a patrol near Batoche in June 1896 recorded that the black flies and mosquitoes bit the horses so much that they would be "used up", exhausted, in the morning. To alleviate their torment the men had to repeatedly apply fly oil to their bodies, and keep smudge pots burning around them all night in an effort to drive the insects away with smoke.[45]

Injuries and accidents involving horses were frequent, sometimes with fatal results. Every year several animals had to be destroyed because of broken legs. These were mostly the result of falls, being kicked by other horses, or catching their feet in gopher holes. There were also a few drownings each year. In 1893, one horse was killed when it fell into a well.[46] Another was gored to death by a cow, and one more got stuck in a snowdrift while on herd and froze to death.[47] At Boundary Creek Detachment in 1897, a remount had to be destroyed after it got tangled in barbed-wire.[48]

Riding or driving horses had its dangers for human beings as well. It was common for men who spent many hours sitting on the back of a horse to develop severe cases of haemorrhoids or varicocele, a varicose condition of the spermatic cord in the scrotum.[49] The source of more serious injuries, however, were the frequent accidents. Runaway horses were common. Between 1886 and 1900, seven members died directly as a result of riding mishaps, and many more were badly injured.

In 1887, the *Regina Leader* reported five serious accidents within a few months. Similar occurrences could be found in newspapers at other locations. One constable was thrown out of a rig and landed on his head. Another was kicked in the face by a horse and permanently disfigured. Sgt. Farmer, the bandmaster, was ejected from a runaway buckboard, the rear wheel passing over his head. It was feared for a while that he would lose his sight. A young recruit was injured after being dragged when his foot caught in a stirrup. Mrs. Moodie, the wife of Insp. Moodie, had ribs broken and a shoulder dislocated when knocked over by a wagon at the barracks.[50]

There were two fatal accidents in 1890. The first involved 28-year-old Sgt. A. E. G. Montgomery, a former school teacher from Quebec's eastern townships. He fell from his horse when it lost its footing during drill at Prince Albert. The animal rolled on top of him causing a severe concussion of the brain from which he died three days later without regaining consciousness.[51] The second occurred under similar circumstances. While exercising his mount on Stephens Avenue in Calgary, Cst. W. T. Reading's horse stumbled. He was thrown to the ground. The horse tumbled on him breaking his spine in three places. He died the following day. A "good reliable man", lamented his commanding officer. He was also "our best cricketer".[52]

Two years later, Cst. Hans Prahl died after his skull was crushed in a fall with a horse at Lethbridge. A native of Prussia, Prahl had formerly served in the 9th Uhlans, a cavalry regiment of the German Army. The reason for his horse's tumble appears to have been the very thing recruits were constantly warned against, pulling on the reins sharply whilst at the same time applying the spurs.[53] A runaway team led to the death of Cst. B. A. Lutz at Battleford in 1895. Thrown from the wagon, he too suffered a concussion from which he did not recover.[54] Cst. John Kingscote was out riding with a woman friend near Wapella that same year. He dismounted to pick up something that had fallen from his companion's saddle. As he was remounting his nervous horse lunged away from him pulling him to the ground. It then struck out with its feet kicking him in the neck. At first he appeared to be just badly shaken, but upon returning to Wapella began to spit blood. The young Irishman from County Galway died a few hours later.[55] Two other deaths, that of Cst. W. A. Buchanan in 1898 and Cst. H. L. Flower in 1899, were at least partly attributable to accidents with horses.

Each year between 20 and 30 horses died from disease, or were destroyed for medical reasons. The veterinarians were constantly on the alert for any signs of serious contagious infections like glanders and typhoid. The latter was the most destructive as far as Mounted Police horses were concerned. Its worst outbreak occurred in 1888 after two horses from Writing-on-Stone Detachment bolted across the border during a severe thunderstorm. They got mixed up with infected horses on the Miller Ranch in Montana, where typhoid among the animals had already reached epidemic proportions. After wandering back to Writing-on-Stone they passed the sickness on to the other police horses there. It soon contaminated the stock at other detachments in the area as well.

Alarmed at its rapid spread, Assistant Veterinary Surgeon T. A. Wroughton at Fort Macleod telegraphed Regina for help and then hurried to the border posts. There he was joined by his superior, Veterinary Surgeon J. Burnett. For a time the nature of the disease baffled the two men. Finally, they determined that it was a virulent form of typhoid fever similar to that which infected humans. Wroughton believed that healthy horses picked it up from grass which had been soiled by the excreta of infected ones. Steps were immediately taken to stop the spread by isolating the sick animals. These either recovered or died in a period of five to seven days. Most of the horses at Writing-on-Stone, Milk River and nearby detachments succumbed to the disease. Elsewhere, eight died at Battleford before it was brought under control.[56] As with glanders and other dangerous communicable maladies the carcasses had to be buried promptly, all articles close to the horse that were likely to harbour infection burned, and the saddlery thoroughly disinfected.

Mounted Police veterinarians laid much of the blame for sickness among the horses to poor stabling or, as in the case of Prince Albert, no stables at all. Several horses died there in 1887 from a lung ailment after being kept in the open tied to lines during an extraordinarily cold and wet summer.[57] Their stables were in the process of being built. Most divisions in 1886 did not have an isolation stable so that animals with infections could be separated from others. Considerable improvements were made in stabling throughout the Force, however, in 1887. By the time John Burnett took up his duties as senior veterinary officer that year, he found all divisions well equipped with stables. His first report stressed the importance of proper light, ventilation, heat and drainage, and praised the newly completed accommodation at Prince Albert as "first class".[58] Burnett also believed firmly that the surface of the front half of stalls should be made of clay. Horses in their natural state, he advised, had few problems with their feet because they obtained a sufficient amount of moisture from the ground to keep them healthy. Once they were kept in a stall with a surface entirely of wooden planks, he argued, their feet became dry and hard, resulting in numerous foot complaints. Planks need only be used at the rear for the sake of cleanliness. His recommendations were eventually introduced in most Mounted Police stables, apparently with beneficial results.

In their annual reports for this period the veterinarians in the divisions, with the odd exception, described the health of the horses under their care as generally good. By far, the two most common medical problems were wounds, a result of minor accidents or kicks, and a wide variety of abrasions, such as collar and saddle galls. Next in order of prevalence were foot, respiratory, digestive and muscular ailments. The total strength of horses for 1893 was just over 800, and 842 treatments were administered by the veterinarians. Twenty horses died or were destroyed.[59]

The horses received the best veterinary care available at the time. The position of Veterinary Surgeon had been abolished in 1877 as part of a policy of financial restraint. The health of the animals was left in the hands of veterinary NCOs. Some of these were qualified, some partly qualified and others simply self-taught in the care of horses. They wore their badge of appointment, a horse shoe, on the right arm. With the doubling of the establishment in 1885, the capital investment in horseflesh rose to well over $100,000. Sir John A. Macdonald evidently decided to protect this asset better by gradually improving the quality of the veterinary service. In 1886, the commissioned rank of Veterinary Surgeon was revived, and Veterinary Staff Sgt. Robert Riddell, a graduate of the Ontario Veterinary College in Toronto, was promoted to it at a salary of $700 a year. His principle task was to oversee the work of the veterinary NCOs in each division. Herchmer argued that given the area to be covered it was too big a job for one man.[60] This seemed to have the desired effect and the new position of Assistant Veterinary Surgeon was created. Another graduate of the Ontario Veterinary College, S/Sgt. John F. Burnett, was moved up to the position at a salary of $600 a year.

A continuing problem with professionals like these was that NWMP pay rates were not always very competitive with the money that could be made in private practice. The more ambitious veterinarians tended to leave once more lucrative opportunities presented themselves. Riddell's pay only amounted to a little over $100 a year more than he had received as a staff sergeant. As an officer he had extra expenses, including the purchase of his uniform. As a result, Riddell resigned at the end of 1887 and headed for greener pastures. Burnett was promoted in his place, and another staff sergeant, T. A. Wroughton, became the Assistant Veterinary Surgeon. In 1890, upon Herchmer's continued urging, their salaries were raised to $1,000, the same rate as an Inspector, and $700 respectively.[61] Both men remained in their positions until well after 1900. The senior veterinary surgeon was based at Headquarters in Regina, and his assistant at Fort Macleod. They regularly inspected the veterinary staff sergeants located at each division. By 1900, all of these were professionally qualified, mostly graduates of the Ontario Veterinary College.

Under the regulations the veterinary surgeons were completely in charge of the care and treatment of all sick or injured animals. They examined all remounts before their purchase, and sat on the boards that decided whether a horse was fit for continued service or should be cast. The farriers came under their supervision, and during the winter months they visited the divisions to give lectures on the rudiments of health care for animals to the men. Veterinary NCOs in the divisions, meanwhile, were required to inspect every horse daily and report any illness to the surgeons. They also administered any medicines or treatment prescribed and oversaw shoeing and branding.[62]

Most shoeing was done by the division farrier, who was also often a blacksmith as well. In his 1893 report, Veterinary Surgeon Burnett spoke well of the ability of these farriers. He found, however, that the detachment men who sometimes had to shoe their own horses did not get enough practice or instruction.[63] As a consequence, local farriers were employed from time to time when detachment men were not able to get to their division headquarters. Farriers wore the same badge of appointment, a crossed hammer and pincers, as blacksmiths. S/Sgt. "Jocko" Robinson was the farrier and blacksmith at Regina for over 30 years. He was one of the colourful and unforgettable "characters" of the time. He projected a fierce exterior and frightened wide-eyed new recruits from the East with stories of man-eating bronchos and scalping Indians. Later they would learn to bring their troubles to him and thank him for his wise and fatherly advice. "Jocko" had a pet poodle to which he was greatly attached. One day the Provost NCO was ordered to collect any dogs he found on the post and impound them. Upon finding that his dog was missing "Jocko" went berserk. A large man, he picked up his hammer and headed across the Barrack Square. The sight of him approaching was enough to scare the Provost and the poodle was soon running free again.[64]

By the 1880s, mass-produced, machine-made shoes had replaced those fashioned by the farriers themselves. Thousands of kilograms of shoes and nails were purchased annually by the Mounted Police from suppliers on the prairies. When Herchmer took over command, the shoes currently in vogue were known as the "Montreal" pattern. There were many complaints about them, the principle one being that they broke easily. As a result the Force switched in 1887 to the "Rhode Island" pattern. Veterinary Surgeon Burnett found them much more satisfactory and they became the standard shoe throughout the Mounted Police for many years to come, although other types like the "Chuler" pattern were used from time to time.[65]

In spite of the regulation calling for monthly shoeing of horses, many of the bronchos were never shod at all. In 1892, Burnett issued instructions to the veterinary NCOs that they could decide whether or not a horse should have shoes. One later reported back that many of the saddle horses in his division had not been shod during the year, even though they had been employed regularly on patrol. There had been no injuries as a result. Even the team horses had gone through the summer months without shoes. In winter they had been shod so that caulks could be applied to the shoes to prevent the animals slipping on ice.[66]

The story of the early saddlery of the NWMP is similar to that of the uniform, a case of the eventual rejection of standard cavalry accoutrements in favour of those that experience showed were more suitable to local conditions and circumstances. The Force had started out in 1873-74 with a variety of military riding tack, most of the saddles of the Universal pattern, usually with Pelham bits. They did not turn out to be entirely satisfactory so there followed several years of trial and experimentation with different types of saddles, including the McClellan, Whitman and Western.

By the 1880s, the consensus of opinion among both officers and men was in favour of the Western, otherwise known as the California, Cowboy or Stock style of saddle, and the Whitman bit. These became standard issue throughout the Mounted Police until well into the twentieth century, although samples of other patterns were tried from time to time. A few officers had their personal preferences and purchased their own equipment, and the Universal saddle was retained for recruit training.

The Western saddle had its origin in Mexico. In some respects it was a modification of the saddles brought to the New World by the Spanish Conquistadors. Its use later spread to the southwestern United States, from whence it became a favourite of the "cowboy".[67]

The distinctive features of the Western were its high pommel, high cantle, the rear arch of the seat, and its long stirrups which extended the rider's legs so that he almost stood in the saddle. Its traditionalist detractors compared it to a rocking chair and heaped scorn on those who used it, claiming that it was almost impossible to fall out of. The police, however, from experience found it better suited to prairie conditions. For example, used with a double cinch it produced fewer galls and sore backs when patrolling in rolling country than other types of saddles did.[68] It was not only more comfortable for the horse, but also easier on the rider on a 37 to 50 miles journey. In addition, its wooden stirrups did not conduct the cold to the feet as easily as metal ones during the winter. Its principal disadvantage was its weight of about 30 lbs. This went up to 45 lbs. when head collar, bit, reins, blanket and saddle wallets were added. Nevertheless, the adoption of the Western saddle, like the "cowboy hat", was another element in the transformation of the

British cavalry trooper of the NWMP into a "Rider of the Plains".

The principal supplier of the first Western saddles was the U.S. company of Main and Winchester. As with other equipment, the police were often under a certain amount of pressure to support local producers by buying Canadian. Saddles made in Canada had been tried in the past but had always proven unsatisfactory. However, when the increase in horses in 1885 resulted in the need for additional saddlery, an order for new equipment was placed with two Canadian manufacturers, Barbridge of Ottawa and MacLaren of Montreal. Their imitations of the American-made saddles were received in Regina in late 1885 and early 1886. They turned out to be of such poor quality, however, that many were soon unserviceable. Herchmer reported, "All imitations of the California saddle as yet made in Canada are unsuitable, and if used on service for a week would not only use up all the men but give sore backs to every horse in the command."[69] Once more, therefore, the police had to return to their old source and buy 100 saddles from Main and Winchester of Portsmouth, New Hampshire.[70] These were found to be quite satisfactory, although the Commissioner suggested that the trees, the frames, might be a couple of inches longer to enable great coats to be carried in a roll behind the saddle. He also came out adamantly in favour of double cinches, and requested that in future no more single cinch saddles be purchased. Eventually, most of the Canadian-made ones were condemned and eliminated.[71] It would only be a matter of time though before Canadian craftsmen would improve the quality of their work.

In the spring of 1887, Comptroller White received a letter from E. F. Hutchings and Company, saddle and harness makers of Winnipeg, seeking an opportunity to compete with the U.S. firms for the Mounted Police custom. It was accompanied by a note supporting the application from a Winnipeg member of parliament. White forwarded it on to Regina, instructing the Commissioner to place a small order.[72] The instance was a good example of how White's position shielded Herchmer from having to make decisions over political patronage.

By the end of the year Veterinary Surgeon Burnett was able to advise his superiors that the Canadian-made saddles had come through their trial period with flying colours. Using two of the best trees available, the Goodall and the Viscillia, the Winnipeg manufacturer, had produced a saddle equal to that of Main and Winchester. He recommended its adoption throughout the Force and the dependence upon American supplies brought to an end.[73] Under similar circumstances Burnett was also able to report in 1887 that veterinary instruments made in Toronto were now just as good as those the police had been importing from England, and only half the price.

By 1891, all of the saddlery and harness supplied to the Mounted Police were being produced in the NWT or Manitoba. Not everyone, however, was entirely satisfied by the Western saddle. Both Supts. Griesbach and Perry considered it acceptable, but too heavy. Superintendent Antrobus, meanwhile, repeatedly complained that "D" rings should be added to the cantle to enable great coats to more easily be carried on the rear of the saddlery. Eventually his recommendations were adopted and a modified saddle was produced by Hutchings.[74] Perry argued that putting 45 lbs. on a horse's back even before it had a rider was too heavy a burden on the animal. He also took issue with those who said it was more comfortable, claiming that while that may be so at the canter or gallop it was certainly not the case when the horse was at the trot.[75] After he succeeded Herchmer in 1900, the search began for a lighter model.

One of the principal reasons for choosing the Western saddle over other types was that it produced fewer sore backs among the horses. This was dependent, however, upon there being adequate protective padding under the saddle. For years the police had complained about the quality of the numnahs, the felt pads placed underneath the saddle, supplied to them. In 1886, Herchmer reiterated the comments of his predecessor, complaining that they only lasted four months and then had to be replaced.[76] Veterinary S/Sgt. J. L. Poett recommended that a saddle blanket be used, either in combination with the numnah, or instead of it on horses prone to sore backs.[77] This advice was generally adopted and with the acquisition of a better supply of felt in 1890 the problem was rectified.

As to horse blankets, there were two types in common use in the period. The first, usually referred to as the "old pattern", was manufactured by Barbridge and Company of Ottawa. It was described as a grey wool blanket lined with No. 18 jute. The second was also lined with jute, but had a check weave. The Commissioner preferred the older pattern. He found it better sewn, had better lines, was warmer and it absorbed the perspiration quicker.[78]

A key figure of the time in keeping the horses equipped for patrol work was the Force's Saddler Major in Regina, who oversaw the repair and maintenance of all saddlery. For years the police had had difficulties obtaining suitable harness, head collars, bridles and other saddlery accessories. Herchmer suggested that the problem might be solved if in future the Force made its own. "We have the required skill," he informed the Deputy Minister, "in the person of Saddler Major Horner, 'a mechanic second to no tradesman in the Dominion'. All we need to carry out the job," he continued, "was a few good stitchers and the leather to do the work".[79] "Of course," he added, "it would be a saving to the public purse."

Ottawa agreed, and by 1889 the Commissioner was able to report that the saddlers were producing all the martingales, pole straps, hopples, reins, head collars, halters, side straps, and even sword and cross belts, holsters and bandoliers that were needed.[80] A variety of saddlery accoutrements still had to be purchased from suppliers in the Territories and Manitoba, but it was a major step towards self-sufficiency at a considerable saving. It was just the kind of administrative innovation that Macdonald and the parliamentary penny-pinchers loved to see. In the process of doing the work, the saddlers discovered through experience that leather which had been tanned with acid obtained from the bark of oak trees had a closer fibre and resisted water better than leather tanned with acid from the bark of other trees.[81]

The man referred to as having outstanding skill in working with leather was Saddler Major Sam Horner. Although born in Schenectady, New York, Horner grew up in Hamilton, Ontario. His military career began quite early. In 1861, at the age of 16, he joined the Canadian Militia when an American invasion was threatened over the "Trent Affair". He saw active service during the Fenian raids of 1866, and four years later went west as a private in the Red River Expedition to seek adventure.

Where Horner served his apprenticeship as a saddler and harness maker is unknown. His reputation was known to Comm. French, however, who persuaded him to join the Mounted Police in Winnipeg in 1875. Horner was the Force's Saddler Major with the rank of staff sergeant from 1875 to 1890. He was easily recognizable around the barracks in Regina by his huge, unkempt black beard. Horner took his discharge to open up his own shop in Lethbridge. It was a move he later regretted. Sam Horner's workmanship was admired and known throughout the Territories for years, but his saddlery and harness business did not thrive.

Approximately a third of the horses in each division were team horses. It was their task to pull the ten heavy wagons, three buckboards, one ambulance, eight heavy sleighs, three light sleighs and two single sleighs allocated to each division by the regulations. These were used to transport a variety of supplies as well as prisoners and personnel. Actually, the regulations were not strictly observed, and the number and type of transport varied from place to place. In 1893, "H" Division at Fort Macleod, for example, had two heavy freight wagons, seven heavy wagons, seven spring wagons, four half spring wagons, often referred to as "Minchin" wagons, seven double buckboards, five single buckboards, four bob sleighs, one jumper and one water wagon with a 600 gallon tank.[82] According to general orders, all heavy wagons, spring wagons and buckboards were to be painted ordinance blue, and all lighter transport black with red running gear.[83] Sleighs were often equipped with bells.

As with other supplies, there was the usual pressure to buy Canadian. Once again it was a question of waiting for transport made locally to equal the quality of those imported from the U.S. By 1891, Herchmer was able to report that all light transport purchased was being produced in the NWT or Manitoba, the principal suppliers being McCurdy and Tucker of Moosomin, Massey, Harris of Winnipeg, Hudson's Bay Company of Winnipeg and W. R. Fish of Prince Albert.[84] The experience of the police with Canadian-made heavy wagons was not quite as satisfactory and they continued to purchase those made in the U.S., particularly Schuttler wagons.[85]

In addition to horses, mules, and oxen, pack ponies and sled dogs had a role in transporting the Mounted Police and their supplies. An ox train was still in use at Fort Macleod in 1886. The commanding officer did not think much of the ponderous beasts. They were too slow and could not be used in snow. He recommended that they be sold and the money obtained put to better advantage by buying mules.[86] The suggestion was approved. Several divisions had one or two mules from time to time. Because of the hilly country in the Fort Macleod area it was decided to put together an ox train again in 1897 for hauling heavy freight. Seven of the animals were purchased. The Commissioner ordered that they were to be worked as long as possible and then destroyed for dog feed.[87] It was no good keeping them through the winter. They would not earn their keep.

The police found pack ponies an asset on long patrols in difficult terrain, where trails were poor or non-existent. The animals used for this purpose were Indian ponies. Like the bronchos they were descendants of the Arabian bred horses brought to America by the Spaniards. Although smaller than their cousins, they were – if anything – tougher. The Mounted Police purchased many of these ponies from the Blood Indians at prices ranging from $12 to $15 a head. Supt. Steele took over 30 pack ponies with him on the expedition to the Kootenays in 1887. In the closing years of the century the police obtained large numbers of both ponies and sled dogs as their operations expanded into the Yukon and the northern regions of the Territories. Many of the dogs came from Labrador. In his report for 1899, the commanding officer for the Fort Saskatchewan district, where there were a growing

number of winter patrols using sled dogs, reported their annual mileage as 2,734 miles.[88]

By the end of the century the total annual mileage patrolled by Mounted Police horses in the Territories had declined to about half of the almost 2,000,000 tallied in 1895. The number of saddle and team animals on strength in December 1899 was 572,[89] the lowest number, by far, since 1886. Patrolling should have increased, given the fact that immigrants were arriving in larger and larger numbers. Each year there were more farms and settlements for the police to visit. The Commissioner continued to complain about poor quality horses and high prices, but this was not the explanation for the reduction. The decrease was a result of the transfer of men to the Yukon beginning in 1897. Strength dropped from 730 on the prairies in 1896 to 501 in 1899. The "Day of the Horse" for the Mounted Police was by no means over, but it had peaked. There would never again be quite as many hours spent in the saddle on western trails asking for "Any Complaints".

The Herchmer years also saw the beginnings of what would, many years later, be the world famous RCMP Musical Ride. Mounted displays by units of cavalry are probably as old as soldiers engaging in mounted tournaments, cavalcades and sports as an occasion to show off their ability to ride and their prowess with weapons. During the last half of the nineteenth century it became popular for cavalry regiments throughout the British Empire to give public demonstrations of their military proficiency. These usually involved a mounted troop being put through its drill movements, and was often followed by a mock battle on horseback, or contests in swordsmanship and the use of the lance.

From the late 1880s, such displays by the NWMP at Regina and other main posts became a regular feature of celebrations on holidays like the Queen's Birthday in May and Dominion Day on July 1st. The 50th anniversary of Queen Victoria's reign in June 1887 was observed in many communities with parades, speeches and sporting events. A troop of Mounted Police was included in the program at Edmonton. Supt. Griesbach put the men through various drill movements at the walk, trot and gallop. To the delight of the crowd of spectators, the mounted display ended with a sham fight.[90] In Regina on the Queen's Birthday in 1890 the public was invited to the Barracks for a program of mounted events. These included tent pegging, Tilting at the Ring, Cutting the Turk's Head, mounted wrestling and a demonstration of lance drill by a troop trained by Insp. Tommy Wattam.[91]

By the 1890s, the entertainment provided by the police had become such a regular feature of Dominion Day celebrations in Regina that it was referred to as the "Annual Athletics and Military

Sports of the NWMP".[92] Two of the most popular events were the Balaclava Melee, named after the site of the famous charge of the Crimean War, and bareback wrestling. In both sports a troop was divided into two opposing teams. During the Melee each team wore padded clothing, face masks, similar to those in fencing, and wielding wooden swords charged their opponents trying to unseat them. These were rough and tumble sports; the participants often suffered scrapes, bruises and sprains, but the settlers enjoyed the events and so did the men.

The program in 1896 started on June 30th with athletic contests before several hundred spectators lining the sports field at the barracks. Among the events were the 100 yard dash, won by Cst. Browning, who also took first place prizes for the quarter mile, the hop, step and jump and the hurdles. There were various races for children. Cpl. Fred Light won the cricket ball throw with a toss of 110 yards. The day concluded with a tug-o-war competition, wheelbarrow and obstacle races.[93]

The biggest attraction for the townsfolk, however, was the military display that took place at the Exhibition grounds on the following day, Dominion Day. The show kicked off with a "Grand Review" of the entire "Depot" establishment in full dress uniform. The Division along with its field guns and transport teams paraded past the reviewing stand at the march, trot and gallop in various cavalry formations. This colourful scene was followed by military sports. Events included Heads and Posts, Tilting at the Ring, Tentpegging, Bareback Wrestling, and Needle and Thread Race, won by Mrs. Margaret Belcher, wife of Insp. Robert Belcher, riding "Ritchie". The Finale was the Balaclava Melee with Cst. A. H. Richardson's team pitted against that of Cpl. Hilliam. Cst. Richardson would later win the Victoria Cross while serving with the Canadian Forces in South Africa. His opponent would become Brigadier General E. Hilliam, C.B., C.M.G., D.S.O. and Bar. The prizes for these contests were presented to the winners by Mrs. Mackintosh, the wife of the Lieutenant-Governor. According to the *Regina Leader* much of the credit for organizing the program was due to Sgt. George Service, the division carpenter.[94]

What distinguished a Musical Ride from exhibitions of cavalry movements and drills was the substitution of a brass band for the orders shouted by an instructor. Instead of responding to words of command, the change from one formation to another was signalled to the mounted troops by a change of tempo or tune in the accompanying music. The result was a non-stop harmonious blend of music, movement and horsemanship. The first known public performance of what was from the start termed a "Musical Ride" was given by the 1st

Regiment of Life Guards at the Royal Military Tournament in London, England, in June 1882.[95]

The Royal Tournament, as it was later popularly known, had its start in 1880 as "A Military Tournament and Assault-at-Arms". The inaugural performance was held in north London at the Agricultural Hall, Islington. At first it consisted largely of competitions between contingents from several British regiments. There were shooting contests, sham battles, jousts with various weapons and riding events like tilting the ring and slicing the lemon. Much later the Royal Navy, Royal Marines and the Royal Air Force added their own contributions to the annual event to turn it into a vast military pageant. The first tournaments lasted for about a week.

It was intended to use the profits to assist the widows of soldiers. Unfortunately, for the first two years, 1880 and 1881, the public stayed away in droves and it was a financial flop.

This all changed in 1882. That year the 1st Life Guards introduced a Musical Ride into the program. It was an instant success and the hall which seated 4,000 persons and had standing room for 10,000 more was packed for every performance. Thereafter the Musical Ride became a permanent and popular part of the spectacle. For many years the 1st and 2nd Regiments of Life Guards took turns annually to put it on. Another popular innovation at the Royal Tournament occurred in 1884 when a display of cavalry movements was presented by the 3rd Hussars. The origins of these first Musical Rides and mounted displays remain very obscure. Tradition links them with tournaments held earlier by British Volunteer regiments. It is also likely that they had some tie with the experience of the British Army in India, where military pageants that included mounted events had been taking place for some years. There are, however, good reasons to link these events in London with the first NWMP Musical Rides in Regina in 1887.

As with so many other developments in the Mounted Police at this time, the Musical Ride owes its appearance to the changes wrought by the Rebellion, the increase in men, the creation of a permanent training centre in Regina and the new construction program. One of the buildings planned for Headquarters was a large wooden indoor riding school. Hitherto, all mounted training had taken place out of doors. Needless to say, it was frequently disrupted during the winter by severe weather. A riding school was essential to the organization of a Musical Ride because it was only during the winter, when the men had been brought in from the summer detachments, that there were sufficient riders available to train. Construction on the riding school began in the summer of 1885. It was not completed until May of the following year.[96]

The riding school provided the necessary accommodation. Two key individuals now entered upon the scene. The first of these was George Kempster, who took his discharge from the Life Guards in London in 1884, and came to Canada and joined the Mounted Police in December of that year. The 30-year-old Kempster had also served for several years in the 11th Hussars. Whether he was involved in the first Musical Rides in London from 1882 to 1884 is unknown, but as a member of the Life Guards stationed there it is unlikely that he would not have known about them. In fact, Kempster turned out to be an outstanding horseman and, by 1885, he was the riding instructor in Regina with the rank of sergeant major.

Finally, and probably most important, there was Insp. William George Matthews, a 40-year-old former Lieutenant and Riding Master of the 3rd Hussars, a regiment which had had a prominent part in presenting mounted displays at the Royal Tournament. Matthews had also spent several years of his service with the regiment stationed in India. He was commissioned an Inspector in the NWMP on 20 October 1886. Shortly after his arrival at Headquarters, Herchmer appointed him Riding Master. He took up his new duties just as the men of "B" Division returned to Regina from their summer detachments to spend the winter at mounted and dismounted drill. Exactly what Matthews and Kempster knew about Musical Rides at this point, no one will ever know for sure. They were certainly experienced and accomplished horsemen and together with the new riding school, the men of "B" Division and the newly organized Headquarters band under Cpl. Jakey Farmer had the expertise that put together the first Musical Rides of the NWMP.

There were five public performances of the Ride during the winter of 1887. The records of the NWMP reveal very little as to the nature of them. Although they sometimes comprised 16 men instead of 32, from the descriptions of them in the local newspaper they appear to have had most of the elements which are to be found in the RCMP Musical Ride later. The first performance took place in the riding school on Saturday afternoon 15 January 1887.

In the spectators' gallery were Commissioner and Mrs. Herchmer, several other officers and their spouses, as well as a number of guests from town who braved a blizzard and sub-zero temperatures to attend. The reporter from the *Regina Leader* described the scene:

> The band, under Mr. Farmer, played a spirited march, and sixteen Mounted Policemen, with lances at rest . . . were putting their equines through a series of

geometrical and other figures with remarkable accuracy and skill, with a most pleasing effect.

> After going through a number of interesting gyrations, radiating circles and other odd figures, now walking, the next minute trotting, and then breaking into a gallop, the horsemen formed into a line at the opposite end of the pit from the gallery, and as the band struck up 'Bonnie Dundee', cantered forward to the other end, keeping exact time with the music, halted abruptly, broke in the centre, wheeled sharply to right and left, formed fours and cantered back along the sides.[97]

Apart from the number of riders it sounds very similar to the present RCMP Musical Ride. "Bonnie Dundee" was to remain a favourite tune with future rides.

The second performance took place on Wednesday the 26th of January but the newspaper did not cover it. The third occurred a month later on the 26th of February. This time it was a state occasion with His Honour Lieutenant-Governor and Mrs. Dewdney in the gallery, and there were 32 riders instead of 16. The newspaper's brief account describes it as being "heartily applauded by the spectators", and reflecting "great credit on the drill officers".[98]

The next Musical Ride was presented a few days later on Saturday, March 5th. Once again the Lieutenant-Governor of the NWT attended, along with deputy ministers from Ottawa, the territorial justices and other local dignitaries. The *Regina Leader* found this Ride similar to the others, but "more interesting and exciting". Once again there were 32 riders. The charge at the end was so warmly received that, at the request of the ladies in the audience, Insp. Matthews had it repeated.[99] The final Ride of 1887 took place on the 5th of April. Unfortunately, the newspaper did not report on the event. A few days later "B" Division headed out for Wood Mountain and its summer detachments.

The only illustration depicting these first Musical Rides is a drawing by the well-known American frontier artist Frederic Remington, which appeared in the 24 December 1887 issue of *Harper's Weekly*, a New York magazine. It shows 16 riders charging with their lances at the engage. The scene, however, is set on the barrack square rather than in the riding school. Whether Remington actually witnessed one of the first performances is not known, although he certainly was in western Canada about that time. The editor of the *Regina Leader*, who did see the Rides, described the drawing as "pretty accurate".[100] Indeed, the detail of the uniform and saddlery is so good it is hard to believe that Remington was not working from real life.

Several years would pass before there would be another performance of the Musical Ride. There were a number of reasons for this. The first and most immediate was that on 26 November 1887 a fire was started in the riding school by a faulty stove in an adjacent harness room. In bitterly cold weather the fire extinguishers were found to be frozen and within minutes the showplace of Headquarters was reduced to a pile of ashes and rubble. In addition, the principals behind the first Rides soon moved on to other things. In October 1887, Sgt. Major Kempster purchased his discharge to try his hand at farming. He eventually died in Calgary in 1920. During the winter of 1888, the band was temporarily suspended due to a lack of musicians. Insp. Matthews, meanwhile, had been transferred to Lethbridge where there was a shortage of officers for field duty. Mrs. Matthews had detested Regina. Lethbridge did not improve her view that life on the Canadian prairies was dull and unsophisticated, a colonial backwater. In 1893, Matthews resigned his commission and returned to England.

More important in the long run, however, was newspaper criticism. A satirical Toronto weekly called the *Grip* saw the Rides as an example of extravagance by the conservative government of Sir John A. Macdonald, which was sensitive to allegations of misuse of public funds. It published a cartoon which labelled the Musical Ride as "Lady Dewdney's Own", and suggested that murder and robbery were taking place while policemen were being used to entertain the Lieutenant-Governor's wife and her friends. The message hit home.

It would be a while before the Mounted Police again engaged in any such "frills". Nevertheless, the 1887 Rides were well received by the citizens of Regina, who, in an age when the horse was still an important means of transportation, were qualified to recognize the skill they represented. They would not be forgotten. Eventually, there would be requests for a repeat performance. As to the Mounted Police, they saw the potential of the Musical Ride for promoting goodwill in the community. A tradition was in the making. The riding school was rebuilt in 1889, but with the departure of Matthews and Kempster it would be a few years before circumstances would again favour the organization of another Musical Ride.

The NWMP had become a colourful part of the pomp and ceremony of state and official occasions on the prairies. They participated in the Opening of the Territorial Legislature, fired salutes on the Sovereign's birthday and provided mounted escorts for Governors General, Prime Ministers and a variety of visiting dignitaries. The appearance and reputation of the Mounted Police were well known at home. With the celebration of Queen Victoria's Diamond Jubilee in 1897 they would make their international debut on the stage of imperial pageantry.

The young Princess Victoria had ascended the throne in 1837 following the death of her uncle, William IV. In June 1897, she would look back upon a reign of 60 years. She had been on the throne so long that only the very old could remember another sovereign. Although unpopular in middle age with many of her subjects, she attracted considerable affection in her later years.

The approach of the Jubilee coincided with a new surge in imperialist thought and sentiment. There were calls for closer ties between the Mother Country and her young cubs, talk of the superiority of the Anglo-Saxon race and the pre-eminence of British political institutions. Schemes were advanced for more cooperation between Britain and the colonies on matters of defence and trade. The Queen's longevity itself seemed to symbolize the endurance of the British Empire. The celebration of her Jubilee in London would provide a unique opportunity of bringing her dominions together in a great display of patriotism that would encourage and advance the imperialist movement. Contingents would come from every corner of the world, from all those places that were shaded red on British printed maps. As the senior dominion, Canada would be expected to have a prominent role.

Ottawa was slow to announce that it would send an official contingent to represent the country. It side-stepped the critics of its tardiness by stating that Canada had not yet received an invitation. What it was really concerned about obtaining was public support for the expenditure. As might be expected, Nicholas Davin, the member from Regina, was the first to try and prod an answer from the government. Speaking in the Commons on 29 March 1897, he asked if the NWMP would be included in any contingent that was under consideration. The Prime Minister replied that the matter was still being studied.[101]

When the matter was raised again in mid-April, several members representing both parties called for the despatch of a contingent at public expense. More than one noted the desirability of including the Mounted Police. Davin referred to them as the "finest body of men to be found in the Empire". Other members suggested that their appearance in London "splendidly equipped" would assure the British that the prairies were securely guarded and thus help to promote emigration.[102] Responding for the government, Sir Richard Cartwright welcomed the unanimity in the House on sending a contingent, and agreed that the inclusion of the NWMP would demonstrate that the West was no longer a lawless frontier.

Comm. Herchmer, meanwhile, had already anticipated that the police would be represented in any official Canadian party. As early as February he had contacted his division commanders asking them to submit the names of their most intelligent men, as well as their height, weight and nationality. He also requested information on their best horses.[103] It was not until April, however, that he got official confirmation from Ottawa that a party of 25 men under Supt. A. B. Perry had been approved. As to horses, White informed him that the Prime Minister was of the opinion that the police should borrow them when they reached England as the representatives of the Canadian cavalry regiments were going to do.[104]

To Herchmer now must go considerable credit for persuading the Minister to change his mind about a number of things that would make the appearance of the NWMP at the Jubilee a Canadian success story. The first issue was the horses. Ottawa was concerned about the cost of transporting them to London. The Commissioner believed that the police would not perform well on English horses. He wanted them to take their bronchos. They would be a great advertisement for western ranches, he astutely suggested to Laurier. To the argument that the bronchos were unused to large crowds and might be difficult to handle in London, he guaranteed to train them to remain calm in any noise or demonstration. The second issue was closely related to the first. It was a matter of saddlery. If the men had to use English cavalry mounts, they would also have to use cavalry saddlery. They were none too familiar with this, he reasoned, and could hardly be expected to become proficient with it in a day or two.

Finally, there was the question of uniform. The two principal functions in which the Canadian contingent would participate were the grand procession of Her Majesty and the other troops to St. Paul's Cathedral on the 22nd of June for the service of Thanksgiving, and the military review before the Queen a few days later at Aldershot. In the Commissioner's view the party should wear the full dress dragoon cavalry uniforms for the procession, and the "Prairie Suits" with the "cowboy hats" at Aldershot. It was the latter outfit that would make a lasting impression upon the British public as something distinctly Canadian. In their cavalry uniforms the police would look little different from many other contingents from around the world.

Herchmer got all he wanted and more.[105] Ottawa agreed to let the men take the bronchos, the western saddlery and their Winchester rifles. New uniforms were to be provided for each member, including prairie suits, cowboy hats and overalls with elastic sided boots and box spurs for walking out (attending off-duty social events). In addition, the Minister approved a grant of $400 from the Fine Fund to meet the personal expenses of the men, and over $500 from the Canteen Fund for the social obligations and entertaining that Supt. Perry would be faced with as the officer in charge.

By the end of April, 28 men had been chosen and sent to Regina to commence training. From these, 24 would be selected to accompany Perry. They ranged in height from 5 feet 10 inches to 6 feet, had average waist measurements of 35 inches and chest measurements of 39 inches. Contemporary photos show a group of largely young men, trim, handsome, sporting the long waxed moustaches which were considered so dashing at the time.

The Commissioner took care that those selected reflected the racial mix of the Force. The final party consisted of eleven English-Canadians, one French-Canadian, three Irish, seven English and two Scots. He was particularly anxious to see that French-Canadians were well represented, but Sgt. J. H. Genereux, a native of Berthier, Quebec, was the only one he could find who was suitable as far as size and experience was concerned.[106]

Perry was a wise choice to put in command. Tall, handsome, only 37 years old, a graduate of RMC and a former officer in the Royal Engineers, he could be expected to hold his end up as far as gentlemanly conduct, social graces and military etiquette were concerned. The snooty British would not find Perry a colonial yokel. The senior NCO was Sgt. Major A. E. C. "Black Jack" McDonell, from Point Fortune, Quebec. Other NCOs included S/Sgt. F. A. Bagley, known for his musical talents throughout the prairies, S/Sgt. A. R. Brook, and Veterinary S/Sgt. H. J. Joyce, a graduate of the Ontario Veterinary College. In addition to the main party of 25 that would participate in the ceremonies, a detachment of 4 men under Insp. R. Belcher was detailed to accompany the horses to London. These all departed from Montreal on the "S. S. Ottoman" a few days earlier. Following the celebrations the horses would be turned over to the British Army.

The Commissioner selected 28 horses to accompany the contingent, three more than the number of men. It was fortunate that he anticipated illness or injury. Three of the mounts developed bronchial pneumonia on the voyage across the Atlantic as a result of bad weather and unhealthy conditions on board ship. Two died at sea, and the third shortly after reaching London. All the horses, except one, had been bred in the West from thoroughbred imported stallions, including Eagle Plume, Scottish Chief, Acrostic (winner at Ascot), Silk Gown and Halton. Apart from one, they had all ranged the prairie freely until four years old, and were both geldings and mares of good but not uniform colours. One was a grey for the bugler, Cst. H. Cobb.[107] The *Calgary Herald* claimed that 13 of them had been bred on the nearby Quorn Ranch. It also took pride in asserting that all the saddlery for the party had been made by Carson and Shore of Calgary.[108] Another of the horses was something of a celebrity. Just a few months earlier while riding this trooper, Sgt. W. B. Wilde had been shot and killed by Charcoal, a Blood Indian, as he heroically attempted to prevent his escape. Following the festivities in London, Sir Wilfrid Laurier presented this horse in memory of Wilde to his old regiment, the 2nd Life Guards.[109]

Herchmer had only about a month to perfect the men and horses in the latest cavalry drill. Apart from recruit training, the Mounted Police had been following the formations laid down for mounted infantry since 1887. In England their every move would be closely watched by officers from the finest cavalry regiments in the Empire. The *Regina Leader* reported that intensive training was going on at the Barracks seven days a week, with many citizens going out to watch.[110] An important part of the schooling was spent preparing the horses for the noise and bustle of large crowds, the sound of guns firing salutes and the crackle of fireworks. A novel way was hit upon to simulate the conditions they could expect to experience in London. While the men and horses went through their drill movements in the riding school, they were serenaded by the band playing loudly in the gallery, rifles being fired, a party from the kitchen armed with metal pots and spoons, and a group of school children from town whose job it was to shout their lungs out and wave flags. The result was the most awful din that Regina had ever heard.[111]

Just as the preparations seemed to be going so well there was sudden discord. On May 16th, a letter from White arrived on the Commissioner's desk. When he read it, he exploded in anger. In the note the Comptroller informed him that Laurier had decided that henceforth the training of the contingent and the final selection of men was to be put entirely in the hands of Supt. Perry.[112] The reasons for this high-handed decision are unclear. In his eagerness to see that the police took their own horses, Herchmer had tactlessly gone behind his Minister's back seeking support from other cabinet members and even the Governor General. There was his known closeness to Sir John A. Macdonald and now new accusations that he had interfered on behalf of the Conservatives in the recent federal election.[113] There were a number of things that could have been held against him by a new Liberal Prime Minister.

Whatever it was, the Commissioner saw it as a breach of trust. His reaction was predictable. In a reply full of indignation, he protested the humiliation and degradation forced upon him by having one of his own subordinate officers placed over his head. He rightly asserted that he had worked hard in organizing and training the police contingent. He demanded to know who had poisoned the mind of the Minister against him, and requested an opportunity to defend himself. Such an accusation was hardly likely to endear him to his new Minister and, not surprisingly, Ottawa did not respond to his emotional outburst. One immediate effect of the decision was to severely strain relations between himself and Perry, who seemed just as surprised as the Commissioner was by it. Before Perry left Regina, however, the two men were back on friendly terms.

The NWMP party assembled with the militia units from many regiments in Quebec City on June 4th. The Canadian Contingent totalled almost 200 men. An order-in-council placed the police under the command of the Department of Militia until their return home.[114] Supt. Perry would be responsible to Colonel M. Aylmer, the commanding officer of the Canadian Contingent. Following an inspection by the Governor General, the Earl of Aberdeen, the pride of Canada's military forces embarked on the "S. S. Vancouver" on the 6th of June to the accompaniment of brass bands and 6,000 cheering spectators.[115] The London *Times* reported that of the 30 different corps represented in the Canadian Contingent the "North West Mounted Police . . . excited great enthusiasm" in the Quebec City crowds.[116]

While in London, the Canadians were billeted at the Royal Hospital with the other colonial troops. The home of retired and invalided soldiers, Chelsea Barracks, as it was commonly known, had been built in 1694 by Sir Christopher Wren. Conditions there were so crowded that some of the visitors had to be accommodated in bell tents on the lawns. The NWMP was one of the few colonial mounted units to bring its own horses. These travelled by train from the Liverpool docks, arriving at Euston Station in London on June 10th. With the help of some of the troops from Chelsea Barracks, Insp. Belcher and his men moved the horses to the stables there. The Canadian contingent arrived a week later.

Crowds of curious Londoners visited the Barracks to watch the strange array of uniforms and men of many colours and creeds training. "The Northwest Police" are getting their horses used to the noise of the city, reported a Canadian journalist.[117] The uniforms of the police especially attracted attention. There was no shortage of entertainment and other diversions for the men when off duty. The London pubs and music halls were close by, and for those a little more cultured some of the greatest artists of the time were performing in the city on the occasion of the Jubilee, actress Sarah Bernhardt, singer Madame Albani and Polish pianist Jan Paderewski.

The official Jubilee program was made public on the 11th of June.[118] The central event was to be the Thanksgiving Service in St. Paul's Cathedral on the 22nd. There were to be two separate processions to the church. The Royal Procession from Buckingham Palace escorting the Queen through the crowded streets would be made up entirely of British Forces. The Colonial procession, comprising all of the colonial contingents, would commence at the Victoria Embankment and proceed by a slightly different route to join the Royal Procession at the cathedral. As the senior dominion, the Canadians led by Sir Wilfrid and Lady Laurier would be at the head of the Colonial procession. The program also called for the colonial forces to travel to Spithead on June 26th to watch the Queen's review of the British Navy, and to participate in the military parade in front of Her Majesty at Aldershot on July 1st.

At dawn on 22 June 1897, the 60th anniversary of the Queen's reign, the London skies were cloudy. By mid-morning they had cleared, much to the relief of the tens of thousands of people who were jamming the parade routes hoping to catch a glimpse of their Sovereign. Originally, it was intended that the Mounted Police would wear their dragoon uniforms for the procession to St. Paul's. At the last minute it was decided, however, that a few of them, dressed in their prairie dress with cowboy hats, would act as an escort to the state landau carrying the Prime Minister and Lady Laurier. These were the men that got most attention from the newspapers. The NWMP escorting Sir Wilfrid Laurier in their prairie uniforms made a "striking appearance", reported the *Edmonton Bulletin*.[119] One London paper described them as "picturesque and soldier like".[120] In Toronto, the *Globe* said, "The Northwest Police made a striking appearance; quite as brave and serviceable looking as the New South Wales Mounted Rifles."[121]

Back in the NWT there were celebrations in almost every town and village. In Calgary, the Mounted Police fired a salute while in Edmonton, Comm. Herchmer took the salute at a parade and march past of the men of "G" Division. A highlight of the Regina festivities was the final of the Jubilee Cup football tournament. It was won by a team of Indians from the Industrial School beating the Regina Town team three to one. The NWMP team had earlier been knocked out of the competition by Grand Coulee.[122]

On June 26th the Mounted Police travelled by train to Portsmouth with the other colonial forces to watch the naval review. After a reception and lunch provided by the city, they boarded a chartered vessel, the "Koh-in-noor", for the short trip to Spithead where the great warships would steam in procession past the vessel carrying the Queen. During the Spithead visit an incident occurred that did not find its way into any official reports.

While at Chelsea Barracks the police had been visited by many former members of the Force living in England. One of these was Roger Pocock, novelist and writer of travel books, who had been invalided in 1885 after his frostbitten toes had been amputated following the dramatic forced march from Regina to Prince Albert during the rebellion. Pocock treated his old comrades to an evening on the town. When one of them later became too ill to make the trip to Portsmouth, it was decided that, for a lark, Pocock should don his uniform and take his place. To do this he would have to shave off his beard, and his fellow conspirators would have to keep him away from the sergeant major. All went well until they were watching the battleships go by. Pocock became so excited about something that he attracted the sergeant major's gaze. The latter quickly grabbed him by the shoulder and whisked him from sight.[123] Pocock later founded the Legion of Frontiersmen.

On the 1st of July the Queen reviewed some 28,000 soldiers at Aldershot. The Mounted Police paraded before her along with the other Canadians. On the following day, the colonial forces were invited to Windsor Castle to enjoy Her Majesty's hospitality. Lunch was provided for Supt. Perry and about 100 other officers in St. George's Hall. The men ate theirs in tents put up in the Castle grounds. In the afternoon, they all marched dismounted past the Queen in Home Park led by the band of the 2nd Battalion, Coldstream Guards.

The last official engagement for the Mounted Police took place at Buckingham Palace on July 5th. There in the presence of the colonial premiers, the Prince of Wales inspected each colonial contingent, and then presented each man with a Jubilee medal, silver for officers, bronze for other ranks. Their horses disposed of, the police, with the exception of Supt. Perry and Sgt. Major McDonell, began their return journey to Regina the next day. Perry spent a week in Ireland looking at the organization of the Royal Irish Constabulary. McDonell took a short course in machine gunnery at the School of Gunnery in Hythe, Kent, and then went to the Cavalry Depot at Canterbury for another one in equitation.[124] The NWMP could be well satisfied with its performance. Its representatives had been admired; its reputation enhanced, and it could look forward to a steady flow of British recruits in the years ahead looking for adventure in the colonies.

During the latter part of the nineteenth century military-style brass bands became very popular in North America. The leading exponent of this development in musical taste was the American virtuoso John Philip Sousa, who in 1880, was appointed bandmaster of the United States Marine Corps Band. A brilliant showman as well as composer, Sousa and his band achieved international renown. His style was widely emulated, and his popular marches became a necessary part of the repertoire of any successful band. Most large towns and almost every military body organized its own brass band. Even religious groups like the Salvation Army recognized their value in attracting converts. As a result, the concert by the town band in the park, and the parades on public holidays led by local military bands became a common feature of community life in both the United States and Canada.

In the days before the record player, radio and television, people had to create their own amusements. The early members of the Mounted Police were quick to organize their musical entertainment. During the March West constables danced a jig to the accompaniment of a fife and a tin dish upon which the beat was banged out with the aid of a spoon. The men knew from experience that music was a welcome diversion that boosted their spirits above the monotony of their daily routine and the sense of isolation that they felt in the early posts. Bands were organized from time to time in several divisions in the years following the March West, whenever there was a sufficient number of men with a musical inclination and the ability to play. Instruments were purchased with money out of their own pockets, or with small grants grudgingly authorized by Ottawa.

The disruption of the 1885 Rebellion brought an end to the last of these early bands, but in its aftermath new ones soon appeared. Behind their organization and artistry, the leadership of two members stands out during this period. One was S/Sgt. Fred Bagley, who had been a 15-year-old bugler on the March West in 1874. Bagley was a born musician who loved to perform. Although he had never had any formal musical training, he became an accomplished clarinetist and a first rate concertmaster. The other was S/Sgt. Harry Walker, who had originally gone west with the Red River Expedition of 1870. For a while he had been bandmaster for the Provisional Battalion of Militia in Winnipeg. After he joined the NWMP in 1878, he took a leading role in more that one of its early musical groups. In 1885, he took his discharge in an attempt to make his living as a professional musician in civilian life, but evidently was not successful enough to support his young family. He re-engaged in 1891, and was soon placed in charge of the Headquarters Band. Walker not only did his own arranging, he also wrote and published his own compositions. By 1900, both Bagley and Walker had established a reputation for musical skill that was known throughout the Territories.

The first of the new bands to appear in the post-rebellion period was in "H" Division at Fort Macleod and "E" Division at Calgary. In both cases the instruments were purchased by the men themselves.[125] Those of the Calgary Band cost over $600.

Comm. Herchmer asked the government for an annual grant of $50 for these divisions to help meet the expenses incurred by the purchase of music and other supplies. The bands endeavoured to defray their costs and pay for their instruments by charging admission at some of their concerts. This was usually 15 cents for unreserved seats and 25 cents for reserved. Both of these bands were capable of performing mounted or dismounted.

One of the first public performances of the Fort Macleod Band was at the Dominion Day festivities in Medicine Hat in 1886. Unfortunately, this musical ensemble turned out to be short-lived. Its instruments were badly damaged since they were used on horseback and they were sold for what they would bring in 1889.[126] One of the difficulties of organizing a mounted band was finding horses that would not react nervously to the noise of the music. Restless horses resulted in broken instruments, when bandsmen were forced to drop them in order to regain control of their mounts. On more than one occasion, a frightened broncho took off, throwing its rider in one direction and his trumpet in yet another.

The "E" Division Band in Calgary also ran into difficulties, but it surmounted them to become one of the finest police bands of the period. The first group formed in 1886 broke up a year later because many of its members were transferred to other divisions. In 1888, however, the commanding officer found 11 new volunteers who were willing to play. All they needed was a leader. This problem was solved when the CO persuaded the Commissioner to transfer Fred Bagley to Calgary from Regina. Bagley had run afoul of Herchmer's temper due to a misunderstanding between the two, and this probably had something to do with the Commissioner agreeing to the move.[127] It was a fortunate one for Calgary. Under his baton the "E" Division Band became a familiar and welcome sight to its citizens for many years.

During the summer months it was customary for the band to perform mounted in the downtown area, playing well-known martial airs. In winter, public concerts were given in Claxton's Skating Rink. In 1890, it gave performances in the Opera House in aid of the school building fund.[128] From time to time it showed its versatility as "Sgt. Bagley's Orchestra", providing dance music at the annual balls given by the Fire Department and the Calgary Curling Club.[129] In 1895, its performance at the New Year's Ball in the Alberta Hotel was described as "excellent", both as to time and selection.[130] The band frequently led the parade through town each year to celebrate the Queen's birthday in May. One of its most memorable performances took place in 1889 when Bagley and his fellow artists were sent to Banff to provide the music for a glittering vice-regal ball in the Banff Springs Hotel in honour of the visit of the Governor General, Lord Stanley of Preston, the first event of its kind in the recently completed mountain resort. In the years that followed the band returned to Banff on several occasions to play at such formal affairs, probably at the request of the CPR. Bagley retired in 1899. The "E" Division group continued for a while until, like all the other Force bands, it was broken up when so many members volunteered to fight in South Africa.

"F" Division at Prince Albert also briefly had a band. In 1889, Supt. Perry informed the Commissioner that the men there had raised $300 themselves for the instruments. He asked for a grant of $50 from the Fine Fund to cover the cost of music and stands.[131] The grant was approved by Ottawa and eventually a band was performing under the leadership of Cst. Bill Halbhouse. It did not last long, however. In 1891, Perry complained that all the good musicians had been transferred to Regina and the instruments had been placed in storage.[132]

The few records that remain of a band at "G" Division, Fort Saskatchewan in this period suggest that it was not continuous. It is first noted as being under the leadership of Sgt. George Purches, when it provided the music at the Fort for the division's first ball of the season in October 1893.[133] A few weeks later at the Annual Ball, however, the entertainment was given by the Edmonton Orchestral Society. Perhaps the discharge of Purches about this time had something to do with the Band's demise. In 1896, it was reported that a newly organized group had played well at a recent concert.[134] It also performed at a picnic that summer, but by the time of the Annual Ball it had been reduced to a violin and a piano played by Csts. Cook and Beaver. Whatever the band consisted of went to Edmonton in May 1897 to take part in the parade celebrating Queen Victoria's Diamond Jubilee.[135] Later that year, however, it seems to have broken up again when some of its members were transferred to the Yukon.

The band at Headquarters in Regina turned out to be the largest and most permanent of the era. Comm. Herchmer soon realized the good effect that a concert by the police could have in promoting harmony between them and the public. In addition, of course, with Regina the territorial capital, the police got caught up in the cycle of government functions, official visits and local celebrations. A police band added to the character of such occasions, and at the same time enhanced the reputation of the NWMP. The Commissioner wanted a first-class band in Regina and he was prepared to steal men from other divisions to see that it remained so.

The idea of a band for headquarters was initially put forward by Supt. Jarvis, the CO "Depot" Division, in June 1886, who felt that it would be a worthwhile source of recreation for the men. He found that a number of them already had experience playing in musical groups, and were enthusiastic about the prospect of organizing a new one. Bandsmen did not get extra pay, but they could expect to be excused some tedious routine duties in order to practice. Herchmer agreed and forwarded the suggestion to Ottawa along with a list of the required instruments, for which he hoped that the government would pay.[136] Probably to his surprise, White approved the expenditure, and a set of French-made instruments was obtained from the well-known music house of A. S. Nordheimer & Company in Toronto at a cost of $335. These arrived in Regina in November 1886. They included four B Flat Cornets, three E Flat Altos, two B Flat Trombones, two B Flat Euphoniums, one B Flat Bass Euphonium, two E Flat Bass Circulars, one Bass Drum, one Snare Drum and a pair of Cymbals.[137] Music was obtained shortly after in the form of copies of the National Band Book, Volumes 1 to 5.

To oversee the running of the band, the Commissioner appointed Insp. W. G. Matthews "Band President". It was this officer who was largely responsible for the first Mounted Police Musical Rides. Matthews eventually procured distinctive items of uniform for the bandsmen with the aid of grants from the Canteen Fund. In 1887, "Scarlet Cloth Forage Caps" with gold bands, similar to those worn by sergeants of the 12th Lancers, and badges with lyres upon them, the standard military symbol denoting a bandsman, were acquired from Hobson & Sons of London, England. The badges were sewn on to the upper right arm of the tunic.[138] Two years later bandsmen were also provided with leather cross belts and music pouches made by the Saddler, and red horse plumes were purchased from Maynard, Harris & Company of London to be inserted into the tops of their white pith helmets.[139] Finally, to complete this ceremonial dress, brass helmet badges, called helmet plates, depicting the buffalo head and motto of the Force, were obtained also from the latter suppliers in 1890.[140]

The first bandmaster of the new group was Cpl. Jacob Farmer who led it during the premier performances of the Musical Ride. Jakey Farmer was a Londoner with an unmistakable Cockney accent. He had served for ten years in the band of the King's Own Regiment before joining the NWMP in 1885. The Commissioner was so pleased with his success in training the band to play mounted and dismounted that he soon rose to the rank of staff sergeant, although he did briefly slip back a couple of times to sergeant as a result of over-imbibing. The first performance of the new band was at a Christmas Concert at the barracks in December 1886. The *Regina Leader* reported that it played 20 pieces.[141] The *Leader* complimented it upon its fast improvement and announced that it was to provide the accompaniment for the Musical Rides planned in the New Year. The band benefited as much from the new riding school as did the equestrian element of the Force. The building contained a band room which gave the musicians a convenient place of their own to practice for the first time. The school itself, meanwhile, was well suited to the holding of balls, concerts and quadrilles, all of which provided opportunities for the band to show its prowess.

In spite of the success, Farmer did not remain bandmaster at Headquarters for very long. In September 1887, he was transferred to Prince Albert and S/Sgt. Fred Bagley was brought in to take his place, probably because the Commissioner considered the latter the better musician of the two. Under Bagley's guidance it showed its versatility later that year, performing as a brass band at the opening of the NWT Council and playing the waltzes for the state ball that followed. "The Orchestra was the best that was heard in Regina," reported the *Leader*. "It was conducted by S/Sgt. Bagley, and consisted of first and second violins, first and second cornets, flutes, piccolo, baritone and piano."[142] Bagley's tenure only lasted a few months, however. Following his dispute with the Commissioner over singing in the choir, he was transferred to Calgary and by May 1888, Farmer was back once more conducting the band.

With Farmer in charge again, it became a familiar sight and sound in Regina in the summer months marching mounted through the streets giving concerts every Thursday during July and August. In April 1890, Farmer took his discharge in order to try his hand as a businessman in Toronto. His place as bandmaster was taken over by Cpl. W. M. Huntly. It was he who was responsible for its splendid performance before the Duke of Connaught, the third son of Queen Victoria, during his visit to Regina in May 1890.[143] Huntly also led it on its first tour later that year, when it journeyed to the big city of Winnipeg to perform during matches between the NWMP cricket and rugby teams and local Manitoba clubs.

The Regina Band underwent a further change of leadership in April 1891 when Harry Walker re-enlisted. The Commissioner soon appointed him bandmaster in place of Huntly. Under his guidance the band became a popular attraction in the entertainment life of Regina for almost a decade. It per-

formed at school picnics, annual balls, race meetings, and on numerous holidays and state occasions. The Mounted Police Band was on duty when the Governor General opened the Territorial Exhibition in 1895. In the summer of the following year, the Commissioner invited the citizens of Regina to cycle out to the Barracks every Friday night to enjoy a band concert.[144] Starting in 1897, it became a regular participant in the Sunday morning church parades, weather permitting. One young recruit later recalled that its repertoire on those occasions seemed to be limited to two tunes – "In the Sweet Bye and Bye" and "Marching Through Georgia".[145] Another practice of this period was for the band at Headquarters to entertain the members and their families by playing Christmas carols outside the houses and barrack rooms on Christmas Eve. Asst. Comm. McIllree noted in his diary for 24 December 1898 that the Band came around the square in the evening with most of the bandsmen "very full".[146]

From the records that survive of the music played by these police bands it appears that the works of Sousa, melodies from the operettas of Gilbert and Sullivan, and other popular marches and waltzes of the age, were frequently on the program. At a skating carnival at the barracks in 1893, the Regina band under the baton of S/Sgt. Harry Walker played several marches, including "Semper Fidelis" by Sousa, and two of Walker's own compositions, a galop entitled "Maria's Wedding Day" and a waltz called "Riders of the Plains".[147] The latter title of course probably derived from the poem of the same name by Cst. Thomas Boys, an epithet often used by westerners when referring to the NWMP. On the afternoon of the Queen's Birthday in 1896 the "E" Division Band under S/Sgt. Fred Bagley gave a concert on the Barrack Square in Calgary. The selections included two very popular Sousa compositions "The Washington Post March" and "The Manhattan Beach March". The enjoyable program concluded, reported the *Calgary Herald*, with a medley of tunes from the "Pirates of Penzance" by Gilbert and Sullivan.[148]

The Herchmer years were important for the NWMP's development as a mounted and ceremonial force. This decade and a half was the final phase of the policy of the policing of the prairie frontier. Herchmer ensured that the police were well mounted to provide the onerous patrol service which provided order to pioneer communities. From this operational role of cowboy policemen flowed a popular image which found expression in ceremonial functions. The Musical Ride originated in the Herchmer era as did Mounted Police bands.

The prairie dress of the NWMP found favour with the public both at home and abroad. This image would soon become set and would endure for the next century.

Chapter 21

From Forts to Barracks: Post-Rebellion Police Quarters

With the arrival of the railway, the growth of new urban centres and the confinement of the Indians to their reserves, the NWMP began to abandon or renovate the fortified military strongholds that had earlier served as their quarters. In their place they constructed an exposed complex of buildings, commonly referred to by the local citizens as the "Barracks", which, in keeping with their changing duties, resembled more the administrative and operational centre of a police force than a garrison outpost. This transformation was well underway before the outbreak of the North-West Rebellion.

The forts had been characterized by one-storey buildings made of logs chinked with mud, that had sod roofs and earth floors which were enclosed by a stockade with defensive bastions strategically placed at intervals. All cooking and heating had been done with wood or coal stoves. The only light came from oil lamps and candles. The living quarters had been dirty and uncomfortable. In wet weather the rain came through the ceiling and, unless the spaces between the logs were kept plugged with mud, dust blew through the walls in summer and snow in winter. The new posts, on the other hand, were constructed from finished lumber. The roofs were shingled and waterproof, the walls and floors made of wooden planks, the interiors finished off with lath and plaster. As the years went by they gradually incorporated the new technology of the period, electric light, running water, central heating and telephones. They were more habitable and permanent, although not without their problems. In 1882, the Headquarters of the Force was moved from Fort Walsh to the new territorial capital and rail centre of Regina. The old fort had outlived its usefulness. The Sioux under Sitting Bull had returned to the United States and the Canadian Indians no longer gathered in the Cypress Hills in large numbers to hunt. In 1883, the site was abandoned by the police altogether. Some of the material from the fort was used in the construction of new posts at Maple Creek and Medicine Hat that year. The original post at Fort Macleod had been built upon an island in the Old Man River. Its foundations were being undermined by the floods which swept down the river every year. It too was abandoned in 1883, and work begun on a new post on higher ground about two and a half miles west of the old site. At Calgary the stockade around the fort was knocked down in 1882 and the construction of new buildings started. The railway reached the town a year later, and the police post became a new divisional headquarters. Similar changes commenced at Fort Saskatchewan in 1885 and Battleford in 1886. In keeping with the changing times it was significant that the new posts did not take upon themselves the appellation "Fort". There was to be no Fort Regina, Fort Lethbridge or Fort Medicine Hat. In 1886, the responsibility for the construction of new police buildings was taken over from the Mounted Police by the Department of Public Works. Earlier the police had included the costs in their own estimates and either contracted for the work to be done by tender or carried out the construction themselves, the men receiving extra pay for their efforts. Under the new arrangement the Commissioner annually submitted a list of his priorities for new quarters and the estimated cost. This was gone over by White and the Minister, then discussed in cabinet or with officials at Public Works before a final figure was approved. This was usually lower than that which Herchmer had requested. Possibly, like many bureaucrats of the day, the Commissioner deliberately inflated his estimates knowing that whatever sum he put in would be inevitably cut. Once the estimates had been agreed upon, Public Works had the work contracted out by tender. More than once Herchmer protested that he could have got the job done more cheaply if left to arrange for the construction himself using police labour. The Department of Public Works, however, was a major dispenser of political patronage, and the police had to wait patiently while the friends and supporters of the government received their rewards. The one exception to this rule was Fort Steele. In 1887, "D" Division under the command of Supt. Sam Steele was despatched to the Kootenay region of British Columbia to maintain order there when trouble developed between the Kootenay Indians and local settlers. The log buildings that the division occupied during its stay were built by the men themselves under Steele's supervision. The post was fittingly named Fort Steele in his honour. After the division left in 1888, the buildings were turned over to the Department of Indian Affairs for use as an industrial school for Indians.[1] In 1893, the government decided to revert to its former procedure. The Minister of Public Works admitted in the House of Commons that using members to carry out the construction was, in fact, cheaper than employing civilian workers.[2] The following year the economy-conscious administration transferred the responsibility back to the police, but by this time the amount of money spent annually on construction on police posts was only a fraction of what it had been earlier.[3]

The doubling of the strength of the Force from 500 to 1,000 men in 1885 as a result of the rebellion greatly accelerated the need for new quarters. As a result, over the next three years there was something of a construction boom on Mounted Police posts. One of Herchmer's first recommendations was for new barracks at Prince Albert, Calgary, Edmonton, Battleford and Wood Mountain. He urged the government to construct them of brick rather than wood because brick buildings were easier to heat, and therefore in the long run cheaper to maintain. Brick structures, he also rightly pointed out, were less susceptible to destruction by fire.[4] The government, however, decided in favour of the less costly wooden edifices, with some dire results. During the fiscal years 1886-87 and 1887-88, expenditures on new buildings amounted to 13 per cent of the total cost of running the Force. This spurt in building activity culminated the following year when the figure dropped to nine per cent. Thereafter, with governments reducing spending and the Opposition calling for the disbanding of the Force, expenditure on the construction and maintenance of buildings declined drastically. By 1897-98, more money was being spent on police posts in the Yukon than on those in the NWT. As a conse-

quence, there was a significant decline in the physical condition of the existing structures there.[5]

As the Headquarters and training centre of the Force, Regina was the main beneficiary of the post-rebellion building boom. It also served as the model for new construction at other large posts. The original site had been laid out on the treeless prairie beside the Wascana (Pile of Bones) Creek about 2 miles west of the new territorial capital in September 1882 by Supt. Steele. In soldierly fashion he had assembled the barrack buildings, most of them were prefabricated and came from eastern Canada, around the perimeter of a large open square in the middle of which a tall flag pole was erected flying the Union Jack. The officers were accommodated together on one area of the square away from the quarters of the other ranks so as to give them and their families privacy. Behind the living quarters, the mess rooms and the guard room situated on the square were the stables, supply, coal and transport sheds, blacksmith's shop, washhouses and latrines. It was many years before this and other posts were enclosed by a fence. As a result, it was not unusual for settlers' cattle and stray horses to be found grazing around the buildings, or for them to be chased off the barrack square.

There were numerous complaints about the prefabricated structures that were first erected as barracks. It was said that the lumber used in them was not sufficiently seasoned. The boards warped, causing gaps in the walls and the doors and windows to hang improperly. They had no cellars which made them particularly cold in winter. The only heat in the barrack rooms occupied by the men came from two iron pot-bellied stoves, one at each end of the room. One member later recalled that in winter it could be so cold inside them that the buckets of water kept in them in case of fire would freeze during the night.[6] By the time Herchmer arrived in April 1886, there was an acute shortage of barrack room space due to the influx of recruits the previous year. Many of these had to be housed in bell tents set up between the barrack buildings. As might be expected, one of the Commissioner's first priorities on assuming office was for new barracks at Regina. He also recommended new houses for himself and the other officers to replace the wooden portable ones. Irvine was a bachelor, and the house which he had occupied was too small for Herchmer, his wife and their four children. "There is not one room big enough," he told White, "for all the family to eat together in." Furthermore, he informed the Deputy Minister, the snow blew in through the walls, which had resulted in him and his children being sick with colds since their arrival.[7] An imposing riding school was already under construction when Herchmer was appointed. Cold weather had forced the contractor to suspend work on the structure during February and March 1886, but the building was finally completed early in May. To Irvine must go the credit for pressing the government to provide one. Such a building, he told Ottawa, was absolutely necessary if equitation and foot drill were to continue during the long winter months when the outside temperature ranged from -20°F to -50°F.[8] The riding school dwarfed all the other buildings at Headquarters. The tower over its main entrance could be seen for miles around. Erected to the southwest of the Square, the structure itself was 232 feet long and 121 feet wide. It was also the most expensive police structure of the period, costing almost $30,000.[9] As well as a large open area for foot and mounted drill, it contained a band practice room and a gallery from which the band could perform and visitors could watch whatever activity was underway below. It was here that the first NWMP Musical Rides were trained and performed before the public in 1887. The size of the riding school also made possible all kinds of social and sporting events. It was big enough for the recruits to play baseball in and became the rendezvous for numerous balls and other musical events during the winter season. Construction on the new barracks for the men that Herchmer had recommended was begun in the fall of 1886. These consisted of 2 two-storey wooden buildings erected side by side on the west side of the Square. They replaced the draughty portable huts that had been assembled in 1882. One of these was salvaged and moved to the outer perimeter of the complex and became the Herchmer District Public School. A Miss O'Flynn was engaged as teacher, and was soon busy trying to pass on the rudiments of education to a small but growing number of barracks' children. In 1891, she was followed by a Mr. C. F. Brears, who was also organist at the Presbyterian Church in Regina.[10]

The new barracks were designated "A" and "B" Blocks. They were constructed with basements and were the first buildings in Regina to have central heating. This consisted of coal fired furnaces connected to a system of pipes through which the hot air rose to the rooms above. Even so, there was to be no waste, no over indulgence. By the spartan standards of the period, regulations required that room temperatures should be maintained at 45°F to 60°F on winter nights. However, like all the other buildings at the post, they had no running water or sewage disposal. Having a bath could be quite a chore. Each bather had to fetch his own water in pails and heat it on a stove before pouring it into the iron tub that served as a bath. Upon completing his ablutions, he had to empty the tub and clean it for the next man. Bath night must have been quite a scramble, when one realizes that there were only two tubs for up to 100 men in each barrack build-

ing. To answer the calls of nature, latrines were dug and enclosed at a respectable distance to the rear. Separate such establishments were provided according to rank. Although urine tubs were kept in the men's barracks at night, at any other time, or if a more complicated personal need arose, they faced a long walk to an unheated latrine. On a bitterly cold winter's day a buffalo coat could be a very welcome companion. Of course, the officers and the NCOs and their families had the option of following the common practice of the time of keeping chamber pots under their beds.

An adequate and suitable supply of water for drinking and other purposes was a serious problem at Regina for many years. The first supplies were hauled by cart from the nearby Wascana Creek, which ran along the north side of the site. This would dry to a trickle, however, in dry weather and before long animal and human waste in one form or another began to pollute it. This in all likelihood had something to do with the recurring outbreaks of typhoid and other diseases at the post. When these epidemics occurred, houses or barracks with their sick occupants were placed in quarantine. Sadly enough, there were often fatalities, not only among the men, but the wives and children as well. The death toll was still high among the latter from a variety of infections. Their bodies, along with those of the men who died, began to fill the large plot at Regina, which like at most other large posts had been reserved as a cemetery. Buried in the cemetery during this period were ten children of members of the Force.

After digging in several places, a well on the barrack square finally succeeded in reaching a reliable underground source of water at a depth of 45 feet. This resulted in an adequate and permanent supply. The water was very hard, however, and its alkali content so high that it had an upsetting effect upon the stomachs and bowels of recruits until they became accustomed to it. The supply was further improved in 1890 when a 65-foot high tower with a water tank on top complete with engine and pumps was erected over the well.[11] By this time the buildings around the square had all been connected by a boardwalk. It was no longer necessary to traipse through so much mud during wet weather. Boots stayed cleaner longer and less dirt was brought indoors. In 1889, the boardwalk was extended to meet the one coming from Regina along what would later be 11th Avenue. The year before, the first substantial bridge was built over the Wascana to link the post with Dewdney Avenue and Government House to the north.[12] Spring flooding had earlier destroyed several make-shift spans over the creek. A permanent source of water led to the greening of Headquarters. Attempts to grow trees sent from the Experimental Farm in Ottawa and to start lawns had hitherto failed because of the arid climate. By 1892, the Commissioner was able to report, however, that native maples taken from nearby creek beds had become firmly rooted on the square and about the post.[13] In addition, lawns and vegetable gardens began to appear beside the married quarters. Some NCOs and officers started to keep chickens, ducks and even the odd cow. There was the devil to pay one morning when it was discovered that someone's dog had got into the Commissioner's hen house overnight. In addition to "A" and "B" Blocks, a larger residence for the Commissioner and a new hospital were completed in 1887. The commodious 12-room home for the Herchmer family was situated on the northeast corner of the square. Like the new barracks it had the comfort of a basement with a furnace and heating system. The house that Irvine had resided in became the new home of the officers' mess.

The hospital was a two-storey structure containing three wards, with five beds in each. The Senior Surgeon, Dr. Jukes, considered the building an advance on the old one, but not all that could be desired. He complained that it was too small. As no provision had been made for a dispensary or surgery, one of the wards had to be used for these purposes, reducing the space for the sick to only tenbeds. Furthermore, he considered the earth closets (indoor latrines) located in each ward to be unsanitary, and the building itself to be too close to the foul water of the Wascana Creek.[14]

In 1888, a bandstand was added to the barrack square. It enabled the band to give open-air concerts on pleasant summer evenings to the residents and their guests from the town. Two years later a bowling alley was put up for the amusement of the men. The cost for this, $1,600, was met by the Canteen Fund. By this time the cuts in expenditure on police buildings had begun to take effect. At Regina, as at most of the other posts, there was little in the way of new construction after 1891. From this point the Commissioner complained year after year about the deteriorating state of the portable "shacks", and of the lack of resources to maintain and repair existing structures. Ways had to be found to economize. Alterations and repairs were done by members. It was in this way that the burned-out canteen was renovated as a chapel in 1895. To paint buildings prisoners from the guardroom and boys from the nearby Indian Industrial School were used as painters at no expense to the public purse except the cost of the paint.[15]

Sometimes there were unforeseen expenses. The foundations of "A" and "B" Blocks had been made of wood not stone. In 1894, the timbers holding up "B" Block had so weakened as they settled that the basement caved in. The building, as a consequence, had to be propped up and temporarily vacated while a stone foundation was constructed under it.[16] Herchmer repeatedly urged Ottawa to do the same with "A" Block because of the danger that it too would collapse. The government, however, was so intent upon reducing spending that it was prepared to gamble on the matter. During the late 1890s, the buildings at Regina, as elsewhere generally, began to deteriorate rapidly. In 1895, Herchmer reported that "the headquarters office is the very worst in the force, is draughty and cold, and unhealthily close in damp weather, and is most depressing to work in, and there is no protection whatever afforded for records of the force."[17] Later, he described his own office, one of the original portables, as "quite rotten at the foundation and leaks badly, and on wet days the smell is most offensive".[18]

In 1900, while Herchmer was serving in South Africa, Asst. Comm. J. H. McIllree submitted an assessment of the state of buildings at Regina. Among other things, he reported that one of the officers' houses was uninhabitable because its cellar was full of water, that Insp. Strickland had just arrived with his wife and two children and the only available building for him only had two small rooms. Not having any choice in the matter, Strickland decided to move in for the present. His own house, he continued, was unsafe because the wooden sills on which it was built were rotten. Furthermore, some days the doors all jammed and some days they swung loosely, and he had to put strips of wood across the ceilings in the rooms to stop the plaster from falling down. The Commissioner's house, he went on, was in much the same condition.

Once again, he expressed the fear that the wooden basement under "A" Block would founder unless replaced by a stone one. As for the building downtown which was supposed to house the Regina Detachment, it too had become uninhabitable and the men were being temporarily quartered elsewhere. It had earlier been described as having holes in the floors, no storm door, a cracked stove, and one window without glass and no toilet. The members were required to use the facilities of the Windsor Hotel farther up the street.[19]

After years of uncertainty and procrastination over the future of the Force and a resulting reluctance to spend money on it, by the turn of century it looked like much of the physical structure of the NWMP was about to disintegrate from neglect. In 1895, a weekly report from "C" Division, Battleford recorded the following occurrence for Wednesday, July 10th. This evening the town was hit by one of the most severe lightning and thunder storms "within the experience of the oldest inhabitant". One bolt of lightning struck the end of the Quartermaster's Store. It then ran along the roof until it came to the Canteen chimney. Upon meeting this obstruction it knocked it through the roof into the room below where several men were sitting. The current then divided into four branches. One went down the stove pipe of the Canteen twisting it into strange shapes, and then tore up the floor before making a hole in the wall of the building through which it departed into the ground. Another went down the stove pipe of the sergeants' mess and found its resting place in the body of a dog which at the time was lying between the feet of S/Sgt. Currier. The third entered Sgt. Macphail's room, tore a blanket and partly melted the barrel of a carbine. The fourth entered the Quarter Master Store, breaking the shutters and knocking the corner off a box of cartridges. "Those in the Canteen at the time have every reason to be thankful for their providential escape," wrote the commanding officer.[20]

Fires caused a great deal of damage every year at Mounted Police posts until the introduction of improvements like electricity reduced the risk. Some of these resulted from violent thunder storms, which were frequent at certain times of the year, some from accidents, and some from negligence. By far the greatest number of them, however, originated from faulty stoves, chimneys or other heating and lighting apparatus. Sometimes the destruction was increased by the lack of efficient fire fighting equipment and water supplies. The following are some, but by no means all, of the fires of the period. They most frequently occurred during the winter months, when stoves and lights were kept burning longer. They were also most dangerous in the colder months because what fire fighting equipment there was on site was likely to freeze and be inoperable.

In February 1886, Stand Off Detachment was completely destroyed by fire. The cause was unknown. The following winter was a particularly bad one. One of the barrack buildings at Fort Macleod burned down in February. The fire was attributed to a faulty chimney. During the same month one of the four barracks at Calgary was mysteriously reduced to ashes. In March, two out of the three remaining buildings were destroyed by fire. The cause in this instance was attributed to a stove which had been kept going all night in the kitchen of one of the barracks so that the food would not freeze. In January 1888, the hospital at Fort Saskatchewan, for reasons unknown, went up in a blaze and the Surgery at Lethbridge caught fire during an inexplicable explosion. Later in the fall of that same year it was the turn of the Quarter Master Store in Regina. In addition to the building, $1,900 worth of supplies were lost. In 1889, another faulty chimney seems to have been behind the loss of the Bake House at Fort Macleod. During the same year a horse kicked over a carelessly placed lantern in the stables at Lethbridge spilling burning oil across its floor. Only the timely action of the members present saved the 30 horses inside. In 1892, another fire at Regina destroyed the Carpenter's Shop.[21]

The most spectacular and most costly fire of the period, however, was the conflagration that consumed the new riding school in Regina, the showpiece of the force, on the morning of 26 November 1887. It had only been completed 18 months before at a cost of $30,000. The "Alarm" was sounded by the bugler at 8:45 a.m. The temperature at the time was -22°F. As a result, neither the fire engine nor the Babcock fire extinguishers would work because they were frozen. The only weapons left were buckets of water carried by hand and passed up ladders and poured on the roof. When it was realized that the blaze was out of control, orders were given to save the transport, stores and artillery in the building. This was accomplished moments before the roof gave in with a crash. It took the fire 33 minutes from the time the alarm was sounded to destroy "one of the finest buildings in the North West Territory", reported the *Regina Leader*. The Regina Fire Brigade was called for, but arrived too late to be of any help. Fortunately there were no horses in it at the time.[22]

As in all cases of fire, a Board of Inquiry was appointed to investigate the cause and make recommendations as to the remedy. In this case it was determined that the blaze had started in a saddle room on the north side of the Riding School. The cause was an improperly placed stove which had been lit by mistake and left unattended.[23] In 1889, the riding school was replaced by an almost identical building at slightly less cost. It too was to be razed by fire, but not until 1920.

In an understatement, Comm. Herchmer remarked in his Annual Report for 1888 that "our greatest weakness at all posts is inadequate fire protection". In the wake of the Riding School fire, he had earlier that year suggested that each division be supplied with one hand fire engine and one hose cart containing 500 feet of hose. He also suggested that water towers be erected at Regina, Calgary, Macleod and Lethbridge.[24] In the meantime, some posts continued to be woefully ill-equipped to fight fires. At Lethbridge, apart from buckets of water, there were only six fire extinguishers. The water supply was over a half mile away and had to be hauled by water cart. In winter, when fires were most common, this had to be emptied at night so that the water did not freeze.[25] From Maple Creek the commanding officer also reported that there, and at Medicine Hat, the only means of fighting fires were water buckets and a few Babcock fire extinguishers. "In the event of a fire gaining headway at either post," he warned, "the whole of the barracks would go."[26] Battleford had acquired a first class fire engine by 1890, but like Lethbridge its water supply was a half mile away in the Saskatchewan River.[27] Most large posts eventually obtained water towers and fire engines that were operated by hand pumps. The continuing problem with the latter, as Herchmer pointed out, was that they would not work in very cold weather.[28]

A considerable amount of time and energy was put into taking other precautions to stop the spread of fire. Metal chimney pipes were replaced with brick. Stove pipes were required to be cleaned monthly, chimneys every six weeks. Roof ladders were placed atop each building. Regulations required that axes and red fire buckets full of water be located in most rooms. It was forbidden to leave oil lamps burning in any room or barracks while no one was present.[29] Each large post was required to organize a fire party of at least 12 men for a monthly tour of duty. It was drilled regularly in the use of the equipment, and practised by responding to false alarms. Better equipment, improved supplies of water and continuing vigilance did reduce the number of fires in the 1890s. The Commissioner was enthusiastic about a new type of fire extinguisher that did not freeze which was obtained in 1892.[30] As he mentioned in numerous reports, however, the ever present fear of fire would not be eliminated until electricity replaced oil lamps, buildings were constructed with brick, and posts were linked up to the local running water supply. Many communities still did not have the latter. The use of bricks and cement over lumber lay well in the future, but in its concern to reduce the financial loss caused by fire the government became increasing willing to replace oil lamps with the more expensive incandescent light bulb.

Electric power was the exciting technological innovation of the time. Its use was spreading rapidly. By 1890, it was supplanting horse drawn buses with power driven tram cars and lighting the streets of Montreal, Toronto and Ottawa. In keeping with the progressive spirit of the local community, the headquarters of "E" division in Calgary was the first NWMP post to have electric lights installed. Deputy Minister Fred White wrote to the Department of Public Works in November 1889 urging it to give the post priority in the matter. The town (it was incorporated as a city in 1893) already had its own supply. White pointed out that electricity not only gave a better light but was safer. It should be remembered that three barracks had been lost there in 1887. "Oil lamps are a constant danger," he continued, "and the post has a poor supply of water."[31] Public Works gave its approval and by March 1890 the Calgary Electric Company had installed 100 lights of 16 candle-power.[32] The commanding officer, who had a dread of fire at the place, described the change as taking a "great load off my mind".[33] In addition to electricity, the Calgary post was also the first to be hooked up to the local supply of running water (1891) and the first to have flush toilets (1895).[34]

Comm. Herchmer considered the experiment in Calgary to be a great success. He recommended that electricity be introduced to all posts as circumstances permitted. It was essential first of all, of course, that the local communities establish a supply. The Commissioner was undoubtedly envious of the police post in the foothills. He wanted Regina lit up too. Like others of the time, Mrs. Herchmer probably had visions of getting rid of the smelly, smoky oil lamps in her parlour. The town had its own system. In 1890, he got an estimate to replace the 300 oil lamps in use at Headquarters with 275 electric lights.[35] The amount was $1,000, which appears to have been more than Ottawa was prepared to spend at the time. In 1894, the posts at Lethbridge and Prince Albert were furnished with the lights. Regina did not get them until 1896. Edmonton followed in 1898.[36] It would be years before they were installed at smaller posts.

As with electricity, the new technical advances in communications were only introduced slowly to the police. American Christopher Soles produced the first practical typewriter in 1868. There had been many earlier such machines, but they had all been slower than handwriting. Soles entered into a contract with the Remington Company and his invention appeared on the market in 1874. During the 1880s, there were numerous improvements to his technology, and many other companies entered into competition to sell the machine that would eventually revolutionize office procedures around the world and provide employment for millions of women. Until the arrival of typewriters in the Force, all reports and all correspondence had to be written by hand with pen and ink. Each year gallons of blue and red ink and hundreds of pens and nibs were used up in the process. Writing letters and memoranda for the Commissioner or commanding officer was an exacting task requiring care and concentration. A slip of the pen, a spelling mistake, or a blot of ink and the page had to be started over again. Members whose penmanship was accurate and legible were much admired and sought after as Division and Headquarters Clerks. They received extra pay for their talents. The first typewriter appears to have been purchased in 1886-87 at a cost of $100. Where it was used is not clear, probably at Headquarters in Regina. Over the next decade or so two or three were bought each year. They included the following makes: Remington, Empire and Smith Premier.[37] By the turn of the century, it appears that every Division Office and Headquarters had one or two of the machines. As for the detachment men it would be many years before they would be able to do away with pen and ink.

The Herchmer years also saw the introduction of the telephone. Actually the first one was installed at Headquarters in Regina in 1885, just a few months before his appointment. At first, the police regarded the invention as just a useful extension of the telegraph. The latter medium of communication had become an important one for them, when it was necessary to send urgent messages relating to criminal or administrative matters. In fact, by 1886, the annual bill for telegrams amounted to a few thousand dollars, most of this going to the Canadian Pacific Telegraph Company. From time to time Fred White would caution Herchmer about the growing cost, and he in turn would remind his commanding officers that the telegraph was only to be used when it was absolutely necessary. To ensure that their communication over the wires was private the police used Slater's Telegraphic Code, a dictionary of some 25,000 numbered words from which a message could be ciphered or deciphered by the use of a key number known to both the sender and the receiver. The number would be changed each month. The Commissioner would notify his commanding officers of the new one by confidential letter.

The weak link in the telegraph system was the distance between the telegraph office, which was usually at the railway station in the centre of town, and the police post which was often on the edge or a short way out of town. Headquarters was a case in point. Through the telegraph office Herchmer could contact his own divisions, Ottawa and every major police department in Canada and the United States, but it was two and a half miles from his office. How was an urgent telegram addressed to the Commissioner going to reach him? The telegraph office did not deliver messages, and the police were not connected to it by telephone. The answer at first was to have the members of the town detachment keep in close contact with the telegraph office. When messages were received, they took them out to the barracks on horseback, and returned with the reply. It would be much quicker, if the detachment was connected to Headquarters by telephone. In an emergency, the contents of a telegram could much more rapidly be passed on to the Commissioner's office, and a reply received and despatched.

In 1888, Herchmer recommended that telephones be installed in all town detachments for the purpose of receiving and sending telegrams. He argued that they would increase police efficiency, and save on the wear and tear on horses and men.[38] Gradually the larger posts were equipped with them, but there were still problems. Many of the early connections were on party lines. The line that was established between Headquarters and Regina Town Station in 1885, for example, was also shared with the Governor's residence and the Legislative Assembly Building. Both places generated a lot of telephone traffic. A lowly constable could hardly ask the wife of the Governor to cease and desist in arranging her upcoming soirée so that he could get through to the Commissioner's office. Insp. Allan complained bitterly in 1886 that the territorial representatives spent so much time on the telephone that he had to send messages into town with a rider on numerous occasions.

As a result of these circumstances, Ottawa later that year gave the police permission to buy their own equipment and put up their own line between Headquarters and Regina.[39] Other police operated lines followed. In 1887, Moose Jaw was connected to Wood Mountain, the summer headquarters of "B" Division, using two receivers made by the commanding officer, Supt. E. W. Jarvis.[40] By 1890, the police had also put up lines directly from the posts at Maple Creek and Medicine Hat to their local telegraph offices. They found, however, that maintaining telephones lines could become a bit of a burden. They did not always have good equipment. The lines came down in bad weather, and constantly needed repairing and inspecting. Consequently, the Commissioner wrote to the Bell Telephone Company in Winnipeg in 1887 urging it to open telephone exchanges in Regina and elsewhere as their present system did not work very well.[41]

Alexander Graham Bell had patented his invention in 1876 and organized the Bell Telephone Company as a means of turning it into a commercial enterprise. During the 1880s, Bell had become the principal supplier of the telephone service in both the United States and Canada. As the company branched out across the Territories, the police rented equipment from it for most major posts. In addition to Regina, Prince Albert was hooked up in 1887-88, Fort Saskatchewan in 1888-89, Calgary, Banff and Edmonton in 1890, and Lethbridge in 1891. By 1900, every division headquarters was on line. At Regina they had acquired three phones by then at a total rental cost of $90 a month. One was located in the Headquarters Office, another in the Pay Office, and the third in the Supply Office. The Commissioner as yet did not rate a telephone of his own.[42]

The frontier period was coming to an end in western Canada through the Herchmer era. Fortified police establishments gave way to more modern facilities. Necessities such as adequate fire protection and clean water were added to accommodations. Conveniences and amenities such as electric light, telephones, running water and toilets were added as technology and government funds allowed. However, conditions can still be best described as spartan. The job of policing the prairies was not for those seeking a life of comfort.

Conclusion

The Herchmer years, 1886 to 1900, were a period of continued transition for the North-West Mounted Police. Responsibilities on the prairie frontier changed. The focus shifted from guarding against an Indian uprising to policing a rapidly growing area of new settlement. The Force moved from a paramilitary garrison posture to the police role of law enforcement. At the same time, many of the resources needed for the West were shifted to the newly developing frontier in the Yukon.

Commissioner Lawrence Herchmer, in command of the NWMP, played the central role in guiding the Force through this period of transition. It was not an easy task. He did not relate easily to his subordinates and could not count on their personal support. Also, many of the problems he faced were intractable. Service on the western frontier was difficult for officers and men alike. The duties were onerous and the rewards were not generous. Still, Herchmer never stopped trying to build a better Force and in his goal he was reasonably successful.

Herchmer's relations with his commissioned officers were never very easy. Appointed and promoted by political masters, these officers were not his own men. And Herchmer was a stern man who sought to exact obedience rather than accommodation from his subordinates. This was resented by his officers and confrontations were frequent, particularly in the early years of his command. Herchmer had no patience for the weaknesses of his fellow humans and came down hard on those who succumbed too readily to drink, indebtedness or indolence. The ultimate confrontation came with the Wetmore Inquiry in 1892, which after it was all over, led to a period of reduced tension between the officers and their leader. Herchmer improved aspects of his officers' lot, including their training and their pension plans.

Like the officers, the men of the Mounted Police were not an ideal group. Herchmer inherited a Force in 1886 in which most of the men were inexperienced and many were unsuitable. There was a high drop out rate due to reasons of ill-health, desertion, dismissal as unsuitable and discharge by purchase. Herchmer responded to this by offering improved training and a probationary period allowing easy exit to those who did not improve. He also implemented a consistent system of discipline which resulted in a greater standard of efficiency.

Conditions of service for the men of the NWMP were adequate if not luxurious. The pay, leave and health care were sufficient for the times. Under Herchmer the men were granted a pension plan and improvements were made in food and accommodation. More diversions were provided in the form of wet canteens, recreation rooms, libraries and sporting activities. The divisional headquarters posts became more efficient and amenable as the buildings were upgraded. Clean water and fire protection were followed gradually by electric lights, running water, toilets and telephones. Better mounts were provided and more efficient patrol routes were devised for the men.

Along side the betterment of the interior economy of the NWMP came the evolution of the ceremonial Force. From the basic serviceable uniform of the original members came transformation to the dashing prairie dress of Stetson, red serge, striped pants and high boots which caught the imagination of an admiring public. The desire to entertain and to give expression to a military ethos spawned the band and the musical ride which would become enduring symbols of the Mounted Police and Canada itself.

Commissioner Lawrence Herchmer interrupted his tenure as the commander of the Force in 1900 to accept a new challenge, leading a battalion of the Canadian Mounted Rifles to service in the South African War. Herchmer fully expected to return as head of the NWMP, but was to be disappointed. The government chose this opportunity to replace the irascible Tory appointee with Aylesworth Bowen Perry, a man of ability and the right political stripe, to remain permanently as Commissioner. The Herchmer era was over.

General Conclusion

The roots of the modern Royal Canadian Mounted Police are firmly embedded in the prairie frontier. In the Herchmer era the paramilitary frontier police force evolved from a garrison between the Indians and the settlers to become a law enforcement agency preoccupied with the detection of crime and the pursuit of criminals. Even in appearance by 1900 the link between the original and the modern Force was forged. The red coat and Stetson was the public perception and the self-image of the Mounted Policeman.

Notes

Chapter 1

A New Commissioner, A New Order

1. Glenbow-Alberta Institute Archives, Dewdney Papers, vol. 3, Macdonald to Dewdney, 20 Nov 1885
2. *Regina Leader*, 17 Feb 1885
3. R. B. Deane, *Mounted Police Life in Canada* (London: Caswell and Company 1916), 29 (hereafter cited as Deane)
4. "Report Upon the Suppression of the Rebellion in the North-West Territories and Matters in Connection Therewith in 1885," in Canada, *Sessional Papers*, no. 6a, 1886, 6
5. John G. Donkin, *Trooper and Redskin* (London: Sampson, Low, Marston, Searle and Rivington 1889), 149 (hereafter cited as Donkin)
6. *Regina Leader*, 9 June 1885
7. Ibid., 23 June 1885
8. *The Weekly Manitoban*, 12 Aug 1885
9. NWMP, Annual Report, 1885
10. In Prince Albert, however, Irvine remained something of a hero. The ladies of the town presented him with a magnificent clock for protecting the town. It can now be seen in the RCMP Museum, Regina.
11. National Archives of Canada (hereafter NA), Caron Papers, vol. 199, Middleton to Caron, 23 June 1885
12. NA, Macdonald Papers, reel C1516, Melgund to Macdonald, 22 May 1885
13. Loc. cit.
14. Deane, 30
15. Ibid., 20
16. NA, Macdonald Papers, vol. 402, Smith to Macdonald, 2 Apr 1884; Campbell Papers, Macdonald to Campbell, 8 Mar 1886
17. *Regina Leader*, 16 July 1885
18. NA, Lansdowne Papers, reel A623, Lansdowne to Macdonald, 30 Dec 1885
19. *Edmonton Bulletin*, 13 Mar 1886
20. NA, Lansdowne Papers, Lansdowne to Macdonald, 1 Feb 1886
21. NA Macdonald Papers, reel C1488, Macdonald to Hutton, 18 Feb 1886. In 1898, Hutton was appointed Officer Commanding the Canadian Militia. He was forced to resign after 18 stormy months in office because of his uncompromising and uncooperative attitude towards his political superiors.
22. Ibid.
23. *Regina Leader*, 23 Feb 1886
24. NA, Macdonald Papers, reel C1597, Herchmer to Macdonald, 23 Feb 1886 (telegram)
25. Ibid.
26. NA, Records of the Royal Canadian Mounted Police, Record Group 18 (hereafter cited as RG 18), vol. 2337, GO 2399, 1 Apr 1886
27. Donkin, 200
28. E. Morris, "Lt. Col. Irvine and the NWMP," in *The Canadian Magazine*, October 1911
29. *Regina Leader*, 30 Mar 1886
30. NA, Macdonald Papers, Dewdney to Macdonald, 23 Feb 1886
31. W. D. Reid, "Johan Herkimer U.E., And His Family", *Ontario Historical Society Papers*, vol. 31, 1936
32. NA, Macdonald Papers, vol. 521, Macdonald to L. W. Herchmer, 22 July 1872; Bill Mackay, Curator, RCMP Museum, Regina
33. RG 18, vol. 3440, service record C-72, L. W. Herchmer
34. Deane, 34-35
35. *Edmonton Bulletin*, 10 Apr 1886
36. NA, Macdonald Papers, Letterbook 23, 440, Macdonald to A. G. Crozier
37. *Regina Leader*, 10 Aug 1886
38. RG 18, vol. 3438, service record 0-49, R. B. Deane
39. Deane, 66
40. Ibid., 34; and RG 18, vol. 1052, Herchmer to White
41. Deane, 34
42. RG 18, vol. 1052, Herchmer to White
43. *Regina Leader*, 13 Apr 1886
44. NA, Records of the Public Service Commission, Record Group 32 (hereafter cited as RG 32), vol. 480
45. *Statutes of Canada*, 1879, 42 Vic., ch. 36
46. Privy Council Order 1041, 19 June 1880
47. D. Creighton, *John A. Macdonald: The Old Chieftain*, (Toronto, 1968), 573
48. Privy Council Order 694, 3 June 1874
49. NWMP, Annual Report, 1878, 20
50. Deane, 5
51. NWMP, Annual Report, 1886, 13
52. Deane, 4
53. Ibid., 13
54. Privy Council Order 1457, 26 June 1889
55. RG 18, vol. 3437, service record 0-37, W. M. Herchmer; see also R. C. Macleod, "William Macauley Herchmer", DCB, XII, 427
56. Ibid.
57. *Statutes of Canada*, 1879, 42 Vic., ch. 36
58. House of Commons Debates, 10 Apr 1885 (hereafter cited as Debates)
59. Ibid., 10 June 1885
60. Ibid., 24 June 1885
61. NWMP, Annual Report, 1880, 6
62. Ibid., 1885, 13
63. RG 18, vol. 1028
64. Donkin, 262-3

Chapter 2

Agents of the National Policy

1. R. C. Macleod, "Canadianizing the West: The North-West Mounted Police as Agents of the National Policy, 1873-1905" in L. H. Thomas (ed), *Essays on Western History* (Edmonton, 1976), 99
2. Carl Betke, "Pioneers and Police on the Canadian Prairies, 1885-1914", Canadian Historical Association, *Historical Papers*, Montréal 1980, 32 (hereafter cited as Betke)
3. NWMP, Annual Report, 1886
4. Ibid., 1887, 45
5. Ibid., 1889, 8 and 1890, 1-2
6. Betke, 11-12
7. David H. Breen, "The Canadian West and the Ranching Frontier, 1875-1922", (PhD thesis, University of Alberta, 1972) 179-182
8. Provincial Archives of Alberta, Memoirs of Supt. P. W. Pennefather, 42-43 (hereafter cited as Pennefather)
9. NWMP, Annual Report, 1887, 72-74
10. RG 18, vol. 32, file 262-1889, Perry to Herchmer, 4 Dec 1888
11. Ibid., vol. 22, file 386-1888
12. Ibid., vol. 33, file 330-1888, parts 1 to 5
13. NWMP, Annual Report, 1891, 12 and 35
14. RG 18, vol, 32, file 262-1889; and NWMP, Annual Report, 1888, 109-110
15. RG 18, vol. 32, file 262-1889
16. NWMP, Annual Report, 1887, 72-74
17. Ibid., 1891, 84-85
18. Ibid., 1889, 109-110; and RG 18, vol. 34, file 463-1889, Relief schedule dated 9 May 1889
19. RG 18, vol. 47, file 59-1891, Cotton to Herchmer, 12 Apr 1891
20. Ibid.
21. RG 18, vol. 58, file 44-1892, White to Herchmer, 8 Feb 1892
22. NWMP, Annual Report, 1888, 19, and 1889, 79; RG 18, vol. 1136, file 151
23. Betke, 29-31; and NWMP, Annual Report, 1888, 75
24. NWMP, Annual Report, 1889, 47-48; Deane, 300-301
25. Sam Steele, *Forty Years in Canada* (Toronto: McGraw-Hill, Ryerson 1972), 259-260
26. NWMP, Annual Report, 1889, 12-13, 35, 91-92, 98 and 119
27. Ibid., 1887, 75
28. Ibid., 1890, 13
29. Ibid., 1891, 9; Annual Report, 1886-91, "Returns of cases tried in the NWT"; *Edmonton Bulletin*, 3 April 1886
30. Charles Lipton, *The Trade Union Movement in Canada, 1827-1959* (NC Press, Toronto, 1973), 114
31. R.C. Macleod, *The North-West Mounted Police and Law Enforcement, 1873-1905* (Toronto: University of Toronto Press 1976), 156 (hereafter cited as Macleod)
32. Ibid., 157
33. Macleod, "Canadianizing the West," 104-105
34. NWMP, Annual Report, 1891, 78
35. Ibid., 1890, 13
36. Ibid., 181
37. Ibid., 44
38. Ibid., 1888, 121
39. A. A. den Otter, "Sir Alexander Tilloch Galt and the Canadian Government and Alberta's Coal," in Canadian Historical Association, *Historical Papers*, 1973, 29-30; and NWMP, Annual Report, 1887, 10, 48, 84-5
40. NWMP, Annual Report, 1883, 34
41. Ibid., 1886, 7a
42. Ibid., 1888, 9
43. Ibid., 1889, 18 and 124
44. Ibid., 1890, 119
45. Ibid., 1890, 118 and 139
46. NA, RG 18, vol. 57, file 738-1891, White to Herchmer, Apr 1891
47. Ibid., Geo. H. Young, Inspector of Customs to W. G. Parmelee, Commissioner of Customs, 5 Sept 1892
48. Ibid., vol. 1049, file 151, Johnson, Commissioner of Customs to White, 28 May 1886
49. Herbert Legg, *Customs Services in Western Canada, 1867-1925* (Creston: Creston Review Ltd. 1962), 57-58, 99-101, 159-162 and 177
50. NWMP, Annual Report, 1888 to 1891 inclusive
51. Debates, 2 July 1891, 1704
52. RG 18, vol. 56, file 638-1891
53. Ibid., vol. 51, file 301-1891; Legg, Customs Services, 57
54. J. P. Turner, *The North-West Mounted Police* (Ottawa: King's Printer 1950), vol. 1, 112, 126, 324 and 326 (hereafter cited as Turner)
55. H. A. Dempsey (ed), R. B. Nevitt, *A Winter at Fort Macleod* (Calgary: Glenbow-Alberta Institute 1974), 24
56. *Calgary Herald*, 3 Feb 1890
57. Report of the Auditor-General, 1885-1886, XX.
58. Deane, 34
59. See Report of the Auditor-General, 1886-1891 inclusive
60. RG 18, vol. 45, file 830-1890
61. See David Breen, "The Cattle Compact in Southern Alberta, 1881-1896 (MA thesis, University of Calgary, 1968) and his "The Canadian West and the Ranching Frontier, 1875-1922" (PhD thesis, University of Alberta, 1972)
62. NWMP, Annual Report, 1886, 34; and Department of the Interior, Annual Report, 1893
63. NWMP, Annual Report, 1888, 55 and 1889, 55
64. RG 18, vol. 68, file 538-1892, J. Lowe, Deputy Minister of Agriculture to White, 15 July 1892
65. NWMP, Annual Report, 1890, 54-55
66. RG 18, vol. 38, file 27-1890, Steele to Herchmer
67. Ibid., vol. 1056, file 41
68. NWMP, Annual Report, 1891, 94
69. F. M. Loew, *Vet in the Saddle* (Saskatoon: Western Producer Prairie Press, 1978), 45, 49 and 50
70. NWMP, Annual Report, 1890, 141
71. Ibid., 1889, 110
72. Ibid., 144
73. Ibid., 1890, 148-149
74. Ibid., 1887, 114
75. RG 18, vol. 1190, file 267
76. Ibid., vol. 46, file 2-1891
77. Ibid., vol. 1116, file 304
78. Ibid., vol. 1190, file 267
79. NWMP, Annual Report, 1890, 37-38
80. RG 18, vol. 30, file 129-1889, White to Herchmer, 25 June 1886
81. NWMP, Annual Report, 1890, 30
82. Ibid., 1893, 112
83. H. A. Dempsey, "One Hundred Years of Treaty Seven", in I. Getty and D. B. Smith (eds), *One Century Later: Western Canadian Reserve Indians Since Treaty 7* (Vancouver: UBC Press 1978), 21
84. RG 18, vol. 48, file 136-1891
85. H. A. Dempsey, *Indian Tribes of Alberta* (Calgary: Glenbow Museum 1979), 48-49; RG 18, vol. 2213, Herchmer to White, 3 Oct 1893
86. NWMP, Annual Report, 1889, 2-3
87. *Regina Leader*, 8 Oct 1889
88. Turner, vol. 2, 441-443
89. NA, Stanley Papers, reel A673, Lady Stanley's Notes, 21 Oct 1889
90. Turner, vol. 1, 259 and 613
91. RG 18, vol. 753, White to Herchmer, 8 May 1886
92. NWMP, Annual Report, 1888, 116
93. Turner, vol. 2, 295-301
94. NWMP, Annual Report, 1886, 17

95. RG 18, vol. 49, file 142-1891, White to Davin, 12 Feb 1891
96. Ibid., vol. 1224, file 326; NWMP, Annual Report, 1891, 92
97. NWMP, Annual Report, 1889, 44
98. RG 18, vol. 15, file 27-1888, Herchmer to White, 26 Jan 1888
99. NWMP, Annual Report, 1888, 20-21 and 1890, 12
100. RG 18, vol. 42, file 528-1890; vol. 1193, file 347
101. Ibid. vol. 41, file 339-1890; NWMP, Annual Report, 1889, 118
102. NWMP, Annual Report, 1890, 122
103. A. S. Morton, *History of Prairie Settlement* (Toronto: Macmillan 1938), 93 and 118
104. NWMP, Annual Report, 1891, 10
105. Klaus Hansen, "The Mormons: Quest for Empire or Quest for Refuge", Westward Movements Conference, Vancouver, 1 Nov 1979
106. RG 18, vol. 41, file 25-1890, Card to A. M. Burgess
107. Ibid., vol. 1127, file 518, W. Herchmer to L. Herchmer, 29 Sept 1888
108. RG 18, vol. 41, file 250-1890
109. Ibid., Burgess to Dewdney 16 Dec 1889
110. Ibid., vol. 1192, file 298
111. Betke, 15-16
112. The government dispensed patronage through the Force just as through other departments of the public service. See P. B. Waite, Canada, 1874-1896, *Arduous Destiny* (Toronto: McClelland and Stewart 1971), 219-221
113. R. Phillips and S. J. Kirby, *Small Arms of the Mounted Police* (Ottawa: Museum Restoration Service 1965)
114. Report of the Auditor General, 1886 to 1891 inclusive
115. RG 18, vol. 1094, file 80, White to Herchmer, 5 Feb 1888
116. Ibid., vol. 1229, file 78
117. Ibid., vol. 1071, file 184
118. Sean Murphy, "Saddlery: North West Mounted Police, 1874-1904" unpublished manuscript, RCMP Historical Branch, 1978, 45 and 61
119. NWMP, Annual Report, 1889, 6-7
120. RG 18, vol. 1220, file 233, White to Herchmer, 31 Jan 1891
121. NWMP, Annual Report, 1891, 5
122. Debates, 19 May 1888, 1608; and *Fort Macleod: The Story of the Mounted Police* (Fort Macleod: Fort Macleod Historical Association 1958), 35
123. Report of the Auditor General, 1890-1891, D207-D210
124. See the *Macleod Gazette*, 28 June 1887, for example
125. RG 18, vol. 125, file 590-1896
126. Report of the Auditor General, 1890-1891, D184-D192
127. NWMP, Annual Report, 1888, 13-17
128. Article from the *Saskatchewan Herald*, reprinted in *Macleod Gazette*, 6 Dec 1887
129. RG 18, vol. 137, file 137-1897
130. Ibid., vol. 67, file 448-1892
131. Ibid., vol. 60, file 111-1892; and Report of the Auditor General, 1890-1891, D188
132. Debates, 19 May 1888, 1610
133. NWMP, Annual Report, 1895, 5
134. Ibid., 1886, 8 and 20
135. RG 18, vol. 82, file 355-1893
136. NWMP, Annual Report, 1889, 4
137. Report of the Auditor General, 1888-1889, E160
138. Saskatchewan Archives Board (Saskatoon), ATG (I) - G Series, file 3162
139. *Prince Albert Times*, 4 June 1886
140. RG 18, vol. 40, file 235-1890, J. Herron to John A. McDonald, 12 Feb 1890
141. Ibid., Herchmer to White, 1 Mar 1890
142. Ibid., vol. 51, file 308-1891
143. John Archer, op. cit., p. 104.
144. Ibid., vol. 33, file 344-1889
145. Ibid., vol. 48, file 111-1891
146. Ibid., vol. 1114, file 271
147. *Regina Leader*, 4 Dec 1888
148. RG 18, vol. 1159, file 321, Herchmer to White, 29 Jan 1889
149. *Regina Leader*, 4 Dec 1888
150. Ibid., 22 Jan 1889
151. Ibid., 4 Dec 1888
152. Ibid., 29 June 1889
153. Ibid., 26 Mar 1889
154. Debates, 15 Feb 1889, 152-153
155. Ibid., 8 Apr 1889, 1082
156. *Regina Leader*, 29 Oct 1889
157. For more on patronage system in this era, see: W. Beahen, "A Citizens' Army: The Growth and Development of the Canadian Militia, 1904 to 1914," (PhD thesis, University of Ottawa 1980), 266 to 308; Gordon Stewart, "John A. Macdonald's Greatest Triumph," *Canadian Historical Review*, March 1982, 3-33; and Stewart's "Political Patronage under Macdonald and Laurier, 1878-1911", *The American Review of Canadian Studies*, spring 1980, 3-36
158. RG 18, vol. 19, file 326-188; and vol. 26, file 36-1889
159. See Report of the Auditor General, 1886 to 1891 inclusive for information on contracts
160. NA, Macdonald Papers, 242901-242902
161. W. Stewart Wallace (ed), *The Macmillan Dictionary of Canadian Biography* (Toronto, 1978), 623
162. J. K. Johnson (ed), *The Canadian Directory of Parliament, 1867-1967* (Ottawa: Public Archives of Canada 1968), 519
163. Ibid., 504-505
164. J. Castell Hopkins (ed), *The Canadian Album: Encyclopedic Canada* (Toronto: Bradley- Garetson Co. 1896), vol. 2, 339 and vol. 5, 37
165. RG 18, vol. 57, file 58-1889; and vol. 65, file 311-1892
166. R. C. Macleod has reached the same conclusion in *The North-West Mounted Police and Law Enforcement, 1873-1905*, 92-94. This conjecture is elevated to fact in later periods where stronger evidence has come to light.

Chapter 3

"Curbing Their Appetites": Enforced Morality on the Frontier, 1886-1892

1. NWMP, Annual Report, 1884, 54
2. *A Chronicle of the Canadian West*; NWMP Annual Report, 1875 (Calgary: Historical Society of Alberta: 1975), 24
3. *Regina Leader*, 17 May 1883
4. NWMP, Annual Report, 1884, 58
5. Canada, *Criminal Code*, 55-56 Vic, ch. 29. s. 195.
6. Ibid., s. 207
7. Ibid., s. 195
8. Canadian Criminal Cases (abridgement 1892-1925), 172
9. *Regina Leader*, 17 May 1883
10. *Edmonton Bulletin*, 27 Oct and 3 Nov 1888; James Gray, *Red Lights on the Prairies* (Toronto: Macmillan 1971) includes a spirited account of this incident, 121-122
11. *Edmonton Bulletin*, 10 Nov 1888
12. Ibid., 3 Nov 1888
13. RG 18, vol. 1217
14. RG 18, vol. 1160, Mayor of Regina to Herchmer, 22 July 1889
15. *Regina Leader*, 30 Sept 1890
16. Ibid., 21 Oct 1890
17. *Calgary Herald*, 22 Jan 1891
18. NWMP, Annual Report, 1891, 156-160
19. RG 18, vol. 1786, file 170
20. Ibid., vol. 86, file 659-93
21. Ibid., Vol. 3339, file 878.

22. Chief English remained head of the Calgary Police Department until 1909 when he fell victim to a crusade for moral reform.
23. RG 18, vol. 69, file 616
24. 38 Vic., ch. 49, s. 74
25. See also: S. W. Horrall, "A Policeman's Lot is Not a Happy One: The Mounted Police and Prohibition in the North-West Territories, 1874-91," in *Historical and Scientific Society of Manitoba, Transactions, Series III*, No. 30, 1973-74, 5-16; and J. G. Bellomo, "The Liquor Question and the North West Mounted Police, 1874-1905," unpublished ms, RCMP Historical Branch
26. NA, RG 18, vol. 1039, file 82, Neale to Herchmer, 30 Nov 1886
27. NWMP, Annual Report, 1888, 67
28. Ibid.
29. RG 18, vol. 1116, file 314
30. NWMP, Annual Report, 1889, 4
31. Debates, 4 Apr 1889, 1016; and NWMP, Annual Report, 1889, 171
32. NWMP, Annual Report, 1890, 51-52 and 201
33. L. H. Thomas, *The Struggle for Responsible Government in the North-West Territories, 1870-97* (Toronto: University of Toronto Press 1978), 159
34. *Regina Leader*, 4 Dec 1888
35. Department of the Interior, Annual Report, Part IV, 7
36. RG 18, vol. 1111, file 195, Lieutenant-Governor's office to Commissioner's office, 24 July 1888
37. Debates, 15 Feb 1889, 152
38. Ibid., 21 Mar 1890, 2347
39. NWMP, Annual Report, 1889, 3
40. RG 18, vol. 1104, file 151
41. Ibid., vol. 1114, file 271, Herchmer to White, 28 Nov 1888
42. NWMP, Annual Report, 1888, 98
43. RG 18, vol. 1050, file 154, White to Herchmer, 15 Apr 1888, and vol. 1075, file 278
44. Ibid., vol. 1141, file 194
45. Ibid., vol. 1194, file 435
46. Debates, 12 Mar 1875, 655; 11 Apr 1882, 800; 11 Mar 1889, 550-553; 17 Apr 1889, 1331 to 1344
47. L. H. Thomas, *The Struggle for Responsible Government*, 68, 108
48. D. M. McLeod, "Liquor Control in the North-West Territories: The Permit System, 1870-1891" in *Saskatchewan History*, autumn, 1963, 81-89 (hereafter cited as D. M. McLeod)
49. NWMP, Annual Report, 1889, 3-4
50. RG 18, vol. 1104, file 151 and NWMP, Annual Report, 1888, 11
51. Ibid., vol. 1112, file 198; and NWMP, Annual Report, 1890, 22
52. RG 18, vol. 1192, file 297
53. NWMP, Annual Report, 1890, 36
54. RG 18, vol. 1177, file 198
55. Ibid., vol. 17, file 204-1888
56. Ibid., vol. 1104, file 151, Herchmer to White, 11 Jan 1888
57. NWMP, Annual Report, 1890, 37
58. RG 18, vol. 1039, file 82 and vol. 1104, file 151
59. Ibid., vol. 1039, file 81
60. NWMP, Annual Report, 1888, 46
61. RG 18, vol. 1039, file 85
62. Ibid., vol. 1039, file 82
63. Ibid., vol. 1141, file 194; vol. 1221, file 257; vol. 1222, file 289
64. NWMP, Annual Report, 1891, 22
65. Ibid., 1888, 58
66. Ibid., 1889, 40 and 176
67. Ibid., 1891, 33-34
68. See Chapter 5, 7-8
69. RG 18, vol. 1077, file 317; NWMP, Annual Report, 1888, 11
70. Ibid., vol. 1112, file 198; NWMP, Annual Report, 1888, 46
71. RG 18, vol. 1064, file 124
72. Ibid., vol. 3380, service file 2225, T. W. Hussey
73. Ibid., vol. 2283, Herchmer to White, 13 Oct 1891
74. NWMP, Annual Report, 1891, 157-158; Hussey service file
75. *Calgary Herald*, 22 Apr 1891
76. Ibid., 29 Apr 1891
77. Ibid.
78. Ibid, 11 July 1891
79. RG 18, vol. 3380, service file 2225, T. W. Hussey
80. *Calgary Herald*, 29 July 1891; 5 Sept 1891
81. *Winnipeg Free Press*, 24 Oct 1891
82. NWMP, Annual Report, 1888, 195
83. RG 18, vol. 1116, file 312
84. NWMP, Annual Report, 1888, 195
85. RG 18, vol. 1116, file 312
86. Ibid., vol. 35, file 843-1888 and vol. 1127, file 507
87. Ibid., vol. 3365, service file 1674, A. Leslie
88. D. M. McLeod, 88-89
89. Pennefather, 12
90. D. M. McLeod, 88-89
91. A. A. den Otter, *Civilizing the West: The Galts and the Development of Western Canada* (Edmonton: University of Alberta Press 1982), 173-174

Chapter 4

Easing the Transition from Frontier to Prairie Settlement, 1893-1900

1. A. F. J. Artibise, *Prairie Urban Development 1870-1930*, CHA Historical Booklet No. 34 (Ottawa, 1981), 31
2. NWMP, Annual Report, 1892, 27, 102, 121
3. RG 18, vol. 82, file 364-1893, White to Burgess, Deputy Minister of Interior, 11 Feb 1893
4. Ibid., file 370-1893, White to L. Pereira, 27 Apr 1893
5. Ibid., vol. 61, file 192-1892, White to Burgess, 13 Feb 1892
6. Ibid., vol. 153, file 344-1889, S/Sgt. Hooper to Herchmer, 26 May 1898
7. Betke, 10-13
8. NWMP, Annual Report, 1895, 4 and 24; 1898, 13 and 89
9. RG 18, vol. 109, file 380-1895, White to Herchmer, 10 Apr 1895
10. Ibid., vol. 61, file 185-1892, Burgess to White, 1 Mar 1892, and vol. 96, file 493-1894, Pereira to White
11. Ibid., vol. 1342, file 194 and NWMP, Annual Report, 1895, 24 and 1896, 39-43
12. Ibid., vol. 1401, file 233 and vol. 145, file 67-1898
13. Ibid., vol. 227, file 131-1902, J. Smart, Deputy Minister of Department of Interior to White, 10 Dec 1902
14. Ibid., vol. 108, file 348-1895
15. *Calgary Herald*, 7 June 1895
16. Ibid., vol. 108, file 348-185
17. NWMP, Annual Report, 1896, 12
18. Ibid., 1899, 5
19. Ibid., 1899, 76
20. Carl Betke, "The Mounted Police and the Doukhobors in Saskatchewan, 1899-1909," *Saskatchewan History*, Winter 1972, 1-14
21. George Woodcock and Ivan Avakumovic, *The Doukhobors* (London: Oxford University Press 1968), 169-181
22. J. F. C. Wright, *Slava Bohu: The Story of the Doukhobors* (Toronto: Farrar and Rinehart 1940), 187-196
23. Simma Holt, *Terror in the Name of God; The Story of the Sons of Freedom Doukhobors* (Toronto: McClelland and Stewart 1964), 27-38

24. Ibid., vol. 96, file 418-1894, Insp. D. A. E. Strickland to OC Prince Albert, 2 June 1894
25. Ibid., vol. 107, file 222-1895, Insp. D. A. E. Strickland to Herchmer, 17 Feb 1895
26. Ibid., vol. 129, file 75-1897, A. M. Burgess, Deputy Minister of Interior to F. White, 12 Nov 1896
27. Ibid., vol. 146, file 96-1898
28. Ibid., vol. 95, file 356-1894, Insp. Bégin to OC Battleford, 20 Sept 1894
29. NWMP, Annual Report, 1899, 74-75
30. RG 18, vol. 166, file 213, 1899
31. NWMP, Annual Report, 1896, 115
32. Ibid., 1899, 75
33. RG 18, vol. 108, file 310-1895
34. NWMP, Annual Report, 1896, 2 and 14; *Edmonton Bulletin*, 23 Mar and 4 May 1896
35. Debates, 23 Apr 1896, 7125 to 7128; and Department of the Interior, Annual Report, 8-9. In previous years the Department of the Interior had itself managed issues of relief grain in quantities as large or larger than in 1896. However, the annual report remarked upon the particular efficiency and accuracy of the program when handled by the police.
36. RG 18, vol. 1291, file 64, Herchmer to Dominion Lands Office, Winnipeg, 8 Sept 1894
37. Debates, 14 June 1897, 4080-4081; NWMP, Annual Report, 1894
38. NWMP, Annual Report, 1894, 50
39. RG 18, vol. 96, file 470-1894; NWMP, Annual Report, 1895, 12
40. Ibid., vol. 73, file 37-1892
41. *Calgary Herald*, 30 Aug 1895
42. Ibid., 2 Oct 1896
43. Ibid., 19 Oct 1896
44. *Edmonton Bulletin*, 23 Sept 1895
45. *Calgary Herald*, 27 Aug 1897
46. Ibid., 30 and 31 Aug 1897
47. *Battleford Herald*, reprinted in *Calgary Herald*, 7 Sept 1897
48. NWMP, Annual Report, 1897, 15
49. *Calgary Herald*, 27 Sept 1897
50. Debates, 23 June 1899, 5832-5833
51. Ordinance No. 6 entitled, "An Ordinance Respecting Infectious Disease" in *The Revised Ordinances of the North-West Territories* (Regina, 1888), 41-42
52. W. Beahen, "Mob Law Could Not Prevail," in *Alberta History*, Summer 1981. This article contains more details on the NWMP's handling of the Calgary mob violence.
53. RG 18, vol. 68, file 516-1892; NWMP, Annual Report, 1894, 36
54. RG 18, vol. 141, file 567-1897; NWMP, Annual Report, 1897, 27
55. RG 18, vol. 212, file 354-1901
56. Ibid., Patterson to Perry, 21 May 1902
57. Ibid., vol. 233, file 219-1902
58. Ibid., Cuthbert to Perry, 31 Aug 1902
59. Ibid., vol. 255, file 401-1903
60. Ibid., vol. 258, file 606-1903, White to Walter Scott, MP, 13 Oct 1903
61. Ibid., vol. 255, file 401-1903, Perry to White, 3 Apr 1903
62. Ibid., vol. 68, file 538-1892, and vol. 80, file 274-1893
63. Debates, 6 Feb 1893, 330-334
64. Ibid., 14 June 1894, 4374 to 4389, and 4 July 1894, 5301-5366
65. RG 18, vol. 80, file 274-1893, Order-in-Council, 22 Mar 1893
66. RG 18, vol. 1281, file 311
67. Ibid., vol. 80, file 274-1893, parts 1 to 3
68. Ibid., vol. 89, file 72-1894
69. Ibid., vol. 94, file 300-1894
70. Ibid., vol. 115, file 38-1896
71. NWMP, Annual Report, 1893 to 1896
72. Ibid., 1897, 48
73. Ibid., 1895, 99
74. RG 18, vol. 105, file 184-1895, and vol. 1336, file 110
75. NWMP, Annual Report, 1895, 50 and 221
76. RG 18, vol. 153, file 374-1898, and vol. 240, file 822-1902
77. Ibid., vol. 235, file 235-1902, and vol. 241, file 862-1902
78. Ibid., vol. 122, file 370-1896, and vol. 112, file 716-1895
79. NA, Records of the Office of the Governor General, RG 7, G 21, vol. 93, file 132
80. Deane, 156
81. RG 18, vol. 235, file 295-1902
82. Ibid., vol. 234, file 277-1902, White to Perry, 17 Mar 1902
83. Ibid., vol. 241, file 862-1902. On file is Deane's annual report which was not published as part of the Commissioner's Annual Report because in the judgement of Perry it was too controversial. Deane finally told the story in *Mounted Police Life in Canada*, 93 and 154-181
84. RG 18, vol. 241, file 862-1902, Sifton to White, Dec 1902
85. Ibid., vol. 240, file 755-1902, R. G. Matthews, Secretary of the Western Stock Growers' Association to Perry, 10 Oct 1902. Matthews was a former Mounted Policeman himself. He was married to Claire, a daughter of Insp. Henry Casey, and he served as best man at the wedding of Supt. Phillip Primrose and Lily Deane, daughter of Supt. R. B. Deane, held at Lethbridge in January 1902.
86. NWMP, Annual Report, 1902, 86
87. RG 18, vol. 242 and 243, file 25-1903, parts 1 and 2
88. F. M. Loew and E. H. Wood, *Vet in the Saddle*. John L. Poett, *First Veterinary Surgeon of the North West Mounted Police* (Saskatoon: Western Producer Prairie Books 1978), 45, 122
89. NWMP, Annual Report, 1893, 171
90. Ibid., 180 and RG 18, vol. 83, file 417-1893. As it turned out, the glanders had not been eliminated from the Oxarart herd and, in succeeding years, spread to other horses in the region (see NWMP, Annual Report, 1897, 225)
91. Loew and Wood, *Vet in the Saddle*, 51
92. RG 18, vol. 124, file 525-1896, W. B. Scarth to White, 17 Oct 1896 and White to Herchmer, 29 Oct 1896
93. NWMP, Annual Report, 1897, 17
94. RG 18, vol. 140, file 543-1897, W. B. Scarth to White, 29 Sept 1897
95. Ibid., vol. 176, file 738-1899 and vol. 1450, file 18
96. NWMP, Annual Report, 1897, 225
97. Ibid., 1899, 61
98. Ibid., 1898, 128
99. J. G. MacGregor, *Edmonton: A History* (Edmonton: Hurtig Publishers 1967), 106-107
100. *Edmonton Bulletin*, 20 June 1892
101. RG 18, vol. 68, file 492-1892, L. Pereira, Assistant Secretary, Department of the Interior to the Commissioner of Dominion Lands, Winnipeg
102. Ibid., Supt. A. H. Griesbach to Herchmer, 23 June 1892
103. *Edmonton Bulletin*, 20 June 1892
104. RG 18, vol. 68, file 492-1892
105. *Edmonton Bulletin*, 23 and 30 June 1892 and B. A. Ockley, "A History of Early Edmonton," (MA thesis, University of Alberta, 1932), ch. 13
106. RG 18, vol. 68, file 492-1892, Report by Supt. A. H. Griesbach, 23 June 1892
107. Ibid., Abbott to White, 13 July 1892
108. Ibid., vol. 1254, file 293
109. NWMP, Annual Report, 108 and *Calgary Herald*, 23 Mar 1892
110. RG 18, vol. 63, file 228-1892
111. Ibid., White to Herchmer, 22 Mar 1892

112. E. Forsey, *Trade Unions in Canada, 1912-1902* (Toronto: University of Toronto Press 1982), 268-269

113. NWMP, Annual Report, 1896, 138

114. Forsey, *Trade Unions in Canada*, 181-182

115. NWMP, Annual Report, 1901, 65-66

116. A. A. den Otter, *Civilizing the West*, 212-213, 275-276 and NWMP, Annual Report, 1894, 91-92

117. den Otter, *Civilizing the West*, 276-278; NWMP, Annual Report, 1897, 57-58; RG 18, vol. 1392, files 126 and 127

118. RG 18, vol. 141, file 580-1897

119. Ibid., vol. 145, file 64-1898

120. NWMP, Annual Report, 1898, 206-209

121. Ibid., 38

122. Ibid., 1897, 63

123. RG 18, vol. 145, file 64-1898, Deane to Herchmer, 5 Nov 1897

124. NWMP, Annual Report, 1897, 283; RG 18, vol. 1401, file 221, Cuthbert to Herchmer, 18 Sept 1897

125. "Return to the House of Commons of the Report of the Commissioners appointed to inquire into complaints respecting the treatment of labourers on the Crow's Nest Pass Railway, Ottawa, 30 April 1898" (Canada, Sessional Papers, no. 90a, 1898), 8-9

126. RG 18, vol. 1401, file 221, Steele to Herchmer, 12 Nov 1897; NWMP, Annual Report, 1897, 40

127. NWMP, Annual Report, 1897, 289-290

128. RG 18, vol. 147, file 120-1898, Cuthbert to Steele, 26 Jan 1898

129. Crow's Nest Pass Railway inquiry, 1-22

130. NWMP, Annual Report, 1898, 24

131. "Report of Mr. R. C. Clute on the Commission to Inquire into the death of McDonald and Fraser on the Crow's Nest Pass Railway, Ottawa, 17 January 1899" (Canada, Sessional Papers, no. 70, 1899, 1-16

132. S. M. Jamieson, Times of Trouble; Labour Unrest and Industrial Conflict in Canada, 1900-66. Study #22, Task Force on Labour Relations Ottawa 1968

133. NWMP, Annual Report, 1898, 39-40

134. Ibid., 1900, 6

135. Ibid., 1894, 52

136. RG 18, vol. 96, file 441-1894 and vol. 150, file 225-1898

137. Ibid., vol. 140, file 512-1897

138. Ibid., vol. 133, file 139-1897 and vol. 233, file 216-1902

139. Ibid., vol. 135, file 261-1897, Macdonell to OC "Depot" Division, 12 Apr 1897

140. NWMP, Annual Report, 1897, 246-256

141. Auditor General, Report, 1892-1902 inclusive

142. RG 18, vol. 110, file 504-1895

143. R. F. Phillips and D. J. Klancher, *Arms and Accoutrements of the Mounted Police, 1873-1973* (Bloomfield, Ont.: Museum Restoration Service 1982), 85-89; RG 18, vol. 1468, file 19

144. Debates, 28 May 1900, 6095-6098

145. RG 18, vol. 108, file 318-1895

146. Ibid., vol. 122, file 312-1896, Steele (with petition enclosed) to Herchmer, 16 Apr 1898

147. Auditor General, Report, 1895-96, M5-M30

148. RG 18, vol. 163, file 172-1899

149. Ibid., vol. 127, file 8-1897, Gagnon to Herchmer, Monthly Report for June, 15 July 1897

150. Ibid., vol. 2285, Herchmer to Perry, 4 Apr 1897

151. Ibid., vol. 347, file 39-1908, patronage list

152. Ibid., vol. 2285, Herchmer to OC "Depot" Division, 21 Sept 1897

153. Auditor General, Reports, 1892-1902 inclusive: Payments to Force Expenditures Fiscal Year

Fiscal Year	R.H. Williams	Force Expenditure
1892-93	$ 253.90	$615,479.21
1893-94	841.98	622,959.22
1894-95	968.43	657,294.46
1895-96	1169.53	545,449.39
1896-97	5835.58	538,671.34
1897-98	2236.86	369,638.88
1898-99	4100.96	402,628.88
1899-00	1527.38	365,933.59
1900-01	3302.32	413,326.07
1901-02	5048.39	449,147.11
1902-03	6865.63	399,098.67

154. Auditor General, Reports, 1892-1902 inclusive:

Fiscal Year	E. F. Hutchings	Adams Brothers
1892-93	$1675.70	00.00
1893-94	1915.19	00.00
1894-95	1312.45	00.00
1895-96	990.44	00.00
1896-97	402.53	130.33
1897-98	00.00	1054.03
1899-00	00.00	2707.74
1900-01	00.00	1140.04
1901-02	00.00	2232.29
1902-03	00.00	558.88

155. RG 18, vol. 347, file 39, Sifton to Laurier, 15 Jan 1897

156. Ibid., White to Herchmer, 27 Jan 1897

157. Debates, 28 May 1900, 6099

158. RG 18, vol. 70, file 649-1892

159. Debates, 28 May 1900, 6093-6100

160. RG 18, vol. 347, file 39, White to Herchmer (private), 15 Sept 1896

161. Auditor General, Reports, 1892-1902 inclusive:

Fiscal Year	J. H. Ashdown	Miller, Morse and Co.
1892-93	$1519.88	00.00
1893-94	4461.08	3693.94
1894-95	00.00	9392.86
1895-96	00.00	5739.96
1896-97	3223.36	3523.19
1897-98	3795.11	00.00
1898-99	2256.24	00.00
1899-00	2583.34	00.00
1900-01	3879.46	00.00
1901-02	1400.42	00.00
1902-03	235.37	00.00

162. Debates, 28 May 1900, 6093-94

163. RG 18, vol. 347, file 39, White to Perry, 6 Mar 1903

164. Debates, 28 May 1900, 6095-96

165. RG 18, vol. 205, file 123

166. Laurier Papers, reel C779, 49647-50, White to Laurier, 29 Sept 1900; Sifton Papers, reel C474, 30721, Laurier to Sifton, 31 Mar 1898

167. NA, Minto Papers, vol. 4, 46-51, Memoranda, 22 Oct 1902

168. Ibid., vol. 2, 18-19, Minto's memo of conversation with Laurier

169. Ibid.

170. Laurier Papers, reel C775, 4476, Jas. Sutherland to Laurier, 14 Apr 1900; see also reel C788, 59096-98

171. Sifton Papers, reel C530, 1055, White to Sifton, 15 Jan 1901

172. RG 18, vol. 347, file 39 and vol. 2285, Herchmer to Rev. Douglas, 27 Jan 1898

173. Saskatchewan Archives Board, W. Scott Papers, MI, V, file 15, White to Scott, 22 Oct 1901

Chapter 5
Adjusting to a New Reality: The Mounted Police and the Indians, 1886-1892

1. Canada, Statistical Abstract and Record (Ottawa: McLean, Roger 1887), 73

2. J. L. Taylor, "The Development of Indian Policy for the Canadian North-West, 1869-79" (PhD, Queen's University, 1975)

3. M. J. Boswell, "'Civilizing' the Indian: Government Administration of Indians, 1876-1896" (PhD, University

of Ottawa, 1977), 229

4. Ibid., 277
5. Ibid., 123
6. A. J. Looy, "The Indian Agent and his Role in the Administration of the North-West Superintendency, 1876-1893" (PhD, Queen's University, 1977), 270-273
7. Boswell, "'Civilizing' the Indian", 415
8. Hugh Dempsey, *Crowfoot: Chief of the Blackfeet* (Norman University of Oklahoma Press 1972), 13-20 (hereafter cited as Dempsey, Crowfoot)
9. NWMP, Annual Report, 1886, 7, 12, 21-28, 33-38, 55-65, 69
10. Ibid., 1890, 75
11. Macleod, 146
12. RG 18, vol. 45, file 953-1890, Reed to Dewdney, 30 Aug 1890
13. John N. Jennings, "The North West Mounted Police and Indian Policy, 1874-1896" (PhD, University of Toronto, 1979), 266-315
14. Dempsey, *Crowfoot*, 207
15. RG 18, vol. 1173, file 158, Cotton to Herchmer, 13 Mar 1890
16. Macdonald Papers, 33262, Lansdowne to Macdonald, 11 Nov 1885
17. Ibid., 146956, H. Reed to Dewdney, 9 Mar 1886
18. Ibid., 90480, Dewdney to Macdonald, 11 Feb 1886; RG 18, vol. 1042, file 95, Report of Supt. S. Gagnon, 3 Apr 1886; Boswell, "'Civilizing' the Indian", 124
19. NWMP, Annual Report, 1886, 31; RG 18, vol. 1037, file 65, Dewdney to Herchmer, 17 May 1886
20. Ibid., 1886, 50
21. RG 18, vol. 13, file 16-1888, L. Vankoughnet to White, 29 Nov 1886
22. Ibid., W. H. Herchmer to L. W. Herchmer, 9 Feb 1887
23. Macdonald Papers, Report of B.C. Executive Council, 26 Apr 1887
24. Ibid., Wm. Smithe to Macdonald, telegram, 21 Mar 1887
25. Ibid., Macdonald to Smithe, telegram, 23 Mar 1887
26. Ibid., Lt. Vol. J. Baker to B.C. Attorney General, 27 Apr 1887; R. Fisher, *Contact and Conflict* (Vancouver: University of British Columbia Press 1977), 203-204
27. Steele, 247
28. Macdonald Papers, 146873-146876, Dewdney to Macdonald, 5 May 1887
29. Ibid., 146887-889, Herchmer to White, 6 July 1887
30. NWMP, Annual Report, 1887, 18-19
31. RG 18, vol. 1115, file 287, Steele to Herchmer, 19 Jan 1888
32. Steele, 245-249; NWMP, Annual Report, 1887, 53-55
33. Macdonald Papers, 146890-893, White to Macdonald, 17 Aug 1887; RG 18, vol. 13, file 16-1888, Neale to Herchmer, 8 Aug 1887
34. Steele, 249; NWMP, Annual Report, 1887, 62-63
35. RG 18, vol. 15, file 60-1888; Fisher, *Contact and Conflict*, 204
36. NWMP, Annual Report, 1888, 84-92; Steele, 249-254
37. NWMP, Annual Report, 1888, 68, 111-112
38. RG 18, vol. 46, file 15-1891, Steele to Herchmer, 24 Dec 1890; vol. 1124, file 431
39. Ibid., vol. 19, file 249-1888, Transcript of meeting of Blood, Peigan Indians, Mounted Police and Indian Department Officials at Fort Macleod, 4 Feb 1888; Jennings, "The North West Mounted Police and Indian Policy", ch. 8
40. RG 18, vol. 1100, file 133
41. R. M. Uttey, *Frontier Regulars: The United States Army and the Indian, 1866-1891* (New York: Macmillan 1973), 407-423
42. RG 18, vol. 1204, file 157
43. Ibid., file 158
44. Ibid., vol. 46, file 15, 1891, White to Herchmer, 14 Jan 1891

45. Stanley Papers, reel A673, Lord Stanley to Sir J. Pauncefort, 10 Jan 1891
46. RG 18, vol. 46, file 15-1891
47. Ibid., vol. 1217, file 220, H Division Monthly Report, Jan 1891
48. Ibid., vol. 50, file 204-1891
49. Ibid., vol. 1204, file 157; *Calgary Herald*, 23 Jan 1891
50. *Regina Leader*, 13 Jan 1891
51. *Calgary Herald*, 16 Jan 1891
52. Boswell, "'Civilizing' the Indian", 391-393
53. NWMP, Annual Report, 1886, 67; Macdonald Papers, 134958, White to Macdonald, 28 Aug 1886
54. RG 18, vol. 1077, file 361, W. Herchmer to L. Herchmer
55. NWMP, Annual Report, 1886, 47, 124
56. RG 18, vol. 1062, file 106, Dewdney to Herchmer, 2 Dec 1887
57. NWMP, Annual Report, 1888, 98
58. RG 18, vol. 1062, file 106, Dewdney to White, 12 Sept 1887
59. Ibid., vol. 1062, files 106, 107
60. Ibid., vol. 1123, file 427, Report of Supt. R. B. Deane, 15 May 1888
61. Ibid., 8 Dec 1888
62. NWMP, Annual Report, 1889, 41
63. Ibid., 1890, 51
64. Ibid., 29; 1891, 24
65. RG 18, vol. 45, file 953-1890
66. NWMP, Annual Report, 1890, 61-62
67. RG 18, vol. 1204, file 163, Sanders to Herchmer, 26 Jan 1891
68. NWMP, Annual Report, 1891, 95
69. The figures were taken from NWMP Annual Reports
70. NWMP, Annual Report, 1890, 178-204
71. Saskatchewan Archives Board, A&G (1), G Series, file 304L, McIllree to Herchmer, 17 May 1886
72. RG 18, vol. 753, White to Herchmer, 31 May 1886 Chastened by this rebuke from the Prime Minister, McIllree later amplified his recommendation, explaining that he meant only those Indians who brandished their guns in a threatening manner when they encounter police should be prepared to suffer the consequences. McIllree's attitude is perhaps more understandable in the context of the uncertainty of the immediate post-rebellion period.
73. Ibid., vol. 1037, file 66
74. NWMP, Annual Report, 1887, 45; Dempsey, *Crowfoot*, 207-208
75. RG 18, vol. 1062, file 107, Report of Insp. Sanders, 25 June 1887
76. Ibid., vol. 1082, file 450
77. NWMP, Annual Report, 1887, 48
78. Dempsey, *Crowfoot*, 207
79. RG 18, vol. 1073, file 343
80. Ibid., vol. 1080, file 401
81. Ibid., file 422
82. NWMP, Annual Report, 1887, 49
83. RG 18, vol. 1173, file 158
84. *Macleod Gazette*, 21 May 1891. In 1893, The Dog was temporarily employed by the Mounted Police as a scout, but his job ended abruptly when he settled a dispute with Mounted Police Constable Currie by stabbing him in the head, neck and face. The Dog was convicted of stabbing with intent and sentenced to two years in jail by Judge Macleod. See NWMP, Annual Report, 1893, 220
85. RG 18, vol. 26, file 43-1889
86. NWMP, Annual Report, 1891, 3-4
87. RG 18, vol. 42, file 481-1890, vol. 50, file 249-1891
88. Ibid., vol. 19, file 249-1888; NWMP, Annual Report, 1890, 75
89. NWMP, Annual Report, 1891, 32, 167; RG 18, vol. 1204, file 158. Medicine White Horse escaped custody a second time in June 1891 while awaiting conveyance to Stony

Mountain Penitentiary. He crossed over into Montana and was a fugitive until 1 November 1893 when he surrendered to Mounted Police in Canada. See NWMP, Annual Report, 1893, 18-19

90. Ibid., 1891, 32-33
91. RG 18, vol. 1204, file 158, Reports of Supt. Sam Steele, Oct 1891
92. Ibid., vol. 56, file 690-1891. No further report has been found on the fate of Steals Fire.
93. NWMP, Annual Report, 1888, 60
94. RG 18, vol. 1124, file 429
95. NWMP, Annual Report, 1888, 60
96. Ibid., 1889, 42-43, 65-66; RG 18, vol. 35, file 379-1889
97. NWMP, Annual Report, 1889, 42
98. RG 18, vol. 39, file 94-1890
99. NWMP, Annual Report, 1886 to 1891, appendices on criminal statistics
100. NWMP, Annual Report, 1887, 92-93
101. *Edmonton Bulletin*, 10 Sept 1887
102. Ibid., 17 Sept 1891
103. Pennefather, 30
104. Ibid., 38-41
105. NWMP, Annual Report, 1887, 9, 20, 92, 143
106. Assistance provided by Hugh Dempsey of the Glenbow Museum in identifying the names of the several individuals involved in this confusing series of events is gratefully acknowledged.
107. Saskatchewan Archives Board, Attorney General (1), G Series, file 409L
108. RG 18, vol. 19, file 249-1888, Transcript of meeting of Blood, Peigan Indians, Mounted Police and Indian Department Officials at Fort Macleod, 4 Feb 1888
109. NWMP, Annual Report, 1888, 59-60; RG 18, vol. 1100, file 132
110. *Regina Leader*, 16 Apr 1888
111. RG 18, vol. 33, file 350-1889, vol. 1140, file 177
112. NWMP, Annual Report, 1889, 181; *Regina Leader*, 11 June 1889
113. RG 18, vol. 54, file 493-1891; *Calgary Herald*, 16 July 1891; NWMP, Annual Report, 1891, 159; 1897, 56
114. Boswell, "'Civilizing' the Indian", 31-32, 123-124
115. NWMP, Annual Report, 1889, 64-65
116. Adolf Hungry Wolf, *The Blood People* (New York: Harper, Row 1977), 36-44
117. Dempsey, *Crowfoot*, 199-200; NWMP, Annual Report, 1891, 31
118. RG 18, vol. 1100, file 132, Report of Supt. Neale, 7 Aug 1888
119. Steele, 264-265
120. NWMP, Annual Report, 1889, 64-65, 179
121. RG 18, vol. 36, file 817-1889, Steele to Herchmer, 12 Aug 1889
122. Ibid., vol. 1139, file 173, Herchmer to White, 20 Aug 1889
123. Ibid., vol. 36, file 817-1889, White to Herchmer, 21 Oct 1889
124. Ibid., Sedgewick to White, 31 Oct 1889
125. J. Gresko, "White 'Rites' and Indian 'Rites'" in A. W. Rasporich (ed), *Western Canada Past and Present* (Calgary: McClelland and Stewart 1975), 163-223; Boswell, "'Civilizing' the Indian", 284-285
126. Hugh Dempsey (ed), Mike Mountain Horse, *My People, the Bloods* (Calgary: Glenbow Foundation and Blood Tribal Council 1978), 15-16
127. Gresko, "White 'Rites' and Indian' Rites'", 170-175
128. RG 18, vol. 1037, file 65
129. Ibid., vol. 1062, file 106, Reed to Herchmer, 29 Nov 1887
130. NWMP, Annual Report, 1888, 38; 1889, 124
131. Ibid., 1890, 108, 179
132. RG 18, vol. 1120, file 351, Neale to Herchmer, 21 Feb 1888
133. Ibid., vol. 753, Comptroller's Letterbook, White to Herchmer, 10 May 1886
134. Ibid., vol. 754, Comptroller's Letterbook, White to Herchmer, 4 Nov 1886, White to Vankoughnet, 4 Nov 1886
135. Ibid., vol. 46, file 15-1891, Steele to Herchmer, 24 Dec 1890
136. Ibid., vol. 1116, file 311, White to Herchmer, 12 Apr 1888; Hugh Dempsey, "The Snake Man", *Alberta History*, vol. 29, no. 4, autumn 1981, 1-5
137. RG 18, vol. 22, file 358-1888
138. Ibid., vol. 1084, file 513
139. NWMP, Annual Report, 1890, 4
140. Ibid., 1887, 51
141. RG 18, vol. 45, file 832-1890
142. NWMP, Annual Report, 1892, 2
143. RG 18, vol. 61, file 120-1892

Chapter 6

A Pragmatic Approach to Law Enforcement: The Police and Western Indians, 1892-1900

1. *Macleod Gazette*, 4 June 1897
2. Boswell, "'Civilizing' the Indian"
3. See the annual reports of the NWMP and the Department of Indian Affairs
4. D. J. Hall, "Clifford Sifton and Canadian Indian Administration, 1896-1905" in *Prairie Forum*, vol. 2, no. 2, Nov 77, 141 and 150. Hall gives the following figures prepared in 1904 by Frank Pedley, Deputy Minister of the Department of Indian Affairs: Quantities of Food Issued

Fiscal year	Nos. on List	Flour	Beef	Bacon
1890-91	12,155	1,745,300 lbs.	2,029,697 lbs.	245,742 lbs.
1896-97	8,853	1,286,100 lbs.	1,409,783 lbs.	149,266 lbs.
1902-03	5,928	991,050 lbs.	1,206,715 lbs.	135,887 lbs.

5. RG 18, vol. 73, file 6-1893, Steele to Herchmer, 21 Dec 1892
6. Ibid., vol. 80, file 258-1893
7. Ibid., A. B. Macdonald to Steele, 6 Mar 1893
8. Ibid., vol. 78, file 233-1893 and vol. 1281, file 296
9. Ibid., vol. 79, file 235-1893
10. Ibid., vol. 80, file 345-1893, Reed to White, 28 June 1893
11. Ibid., vol. 2284, McIllree to Herchmer, 11 June 1894
12. Ibid., vol. 101, file 38-1895, Herchmer to Department of Indian Affairs, 30 Sept 1894
13. Ibid., vol. 2284, Herchmer to Forget, Indian Affairs
14. Ibid., vol. 101, file 38-1895
15. Ibid., Wadsworth to A. E. Forget, Indian Affairs, 22 July 1895
16. Ibid., White to Ives, 6 Oct 1894
17. Indian Affairs, Annual Report, 1895, xxi
18. NWMP, Annual Report, 1895, 6 and 129; *Calgary Herald*, 4, 5, and 6 Apr 1895. This account of the circumstances of Skynner's death came from police and news reports made at the time. Hugh Dempsey describes this version of the incident in his book Charcoal's World (36), but then offers a differing story which he prefers. Dempsey gives the Indian's name as "Scraping Hide" and says that after his son's death, the man, after brooding for some time, decided to take revenge by killing a white man. His first target was G. H. Wheatley, the farm instructor, but when he was not at home, Skynner was selected as an alternative. Unfortunately, the only source Dempsey gives for his information is a 1962 story in the *Calgary Herald Magazine*.
19. RG 18, vol. 110, file 517-1895 and vol. 1342, file 191

20. Debates, 4 July 1895, 3897
21. NWMP, Annual Report, 1896, 138 and 267
22. John Jennings, "The North-West Mounted Police and Indian Policy, 1874-1896"
23. NA, RG 18, vol. 1038, file 68, Cuthbert to Perry, 19 Feb 1886
24. David Lee, "Almighty Voice," unpublished paper prepared for the Historic Sites and Monuments Board of Canada, Canadian Parks Service
25. Ibid.; W.B. Cameron, Scarlet and Gold, 2nd annual, 1920, 46
26. NWMP, Annual Report, 1895, 233
27. RG 18, vol. 107, file 224-1895, Colebrook to Moffatt, 22 Oct 1895
28. Ibid., vol. 2217, Moffatt to Herchmer, 13 Mar 1896
29. Ibid., vol. 121, file 269-1896
30. RCMP Museum, Prince Albert Letterbooks, Moffatt to Herchmer, 3 Nov 1895 (hereafter cited as Prince Albert Letterbooks)
31. RG 18, vol. 3331, file 605, Transcript of Testimony of François Dumont at Coroner's inquest into the death of Sgt. Colebrook, n.d.
32. Ibid.
33. Ibid., vol. 3331, file 605, Transcript of Testimony of Small Face at Cornoner's inquest into the death of Sgt. Colebrook, n.d.
34. Prince Albert Letterbooks
35. RG 18, vol. 3331, file 605, Herchmer to White, 30 Nov 1895
36. Prince Albert Letterbooks, Moffatt to Herchmer, 4 Dec 1895
37. Lee, "Almighty Voice," 7
38. RG 18, vol. 2284, Herchmer to White, 21 Jan 1896
39. Prince Albert Letterbooks, Moffatt to Herchmer, 13 Mar 1896
40. RG 18, vol. 1398, file 186, affidavit of Oo-spok-un-ace; H. S. Kemp, "Almighty Voice - Public Enemy No. 1," in RCMP Quarterly, July 1957, 5
41. Lee, "Almighty Voice," 7
42. Cameron, Scarlet and Gold, 2nd annual, 1920
43. John B. Allan, "A Chapter in R.N.W.M.P. Annals," in Scarlet and Gold, 6th annual, 1924, 34-6
44. Prince Albert Letterbooks, Gagnon to Herchmer, 3 June 1897
45. Regina Leader, 3 June 1897
46. Prince Albert Letterbooks, Gagnon to Herchmer, 3 June 1897
47. NWMP, Annual Report, 1897, 23-4
48. RCMP Historical Branch, Manuscript copy of a memoir written by Joseph Walton on the Almighty Voice affair
49. Lee, "Almighty Voice," 12
50. Pierre Berton, "The Legend of Almighty Voice" in The Wild Frontier: More Tales from the Remarkable Past (Toronto: McClelland and Stewart 1978), 211
51. Mike Mountain Horse, My People, the Bloods, ed. by H. A. Dempsey (Glenbow-Alberta Institute and Blood Tribal Council 1979), 119-131; and Mike Mountain Horse, "Charcoal and How He Grew Blacker," RCMP Quarterly, July 1941, 30-38
52. Hugh Dempsey, Charcoal's World (Saskatoon: Western Producer Prairie Books 1978), 28-33
53. There are several major sources for the following chronological treatment of the Charcoal case. To avoid repetitive notes, the most important sources will be cited here and other sources will only be cited as they are used. The major police sources are: RG 18, vol. 1374, file 212 and vol. 1376, file 212; NWMP, Annual Report, 1896, 2, 8-9, 16, 18, 22-31, 44-58, 270, 273 and 1897, 38. Transcripts of the proceedings of Charcoal's trial can be found in MG 30, E87, Horace Harvey Papers, vol. 42. Most of the psycho-historical dimension of Charcoal's world is derived from oral tradition in a manner which does not appear to meet conventional historical standards. For this reason, the material in Dempsey's book is used with care. However, some of the information is used because it came from documentary sources in the author's possession and is consistent with material in archival sources.
54. NWMP, Annual Report, 1883, 48
55. Steele, 277-278
56. The evidence from most sources strongly suggests that Charcoal was inclined to be wild and troublesome. It is curious to note, however, that in the course of Charcoal's trial, Cliff Clark, a farm instructor on the reserve, stated: "I know prisoner and have known him for about two years. Up to the present his character has been very good." Perhaps after marrying Pretty Wolverine Woman, he had settled down until he was cuckolded. Source: Harvey Papers, vol. 42, Transcript, Queen vs Charcoal, 20
57. Macleod Gazette, 22 Jan 1897; RG 18, vol. 1374, file 212, Steele to Herchmer, 25 Jan 1897
58. NWMP, Annual Report, 1896, 58
59. RG 18, vol. 125, file 572-1896
60. Ibid., vol. 1356, file 87
61. Indian Affairs, Annual Report, 167
62. NWMP, Annual Report, 1892, 191-192; Calgary Herald, 14 May 1892
63. RG 18, vol. 124, file 480-1896
64. Ibid., vol. 195, file 667-1900
65. NWMP, Annual Report, 1894, 51-52
66. RG 18, vol. 1484, file 166
67. Regina Leader, 22 May 1902
68. NWMP, Annual Report, 1902, 4
69. RG 18, vol. 96, file 514-1894
70. NWMP, Annual Report, 1897, 128-129, 301
71. RG 18, vol. 134, file 1889-1897
72. NWMP, Annual Report, 1898, 110
73. Ibid., 1896, 138-139
74. The principal sources for this account of the Blood dance crisis of 1898 are: NWMP, Annual Report, 1898, 26-27, Supt. R. B. Deane's annual report on the Macleod district, and H. A. Dempsey, Red Crow, 207-211. The two sources differ is some details and we have chosen to follow Deane's version in these instances. Deane wrote his report with the affair fresh in his mind, while Dempsey does not adequately document his sources of information.
75. RG 18, vol. 205, file 136-1901, J. Smart to White, 30 Jan 1901
76. Ibid., White to Smart, 22 Feb 1901
77. NWMP, Annual Report, 1892, 135-136
78. Debates, 9 July 1894, 5552-5554
79. RG 18, vol. 103, file 63-185, Herchmer to White, 22 Feb 1895
80. Ibid., various correspondence
81. J. F. L. Prince, "The Education and Acculturation of the Western Canadian Indian, 1880-1970, with reference to Hayter Reed," MA thesis, 1974, 48-49, 83-85
82. Hall, "Clifford Sifton and Canadian Indian Administration, 1896-1905," 133-135; Gresko, "White 'Rites' and Indian 'Rites'", 172-173
83. NWMP, Annual Report, 1892, 49
84. RG 18, vol. 218, file 763-1901, Herchmer's circular memorandum, 26 May 1893
85. NWMP, Annual Report, 1893, 83 and 1896, 34
86. Calgary Herald, 20 July 1892
87. NWMP, Annual Report, 1892, 128
88. Ibid., 1899, 88
89. Ibid., 1896, 2
90. Ibid., 1895, 6
91. RG 18, vol. 2217, Herchmer to White, n.d.
92. Ibid., vol. 84, file 465-1893
93. NWMP, Annual Report, 1896, 14, 91-97; Calgary Herald, 18 July 1896

94. NWMP, Annual Report, 1894, 52; RG 18, vol. 95, file 403-1894
95. Indian Affairs, Annual Report, 1900, 128
96. NWMP, Annual Report, 1897, 5

Chapter 7

Mountie Justice on the Canadian Frontier, 1886-1891

1. Robert Dykstra, *The Cattle Towns* (New York: Alfred A. Knopf 1968)
2. T. D. Phillips, "The Multi-purpose Army," in A. G. Bogue, T. D. Phillips and J. E. Wright (eds), *The West of the American People* (Itasea, Ill.: F. E. Peacock Publishing 1970), 415-420
3. Frank R. Prassel, *The Western Peace Officer: A Legacy of Law and Order* (Norman: University of Oklahoma Press 1972)
4. W. E. Hollan, *Frontier Violence: Another Look* (London: University of Oxford Press 1974)
5. David Breen, "The Turner Thesis and the Canadian West: A Closer Look at the Ranching Frontier," in L. H. Thomas (ed), *Essays on Western History* (Edmonton: University of Alberta Press, 1976)
6. Arthur Schlesinger, "What Then is the American, This New Man?" in Bogue, Phillip and Wright, *The West of the American People*, 525-530
7. R. M. Maxwell, "Historical Patterns of Violence in America," in *The History of Violence in America: Historical*
8. S. W. Horrall, "Sir John A. Macdonald and the Mounted Police Force for the Northwest Territories," CHR, June 72, 179-200
9. David Breen, "The Canadian West and the Ranching Frontier, 1875-1922," PhD thesis, University of Alberta, 1972, 177-178
10. T. M. Reynolds, "Justices of the Peace in the North-West Territories, 1870-1905," MA thesis, University of Regina, 1978
11. Ideally, an assessment of the effectiveness of the Mounted Police would include quantitative analysis of the Force's success in combatting crime. The authors have made forays into the bewildering realm of crime statistics and have been frustrated in their attempts to extract significant data. Many records are missing and what figures are available are erroneous or incomplete. To build an adequate research base, a labourious sorting is required of the existing judicial records of the territorial and provincial west. Such a task is of the magnitude of an ongoing commitment by a university graduate program. It is much beyond the scope of this study. Exacerbating the lack of confidence in the adequacy of sources are difficulties in interpretation. Based on statistics alone it would be impossible to say, for instance, if a small number of cases of serious crime being heard in court was a reflection of the lawfulness of society or the inefficiency of the police. Sense would only be made out of these data by studying them in connection with police handling of sample cases and the community's judgement of the work of the police. It is to these last two aspects that the authors will address themselves.
12. *Fort Benton Record*, 13 Apr 1877
13. Debates, 16 July 1885, 3427-3433
14. *Revised Statutes of Canada*, 1886 (numbers 147-149, 151-152)
15. NWMP, Annual Report, 1891, 192-193
16. Ibid., 170 and 1890, 140
17. In addition to the four murders in Assiniboia dealt with in the text, there were three other victims: Scott Krenger, near Calgary in 1886; Peter Dacotah in 1891; and a young girl named Westerlund, also in 1891. The Krenger murder was never solved, but police suspected the crime was committed by the Calgary stagecoach robbers. An American named Edward Fletcher was convicted of manslaughter in the death of Dacotah and sentenced to 20 years in prison. The Westerlund girl was killed by her father who was acquitted of murder by reason of insanity. See NWMP, Annual Report, 1886, 68; 1891, 44, 97-98; and RG 18, vol. 48, file 140-1891
18. RG 18, vol. 14, file 17-1888; NWMP, Annual Report, 1887, 17-18, 33, 35-36, 39-44, 88
19. RG 18, vol. 1080, file 426
20. *Regina Leader*, 7 June 1887
21. NWMP, Annual Report, 1887, 9
22. Ibid., 1886, 51-53
23. Ibid., 1886, 19, 67-68, 127, 136; *Calgary Herald*, 14 Aug 1886
24. *Calgary Herald*, 14 Aug 1886
25. Ibid., 11 September 1886
26. *Calgary Tribune* article (date unknown) reprinted and endorsed by the *Regina Leader*, 26 July 1887
27. NWMP, Annual Report, 1886, 13
28. RG 18, vol. 22, file 383-1888, White to Macdonald, 24 Aug 1887
29. Ibid., White to Herchmer, 5 Aug 1887
30. Ibid., Constantine to Herchmer, 14 Aug 1887
31. Ibid., vol. 1121, file 384, Herchmer to White, 17 Aug 1887
32. Ibid., vol. 22, file 383-1888, White to Macdonald, 24 Aug 1887
33. Ibid., vol. 1121, file 384, Constantine to Herchmer, 23 June 1888
34. Ibid., Herchmer to W. Whyte, Chief Superintendent, CPR, 21 May 1888
35. Ibid., vol. 1140, file 194, Herchmer to McIllree, 22 Mar 1889
36. Ibid., vol. 1121, file 384, Antrobus to Herchmer, 19 July 1888, enclosing Moodie to Antrobus, 14 July 1888
37. Ibid., vol. 32, file 202-1889, Monthly reports from Regina District
38. Breen, "The Canadian West and the Ranching Frontier, 1875-1922," 170-182
39. NWMP, Annual Report, 1886, 7, 140-141
40. Ibid., 1891, 63
41. Ibid., 69-70
42. Ibid., 1886, 33, 118; *Regina Leader*, 16 Feb 1886; RG 18, vol. 1117, file 317
43. NWMP, Annual Report, 1886, 27, 117
44. Ibid., 1888, 8
45. Ibid., 119, 122
46. Ibid., 64 and 1889, 174
47. Ibid., 1889, 93-94
48. Ibid., 1890, 49
49. Sharon A. Williams and J. G. Castel, *Canadian Criminal Law: International and Transnational Aspects* (Toronto: Butterworths 1981), 337-431
50. G. V. La Forest, *Extradition To and From Canada* (New Orleans: Hanser Press), 1-14, 164-165; MG 16, Foreign Office Records, vol. 414, files 42, 51 and 71; RG 18, vol. 249, file 149-1903
51. RG 18, vol. 1124, file 440
52. Ibid., vol. 1134, file 134; NWMP, Annual Report, 1889, 35, 98. Rewards offered by American authorities for the arrest of criminals were only occasionally claimed by Mounted Policemen. Wanted circulars, sometimes offering rewards, were received by NWMP posts on a sporadic basis from a wide variety of U.S. sources, including local sheriffs, private detective agencies and eastern police forces. In all probability, they were sent only when it was suspected that the individual sought was headed for the that region of the NWT. See also RG 18, vol. 1117, vol. 317

53. NWMP, Annual Report, 1890, 61
54. Macleod, 34-35
55. Horace Harvey, "The Early Administration of Justice in the North West," and "Some Further Notes on the Early Administration of Justice in the North West," *Alberta Law Quarterly*, vol. 1, 1935, 1-15 and 171-196. Wm. P. Ward, "The Administration of Justice in the North-West Territories, 1870-1887," MA thesis, University of Alberta, 1966
56. Reynolds, "Justices of the Peace in the North-West Territories"
57. Ibid., ch. 4
58. See P. Michael Bolton, Procedure and Practice in Canadian Criminal Trials (Toronto: International Self-Counsel Series 1974). This volume gives a more detailed explanation of procedures with references to historical notes.
59. *Calgary Herald*, 21 Mar 1889
60. Reynolds, "Justices of Peace in the North-West Territories"
61. RG 18, vol. 1053, file 282
62. NWMP, Annual Report, 1889, 96
63. Ibid., 1891, 51, 61, 146-151
64. Officers at Calgary were kept busy with criminal justice work. In 1891, the NWMP reported on 180 cases cleared through the work of the Force in the Calgary district courts. Of that total, only 18 were handled by one of the superior court judges and none by civilian J.P.s alone. Of the remaining 162, 22 were trials with both a police justice and a civilian justice presiding. NWMP, Annual Report, 1891, 16-17, 156-163
65. *Regina Leader*, 16 Nov 1889
66. *Macleod Gazette*, 12 Sept 1889
67. RG 18, vol. 36, file 801-1889
68. Saskatchewan Archives Board, ATG (1), G Series, Herchmer to R. B. Gordon, Secretary to the Governor, 28 June 1889, and Gordon to Herchmer, 10 July 1889
69. See Chapter 9 for details
70. Edward Mills, "The Early Court Houses of Alberta," Manuscript Report No. 310 (Ottawa: Parks Canada 1977), 8-9 and Debates, 26 Apr 1888, 1025
71. NWMP, Annual Report, 1890, 24. Presumably, the 34 prisoners which McIllree does not account for were held in the guardroom awaiting trial or were policemen imprisoned for breaches of discipline.
72. Ibid., 1891, 8
73. Ibid., 1890, 42
74. Mills, "Early Court Houses," 10
75. Saskatchewan Archives Board, ATG (1), G Series, file 521D, Wetmore to Gov. Dewdney, 17 June 1887; RG 18, vol. 1067, file 150
76. Ibid., NWMP, Annual Report, 1887, 41-42
77. Auditor General, Report, 1888-89, D189-193; 1889-90, B369-373; 1890-91, C157-163; 1891-92, C144-147
78. Mills, "Early Court Houses," 12-13, 50-51
79. *Calgary Herald*, 24 Sept and 23 Oct 1891
80. *Canada, Regulations and Orders for The Government and Guidance of the North-West Mounted Police* (Ottawa: Queen's Printer 1889), 13, 16, 27-29
81. RG 18, vol. 2282, Herchmer to Griesbach, 5 Nov 1887
82. Ibid., vol. 1041, file 93, Griesbach to Herchmer, 18 May 1886
83. RCMP Historical Branch, J. D. Nicholson to J. P. Turner, 2 Mar 1944
84. NWMP, Annual Report, 1886, 141
85. *Edmonton Bulletin*, 15 May 1886
86. Ibid., 29 May 1886; *Calgary Herald*, 29 May 1886; NWMP, Annual Report, 1886, 66
87. *Edmonton Bulletin*, 27 Nov 1886
88. *Calgary Herald*, 24 Sept 1891
89. Ibid., 6 Oct 1891
90. Ibid., 29 Sept 1891
91. NWMP, Annual Report, 1891, 160
92. See chapter
93. RG 18, vol. 3353, service file 1242, C. A. Fisher
94. Ibid., vol. 1122, file 399, Herchmer to McIllree, 7 May 1888

Chapter 8

"An Iron Fist in a Velvet Glove": The Mounted Police and Crime, 1892-1900

1. NWMP, Annual Report, 1900, pt.I, 2
2. Ibid., 1892, 142, and 1900, pt. I, 4-5, and pt. II, 8
3. Macleod, *The North-West Mounted Police*, 178
4. There is considerable peril in citing crime statistics as measurement of social evils lurking in particular communities. It is commonplace that many crimes go unreported and that fact alone may tell much about a society. As seen in this chapter, the small number of convictions obtained by the Mounted Police from stock thefts each year in no way demonstrated the prevalence of the crime nor the effort made by police to counter the threat. Moreover, in Canada during the entire period covered by this history there was no scientific approach to the compilation and analysis of crime statistics. A very misleading effort was made by the Canadian Government's Census and Statistics Office to publish crime figures from 1886 in an annual report. This office gathered information on crimes, convictions and criminals from judicial districts across Canada. There is the occasional disquieting reference in the annual reports that the figures are not complete due to the failure of some districts to forward their returns. A contemporary analyst has warned that "the figures must be used in extreme caution" due to the incompleteness of returns and the lack of uniformity and consistency in reporting and presentation. But this analyst was evidently unaware of how extensive was the under-reporting of criminal charges and convictions for the North-West Territories. A comparison of the figures presented by the statistics office with those supplied by the Mounted Police show that year after year in the 1890s and 1900s the NWMP were handling far more cases than statistics office reports showed for the combined efforts of all the police forces in the territories. In later correspondence with the Deputy Attorney General of Alberta, the Secretary of the Census and Statistics Office admitted that the information received from the clerks of the western judicial district were seriously incomplete. By contrast, the Mounted Police kept a fairly good record of cases in which they were involved, either laying charges or deciding in a judicial capacity. During Herchmer's term as Commissioner figures were often presented in annual reports but only in 1886, 1887 and 1888 did the reports present totals for the entire Force on cases in which charges were laid with which the NWMP was involved. Thereafter figures were presented, or not, in varying forms of completeness by the officer commanding each police district. Even a cursory examination of the figures shows that there was a rather slow growth in criminal investigatory work of the Force during this period. A more sophisticated analysis of this growth is possible from police returns in the annual reports and archival records in RG18, Public Archives of Canada. However, the effort may not reveal much more than the cursory examination.
5. William Pinkerton, "Yeggmen," in D. C. Dilworth (ed), *The Blue and the Brass* (International Association of Chiefs of Police 1976), 85-90

6. Provincial Archives of Alberta (hereafter cited as PAA), Records of the Deputy Attorney-General, box 3, item 38, file 42; and RG 18, vol. 2283

7. *Edmonton Bulletin*, 14 and 17 Nov 1892, and May 15, 1893; NWMP, Annual Report, 1892, 96

8. *Edmonton Bulletin*, 21 Nov 1892

9. Ibid., 24 Nov 1892, quoting the editorial position of the *Calgary Herald*

10. RG 18, vol. 2283, Herchmer to White, 13 Feb 1893

11. PAA, Records of the Deputy Attorney-General, box 3, item 38, file 42

12. *Edmonton Bulletin*, 14 May 1893

13. RG 18, vol. 2213, Herchmer to White, 18 Oct 1893; vol. 3416, service file 3468, Cst. C. E. Bleakney

14. *Edmonton Bulletin*, 16 Mar 1893

15. RG 18, vol. 2283, Herchmer to Griesbach, 16 Mar 1893

16. NWMP, Annual Report, 1893, 40 and 1894, 49

17. RG 18, vol. 2284, Herchmer to William Whyte, 11 Apr 1895

18. Ibid., vol. 1346, Whyte to Herchmer, 5 May 1895

19. Ibid., Herchmer to Whyte, 16 May 1895;

20. Ibid., circular memorandum 113, 16 May 1895

21. NWMP, Annual Report, 1895, 58-60, and 1896, 7, 77

22. Ibid., 1896, 62, 180

23. *Calgary Herald*, 12 Sept 1898

24. RG 18, vol. 110, file 507-1895, and vol. 1344, file 193

25. *Calgary Herald*, 12 Sept 1898

26. Wm. Pinkerton, "Train Robbers and Holdup Men," [1907], in Dilworth, *The Blue and the Brass*, 20-22

27. NWMP, Annual Report, 1895, 93-94

28. Ibid., 90

29. Ibid., 2, 34

30. RG 18, vol. 125, file 586-1896, Shaughnessy to White, 20 Nov 1896

31. See NWMP, Annual Report, 1903, 57-58 and 1904, 29-34

32. To simplify matters, it was decided not to include deaths resulting from conflicts among Indians and between Indians and authorities. The Indian situation is studied separately in this volume.

33. Statistics on murders were compiled from the annual reports of the Commissioner of the Mounted Police for the years 1892 to 1900. Additional information used to analyze the circumstances of these deaths came mainly from police reports in RG 18 and newspapers.

34. NWMP, Annual Report, 1900, 44

35. *Regina Leader*, 17 Jan 1901

36. RG 18, vol. 1177, McIllree to Commissioner, 23 July 1900; NWMP, Annual Report, 1891, 156-162

37. *Edmonton Bulletin*, 3 and 10 Nov 1888; NWMP, Annual Report, 1888, 198

38. NWMP, Annual Report, 1894, 109; RG 18, vol. 88, file 45-1888

39. *Edmonton Bulletin*, 21 May 1894

40. NWMP, Annual Report, 1897, 113

41. Turner, vol. I, 165, 202, 210, and vol. II, 427, 489, 574

42. NWMP, Annual Report, 1894, 93; A. Johnston and A. den Otter, *Lethbridge: A Centennial History* (Lethbridge: Historical Society of Alberta, Whoop-Up Country Chapter 1985), 119

43. NWMP, Annual Report, 1895, 61 and 1896, 63-82

44. RG 18, vol. 1251, file 257; NWMP, Annual Report, 1892, 38

45. NWMP, Annual Report, 1894, 109

46. Ibid., 1899, 85

47. E. L. Silverman, *The Last Best West: Women on the Alberta Frontier, 1880-1910* (Montreal: Eden Press 1984), 59-65

48. NWMP, Annual Report, 1892, 194; *Calgary Herald*, 21, 22 and 25 Nov 1892

49. *Calgary Herald*, 19 Apr and 3 May 1893; RG 18, vol. 75, file 127-1893, Insp. Cuthbert's monthly report from

50. *Edmonton Bulletin*, 8 May 1893

51. *Calgary Herald*, 6 and 10 July 1894; NWMP, Annual Report, 1894, 231

52. NWMP, Annual Report, 1894, 230, 233

53. *Calgary Herald*, 15 Mar 1895

54. S. R. Clarke, *The Magistrate's Manual Founded on the Criminal Code, 1892*, (Toronto: Carswell Co. 1893), 385-387 (hereafter cited as Clarke, Magistrate's Manual)

55. RG 18, vol. 126, file 2-1897, Supt. J. Howe's monthly report for Oct 1897

56. Ibid., Howe's monthly reports for May and June 1897

57. Ibid., vol. 184, file 219-1900, Supt. Constantine's monthly report for Sept 1900

58. Ibid., vol. 126, file 2-1897, Howe's monthly report for Oct 1897

59. NWMP, Annual Report, 1897, 124

60. The figures are derived from Mounted Police annual reports and are approximate only. For instance, one difficulty is that in one year, 1899, Headquarters District entered as one figure prosecutions for rape and criminal seductions, and in other districts, numbers were given for offences against persons without further breakdown. Thus, sexual offences may have occurred which are not accounted for in this rough statistical analysis. Given this obvious shortcoming, it can still be said that 18 persons were convicted of sexual assaults against women or children, 40 were acquitted or had their cases quashed at some point in the proceedings and in 4 cases, the outcome was not recorded.

61. C. Backhouse, "Nineteenth Century Canadian Rape Law," in D. H. Flaherty (ed), *Essays in the History of Canadian Law*, vol. II (Toronto: Osgoode Society, University of Toronto Press 1983), 200-247; J. G. Haskins, "The Rise and Fall of the Corroboration Rule in Sexual Offence Cases," *Canadian Journal of Family Law*, vol. 4, no. 2, Oct 1983, 173-214

62. NWMP, Annual Report, 1900, 51

63. Ibid., 1901, 89 and 1902, 72

64. Ibid., 1896, 17

65. Ibid., 260

66. Ibid., 1898, 150; *Regina Leader*, 23 June 1898

67. RG 18, vol. 208, file 213-1901, Insp. Casey's monthly reports for Lethbridge for Jan and Mar 1901; NWMP, Annual Report, 1901, 98

68. Clarke, *Magistrate's Manual*, 403-404

69. NWMP, Annual Report, 1895, 199

70. *Calgary Herald*, 22 May 1895

71. RG 18, vol. 102, file 54-1895, Perry's monthly report for June 1895

72.` Ibid., vol. 188, file 303-1900, Griesbach's monthly report for May 1900

73. Clarke, *Magistrate's Manual*, 356

74. Figures on family abuse are derived from annual reports of the Commissioner, 1892 to 1900, and from individual cases treated in more detail in police reports found in RG 18, various volumes.

75. RG 18, vol. 184, file 219-1900, Supt. C. Constantine's monthly report for Oct 1900

76. NWMP, Annual Report, 1904, 115

77. Figures on stock thefts are derived from annual reports of the Commissioner and should be regarded as approximate representation of cases investigated by the Mounted Police.

1892

Cattle Thefts

Cases	2
Withdrawn, dismissed or acquitted	2

Horse Thefts

Cases	13
Withdrawn, dismissed or acquitted	8
Convicted	5*

*(sentences ranged from 2 to 5 years)
1893
Cattle Thefts
Cases	11
Withdrawn, dismissed or acquitted	11
Cattle Killings
Cases	2
Withdrawn, dismissed or acquitted	2
Horse Thefts
Cases	6
Withdrawn, dismissed or acquitted	4
Outcome not known	2
1894
Cattle Thefts
Cases	18
Withdrawn, dismissed or acquitted	15
Convicted	3*

*(sentences ranged from 1 month hard labour to 2 1/2 years hard labour)
Cattle Killings
Cases	1
Dismissed	1
Horse Thefts
Cases	13
Withdrawn, dismissed or acquitted	9
Convicted	3*
Outcome not known	1

*(sentences were $10.00 fines; 10 days hard labour; and 5 years hard labour)
1895
Cattle Thefts
Cases	16
Withdrawn, dismissed or acquitted	7
Convicted	5*
Outcome not known	4

*(sentences ranged from $1.00 fine to 3 years in prison)
Cattle Killings
Cases	1
Withdrawn, dismissed or acquitted	1
Horse Thefts
Cases	20
Withdrawn, dismissed or acquitted	12
Convicted	6*
Outcome not known	2

*(sentences ranged from pay court costs and return horse to 12 months hard labour)
1896
Cattle Thefts
Cases	3
Dismissed	3
Convicted	7*

*(sentences ranged from pay court costs to 2 years hard labour)
Cattle Killings
Cases	3
Dismissed	1
Convicted	2*

*(sentences were: sentence suspended and 1 year hard labour)
Horse Thefts
Cases	18
Dismissed	13
Skipped bail	1
Convicted	4*

*(sentences were: bonded for good behaviour for 6 months; and 2 and 3 year terms of hard labour)
1897
Cattle Thefts
Cases	15
Withdrawn, dismissed or acquitted	12
Convicted	3*

*(sentences were: sentence suspended; 2 months hard labour; and 5 years in prison (convicted on combined charge of horse and cattle thefts))
Cattle Killings
Cases	4
Dismissed	2
Convicted	2*

*(sentences were: 3 months hard labour and 12 months hard labour)
Horse Thefts
Cases	19
Withdrawn, dismissed or acquitted	14
Convicted	5*

*(sentences ranged from $30.00 fine to 3 months hard labour exclusive of 5 year sentence on combined charge of horse and cattle thefts)
1898
Cattle Thefts
Cases	15
Withdrawn, dismissed or acquitted	12
Convicted	3*

*(sentences were: suspended sentence; 12 months hard labour; and 1 year hard labour)
Cattle Killings
Cases	1
Withdrawn, dismissed or acquitted	1
Horse Thefts
Cases	12
Withdrawn, dismissed or acquitted	4
Convicted	8*

*(sentences ranged from paying court costs to 2 years hard labour)
1899
No overall criminal statistics compiled by NWMP this year.
1900
Under Commissioner Perry a less detailed system was used in publishing criminal statistics. Comprehensive details on sentencing are not available after 1900. Also cattle killing was not reported as a separate category.
Cattle Thefts
Cases	12
Withdrawn, dismissed or acquitted	11
Convicted	1
Horse Thefts
Cases	54
Withdrawn, dismissed or acquitted	41
Convicted	13
1901
Cattle Thefts
Cases	13
Withdrawn, dismissed or acquitted	10
Convicted	0
Outcome not known	3
Horse Thefts
Cases	43
Withdrawn, dismissed or acquitted	23
Convicted	10
Settled out of court	1
Outcome not known	9
1902
Cattle Thefts
Cases	19
Withdrawn, dismissed or acquitted	12
Convicted	4
Outcome not known	3
Horse Thefts
Cases	74
Withdrawn, dismissed or acquitted	35
Convicted	38
Outcome not known	1

1903

Cattle Thefts

Cases	29
Withdrawn, dismissed or acquitted	11
Convicted	12
Outcome not known	6

Horse Thefts

Cases	88
Withdrawn, dismissed or acquitted	45
Convicted	34
Outcome not known	6

1904

Cattle Thefts

Cases	47
Withdrawn, dismissed or acquitted	16
Convicted	19
Outcome not known	6

Horse Thefts

Cases	70
Withdrawn, dismissed or acquitted	36
Convicted	25
Outcome not known	9

1905

Cattle Thefts

Cases	17
Withdrawn, dismissed or acquitted	10
Convicted	5
Outcome not known	2

Horse Thefts

Cases	71
Withdrawn, dismissed or acquitted	27
Convicted	34
Outcome not known	2

78. NWMP, Annual Report, 1897, 60-61
79. RG 18, vol. 136, file 288-1897
80. Ibid., vol. 140, file 483-1897, White to Newcombe, 25 Aug 1897
81. Ibid., vol. 3413, service file 3383, Cst. H. R. Forsythe
82. NWMP, Annual Report, 1900, 8
83. Canadian Criminal Cases, vol. 5, *The Queen vs. Forsythe*, 475-484
84. RG 18, vol. 255, file 394-1903; NWMP, Annual Report, 1903, 16-18
85. Stan Hanson, "Policing the International Boundary Area in Saskatchewan, 1890-1910," *Saskatchewan History*, spring 66, 61-77 (hereafter cited as Hanson)
86. RG 18, vol. 1422, file 169-10, Geo. Dunnell to Herchmer, 19 Jan 1898
87. Ibid., vol. 143, file 16-1898, Howe's monthly report for Regina, Jan 1898
88. *Regina Leader*, 17 Feb 1898
89. Ibid., 2 Aug 1905
90. NWMP, Annual Report, 1902, 71-72, 78-79; *Regina Leader*, 19 June and 17 July 1902
91. Sifton papers, reel C546, 108170-1, White to Sifton, 26 Nov 1902
92. RG 18, vol. 3424, service file 3818, Cst. L. Lachapelle. Most of the information on the Lachapelle incident is derived from this file.
93. Ibid., Insp. Moodie to OC, Regina District, 5 Dec 1902
94. Ibid., 31 Dec 1902
95. Ibid., 19 Dec 1902
96. Ibid., vol. 3343, service file 1007, Cst. P. Waller, report written by S/Sgt. C. Hilliard, undated
97. Ibid., vol. 3444, service file, O.128 Insp. Henri LaRoque
98. RG 18, vol. 274, file 353-1904; NWMP, Annual Report, 1903, 101; Hanson, 70
99. RG 18, vol. 274, file 353-1904, Sheriff Harry Casner to CO, Regina District, 27 Feb 1904
100. NWMP, Annual Report, 1904, 78
101. *Regina Leader*, 2 Aug 1905
102. RNWMP, Annual Report, 1905, 73; *Regina Leader*, 5 July and 2 Aug 1905
103. RNWMP, Annual Report, 1906, 41; Monty Star, "The Amiable Outlaw," *Scarlet and Gold*, vol. 54, 1972, 86-88
104. RCMP Historical Branch, Dutch Henry Leuch reference file, McIllree to Comptroller, 12 Jan 1910
105. RG 18, vol. 168, file 241-1899, Sgt. G. W. Byrne to Supt. J. Howe, 12 Mar 1899
106. Ibid.
107. NWMP, Annual Report, 1899, 66
108. Ibid., 1897, 162
109. RG 18, vol. 1454, file 63, various letters, 1900
110. Ibid., vol. 218, file 814-1901, various letters; NWMP, Annual Report, 1901, 25
111. RG 18, vol. 199, file 897-1901
112. NWMP, Annual Report, 1901, 99
113. Deane, 93
114. NWMP, Annual Report, 1895, 124, 127-128, 231
115. Ibid., 1903, 57. Z. McIlmoyle left the Force in 1903 to take up farming at Didsbury, Alta. In 1913, he was appointed Assistant Deputy Minister of Agriculture, a post he held until his death in 1928.
116. Ibid., 1900, 45
117. The following figures are derived from annual reports of the NWMP, 1892 to 1905 inclusive:

Cases Entered

Year	Where outcome is known	Convictions	Conviction Rate
1892	67	32	47.76%
1895	122	56	45.90%
1898	150	71	45.51%
1900	122	57	46.72%
1901	187	79	42.25%
1902	294	158	53.74%
1903	390	230	58.97%
1904	634	424	66.88%
1905	672	451	67.11%

118. *Edmonton Bulletin*, 20 Oct 1892
119. NWMP, Annual Report, 1901, 49
120. Ibid., 89
121. RG 18, vol. 118, file 122-1896
122. *Edmonton Bulletin*, 12 Nov 1894
123. *Manitoba Free Press*, 2 Feb 1906
124. RG 18, vol. 98, file 671-1894; NWMP, Annual Report, 1894, 67 and 1895, 61; Macleod, 122
125. *Directory of the Council and Legislative Assembly of the North-West Territories, 1876-1905* (Regina and Saskatoon: Saskatchewan Archives Board 1970), 43
126. RG 18, vol. 140, file 493-1897; NWMP, Annual Report, 1897, 52
127. RG 18, vol. 1442, file 166; NWMP, Annual Report, 1899, 51-52
128. Artibis, op. cit., 35
129. RG 18, vol. 85, file 620-1893 and vol. 2213; Macleod, 91-92
130. RG 18, vol. 97, file 632-1894
131. NWMP, Annual Report, 1895, 91-92; Deane, 266-276
132. Macleod, 120-121
133. NWMP, Annual Report, 1896, 117-118, 281-283
134. Macleod, 141-142; James Gray, *Booze: The Impact of Whisky on the Prairie West* (Toronto: Macmillan 1972)
135. D. M. Mcleod, "The History of Liquor Legislation in Saskatchewan, 1870 to 1947" (MA Thesis, University of Saskatchewan, 1948), 44-53; R. F. McLean, "A 'Most Effectual Remedy': Temperance and Prohibition in Alberta, 1875-1915" (MA Thesis, University of Calgary, 1969)
136. den Otter, A.A., op. cit., 242
137. RCMP Historical Branch, J. G. Bellomo, "The Liquor Question and the North-West Mounted Police, 1874-1905," unpublished manuscript

138. Figures derived from annual reports of the NWMP
139. NWMP, Annual Report, 1896, 180
140. Figures derived from annual reports of the NWMP
141. RG 18, vol. 1455, file 188
142. *Regina Leader*, 10 May 1900
143. Figures derived from the annual reports of the NWMP, 1892, 1896 and 1900
144. J. H. Carpenter
145. RG 18, vol. 1269, file 220, McKillon to Herchmer, 12 June 1894
146. Ibid., vol. 91, file 148, Monthly report, K Division, July 1894
147. NWMP, Annual Report, 1892, 51
148. RG 18, vol. 91, file 148, Monthly report, K Division, July 1894
149. Ibid., vol. 1416, file 120, Monthly report, D Division, Sept 1898
150. NWMP, Annual Report, 1891, 168-169, and 1892, 206-207
151. RG 18, vol. 1463, file 166
152. Figures derived from the annual reports of the NWMP, 1892, 1896 and 1900
153. NWMP, Annual Report, 1893, 200-202
154. Ibid., 1894, 62
155. RG 18, vol. 1315, file 182
156. *The Consolidated Ordinances of the Territories* (Regina: The Leader Company 1898), 877
157. Figures derived from the annual reports of the NWMP, 1892, 1896 and 1900
158. *Calgary Herald*, 1 Oct 1895; NWMP, Annual Report, 1895, 229
159. RG 18, vol. 1396, file 167
160. RG 18, vol. 1313, file 151, Insp. E. G. Hopkins to HQ, Oct 1894
161. Ibid., vol. 121, file 269-1896
162. Ibid., vol. 128, file 52-1897
163. Ibid., vol. 217, file 713-1901
164. Clarke, *The Magistrate's Manual*, 90
165. *Rex vs Thompson*, 1893, *All England Law Reports Reprint*, 1891-1894, 376
166. *Canadian Criminal Cases*, 1898, vol. 1, 397-401
167. RG 18, vol. 143, file 19-1895, Deane's monthly report for Lethbridge, Dec 1898
168. D. C. Dilworth (ed), *The Blue and the Brass*, 63-67
169. D. C. Dilworth (ed), *Identification Wanted: The Development of the American Criminal Identification System, 1893-1943* (Gaithersburg: International Association of Chiefs of Police 1977), 1-20
170. Garry Saunders, "The 75th Anniversary of Fingerprinting in Canada," *RCMP Quarterly*, Summer 86, 8-11
171. Debates, 8 June 1898, 7488
172. RG 18, vol. 210, file 361-1901, vol. 323, file 708-1906
173. Ibid., vol. 431, file 9-1913
174. Ibid., vol. 1526, file 133
175. F. E. Heron and A. R. Pike, *A Brief History of the Metropolitan Police* (Metropolitan Police nd), 29
176. RG 18, vol. 1547, file 133, Perry to Commissioner, Scotland Yard, 28 Sept 1904
177. S. W. Horrall, "Foster's First Case," *RCMP Quarterly*, spring 81, 25-26
178. RG 18, vol. 431, file 9-1913
179. Dilworth, *Identification Wanted*, 54-161
180. Sifton Papers, reel C469, 23991-3, White to Sifton, 20 Jan 1897
181. RG 18, vol. 2212, Herchmer to White, 10 May 1893
182. *Calgary Herald*, 24 Apr 1895
183. RG 18, vol. 120, file 200-1896, J. B. Smith, Acting Crown Prosecutor, to Minister of Justice, 17 July 1895
184. T. M. Reynolds, "Justices of the Peace in the North-West Territories, 1870-1905" (MA Thesis, University of Regina 1928), ch. 4 (hereafter cited as Reynolds, "Justices of the Peace"). In 1890, 27 J.P.s sent a total of $497.80 to the NWT government in fines for ordinance violations; 8 of these were NWMP officers whose fines totalled $247. In 1901, 10 policemen sent in $737.75 and 57 civilians sent in $1771.08 in ordinance fines.
185. Saskatchewan Archives Board (Saskatoon), Records of the Attorney General, Justice of the Peace Files. See also finding aid GS 49 to this collection.
186. Ibid., file A5, Records for Supt. R. B. Deane
187. Ibid., file 108, Records for William Trant
188. Ibid., file 106 and 381, Records for W. C. Sanders
189. Debates, 20 June 1897, 4667
190. Ibid., 4668
191. Reynolds, "Justices of the Peace," ch. 2
192. RG 18, vol. 225, file 96-102
193. Judge T. H. McGuire, *A Handbook for Magistrates in Relation to Summary Convictions and Orders and Indictable Offences* (Toronto: Carswell and Company 1890)
194. Reynolds, "Justices of the Peace," ch. 3
195. Sifton Papers, reel C497, 55560-62, Report of Insp. W. H. Irwin, 10 May 1899
196. RG 18, vol. 1435, file 81, statement of Cpl. Balderson
197. *Calgary Herald*, 20, 24, 29 and 30 Apr, 1, 2, 8 and 9 May 1895
198. RG 18, vol. 1237, file 172, Report of S/Sgt. Fyffe, 16 Jan 1892
199. Ibid., vol. 1296, file 87, Report of Cst. McCusig, 2 May 1894 and Report of Supt. Griesbach, 10 Sept 1894
200. Ibid., Report of Sgt. Forrester, 15 Sept 1894
201. Ibid., vol. 1400, file 211, Report of Insp. Davidson, May 1897
202. Sifton Papers, reel C497, Report of Insp. W. H. Irwin, 19 May 1899
203. RG 18, vol. 101, file 39-1898
204. Auditor General's Report 1897-98, I6, I36-37
205. NWMP, Annual Report, 1898, 91
206. *Calgary Herald*, 5 July 1895
207. Ibid.
208. NWMP, Annual Report, 1895, 135-136
209. RG 18, vol. 1359, file 106, Insp. Z. T. Wood to Herchmer
210. RG 18, vol. 123, file 404-96, vol. 218, file 821
211. NWMP, Annual Report, 1893, 100
212. Ibid., 1894, 24
213. Ibid., 1893, 29
214. RG 18, vol. 2213, Herchmer's answer to question posed by the Minister, Oct 1893
215. Ibid., vol. 150, file 211-1898
216. Ibid., vol. 191, file 442, Insp. J. O. Wilson, Monthly Report for Nov 1900
217. Ibid., vol. 257, file 531-1903
218. Ibid., vol. 59, file 66-1892
219. NWMP, Annual Report, 1897, 56
220. RG 18, vol. 117, file 79-1896
221. Ibid., vol. 1359, file 106
222. NWMP, Annual Report, 1894, 172
223. RG 18, vol. 209, file 246-1901
224. NWMP, Annual Report, 1894, 172
225. *The Consolidated Ordinances of the North-West Territories*, 1898, ch. 90, "An Ordinance Respecting Insane Persons," 875-876
226. Debates, 4 June 1900, 6683
227. NWMP, Annual Report, 1897, 56
228. Ibid., 1896, 144
229. *Calgary Herald*, 22 Oct 1895
230. NWMP, Annual Report, 1898, 100
231. RG 18, vol. 134, file 164-1897; NWMP, Annual Report, 1896, 97
232. RG 18, vol. 323, file 763-1906
233. Ibid., vol. 1359, file 106
234. *Calgary Herald*, 17 July 1894
235. RG 18, vol. 109, file 403-1895

236. Ibid., vol. 1266, file 208, White to Herchmer, 10 May 1893
237. NWMP, Annual Report, 1895, 70 and 1898, 90
238. RG 18, vol. 1429, file 230
239. Ibid., vol. 3403, service file 3015

Chapter 9

The Herchmer Scandals

1. Deane, 67
2. Ibid.
3. Macdonald Papers, vol. 395, Dewdney to Macdonald, 24 Aug 1883
4. Ibid., vol. 397, Davin to Macdonald, 8 Nov 1883
5. *Regina Leader*, 11 Jan and 23 Aug 1887
6. Ibid., 19 June 1888
7. Ibid., 25 Dec 1888 and 1 Jan 1889
8. Ibid., 22 Jan 1889
9. Ibid., 8 Jan 1889
10. Ibid., 29 Oct 1889
11. RG 18, vol. 2282, Herchmer to White, 9 Oct 1889
12. 49 Vic., ch. 45, s.18
13. Debates, 4 Mar 1889
14. Ibid.
15. *Regina Leader,* 10 Sept 1889
16. RG 18, vol. 3332, service file 643, Thomas Craig
17. Ibid.
18. *Regina Leader,* 1 Nov 1887
19. RG 18, vol. 2282, Herchmer to White, 10 Jan 1888
20. Ibid., vol. 758, White to Herchmer, 11 Feb 1888
21. RG 18, vol. 3367, service file 1762, J. D. Somerville
22. Debates, 31 Mar 1890. Deliberately or erroneously, Davin stated that Somerville had received 3 months imprisonment.
23. RG 18, vol. 761, White to Herchmer, 28 Nov 1889
24. Ibid., vol. 3367, service file 1762, J. D. Somerville
25. *Regina Leader*, 3 Dec 1889 reprints editorials on the subject from various newspapers.
26. Ibid., 26 Nov 1889
27. Ibid., 29 Oct 1889
28. Ibid., 3 Dec 1889
29. RG 18, vol. 2282, Herchmer to White, 31 Aug 1891
30. *Regina Leader*, 5 Nov 1889
31. Ibid.
32. RG 18, vol. 2282, Herchmer to White, 14 Dec 1889
33. Debates, 5 Mar 1890
34. Ibid., 31 Mar 1890
35. Ibid., 14 Apr 1890
36. *Regina Leader*, 22 July 1890
37. *Macleod Gazette*, 19 Aug 1890
38. *Regina Leader*, 26 Aug 1890
39. Ibid., 24 Mar and 21 Apr 1891
40. RG 18, vol. 2282, undated, but from contents between 27 Mar and 7 Apr 1891
41. Ibid., Herchmer to White, 29 Apr 1891
42. Debates, 20 May 1891
43. Ibid., 1 and 22 July 1891
44. Ibid., 27 July 1891
45. Ibid.
46. Ibid.
47. "Departmental Report of the Charges preferred against the Commissioner of the NWM Police" (Canada, House of Commons, Sessional Papers, no. 69, 1891)
48. *Regina Leader*, 18 Aug 1891
49. Debates, 24 Aug 1891
50. Ibid.
51. Privy Council Order 2651, 26 Nov 1891
52. Donald Smith, "The Herchmers' Secret," The Beaver, spring 1980, 52-58
53. *Regina Leader*, 29 Mar 1892
54. *Calgary Herald*, 4 Feb 1892
55. Ibid., 5 Feb 1892
56. *Macleod Gazette*, 11 Feb 1892
57. *Calgary Herald*, 17 Feb 1892
58. *Regina Leader*, 15 Mar 1892
59. RG 18, vol. 2283, Herchmer to White, 26 Mar 1892
60. Debates, 18 Mar 1892
61. *Calgary Herald*, 23 Feb 1893
62. RG 18, vol. 79, file 241, *Report of the Inquiry into the conduct of Commissioner L. W. Herchmer*
63. Ibid.
64. Debates, 15 Mar 1893
65. Deane, 67
66. NWMP, Annual Report, 1892, 72
67. RG 18, vol. 125, file 660, Circular memorandum to officers of the NWMP, 24 Nov 1893

Chapter 10

Herchmer, The Final Years

1. Debates, 16 May 1892
2. Ibid.
3. Ibid.
4. L. H. Thomas, *The Struggle for Responsible Government in the North-West Territories, 1870-97* (Toronto 1956), 254
5. Debates, 10 Mar 1893
6. NA, RG 18, vol. 1281, Herchmer to White, 8 Mar 1893
7. Ibid, vol. 1281, White to Herchmer, 17 Mar 1893
8. Ibid, vol. 2213, Herchmer to White, 3 Oct 1893
9. Ibid.
10. *Edmonton Bulletin*, 2 Oct 1893
11. *Regina Leader*, 21 Sept 1893
12. RG 18, vol. 85, 21 Nov 1893
13. NWMP, Annual Report, 1893, 10
14. Debates, 19 June 1894
15. The figures used in Parliament by both parties for the total strength of the police during these years are confusing. They may refer to the actual strength, the established strength, or the strength including or omitting commissioned officers and special constables.
16. The figure given here is for NCOs and constables. It does not include about 40 officers and 60 special constables.
17. RG 18, vol. 96, White to Herchmer, 20 June 1894
18. NWMP, Annual Report, 1894, 13
19. *Calgary Herald*, 15 Jan 1895
20. Ibid, 12 Feb 1895
21. RG 18, vol. 108, file 318/95
22. *Edmonton Bulletin*, 18 Feb 1895
23. *Calgary Herald*, 26 Mar 1895
24. Ibid, 28 Mar 1895
25. RG 18, vol. 109, White to Herchmer, 10 Apr 1895
26. RG 18, vol. 109, Herchmer to White, 15 Apr 1895
27. J. H. Carpenter, *The Badge and the Blotter* (Lethbridge: 1974), 15
28. NWMP, Annual Report, 1895, 13
29. Ibid, 1894, 169
30. RG 18, vol. 1330, Herchmer to White, 26 Jan 1895
31. Debates, 2 July 1895
32. Ibid.
33. RG 18, vol 2284, Herchmer to White, 22 Nov 1895
34. NWMP, Annual Report, 1895, 157
35. Ibid., 1
36. *Macleod Gazette*, 1 Mar 1896
37. C. B. Koester, Mr. Davin, MP (Saskatoon: 1980), 149
38. *Edmonton Bulletin*, 18 Feb 1895
39. *Calgary Herald*, 5 June 1896
40. Ibid, 29 May 1896
41. Koester, Davin, 152
42. *Regina Leader*, 23 July 1896
43. Laurier Papers, reel 743, Walsh to Laurier, 15 Sept 1896
44. Debates, 25 Sept 1896

45. Ibid, 23 June 1899
46. NWMP, Annual Report, 1896, 1-10
47. *Calgary Herald*, 13 Nov 1896
48. RG 18, vol. 1355, Herchmer to White, 6 Nov 1896
49. Debates, 4 May 1897
50. Ibid, 4 June 1897
51. NWMP, Annual Report, 1897, 5
52. *Macleod Gazette*, 18 May 1886
53. RG 18, vol. 1399, White to Herchmer, 4 Dec 1896
54. Ibid, Circular Memorandum 223, 25 Jan 1897
55. Sifton Papers, White to Sifton, 5 Mar 1897
56. RG 18, vol. 1401, Herchmer to White, 16 June 1897
57. *Regina Leader*, 2 Sept 1897
58. *Calgary Herald*, 15 Nov 1897
59. Laurier Papers, reel 754, 31 Jan 1898
60. Ibid., 28 Jan 1898
61. Debates, 11 Feb 1898
62. Ibid, 23 June 1899
63. NWMP, Annual Report, 1897, 17
64. Ibid, 1886, 1899

Chapter 11

The Officers' Life in the North-West Mounted Police

1. Debates, 11 Apr 1889
2. *Regina Leader*, 18 Jan 1887
3. RG 18, vol. 3440, service file O.80, Insp. H. Casey
4. Macdonald Papers, 215019-021, Casey to Macdonald, 5 Feb 1887
5. RG 18, vol. 3438, service file O.55, J. B. Allan
6. Ibid., vol. 22, White to Macdonald, 24 Aug 1887
7. Ibid., vol. 3438, service file O.54, Z. T. Wood
8. Ibid., vol. 38, file 17, Herchmer to White, 10 Oct 1889
9. Dwight, *Life in the NWMP and Other Sketches* (Toronto: National Publishing 1892), 106 (hereafter cited as Dwight)
10. R. A. Preston, *Canada's RMC: A History of the Royal Military College* (Toronto: University of Toronto Press 1969), 74
11. NA, MG 25, G205, Perry Family History
12. Revised Statutes of Canada, 1886, 49 Vic., ch. 17
13. RG 18, vol. 1225, file 380
14. Ibid., vol. 130, file 76
15. Ibid., vol. 82, file 349
16. Auditor-General's Report, 1886-87, XX
17. Deane, 60
18. RCMP Museum (Regina, Sask), Journal of Lily McIllree
19. 49 Vic., ch. 17
20. RG 18, vol. 3445, service file O.134, George Stevens
21. *Regulations and Orders of the North-West Mounted Police* (Ottawa: 1889), 47 (hereafter cited as Regulations and Orders, 1889)
22. Steele, 268
23. RG 18, vol. 755, White to Herchmer, 29 Jan 1887
24. Ibid.
25. Ibid., vol. 2282, Herchmer to White, 20 Oct 1890
26. Ibid.
27. Ibid., vol. 2337, General Order 1186, 1 May 1887
28. *Regina Leader*, 13 May 1890
29. *Calgary Herald*, 24 Nov 1893
30. RG 18, vol. 91, White to Ives, 19 June 1893
31. *Regulations and Orders*, 1889, 29
32. RG 18, vol. 2338, General Order 22, 10 Apr 1886
33. Ibid., vol. 1205, file 174
34. Ibid., vol. 753, White to Herchmer, 10 May 1886
35. Supt. John Cotton and Insp. J. O. Wilson, among others
36. RG 18, vol. 3437, service file O.40, Sam Steele
37. Ibid., service file O.42, J. Cotton

38. RCMP Historical Branch, McIllree reference file, White to Thompson, 26 Oct 1892
39. *Regulations and Orders*, 1889, 4
40. RG 18, vol. 2192, Herchmer to White, 22 Apr 1886
41. Ibid., vol. 753, White to Macdonald, 10 May 1886
42. Ibid., vol. 2286
43. *Winnipeg Free Press*, 7 Oct 1890
44. RG 18, vol. 2288, Starnes to White, 19 May 1892
45. Ibid., vol. 2200, Herchmer to White, 23 Oct 1888
46. Debates, 29 May 1886
47. RG 18, vol. 97, Memo by White, 16 July 1894
48. Ibid., vol. 1108
49. Deane, 37
50. Steele, 272
51. RG 18, vol. 8, General Order 4397, 2 Nov 1889
52. *Regina Leader*, 21 June 1887
53. Ibid., 29 June 1886
54. Ibid., 29 Nov 1883
55. *Calgary Herald*, 26 Oct 1892
56. Steele, 270
57. *Calgary Herald*, 12 Dec 1889
58. Ibid., 12 Dec 1890
59. Ibid., 11 March 1892
60. *Regulations and Orders*, 1889, 4
61. Steele, 240
62. 37 Vic., ch. 22, 38 Vic., ch. 50
63. Deane, 36
64. RG 18, vol. 2282, Herchmer to White, 20 Dec 1888
65. Ibid., vol. 2283, White to Herchmer, 21 Aug 1891
66. Ibid., vol. 3437, service file O.39, A. R. Macdonell
67. Ibid.
68. T. Morris Longstreth, *The Silent Force* (New York: Century Company 1927), 108, 131
69. RG 18, vol. 3437, service file O.40, Sam Steele
70. Ibid., vol. 3440, service file O.85, W. H. Routledge
71. Deane, 71
72. *Regina Leader*, 21 May 1889
73. RG 18, vol. 2282, Herchmer to Steele, 16 Oct 1887
74. Ibid., Herchmer to Deane, 8 Oct 1887
75. Ibid., Herchmer to White, 2 Oct 1887
76. Ibid., Herchmer to White, 5 Nov 1887
77. Ibid., Herchmer to Antrobus, 20 Feb 1888
78. Ibid., Dodd to Herchmer, 20 Sept 1888
79. Ibid., Herchmer to McIllree, 20 Dec 1888
80. Ibid., vol. 2323, General Order 2270, Feb 1887
81. Deane, 42
82. RG 18, vol. 2282, Herchmer to Dewdney, 6 May 1888
83. Ibid., Herchmer to Dewdney, 7 May 1888
84. Ibid.
85. Ibid., Herchmer to White, 21 May 1888
86. Ibid., Herchmer to White, 21 June 1888
87. Ibid., vol. 2323, General Order 2941, Sept 1888
88. Ibid., vol. 2282, White to Herchmer, 20 Feb 1889
89. Ibid., Herchmer to White, 4 Apr 1889
90. Ibid., Herchmer to White, 6 Dec 1889
91. Ibid., Herchmer to White, 12 Aug 1890
92. Ibid., Herchmer to White, 6 Oct 1890
93. RCMP Historical Branch, J. Howe reference file
94. RG 18, vol. 2282, Herchmer to Herchmer, 27 Mar 1891
95. Ibid., Herchmer to White, 7 Apr 1891
96. Ibid., Herchmer to White, 10 Apr 1891
97. Ibid., vol. 3437, service file O.36, W. D. Antrobus
98. Ibid., vol. 2282, Herchmer to Draynor, 20 July 1887
99. Ibid., Herchmer to Draynor, 13 Mar 1890
100. Ibid., Herchmer to White, 28 Dec 1888
101. Ibid., Herchmer to White, 6 July 1889
102. NWMP, Annual Report, 1894, 26
103. RG 18, vol. 2282, Herchmer to Starnes, 14 Apr 1888
104. Ibid., Herchmer to Griesbach, 10 Oct 1889
105. Ibid., Herchmer to Attorney General for British Columbia, 7 July 1887

106. Ibid., vol. 2283, Herchmer to White, undated, but from the contents it was written between 27 Mar and 7 Apr 1891
107. Ibid., vol. 1973, White to Macleod, 15 Nov 1876
108. RCMP Museum, Regina, Sask.
109. RG 18, vol. 16, Maynard, Harris and Co. to White, 10 Mar 1887
110. Ibid., vol. 1082, Norman to Herchmer, 20 June 1887
111. Ibid., vol. 1105, Antrobus to Herchmer, 27 May 1888. Insp. Bradley obtained permission for his uniform to be made by a military tailor in Kingston, Ontario.
112. Ibid., vol. 2197, Herchmer to White, 16 Oct 1887
113. Ibid., vol. 2198, Herchmer to White, 22 Feb 1888
114. Ibid., Herchmer to White, Apr 1888
115. Ibid., vol. 1105, Antrobus to Herchmer, 27 May 1888
116. RCMP Historical Branch
117. For a detailed explanation on the origin of khaki uniforms refer to pages 219-220

Chapter 12

All Sorts and Conditions of Men

1. Donkin, 37. Among the medal winners were Csts. John Albert, Charles Baines, George Martin, John Turnbull and William McNair who held the Khedive's Egyptian Star and Cst. Patrick Scanlan who held the Afghan Medal with a bar for Ahmed Khel.
2. J. A. G. Creighton, "The Northwest Mounted Police of Canada," *Scribner's Magazine*, October 1893
3. RG 18, vol. 3394, service file 2736, John Temple
4. Ibid., vol. 3403, service file 3046, Ralph Coote; vol. 3344, service file 1010, M. Blomefield; vol. 3400, service file 2924, Lionel Palmer; vol. 3406, service file 3147, Robert Baillie
5. Ibid., vol. 3376, service file 2079, Reginald Gwynne
6. Ibid., vol. 1035, CO, "E" Division to Herchmer, Dec 1885
7. Ibid., vol. 3378, service file 2150, John Mackie and vol. 3376, service file 2067, James Warren
8. *Regina Leader*, 16 June 1891
9. RG 18, vol. 1201, Jarvis to Herchmer, 6 Mar 1891
10. Frances G. Halpenny, Gen. Editor, Dictionary of Canadian Biography, vol. X1, (Toronto, 1982), p.266.
11. RG 18, vol. 1326, file 56
12. Ibid., vol. 1379, file 56
13. Ibid., vol. 3375, service file 2029, William Van Pettius; vol. 3355, service file 1321, John Von Hemert; vol. 3361, service file 1556, Hans Kjosterud; vol. 3348, service file 1149, L. Monjeau; vol. 3357, service file 1380, Vincent Miniszowsky; vol. 3385, service file 2429, Paul Wolters; and vol.1326, file 56
14. Ibid., vol. 3447, service file 0.149, Christen Junget
15. Ibid., vol. 240, file 783
16. Ibid., vol. 1083, file 492
17. NWMP, Annual Report, 1887, 15
18. Ibid., 1885, 13
19. RG 18, service files 1695 to 1735
20. *Regina Leader*, 7 Feb 1896
21. Debates, 7 Feb 1896
22. RG 18, vol. 2284, Herchmer to White, 23 May 1896
23. NWMP, Annual Report, 1888, 17
24. Ibid., 1886, 11
25. RG 18, vol. 1035, Herchmer to Moodie, May 1886
26. Ibid., vol. 753, Moodie to White, 4 June 1886
27. Ibid., vol. 756, White to Deane, 23 May 1887
28. Ibid., service file 2031
29. Ibid., vol. 756, White to Deane, 3 June 1887
30. NWMP, Annual Report, 1891, 6
31. RG 18, vol. 2282, Herchmer to Mowatt, 8 Aug 1887
32. Ibid., Herchmer to White, 6 Nov 1887
33. Ibid., vol. 2197, Herchmer to White, 7 Oct 1887 and service files 1867 and 3584
34. NWMP, Annual Report, 1888, 15
35. RG 18, vol. 1122, Herchmer to Sanders, Mar 1888
36. Ibid., vol. 760, White to Bremner, 31 Oct 1888
37. NWMP, Annual Report, 1889, 9
38. Debates, 19 Apr 1887
39. NWMP, Annual Report, 1889 and 1891
40. Ibid., 1890, 9
41. RG 18, service file 2910
42. NWMP, Annual Report, 1895, 13
43. Ibid., 1896, 13
44. Ibid., 1898, 16 and 1899, 55
45. RG 18, vol. 187, Constantine to McIllree, 22 Feb 1900 and McIllree to White, 13 Mar 1900
46. Ibid., vol. 125, White to Herchmer, 11 Nov 1896
47. *Regina Leader*, 6 Jan 1898
48. RG 18, vol. 2285, Herchmer to White, 20 Aug 1898
49. Ibid., vol. 1433, file 56
50. *Regina Leader*, 15 Mar 1900
51. Donkin, 19
52. Dwight, 24
53. RCMP Museum (Regina), Letters of Cst. Vernon Shaver
54. RCMP Historical Branch, Reminiscences of Cst. James Tinsley
55. Shaver letters
56. *Regina Leader*, 13 Apr 1886
57. Debates, 17 June 1887
58. *Regulations and Orders*, 1889, 29
59. W. D. Otter, *The Guide; A Manual for the Canadian Militia*, (Toronto: 1880), 120
60. Tinsley reminiscences
61. RG 18, vol. 2338
62. Steele, 241
63. NWMP, Annual Report, 1892, 8
64. RCMP Museum (Regina, Sask)
65. NWMP, *Manual and Firing Exercise for the Winchester Carbine and the Enfield Revolver*, (Ottawa: 1886)
66. NWMP, Annual Report, 1891, 51
67. RG 18, vol. 1201, Herchmer to White, 12 Mar 1891
68. Ibid., vol. 2213, McIllree to White, 9 Jan 1894
69. *Royal Northwest Mounted Police Constables Manual*, (Ottawa: 1907)
70. RCMP Museum (Regina, Sask), Notebook of Cst. W. S. Clarke
71. NWMP, Annual Report, 1900, 10
72. Ibid., 1886, 44
73. Ibid., 1894, 33
74. RG 18, vol. 2337, General Order 1024, Mar 1887
75. Ibid., vol. 97, Herchmer to White, 24 Jan 1895
76. NWMP, Annual Report, 1891, 28
77. RG 18, vol. 172, file 465

Chapter 13

Health and Happiness: The Benefits of Service

1. Auditor General's Reports, 1886-87 to 1900-01
2. RG 18, vol. 118, file 102
3. NWMP, Annual Report, 1894, 49
4. S. R. Clarke, *The Magistrate's Manual* (Toronto: 1893), 205
5. NWMP, Annual Report, 1887, 50
6. Debates, 17 June 1887
7. NWMP, Annual Report, 1889, 10
8. Ibid., 1898, 13
9. 49 Vic., ch. 41
10. G. Torrance, *The Hamilton Police Department* (Hamilton: 1967), 20

11. K. A. Buckley and M. C. Urquhart, *Canadian Historical Statistics* (Toronto: 1965), 87, 95
12. Pennefather
13. Donkin, 219
14. RG 18, General Order 5225, July 1890
15. Ibid., vol. 3332, service file 641, Alfred Coulson
16. NWMP, Annual Report, 1886, 57
17. Ibid., 90
18. Ibid., 1888, 18
19. RG 18, vol. 1197, file 86
20. NWMP, Annual Report, 1889, 11
21. Ibid., Auditor General's Report, 1889-90, C-213
22. RG 18, vol. 129, file 60
23. Ibid., vol. 1336, file 114
24. Regulations and Orders, 1889, 47
25. Steele, 267
26. RG 18, vol. 125, file 565
27. Ibid., vol. 1050, White to Herchmer, 17 Apr 1886
28. Debates, 19 Apr 1887
29. Ibid., 21 Mar 1889
30. Ibid., 15 Apr 1889
31. 52 Vic., ch. 26
32. 61 Vic., ch. 33
33. RG 18, vol. 3343, service file 992, William Perrin
34. Ibid., vol. 3356, service file 1342, Phillipe Casault
35. Privy Council Orders 1016 12 June 1880 and 899, 15 May 1880
36. RG 18, vol. 1078, file 355
37. Ibid., vol. 2284, Herchmer to Colebrooke, 20 Dec 1895
38. Ibid., vol. 1360, file 107
39. Ibid., vol. 1334, Herchmer to Moffatt, 18 Nov 1895
40. Ibid., service file 3513, Seymour Farquharson
41. Ibid.
42. Debates, 19 Apr 1901
43. Privy Council Order 1134, 30 Aug 1873
44. 36 Vic., ch. 35
45. 37 Vic., ch. 22
46. For an account of Nevitt's service in the NWMP as well as some of his artistic work while in the West, see Hugh Dempsey (ed), *A Winter at Fort Macleod* (Calgary: Glenbow-Alberta Institute 1974)
47. S. W. Horrall (ed), *A Chronicle of the Canadian West: North-West Mounted Police Report for 1875* (Calgary: 1975), introduction, 20
48. Hugh Dempsey (ed), *William Parker, Mounted Policeman* (Edmonton: Hurtig 1973), 10
49. Deane, 12
50. George Stanley, *Louis Riel* (Toronto: 1963), 367
51. NWMP, Annual Report, 1886, 87
52. J. B. Ritchie, "Early Surgeons of the NWMP," *Historical Bulletin of the Calgary Associate Clinic*, vol. 22, Aug 1957
53. RG 18, vol. 3344, service file 1025, E. A. Braithwaite
54. NWMP, Annual Report, 1886, 109
55. Ibid., 89
56. Ibid., 82
57. Ibid., 1900, 75
58. Ibid., 1893, 156
59. Ibid., 1886, 87
60. Ibid., 1895, 167
61. Ibid., 1889, 136
62. Auditor General's Report, 1887-88, 80
63. Dr. M. T. Tory, "Surgery and Chirurgeons of Calgary 100 Years Ago," unpublished paper, Calgary, 1975
64. NWMP, Annual Report, 1886, 84-85
65. Ibid., 1887, 114
66. Ibid., 1880, 45
67. Ibid., 1886, 93
68. *Edmonton Bulletin*, 10 Sept 1887
69. RG 18, vol. 1170
70. *Macleod Gazette*, 7 Mar 1891
71. RG 18, General Order 1539, 1884
72. Ibid., vol. 1065, file 133
73. Debates, 18 Apr 1886
74. RG 18, vol. 1065, White to Herchmer, 30 Sept 1887
75. NWMP, Annual Report, 1889, 126
76. Ibid., 148
77. RG 18, vol. 2283, Herchmer to Davidson, 8 Apr 1892
78. Ibid., Herchmer to White, 27 Apr 1893
79. Hendryx, James B., *Downey of the Mounted* (New York: 1925), 101
80. NWMP, Annual Report, 1877, 22
81. RG 18, vol. 2282, Herchmer to White, 22 Dec 1887
82. NWMP, Annual Report, 1888, 18
83. *Regina Leader,* 2 Oct 1888
84. RG 18, vol. 758, White to Mcdowall, 14 Jan 1888
85. *Regina Leader*, 16 June 1891
86. Ibid., 21 July 1898
87. RG 18, vol. 2282, Herchmer to Griesbach, 27 Dec 1889
88. *Regina Leader*, 18 Dec 1888
89. Ibid., 25 Dec 1888
90. RG 18, vol. 2285, Herchmer to White, 11 Oct 1897
91. Ibid., vol. 1357, file 104
92. *Edmonton Bulletin*, 25 Jan 1897
93. RG 18, vol. 1191, file 277
94. Ibid., vol. 1225, White to Herchmer, 27 May 1891
95. Ibid., vol. 1298, Herchmer to White, 22 Feb 1894
96. Ibid., General Order 9644, 14 June 1894
97. Debates, 20 June 1894
98. RG 18, vol. 1408, file 88
99. Ibid., vol. 1436, Herchmer to White, 20 Nov 1899
100. Ibid., vol. 3366, service file 1716, J. A. Smith
101. Ibid., vol. 1475, file 88
102. Rules and Regulations of the RNWMP (Ottawa: 1909), 88, 96

Chapter 14

Room and Board and the Pleasures of Mounted Police Life

1. RG 18, General Order 9491, 23 Apr 1894
2. Ibid., vol. 1092, file 71
3. Debates, 19 May 1888
4. Dwight, 28
5. Ibid., 32
6. Pennefather
7. Donkin, 26
8. NWMP, Annual Report, 1895, 14
9. Ibid., 1899, 98
10. NWMP, Annual Report, 1895, 14
11. Interview by S. W. Horrall with A/Comm. Christen Junget (Rtd), Victoria, B.C., 21 Jan 1969
12. Donkin, 212
13. NWMP, Annual Report, 1888, 31
14. Donkin, 276
15. RCMP Historical Branch, "The Story of Corporal John Moore Rupert"
16. NWMP, Annual Report, 1890, 68
17. Ibid., 1893, 26
18. Steele, 275
19. RG 18, vol. 758, Fortescue to Herchmer, 15 Dec 1887
20. Ibid., vol. 1226, file 401
21. R. G. Matthews, "An Ex-Corporal's Diary," *Scarlet and Gold*, 1942
22. Ibid.
23. Pennefather
24. NWMP, Annual Report, 1888, 15
25. Auditor General's Report, 1894-95, 14
26. NWMP, Annual Report, 1896, 7
27. Ibid., 1892, 70
28. RG 18, vol. 1056, Herchmer to Paskett, Aug 1887
29. Donkin, 262-270

30. S. W. Horrall (ed), *A Chronicle of the Canadian West*, introduction, 23
31. Matthews, "An Ex-Corporal's Diary"
32. RG 18, vol. 2210, Herchmer to White, 13 Aug 1892
33. Ibid., vol. 1260, file 73
34. Debates, 15 Feb 1889
35. Donkin, 39
36. RG 18, vol. 1114, file 271
37. Ibid.
38. Ibid., Circular Memorandum 108, 15 Mar 1895
39. RG 18, vol. 95, file 351
40. NWMP, Annual Report, 1890, 40, 59, 79
41. Ibid., 1891, 8
42. Ibid., 1892, 46
43. Ibid., 1890, 11
44. Dwight, 67-68
45. NWMP, Annual Report, 1890, 7-8
46. RG 18, vol. 1044, file 107
47. Donkin, 39
48. NWMP, Annual Report, 1888, 62
49. RG 18, vol. 1262, file 136
50. NWMP, Annual Report, 1898, 81
51. Ibid., 1899, 89
52. RG 18, vol. 1351, file 57
53. Ibid., vol. 1262, file 136
54. *The Canadian Encyclopedia* (2nd ed), vol. 3, 1715
55. NWMP, Annual Report, 1891, 36
56. Nevitt, *Winter at Fort Macleod*, 67
57. Ibid., 111
58. Dempsey, *William Parker: Mounted Policeman*, 103
59. RG 18, vol. 3319, service file 57, E. Warren
60. *Saskatchewan Herald*, 25 Aug 1879
61. *Regina Leader*, 7 June and 11 Oct 1883
62. RG 18, vol. 1070, file 179
63. Ibid., vol. 3364, service file 1659, J. M. Rupert
64. W. McLennan, *Sport in Early Calgary* (Calgary: 1963), 136
65. *Calgary Herald*, 18 Aug 1890
66. Ibid., 7 Nov 1890
67. Ibid., 20 Mar 1896
68. Ibid., 28 Mar 1891
69. Ibid., 14 Mar 1891
70. Ibid., 12 Dec 1889
71. Ibid., 12 June 1886
72. Ibid., 18 Dec 1886
73. Ibid., 23 Jan 1893, 17 Feb and 14 Mar 1896
74. *Edmonton Bulletin*, 28 Jan 1895
75. *Manitoba Free Press*, 29 Sept 1890
76. Ibid., 2 Oct 1890
77. D. Sturrock, "A History of Rugby Football in Canada" (MA thesis, University of Alberta, 1971), 74
78. P. Lamb, "The North West Mounted Police and the Development of Rugby Football in Western Canada, 1873-1908," unpublished paper, University of Alberta, 1987
79. *Regina Leader*, 1 Jan 1889
80. RCMP Museum, Diary of J. H. McIllree, 7 Dec 1895
81. *Regina Leader*, 21 July 1898
82. *Regina Leader*, 17 May 1887
83. S. W. Horrall, interview with Insp. Christen Junget (ret), Victoria, B.C., 21 Jan 1969
84. RG 18, vol. 2339, General Order 2785, 13 Aug 1888
85. Ibid., vol. 1156, Griesbach to Herchmer, 17 Aug 1889
86. *Regina Leader*, 12 Apr and 15 Dec 1887
87. RG 18, vol. 752, White to Irvine, 10 Feb 1886
88. Ibid., vol. 2210, Herchmer to White, 18 Apr 1892
89. Ibid., vol. 108, file 300/95
90. RCMP Historical Branch, Cunning to Howard, 16 June 1941
91. RG 18, vol. 1292
92. *Regina Leader*, 19 Dec 1970
93. RG 18, vol. 123, McIllree to White, 28 Oct 1895
94. *Scarlet and Gold*, vol. 20, 36
95. Horrall interview with Insp. C. Junget
96. RCMP Museum, McIllree diary, 7 Jan 1900

Chapter 15

Without "Fuss or Feathers": Kit and Clothing

1. Donkin, 10. For a comprehensive illustrated study of Mounted Police uniforms, see James J. Boulton, *Uniforms of the Canadian Mounted Police* (North Battleford: Turner-Warwick Publications 1990).
2. *Regina Leader*, 8 Oct 1889
3. J. A. G. Creighton, "The Northwest Mounted Police of Canada," *Scribner's Magazine*, Oct 1893
4. Ibid., and *Harper's Weekly*, 16 Dec 1887
5. RCMP Museum, E. A. Braithwaite, "Early Days of the RNWMP" (unpublished manuscript, 1941)
6. Pennefather
7. RG 18, vol. 2214, Steele to Herchmer, 5 June 1894
8. Ibid., vol. 1348, McIllree to CO, E Division, May 1896
9. Ibid., vol. 1051, file 216
10. Privy Council Order 90, 24 Jan 1882
11. *Regulations and Orders,* 1889, 37-39
12. Auditor General's Report, 1888-89, 157-159
13. RG 18, vol. 1133, file 117
14. Auditor General's Report, 1886 to 1900
15. RG 18, vol., General Order 7594, July 1892
16. *Regulations and Orders*, 1889, 32
17. RG 18, vol. 2352, General Order 10563, 12 Aug 1895
18. S. W. Horrall, "Maintien(s) Le Driot," *RCMP Quarterly*, April 1974
19. RG 18, vol. 1422, file 172
20. Ibid., vol. 2328, General Orders 9628-9629
21. Ibid., vol. 755, White to Herchmer, 10 Dec 1886
22. NWMP, Annual Report, 1886, 11
23. Auditor General's Report, 1889-90, 221
24. W. D. Otter, *The Guide: A Manual for the Canadian Militia*, 183
25. RG 18, vol. 755, White to MacLaren, 7 June 1887
26. NWMP, Annual Report, 1889, 6
27. Auditor General's Report, 1891-92
28. RG 18, vol. 1438, Cotton to Herchmer, 17 June 1896
29. Ibid., vol. 1404, file 44
30. Ibid., vol. 1470, file 1
31. Ibid., vol. 2329, General Order 225, 18 June 1886
32. Ibid., vol. 755, White to Herchmer, Nov 1886
33. Ibid., vol. 1057, file 54
34. NWMP, Annual Report, 1888, 17
35. RG 18, vol. 758, White to Herchmer, Nov 1888
36. Ibid., vol. 1169, file 107
37. Ibid., vol. 1199, General Order 6843, 3 Nov 1891
38. NWMP, Annual Report, 1898, 21
39. Ibid., 1887, 69
40. RG 18, vol. 1123, Steele to Herchmer, Sept 1888
41. Ibid., vol. 1133, Herchmer to White, May 1889
42. Ibid., vol. 1261, file 106
43. Ibid., vol. 755, White to Shorey & Co., 27 Apr 1886
44. Ibid., vol. 1169, file 107
45. NWMP, Annual Report, 1885, 9
46. Ibid., 1888, 17, 40, 49, 114
47. RG 18, vol. 2214
48. NWMP, Annual Report, 1888, 40
49. RG 18, vol. 2217, Herchmer to White, 20 May 1886
50. Donkin, 223
51. NWMP, Annual Report, 1891, 14
52. RG 18, vol. 1437, file 107
53. Ibid., vol. 1169, file 107
54. Ibid., vol. 1163, Perry to Herchmer, 18 May 1889
55. Ibid., vol. 755, White to Herchmer, 15 Dec 1886

56. John Martin, "Reminiscences of One of the Originals," *RCMP Quarterly*, July 1933
57. *Regina Leader*, 20 Aug 1889
58. Donkin, 223
59. NWMP, Annual Report, 1891, 7
60. Ibid., 1888, 17
61. RG 18, vol. 2209, Herchmer to White, 29 Sept 1891
62. Ibid., vol. 2288, Starnes to Dineen, 12 Apr 1893
63. Ibid., vol. 1315, file 184
64. Ibid., vol. 2285, Herchmer to Laurier, 27 Apr 1897
65. *Edmonton Bulletin*, 3 May 1897
66. RG 18, vol. 1399, Herchmer to White, 29 Apr 1897
67. Ibid., Perry to White, 6 June 1897
68. Ibid., vol. 2219, Herchmer to White, 4 July 1899
69. Ibid., vol. 1492, file 44
70. NWMP, Annual Report, 1898, part III, 12 and Auditor General's Report, 1895-96 to 1898-99
71. RG 18, vol. 1289, file 49
72. NWMP, Annual Report, 1900, 9
73. Ibid.
74. *Regina Leader*, 25 May 1886
75. Privy Council Order 1428, 10 July 1886
76. *Regina Leader*, 9 Nov 1886
77. Debates, 26 Apr 1894
78. Ibid., 3 May 1899
79. Privy Council Order 2043, 20 Aug 1900
80. *Edmonton Bulletin*, 1 Oct 1900
81. Debates, 30 July 1931
82. *RCMP Quarterly*, Jan 1935, 18
83. D. J. Klancher, "NWMP Issues of Northwest Canada Medals," *RCMP Quarterly*, Oct 1975

Chapter 16:

Mounted Men at Arms

1. P. Stevens and J. T. Saywell (eds), *Lord Minto's Canadian Papers: 1898-1904*, vol. 1, (Toronto: Champlain Society 1981), 206
2. For a thoroughly expert and detailed description of the arms and accoutrements of the NWMP, see Roger F. Phillips and Donald J. Klancher, *Arms and Accoutrements of the Mounted Police 1873-1973* (Bloomfield: 1982)
3. R. Phillips and S. J. Kirby, *Small Arms of the Mounted Police* (Ottawa: 1965), 10
4. NWMP, Annual Report, 1883, 31
5. Auditor General's Report, 1885-86, 480
6. RG 18, vol. 2216
7. Ibid., vol. 1376, file 18
8. Ibid., vol. 2190, Irvine to White, 5 Aug 1885
9. Donkin, 229
10. NWMP, Annual Report, 1887, 12
11. RG 18, vol. 1167, file 79
12. Ibid., vol. 3341, service file 922, John MacNamara
13. Ibid., vol. 1197, Hooper to White, 13 May 1891
14. Privy Council Order 3254, 30 Oct 1894
15. Auditor General's Report, 1894-95, M-19
16. NWMP, Annual Report, 1895, 11
17. Ibid.
18. RG 18, vol. 2216, Herchmer to White, 14 Oct 1895
19. Ibid., vol. 1468, file 18
20. Ibid., vol. 1518, file 22
21. Auditor General's Report, 1885-86, 480 and 1887-88, E-79
22. NWMP, Annual Repport, 1886, 10
23. Ibid., 1896, 171
24. Ibid., 1897, 12
25. Phillips and Klancher, *Arms and Accoutrements*, 22
26. RG 18, vol. 1491, file 18, and Auditor General's Report, 1900-01, R-26 and RG 18, vol. 1518, file 22
27. NWMP, Annual Report, 1887, 12
28. RG 18, vol. 2206, Herchmer to White, 2 Oct 1890
29. Auditor General's Report, 1886-87, 565
30. Ibid., 1887-88, E-79
31. RG 18, vol. 759, White to Herchmer, 8 Oct 1888
32. Auditor General's Report, 1890-91, D-201
33. Ibid., 1901-02, R-35
34. Rudyard Kipling, "The Young British Soldier," in *Barrack Room Ballads* (New York: n.d.), 50
35. NWMP, Annual Report, 1878, 25
36. Ibid., 1880, 24
37. Ibid., 1881, 21
38. Phillips and Klancher, *Arms and Accoutrements*, 85
39. RG 18, vol. 1094, White to Herchmer, 5 Feb 1888
40. NWMP, Annual Report, 1889, 113
41. Ibid., 1890, 100
42. RG 18, vol. 1229, file 78
43. NWMP, Annual Report, 1893, 95
44. RG 18, vol. 1229, Herchmer to White, 1 Sept 1892
45. NWMP, Annual Report, 1896, 11
46. RG 18, vol. 2220, Perry to White, 4 Mar 1901
47. NWMP, Annual Report, 1890, 65
48. Ibid., 1890, 56
49. Ibid., 1887, 66
50. Ibid., 1888, 70 and 1891, 88
51. Ibid., 1893, 6
52. Ibid., 1895, 101
53. Ibid., 1887, 12 and 1890, 23
54. RG 18, vol. 2328, General Order 9629, 9 June 1894
55. NWMP, Annual Report, 1894, 7
56. RG 18, vol. 2284, Herchmer to White, 17 Aug 1896
57. Ibid., vol 1420, file 142
58. *Regina Leader*, 18 Sept 1897
59. Ibid., 10 June 1890
60. *Calgary Herald*, 3 Nov 1896
61. *Regina Leader*, 20 May 1890
62. NWMP, Annual Reports, 1897, 29 and 1899, 21
63. Ibid., 1897, 65
64. Ibid., 1899, 42, 79, 97
65. Horrall (ed), *A Chronicle of the Canadian West*, 35
66. R. M. Utley, *Frontier Regulars, 1866-1891* (New York: 1973), 73
67. NWMP, Annual Report, 1880, 11
68. Phillips and Klancher, *Arms and Accoutrements*, 121
69. *Regina Leader*, 1 Mar 1887
70. For a detailed account of 7 pounder field guns in the NWMP, see Corps Sergeant Major H. M. Gilbey, "Seven Pounders of the Force," *RCMP Quarterly*, July 1972
71. RG 18, vol. 3319, service file 57, Edward W. Warren
72. Phillips and Klancher, *Arms and Accoutrements*, 115
73. G. F. G. Stanley, *The Birth of Western Canada* (Toronto: 1960), 328
74. RCMP Historical Branch, Supt. J. Howe to Herchmer, 27 Dec 1899
75. NWMP, Annual Report, 1886, 10
76. RG 18, vol. 752, White to Tupper, 23 Apr 1886
77. RCMP Historical Branch, White to Steele, 3 Mar 1886 (telegram)
78. RG 18, vol. 760, White to Herchmer, 20 Nov 1888
79. Ibid., White to Sir John A. Macdonald, 3 Jan 1889
80. Ibid., vol. 2189, Irvine to White, 5 Aug 1884
81. Auditor General's Report, 1897-98, M-53
82. Ibid., M-49; Phillips and Klancher, *Arms and Accoutrements*, 77
83. Some of these artillery pieces and machine guns are now on display in the RCMP Centennial Museum, Regina.

Chapter 17

Desertion

1. NWMP, Annual Report, 1874, 9
2. 38 Vic., ch. 50, sec. 23.2

3. 45 Vic., ch. 29, sec. 19
4. NWMP, Annual Report, 1881 to 1886
5. Ibid., 1886, 16
6. Ibid., 41
7. Ibid., 1887, 16
8. Ibid., 67
9. Ibid., 1888, 125
10. *Ottawa Journal*, 14 May 1935
11. *Regina Leader*, 2 Nov 1886
12. RG 18, vol. 1034, file 37
13. *Macleod Gazette*, 30 Oct 1890
14. NWMP, Annual Report, 1892, 91
15. Ibid., 1890, 33
16. Ibid., 1892, 91
17. Ibid., 1893, 26
18. Ibid., 89
19. Ibid., 26
20. Ibid., 1889, 114
21. RG 18, vol. 3366, service file 1718, C .D. Seals
22. Ibid., vol. 3361, service file 1536, G. Wilson
23. Ibid., vol. 3344, service file 1023, J. Albert
24. NWMP, Annual Report, 1893, 64
25. *Calgary Herald*, 29 July 1896
26. NWMP, Annual Report, 1890, 100
27. *Regina Leader*, 7 June 1887
28. NWMP, Annual Report, 1888, 56
29. Ibid., 1887, 67
30. RG 18, vol. 3369, service file 1815, S. Owens
31. *Ottawa Free Press*, 21 Oct 1886
32. *Victoria Daily Colonist*, 18 Nov 1886
33. NWMP, Annual Report, 1888, 16
34. Ibid., 79
35. RG 18, vol. 3369, service file 1824, Samuel Sutton
36. Ibid., vol. 756, White to Bowell, Apr 1887
37. Ibid., vol. 3356, service file 1357, Philip Short
38. Ibid., vol. 3406, service file 3147, Robert Baillie
39. Ken Cruikshank, "Sir David Lewis Macpherson," DCB, vol. XII (1891-1900), 682-689
40. RG 18, vol. 2338, General Orders, 1886
41. *Calgary Herald*, 23 Oct 1890
42. RG 18, vol. 2338, General Order 366, 29 July 1886
43. Ibid., vol. 3368, service file 1796, George Brocklehurst
44. Ibid., vol. 79, file 241
45. 49 Vic., ch. 45
46. *Edmonton Bulletin*, 31 Dec 1887
47. RG 18, vol. 2197, Herchmer to White, Oct 1887
48. *Halifax Acadian Recorder*, 6 Oct 1888
49. RG 18, vol. 3444, service file O.121, William James Walke
50. Ibid., vol. 3365, service file 1699, W. P. Crockett, I. A. Sedgewick to Herchmer, 29 Oct 1888
51. Ibid.
52. Ibid., vol. 760, White to Deputy Minister of Justice, Apr 1887
53. 52 Vic., ch. 25, sec. 24
54. RG 18, vol. 163, White to McIllree, 30 Jan 1899; Senate, Debates, 23 April 1889
55. Debates, 30 April 1889
56. RG 18, vol. 163, White to McIllree, 30 Jan 1899
57. 57-58 Vic., ch. 27, sec. 24
58. 55 Vic., ch. 29, sec. 75
59. RG 18, vol. 163, White to McIllree, 30 Jan 1899
60. Ibid., vol. 3353, service file 1242, Clarence A. Fisher
61. 2 Edw. II, ch. 21, sec. 5

62. William Beahen, "A Citizen's Army: The Growth and Development of the Canadian Militia, 1904 to 1914" (PhD thesis, University of Ottawa: 1979), 162

Chapter 18

Discipline

1. Debates, 21 and 27 Apr 1880
2. Ibid., 10 Mar 1881
3. Pierre Berton, *Hollywood's Canada: The Americanization of Our National Image* (Toronto: 1975), 111
4. Harwood Steele, *Policing the Arctic* (Toronto: 1936), 22
5. RG 18, vol. 3437, service file O.25, C. E. Denny
6. Macdonald Papers, 90524-34, Vankoughnet to Macdonald, 16 Jan 1886
7. NWMP, Annual Report, 1888, 204
8. Ibid., 1892, 205
9. Ibid., 1893, 18
10. Berton, *Hollywood's Canada*, 124
11. Charles Reith, *A Short History of the British Police* (London: 1948, 20
12. Brian Grosman, *Police Command* (Toronto: 1975), 34
13. Macdonald Papers, vol. 516, Macdonald to Cameron, 21 Dec 1869
14. Ibid., vol. 517, Macdonald to Sir John Rose, 23 Feb 1870
15. 36 Vic., ch. 35
16. 37 Vic., ch. 22
17. *Standing Rules and Regulations for the Government and Guidance of the Royal Irish Constabulary* (Dublin: 1888), 279
18. 38 Vic., ch. 50
19. RG 18, vol. 8, file 480
20. Ibid.
21. Debates, 25 Feb 1875
22. Ibid., 8 Mar 1875
23. 42 Vic., ch. 36, sec. 14
24. 45 Vic., ch. 29, sec. 14
25. *Regulations and Orders*, 4
26. Otter, *The Guide*, 147
27. Pennefather, 14
28. Dwight
29. NWMP, Annual Report, 1887, 15
30. Ibid., 1886, 12
31. Ibid., 1887, 15
32. Otter, *The Guide*, 120
33. NWMP, Annual Report, 1886, 44
34. RG 18, vol. 1049, Circular Memorandum, 14 Apr 1886
35. *Standing Rules and Regulations of the Royal Irish Constabulary*, 132
36. RG 18, vol. 2197, Herchmer to White, 10 Sept 1887
37. Ibid., vol. 756, White to W. R. Meredith, 14 June 1887
38. Ibid., vol. 2282, Circular Memorandum, 24 June 1887
39. Ibid., vol. 2321, General Order 2524, Apr 1888
40. Ibid., vol. 2282, Herchmer to MacDonell, 9 Oct 1887
41. NWMP, Annual Report, 1887, 15
42. RG 18, vol. 1144
43. Debates, 11 Apr 1882
44. NWMP, Annual Report, 1888, 77
45. RG 18, vol. 2286, Acting Adjutant's Letterbook, 26 Jan 1889
46. NWMP, Annual report, 1892, 92
47. Pennefather, 22
48. *Regulations and Orders*, 8
49. RG 18, vol. 2282, Herchmer to Antrobus, 29 Nov 1888
50. Ibid., Herchmer to White, 6 Nov 1887
51. *Edmonton Bulletin*, 13 and 27 Feb 1886; *Calgary Herald*, 27 Feb 1886; RCMP Archives (Ottawa), J. D. Nicholson to J. P. Turner, 2 Mar 1944 and 5 Apr 1944; Sen. W. A. Griesbach to J. P. Turner, 22 June 1944
52. NWMP, Annual Report, 1886, 60

53. T. Morris Longstreth, *The Silent Force* (New York: 1927), 162
54. RG 18, vol. 3348, service file 1139, John Henry Beggs
55. Ibid.
56. Pennefather, 56
57. The circumstances of this incident are fully described on page 96
58. *Edmonton Bulletin*, 15 and 29 May 1886
59. RG 18, vol. 2337
60. Ibid., General Order 12311, Aug 1897
61. Ibid., vol. 2338
62. Ibid., vol. 1386, file 104
63. Ibid., service file 3148
64. Ibid., vol. 2338
65. NWMP, Annual Report, 1889, 188
66. RG 18, vol. 2338, General Order 1377, 28 May 1887
67. Ibid., vol. 1074
68. Ibid., vol. 2500
69. Ibid., service file 1804
70. Ibid., service file 1909
71. 55-56 Vic., ch. 29
72. RG 18, vol. 1070, Monthly Reports, "Depot" Division, Apr 1887 and vol. 2338, General Order 1138, 12 Apr 1887
73. Ibid., service file 2674
74. Ibid., service file 1125
75. This incident is described in full on pages 73-75
76. *Calgary Herald*, 12 Nov 1895
77. Ibid., 7 Mar 1896
78. *Edmonton Bulletin*, 9 Mar 1896
79. RG 18, vol. 128
80. Ibid.
81. Ibid., vol. 121, file 269/97
82. William Beahen, "For the Sake of Discipline: The Strange Case of Cst. Basil Nettleship - Deserter," *RCMP Quarterly*, summer 1984
83. Ibid.
84. RCMP Archives, Writ of Prohibition, Cst. Basil Nettleship
85. Deane, 137-138
86. Ibid.
87. Debates, 20 June 1894
88. Ibid.
89. RG 18, vols. 2352-2353, General Orders 1894-95
90. Ibid., vol. 1262, file 136
91. Ibid., vol. 755, Herchmer to White, Dec 1886
92. Ibid., General Order 9628, 7 June 1884
93. Ibid., General Order 10597, 26 Aug 1895
94 Ibid., General Order 10598, 27 Aug 1895
95. NWMP, Annual Report, 1898, 13

Chapter 19

The Officer Cadre, 1893-1900

1. *Regina Leader*, 13 Apr 1893
2. Deane, 37
3. *Regina Leader*, 16 Feb 1893
4. Ibid.
5. *Canadian Military Gazette*, 1 Mar 1894
6. RG 18, vol. 94, file 322
7. Debates, 9 May 1894
8. RG 18, service file O.105
9. Ibid., service file O.107
10. Ibid., vol. 132, White to Herchmer, 21 Jan 1897
11. Debates, 26 Apr 1897
12. Ibid., 10 May 1897
13. Ibid., 5 Apr 1897
14. Privy Council Order 1686, 14 June 1897
15. Minto Papers, vol. 2, 18-19, Memo, Minto in conversation with Laurier, 24 Oct 1902
16. *Calgary Herald*, 23 Aug 1897
17. Laurier Papers, Walsh to Laurier, 15 Sept 1896
18. Privy Council Order 2501, 26 Aug 1897
19. RG 18, vol. 172, White to Herchmer, 25 Sept 1897
20. Ibid., vol. 3443, service file O.116, F. J. Horrigan
21. Ibid., vol. 2284, Herchmer to White, 14 May 1894
22. E. J. Chambers, *The Royal North-West Mounted Police* (Montreal: 1906), 159
23. Ibid.
24. RG 18, vol. 1346, file 202
25. Ibid., vol. 319, file 253
26. Ibid., vol. 3436, service file O.4, J. F. Macleod
27. Ibid., vol. 1300, file 122
28. Ibid., vol. 137, file 323
29. Ibid., vol. 134, file 163
30. Ibid., service file O.50A
31. Debates, 26 Apr 1897
32. Ibid., May 1898 and 7 Feb 1900
33. 2 Edw., ch. 22
34. RG 18, vol. 2285, Herchmer to White, 25 Apr 1899
35. *Regina Leader*, 11 May 1899
36. Laurier Papers, vol. 767, Frank Oliver to Laurier, 17 July 1899
37. RG 18, vol. 168, Herchmer to White, 10 May 1899
38. Ibid., service file O.125, Perry to Heffernan, 18 Aug 1904
39. 57-58 Vic., ch. 27, 23 July 1894
40. RCMP Historical Branch, Research Notes
41. RG 18, vol. 133, White to Herchmer, 21 Jan 1897
42. 57-58 Vic., ch. 27, sec. 21
43. RG 18, vol. 2284, Herchmer to White, 9 Jan 1895
44. Ibid., vol. 103, Herchmer to White, 23 Sept 1894
45. Ibid., vol. 2283, Herchmer to White, 4 Mar 1893
46. Ibid., vol. 2284, Herchmer to Steele, 1 Dec 1894
47. Ibid., vol. 154, file 419/1898
48. Ibid., vol. 2284, Herchmer to CO, "E" Division, 20 July 1895
49. M. W. Lender, *Dictionary of American Temperance Biography* (London: 1984), 271-272
50. RG 18, vol. 1297, Herchmer to Hunt, 16 Feb 1894
51. Ibid., Herchmer to Starnes, 20 Apr 1895
52. *Regulations and Orders*, 4
53. RG 18, vol. 2284, Herchmer to Gagnon, 5 Nov 1894
54. Ibid., vol. 1319, Circular Memorandum, 28 Dec 1894
55. Ibid., vol. 2284, Herchmer to Howe, 3 Nov 1894
56. Ibid., vol. 2285, Herchmer to Fraser, 25 Jan 1897
57. *Calgary Herald*, 30 Nov 1896
58. RG 18, vol. 2285, Herchmer to Steele, 11 Dec 1896
59. Ibid., vol. 132, White to Herchmer, 19 Jan 1897
60. Ibid., vol. 2285, Herchmer to Steele, 28 Jan 1897
61. See *Calgary Herald*, 22 July and 30 Aug 1897
62. RG 18, vol. 130, file 76/1897
63. Ibid., vol. 2284, Herchmer to Howe, 3 Dec 1896
64. Ibid., vol. 3347, service file 1125, Frank Perry
65. Ibid., vol. 2285, Howe to White, 4 Jan 1897
66. *Calgary Herald*, 22 Dec 1896
67. *Edmonton Bulletin*, 28 Jan 1897
68. Laurier Papers, vol. 746, Oliver to Laurier, 25 Jan 1897
69. RG 18, vol. 2285, Herchmer to White, 4 Feb 1897
70. Ibid., vol. 2284, Herchmer to Macpherson, 12 Oct 1897
71. NWMP, Annual Report, 1895, 19

Chapter 20

Horses and Music: The Force's Evolution from Function to Ceremony

1. NWMP, Annual Report, 1887, 127
2. Ibid., 1885, 12
3. Canada, *Regulations and Orders of the North-West Mounted Police*, 1889 (Ottawa, 1889), 42-44
4. *Lethbridge News*, 16 Dec 1890
5. NWMP, Annual Report, 1899, 116

6. Ibid., 98
7. RCMP Historical Branch, "A Brief Outline of the History of the RCMP Musical Ride," (Ottawa, 1978), 7
8. RG 18, vol. 1194, file 518
9. Ibid., vol. 1036, file 52
10. *Regulations and Orders*, 1889, 43
11. NWMP, Annual Report, 1889, 6
12. RG 18, vol. 1074
13. NWMP, Annual Report, 1886, 8
14. *Regina Leader*, 15 Sept 1891
15. *Calgary Herald*, 27 June 1892
16. Ibid., 15 Apr 1891
17. NWMP, Annual Report, 1887, 127
18. Ibid., 1888, 13
19. Ibid., 1889, 5
20. *Calgary Herald*, 26 Apr 1893
21. NWMP, Annual Report, 1892, 5
22. Ibid., 1894, 3
23. Ibid., 1892, 5
24. NWMP, Annual Report, 1895, 7
25. Ibid., 1896, 3
26. RG 18, vol. 3350, service file 1202
27. NWMP, Annual Report, 1892, 132
28. Dwight, 61
29. *Regina Leader*, 29 May 1888
30. Marquis of Anglesey, *History of the British Cavalry*, vol. 2 (London, 1975), 57
31. RG 18, vol. 1037, file 60/86
32. NWMP, Annual Report, 1888, 53
33. Dwight, 43
34. Ibid., 45
35. Ibid., 49
36. H. D. Dempsey (ed), *William Parker: Mounted Policeman*, (Edmonton: Hurtig 1973), 55
37. Pennefather, 55
38. Dwight, 239
39. RG 18, vol. 2328, General Order 2115
40. Ibid., General Order 2591
41. NWMP, Annual Report, 1895, 68
42. Ibid., 102
43. Ibid., 1887, 11
44. Donkin, 232
45. RG 18, vol. 1368
46. NWMP, Annual Report, 1893, 172
47. Ibid., 1896, 223
48. Ibid., 1897, 42
49. Ibid., 1895, 164
50. *Regina Leader*, 1 Feb, 5 Apr, 21 June and 4 Oct 1887
51. NWMP, Annual Report, 1890, 26
52. Ibid., 1891, 18
53. Ibid., 1892, 90
54. Ibid., 1895, 23
55. Ibid., 23
56. Ibid., 1888, 177-179
57. Ibid., 1887, 76
58. Ibid., 126
59. Ibid., 1893, 172
60. Ibid., 1886, 14
61. Privy Council Order 1669, 27 June 1890
62. Canada, *Regulations and Orders of the North-West Mounted Police*, 1889, 22
63. NWMP, Annual Report, 1893, 172
64. D. Wallace, "Old Timers in Regina", *RCMP Quarterly*, Jan 1934, 103
65. NWMP, Annual Report, 1887, 127
66. Ibid., 1892, 172
67. S. T. Murphy, "Saddlery of the North-West Mounted Police, 1874-1904," unpublished ms, (RCMP Historical Branch, Ottawa, 1978)
68. Ibid.
69. NWMP, Annual Report, 1886, 9
70. RG 18, vol. 752
71. Ibid., vol. 109, file 466/95
72. Ibid., vol. 1071, White to Herchmer, 18 May 1887
73. NWMP, Annual Report, 1887, 128
74. Ibid., 1890, 111
75. Ibid., 1900, 9
76. Ibid., 1886, 38
77. Ibid., 1889, 93
78. RG 18, vol. 1294, file 71
79. NWMP, Annual Report, 1886, 9
80. Ibid., 1889, 6
81. RG 18, vol. 1157, file 287
82. NWMP, Annual Report, 1893, 28
83. RG 18, vol. 2328, General Order 5079, 6 May 1890
84. NWMP, Annual Report, 1891, 18
85. Ibid., 1892, 90
86. Ibid., 1886, 30
87. Ibid., 1897, 11
88. Ibid., 1899, 30
89. Ibid., 5
90. *Edmonton Bulletin*, 25 June 1887
91. *Regina Leader*, 27 May 1890
92. Ibid., 21 July 1898
93. Ibid., 2 July 1896
94. Ibid.
95. Bis, P. L., *The Story of the Royal Tournament* (Aldershot, 1952), 1
96. *Regina Leader*, 11 May 1886
97. Ibid., 18 Jan 1887
98. Ibid., 1 Mar 1887
99. Ibid., 8 Mar 1887
100. Ibid., 10 Jan 1888
101. Debates, 29 Mar 1897
102. Ibid., 13 Apr 1897
103. RG 18, vol. 1399, file 195
104. Ibid.
105. Ibid.
106. Ibid.
107. Ibid.
108. *Calgary Herald*, 5 July 1897
109. NWMP, Annual Report, 1897, 286
110. *Regina Leader*, 20 May 1897
111. Ibid.
112. RG 18, vol. 133, file 349
113. Laurier Papers, reel C741
114. Privy Council Order 1432, 24 June 1897
115. *Toronto Globe*, 7 June 1897
116. *London Times*, 7 June 1897
117. *Toronto Globe*, 21 June 1897
118. *London Times*, 11 June 1897
119. *Edmonton Bulletin*, 28 June 1897
120. *London Times*, 23 June 1897
121. *Toronto Globe*, 23 June 1897
122. *Regina Leader*, 24 June 1897
123. *RCMP Quarterly*, Apr 1948, 379
124. RG 18, vol. 141, file 622
125. NWMP, Annual Report, 1886, 12
126. RG 18, vol. 1161, file 357
127. Ibid., vol. 1117, CO, E Division to Herchmer, 17 Aug 1888
128. Ibid., 21 Feb 1896
130. Ibid., 5 Jan 1895
131. RG 18, vol. 1161, file 357
132. *Edmonton Bulletin*, 26 Oct 1893
133. *Edmonton Bulletin*, 26 Oct 1893
134. Ibid., 13 Feb 1896
136. RG 18, vol. 1050, file 194
137. Ibid., vol. 754, White to Herchmer, 2 Nov 1886
138. Ibid., vol. 1055, file 17
139. Ibid., vol. 2286
140. Ibid., vol. 2287

141. *Regina Leader*, 28 Dec 1886
142. Ibid., 1 Nov 1887
143. Ibid., 27 May 1890
144. Ibid., 10 July 1896
145. C. Junget, interview with S. W. Horrall, 24 Jan 1969
146. RCMP Museum, Regina, Diary of Asst. Comm. J. H. McIllree
147. *Regina Leader*, 16 Mar 1893
148. *Calgary Herald*, 26 May 1896

Chapter 21

From Forts to Barracks: Post-Rebellion Police Quarters

1. RG 18, vol. 1160, file 339
2. Debates, 10 Mar 1893
3. Ibid., 20 June 1894
4. NWMP, Annual Report, 1886, 12
5. Auditor General's Reports, 1886-87 to 1899-1900
6. Donkin, 43
7. RG 18, vol. 2192, Herchmer to White, 27 Apr 1886
8. NWMP, Annual Report, 1884, 23
9. Auditor General's Reports, 1885-86, 253
10. *Regina Leader*, 9 Oct 1891
11. NWMP, Annual Report, 1890, 8
12. Ibid., 1889, 8 and 1888, 53
13. Ibid., 1892, 10
14. Ibid., 1887, 99-100
15. Ibid., 1895, 12
16. Ibid., 1894, 8
17. Ibid., 1895, 12
18. Ibid., 1898, 12
19. RG 18, vol. 1451, file 25
20. Ibid., vol. 1336, file 114
21. Annual reports of the NWMP, 1886 to 1892
22. *Regina Leader*, 29 Nov 1887
23. RG 18, vol. 1087, file 638
24. Ibid., vol. 1105, files 164, 165
25. NWMP, Annual Report, 1888, 73
26. Ibid., 1887, 36
27. Ibid., 1890, 112
28. Ibid., 1892, 9
29. RG 18, vol. 2343, General Order 3242, 10 Dec 1888
30. NWMP, Annual Report, 1892, 9
31. RG 18, vol. 761, White to Public Works, 2 Nov 1889
32. Ibid., vol. 1165, file 18
33. NWMP, Annual Report, 1890, 32
34. Ibid, 1895, 132
35. RG 18, vol. 1165, file 16
36. Annual reports of the NWMP, 1894 to 1898
37. Auditor General's Reports, 1886-87 to 1899-00
38. NWMP, Annual Report, 1888, 21
39. RG 18, vol. 1053, file 275
40. Ibid., vol. 1108, file 183
41. Ibid., vol. 1074, file 245
42. Auditor General's Reports, 1886-87 to 1899-00

Annotated Bibliography

The best general introduction to Force history, with a more comprehensive text than the title indicates, is S. W. Horrall's *The Pictorial History of the Royal Canadian Mounted Police* (Toronto: McGraw-Hill Ryerson 1973). The period of the North-West Mounted Police has been covered by many authors. Among the best are R. C. Macleod, *The North West Mounted Police and Law Enforcement, 1873-1905* (Toronto: University of Toronto Press 1976); Ronald Atkin, *Maintain the Right* (New York: John Day Company 1973); Hugh Dempsey (ed), *Men in Scarlet* (Calgary: McClelland and Stewart 1974); J. P. Turner, *The North-West Mounted Police, 1873-1893*, 2 vols (Ottawa: King's Printer 1950); Sam Steele, *Forty Years in Canada* (Toronto: McGraw-Hill Ryerson 1972); and W. R. Morrison, *Showing the Flag: The Mounted Police and Canadian Sovereignty in the North, 1894-1925* (University of British Columbia Press 1985).

The Commissioner's annual reports were regularly published in the *Sessional Papers of Canada*. To complement the official record, one should also consult several good first-hand accounts of life in the NWMP. These include, in addition to Steele's memoirs mentioned above, Jean D'Artigue's *Six Years in the Canadian North-West* (1882); R. B. Nevitt, *A Winter at Fort Macleod*, edited by Hugh Dempsey (Calgary: Glenbow-Alberta Institute 1973); Hugh Dempsey (ed), *William Parker: Mounted Policeman* (Edmonton: Glenbow-Alberta Institute/Hurtig 1973); Cecil Denny, *The Law Marches West* (Toronto: J. M. Dent and Sons 1972); R. Burton Deane, *Mounted Police Life in Canada* (1916); John Donkin, *Trooper and Redskin in the Far North-West* (1889); and M. H. E. Hayne, *The Pioneers of the Klondike* (London: Sampson, Low, Marston and Company 1897).

The more recent past has not been studied in as much detail. Lorne and Caroline Brown, *An Unauthorized History of the RCMP* (Toronto: James Lewis & Samuel 1973) and Nora and William

Kelly, *The Royal Canadian Mounted Police* (Edmonton: Hurtig 1973) are two vastly different centennial treatments of Force history. Among the best modern reminiscences are Vernon Kemp, *Without Fear, Favour or Affection* (Toronto: Longmans-Green 1958), C. W. Harvison, *The Horsemen* (Toronto: McClelland and Stewart 1967); and Henry Larsen, *The Big Ship* (Toronto: McClelland and Stewart 1967). For a topic usually untouched, see Joy Duncan (ed), *Red Serge Wives* (1974).

For a comprehensive survey of the history of uniforms, J. J. Boulton's *Uniforms of the Canadian Mounted Police* (North Battleford: Turner-Warwick 1990) is indispensable. Those interested in firearms and equipment will find a wealth of information in R. F. Phillips and D. J. Klancher, *Arms and Accoutrements of the Mounted Police* (Bloomfield: Museum Restoration Services 1982). William and Nora Kelly's *Horses of the Royal Canadian Mounted Police* is a handsome pictorial history which tells the tale of the essential contribution made by these animals.

John Sawatsky explores the development of the RCMP Security Service in *Men in the Shadows* (Toronto: Doubleday 1980); this should be supplemented by S. W. Horrall's article "Canada's Security Service" which appeared in the *RCMP Quarterly* (Summer 1985). The Force's place in Canadian culture is given a scholarly appreciation in Keith Walden's *Vision of Order: the Canadian Mounties in Symbol and Myth* (Toronto: Butterworth Press 1982).

Original archival records of the NWMP, the RNWMP and the RCMP are in the custody of the Government Archives Division, National Archives of Canada, Ottawa, Ontario.

Index

344

Other RCMP-Related Books
published by Centax Books/PrintWest Publishing Services

Policing the Fringe: One Mountie's Story
William Kelly and Nora Hickson Kelly

Policing in Wartime: One Mountie's Story
William Kelly and Nora Hickson Kelly

My Mountie and Me: A True Story
Nora Hickson Kelly

Sam Steele: Lion of the Frontier
Robert Stewart

Headdress of the Canadian Mounted Police, 1873-1998
James J. Boulton